D1741012

The Edinburgh Review
by Sydney Smith

Copyright © 2019 by HardPress

Address:
HardPress
8345 NW 66TH ST #2561
MIAMI FL 33166-2626
USA
Email: info@hardpress.net

NRLF

622 965

SIGILLVM · VNIVERSITATIS · CALIFORNIENSIS

FIAT LVX

MDCCCLXVIII

EX LIBRIS

COLLEGE OF AGRICULTURE
DAVIS, CALIFORNIA

THE

EDINBURGH REVIEW,

OR

CRITICAL JOURNAL:

FOR

JULY, 1866. . . . . . . OCTOBER, 1866.

TO BE CONTINUED QUARTERLY.

JUDEX DAMNATUR CUM NOCENS ABSOLVITUR.

PUBLIUS SYRUS.

VOL. CXXIV.

LONGMANS, GREEN, READER, AND DYER, LONDON.

ADAM AND CHARLES BLACK, EDINBURGH.

1866.

UNIVERSITY OF CALIFORNIA
LIBRARY
COLLEGE OF AGRICULTURE
DAVIS

LONDON
PRINTED BY SPOTTISWOODE AND CO.
NEW-STREET SQUARE

CONTENTS OF No. 253.

Page

ART. I.—1. Essai sur l'Histoire des Arabes avant l'Islamisme, pendant l'Époque de Mahomet et jusqu'à la Réduction de toutes les Tribes sous la Loi Mussulmane. Par A. P. Caussin de Perceval. 3 vols. Paris: 1847-48.

2. Mohammed der Prophet, sein Leben und seine Lehre. Von Gustav Weil. Stuttgart: 1844.

3. Life of Mahomet, and History of Islam to the Era of the Hegira. By William Muir. 4 vols. London: 1861.

4. Das Leben und die Lehre des Mohammed's. Von Adolf Sprenger. 3 vols. Berlin: 1855–65.

5. Mahomet et le Coran. Par J. Barthélemy Saint-Hilaire. 1 vol. Paris: 1865.

6. Études d'Histoire Religieuse. Par E. Renan. 1 vol. Paris: 1862.

7. Histoire Générale et Système comparé des Langues Sémitiques. Par E. Renan. 1 vol. Paris: 1861, ... 1

II.—1. Report of a Committee appointed by the Royal Society, the Admiralty, and the Board of Trade, to consider certain Questions relating to the Meteorological Department of the Board of Trade. Presented to Parliament, April, 1866.

2. The Law of Storms considered in connexion with the ordinary Movements of the Atmosphere. By H. W. Dove, F.R.S. With Diagrams and Charts of Storms. Second Edition. Translated by Robert H. Scott, M.A. London: 1862.

3. Proceedings of the British Meteorological Society. Edited by James Glaisher, F.R.S., Secretary. London: 1865.

4. Meteorographica, or Methods of Mapping the Weather. Illustrated by upwards of 600 printed and lithographed diagrams referring to the weather of a large part of Europe during the month of December 1861. By Francis Galton, F.R.S. 1863, . 51

III.—1. Bulletin de la Société de l'Histoire du Protestantisme Français. Documents Historiques inédits

65345

Page

et originaux, XVIe XVIIe et XVIIIe Siècles.
Tomes I.—XIII.   Paris : 1852–1864.

2. Correspondance des Réformateurs dan les Pays de
la Langue Française, recuillie et publiée avec
d'autres Lettres relatives à la Réforme et des Notes
historiques et biographiques. Par A. L. Herminjard. Tome premier. (1512–1516.) Genève et
Paris : 1866, ...   86

IV.—An Examination of Sir William Hamilton's Philosophy, and of the principal Philosophical Questions
discussed in his Writings. By John Stuart Mill.
London : 1865, ...   120

V.—The Albert Nyanza, Great Basin of the Nile, and
Explorations of the Nile Sources. By Samuel
White Baker, M.A., F.R.G.S., and Gold Medallist
of the Royal Geographical Society. With Maps
and Illustrations. 2 vols. 8vo. London : 1866, .   151

VI.—1. Report of the Assistant-Secretary to the Navy on
the Attempt to relieve Fort Sumter in 1861. New
York : 1865.

2. Reports of the Secretary for the Navy, with Appendices. Washington : 1861–5.

3. Diary of the War for Separation. Vicksburg :
1862.

4. Reports on the Fall of New Orleans presented to
the Confederate Congress. Richmond : 1862, .   185

VII.—1. The Natural History, Ancient and Modern, of
Precious Stones and Gems, and of Precious Metals.
By C. W. King, M.A., Fellow of Trinity College,
Cambridge. London : 1865.

2. Handbuch der Edelsteinkunde für Mineralogen,
Steinschneider und Juweliere. Von Karl Emil
Kluge. Leipsic : 1860.

3. Gems and Jewels, their History, Geography, Chemistry, and Ana, from the earliest years down to
the present time. By Madame de Barrera. London : 1860.

4. Diamonds and Precious Stones, their History,
Value and Distinguishing Characteristics, with
simple Tests for their Identification. By Harry
Emmanuel. London : 1865, ...   228

VIII.—Charles Lamb : a Memoir. By Barry Cornwall.
London : 1866, ...   261

IX.—International Policy. Essays on the Foreign Relations
of England. 8vo. London : 1866, . . .   275

CONTENTS of No. 254.

Page

ART. I.—1. The History of the Sepoy War. Vol. I. By John
W. Kaye, Esq. London : 1864.

2. Notes on the Revolt in the North-Western Provinces of India. By Charles Raikes, Judge of the
Sudder Court at Agra, late Civil Commissioner
with Sir Colin Campbell. London : 1858, . . 299

II.—Causeries d'un Curieux : Variétés d'Histoire et d'Art ;
Tireés d'un Cabinet d'Autographes et de Dessins.
Par F. Feuillet de Conches. Tomes Premier et
Second, 1862 ; Tome Troisième, 1864 : Paris, . 341

III.—1. Les Métaux precieux. Par M. Roswag. Paris :
1865.

2. Etat de la question de l'uniformité des Poids et
Mesures. Par M. Nahuys. Utrecht : 1865.

3. Production der edlen Metälle. Von Soetbeer.
Berlin : 1865.

4. Revue Contemporaine. Articles on International
Coinage, by M. de Parieu : published in 1858, 1860,
1861, and 1865. Paris.

5. Eighth Report of the International Association for
obtaining a uniform decimal system of measures,
weights, and coins. London : 1865.

6. Decimal Coinage. By Frederic Hendriks. London :
1866.

7. Rapport adressé à S.M. l'Empereur par M. le
Ministre des Finances sur un Projet de Loi relatif
à la Convention Monétaire passée entre la France,
la Belgique, l'Italie et la Suisse. 14th Avril, 1866, 383

IV.—Histoire de Jules César. Par Napoleon III. 2 vols.
8vo. Paris : 1865–66, ... 399

V.—Felix Holt, the Radical. By George Eliot. 3 vols.
post 8vo. London : 1866, ... 435

VI.—1. Das Leben Jesu : für das deutsche Volk bearbeitet.
Von D. F. Strauss. Leipzig : 1864.

Page

2. Dr. D. F. Strauss's 'New Life of Jesus:' the authorised English Edition. 2 vols. London: 1865.

3. Histoire des Origines du Christianisme; Livre deuxième: 'Les Apôtres.' Par Ernest Renan. Paris: 1866.

4. 'Ecce Homo:' a Survey of the Life and Work of Jesus Christ. Fifth Edition, with a new Preface. London: 1866, ... 450

VII.—History of England, from the Fall of Wolsey to the Death of Elizabeth. By James Anthony Froude, M. A., late Fellow of Exeter College, Oxford. Reign of Elizabeth. Vols. III., IV. London: 1866, . 476

VIII.—1. Antique Gems: their Origin, Uses, and Value as Interpreters of Ancient History, and as illustrative of Ancient Art; with Hints to Gem Collectors. By the Rev. C. W. King, Fellow of Trinity College, Cambridge. London: 1860.

2. Pyrgoteles: Die edlen Steine der Alten im Bereiche der Natur und der bildenden Kunst, mit Berucksichtigung der Schmuckund Siegelringe insbesonders der Griechen und Römer. Dr. Johann Heinrich Krause. Halle: 1865, ... 511

IX.—1. Preussen als Militärstaat: eine historische Skizze. Vienna: 1866.

2. Der einjährige Freiwillige im Preussischen Heere. Berlin: 1862.

3. Allerhöchste Verordnungen über die grösseren. Truppenübungen. Berlin: 1661.

4. A Military Memorial, translated from the German of Prince Frederic Charles. London; 1866.

5. Military Correspondence of the Times during the late Campaign. London: 1866, ... 553

INDEX TO VOL. CXXIV., ... 597

THE

EDINBURGH REVIEW,

JULY, 1866.

Nᵒ· CCLIII.

ART. I. — 1. *Essai sur l'Histoire des Arabes avant l'Islam-isme, pendant l'Époque de Mahomet et jusqu'à la Réduction de toutes les Tribes sous la Loi Mussulmane.* Par A. P. CAUSSIN DE PERCEVAL. 3 vols. Paris: 1847–48.

2. *Mohammed der Prophet, sein Leben und seine Lehre.* Von GUSTAV WEIL. Stuttgart: 1844.

3. *Life of Mahomet, and History of Islam to the Era of the Hegira.* By WILLIAM MUIR. 4 vols. London: 1861.

4. *Das Leben und die Lehre des Mohammed's.* Von ADOLF SPRENGER. 3 vols. Berlin: 1855–65.

5. *Mahomet et le Coran.* Par J. BARTHÉLEMY SAINT-HILAIRE. 1 vol. Paris: 1865.

6. *Études d'Histoire Religieuse.* Par E. RENAN. 1 vol. Paris: 1862.

7. *Histoire Générale et Système comparé des Langues Sémitiques.* Par E. RENAN. 1 vol. Paris: 1861.

THE sudden appearance of the Arabs on the scene of human affairs immediately after the decease of Mahomet, the rapid expansion of their power, the brilliant and fugitive bloom of civilisation which embellished their dominion, and the abrupt collapse of their empire, are events in history without a parallel. The reason of this surprising and sudden efflo-rescence of national character has only been adequately ex-plained by the writers of our times, whose works are now before us. An imaginary creative and exciting power had been supposed to reside in the religion of the Arabian Pro-phet, but modern criticism has shown from the state of the Arab mind and character in the period antecedent to the coming of Mahomet, that the race was fully prepared for its mission, as soon as some principle should unite in one nationality the straggling and divided tribes of the peninsula. That principle was provided by the religion of Mahomet, and the Arabs grasped its political significance with marvellous rapidity, although then, as now, the most sceptical and incredulous of mankind, and caring little for the faith of Islam except in so far as it led to conquest and dominion. The researches of M. Caussin de Perceval have rendered an inestimable service in revealing this pre-Mohammedan state of Arabia; and the condition of the Arab race before the coming of Mahomet is described in his pages with a clearness and fidelity of detail which leaves nothing to be desired. We are further indebted for the greater portion of the materials we are now about to use, to the great and admirable work of Dr. Sprenger, who has thrown an entirely new light upon the character of Mahomet and the sources of his religion, derived from the closest study of the subject in the East.

The Arabs had attained, in spite of their predatory habits and their internecine wars, to a high degree of intelligence for so nomadic and barbarous a race. The growth of a language affords strong evidence of the mental and moral condition of a people, and its poetry is a trustworthy record of its favourite passions and pursuits. The sudden appearance of the Arab language in full perfection, endowed with such perfect flexibility, capacity, and richness of vocabulary that it has not suffered any perceptible change down to the present time, and has thus never exhibited the slightest trace of either infancy or decrepitude, is in itself a unique fact in the history of mankind. The poems of the *Moallakat,* which were written in gold letters and suspended in the Caaba, prove that the Arabian mind had attained not only to grammatical refinement but to great subtlety of thought, expression and feeling. War and love, the valour of tribes and of chieftains, the praises of wine and of women, of joyous living, of a roving life, and of the finer pleasures of Baalbec and Damascus, the swiftness and beauty of the horse, the speed and strength of the camel— form the chief topics of these poems; but some touch of nature, some delicate detail of observation or ingenious metaphor adds freshness to the description; and evidently the Arabs who, as judges, gave these competitive poems supereminent rank, must have been acquainted with every delicacy and artifice of poetical expression. Some of the scenes come as vividly before the eyes as the art of language can possibly bring them. Thus we see the lover lingering with a lover's attachment over the spot from which the camp of his mistress has been raised, the circular depression left by the tent of his beloved is not effaced from the sand, the stones which sustained the cauldron are yet black with fire, and the fringe of her litter has left behind it little tufts of red on the thorn, like crimson blossoms; when he arrives in the presence of his mistress he feels as though the breeze had wafted to his senses the perfume of the pink; and when he prevails upon her to fly with him by midnight, he approaches the tent, while the Pleiades are glittering in the heavens like a girdle studded with ,gems; the maiden is waiting with beating heart behind the folds of the tent-door, and as they fly together she lets her robe sweep down behind her to efface the marks of their footsteps on the sand. It is not possible to surpass the minute observation of natural objects contained in some of these poems; thus a poet describes ' a fly settling on a blade of grass and rubbing its ' fore-legs together, just as a man with mutilated arms would ' roll a stick in the round orifice of wood to produce a flame.'

The *Moallakat,* moreover, as well as the narrative of M. Caussin de Perceval, bear ample testimony to the inveterate hostility of tribe to tribe among the Arabs. This ferocious hatred has lasted for now something like three thousand years, and without some knowledge of its character, their history is entirely unintelligible. From time immemorial the Arabs have been divided into two great races; the elder, called the Yemenites, or Kelbites,* claim descent from Joktan, or Cahtan, the son of Heber, who gave his name to the Hebrew race. The other, and younger race, known as Maadites, Modharites, or Caisites, own as ancestor Adnan, one of the descendants of Ishmael, although they probably derived their origin from various Biblical patriarchs, all comprised under the name of Adnan. The animosity of these two races to each other is unaccountable, but invincible; like two chemical products which instantly explode, when placed in contact, so has it always been found impossible for Yemenite and Maadite to live quietly together. At the present day the Yemenite in the vicinity of Jerusalem detests the Maadite of Hebron, and when questioned as to the reason of their eternal enmity, has no other reply but that it has always been so from time immemorial. In the time of the Caliphs

---

* It is very puzzling often to make out of which party a tribe is, since the parties change their denomination in every district—both Kelbite and Maadite using as a party name in that district the name of their own local leading tribe.

the territory of Damascus was desolated by a murderous war for two years because a Maadite had taken a melon from the garden of a Yemenite. The province of Murcia in Spain was deluged with blood for seven years because a Maadite inadvertently plucked a Yemenite vine-leaf. It was a passion which surmounted every tie of affection or interest. 'You 'have prayed for your father, why do you not pray for your 'mother?' a Yemenite was asked in the Caaba. 'For my 'mother!' said the Yemenite, 'how could I? she was of the 'race of Maad.' And Mahomet himself, notwithstanding that he owed everything to the Yemenite, never ceased to congratulate himself that he was of the race of Maad. The conquest of Islam, so far from diminishing the instinctive hatred of these two races, gave it renewed vigour and intensity. The Yemenites and Maadites, after each conquest, were often obliged to live on the same soil and divide the fruits of conquest between them. Incessant contact engendered incessant dispute, and the animosity of the two tribes bathed in blood at the same time the plains of Irak and Mesopotamia, the oases of the Sahara, the valleys of Mount Atlas, the banks of the Guadalquivir, and the regions watered by the Indus and the Ganges.

The Yemenites, however, preceded the Maadites by some two thousand years in the history of the world. The Yemenite Himyarite empire, which existed in the very dawn of civilisation in the southern extremity of the Arabian peninsula, has recently received the attention of many learned investigators. The Yemenite evidently has a superior aptitude for social organisation and the life of towns, and this diversity of character from the Maadite, by whom inhabitants of towns are held in contempt, is doubtless one of the reasons of their mutual aversion.* It is clear, from many passages of the Hebrew prophets, that the inhabitants of Yemen and its cities held rank as one of the first mercantile and manufacturing communities then known; and from their being frequently mentioned in connexion with the kingdom of Ethiopia, it was surmised that a near relation existed between the two countries. Recent discoveries have verified these conjectures. M. Fresnel, a French consul in those parts, with other travellers, has visited the extensive and imposing remains of ruined Himyarite cities, and has discovered inscriptions of the ancient Himyarite

---

* Mahomet, like a true Maadite, regarded everything indicating a settled life with contempt. He once said, looking at a plough, 'Whosesoever house that enters, it brings shame with it.'

language. This language appears, on examination, to have been a sister of the *Ghez* or Abyssinian, another member of the Semitic family. Indeed, the people of Hadramaut and Oman, with their great cities of Mareb, Saba or Sheba, Aden or Eden, Saana and others, seem in the days of Solomon and the kings to have stood towards Egypt, Palestine, and Assyria, in the same position as Venice towards Europe in the Middle Ages; for the sailors of Hadramaut and Oman carried on the maritime trade between the coasts of Africa, India, and Malabar, and the mighty empires of the Euphrates and the Nile.*

While this Himyarite Yemenite empire was thus early the chief seat of commercial and manufacturing activity, their Maadite brethren occupied themselves with the land or caravan trade, a business which they have never abandoned since their first appearance in that capacity in the book of Genesis. The brethren of Joseph, after they had thrown him into the pit, sat down by its side to eat bread, and saw ' a com- ' pany of Ishmeelites coming from Gilead with their camels ' bearing spices, and balm, and myrrh, going` to carry it down ' to Egypt.'

The great distinguishing feature of ancient commerce, as Heeren has remarked, is that it was carried on chiefly by land. Commercial operations at sea were usually confined to small coasting voyages. The immense steppes of Asia and the sandy deserts of Africa and Arabia were the oceans of ancient commerce, across which the long caravans of camels with their bales and ' chests bound with cords,' as described

---

* A passage in Ezekiel (xxvii. 19–24) is curiously illustra- tive of the state of the commerce of that time, and the nomad character of the princes of Kedar is clearly distinguished from the merchants of Sheba by the character of the commodities they dealt in : ' Dan also and Javan going to and fro occupied in thy fairs : ' bright iron (sword blades), cassia, and calamus, were in thy market. ' Dedan was thy merchant in precious clothes for chariots. Arabia, ' and all the princes of Kedar, they occupied with thee in lambs, and ' rams, and goats: in these were they thy merchants. The mer- ' chants of Sheba and Raamah, they were thy merchants : they oc- ' cupied in thy fairs with chief of all spices, and with all precious ' stones, and gold. Haran, and Canneh, and *Eden*, the merchants of ' *Sheba*, Asshur, and Chilmad, were thy merchants. These were ' thy merchants in all sorts of things, in blue clothes, and broidered ' work, and in *chests of rich apparel, bound with cords,* and made ' of cedar, among thy merchandise.' The wealth of southern Arabia continued to be an object of marvel with foreign nations till the days of Horace, who in five passages celebrates the wealth of Arabia : *Od.* i. 27 ; iii. 12, 24 ; iii. 24, 2 ; *Ep.* i. 6, 6 ; i. 7, 36.

in Ezekiel, trailed their long lengths like fleets of ships. In the days of Augustus, Aulus Gellius described the caravans of Arabia as being like armies in magnitude. The time and course of each caravan was marked by the convenience of merchants and the occurrence of watering places. Each had its fixed time of starting— so often in the course of the year — its invariable daily halting-places, its *entrepôts*, and its points of ' junction ' with other caravans who would join it for protection. To each city through which it passed it was like the railway train of our own! times, or a fleet for a seaport, a source of wealth and daily topic of interest, and the distant signs of its arrival would be anxiously awaited outside the walls by merchants and citizens. The increased use of shipping, and more especially the establishment by the Romans of a direct trade with India by sea from Suez, ruined the caravan trade, and consequently those vast cities which maintained their enormous prosperity by the passage of caravans fell into decay. This is the reason of the otherwise inexplicable existence of the magnificent remains of colonnades, temples, and amphitheatre, which excite the traveller's admiration and surprise amid the sands of the Hauran and the deserts east of the Dead Sea and the Lake of Tiberias. Palmyra, Philadelphia, and the cities of the Decapolis were the northern stations or *termini* of the great caravan road from Petra to Damascus. But the position of Petra was peculiarly adapted to advance it to that incredible degree of opulence which won the admiration of visitors in the days of Greece and Rome, which was described by Athenodorus the stoic, and which after having been forgotten in the desert for centuries, still exists within its rock ramparts and its richly chiselled and stately pillars and edifices, to astonish and instruct the modern traveller. Petra in fact was one of the chief points of junction of the great caravan traffic, and it was here that the cargo of the caravan changed hands from the carriers of the Southern to those of the Northern merchants.*

---

* Not only the populous kingdom of the Nabathæans, of which Petra was capital, but probably the kingdoms of Hira and Ghassan owed a great portion of their prosperity to being traversed by the ancient arteries of trade. When, however, the caravan trade fell into ruin, these countries lost the means of supporting the numerous settled populations of Arabs who had found occupation among them, and one by one the tribes again betook themselves to the life of the desert, and the disturbances into which these wandering tribes in search of a locality for settlement threw Arabia and the adjacent country were followed by a series of commotions which evidently lasted very nearly to the time of Mahomet.

Two great lines of caravans started from Yemen : the one proceeded from Hadramaut by Oman and took the line of the Persian Gulf, the other came by the Hidjaz along the coast of the Red Sea, and arrived at Petra, and from hence bifurcated off into two roads, the one going to Gaza and the other to Damascus. From Yemen to Petra the time of caravan march was seventy days, and the stations of the present day are the same as those described by Athenodorus, and were probably the same in the days of Ishmael and Abraham. The Maadite tribes found in this occupation an immense field of employment. Some let their camels for hire, some acted as guides, some secured protection in return for payments of money, some engaged themselves in traffic. These Maadite Arabs all for the most part trace their origin from Abraham, although according to Genesis some must be descended from Abraham's brother Nahor and his nephew Lot. The nations mentioned in Genesis under the name Ishmaelite, ' the rams of ' Nebaioth,' ' the tents of Kedar,' the Kedarenes, the Edomites or Idumæans, the Amalekites, the descendants of Uz and Buz, sons of Nahor, the Moabites and the Ammonites (descended from Lot), the Midianites, were all of this Arab branch of the Semitic family.

The Arabs long acknowledged the ascendency of their neighbours and kinsfolk the Jews, and the kings of Israel made their power felt across the Arabian peninsula. David fortified Petra ; Solomon had a fleet at Akaba (Eziongeber) on the Red Sea, and sent fleets to Ophir (Malabar) ; Jehoshaphat also occupied the same place as a naval station. In the decline of the power of the kings of Israel the Edomites got possession of Petra and the naval stations of the Hebrews on the Red Sea, but they were in their turn expelled by the Nabathæans. During the dominion of the Nabathæans and in the time of the prosperity of Petra, the expedition led by Ælius Gallus, the friend of Strabo, still affords some slight knowledge of the state of the peninsula, when after a march of six months, protracted by the duplicity of the Arab guides, the Roman legions penetrated into Yemen and took Mareb.

Mecca had always been an emporium of the great caravan road from Yemen; but although the valley in which it is situated is desolate and barren, the presence of water, and its position between Jeddah and the fertile district of Tayif, rendered it an advantageous halting-place and commercial station for merchants, so that before the decline of the caravan trade it was a city of some importance. Mohammedan tradition first places Mecca in the possession of a race called by them the ' Amalica,' a name which naturally suggests the Amalekites of Scripture. Subsequently a Yemenite race of Djorhomites dwelt there, and immediately before the advent of the Coreishites on the scene, another Yemenite tribe, named Khoza, had obtained possession of the holy spot. The Coreishites, whose name was destined to supplant those of the previous occupiers of the valley, were a Maadite tribe, enriched by the caravan trade, which they continued to prosecute with great success in the days of Mahomet. The first chief of the tribe who appears in prominent connexion with the Caaba is Cossai—the ancestor of Mahomet four times removed. The occupation of the Caaba and its *Haram* or sacred precincts by Cossai forms an initial point in the history of Mohammedanism, and successively the several ancestors of Mahomet so modified the regulations and institutions of the worship of the Caaba, that Mahomet really did little more than purify the institutions of his ancestors of idol-worship, and of some barbarous customs, retaining all their ceremonies and institutions, and adding to them some practices of his own invention or importation.

From time immemorial the temple of the Caaba had been an object of reverence. It was said indeed to have been raised by the hands of Abraham. The monotheism of Abraham was, however, in time depraved by the addition of idol and fetish worship. The idols were *Djinn* (Genii), or spirits, divided into household penates and national deities of the tribes ; the fetishes were trees and stones.* Of these the Caaba is the last surviving representative, and the worship of that venerable stone Mahomet himself did not venture to abolish. Some of these idols were unquestionably of the very highest antiquity. Herodotus himself mentions (under the name of Alilat) the Al-Lat, so often spoken of in the Coran. The chief Djinn, however, was Hobal, who was represented as a venerable old man with a beard, and a sheaf of arrows in his hand. The temple of the Caaba had become in the days of Cossai a sort of Pantheon for all Arabian divinities, and numbered no less than four hundred tutelary deities ; when the idols were destroyed by Mahomet a Byzantine virgin was even found among them, so anxious were they to include all divine influence under the roof of their temple. Mecca, besides having the reputation of being the most holy place in Arabia, was the greatest emporium of commerce in the peninsula.

---

* One tribe worshipped a loaf of bread, and during a famine ate their divinity. The *teraphim* of Laban stolen by Rachel were probably *djinn*.

The policy of the merchant tribes who obtained possession of the holy city was to make it as great a place of resort as possible, by including in their list of deities the tutelary gods of all the tribes, so that in fact they formed at Mecca a sort of federative religion in which each tribe found itself represented. Hence it was that Mahomet encountered but little opposition so long as he merely attacked the worship of the *Djinn* or household penates. It was when he began to assail the national deities of the surrounding tribes, that he excited the bitter animosity of the Coreishites, for these tribes were attracted to the markets and pilgrimages of Mecca by such deities as Al-Lat and Al-Ozza, whence not only were great commercial profits secured, but the revenues of the Coreishites, as keepers of the Caaba and as purveyors to the pilgrims, were largely increased.

Cossai died about the end of the fifth century in extreme old age, and held almost supreme power in Mecca for nearly forty years. Tradition says that he drank the Khozaite keeper of the Caaba into a state of intoxication, and then obtained possession of the keys; he did not retain them, however, without a severe struggle, which ended by his being enabled to transfer the dominion of Arabia with the possession of Mecca to his tribe. Cossai had, moreover, the true spirit of a founder, and he established institutions destined to perpetuate the supremacy of the Coreishites, which remain in force to the present day. Before his time, the valley of Mecca, and the precincts of the Caaba, known by the name of the Haram, had been considered so sacred, that none of its possessors had dared to erect any fixed habitations in the neighbourhood of the sanctuary, which was surrounded by a grove of trees. The worshippers of the Caaba and its guardians dwelt in tents outside the holy ground. Cossai determined to take permanent possession of the soil by building houses upon it, and when his fellow tribesmen hesitated to hew down the sacred trees, he himself seized an axe and commenced their demolition. By that blow of the axe, Cossai showed himself a true ancestor of his better known descendant. Not only did Cossai thus found the city of Mecca, but in the immediate neighbourhood of the Caaba he built a council-house for the Coreishites called the Dar-el-Nadwah. As guardian of the Caaba and founder of the council of his tribe, Cossai organised the following institutions : the *liwa,* or right of presenting the flag to the leader of forays and expeditions ; the *sicaya,* or right of managing the water supplies, an institution of great importance in a country like the neighbourhood of Mecca;

the *rifada*, or distribution of alms and provisions to the pilgrims at Mecca; the *nasaa*, or intercalation of days in the calendar, an office likewise conveying great authority, since it determined the time of the sacred month; the *ijaza*, or right of marshalling the tribes in procession, necessarily also an office of great authority among a race so tenacious of right to precedence as the Arabs; and the *nidjaba*, or guardianship of the keys of the Caaba. Of these institutions the *nasaa* was perhaps the most important of all, since the Arabs reckoned time by the lunar calendar; the months of the year were constantly changing their seasons, consequently the dates of the time of pilgrimage changed likewise; and as it was a matter of life and death with the majority of the tribes not to have the time of pilgrimage fixed during the harvest months, the privilege of deciding the season of pilgrimage alone conferred supereminent authority on the Coreishites.

The successors of Cossai followed in his steps. Haschim,* the great-grandfather of Mahomet, discharged the functions of the *rifada* and *sicaya* with a generosity which remained proverbial, and established the two great yearly caravans of the people of Mecca; the one in winter for Yemen, and the one in summer for Syria. Abd-al-Mouttalib, the grandfather of the prophet, filled the same position with equal magnificence; he rebuilt the sacred well of Zemzem, and restrained the privilege of its use to the Coreishites alone. Abdallah the son of Abd-al-Mouttalib and father of Mahomet, died a youth, leaving his wife then *enceinte* with a posthumous child.

Such were the institutions which were the work of Mahomet's ancestors, and which he incorporated into his own system, as well as those various rites and ceremonies which had existed from time immemorial before the time of Cossai. These were the *Ihrâm*, the shaving of the head, the paring of the nails, the casting away the clothes and assuming a new garb before performing the great pilgrimage; the *Hajj el Akbar*, the great pilgrimage; the *Omra*, the lesser pilgrimage; the *Dzal Hajj* or pilgrimage to Arafat, the casting of stones into the valley of Mecca, the seven peregrinations round the Caaba, the kissing the black stone, the sacrifices of sheep and camels, and the burial of their hair and nails in the sacred ground—all practices derived from idolatrous worship. All this large body of ceremonies and institutions, Mahomet found established antecedently

* It was from Haschim Mahomet's party were afterwards named Haschimites, in opposition to the Ommeyades, so called from Ommeyah, another son of Cossai.

to himself. The practice of abstaining from swine's flesh and the rite of circumcision had been observed by the Arabs from time immemorial, and the latter they believed to have been instituted by Abraham himself.

It remains to be seen what originality there was in the religious doctrines which he promulgated. For even in his monotheistic creed, Mahomet was by no means in advance of the most enlightened Arabs of his own time. The Semitic mind, in the very earliest recorded ages, was by its very constitution carried with a rapidity beyond all example among other nations to the adoption of monotheism in its conception of the divine government of the world. Apart from the Hebrew patriarchs and prophets, we know of Melchisedec, Jethro the Midianite, and Job, who dwelt in Arabia; and, doubtless, among the Semitic races, there were at all times many worshippers of the one true God. The distinguishing character of the Semitic mind is simplicity, not to make use of the word monotony. The complex organisation of the Indo-European mind is entirely unintelligible to them. There is, as M. Renan well observes, no example in Semitic literature of any composition resembling the complex structure of the drama and the epos. That exuberant imagination of the Greeks which conceived a thousand graceful and majestic male and female impersonations of the forces and elements of nature, is utterly wanting to the Semitic race, and differs from it as much as the vale of Tempe, overhung by Ossa and Pelion, differs from the expanse of the Arabian deserts and the wastes beyond Jordan. 'The desert,' as M. Renan says, 'is monotheist.' The Djinn and idols of the tribes were not so much divinities as attendants and ministers of the great Divinity (the *Allah ta-Allah*), who was always the predominant object of worship. These Djinn, idols and fetishes, stood in the same relation to him as saints and relics stand in the Romish hagiology to the Almighty. Another institution which Mahomet found ready prepared for his use was that of prophecy. Among all the Semitic tribes, the *nebi* has ever been a public character. Prophecy is a necessary consequence of Semitic monotheism. There are traditions of prophets to be found among all the Semitic nations. Not to speak of Balaam the prophet of Mesopotamia, among the Arabs in Mahomet's own time the story of the punishment of the tribes of the Thamudites and the Adites, for not listening to the warnings of the prophets Houd and Saleh, was universally received.

Such, indeed, were the institutions and doctrines which Mahomet found ready prepared for him among his own race;

it remains an equally interesting subject of investigation what was the state and prevalence of the Jewish and Christian beliefs in the Arabian peninsula and what influence these exercised on Mahomet. Even before the destruction of Jerusalem, the burning and desolate solitude east of Jordan and around the Dead Sea became the refuge of Judaic sects who fled from the despair and degradation of their race and found consolation in austere observances and separation from the world. The religion of the Jews was then fast becoming what it has ever since remained— a religion of mystic hope and lamentation. One of the chief of these sects was that of the Essenes, who exercised a larger influence on the subsequent course of theological belief than it is easy now to appreciate. They were a fraternity sprung from the Jews, who formed an ascetic community on the west side of the Dead Sea; a distaste for worldly life, frequent prayer, much fasting, daily ablution, allegoric interpretation of the Bible, belief in the Persian hierarchy of angels, severe observation of the Sabbath, together with a conviction of the immortality of the soul, and a wider love of humanity than was common to the Jews, formed the chief body of their tenets and practices. The general philanthropy of their principles and practices seems to have exercised great influence over the surrounding Semitic and heathen races, and they had a prophet named Elxai, who is supposed to be identical with Lokman of the Coran.* Near them subsequently, in Moabitis, settled the Ebionites or Nazarenes, who must have impressed the Arabic mind strongly with their influence, since the name up to the present time for a Christian is Nazara. Among the obscure heresies of which an account is left by Epiphanius, a Greek bishop who lived in the fourth century, the tenets of the Ebionites or Nazarenes find place; the doctrines of this sect are also expounded in the Homilies of Clemens, a learned Greek Ebionite, and the theory of revelation there set forth is precisely that which was adopted by Mahomet. They supposed that there was an original primary revelation, the text of which was preserved in Heaven. Adam received the first communication of this revelation, which was handed down among his progeny by tradition, but as it grew corrupted in course of time by adventitious inventions, it became necessary to promulgate it afresh to the world, and thus a new prophet was chosen

---

* In addition to their identification of Elxai with Lokman, the Essenes are said by Epiphanius to have sworn by salt, by water, by earth, and by bread and wine, sky and wind, all oaths which occur constantly in the Coran.

to be the depository of the original faith. The long line of prophets thus sent was closed by John the Baptist and by Christ. Christ called out in his cradle, according to the Coran, ' I have the book, and am chosen to be a prophet.' The same incident is found also in the spurious Gospel of the Childhood of Christ, which has only been preserved in an Arabic version, and indeed superseded all the other Gospels among the obscure sects settled in the extreme south of Palestine and in Arabia. Epiphanius, moreover, says that remains of the ark were still believed by the Nazarenes to exist in Mount Ararat, a circumstance also to be found in the Coran, and forming an additional proof of the knowledge of the Ebionite and Nazarene doctrines possessed by Mahomet or his prompters.

Another of the sects enumerated by Epiphanius are the Hemero-baptistæ, from their practice of daily washing, in the mystic sense of cleansing from sin, who are supposed to have been classed by the Arabs among the Sabians—whose appellation is also derived from the practice of ablution. As the Arabs appear to have confounded under this title various sects, the Essenes likewise possibly were comprised also under the term of Sabians or Sabæans, since the Essenes also paid adoration to the rising sun and also used rites of ablution. It was no wonder that these various doctrines should be floating about the peninsula, for long before the advent of Mahomet it had been a practice for all the strange heretical sects who could find no toleration in the Byzantine empire, either to escape and settle down on the border of Palestine, whence they could easily fly into the trackless deserts of Arabia, or to betake themselves to the oases of the desert itself, a place of refuge more secure than Holland to the Protestant refugees in the days of Louis XIV., and more accessible than America to the discontented European spirits of the present day. Christianity had, however, found little favour in Arabia. The free-spirited Bedouins stigmatised it as the ' *maliki,*' the state religion, the orthodox, and appear to have regarded it as synonymous with slavery. Besides which, the religion of humility—the worship of sorrow—the adoration of the mystery of the Divinity taking upon Him the burden of human affliction—the doctrine of the Trinity—has gained fewer converts among the proud self-reliant impetuous sons of the desert than among any other nation. For Christianity, although there were Christian tribes in Arabia, and one large Christian city Nadjran in the days of Mahomet, has rarely been received by them but with incredulity and ridicule, as in the case of one of the Arab kings of Hira whom some

Christian missionaries attempted to convert. While they were speaking to him an officer of the court whispered in the king's ear. The monarch immediately assumed an aspect of intense sorrow; his religious instructors inquired the reason. 'Alas!' he said, 'I have had dreadful news; the archangel Gabriel is 'dead.' 'But, prince, you are deceived; an angel is immortal.' 'What! and yet you tell me that God himself could die.'

The Jews were, on the contrary, established in a powerful position in the peninsula. There were two strong tribes of them settled at Medina; they had a fortified capital in Chaibhar, and in the third century of the Christian era they succeeded in converting one of the *tobbas* or kings of Yemen to the Jewish faith. A subsequent *tobba*, Dhou Nowas, became so ferocious a bigot in the cause of the Jewish religion, that he declared a holy war for the propagation of his creed, and took and destroyed the Christian city of Nadjran. On the complaint of the victims, and at the suggestion of Justin I., the *nedjachi* or king of Abyssinia undertook to avenge the cause of his coreligionists and conquered Yemen, which thus became an Abyssinian dependency until it was reconquered for the Yemenites by the Kesra or Chosroes of Persia and governed by a Persian viceroy. During the reign of the Abyssinian kings, however, one of them, Abraha-el-Achram, built a magnificent church at Sana, and endeavoured to divert the reverence of the Arabs from the Caaba to worship and pilgrimage to his new cathedral. The Arabs flew to arms in honour of their national shrine, and in the course of hostilities Abraha laid siege to Mecca, but retired in great discomfiture and died shortly afterwards. His assault of Mecca formed not only a crisis in the history of the Arab races, but the year, 570 A.D., of his expedition has become ever memorable as the year of Mahomet's birth, who was thus said to be born in the year of the Elephant, from the animal on which the king rode in his expedition.

But of all the various Jewish, Christian, and other sects scattered throughout the peninsula, there was one with which Mahomet was most closely associated, and on which a great deal of new light has been thrown by the researches of Dr. Sprenger, and this was the sect of the Hanyfs. The Hanyfs were the immediate forerunners of Mahomet, and it was from them that the religion of Islam in part proceeded. Mahomet calls himself a Hanyf, and the name Hanyf occurs twelve times in the Coran. The word is of Hebrew origin, and appears to have been among the Jews synonymous with freethinker; among the Arabs, however, the name came into honour. There is also frequent mention in the Coran of the Sohof, or rolls of Abraham, an expression equally obscure with the word Hanyf, until the following explanatory passage was discovered in the Arab historian Fihrist: ' This book,' says Fihrist, ' I have taken from the Bible of the Hanyfs, the ' Abrahamite Sabæans, who believed in Abraham, and from ' him have received the rolls which God gave to the patriarch.' Up to the discovery of this passage, no one knew what was meant by the rolls of Abraham; from researches made in other quarters it is now manifest that the Hanyfs had a series of rolls, said to have reached the number of 140, all of which were fabrications, though attributed to the various prophets and patriarchs.

The Hanyfs were, however, a monotheistic sect, descended probably from the Jews, without other veritable records of their race than such as they maintained by oral tradition, and their doctrines were then in great vogue among the most enlightened of the Arabs. A dozen Hanyfs are named as companions of Mahomet, and he himself was continually reproached by the people of Mecca with being a Sabæan. In the language of the Hanyfs, somewhat altered by tradition, the biblical names assumed the forms now common in the East. Thus, Noah became Nuh; Lot, Lut; Abraham, Ibrahym; Moses, Musa; Pharaoh, Firaun; and Aaron, Haroun. The Hanyfs regarded Abraham as the founder of their religion; he was the first Hanyf; and Abraham was also with all the patriarchs, and Christ himself, not only a Hanyf but a ' Moslem,' a man resigned to the will of God—' Moslem' being the participial appellation of those whose faith has the quality ' Islam,' ' resig- ' nation,' which, indeed, has the same root with ' Salam,' peace, prosperity. A dozen prophets of this sect were precursors of the prophet at Tayif, two days' journey from Mecca east among the mountains, and at Nadjran. At Tayif, Omayya was a celebrated Hanyf, and also an esteemed poet. Omayya never acknowledged the divine mission of Mahomet, in consequence of which three chapters of the Coran were directed against him; and Mahomet was wont to inveigh against him for his incredulity, as having a good tongue but a bad heart. One of the most striking passages to be found about the Hanyfs in the Arabian historians, is found in Ibn Ishac. It is there stated that on one occasion when the Coreishites were collected around one of their idols and offering sacrifices, four persons kept themselves apart from the ceremony; these were Waraka, a nephew of Khadidja, the first wife of the prophet, Othman, his cousin, and Obeidallah, cousin-german of Mahomet. These men talked together and said: ' Our tribe ' has fallen into error; they pervert the true religion of their

' father Abraham. Let us each seek a better path than
' theirs.' All four departed into foreign lands to endeavour
to discover the source of the religion of the Hanyfs, the true
creed of Abraham. But the greater part of them became
ultimately Christians. Waraka attained to some knowledge of
the Scriptures of both Jews and Christians; saw the first beginning of Mahomet's career, and died. Obeidallah, after a temporary conversion to Islamism, became and died a Christian.
Othman went to Constantinople and became a Christian, lived
in honour at the court, and filled office there. The most
interesting character of the four was Zeid ben Amr, who has
been called the John the Baptist of Islam, and for whose
memory Mahomet always evinced the most intense respect.

Zeid was the leader of his three companions, and Mahomet
said that Waraka was surely destined to eternal paradise,
because he professed no other religion than the religion of
Zeid. Zeid lived and died a pure Hanyf. He gave out his
utterances in the same rhymed prose as that in which the
Coran is composed, and in this also he was a forerunner of
Mahomet. It is supposed, indeed, that some of Zeid's verses
are to be found in the Koran; in any case, verses of Zeid's
have been preserved by Ibn Ishac and Ibn Hishan, which
would not be out of place in the Coran. In these compositions
Zeid celebrates the glory of the one true God, the merciful,
the forgiver of sins, the support of the good, and the punishment of the wicked. He attacks the worship of the idols,
which he had abandoned; he believes no longer either in Lat
or in Ozza; and, indeed, the whole of the purer doctrines of
the Coran are to be found in the poems of Zeid, with the
exception that Zeid made no pretence to prophecy and spoke in
no other name than his own. Alone with his back against the
Caaba he used to declaim to his fellow tribesmen on the folly
and wickedness of idolatry; and, indeed, he was banished to the
hill of Hira, outside the city, for his disbelief in the divinities
of the Caaba. He was especially vehement against the practice
of burying female children alive, a barbarous habit which
Mahomet alone was able to put down. During one of his
journeys, undertaken like those of his three friends for the
purpose of religious instruction, he was killed by a party of
Bedouins; from the praise which Mahomet bestowed upon
him and his doctrines, he clearly considered himself as professing the same religion as Zeid, which, indeed, was identical
with that of Omayya, against whom Mahomet inveighed so
bitterly for want of belief in his own mission. All these four
men were either related to or in constant communication with

Mahomet, and he doubtless profited largely both by their example and precepts.

The melancholy incidents associated with almost every step of Mahomet's birth and parentage deepened the seriousness and heightened the sensibility of his character. He was a posthumous child, orphan of both father and mother at five years of age, among a people with whom to be an orphan was a disgrace. How deeply he felt his unprotected state is evident from the earnestness and frequency with which he recommends in the Coran orphans to the care of the faithful. The life and destiny of his father Abdallah was also peculiar, for he narrowly escaped being offered in sacrifice to an idol, in consequence of a rash vow of Abd-al-Mouttalib, and was only rescued at the price of a hundred camels. Mahomet was born during the period of tears and desolation of his mother, Amina, after the death of her young husband, at the age of twenty-five, on a caravan journey ; when born, he was carried by his grandfather before an idol, and received his name. Unable to nurse her own infant, his mother, after Arab fashion, wished to send him to the desert to be reared ; but the Bedouin nurse who ultimately took him at first refused to have charge of a fatherless boy. At six years of age Mahomet lost his mother also, and was taken care of by his grandfather, and on the death of the latter three years later, by Abou Taleb, his uncle, who as long as he lived gave him his protection. The events known of his youth are few. He appears to have accompanied his uncle to Syria, and on that journey Mohammedans place the absurd legend of Sergius, Djerzi, or Bahyra recognising the boy as the future prophet by a mark between his shoulders. During the wars of the tribes known as the wars of the Fidjar, he is reported to have been present at one battle when he was fourteen, and to have picked up arrows for his uncle; at twenty he was keeping sheep for something like a farthing a day—an occupation considered disgraceful by the Arabs, and abandoned to slaves and women. But Mahomet always loved to dwell on the fact that Moses, and Jacob, and David had been shepherds before him, and indeed the race of visionaries and prophets has generally been largely recruited among shepherds and herdsmen. Not long afterwards he entered the service of Khadidja, a wealthy trading widow with three children, as camel-driver of the caravans which she despatched to the different markets of Arabia and Syria,*

* Many illustrations are taken in the Coran from the camel-driver's and the caravan merchant's vocabulary, such as the necessity of having *Hoda* or guidance in difficult passages.

and rose by his good conduct to be master of the caravan, a position of confidence. He was found a good man of business, and to have an acute perception of the market value of the striped stuffs and incense of Yemen, and the leather of Arabia, which he exchanged in the markets of Syria for corn and oil, and the silk goods of Damascus, while his long monotonous marches across the desert with his long file of camels were perhaps spent in meditation. His good qualities gained him the title of '*El Amin*'—the honest fellow. He was of comely appearance, and Khadidja, in spite of being fifteen years older than Mahomet — an immense difference in a country like Arabia—conceived the project of marrying him, and carried it into execution. For such a marriage, Mahomet seems to have been an exemplary husband. He married another wife, it is true, in two months after Khadidja's death ; but he never ceased to speak of his deceased wife in such terms of praise, that Ayesha declared she was the only one of the Prophet's wives of whom she had ever felt jealous. Seven children were the result of this marriage; and throughout the East crowds of green turbans claim to be descended from some one of the three daughters who survived. There were three sons, who all died young—one was called Abd Manaf, after the idol, which proves that Mahomet was at that time still an idolater. The last daughter, Fatima, was born eleven years after the marriage—when Khadidja was beyond fifty.

Four years after the birth of Fatima he had his first vision, and in connexion with that event some considerations are necessary respecting his mental and bodily constitution.

Whatever may have been the superiority of his moral character, it is certain that he was as unlike the most esteemed type of Arab manliness as it is possible to conceive. Nowhere in the world does man reach such a degree of dauntless independence as the Arab, educated in the freedom of the desert, and exposed to its hourly and daily vicissitudes of destiny. The ideal of the Arab was a fiery-souled irresistible warrior, always in sight of his tribe, bold in speech, rapid with song and repartee, indulging in wine, feasting, gambling, and love of women, holding tears to be disgraceful, with limbs as iron as his armour, supporting without suffering the heat of the desert under an Arabian sun, delighting in the beauty and swiftness of his steed or of his camel, impassioned for the chase, a match unarmed for the lion, indefatigable in combat, and routing like Antar whole armies with his single spear and shield. Recent travellers have confirmed the experience of ages, that the Bedouin have the least religious sensibility of any known race—at the present time they are mere Mohammedans in name, and never utter a prayer, or if they perform any religious rites at all, these may possibly be some lingering relic of the old Sabæan adoration of the rising sun. In the days of Mahomet, the people of Mecca upheld the worship of their idols from motives of gain, but Arabs in general had little respect for them, and treated them worse than Neapolitans have ever treated a refractory saint. If the prophecies of their *kalim*, seers or holy men, did not concur with their wishes, they often put them to death. When Amrolcais commenced an expedition to avenge the death of his father, he entered, according to custom, the temple of the idol Dhou-l-Kholosa, to obtain his approbation by means of the divining arrow. Drawing the wrong arrows three times in succession, he broke them all, and threw them at the head of the idol, saying : ' Wretch ! if your father had been killed, you would ' not forbid revenge for his death !'

Mahomet was directly the opposite of such an ideal ; he had inherited from his mother a delicate, nervous, and extremely impressionable constitution. He was gifted with an exaggerated and sickly sensibility ; he had a woman's love for fine scents and perfumes ; he was melancholy, silent, fond of desert places, solitary walks, and lonely meditations at set of sun in the valleys; full of vague restlessness, weeping and sobbing like a child when he was in pain; subject to attacks of epilepsy, and without courage in the field of battle. In addition to all which he had religious exciteability of the most acute character.

Dr. Sprenger goes at great length into an investigation of the physical and psychological nature of Mahomet; as a member of the medical profession his opinion is of value, the more so as he supports it with the authority of Schönlein, one of the most learned and patient investigators of the phenomena exhibited by hysterical persons, among whom he classes Mahomet. We can do no more than state the results of his diagnosis respecting Mahomet. His opinion is, that the Prophet suffered from two distinct kinds of *hysteria*, —the *hysteria muscularis*, and the *hysteria cephalica*. Concordant testimony proves that Mahomet had occasional fits; that he fell to the ground without sense, turned red in the face, and ' snored like a camel.' This, according to Dr. Sprenger, was the result of the *hysteria muscularis*, in its most violent form. In these severe attacks the will was entirely overpowered, and utter insensibility ensued; but there are lighter forms of this disease, in which the will is still able, after a severe struggle, to maintain its mastery. The *hysteria cephalica* announced itself by pains in the head and immense oppression, followed by illusions and fancies of the most vivid character. *Hysteria*, in its general form, although more prevalent among women than men, is by no means confined to the former—all visionaries of all ages have been for the most part hysterical: and it is an acute observation of M. Renan, in treating of the saints of the middle ages, that visionaries always reflect the character of the prevalent superstitions, and illusions of their time. 'Being a lady's disease,' Dr. Sprenger says, ' like a lady, it follows the fashion.' In the middle ages visionaries were beset with evil spirits, or had celestial visitants. In the days of witchcraft, some believed themselves to be witches. A short time back animal magnetisers, clairvoyants, and *somnambulists*, found plenty of disciples and subjects; and in our own days still more absurd spiritual hallucinations have prevailed.

Indeed, a tendency to hallucination is the almost invariable concomitant of the hysterical affection. Hallucination is turned by the hysterical patient into an indisputable and cardinal fact; becomes a part of his theory of life and consciousness, and all other considerations and evidences are made to support it. From being self-deceived, the patient proceeds by inappreciable modes of reasoning, to the deception of others. Schönlein even goes so far as to say, ' all hysteric persons have more or less a tendency ' to lying and deception, and this tendency becomes inve- ' terate.' In support of this statement, Dr. Sprenger cites a number of instances of the extreme amount of suffering which people have undergone to make other people believe in their hallucinations — of girls, young and apparently innocent, who have thrust needles under their nails; of both men and women who have counterfeited the mark of the *stigmata;* and of the prevalence of a particular fashion of deceit in consequence of the success of one striking example. But what is equally distinctive of this form of disease is the belief in inspiration and in the habitual society of spirits and demons. Socrates had his demon; Tasso had his demon, with whom he was heard continually to converse; Swedenborg was habitually overheard talking to his celestial visitant. As to Socrates, we have not perhaps sufficient data; but as to Tasso and Swedenborg there can be little doubt, and the description of the cataleptic fits into which the latter fell, and out of which he awoke with a face bathed in perspiration, forms the exact parallel of the description of the cataleptic attacks of Mahomet. To these mental phenomena the German writers to whom we have referred, add a multitude of considerations on the physical constitution of Mahomet, which it would here be out of place to discuss.

With such a nature, so morbidly sensitive to emotion, and especially those of a religious character, Mahomet was thrown into contact with Zeid and Waraka, and others in search of a purer faith. From what we have stated of Zeid and the poetry he has left behind him, it may be concluded that he possessed the evangelical nature in a far higher degree than Mahomet; a romantic and almost saintly interest attaches to his premature death in the search after a purer faith. He was, as we have said, banished to the hill of Hira, which was also a favourite retreat of Mahomet; and there is a trustworthy tradition of their meeting on one occasion, when Zeid fervently exhorted Mahomet not to weary in the search after the true God. In addition to this, the feeling of retribution, and the awe accompanying the growing conviction of a future state, had peopled the deserts and Thebaids with anchorites and penitents; and in Mahomet's journeys into Syria it was impossible that he should escape the influence of these ideas. Under such predisposing circumstances, and after a terrible conflict in his soul of religious doubts and enthusiasm, which had lasted for six months, it happened in the year 612 that Mahomet, in the course of one of his solitary wanderings in Mount Hira, entered a cave where he used to seek refuge from the heat. In order to form a conception of his state of mind, it is necessary to realise not only the condition of the man, but the scene and tenor of his first revelation. A hill looking like a fragment of a burnt volcano—not a sound of insect or murmuring stream—no grass or flower or shade—the rocks all herbless and black, as though recently ejected from the central fire of the earth—here and there abysses and steep precipices—ravines whose depths were strewn with hot rubble and fragments of stone, and the whole calcined soil heated to a degree capable of scorching the eyes of the head, of blistering the soles of the feet, and of making every nerve quiver with preternatural excitement. In such circumstances the Arabian prophet had his first vision, a vision of a supernatural being—he was not clear for a long time whether it was a Djinn or an angel—who said :—

    ' Recite in the name of the Lord, thy Creator.
    He hath made man out of clots of blood.

Speak out, for thy Lord is the mightiest
Of all who have instructed through the pen.
He taught man what he did not know.' *

This revelation, however, by no means made more light the
state of religious oppression under which Mahomet was labouring. On the contrary, his gloomy doubts and frenzied state of
mind were only increased by it. It was two years before a second
revelation occurred to him, a period called by the Mussulmans
the Fitreh or Pause ; and during all that time he was su-
premely miserable. So far from ascribing the visit in the cave
at Hira to an angel, he imagined that he was pursued by
djinn ; and he wandered about the hills like a madman, striding up and down the mountains of Thabyr and Hira, and
determining from time to time to throw himself off some preci-
pice and end a dreadful existence. He heard the voices of
spirits calling him, and the rocks and stones addressed him by
name. In this state of mind he had a second vision, but this
time the hallucination was one of sight only ; wandering about
on those desolate, burning hills, the unhappy man's eyes were
cheered by the sight of the ' *Sidra-tree,*' the Lote-tree, which

---

* The singular expression, 'the mightiest of all who have in-
' structed through the pen,' has, so far as we are aware of, excited no
remark. Such an expression must have been elicited from Mahomet
by some predisposing train of circumstances ; indeed there are numbers of singular expressions of the Coran which are explained only
by the consideration of the events which brought them forth. In the
present case we imagine the explanation to be this :—Mahomet
was full of religious yearning for the immediate knowledge of the
one true God ; but he was an uneducated man, and did not know
how to write or read, while he had been in contact with the
Jews, called commonly the 'people of the book,' with the Hanyfs
who had their 'rolls,' and with the Christians who had also their sacred
books. The religious crisis through which Mahomet had passed must
have been rendered more intense by the conflicting claims of these
three 'people of the book,' taught by those who 'instructed
'with the pen.' Moreover, as an Arab of a noble race, he would
naturally feel humiliated and oppressed at having to appeal to other
tribes and nations for a knowledge of the one true God. Hence the
spirit relieves his mind of the first distressing doubt and tells him
that his Lord is the true Lord, mightiest of all who have 'instructed
'with the pen.' It is singular also that the word he uses here for
'Lord' is not Allah, the most usual Arabian expression, and which
occurs three thousand times in the Coran, but Rabb. Now the
word used by the Christians was Al-Rabb, which expression
Mahomet carefully avoids ; he does not use ' Al-Rabb,' that expression denoting the God of the Christians. But the angel says ' thy
' Rabb ' in this place.

stands on the outer border of Paradise; and then at last a celestial visitor appeared with these ever-memorable words:—

> Now, by the pen, and what can be written therewith,
> Thou art, by the grace of God, no '*majnun*' (no possessed person),
> But an endless reward awaiteth thee.

After this third revelation Mahomet fell to the ground as though dead. On recovering his senses, he still remained utterly exhausted, and was aware that he was going to have another hysteric attack. His first words to Khadidja and a friend who was with her on entering were, ' Cover me up, ' cover me up.' They covered him up and threw water on his face. Then an angel awoke him from trance with these words of a Sura, one of the most remarkable in the Coran:—

> ' O thou covered up,
> Arise and give warning
> And praise thy Lord,
> And cleanse thy garment,
> Avoid the abomination (of idol-worship),
> Be not selfish in your going forth,
> Suffer for the Lord.'

After this he was convinced of his mission. He with his wife, Khadidja, went for advice to Waraka, the Hanyf, who had buried himself in the Jewish and Christian Scriptures, in searching for the true God; and Waraka told him he had been visited by the great ' Namous,' which is supposed to be Waraka's Arabic for the Greek ' Nomos,' or the Law. Relieved thus from the terror of being possessed by demons, his spirit was full of joy and thankfulness, and then ensued revelations like the following, which is a kind of Moslem ' *Magnificat*,' after the reading of which in the mosques all the congregation cry aloud ' *Allah akbar*.' The rhymes will give some notion of the peculiar rhymed prose so grateful to an Arab ear.

> ' I swear by the splendour of light,
> And by the silence of night,
> Thut the Lord shall never forsake thee nor in his hatred take thee,
> Truly for thee shall be winning, better than all beginning,
> Soon shall the Lord console thee, grief no longer control thee, and fear no longer cajole thee.
> Thou wert an orphan-boy, yet the Lord found home for thy head,
> When thy feet went astray, were they not to the right path led?
> Did he not find thee poor, yet riches around thee spread ?
> Then on the orphan-boy let thy proud feet never tread,
> And never turn away the beggar who seeks for bread,
> But of the Lord's bounty ever let praise be sung and said.'

His first converts after Khadidja, his wife, were the faithful and affectionate Zeid, one of his slaves, and Ali his cousin, a bold spirited youth then only ten years of age ; but the most important acquisition was Abubeker, a man a few years younger than himself, a merchant of good repute and having a fortune amounting to 40,000 dirhems. In obedience to the commands of the angels, he and his disciples now passed whole nights in prayer, and in repeating the ' *la illa illa illah,*' ' there is no God ' but Allah,' without intermission, a mechanical exercise which, like the whirling of the dervishes and the passes of the animal magnetiser, ends by throwing the neophyte into a highly nervous condition. Mahomet and his disciples practised this night discipline with such assiduity that their feet became swollen and their health suffered. When he began to make open claims, however, to inspiration, the assumption of the prophetic character was at first treated by his sceptical tribesmen with unrestrained ridicule and contempt. ' Here comes the ' son of Abdallah,' they would say, ' with the last news from ' heaven.' They would ask him ' what the weather would be a ' week hence,' ' what the prices of the markets would be next ' fair-time,' and tell him he had a fine opportunity of making a fortune. They would also bring him a pregnant woman, and ask him whether the child would be a male or a female; and they would offer, with an air of too benevolent interest, to send for a doctor for him to take care of his health. When, to make more impression on their incredulity, Mahomet began to talk of the Resurrection, they said, ' If our fathers are going to live again, ' bring us back one or two of them and we will believe.' He then began to recite stories of the destruction of wicked races who had refused to listen to their prophets—of the destruction of the world in the time of Noah—of the destruction by showers of stones of the Thamudites, a race recorded in the Rolls of the Hanyfs, for refusing to listen to the voice of Houd their prophet—of the similar destruction of the Adites, a race equally celebrated in the books of the Hanyfs. To such reasoning, and to actual menaces of temporal punishment, they would reply, ' Let it rain stones, let the sky come down, and then we will see.' When the temporal punishments with which he menaced them were so long in coming that their incredulous spirits grew more sarcastic still, he began to talk of the approach of the day of the last judgment; * and for this topic, by the aid of the poetry

---

* He used to say 'My mission and the day of resurrection are ' as far apart as my thumb from my forefinger.'

and vigour of his style, he obtained a greater degree of attention, for no race were ever more carried away by beauty of language and grace of style than the Arabs. He met, however, with no open persecution till he openly attacked the idols of the Caaba. And when he began to do this the governing class of Mecca, the ' *Mala*,' at first reasoned with him in a serious and considerate manner as to the impropriety of his conduct; but when they found his pertinacity was invincible, and perhaps somewhat ashamed themselves of the heterogeneous population of the Caaba, they were willing to make a bargain. At first they offered that in alternate years he should worship the idols, and they should give them up, and be decided by the most prosperous result. At last they offered as a compromise, to let all the rest of the idols go if he would retain Lat, Ozza, and Manah. Without the aid of these divinities the Meccans hardly considered existence possible.

For these were the favourite deities of the surrounding tribes, who might at any time place Mecca in a state of blockade, put an end to the caravan trade, ruin its fairs, and stop its pilgrimages and revenues. The wild Kinana races, that swarmed between Mecca and the Red Sea, of which the tribe of the Coreish was itself a member, were adorers of Ozza, an idol which was in reality a tree at Nackla. Various tribes of Yemenite origin to the south-east of Mecca adored Manah, which was a rock, and Lat was the idol of the people of Tayif, the nearest and most important town near Mecca. If Lat, Ozza, and Manah were treated with indignity, retaliation would evidently be made upon the black stone of the Caaba. Mahomet himself at last yielded to the force of this line of argument, and consented to allow Lat, and Ozza, and Manah, to have representatives in the Caaba; and, moreover, he agreed to have an inspiration which should say a good word for these popular divinities. Accordingly, on one of the days of his public preaching, he inserted these words in a reading of the Coran: ' Lat, Ozza, and Manah, are illustrious (*Gharanyk*) ' intercessors.' At these words, the Coreish cried out in a body in applause; and when at the conclusion he called all his hearers to prostrate themselves at the name of Allah, they all did so with extreme enthusiasm; one fat and aged devotee, unable to kneel with the rest, in his desire to show his perfect acquiescence, took up dust in his hand from the ground and placed it on his forehead. Either from the remonstrances, however, of his friends and advisers, or stung by the contemptuous expressions of his enemies, or from unassisted repentance, or because he saw this concession would ruin his whole career as Prophet, Mahomet soon withdrew these words; and shortly after in the pulpit declared that the passage had been whispered to him by Satan, whose voice he had mistaken for Gabriel's, and said that he utterly repudiated Lat, and Ozza, and Manah, thenceforth and for ever. This made matters with the Coreish far worse than before; and it would have fared ill with Mahomet had he not been under the protection of his uncle, Abou Talib. Abou Talib was a poor man, but he rejoiced in the strength of eight strong sons, all in fighting condition; and the possession of so much combative power entitled him there and then, as it would now in the western settlements of America, to much respect. Abou Talib, although he lived and died a heathen, was not only inclined to protect his nephew, as he had done from childhood, but he was bound to do so by the custom of his tribe. In a lawless state of society like Arabia, to grant protection to those who sought it was, with hospitality, one of the chief duties of man. As soon as any one confessed his weakness, so far as to claim protection of another, the latter was bound to defend him at the cost of his own life, and of that of the lives of his family; another corollary to this rule was, that it was considered disgraceful to a family for any member of it to have to seek for protection out of the family. Consequently, if a member of any family felt himself oppressed by his own kinsfolk, he had generally only to threaten to seek for protection elsewhere, in order to secure good treatment.

- When the Coreish found that Mahomet was intractable in the matter of Lat, Ozza, and Manah, they came to Abou Talib in deputation, and asked him courteously either to make his nephew desist from throwing contempt on the ways of their ancestors, or to withdraw his protection from him. To which Abou Talib replied, ' I believe in him just as ' little as you do; but I have no power to make him leave off.' Seeing how troublesome the Prophet was likely to be, one of the members most in repute in the Coreish, Otba Ebn Rebia, came courteously up to Mahomet as he was sitting in the court of the Caaba in the presence of other members of the Coreish, and said, ' Son of my friend, you are a man distin- ' guished for your talents and your truth. Although you are ' stirring up discord in your country and division among fami- ' lies; although you insult our gods, and accuse our ancestors ' and sages of impiety and folly, we wish to deal gently with ' you. Listen to the propositions which I have to make to

' you, and reflect if you cannot accept some of them.' ' Speak,'
said Mahomet, ' I listen.' ' Son of my friend,' said Otba ; ' if
' your aim be wealth, we will all put our purses together, and
' make you rich ; if you would have honour, we will elect you
' chief; or if the spirit who attaches itself to you still perse-
' cutes you, able physicians shall be sent for, and we will pay
' them to cure you.' To which Mahomet replied that he
wanted none of these things, but that he was the chosen prophet of Allah. ' Well then,' said the Coreishites, coming round
him, ' since you do not accept our proposals, and you pretend
' to have a mission from Allah, give us some proof that such is
' the case. Our valley is narrow and barren, ask God to
' make it wider—that he thrust back the two chains of moun-
' tains which close it up—that he make rivers flow here equal
' to the rivers of Syria and Irak—or that some of our ances-
' tors, with Cossai among them, shall revive to recognise you
' as a prophet, then we will do so too.' Mahomet said that
God had not entrusted him with any such power, but only to
preach the law. ' At least,' continued the Coreishites ; ' de-
' mand of thy Lord that some one of his angels shall come and
' bear witness to your truth, and order us to place belief in
' you ; or ask him to dispense you from being obliged to seek
' your daily bread like the least of us.' ' No,' said Mahomet,
' I will make no such request ; my duty is only to preach !'—
' Well then, let thy Lord cause the heavens to fall upon us, as
' thou sayest he can ; but we will not believe thee.'

In fact the only ruse which Mahomet practised in order to
convince people he was a prophet was a very simple, not to say
clumsy device, for it was open to easy detection, and the use
of such practices is sufficient proof that imposture had begun
to mix itself up largely with his religious enthusiasm. He
gave out accounts, from the histories of former prophets, as
having been received by inspiration, when he was in fact
prompted by the Hanyf or Jew Christian, Bahyra, who remained behind the scenes, and then called upon either his
mentor or some one else to state if it was not true. Mahomet's
argument was how could an ignorant Arab know such minute
events of past times except by inspiration—and these accounts
of mine, are they not in good Arabic, while the original stories
are in Hebrew or Aramaic ? Such arguments, however, made
little progress, and, moreover, there is reason to believe that
he was convicted before the most acute members of the Coreish of having confounded the books of the Hanyfs, which
were recent forgeries, with the Bible of the Jews ; and he

incurred increased contempt in consequence. Nevertheless the number of his disciples increased in spite of persecution, which now began in earnest. Slaves at first formed the greater proportion of converts, and as these, from their defenceless condition, were more subject to persecution than the rest, the wealthy man of the new religion, Aboubekr, purchased their manumission. Persecution soon grew so severe that a portion of the disciples made a temporary emigration into Abyssinia. Slaves were at this time taken and placed naked on the scorching sand at midday, others were prevented from obtaining water during the raging heat. The free men of the new religion were subject to every public insult. Boys were encouraged to follow Mahomet and torment him as he walked abroad—they pelted him with stones till his feet bled, and passers-by spat in his face. Sometimes they seized him by the throat till he was nearly strangled, and dirt and filth were heaped at his door, which he was obliged to remove himself. It cannot be wondered, indeed, that all Meccans who did not believe in the Prophet should have little friendly feeling towards him, since his favourite argument to persuade men to his belief was that all worshippers of idols, including his own ancestors, were in hell, an argument which Abou Djahl, his most malignant persecutor in Mecca, turned against him to deprive him of the protection of his uncle Abou Lahab. After the death of Abou Talib, Abou Lahab came to Mahomet and told him to have no fear, he would now take upon him his protection, and take the place of Abou Talib. Whereupon Abou Djahl went about crying, ' Abou Lahab is become a Sabian ' (the name they gave the disciples of Mahomet). As this, however, had no effect, he went to Abou Lahab and said, ' How can you protect a ' man who says your father is in hell?' Upon which Abou Lahab went to Mahomet and said, ' Where is my father?' to which Mahomet replied, evasively, ' With his people.' Abou Lahab went away contented, but returned again at the suggestion of Abou Djahl, and said, ' Where are my father's ' people?' Mahomet answered, ' In hell.' Then Abou Lahab said, ' Now, Mahomet, I will never cease to be thy enemy.' And this he became in future, following Mahomet about and calling upon the people and pilgrims as he preached not to be seduced by his follies. Aboubekr at this time was Mahomet's chief support, and Aboubekr recited the Coran publicly in front of his own house day by day, and visited Mahomet in his own house twice daily.

But now the members of the Coreish made a league against the Haschimites, Mahomet's branch of the Cossai family. In this league the Ommeyades, with Abou Sophyan for their head, bound themselves not to intermarry with the Haschimites, not to trade with them, and not to permit them to join their caravans, which, as the Haschimites were not strong enough to form caravans of their own, and there was no other source of income open to them, was equivalent to placing them in a state of siege, in which condition they remained for three years, the Haschimites, to avoid further persecution, betaking themselves to the Sheb, or quarter of Abou Taleb, and there shutting themselves up, subject to every privation. At length, however, their moans of hunger and the lamentations of their women and children wrought the Coreishites to pity, and the persecution of the Haschimites was relaxed. Mahomet, however, was still so hardly used that he fled to Tayif and tried to obtain a hearing there. He was, however, treated with contumely and scorn, and driven out of the town amid a shower of stones, and departed with his legs streaming with blood.

Amid all these persecutions he had received the adhesion of one strong spirit, who was indeed the virtual founder of Islam; for it may be said that the name of Mahomet would not now be heard of had it not been for the vehement energy which Omar, a young man of twenty-six, threw into the creed, and the watchfulness and unhesitating decision with which he maintained its integrity to his death. Like St. Paul, he too previous to his conversion had been known only as a violent persecutor of the new creed. For tradition says that on one occasion, in the height of his wrath against the Prophet, when he had already resolved, sabre in hand, to kill him, he was overcome by the beauty of a passage of the Coran, which was read to him by some members of his family. Henceforth Omar, in company with Aboubekr, kept watch over Mahomet like a child. Aboubekr was the calm prudent man of business, the cool head of the new sect, while the fiery Omar, whose whole body was full of irresistible energy, whose left arm was as strong as his right, provided all the vigour and decision. His impassioned straightforward course of action saved the Prophet from many a weakness and many ignominious concessions. Nor did he confine his attention to public matters. For in later time, when a revolt took place in the Prophet's Hareem, he would break in among the affrighted women stick in hand and reduce them to order and submission.

Ten long years, however, thus passed while Mahomet and his disciples were undergoing the terrible ordeal of persecution. Khadidja died; her death was speedily followed by that of Abou Taleb, and Mahomet's life was no longer safe.

Assassination had frequently been proposed to Abou Taleb as the simplest way of settling the difficulty, but he had always replied, ' You lie, by the Holy Temple, if you say that we will ' allow the blood of Mahomet to be shed without fighting ' with the bow and lance.' After Mahomet had told his other uncle Abou Lahab that his father was in hell, he had nothing but persecution to look for in that quarter, and things for him appeared to be at their very darkest, when an unhoped-for asylum for the new creed was offered by another and a fairer city, which was destined to be and to pay the penalty for being the foster-city of Islam and the Defender of the Prophet.

About a mile and a half from Mecca, on an eminence on the road to Mina, stands a small mosque, erected in celebration of an event which has had no small influence on the history of mankind, and through which Mahomet's teaching was emancipated from the confinement and persecution of Mecca, and took its place among the great religions of the world. On the day when the pilgrims flocked to the valley of Mina to throw the customary stones there, at a turning of the hill below the present mosque, called *Akaba* (as being a corner), Mahomet came suddenly upon a troop of six pilgrims. ' Of what tribe are you?' said Mahomet. ' Of the ' tribe of the Khazradjs.' ' Then you are allies of the Jews?' ' Yes.' ' Then let us sit down and talk.' To be oppressed by the Maadites was a recommendation to a Yemenite, even on behalf of a Maadite. Consequently the Khazradjs, who were Yemenites, listened with interest to Mahomet's exposition of his creed and to his exhortations, which they were more capable of comprehending and taking to heart than the Meccans, from their peculiar position at Medina.

Medina, or the city called Yathrib before the time of Mahomet, and known to Ptolemy as Jathryppa, is situated in a hollow among the hills, one of the few sporadic fertile oases which dot—at immense distances apart—the sandy stony soil of Arabia—situated in the skirts of the bare volcanic region of Harra, and twelve days' camel-journey from Mecca. Its inhabitants have from time immemorial been agriculturists, and cultivation is probably here almost as old as the human race. The spot is famed for its sweet waters, for the size and flavour of its dates and the smallness of their stones. Arab tradition declares the earliest inhabitants of Medina to have been ' *Amalika*,' Amalekites, the descendants of Esau. They possessed at one time the whole of the northern part of the peninsula of Arabia, extending some way out of Syria, and bordering on Egypt in their possession of Petra. Chaibhar was the strongest capital city of this part of Arabia, and in its neighbourhood Job appears to have lived. This position of the Amalekites accords with Scripture, which always places that warrior race in the south. The supremacy of the country passed into the hands of the Jews, who began to settle there after the successful campaign of Saul and David, when ' Saul ' smote the Amalekites from Havilah unto Shur which is over ' against Egypt.' The Amalekites were, probably, absorbed by the more powerful nationality of their conquerors. The Jews remained there in great numbers even after the cruel per-secutions of Mahomet, until in accordance with his policy that the Arabian peninsula should be inhabited by none but his own followers, Omar in his caliphate drove the whole of them over the borders into Syria.

Three Jewish tribes, the Benou Kainoka, the Benou Nadhyr, and the Benou Coraitza, though always involved in discord and warfare, shared Medina between them until the tribes of the Awzs and the Khazradjs appeared upon the scene in the fourth century, and after wandering about the country for some time in a starving condition, by treachery and mas-sacre overcame the Jews, and assumed the supremacy in Medina, then called Yathrib.* The tribes of the Awzs and Khazradjs were themselves noted throughout all Arabia for the inveterate and sanguinary character of their wars with each other, and had been for the forty years immediately preceding Mahomet's mission in a constant state of war-fare. The Benou Kainoka, Nadhyr and Coraitza, far from taking advantage of this state of things to unite against their invaders, were themselves divided by so many sangui-nary feuds and memories of ancient hatred, that they ranged themselves in the opposite ranks of the hostile Yemenite tribes, a short-sighted policy which ended in their destruction. These Yemenite Arabs and idolaters were thus living among a race of Jews possessing the majestic records of the Hebrew people, proud of their superiority as the chosen race and as

---

* Dr. Sprenger thinks the Awzs and the Khazradjs came to Medina in the fourth, M. Caussin de Perceval in the second century. Their immigration took place probably about the same time that the Yemenite Khoza tribe settled at Mecca. Arabia was evidently plunged into great disorder at various epochs by the failure of the commercial wealth which had maintained the immense populations of Yemen and Petra, as well as by the decline of the caravan trade which cast thousands of Arabs adrift without resources and without occupation.

worshippers of the one true God, and in all probability quite as enlightened as the wealthy communities of Jews settled at Damascus or Aleppo at the present day, where the rich display and decorations of their houses form an object of curiosity to the traveller. The Arabs of Medina, nevertheless, lived in close communion with their Jewish townsmen. Proselytism was not uncommon, and intermarriages took place between the Jews and their outside Semitic brethren as they did in the days of Ruth. But the Yemenite Arabs had their pride constantly humiliated not only by the claims of the Jews to superiority as the chosen people of the one true God, of whom Mahomet now spoke to them; but in dispute with their Jewish townsmen, the latter would constantly triumph over them, with a threat of their approaching Messiah, saying, 'Wait till our Messiah appear and he will strike you dead.' Therefore, when Mahomet began to preach to them the '*Allah ta-Allah*,' they not only were inclined to believe in him on account of having often heard the same doctrine before; but they conceived the notion that this must be the Messiah the Jews spoke of, and they determined to be beforehand with their Jewish allies in securing his favour. They listened then eagerly to the words of Mahomet, agreed to spread his doctrine among their townspeople, and with sensible reflection on their own long and sanguinary hostilities, said, 'There has been 'more disunion among our tribes than among any other, and 'if you can unite us you must be the greatest man on earth.'

In the following year more Khazradjs came to Mecca to the pilgrimage, accompanied by the original six. They swore at a midnight meeting at the hill of Akaba, to receive and remain faithful to the doctrine of Mahomet, and asked for a disciple who should instruct themselves and their fellow-citizens in the faith. The next year a greater number of pilgrims from Medina held with Mahomet another midnight meeting at the same hill of Akaba, and amid great enthusiasm, swore to adopt and maintain his faith, to receive him in their city, and to defend his life and doctrine with the utmost sacrifice of life and property. The first of these midnight oaths at Akaba is called the woman's oath, and the second the man's, because fighting was undertaken by the second and not by the first, and it is most probable that during the course of the year that intervened between the two oaths Mahomet had resolved on that change of policy with respect to his doctrine which signalised his flight from Mecca. The Meccans had full information of the proceedings at the second midnight meeting at the Akaba, as their spies were present. They were furious at the notion of their persecuted tribesman finding protection in hostile clans, whom they hated the more as being in close amity with Jews, and they feared that he might find means to exact retribution for past sufferings by the ruin of their commerce, and the degradation of the holy city. It is even said that they determined in public council, under the presidency of Abou Sophyan the Ommeyade chief, in the very hall of Cossai, to have him assassinated. Meanwhile Mahomet with his followers was making daily preparations to escape to Medina. One by one they got away, till no Moslems were left in Mecca but Mahomet, Abubekr and Ali. For four months a camel had been waiting in readiness for the flight of the Prophet. At last he escaped, on the very night, as it is said, that they had resolved to assassinate him, and after the famous sojourn for three days in a cave to baffle pursuit, reached Medina with Abubekr, in sixteen days after his escape from Mecca.

The Moslems have been guided by a true instinct in dating their religion from the *Hijra*, the flight to Medina, for the religion of Mahomet changed its complexion completely in changing its abode. The different character of the two oaths which he tendered to the deputies of Medina, on the hill of Akaba, indicates that his ideas of the policy necessary to establish his prophetic ascendency had undergone an entire change in the interim; and when we consider both human nature at large and his own special idiosyncrasy, does it seem possible that it could be otherwise? After ten years of incessant persecution, ignominy, contempt, degradation, and defilement, after being shut up with sceptics, scoffers, and tormentors, amid the burning hovels of Mecca, an offer was made to him of assistance and protection in the most cultivated and civilised town of Arabia; and it was not possible but that a man of his great political genius and perspicacity should at once see the immense new horizon thus laid open to the prospects of his ambition. To escape from the midst of his fiendish enemies, harass their caravans by Bedouin *razzias*, unite the wild tribes of the desert with the friendly tribes of Medina, and come back to impose his creed on the scoffing and sceptical guardians of the holy temple, must have been his dream day and night, from the moment that overtures were made to him by the Khazradjs, and such a result the Meccans themselves apprehended.

From that date Islam became another creed. Before the *Hijra*, *Taksa*—patience, resignation to the wrongs inflicted by man in submission to God, was the cardinal virtue of Mahomet's religious morality. After the *Hijra*, the merit of fighting for it with the sword surpassed all other merit whatsoever. The sword henceforward was the key both of heaven and hell; and a drop of blood shed in the cause of God was to be of more avail than two months' fasting and prayer: to the slain in battle all sins were immediately forgiven, and the wretch whose life had been sullied by every crime and iniquity was at once wafted up to Paradise, and there enjoyed in the arms of dark-eyed houris an eternal round of sensual felicity.

The authority which Mahomet enjoyed in Medina was unbounded; from a poor persecuted wretch stoned, jeered at by boys, and spat upon by men, he became at one leap the irresponsible head of a theocratic government. His first measures were taken with great wisdom. It cannot be denied that however much a critical examination of his career may lessen his character for sincerity, the estimate of his ability as a crafty politician must be increased by it. For example, on his entry into Medina, it was a difficult matter to decide at whose house he should first alight; he could not name any one individual among so many aspirants of equal rank without wounding many susceptibilities. Mahomet avoided the difficulty by telling them to let his camel find her own way through the streets, that she had the command of God to stay at whatever house might please them best. This, though a trifling example, manifests sufficiently the subtlety of policy which he had ever at command for the solution of every difficulty. The angel Gabriel was the *deus ex machinâ*, who settled every doubt and every dispute. Thus if the question were asked whether or no a plundering expedition should be undertaken—in what way the booty was to be divided—whether a whole tribe was to be put to death—what prayer and ceremonies should be used in Moslem worship—whether or no he should add a new wife to his bevy—either the angel Gabriel was close at hand with a verse or two of the Coran, or he was able to get up an inspiration at a moment's notice; and not only could he thus improvise fresh inspirations, but he could make amendments in the old in the same manner. Thus, on one occasion, after he had promulgated a verse of the Coran denouncing future punishment against those who remained at home and kept away from the field of battle, some of the Moslems brought him a blind old man, and asked him if it were just that such should suffer the punishment. 'Insert,' he said, turning to Zeid, his secretary, 'except such as suffer from infirmity.'

His first care on arriving at Medina was to settle the rites of the new creed; he built a humble mosque of burnt tiles with a roof of palm leaves which leaned over and formed a verandah supported by palm-tree trunks; round a court on one side of the mosque, habitations were erected for his thirteen wives as they arrived one after the other; he changed his wife every day, and lived for the day in the habitation of the wife thus honoured. Hangings in these huts took the place of doors; their roofs might be touched with the hand; and under their verandahs and that of the mosque slept about thirty or forty fugitives from Mecca, who had no roof to their heads, and were called the companions of the Prophet. These men were styled the *Ahl-el-soffa*, the people of the bench, and as they lived much with Mahomet, eating and drinking with him and at his expense, they became the sources of innumerable traditions respecting his habits and manner of life. For the *Mohadjir*, as the fugitives from Mecca were called, arrived for the most part at Medina in an utterly destitute condition; some thirty or forty of them were seen for a long time walking about destitute of all clothes but mere rags held together by thorns. Ayesha said that at this time the Prophet and his wives suffered much from want of sufficient food. Once he was three days without tasting bread. The *Ansar*, however, or the 'Defenders,' as the people of Medina were called, extended towards the followers of Mahomet the utmost hospitality; and one of the first cares of the prophet was to draw up a regular treaty in which the mutual duties of *Ansar* and *Mohadjir* were defined, and the inner constitution of Medina set forth in a series of provisions which evinced no mean capacity as a lawgiver.

Nothing, indeed, could exceed the singleness of heart and devotion with which the people of Medina gave themselves and their destiny into the hands of the Prophet; the *Ansar* were, under the guidance of Mahomet, the true founders of Islam, and they at least were sincere believers; yet such is the astonishing irony of destiny, that all the gathering evils, all the accumulating penalties of imposture and infidelity comprised in the Mahometan religion, were destined in less than sixty years from the Hijra to descend in one fell swoop on the very foster-city of Islam, and almost to blot it from the face of the earth. After the disastrous battle of Harra, in which the army of the infidel and voluptuous Yezid, the Caliph of Damascus, commanded by the cruel and one-eyed Moslim, a man not only not a Moslem, but a believer in the worst superstitions of pre-Mohammedan Bedouin heathenism, overthrew the army of Medina, slaughtered the sacred band of the aged companions of the Prophet, and left not alive a single representative of the victors of Badr, the foster-city of

Islam was given up to sack. The Syrian victors stabled their horses in the holy mosque itself, built by the hands of Mahomet, and fastened their halters in the very tomb and pulpit of the Prophet. The men of the town who refused to swear submission to the infidel Yezid were either slaughtered or branded with hot irons; the children were massacred or sold into bondage; the women violated, and the progeny of that horrible night are remembered in Arab history as the ' children ' of Harra.' The *Ansar* never recovered from that fatal day; their town remained for some time abandoned to dogs, their fields to the wild beasts; for the majority of the inhabitants sought a new country and a new fate in the army of Africa, and many of them had illustrious descendants among the Moors of Spain, for nearly all that remained of the ' defenders of the ' Prophet' crossed with Mousa over the Straits of Gibraltar. When a traveller of the thirteenth century, on passing through Medina, demanded if any of the descendants of the celebrated *Ansar* were still to be found in Medina, he was shown one decrepid old man and one old woman. Such was the recompense which the hospitality of the people of Medina was destined to receive.

After six months' repose, occupied in making political and religious ordinances, Mahomet proceeded to make open war upon his native city by attacking its caravans. The reasons of this policy were all-powerful—the desire of avenging his own injuries, of securing booty for the maintenance of his indigent companions in exile, and, above all, of keeping the spirit of the young religion in constant activity. Medina did not lie in the direct line of march of the caravans from Mecca to Syria, but a three days' journey from Medina was necessary to cut across their track. After some unsuccessful attempts, at length several caravans were plundered; and one rich column of a thousand camels, led by Abou Sophyan, on its return from Syria, ran a similar risk, when the Meccans marched with an army of about one thousand men to its support. Mahomet met them with only 324 combatants. The Ansar and the Mohadjir fought desperately. Mahomet had a cataleptic attack in the field, but recovered, and threw a handful of dust at the enemy; this, and his assurance that three thousand angels were fighting on the side of the Moslem, wrought such marvels that they utterly routed the Coreishites, and Mahomet had the satisfaction of being presented with the severed head of his lifelong and bitterest enemy, Abou Djahl. He exclaimed the present was dearer to him than the choicest camel in Arabia, fell on his knees, and thanked God for his mercies.

This was Mahomet's first victory; and just as it is clear that the certainty of material aid from Medina changed the whole character of his system of religious ethics, so this first victory of Badr inaugurated a new period of sanguinary and ruthless policy. Hitherto his hands had been soiled with no man's blood, but he scrupled not henceforward to shed it on any occasion when he could safely do so for the furtherance either of his ambition or revenge. Immediately after Badr, he signalised this change of policy by two cold-blooded murders, the one on a woman, and the other on an old man, against neither of whom had he any other ground of complaint than that they had attacked him in satirical verses. The woman's name was Asma. She was, it appears, a poetess. 'Who will rid me of 'this woman?' he inquired among his disciples; and he was accustomed henceforward to make a similar inquiry whenever he wanted to be rid of an enemy. A blind man of her tribe made the offer; he slunk to her house at dead of night, where, with the security of the Arabs, she was sleeping with unbolted doors; she was lying in slumber with her children. The blind man groped with his hand and found a babe lying across her breast; he removed the child and stabbed the mother as she slept, so that the sword pierced through her back bone. The murderer joined the Prophet at the mosque for morning prayer at daybreak; he told him what he had done, and on his expressing some anxiety lest her kindred should attempt to revenge the murder, the Prophet replied, 'Two goats will not 'butt together about her.' Turning to the congregation, he said, 'Behold a man who has served God and his Prophet 'well.' The murder of the old man was equally cruel. He was a Jew, and against the Jews Mahomet nursed a feeling of spite and revenge which knew no rest till he had compassed the destruction of the whole race in Northern Arabia. His treatment of the Jews became henceforward one of the most characteristic features of his policy.

Mahomet, in his pretensions as Prophet, could not but regard the Jews as a highly-favoured race, since God had himself raised a long line of prophets from among them; nor could he avoid respecting them as the only people in the peninsula who possessed a literature. It is clear from the chapters of the Coran composed at Medina, that their presence in that city exercised a salutary restraint on his inspirations. He no longer ventured to give out long mytho-biblical narratives as inspirations, when the 'people of the book' were there ready to confront him and convict him of imposture. Nevertheless he was bent on obtaining their recognition, and the

Jews were, on their side, ready to recognise him as a prophet for the heathen.   But Mahomet was not satisfied with this; he felt as long as there was a people dwelling side by side with his disciples, possessing superior knowledge and an older revelation embodied in writings whose authenticity none had even dared to place in doubt, his own religion could never stand on secure ground; and he determined to secure their adherence or to annihilate them.   Of his wish to conciliate them no higher proof is conceivable than his adopting Jerusalem as the *Kebla* for prayer for the first fifteen months of the Hijra.   To his claim to be considered as a prophet for the Jews, and his clumsy proofs of his mission, the learned rabbis of the Jewish tribes, one of which still claimed to be descended from Aaron himself, listened with supercilious contempt; and slights of this nature the Prophet was utterly unable to forgive or to forget. Unfortunately for the Jews, the divisions of their tribes and their mutual jealousies were so great, that they did not permit them to unite in self-defence; consequently the Prophet was enabled to destroy their tribes one after another without opposition.

Immediately after Badr he commenced with the Benou Kainoka, who, unlike the other Jews in the peninsula, did not devote themselves to agriculture, but were dexterous workers in gold and silver.   Summoned to surrender at discretion, they shut themselves up in the quadrangular fortified houses in which the Jews lived within and without the city, and there they stood a siege of fifteen days, at the end of which time they were compelled to give themselves up.   The lives of the men, 700 in number, for some time trembled in the balance of life and death; and they were only saved from destruction by the energy of Abdallah ebn Obay, the noblest Khazradj in Medina —a man who would have held the supreme authority in the city had it not been for the arrival of Mahomet, and who passed as the chief of the celebrated party of the Mounaficon, stigmatised in the Coran as the party of the Hypocrites, and who were in fact mere conventional believers.   Abdallah had contracted a strict alliance with the Benou Kainoka, and in recent battle they had fought bravely on his side against the Awzs.   While the Prophet was gloomily meditating the slaughter of the Kainoka, Abdallah came and asked for mercy to be shown to his allies; but Mahomet turned away in sullen silence, upon which Abdallah seized him by the cuirass under the throat and forced him to listen to him, saying, ' By heaven ! ' it shall never be said that I tamely allowed the men who ' fought for me at Boach to be murdered.'   Overcome by his energy, Mahomet gloomily ordered the lives of the tribe to be spared, but adding as he turned away, ' God curse him and ' them too !' and confiscating all their property, he dismissed them into perpetual exile.

He now gave his followers permission to slay a Jew wherever they met one; and not long afterwards he proceeded to the extirpation of· the second tribe, the Nadhyrites. His pretext for attacking the Nadhyrites was that it had been revealed to him that they meant to assassinate him ! Their brave and energetic defence secured them, however, terms more favourable than those of the Benou Kainoka; and they departed with all their arms and property, leaving the city behind them for ever, going forth from the gates defiantly to the music of pipes and timbrels, and taking the road to Syria, where they settled. And now the unhappy Coraitza were left alone to bear the whole weight of his jealous revenge. The Benou Coraitza claimed to be descended from Aaron, and were the most powerful of the three tribes; they had exposed themselves more to his anger than the other two tribes, for they held communication with the Coreish while Medina was undergoing the famous siege of the ditch, in which the united tribes, under the leadership of the Coreish, made their last unsuccessful attempt at aggressive warfare. No sooner had the besiegers departed and the army of the besieged retired from the ditch than the herald cried through the streets that no soldier should resort to midday prayer before he had betaken himself to the quarter of the Coraitza. And the Coraitza now, like its sister tribes, was shut up in its quadrangular houses. They stood a siege of twenty-four days, reduced to every extremity of famine. The unfortunate people asked in vain for permission to follow their brethren the Benou Nadhyr into exile. Mahomet refused to hear of anything else but surrender at discretion pure and simple.

Meantime the Coraitza within their fortified quarters were going through all the agonies and useless discussions and resolves of despair. They obtained an interview with a chief of the Awzs, an old ally; he visited them, but overcome by the desolation around him could utter no word, only significantly drew his hand across his throat as a sign of what they must expect, and departed. One desperate man then said, ' Let us ' kill our wives and children, and fall on our foes, and die like ' men or cut our way out.' But no resolution could be made ; the men sullenly awaited their destiny, while the children wept and cried and the women rent their hair : the only consolation that any could find was the one which hardly ever fails on such occasions—that it was the will of God. At length they gave themselves up; they might all have purchased their lives at once with apostasy; three or four only did so. The Awzs, however, their allies, besought that their lives should be spared. Mahomet asked them if they would be satisfied with the decision of one of their number; they said ' Yes,' and he named Sad. Now Sad had been severely wounded at the siege, and was, as Mahomet well knew, in a state of fury against the Coraitza. Mahomet sent for the wounded man, and sat by him as he proposed to him the decision of the fate of the Coraitza. Sad said first to his tribe, ' Will ye swear to be bound ' by my decision ?' The Awzs cried ' Yes.' ' Then,' said Sad, ' the men shall be executed, and their wives and children sold ' as slaves.' Mahomet cried with savage joy, ' It is a decision ' dictated by God from the height of the seventh heaven.' The men, 600 in number, had their hands bound behind their backs, and were confined in one of their immense houses; the women and children were confined in another; both were provided with dates for food, and passed the night in reciting psalms and in prayer. The next morning, Mahomet went to the market-place and ordered deep graves to be made. When these were finished, the men were led to the brink one by one, with their hands tied behind their backs; their heads were hewn off with sabres, and they were thrown into the pits. The slaughter lasted the whole day, and was carried on by torchlight.

There were two notable instances, however, in the tribe of fortitude and contempt of their oppressors; one high-souled woman, the wife of a Jew, refused to outlive the death of her husband, and accused herself of having endeavoured to destroy a Moslem soldier by throwing a millstone from her roof on his head during the siege, demanded execution, and went in pride to the place of slaughter. Another Jew, an old man, had formerly saved the life of Thabit, one of Mahomet's favourite disciples. Thabit, by earnest entreaty, obtained the life of his benefactor; he went and gave him the intelligence, which was received in silence; and then the old man asked : ' What is become of the beautiful Asad ben Kad, whose face ' was a mirror in which girls saw their own modesty ?' ' He is ' dead.' ' What is become of him who was held as a prince by ' the tribes of the city and of the desert, who nourished them ' in peace and was their leader in war—Hoyaz of the Benou ' Adab ?' ' Dead.' ' What is become of him of the keen ' mind—of him before whom no riddle remained unsolved, and ' before whose pursuit no tribe could hide their traces—Nabbash

' of the Benou Kays?' 'Dead.' 'Where is the standard-
' bearer of the Jews and of the host, Wahb ben Zayd?'
' Dead.' 'Where is the princely head of Jewish hospitality,
' the father of the orphans and of the poor, Okba ben Zayd?'
' Dead.' 'And the two Amr, where are they, they who walked
' like brothers in the light of the law?' 'Dead.' 'Then, O
' Thabit, life has no more charm for me; I will follow them
' to the home where they are gone before. I pray thee by all
' the influence I possess upon thee, lead me not before that
' bloodthirsty man who has shorn off the heads of the chiefs of
' the Coraitza—lead me to the place of slaughter. I wait
' with impatience till the pitcher of life is poured forth, and
' I am reunited with my companions.' Mahomet was told of
his last speech, and exclaimed, ' He will be reunited to them
' in hell.' The Jew walked of himself to the pits piled
with the yet warm bodies of his comrades, asking of Thabit
only to secure liberty for his wife and children; and these
the Arab received and nourished in his own house. The
spoils of the Coraitza were great in armour, spears, vessels
of gold and silver, carpets, clothes, camels, mules, and lands
and slaves. These Mahomet, with the consent of the Ansar,
divided among the naked exiles who had preceded him from
Mecca, reserving for himself a beautiful Jewess, Rihana,
whom he kept as concubine and as a relic of the murdered
Coraitza.

Thus was the last remnant of Jewish civilisation extinguished in Medina; but the strong Jewish city of Chaibhar,
at six days' journey from Medina, still remained rich in cultivated lands and in the industrial arts of peace. After the truce
struck with the Meccans at Hodeibaya, which caused such indignation to Omar, and which lowered Mahomet's character in
the eyes of his whole host, he could imagine no better way of
recovering his position than by the overthrow of Chaibhar and
the distribution of its wealth among his dependants. He had
no complaint against Chaibhar, except that some of the exiled
Benou Nadhyr had found refuge and honourable treatment
there. He commenced operations by having the chief of the
place assassinated in secret. His successor he invited with
fair pretences to Medina, and then caused him with thirty of
his followers to be waylaid and murdered on the road. He
then marched against the place, and took it after a month's
siege. The property of the whole population was confiscated,
though their lives were spared with the exception of one man
who was put to death because the Prophet coveted his wife. The
revenues derived from the spoils of Chaibhar were very great—

the Prophet's share of the spoil alone brought him in 30,000 wasks of dates yearly—a quantity sufficient to maintain 30,000 men in the field for three months.   His wives and followers were all provided with revenues out of the agricultural district of Chaibhar ; and by the politic and careful administration and application of the spoils thus obtained from the destruction of these wealthy communities of Jews, he was enabled to seduce whole tribes of savage Bedouins and adventurers to his standard, and form the army who established the ascendency of his faith.

To form a conception of the reason of the rapid expansion of the creed of Islam amid the Arabs and wild Bedouins of the desert, it must be remembered that the religion of Mahomet had innumerable advantages for combination over every league which could be brought to oppose it.   The chief reason of the obscurity in which the Arabs had so long lain hidden from the knowledge of the world was its then divided and anarchical condition.   No principle, political or religious, existed by which any portion of the Arab tribes could be congregated together.   The son of Ishmael, from the very commencement of his desert life, had been little else than ' a wild ' man ; his hand was against every man, and every man's hand ' had been against him.'   Now one of the leading principles of Islam was to hold every Moslem as a brother, to consider themselves as one fraternity for defensive and offensive purposes.   The jealousies and hatreds of centuries were to be abandoned in the profession of faith of the Prophet of God, and Yemenite and Maadite were bound in one holy league.   Add to this that numbers of the weaker tribes flocked to the standard of the Prophet to acquire a protection and security attainable in no other way, and that the greater portion of his followers thus professed the religion for mere political purposes, without any real belief at all ; and moreover, that when any member of a tribe, or a tribe in alliance with another tribe, professed his faith from motives of sincerity, they necessarily brought along with them crowds of heathens and infidels who cared nothing about Mahomet or his creed, but adopted it from reasons of clanship and of ties of alliance. Besides this, since he had raised the standard of a freebooter, of aggressive warfare, of rapine, murder, and confiscation, the conquest of booty had been enormous.   The division of plunder was of monthly, weekly, and sometimes of daily occurrence, and drew to his standard the fine scent of every roving Bedouin from the banks of the Euphrates to the most southern shores of Hadramaut; for where the prey was, there such eagles were certainly gathered together. The accretive and adhesive power of Islam over the loose communities of Arabs was thus without limit, and did not rest until it had absorbed into itself the whole of the roving and settled communities of the peninsula; and thus it was that the military power of Mahomet increased with such astounding rapidity—commencing with the 324 infantry and two horsemen who won the battle of Badr, and expanding into the host of 114,000 infantry and cavalry who accompanied him seven years later in his last pilgrimage to Mecca.

That last great scene in Mahomet's life is assuredly one of the most imposing in history. Mahomet played his part of a prophet well, and all he then spoke was truly worthy of the occasion. For indeed that day saw the solemn appearance on the theatre of the world of the Arab race as a nation; the tribes of the Amalekites, the Edomites, the Midianites, the Moabites, and all the obscure clans who for some twenty-two centuries had been wandering about the deserts of Arabia and Syria, without a history, and seemingly without any possibility of union, had been united into one body in seven years by the genius of one man. This, indeed, was Mahomet's great work.

As to the conquest of Mecca, that too was the result not of violence but of circumstances; and the city fell naturally into his hands with the increase of his power. The interruption of their caravan trade, the defection of some of their chief allies, and the growing strength of Islam, were certainly powerful arguments for conversion with the merchants of Mecca. Finding that the old caravan road by the coast to Syria was completely at the mercy of Mahomet, they had in vain attempted to send a caravan to Syria by the old east road across the plateau land of the Nejd, but that too was intercepted. They had been unable to follow up their victory at Ohod, and when they retired in disorder from the famous trench of Medina at the suggestion of Abou Sophyan, it was easy to see that Mecca must ultimately fall into the hands of its own fugitive son. Year by year more and more of the Meccan chiefs gave in their adhesion to the design of the Prophet; but with the exception of the terrible Khaled, afterwards known as the sword of God, and one or two others, there is no probability that any of them were sincere converts. If Henry IV. could say *Paris vaut bien une messe*, they felt that the guardianship and prosperity of the holy city was well worth a profession of Islam. In the two negotiations by which Mahomet acquired the sovereignty of his native city, the spirit of his adversaries is easily recognisable. By the truce of Hodeibaya made in the vicinity of Mecca, they recognised him as a belligerent power, and the right of himself and his followers to make the pilgrimage to the Caaba. But the spirit in which it was made is evident from the words of Sohayl, the negotiator on the part of the Meccans. After the preliminaries had been arranged, Mahomet proceeded to dictate the text of the treaty. 'In the name of Allah Rahman'* —'I know nothing of Rahman,' said Sohayl; 'write simply " In the name of Allah"'—' These are the conditions which ' Mahomet the Prophet of God makes.' 'If I believed you ' were the Prophet of God,' said Sohayl, 'I could not fight ' against you: write in the name of Mahomet son of Abdallah.' Such was the style of the truce which Mahomet concluded at Hodeibaya with the Meccans, the character and tenor of which so disgusted Omar and followers of similar sincerity and vehemence, that the Prophet was obliged instantly to lead his army against Chaibhar, to dispel their indignation with active fighting and a plentiful share of booty.

The truce of Hodeibaya, however, led by its breach to the second march upon Mecca, when the city was delivered up evidently through the collusion of Abou Sophyan, the old hostile chief of the Ommeyades, who was now convinced that submission to Mahomet was the only advantageous policy. When the Coreish then were startled with the appearance of the ten thousand fires in Mahomet's camp, as they halted for the night on the hills above Mecca, Abou Sophyan slunk over to the enemy and made arrangements for delivering up the city.† 'Dost believe there is but one God?' said Mahomet on their meeting. 'This I believe,' said Abou Sophyan. 'Dost ' believe that I am his prophet?' 'Excuse me,' said Abou Sophyan; 'on this point I have still a few doubts.' And the next day, when the chief of the Ommeyades saw the Prophet's troops defiling past him in state with their banners, and beheld the famous body-guard of Mahomet, he said to Ali, 'Truly my ' uncle has made for himself a fine kingdom.' 'He is a pro-' phet,' said Ali, 'and a prophet is greater than a king.' 'Yes, ' no doubt,' sarcastically replied Abou Sophyan.

When Mahomet proceeded from Mecca to the siege of Tayif, and the Thakifs proposed to surrender by treaty, the spirit of the negotiation was precisely the same. The deputies of the Thakifs announced that their tribe were willing to become Mussulmans

---

* 'Allah the Merciful,' an epithet considered by Mahomet distinctive of his doctrine.

† Mr. Muir is of the opinion that Mecca was delivered up by arrangement with Abou Sophyan, and we think he is right in his conjecture. The strange hazard of the meeting, and the subsequent treatment of the city, speak in favour of the fact.

on condition that they should be allowed *to keep their favourite idol Lat three years longer and to say no prayers.* ' Three years of idolatry is too much,' said ' Mahomet, and ' what is a religion without prayer?' After much bargaining on both sides, it was arranged that the tribe should keep their beloved Lat for one year longer, should not be called upon to take part in the holy war, should pay no tithes, ' and ' should pray but make no prostrations at prayer.' Mahomet, however, still hesitated; he was afraid of ' what people would ' say.' ' Never mind about that,' said the Thakif deputies; ' if the Arabs ask you about the treaty, you have only got to ' say, *God dictated it.*' This argument convinced the Prophet, and he proceeded to give out the terms of the agreement. ' In ' the name of Allah, the Mild and Merciful, these are the terms ' of treaty agreed upon between Mahomet, prophet of God, ' and the Thakifs. The Thakifs shall be called upon to pay no ' tithes, to take no part in the holy war, &c.' So far the Prophet proceeded, and hesitated, when Omar broke out with his usual fiery vehemence, and with drawn sabre menaced the deputies. The Prophet, recovering himself, said, ' Islam pure ' and simple, or war.' ' Well, let us keep Lat another six ' months?' ' No.' ' A month, then?' ' Not an hour.' The deputies returned to their tribe, and Lat was instantly demolished amid the wailing of the women of the tribe.

Where he could be vindictive without danger — towards women, towards makers of verses, towards defenceless Jews, towards all who did not submit to him, Mahomet was without a tinge of mercy. To subdue the haughty *Mala*—the scoffing and sceptical aristocracy of Mecca—was the crowning and great triumph of his life, and without this all victory would have been incomplete; after the surrender of Mecca he omitted no cajolery to gain them over thoroughly to his side. In the division of spoil at the end of the campaign of Tayif, the chiefs of the Meccan aristocracy received one hundred camels each and forty ounces of silver. The men of Medina were loud in their disapproval; upon which Mahomet made them a fine speech, such as he always had at command, to the effect that what he gave the Meccans was but perishable goods, but that to them, to the *Ansar*, he owed the eternal gratitude of his heart, and that with them he would live and die. The noble-hearted men of Medina accepted his explanation with tears and renewed cries of devotion; but nevertheless the policy inaugurated by Mahomet on that very day was in the end the destruction of the house of Ali, and the ruin of the *Ansar*, their families, their homes, their whole city, and their descendants. The conquest of the faithful became the spoil and the heritage of the infidel Ommeyades, the descendants of Abou Sophyan and of Hind, and the enemies and persecutors of the Prophet obtained supreme power in every theatre of conquest, to the confusion of the true believers. Moawiyah, the son of Hind, became caliph of Syria; his son Yezid, who succeeded him, was noted for his impiety and debauchery, and he it was who ordered the destruction of the City of the Prophet—*Medinet-en-nebi.*

Walid, who became governor of Cufa, was the son of the very Ocba who was known to have spit in the face of the Prophet and to have nearly strangled him, and who was condemned to death by the Prophet himself. His son, called ' the Son ' of Hell,' nevertheless became governor of Cufa. His character is sufficiently portrayed in the following anecdote. Having spent the night in an orgy of wine and singing women, he heard in the dawn the voice of the Muezzin calling to prayer from the top of the minaret. In the loose dress of his revel, and hot with wine, he went to the mosque, mounted the pulpit, and recited as *imam* the customary prayer; when he had gone through it, thinking probably of the songs he had just been singing, he turned to the assembly and said, ' Shall I give ' you another ?' ' By *Allah !*' said a pious Mussulman, ' I ex- ' pected nothing better from thee ; but I little thought ever to ' see such a governor here;' and, joined by the rest of the congregation, he began to tear up the paving-stones of the mosque to hurl them at the head of the profane governor. Walid slipped away and got back to his drinking party, singing from a profane poet, ' Wherever there are wine and female ' singers, there am I to be found; for I am not a dry flint ' without a feeling for what is good.' A poet of the day, Ho- taia, thought the adventure so good that he sang of it thus : ' On the day of the last Judgment, Hotaia will bear witness ' that Walid does not deserve the fault men now find with ' him. What has he done when all is told? As soon as he finished saying his prayer, he asked " Do you want any ' " more ?" It is, however, fortunate that they stopped thee, ' Walid, or thou wouldst have gone on praying till the end of ' the world.'

Such were the men who were advanced to power by the policy of the Prophet. The throne of Egypt was filled with a treacherous renegade, the especial object of the Prophet's de- testation in his lifetime, whom he had wanted to put to death ; indeed the conquest of the world by Islam was made in fact by infidels who had no more religion than their savage forefathers,

or than a Bedouin of the present day, but who were its chiefs
in the same way and for the same reason as Alexander VI.
or Leo X. became the chiefs of Catholic Christianity. Nor
indeed was it much better with the masses. Under the terror of
the sword of the ferocious Khaled, whole tribes of Bedouins
professed Islam, it is true, but it was a mere profession which
passed away with the terror of the sword that caused it, and
the majority of the tribes endeavoured to cast it off as soon as
the Prophet was dead. Thousands of Arabs knew nothing
more of the creed than the first five words of the Coran—' In
' the name of Allah, the Clement and Merciful.' And in the
next century the Arabs who conquered Egypt and scattered
themselves along the borders of the Sahara, were found by
travellers and missionaries of the caliph to have forgotten the
religion of Mahomet, to be drinkers of wine, and to have re-
verted to the rites and practices of Arab heathendom as if the
Prophet had never existed. Under the caliphate of Omar an
Arab was brought before the Caliph accused of having married
two sisters. On being questioned by the Caliph, he said he
knew of no law to the contrary ; and when told he must repudiate one of the sisters, he cried, ' What an abominable
' religion ! I have never got the slightest good from it,' ignorant
that in saying this he was exposing himself to the punishment
of death as a blasphemer and a renegade.

So far as the Arab race is concerned, Mohammedanism, as
a religion, has had no root and no vitality. There is no ground
for supposing that Mahomet's design of a future for his creed
extended beyond his own race, yet it was altogether beyond
the pale of the Semitic nations that Islam was destined to
have its most astounding success. What Mahomet really did
was to invent a religion for the nomad hordes of Asia : it was
to the cry of ' *Allah Akbar* ' that the swarms of Turks and
Tartars, the hosts of Alp Arslan, Othman, Genghis Khan,
and Tamerlane, surged up from the vast steppes of Asia, and
overran the most ancient seats of civilisation, and spread desolation around them. With nomad and semi-barbarous Asiatic
hordes it will remain a religion until they, in their turn, if possible, are drawn within the sphere of a purer civilisation.

With the Arabs Islam was simply a means of banding
together those wild, dispersed and predatory tribes, and forming
them into a nation. It gave them a consciousness of their
collected strength, which was really immense, and no power
in the world at that time was capable of resisting it.

As for the extraordinary man who thus succeeded in giving
a new creed to the world, his mission was fitly terminated by

his last triumphant procession to Mecca with his immense *cortége* of adherents, and three months afterwards he died at Medina; the immediate cause was a fever, though he believed his health was undermined by the attempt of a Jewish woman to poison him at Chaibhar. It was characteristic of his character and of his creed that among his last prayer was one of great fervency for the entire destruction of Jews and Christians. In other respects he died in a manner not unbecoming the character he assumed, and in the full conviction that he was immediately to be taken up to Paradise.

To form a correct appreciation of such a man is one of the most difficult tasks of history, and in order rightly to do it it is necessary to fathom the abysses of the human conscience itself, and to endeavour to discriminate between the confused boundary-lines of good and evil which lie within it. Every one is aware how insidiously the promptings of self-advantage, vanity, or ambition, are apt to mix themselves up with nobler passions, and ultimately to supplant them altogether. The beginnings of self-deception in such cases are always difficult of apprehension. If such is the case with ordinary persons, in the case of a career like Mahomet's it is impossible to separate entirely real enthusiasm from self-deception and imposture. That he went through these stages no candid inquirer can doubt. Perhaps it may be an approximation to the truth if we said that while in a state of oppression at Mecca his career was made up of much real enthusiasm and little deceit, but that at Medina, inflated by the possession of absolute power, urged on by the insatiable promptings of ambition, and intoxicated with the fumes of sanguinary and merciless vengeance, his career was a mixture of immense and shameless imposture, still leavened with bursts of the old enthusiasm.

As he assumed the character of a prophet, one is naturally led to compare him with the mighty spiritual leaders of the chosen people of his own Semitic race, whose majesty Michael Angelo alone has fitly been able to interpret, with Moses, with Elijah, with Isaiah, and with Ezekiel; yet the Arabian is but a sorry and barbarous counterfeit of these grand types of humanity. One chapter of Hosea or Amos contains more grandeur of soul and more literary value than the whole of the Coran. Thus, in his highest flights, Mahomet never rises above the dignity of a coarse and ignorant imitation of a Hebrew prophet; while in his lowest abasement, as in the scene of the massacre of the Coraitza, for example, he looms through history with the sanguinary darkness of a king of Dahomey or Ashantee. As the founder of a religion, it would be blasphemy to name him in the same breath with one to whom he presumed to declare himself a rival, of whose mission and incarnation he could appreciate neither the beauty, the spotlessness, nor the truth. Place side by side a narrative of the origin of Christianity and a narrative of the origin of the faith of Islam, and without another word of argument the divinity of the one and the humanity of the other are apparent. But if we compare Mahomet with another founder of a religion, Bouddha, Bouddha appears, in his doctrine of self-abnegation and in his spiritual conception of human nature and the destinies of man, to stand as much above Mahomet as Mahomet does above the founder of American Mormonism. As in Mahomet's moral conduct of life, so in all his religious conceptions, there is a coarseness and grossness suited only to the semi-barbarous nations who have remained faithful to his creed. The distinguishing mark, however, of Mahomet's whole life and character is a savage incongruity; he was a strange mixture of barbarity and gentleness, of severity and of licentiousness, of ignorance and elevation of character, of credulity and astuteness, of ambition and simplicity of life, of religious conviction and low imposture; but the most astonishing trait of his character, and that which made him indeed a great man, was an invincible belief in himself, in the ever-present protection and favour of God, and in the destiny of the religion he was to found. The indissoluble tenacity of his belief in spite of the tremendous difficulties which beset his career forms the real grandeur of his character.

Mahomet is the only founder of a religion of whose personal appearance we possess authentic details. He was a little above the middle height, strongly but sparely made, with broad shoulders and a slight stoop; his hair was black, and in the prime of life clustered over his ears; his moustache and beard were also black, the latter abundant and reaching some way down his chest; his forehead was large with a vein on it which swelled when he was angry; his complexion was fair for an Arab; his eyes were large, black, and piercing, but bloodshot and restless; his teeth were white and well formed, but stood apart; his walk was so rapid that people had to run to keep up with him, and his gait is described as being like that of a man striding downhill. He was simple in his apparel; he never wore silk but once in his life, and then threw it aside in disgust, saying it was no fit dress for a man. His general attire was white and red or striped cotton; like all Arabs, he had no taste for comfort, and the luxurious refinements of artificial life were not known to him, or would have been despised had they become so; a bed of palm-tree fibre, a low hut of burnt tiling with a palm-tree roof, would have been by him preferred to a palace. Still he was in some things of extremely delicate and sensitive taste, as in the use of perfumes and in his distaste for unpleasant odours. At Medina he once sent back a dish of mutton to the sender untouched, because it was flavoured with onions, saying that they were disagreeable to the angel who visited him; he never travelled without toothpicks and antimony for his eyes; he was a good listener in conversation, and never in shaking hands was the first to withdraw his own; he was not addicted to any of the games or sports of which the Arabs were passionately fond, and was, in all things, most unlike the heroic ideal of Arab character.

The Prophet could little foresee in the triumph of his later years that his own country of Arabia would, as later travellers have verified, be the country of all the East in which Mohammedanism occupies the least place in the belief of the inhabitants. The Arab race, however, will ever have a romantic and intellectual interest for the observer of history, as the last surviving nationality of that great Semitic family so mysteriously and prodigiously active in the obscure dawn of civilisation, who built stupendous cities and engaged in the work of industry and commerce on a gigantic scale; who were inspired by the sublimest conceptions of religious belief and of the theocratic government of the universe before the Indo-European race had even made its appearance upon the theatre of the world. It was the Semitic family which covered the plains of Mesopotamia and the valley of the Euphrates with cities fit rivals of the Aramaic capitals of Nineveh and Babylon; which laid the foundations of primeval civilisation in Æthiopia and Southern Arabia; which from Tyre and Carthage crossed the most distant oceans with their fleets; which have left behind in the Hebrew Scriptures a monument of their former spiritual supremacy more venerable and more imperishable than any structure raised by the hands of man. They are the only race besides the Indo-European who have had any important share in the dominion of the civilised world, in the evolution of spiritual and religious truth, and they alone share with the Aryan races the possession of the highest type of physical beauty and intellectual culture.

Art. II.—1. *Report of a Committee appointed by the Royal Society, the Admiralty, and the Board of Trade, to consider certain Questions relating to the Meteorological Department of the Board of Trade.* Presented to Parliament, April, 1866.

2. *The Law of Storms considered in connexion with the ordinary Movements of the Atmosphere.* By H.W. Dove, F.R.S. With Diagrams and Charts of Storms. Second Edition. Translated by Robert H. Scott, M.A. London : 1862.

3. *Proceedings of the British Meteorological Society.* Edited by James Glaisher, F.R.S., Secretary. London : 1865.

4. *Meteorographica, or Methods of Mapping the Weather.* Illustrated by upwards of 600 printed and lithographed diagrams referring to the weather of a large part of Europe during the month of December 1861. By Francis Galton, F.R.S. 1863.

THE Science of the Weather, taking that term in its largest sense, as comprehending the fruits of daily meteorological observation, is the most popular of all topics and the most familiar of all inquiries, yet it is the least systematic and the most backward of all the sciences founded on induction. In one view all mankind are making loose observations and vague prophecies about the weather, for the business and the enjoyments of each day are continually affected by it. This is pre-eminently the knowledge which ' comes home ' to men's business and bosoms.' The child with his toys and projects, the youth with his sports and holidays, the man with his infinite variety of pursuits and undertakings, each and all look at the skies, note the winds, and observe the clouds. What these presage is the first theme of the morning, the proverbial sequence to an Englishman's greeting, the earliest and latest topic amongst cultivators of the soil and sportsmen in the field. So long have such habits prevailed, that it might be fairly presumed that some precise and undisputed results of so much weather-wisdom and weather-colloquy must have been attained. We ought by this time to have settled upon some broader basis than a shepherd's proverb what are the trustworthy signs and indications of the immediate future. We must have learned something worth recording of atmospheric causes and effects. So many thousand blasts have not blown, so many thousand storms have not raged, so many thousand showers have not fallen, without at least arousing us to record their varied phenomena, and enabling us to foretell their recurrence. These are phenomena that strike all men. They are not merely to be found in the laboratory or the remote and studious observatory, but they appeal to the senses of the entire communities where they occur. Literally they speak to us in tones of thunder and in winged words. The fruits of the earth, the flocks of the field, the food and raiment of mankind, in a large manner depend upon aërial conditions and oppositions. Confining our attention thus far to the land, how momentous are the consequences of the weather; and yet, after all the years that have elapsed, the manifold phenomena which have been observed, the desolation and destruction with which we have been afflicted, our ignorance of the true causes of these things, or rather of their times and conditions of visitation, is almost as great this day as it was centuries ago. Weather prophets still hold amongst us about the same rank as astrologers. A clever charlatan may even now make a profit of a silly weather almanac, and the common people still believe in antiquated weather proverbs. Yet all these pretensions to a knowledge of the weather are purely empirical. Not seldom the instincts of the lower animals are a surer guide to approaching atmospheric changes than the knowledge and experience of man. For in truth the *causes* of these phenomena are still most imperfectly understood; and although it is certain that every change of the weather, even in our own variable climate, must be the result of certain physical laws, no successful attempt has yet been made to reduce them to a theory capable of explaining their effects.

To ascertain if any, and what amount of faith may be put in the mass of popular prognostics which have been handed down traditionally from age to age and generation to generation, they should be locally collected, and then submitted to the scrutiny of science and the comparisons of experience. The ancient and still extensively prevailing belief in lunar influence upon the weather can only be established or eradicated by rigorous scientific reasoning and observation. Dr. Marcet examined a register of the weather kept at Geneva for thirty-four years to test the popular opinion that changes of weather (limiting the expression to changes ' from clear ' weather to rain, or from rain to clear weather') occurred more frequently on the four principal days of the lunar phases than on other days. The results which he obtained seemed ' upon the whole to lend some support to the vulgar opinion of ' the influence of new and full moon, but none whatever to any ' special influence of the first and third quarters.' Against this slight support must be brought the results of observations made at the Greenwich Observatory since 1840, from which it seems that changes of weather have been found to be as frequent at every age of the moon as when she is seven, fourteen, twenty-one, or twenty-eight days old.

We by no means deny that solar and lunar influences may affect our atmosphere in modes at present uncertain. M. Wolf, Director of the Observatory at Berne, in connexion with his laborious study of the solar spots, conceived a connexion between them and the weather, believing that the years in which the spots are more numerous are drier and more fertile than others, while those years in which the spots are few are more moist and stormy. Other astronomers have propounded theories of solar influence in the production of meteorological phenomena, and have expended an amount of labour in their pursuits and speculations of which the world at large has no conception. All their theories, however, demand as a basis registers of long meteorological periods; and from the comparatively recent establishment of correct thermometrical and barometrical registrations, such theories must be vague and incomplete, though they may perhaps contain the germ of truths yet to be completely discerned and established upon a sound induction from more abundant observations.

We are here adverting principally to ordinary observations such as any individual or body of individuals may regularly make, and not to more important matters such as public storm warnings, which, being derived from numerous observations over large oceanic and terrestrial areas, can only be regularly and successfully accomplished by a Government department, or by arrangements made under Government supervision and paid for by public funds. Private scientific societies or even private individuals, however, may perform their appropriate work, and at a small expense, the chief outlay being for instruments, which should always be of the best order, and not infrequently compared with the ' standards.'

Amongst several societies of this character, we are pleased to see that one has been established in Switzerland, and that the Helvetic society now numbers eighty-six meteorological stations. In that land of huge mountains every important atmospheric phenomenon may be well studied. The increase of stations, members, and funds in such societies will soon extinguish the race of prognosticating empirics. Yet it is disheartening to see how obstinately vital they still are. If a Murphy is consigned to oblivion in this country, a Mathieu springs up in France; and, curiously enough, though this same Mathieu (de la Drôme) is dead, it is reported that he communicated his system to his heir, who continues the profitable speculation on the inexhaustible credulity of mankind, in spite of the masterly exposure of the absurdity of his pretensions, which was made by M. Le Verrier and published in the ' Moniteur ' of April 1863, by order of the French Government.

But, it may be asked, if we discover the vanity and discard the fallacies of such prognosticators as these—if we divest ourselves of the illusions of vulgar proverbs, prevalent prejudices, and provincial superstitions—what remains?   And is there in reality any ground for attempting to prognosticate the weather at all?   After so many failures, and with only occasional successes, which may apparently be regarded only as fortunate conjectures, can we look for any scientific basis on which to found future forecasts?

In reply, we must first define the intervals between the prognostication and the actual subsequent weather.   For short intervals of time there can be no question that many natural signs are good prognostics, simply because they are nearly adjoining terms of a natural series.   For instance, certain forms of cirrus in the clouds, if accompanying a falling barometer, pretty surely indicate rain shortly afterwards.   In mountainous countries, when the air is very clear, and the mountains appear quite close, and the falling of water in cascades is more distinctly heard than at other times, the observing inhabitants are confident of coming rain ; and not without reason and a philosophical cause, though it be quite unknown to the observers. When the atmosphere is warm and dry, the outlines of distant objects are hazy and indistinct, owing to the dust which is suspended in the air, the sun at such times appearing particularly red.   But when a moist wind sets in, its aqueous vapour condenses itself at once in the dust in the air, which thus becomes heavy and sinks to the ground.   The air then becomes unusually clear, and the moist wind will in all probability speedily occasion rain.   Again, a clear sunset is generally accepted as a sign of fair weather.   The reason is that rain generally comes from the west, and if the sunset be clear and golden, it is a proof that at least for some time no rain is coming from that quarter.   Such tokens as these have been approved by long experience, and are explicable upon such sound principles as those mentioned.

So likewise at sea there are similar trustworthy prognostics of weather-changes, and these have been noted by seamen who knew little of their philosophy.   For example, it is a prevalent opinion amongst seamen that lightning, when seen in the Atlantic during winter, indicates the approach or con-

tinuance of bad weather; and such is generally the result.   It
may not be easy to trace the cause, which, however, may be
the contact of two gales, and the advance of a new storm in
the steps of one receding.   Flashes of lightning may be caused
by the passage of the electric current through the intervening
air from one gale to another.   As a general rule, the closer
storms are to one another, and the more they overlap each
other, the more lightning will flash.

From the nature of their calling, seamen are commonly
familiar with the usual indications of the near approach of bad
weather, and even a casual voyager soon becomes acquainted
with them.   The most frequent antecedents of a great storm
at sea are calm and close sultry weather, with a falling barometer; clouds assuming the appearance of dark wool, and
stretching across the sky in deep folds, the edge of each fold
being fringed with deep red; masses of cirrus rolled up into
balls like big heaps of cotton, or torn and dragged into a
thousand odd shapes; sudden gloom, with rain and occasional
gusts of wind, low scud flying rapidly across the sky, and now
and then forming into long bands or belts; a peculiar moaning
sound in the air, and sometimes a long heavy swell from the
direction whence the storm is coming.   All these are tokens
which no experienced seaman disregards.

These are the signs of imminent changes and storms, and
merely require minute observation; but when we have to consider *forecasts* for longer intervals and over extended areas,
the case is very different, and we pass from common observation
to science and calculation.

Meteorological science, strictly as a science, is so comparatively young and undeveloped that it has been chiefly concerned in the observation and collection of phenomena and
facts; and hitherto the laws of atmospheric phenomena have
been almost exclusively determined and explained in relation
to general causes, while the order in which these phenomena
follow one another, and the causes of their changes in different
localities, have been very partially investigated.   We know,
for instance, that the direction and force of winds are generally
explained as the consequence of continual atmospheric currents
from the equator to the poles, and from the poles to the equator, or by the diurnal motion of our globe, by various conditions
of the atmosphere over the seas and the continents, by the
line of coasts of those seas, by chains of mountains, and by the
form of the earth's surface.   We know also that a decrease
of temperature condenses vapour, and that such condensa-
tion produces showers which are often followed by electrical

phenomena, and that in consequence of these showers a certain vacuity is produced, and then the surrounding air rushes towards this vacuity. But when we proceed to inquire why such phenomena occur in one place and not in another, why at this time and not at another, why at the same time at other places other phenomena are observed, and in what relation these phenomena stand to each other in order, in time, and in place, then we have at present few satisfactory answers, and it is probable that science will be long in presenting them.

It is manifest also that the more we narrow our area of observation the greater is our chance of error. An intimate connexion subsists between all parts of the atmosphere; it is a landless and uninterrupted aërial ocean, and therefore even a tolerable solution of local atmospheric problems can only consist with an acquaintance with the state of the weather over a large portion of the earth. What may appear to be the minor difficulties of this science are, in fact, parts of great difficulties; and even to foretell the character of the weather after an interval of a few hours would demand a considerable knowledge of important atmospheric conditions. Meteorologists have learned by experience that the changes of weather in England, and even in all Europe, are but the effects of widely operating causes, and bear relation to immense systems. These systems reach southward to the trade winds, and with them far in the direction of the Gulf of Mexico; while to the north they are of unknown extent. The area of the North Atlantic, and especially of the Gulf Stream, appears to exercise a most important influence upon the generation of storms and the weather changes which affect England. It has become obvious, therefore, that the only way of arriving at a true science of weather is by a rigorous induction from a large number of trustworthy observations made over a broadly extended basis. Le Verrier is now acting upon this conviction in preparing charts of a portion of the Northern Hemisphere for each day of the year 1864.

In order to determine what will be the character of any following season, we ought to know at the time of inquiry what the weather is at all other places; for the irregularities occurring in one quarter of the globe are in time transmitted to other quarters, and extremes in one country are compensated by opposite extremes in another. The general equilibrium is maintained in this manner, and the frequent shiftings of the wind which disturb weather previously settled and apparently likely to continue so, while they render such a climate as our own provokingly variable, at the same time

prevent an unhealthy uniformity.   So important is the agency
of the winds that all changes of weather may be attributed to
them.   The quarter from which they come, and the steadiness
with which they blow, govern our atmospheric conditions
and our scientific conclusions.   Æolus is indeed a king,
and Virgil's description of this king and his furious servants
in the first book of the Æneid is not more true to poetry
than to nature.   Meteorological science is ever aiming to emu-
late Æolus, and in some degree to render the ancient fiction a
modern fact.   Though science may never hope actually to sway
the sceptre of the winds, or to imprison them in rocky cells, or
to direct their courses, yet, by foreseeing and foretelling, by
evading and escaping, by measuring force and anticipating
rage, she may so far understand as by human sagacity to control
or avoid the malice of the fiercest winds.   To science prospec-
tively we may apply the words in which the poet depicts the
restraining power of King Æolus :—

> ' mollitque animos, et temperat iras.
> Ni faciat, maria ac terras cœlumque profundum
> Quippe ferant rapidi secum, verrantque per auras.'

What has already been accomplished in reducing to shape
our knowledge of the winds sweeping over the globe, may be
found in the important volume of Professor Dove, of Berlin, a
translation of which we have cited at the head of this article.
The motions of the atmosphere in the different zones are now
classed under three typical forms :—1. Permanent winds, as
the trade winds of the torrid zone ; 2. Periodical winds, as
the monsoons of the Indian Ocean ; 3. Changeable winds, as
the winds of the temperate and frigid zones.   To classify and
discuss the phenomena connected with these winds is a very
onerous task, and one which cannot be said to be completed,
though Dove has done much in this direction.   The atmosphere, as he remarks, is continually striving to obtain equilibrium without ever succeeding.   The character of the disturbance and the process of restoration of the equilibrium exhibit
in every case a distinct type, so that the problem which presents
itself to the meteorologist is to discover the typical form of the
phenomenon, which presents in each several case of its occurrence variations of more or less extent from the original type.
When we reflect how many agencies are at work disturbing the
atmospheric equilibrium—the radiation whose extent varies
from day to day—the infinite variety in the surface of the
ground—the mountainous barriers and extensive deserts—the
oceanic currents, and the different forms in which aqueous
vapour presents itself—we are disposed to marvel how any such

diagram of the winds of the globe as Maury has presented can be constructed out of so many complexities. The calms, indeed, in the face of all these endless mobilities, may excite our astonishment in a greater degree than the winds. Nevertheless, without some approximation to an understanding of the winds, without charting them carefully, and noting their phenomena continually, all weather-warnings must be unsatisfactory and useless; and in respect of storms, the law of storms is but another term for the law of winds.

We now see how numerous must be the observations, how wide the area, how sound the inductions, in order to qualify any meteorologist to enter upon the field of forecasts, and to warrant a hope of final success.

The whole kingdom—we might almost say the whole of educated Europe—knows that in this country we have for some years past been making official attempts at weather forecasts and storm warnings. Visitors to the sea-coast have beheld mysterious drums and cones hoisted to view, and significantly varied or combined; and even the common people have had ocular evidence that certain Government officers were engaged in studying the signs of the weather on behalf of the seafaring community. The public have also long been familiar, through announcement in the daily journals, with the weather prognostications of the late Admiral Fitzroy, and it is desirable at the outset to explain how all these proceedings came to bear an official stamp.

Impressed with the importance of a well and widely concerted plan of meteorological observations at sea, a conference, consisting of representatives from different maritime countries, met at Brussels in 1853. They made recommendations to secure accuracy of instruments, and prepared a form of meteorological register, and subsequently the Meteorological Department of the Board of Trade was constituted, with the late Admiral Fitzroy at its head. The avowed main object of this Department was the discussion and utilisation of meteorological observations made at sea in all parts of the globe, and the opinion of the Royal Society was sought as to those *desiderata* of meteorological science to which the Department should direct its attention. The President and Council of the Royal Society replied in detail, enumerating the chief *desiderata*, and expressing their opinions. In the course of subsequent correspondence, they stated that it would be most important, both in a theoretical and practical point of view, to procure statistics of the direction and force of the wind in those parts of the Atlantic Ocean which are usually traversed by ships. In short, they specified such points of inquiry as amounted to a summary of instructions according to which the Meteorological Department should pursue its labours. It cannot, therefore, be said that its objects were undefined, or left to caprice, or fancy, or theory. There is no indication that it was a part of the functions of this Department, as originally instituted, to publish undiscussed observations, or to speculate in meteorological theories. Nothing at all was proposed respecting prognostications of the weather, although these might be included in the ultimate issue and ripest fruit of such discussions.

It appears that when this Department was first established, its superintendent, the late Admiral Fitzroy, took efficient measures to give effect to the wishes of the Royal Society, by distributing information on the methods of observing, by procuring verified instruments, by lending them with discrimination to the captains of merchant ships, and by supplying the Royal Navy with more than one thousand sets of instruments, while nearly the same number were lent to captains in the merchant service. As the result, no less than 1,298 registers were received, made during voyages averaging 140 days at sea, and containing in the aggregate about 550,000 separate sets of observations. The steadily increasing number of these registers was highly encouraging, and the more so as the large majority of them seem, from internal evidence, to have been executed with scrupulous care and assiduity. But the silent and unpretending accumulation of these data did not satisfy the aspirations of the superintendent; for the Admiral's attention became gradually diverted from the legitimate and commendable pursuits of his position, and fearing an accumulation of ocean statistics far beyond the divided powers of the office to reduce, he felt himself justified in ceasing to accumulate further contributions of meteorological observations taken at sea. To their available value and prospective advantages we shall presently return.

In his report of 1862 the Admiral remarks :—

'By continued and consecutive series of charts, several hundred in number, constructed on the simultaneous or synchronous principle, an insight into the laws of our atmosphere, into meteorological dynamics (distinct from statistical results previously obtained at observatories and elsewhere) has been gained, *which has enabled us to know what weather will prevail during the next two or three days, and, as a corollary, when a storm may occur.* These seem satisfactory and rewarding results.'

The Council of the British Association had recommended in 1859 occasional telegraphic communication between a few widely separated parts of Great Britain and Ireland, by which warnings of storms might be given ; and certain resolutions to this end were drawn up in concert with the Admiral. Meanwhile M. Le Verrier, the well-known astronomer, and director of the Imperial Observatory at Paris, had established a system of daily telegraphing the state of the weather, not only from various ports in France, but also from other ports in Europe, to Paris, and also from port to port in France ; and he invited the British Government to join in this system, which was expressly confined to the communication of the actual state of the weather, and in no way committed to prediction. It appears, therefore, that while acting in consequence of these requests, and in concert with these parties, Admiral Fitzroy went beyond them all, and conceiving that sufficient information had been collected and digested in his office during five years to enable him to foretell the weather, and desiring also that practical results should now follow so much toil and time devoted to registrations, he persevered in his expressed intention of ' forecasting ' (to employ his own expression) not only storms announced by telegraph as already raging, but also weather generally.

Accordingly, in the summer of 1860, arrangements were made for the regular daily communication by telegraph to London of the state of the weather at fifteen stations in the United Kingdom, for receiving daily telegrams of weather from various places in Europe through Paris, and for the daily communication to Paris of the state of the weather at certain points in the United Kingdom. The public were acquainted with the results in the daily newspapers.

Storm signals and weather warnings were hoisted for the first time at certain ports in February 1861. In August of the same year the weather predictions were greatly enlarged, first by extending the storm signals to many places not previously warned, and next by publishing daily forecasts of the weather in the newspapers. All these made the name of Admiral Fitzroy famous, and they have been continued by his principal assistant since his lamentable death. That the storm warnings have become very popular at the ports, and have greatly interested the public, is admitted, but not as a proof of their value or accuracy. They may, moreover, have exercised some influence on foreign observers, the predictions of the English office having been daily sent to Paris. M. Le Verrier organised a similar system of storm warnings, and also published daily a very full bulletin of the actual weather, illustrated with maps of barometric pressure and of wind. For some time his bulletins contained predictions of the probable weather for different parts of France, but these have recently been discontinued.   At Berlin Professor Dove has of late established a system of storm warnings like our own; while in Italy a system has been in process of establishment on an independent plan.   Holland has done, and Prussia is doing, the same, and there are prospects of like proceedings in some countries of less importance.   We shall presently refer more at large to Russia.

In this state of meteorological proceedings, the death of Admiral Fitzroy appeared to present a suitable opportunity for instituting investigations which could scarcely have been made in his lifetime so independently and so completely.   The result of a correspondence between the Board of Trade and the Royal Society was the appointment of a Committee, consisting of Francis Galton,* Esq., F.R.S., who was nominated by the President and Council of the Royal Society; Staff-Commander Evans, R.N., F.R.S., nominated by the Admiralty; and T. H. Farrer, Esq., one of the secretaries of, and nominated by, the Board of Trade.   These gentlemen were instructed to consider and report upon five questions proposed to them, which were so framed as to occasion a thorough examination of what had been done and what had been left undone by the Department, and, as a consequence, what remained to be done, how it should be executed, and with what staff.

These gentlemen are the only persons unconnected with the Department who have examined into its system and its work. We must therefore necessarily acquire our information on the subject from them; and although we have endeavoured to disentangle it from some of the complexities in which it is involved, and to present to our readers some of the results in a simpler form, the verdict is substantially that of the Committee, and our remarks are founded upon their verdict, which there is no apparent good reason for doubting, and which is fortified by details and figures sufficient, we think, to uphold and corroborate it.

Taking first and separately the subject of Weather Forecasts,

---

* Mr. Galton's 'Meteorographica,' quoted at the head of this article, displays both his competence and zeal as a meteorologist; whatever opinion may be entertained of his method of mapping. He joins in the desire for combined observations and a union of separate activities. 'The labour,' he remarks, 'of a meteorologist ' who studies the changes of the weather is enormous, before he can ' even get his materials into hand, and arrive at the starting-point of ' his investigations.'

it immediately occurs to an inquirer that it would be highly instructive to collect and compare from the foreign Observatories, as well as from our Board of Trade, both the plans of their procedure in forecasting the weather, and the results so far as experience has gone. While, however, we can at present learn nothing of this kind from abroad, the report of the Committee now before us fortunately, or unfortunately, to some degree acquaints us with the practice and results at home.

Although Admiral Fitzroy during several years collected a number of observations, and prepared a number of charts with a view to weather forecasts, they do not appear to have been continued and completed so as to bring out clear and definite conclusions, nor have any fixed rules or principles been deduced from them. Admitting that it might be premature to expect at present a precise and full statement of definite principles or laws, still we are fairly entitled to know the conditions of the atmosphere, and the probabilities of future weather arising therefrom as they presented themselves to the Admiral. Doubtless such probabilities are considerable, and capable of arrangement, especially in the important cases of sudden and violent changes of weather, and it is upon these alone that forecasts can be safely founded and sound instruction can be communicated. The very first step and aim of official action should be to take weather forecasts out of the domain of loose conjecture and personal guesswork, and to elevate it into a science of induction. This alone will distinguish it from vulgar prophecy, and win for it the attention and co-operation of men of science. But the more the past procedure of this Department is investigated, the more unsatisfactory in these respects does it appear. Little has been done alone, and scarcely anything in combination with other meteorologists, so as to compare and contrast, and thus establish maxims upon which all agree, or to estimate the value of the compound probabilities arising from the application of each separate combination of maxims to the ever-varying and complicated phenomena of the weather.

That there are already sufficient observations for the deduction of some results, the Committee show by attempting a digest of maxims employed by the Office in forecasting weather. Twenty-three maxims are presented. These naturally comprise some mere elementary truths amongst several important principles and several assumptions, upon all which the Office has hitherto acted. But the manner in which it has employed these maxims is undefined and obscure. It appears that in making forecasts, the area of the British Isles is divided into six districts; and the average state of the weather in each district is deduced from the weather reports received from the stations contained within it. A forecast for each district is then made provisionally upon the basis of the maxims already alluded to. The separate forecasts are next collated and revised, regard being paid to the following particulars:—

(*a*) The mutual action of the estimated weather in each of the six districts of the British Isles.

(*b*) Scattered information in respect to such distant areas of high and low barometer as the limited number of continental stations can afford.

(*c*) Geographical conditions of mountain, plain, or sea, by which the free movements of the air can be affected.

The Committee, however, are unable to offer any satisfactory account of the method in which the particular (*a*) is discussed, and they add that ' it is the custom of the Office to perform the ' whole of the foregoing operations and to determine the fore-' cast after a simple inspection of the list of weather returns. ' No notes or calculations upon paper are ever made. The ' operation occupies about half an hour, and is conducted ' mentally.'

They also very properly remark upon the importance of obtaining a precise value for each of the maxims acted upon, and show by an example what the forecast would be under certain conditions. The probability of the correctness of such forecast must clearly be compounded of the value of each separate probability, and if we are ignorant of the nature of each of these values a very great uncertainty must attach to the value of the forecast. Working out a case or two upon common doctrines of the science of probabilities, they prove the varying and diminished values of attempted forecasts. The whole value of the forecast must so directly depend upon that of the maxims, that the one is obviously proportionate to the other; and if, as seems very possible, some of the maxims should possess no value whatever, then the introduction of any such proposition into a chain of contingencies will diminish the value of the forecast by one half. The Committee refer to some of the maxims as doubtful. Take, for illustration, two of them. No. 9 : ' The whole body of the atmosphere ' in our country travels in an E. direction, at the rate of from ' two to eight miles an hour.' And No. 17 : ' The barometer ' frequently continues high during a N.E. storm, but there is a ' fall of the thermometer.' Meteorologists who scrutinize these maxims might not attach much value to forecasts of weather founded upon uncertain, incomplete, and sometimes questionable rules. The simple and elementary propositions count for nothing as official gain.   Who requires to be authoritatively told that ' rapid changes of all kinds commonly presage violent ' atmospheric commotion; ' that ' strong winds are more steady ' in direction than light or moderate winds; ' and that ' sea ' disturbance often precedes gales '?   These are mere meteorological truisms.

Distinguishing for a moment, for the sake of simplicity, between the weather forecasts and the storm warnings, let us inquire whether the Office kept a careful register of the actual weather as a corroboration or correction of its plans and principles.   The Committee certainly found that a book had been kept from the commencement, in which the daily reports of weather from the stations, as published, were entered, with the appended forecast for the subsequent day or days, so that, by collating the report made on the one day with the forecast for that day made on the previous day or days, some kind of comparison of forecast with fact might be made.   From these and other diligently collected but miscellaneous materials, an attempt was at one time made to compare the daily forecasts with the facts.   This seemed promising enough, but a careful examination disclosed several fatal defects.   In the first place, the forecasts themselves were expressed in such general terms that they cannot readily be compared with the facts; and in the second place, the times for which the forecasts were made were often changed in practice.   Sometimes they were made for the succeeding day, sometimes until the next report, sometimes for the next two days together, and sometimes for each of the next two days separately.   In the third place, the facts given by the daily weather reports, as collected and published, are not sufficient to afford accurate information of the actual weather.   In the fourth place, most of the daily observations were made but once in the twenty-four hours, and only at a few places.   In fact, the whole of the collected materials were found to be inapplicable to any purposes of exact comparison or corroboration.   The page which the Committee append by way of example completely bears out these statements.   They selected certain forecasts at haphazard to illustrate a comparison of the daily forecasts with facts, and these certainly serve to display the vagueness of the official language and the inadequacy of the observations collected, even when the Department concluded that the particular forecast had been good.

Happily we have some definite and decisive tests in the arrangements made by the Wreck Department of the Board of Trade in 1864 for instituting a comparison of the actual weather with the daily forecasts and the storm warnings; but here again the result of the application of the tests is very far from encouraging. Diagrams were prepared by means of which an exact comparison could be instituted of the forecasts with each other; so that, for instance, a forecast for Thursday made on the Tuesday previous could be compared with a forecast for Thursday made on the previous Wednesday, with reference to direction and force of the wind. It was shown that ' not only was there no correspondence, but no determinate ' relation of any kind, between them. The forecasts made on ' two succeeding days for the third day differ from one ' another in every possible way.'

The daily forecasts for the month of December 1865 were compared with each other and with the storm warnings issued for that month ; and from this comparison it appears that, taking the daily forecasts for each district of the United Kingdom, North, West, South, and East, as published in the newspapers, there were in that month eighty-four sets of reiterated forecasts, or, in other words, there were twenty-one days for which in respect of each of the four districts two forecasts were issued, one on the previous day and the other on the day before that one. Yet of the eighty-four sets of double forecasts there were only eleven in which the two forecasts agree with each other verbatim, while there are twenty-seven which agree with each other substantially, and forty-six which do not. The verbatim agreements, therefore, are 13 per cent., the substantial agreements, 32 per cent., and the total disagreements no less than 55 per cent. of the whole number. Furthermore, with relation to certain storm warnings issued in the same month by the same Department, there were only ten daily forecasts out of thirty-two which agreed with the storm warning—that is, 31 per cent.—while the disagreements amounted to 69 per cent. As a rule, therefore, the daily forecasts agreed neither with each other nor with the storm warnings, although they formed parts of the same system, and were issued by the same Department within a short time of each other. With these failures in view, of what value are the late Admiral's words already cited?—' We ' are enabled to know what weather will prevail during the ' next two or three days, and, as a corollary, when a storm will ' occur.' That we may ultimately arrive at this knowledge is possible and even highly probable, but whether the Admiral had attained it the above statements must determine.

The occasional storm warnings have made this Department better known and more popular than its other labours, and they therefore deserve a separate consideration. The Admiral devised a system of day and night warning and cautionary signals, and circulated a description and explanation of them among mariners. In this official circular the Committee point out ambiguities of description which, together with others belonging to the signals themselves, render it difficult to compare the storm warnings with subsequent facts, particularly in the case of a combination of signals. There is little difficulty in ascertaining whether a storm warning has been followed by a gale, but much in discovering whether the different characteristics indicated by the signals as to the direction of gales and dangerous winds, either singly or in combination, have been verified by facts or not. Premising then that these ambiguities impede the application of precise tests to warnings which are themselves wanting in precision—premising further that the Department has not kept any precise record of storms, or of the weather which followed the storm warnings—the Committee proceeded to make such examination as they best could from the accumulated extracts from newspapers before referred to, and a laborious digest of them extending from the 31st July, 1861, to the 27th February, 1862, published by the Meteorological Department as the eleventh of its meteorological papers.

Having due regard to the want of precision in the forecasts themselves, and of completeness in the specified digest, we are nevertheless presented with at least an approximate test of the value of the warnings issued, in respect of the force of the wind, and of the direction as well as force. As the result it is found that in 160 warnings issued in 1862–3 during three months, 81 per cent. of them were right as to force, while only 34 per cent. were right as to direction. In 125 subsequent warnings issued in 1863–4, 68 per cent. were right as to force, and 48 per cent. right as to direction. In 120 warnings issued in 1864–5, 75 per cent. were right as to force, and only 33 per cent. as to direction. Summing up the results of the whole of these 405 warnings, in respect of force alone 75 per cent. were right, while in respect of direction as well as force but 38 per cent. were right, and of course 62 per cent. wrong. Those warnings of direction were treated as wrong in which no gale followed the warning, as well as those in which there was a gale, but not from the direction indicated by the signal.

While it thus appears that only three out of every eight warnings were right in relation to direction, it is noted that the result would probably be still more unfavourable if the ambiguities had not rendered it necessary to give a great latitude to the meaning of the storm warnings; and, again, while about six out of every eight of the warnings were right as regards force, yet if from these were deducted the cases in which a gale was blowing when the signal was hoisted, the proportion of those to be deemed successful would be less.   A rigorous criticism then would diminish the successes and aggravate the failures.   Another failure by way of lack of vigilance is discovered in the fact that between April 1, 1862, and March 31, 1863, the digested returns include several gales, some of which were severe and long, for which no storm warnings at all were issued.

The facts recorded for the same period by the Wreck Department afford a rather better test than those just adverted to, as they were collected independently and with greater completeness, and are gathered from returns locally made by officers of the Customs or the Coastguard in conformity with notices received at the time of the issuing of a storm signal.   These returns being sent to the Wreck Department of the Board of Trade, there exists in that office a complete history of every gale which has followed a storm warning since July 1861, at all those places where such a signal has been hoisted.   These were submitted to the Admiral, but he raised objections to them, which were not well founded and are refuted *seriatim* by the Committee, who observe that although those returns are far from perfect, they nevertheless afford the most valuable data now in hand for checking the correctness of the storm warnings, and for tracing the course and progress of violent gales in the British Isles,—and add, ' we regret that they have ' not been duly made use of for this purpose, since if they ' had, the Meteorological Department would probably by this ' time have been in possession of much precise and valuable ' information on the subject, which might possibly have placed ' the practice of predicting gales on a sound inductive basis.'

The results of a comparison with these despised documents, tabulated with respect to force and direction of winds, are by no means favourable to the efficiency of the warnings.   First as to force, we may just give a summary of their results in the shape of a per centage of total success and total failure.   From July to December 1861, there were issued 413 warnings as to force of wind, of which the total successes were 52 per cent., and of course the total failure 48 per cent.; but upon the supposition that in 20 per cent. of the warnings the wind was blowing a gale when the signal was hoisted, the total successes are reduced to 32 per cent.   In the year 1863 out of 2,288 warnings 36 per cent. are estimated as total successes, leaving 64 per cent. of total failures.   As the analysis of the whole returns is a work of great labour it has not been carried on regularly since 1863, but partial analyses were framed for the months of December in the three years 1863, 1864 and 1865, from a comparison of which similar conclusions were obtained, the total failures ranging from 36 per cent. as the minimum to 86 per cent. as the maximum. Putting the general results of the whole analyses together in respect of force of wind, and turning them into per centages, we find that the total failures, in all places warned, range from 36 to 68 per cent., and that the total failures in seven selected ports named, range from 54 to 60 per cent. ; the period concerned extending from 1861 to 1865. All that can be noted in favour of the warnings is that on the whole there is an improvement in the later as contrasted with the earlier ones.

The force of wind is perhaps the easier field of forecast, and when we come to comparisons of direction, as well as force, the tests become far less precise, and even less satisfactory. Here, again, the inherent ambiguity of the signals increases the difficulty of comparison, and it is impossible to make a perfectly satisfactory selection of the facts with which many of these indeterminate predictions can be compared. Proceeding, however, on the best discernible ground, and putting the best interpretation possible on the official explanations of the signals, the following result is arrived at. During parts of the years 1863, 1864, and 1865, warnings to the number of 244 were issued in relation to direction combined with force of wind, and of those not more than 22 per cent., or less than one quarter, have proved right, while the remainder, being more than three quarters, have proved wrong. One might almost have imagined that mere sagacious conjecture would have achieved equal success, without any pretensions to science. As the Committee remark, ' The chances of success due to mere ' haphazard are considerable in the six winter months of the ' year, for at that time it is probable that gales are blowing to ' a sufficient extent to justify a storm warning in every ten days ' on an average; and, on the other hand, four days in every ' ten are placed under warning by the storm signals.' From the incompleteness of the data for comparison, it could only be ascertained if the weather that *succeeded* the warnings justified them, while nothing is known of the weather that *preceded* them, and there is nothing to show *when* the warnings ought to have been sent, and when they were actually sent.

The utility of the signals manifestly depends in many cases on the precision and correctness with which they indicate direction. A collier, for instance, sailing from the Tyne or Wear will disregard a westerly gale, while an easterly gale might be fatal to her.   It is in vain to tell her that a gale is expected from the Tropical or Polar quarter, and to indicate only a wide range.   Even if such predictions correspond with subsequent facts, they are of little use, and worse than useless if they do not.

The practical utility of these warnings has been inquired into at several ports, and divers, but, on the whole, favourable, opinions have been expressed concerning them.   At Yarmouth it has been found that in some cases fishing-vessels have refused to put to sea when the warning signal was hoisted, although no local circumstances indicated danger or warranted apprehension.   The voyages of such vessels not exceeding twenty-four hours, they might often have put to sea on such occasions, but, not doing so, much time and profit were lost.   A vessel whose destination could be reached in twenty hours, if in a direction contrary to that from which the storm is anticipated, might make her voyage, whilst delay would allow the storm to overtake her.   An illustrative case actually occurred last autumn : Of two vessels ready to sail when the storm signal was hoisted, one set out, and the other delayed.   The former reached her destination in perfect safety ; the latter, by delaying to sail, was afterwards caught in the storm, and was lost.   The signals, then, may make sailors timid in putting to sea, yet they must have the good effect of inducing forethought, precaution, and preparedness under the expectation of a storm.   The sea-faring community look with increasing confidence to these signals, and now more fully credit their correctness.   That they are, with some exceptions, popular, is undeniable, and their discontinuance would cause general regret :—

‘ The existence,’ say the Committee, ‘ of this feeling is strong evidence of the utility of these storm warnings.   But in estimating this at its true value, it must not be forgotten how eagerly the world at large is disposed to base an unreasoning belief on the occasional successes of weather predictions, and how easily it forgets the failures.   We need not say that we do not wish for a moment to compare the efforts of the Department with the predictions of the ordinary weather prophets who attempt to connect the changes of weather with the stars or the changes of the moon.   It is not, however, irrelevant to refer to these prophecies, and to the belief which has been so often placed in them, when we are estimating the value of popular feeling as the evidence of the value of storm warnings.’

Even allowing for such drawbacks, we cannot peruse the ‘ Abstract of Opinions from the Ports concerning the Value ‘ attached to the Storm-Warnings at the present Time (1866) ’ without attaching considerable weight to them.   Take the last,

from Liverpool, as a sample: ' There exists an universal
' opinion that these signals are very valuable ; that the amount
' of accuracy has gradually increased.'   In our view the testimony in their favour is decisive, so far as common opinion
has weight.

It was and is the opinion of the officials of the Meteorological Department that their weather forecasts and their
storm warnings are so intimately associated as necessarily to
stand or to fall together.   The Committee do not think so,
neither do we.   No doubt, in order to give occasional warnings
of violent storms, it is necessary to obtain as constant and as
frequent observations as for daily weather forecasts.   But it
is only natural to suppose that the more sudden and violent
changes of wind and weather which are the subject of the occasional storm warnings are preceded by more decided indications
than the more common and less violent changes of our variable
climate, and that the observations made of a sudden fall of the
barometer may afford a trustworthy indication of approaching
storms, while the sudden daily changes of barometer and thermometer during ordinary weather may have no meaning which
we are at present able to interpret accurately.   It would,
therefore, be unfair to the storm warnings to class them with
the daily forecasts, which latter have already been shown to be
very faulty in every test applied to them.   If they have been
founded on an unsound basis, and if there is no evidence of their
correctness, they are surely wanting in all that can give them
practical value.   These forecasts merely manifest the opinion
of the Department (as it has repeatedly stated) concerning a
probability, and they extend to large districts, without attempting to describe the varied particulars of weather in different
parts of those districts, which alone would be of service to the
sailor in a particular port, or the agriculturist on his own farm.

From the foregoing statements, notwithstanding the unavoidable imperfection of the Committee's examinations, it appears
that they have tested the system of forecasts of weather and
storm warnings under numerous aspects,' and therefore the
conclusions they draw as to the correctness and utility of daily
forecasts and storm warnings are entitled to all attention.   To
employ their own words :—

' The conclusions we draw from this discussion are the following,
viz. :—

' That the maxims on which the Department acts in foretelling
weather have not been reduced into any clear or systematic form, and
are not shown to have been established by sufficient induction from
observed facts.

' That as a matter of fact the Daily Forecasts are not shown to be correct, and that they are not, in our opinion, useful.

' That the Storm Warnings, so far as they indicate the Force of coming gales, have been sufficiently correct to be of some use, and that their utility is widely admitted.   Also that they have improved ; and that they are probably capable of still greater improvement.

' That the Storm Warnings, so far as they indicate the Direction as well as Force of coming gales, are not shown to have been so far precise or correct as to be of use.'

Having gone through all the details which the Committee have presented in the Report, we cannot see how they could have come to any other conclusions, and they would apparently have been justified in putting them in more forcible terms.   It almost seems as though their examinations and comparisons cost greater toil, vigilance, and thought than some of the original forecasts and warnings, just as it often costs more to mend a bad mechanism than to make a good one.   Even to follow minutely the proceedings of this Committee taxes the reader's patience and exercises his ingenuity, thereby compelling him to marvel at the continual inexactitude and confusion of the late Superintendent, while he commends the patient assiduity of those who found themselves involved in a labyrinth of perplexities, to which, if there ever were a clue, it is now irrecoverable.   No official business should be so conducted as to lack inherent evidence of the manner in which important results have been arrived at.   Especially in so tentative and complex a business as that now under investigation, every step of progress should be clear, and every process of reasoning be noted, otherwise the sudden loss of the official head may, as it has now done, involve the loss of very much that judgment and experience have acquired, notwithstanding the labours of an able and diligent chief-clerk.   Not less important are checks and corrections, or confirmations by actual and subsequent atmospheric occurrences.   It is clearly as important to record the results as to issue the forecasts and the warnings, and the collection of the former should be as carefully arranged as the publication of the latter.   As to the daily weather reports previously alluded to, their insufficiency has been noted, and it may be added that miscellaneous facts gathered by the Department itself from miscellaneous sources, without knowledge of the observers, and without order or method in the observations, can be of little value.   They must mark the precise correspondence of the natural phenomena with the forecasts or warnings.   Precision in the one must be met by precision in the other.   Without a careful pre-arrangement of particulars and persons, of ˋbservers and hours of observation; without, in short, an adaptation of all circumstances connected with the actual phenomena to the terms and times of that indication, so that the one may form a complete counterpart of the other, no confidence will be inspired, and little benefit will accrue.

There can be no utility in such vague, uncorroborated, and often unsuccessful daily forecasts of weather as have hitherto been issued by the Department. The Committee, therefore, wisely recommend the discontinuance of their publication, and they believe that in so doing they are borne out by the best practical meteorologists. M. Le Verrier, of Paris, who had attempted something of a like nature, has, it is said, given it up. M. Dove, of Berlin, is confining himself to a system of storm warnings, and even in this appears to find some difficulty. M. Matteucci, of Turin, was obviously in difficulty, even as regards the storm warnings, and the Committee ' can find no evidence that any ' competent meteorologist believes the science to be at present ' in such a state as to enable an observer to indicate day by day ' the weather to be experienced for the next forty-eight hours ' throughout a wide region of the earth's surface.' To this it might be added that competent meteorologists are by their aversion to vulgar and fallacious pretensions indisposed to take serious steps in this direction. They are now labouring to constitute this science as one of precise observation, and to disentangle it from popular prejudices and misconceptions. They relinquish the rod of the prophet for the pen of the recorder. They multiply observations, and diminish conjectures. By their present actions they say in effect,—We are busy enough with the work of to-day and will not concern ourselves about the probabilities of to-morrow. Discredit has been cast upon our studies by almanac-makers, and weather prophets. With such we have no connexion, nor, whatever they may pretend, have they any with us. In the philosophical application as well as the etymological, of the word, such men may rightly be termed *lunatics,* and those who trust them may bear the same appellation.

The recommendations which the Committee make on the whole subject of Daily Forecasts, Weather Telegraphy, and Storm Warnings, and upon Observations of Weather within or affecting the British Isles, amount to fifteen in number, and appear to be generally judicious and warranted by their preceding statements. While they recommend that the publication of daily forecasts of weather probable on the North, East, South and West coasts shall be discontinued, they desire the continuance of the general results of the telegrams, not for frequent publication, but only for issue on special occasions. Every one will agree with them in desiring also that the system of telegraphing the weather from distant stations should be continued, with an addition or diminution of places, as advancing knowledge may require. These telegrams should be published as at present, but arranged in geographical districts.

On the topic of Storm Warnings it will be advisable to present the suggestions of the Committee in their own words, and therefore we quote the 6th, 7th, 8th, and 9th of their recommendations :—

'6. That the practice of issuing Storm Warnings shall be continued, but with the following modifications :—

'(*a.*) That the Signals shall for the present be confined to the indication of a probable gale, without attempting to indicate from what quarter.

'(*b.*) That they shall not be hoisted unless there is reason to expect the gale within 36 or at the outside 48 hours.

'(*c.*) That when hoisted, they shall continue up until all immediate expectations of further gales has ceased.

'(*d.*) That whilst the Signals indicating Direction are discontinued for the present, care shall be taken so to arrange the Signals for Force as to enable the Signals for direction to be added hereafter.

'7. That the officer of the Meteorological Department issuing the Storm Warning for Force should also at the same time, so far as he is able so to do, make, but not issue or publish, a prediction of the probable Direction of the coming gale, endeavouring in so doing to render it as specific as possible, e.g., whether within any particular quarter of the circle.

'8. That this officer shall note down at the time, and reduce into an exact shape afterwards, the maxims or principles which have guided him in making the Signal of Force or Prediction of Direction ; the facts to which those maxims are applied ; the mode in which he has applied and combined them, the value he has attached to each of them, and the value of the probability which he has thus obtained, and which is indicated by the Signal or Prediction.

'9. That the maxims so acted upon shall be reduced into a clear and definite shape, and kept in the office ready for reference.'

Both in respect of weather telegraphy and storm warnings there appears to be no insuperable difficulty, as far as we can judge, in the way of bringing about a system of combined European communications and publications. Why should there not be something approaching to uniform weather bulletins, of which the present form adopted by Le Verrier might almost serve as a model ? Certainly by such a method alone can any considerable body of observations of various states of European weather be grouped under definite categories. By studying such categories we should discover if there be any law regulating the change from one state into other definite states, and consequently if there be any mode of gaining an acquaintance with coming changes of weather. At least the knowledge derived from such observations would furnish a complete check upon predictions. The gathering together, arranging and preserving a complete series of nearly uniform European weather bulletins for a series of years, would obviously be the most expedient course towards the settlement of the possibility of weather prophecy. The extension of the electric telegraph renders the necessary communications rapid and simple. There can be no valid cause why vague and illusory forecasts should not be speedily replaced by trustworthy and well concerted observations.

There is every reason to believe that Foreign Government Officials will gladly co-operate with us, as may be judged from what has already been said, and from the friendly tone of the correspondence that has passed between observers of different countries. The action of one leading country communicates an impulse to others, generally by means of the instigation of eminent meteorologists. In illustration of this observation we are pleased to note the extended series of Meteorological observations recently inaugurated in Russia, and which are as yet only known in our country to meteorologists. We are informed by Lieutenant Rikatcheff, of the Imperial Russian Navy, that the Ministry of that Navy, in order to adopt on the Russian coasts the system in operation in England, had established seventeen new meteorological stations in their principal ports, and had proposed to the Ministry of Public Instruction to establish similar stations over the whole area of the interior of Russia. After careful consideration the Minister of Public Instruction laid before the Council of the Empire a proposal, to carry out which it was necessary to establish thirty meteorological stations. In consequence of this the Council of the Empire, with the approbation of His Majesty, ordered : 1st. that the observatories are to be intrusted to persons recommended by the authorities of public instruction ; and, 2ndly. that the necessary funds for establishing those stations in the interior of the empire are to be taken from the public purse. Fortunately for Russia, the Director of its Central Physical Observatory to whom the execution of this work was entrusted, is the able and widely known Professor Kuppfer, who being thus authorised formed a list of thirty-nine new stations which he believed it was necessary to establish, besides the sea-stations and four stations in Moscow, Dorpat, &c. Instruments were prepared for chosen stations and adjusted in July of last year. From the same informant we learn that the synoptic charts of several storms which have been prepared in our own meteorological Department are approved, and that Admiral Fitzroy's Weather Book is translated into the Russian language by a Russian Captain. The Governors of all European provinces of Russia are requested to give assistance for the institution of regular Meteorological Observations in the capital of each province, and to publish the results in the provincial papers.

The details of the plans are excellent though simple. It is proposed to provide all stations with instruments carefully examined before use at the Central Physical Observatory. At present secondary stations will be furnished only with barometers and thermometers. Observations are to be taken three times every day, and these will be daily sent at eight o'clock A.M. to the Central Physical Observatory, where from all the observations received, the most probable state of the weather for the following day will be declared. The deviation will then be sent by telegraph to all seaports. When the stations shall be finally settled, and the meteorological correspondence by telegraph is in full operation, it is intended to print a daily paper with meteorological intelligence, accompanied by a meteorological chart, and to send this paper by post to every seaport, as well as to correspondents and other persons who are interested in meteorology.

To render the system of telegraphic correspondence of meteorological observations more complete, and taking into consideration that all great storms come from the west, Kuppfer considered it necessary to receive by telegraph the observations made at several stations in Western Europe. With this view he was sent in December 1864 to France, Prussia, Italy, Austria, and Holland, to consult scientific men about the choice of the best points of observation, and to arrange a gratuitous transmission by telegraph of these observations. The proposed plan was well received by all the scientific meteorologists; by Dove, at Berlin; by Le Verrier, at Paris; by Matteucci, at Turin; by Jelinsky, at Vienna; and by Buys-Ballot, at Utrecht (these being, in fact, the most able of foreign meteorologists), as well as by several telegraphic companies, which, for the most part, promised to send the meteorological despatches to Russia gratuitously.

To make the system of daily telegraphic communication of meteorological observations more extensively useful, it was considered necessary to combine them with others made at sea, to prepare charts of the currents of the seas, and of the direction and strength of the wind, by the combination of wind and sea observations. To follow and somewhat extend the instructions given by the Royal Society of London to our Meteorological Department, it was thought desirable to collect, arrange, and discuss the meteorological observations which have already been made.

Recognising the importance of having a knowledge of meteorological changes in particular places in order to determine the laws which regulate them, and the future changes of the atmosphere in such places, the Hydrographical Department resolved to prepare charts of winds from the observations which have been made on Russian seas, and to begin this work at once by collecting all observations, from ships of all kinds, made in the Baltic Sea and near to it for many years past. This work is intrusted to a captain attached to the Hydrographical Department, who has divided the Baltic Sea into spaces of 1° in latitude and 2° in longitude, and the adjacent gulfs into spaces of ½° in latitude and 1° in longitude. He has commenced his labours, with the assistance of two officers, by first extracting from the log-books of all ships, merchantmen and others, the meteorological observations which have been made since the year 1844.*

Plans so excellent, inaugurated in a country so extensive as Russia, cannot but excite the highest hopes for their success; nor is it an insignificant result of our own activity if we may fairly conclude that it communicated the original impulse to the Russians. To them as well as to us the report now before us will prove of considerable interest.

To return from our Russian digression to the matter of storm warnings, it may be fairly assumed that all foreign observatories, or, at least, the principal of them, will co-operate with us and one another. The principles on which we proceed in our prevision of approaching storms are now understood and acted upon by the most advanced European observatories. As to what is known, performed, and observed at Paris, let us hear what M. Marie Davy, of the Imperial Meteorological Observatory, says, in a communication to the Academy of Sciences, in the autumn of 1863:—

'We discern the first symptoms (of coming storms) displaying themselves some days in advance on the Western coasts of Europe,

---

* Proceedings of the British Meteorological Society, vol. iii. No. 21.

by an inflexion of the curves of equal barometric pressure.   Then the wind rises more or less rapidly on the north-west coasts of France and England, manifesting a very distinctly marked tendency to turn round a centre of depression which forms the centre of the tempest.   This centre disperses itself, at one time in a regular manner, and progressively from west to east, lifting itself at first towards the north to descend afterwards towards the south, after having traversed England ;   at another time, on the contrary, there seems to be some hesitation which for a moment keeps back the storm.

' The study of these perturbations possesses great interest, whether in a purely scientific point of view or in view of the probabilities which we may thence deduce relative to the particular parts menaced by a tempest in preparation, or to the place where it has commenced to rage.   This study is regularly carried on in the Observatory at Paris by means of our maps ; but up to the present time these maps have remained in manuscript.   We consider that we shall perform a useful and acceptable service to meteorologists by inserting them in the daily bulletin of the Observatory.

' An examination of our meteorological maps shows that generally it is possible to perceive twenty-four or forty-eight hours before-hand the approach to our coasts of a storm lasting for a mode-rate length of time.   We merely regard these maps as the first sketch serviceable for our guidance as to the probabilities of the morrow or the day after.   Too often our information arrives too late or is incomplete.   But since the 12th of October the documents which have come to us from England, have received from Admiral Fitzroy a very useful complement by additions from Nairn and Greencastle.

' The unquestionable utility of this kind of work for the science of Meteorology makes us ardently desire to extend it over a larger basis.   If our maps would enable us to foresee a storm, and would permit us to follow its course over Europe, still they would indicate to us nothing, or next to nothing, of the place of its origin, or of the mode of its formation.   This, however, is one of the most essential points, not only for science itself, but for its applications. We attach the greatest importance to the construction of daily charts extending over the whole northern hemisphere, and to an annual reunion of the elements of each of them.   In the incessant movements of the atmosphere, it is very certain that there are grand general laws which we should disengage, and which we must search for by a comparison of the observations of preceding and sub-sequent years.   The principal of these maps might be published in our bulletins in a convenient form.'

It were well if our actual attainments in relation to the laws of storms could be precisely known and practically applied. Any casual and partial reader of the great number of separate papers written by Redfield in America ; of General Reid's imposing ' Attempt to develope the law of storms by means of

' facts arranged according to place and time, &c.; '* of Dove's volume now before us, not to mention minor works, would probably be misled in respect of the available and practical services of these several publications. They are all of considerable value, especially that of Dove, who gives a useful section on ' Practical Rules.' Still, the entire results applicable to ordinary navigation are not abundant and decisive. The literature of cyclones is fruitful, for there exists a bibliographical list of 450 authors' books and periodicals, where some interesting accounts of such storms may be found, and especially of West and East India hurricanes; but the application of this literature to practice and voyages is more doubtful and difficult. Piddington has attempted it in his ' Sailor's Horn ' Book of the Law of Storms; ' and Mr. Birt, with less pretension, in his ' Handbook of the Law of Storms.' Yet such books are not well received by all, for we read in the publication of a master mariner, Mr. Jinman, on Winds :—' Should ' this meet the eye of Mr. Piddington, I beg leave to tell him ' that if the junior, or even the senior officers of the Penin- ' sular and Oriental Company's service, and first-rate passenger ' ships, know no more about the law of storms than can be learnt ' by studying such works as the " Horn or Handbook of the ' Law of Storms," they have yet *much* to learn.' Even Maury remarks on this topic,—' After much study, some few principles ' or laws seem to be fairly established, but even these are not ' incontrovertible, though they are sometimes cited as if in- ' controvertible.'

It is true that great cyclones do not often visit us, but the late Admiral Fitzroy believed in the existence of small cyclonic storms in England itself, originating in or near our islands, and generated in the brushing against each other of the N.E. and S.W. currents. These small signs are not frequent, and seldom number more than three or four in a year. This direction of their motion is almost invariably towards some point between N.N.E. and E.S.E. and they take about forty-eight hours to pass from Ireland to the Baltic. These small cyclones constitute a class of phenomena well suited for telegraphic advertisement. Although we are not scourged by violent cyclones, we are bound, in the interests of humanity, to give all possible aid to the discovery and discussion of their laws, for our seamen in their voyages are frequently exposed to them, like the far-sailing seamen of other countries.

---

* Noticed in this Review in an article on the ' Statistics ' and ' Philosophy of Storms,' January 1839.

It is also important to notice that though we are by our situation exempt from great hurricanes, by our situation we are able to act as monitors to Europe; for extensive atmospheric disturbances, which first invade Ireland and England, are those which, more especially in winter, extend to and pass over the Alps (although these great mountains somewhat retard them), and spread over Italy, as M. Matteucci has noted.

We have given more prominence to storm warnings and weather forecasts than, perhaps, mere meteorologists would themselves allot. But Admiral Fitzroy has made them most prominent, and they are certainly the most popular parts of our theme, as well as especially important to seamen. Ere we pass away from them we must draw attention to what is not a scientific topic, but one which intimately concerns the administration of the Department.

Economists will naturally inquire what the expenditure of the Department has been, and the reply is as follows:—At the end of the financial year 1865 the aggregate outlay since 1856, the date of the establishment of this office, has been about 45,000*l.* The annual expenditure has increased from 3,240*l.* to (say) 5,500*l.* In one year, 1863–4, it was as much as 7,100*l.* The sums expended on instruments and other requirements of ocean-statistics, from an average of 2,216*l.* in the years 1856 to 1864, have, for the years 1860 to 1865, diminished to an average of 1,613*l.* In the latter years the expenditure has been increased by a sum averaging 2,011*l.* a year, which has been spent upon telegraphy and storm warnings. For 1864–5 the expenditure on instruments was 1,144*l.* 14*s.* 8*d.*; on telegraphy and storm warnings, 2,735*l.* 10*s.*; for salaries, 1,134*l.* 17*s.*; making in all 5,460*l.*

Against these items in particular and this aggregate of 45,000*l.*, what meteorological advances, what precise records, what available experience, what fully tabulated results, what established maxims, what discovery of principles, have we to set off? Although it may be pleaded that scientific and especially meteorological results are of too delicate a nature to be weighed against so much coin, or of too fine an essence to be rendered appreciable at the bank, it may yet very fairly be asked, What remains in the Department in any form as an equivalent for so large an outlay? It is easy to see the defects which the examinations of the Committee have brought to light, but it is not easy to discern counterbalancing benefits to the extent of the expenditure. Moreover, the Committee now contemplate an increasing expense in the execution of their recommendations; but this they declare to be unavoidable, unless either the original object of the Meteorological Department or the system of Storm Warnings is to be abandoned. There is, however, this great difference between past and future expenditure: the former has been for results which have been shown to be largely unsuccessful, the future may be attended with adequate and accurate returns.

One radical defect has been the absence of all checks upon the work and officers of the Department. Little or nothing of the kind was devised internally, and externally there was no provision for any inquiry. But for the melancholy event which every one deplores, this system, or rather want of system, might have continued to this day. No head of a scientific department should be allowed, or should allow himself, to pursue his course unexamined or unapproved. In such circumstances unaided success is difficult of attainment, and conscious failure is a burden too heavy to be borne.

Much money has been spent, fine opportunities have been lost, valuable records have been neglected. It is, however, now vain to lament, and it behoves us rather to inquire how past omissions and failures may be utilised as warnings, and thus become the motives to amendment.

Considerable amendment may be effected by recalling this Department to its original constitution and functions, to the detailed suggestions made by the Royal Society, and to its own actual procedure in part before its unprofitable diversion to daily weather forecasts; and it is to these that the Committee draw particular attention. ' The meteorology of the ocean,' they remark, ' is as important an object now as it was in 1854, and we ' feel ourselves justified in believing that the Government and ' Parliament will not now abandon an object taken up by them ' after much consideration in 1854, and that they will not be ' satisfied to leave the matter in its present incomplete and ' useless condition. If the grant originally made had been ' steadily applied to this object, and had not been diverted to ' other objects, the work would by this time have advanced far ' towards completion.'

There are now in the Department about 550,000 meteorological observations at sea, mostly, if not entirely, of good quality, which are contained in 1,298 registers. The remaining data are of a miscellaneous and doubtful character. The great body of good observations seems to be the principal scientific result hitherto obtained by the Department, and it is highly desirable that they should be rendered available in the best practicable method. The Committee of the Royal Society—which included Professor Dove of Berlin, one of the most zealous as well as the most eminent of meteorologists—in their letter of 1855, specified the desiderata in detail, and the present Committee of Investigation indicate what is lacking to meet the requirements of the Committee of the Royal Society.   They show that the method of extracting the observations already made is not satisfactory, and that the publication of Meteorological Papers is not based on a well-considered and uniform plan.   Such publications should generally, if not exclusively, be confined to results so carefully digested as to be easily understood and readily handled, and these results, consisting in the main of the Means of barometric pressure, vapour tension, temperature and wind, together with the variability of each of them, should be systematically and uniformly tabulated.

The method pursued is to prepare a chart in which the surface of the globe is divided into spaces ranging between 80° N. lat. and 70°⁄S. lat., and bounded by each tenth meridian and tenth parallel.   These spaces, because of their uniformly rectangular appearance in the charts drawn upon Mercator's projection (those employed by navigators), were named ' ten- ' degree squares.'   Each of these has received a special number, and every one of them admits of a quarterly subdivision into smaller squares of five degrees.   When those of the ten-degree squares are omitted which are now occupied by land or ice, there do not remain more than 330 (approximately) with which the Meteorological Department would have to deal.   According to the present plan of the Department, all the observations have to be copied out of the registers, and sorted on some determinate plan into those of the 330 ten-degree squares to which they severally belong.   But the way in which this is done admits of many improvements suggested by the Committee, and it is important that something should indicate the probable precision of the several results entered.   Wide differences in probable precision clearly prevent uniformity.   Without entering upon the details of procedure, it will be manifest that the aim should be to fill up each of the squares with results of a certain value in probable precision.   What remains, then, to be effected in order to attain this end ?   The requirements of the most variable climate would probably not exceed 200 observations for each quarterly division of each ten-degree square in each of the twelve months.   That is to say, in a variable climate, about 10,000 observations in each of the 330 ten-degree squares would be required to supply the necessary material for determining its meteorological means.   But some squares would perhaps require fewer observations, and much has already been effected by foreign Governments and by private individuals. Proportionate abatement being made, the Committee consider that there remains a grand total of 1,630,000 observations to be collected and discussed. One-third of these may possibly be found in the registers now in possession of the Board of Trade.

All the observations required can be made in ordinary voyages ; therefore the issue of meteorological registers and the loan of instruments should be recommenced and continued as rapidly and widely as convenient. A chart should be annexed to each register, showing the track of the ship through the squares, and an index should be kept in the office, referring, under the head of each square, to each register containing observations relating to that square. The detailed recommendations of the Committee upon all kindred arrangements appear to be well considered, and to be marked improvements upon the method or want of method hitherto prevailing in the Department.

If the letter of the Royal Society, dated Feb. 22, 1855, was to be regarded as an epistolary draught of instruction—and as such the Committee regard it—it is lamentable to compare it with the representation of what has been done by the Department, and to contrast it with what might have been done. This letter also displays the lively interest taken by the Society in the establishment and objects of the Department, and it is but a fair inference to presume that this interest would have been continued, and that, if the late head of the Department had worked hand in hand with the Royal Society, all the resources and knowledge of the latter might have been rendered available for the public benefit. By such a combination the stores of science and the means of Government would have supplied knowledge on the one side and power on the other. This, moreover, would have led to that international scientific fraternity which we have already indicated, and which must be the determinate direction of future efforts.

We are precluded, by the nature of this article, from entering into several meteorological details of a purely scientific character. Were we to enter upon them, we should only, by the result, render still more conspicuous the defective conduct of the Department. In closing this Report of the Committee, we will only add that it appears to us like a business investigation into the *scientific effects* of the late Admiral Fitzroy, as head of the Meteorological Department of the Board of Trade, and it suggests to us a parallel unhappily not uncommon of late years in ordinary circles. A gentleman of some ability and tact, we will suppose, as well as of much self-confidence, finds himself in a high social position, and is the possessor of a fine estate and of considerable reputed wealth. He assumes all that belongs to such a position, manages his own estate, asks little advice, believes he can show his neighbours how to manage their estates, keeps up all the social habits befitting his reputation, and maintains his name amongst the foremost of his class. He becomes an oracle and a monitor, and is listened to with deference, for no one doubts his sagacity. His affairs seem to prosper, his property to increase, his estate to flourish. His lands are productive, his garden and conservatories gay with choice flowers. All goes on for some years as smoothly as his own after-dinner speeches, and he is the envy of some and the admired of others.

One morning the astounding intelligence runs round the neighbourhood that this same gentleman has suddenly died. All alike lament and mourn for him. In due time comes an independent and rigorous investigation of his affairs. The public have felicitated his family upon their pecuniary prospects, and have privately made their estimates of the value of the estate. So deluded have they been, that, when the true condition of affairs transpires, they can with difficulty credit it. This same seemingly prosperous, happy, opulent gentleman, as it now turns out, was all the while insolvent! Everything is now appraised at its true and not its nominal value, and the result is ruinous. He meant well, but he managed ill. He began wisely, but continued foolishly. He spent far more upon his conservatories and flower parterres than upon his kitchen-garden. He wasted his substance, not in riotous living, but in show, in fancies and flowers. What he gained on the one hand he lavished and lost on the other. He died in the midst of his fancies and in the illusions of his dreams. His family, however, wake up to a sad and sober consciousness of disordered affairs and disastrous finance. Will they put in practice the lesson so painfully taught to them? Will they be wise enough to retrench the unprofitable and the showy, and to cultivate and prudently farm out the estate? Will they confess past follies, and accept well-meant advice? If they will, then their affairs may yet be rehabilitated, the estate may yet be made remunerative. Away, however, for ever with flowers, and fancies, and fond theories! For the future, only sound practice and sagacious management. Such is the parallel which has occurred to us, and those who will patiently read the Report we have analysed will admit the justice of this illustration.

As arising out of the whole subject, and not specially out of the Report before us, we may conclude with a few lines upon the great importance of imparting the principles and application of what we may term Oceanic Meteorology to all young naval officers and young seamen in general, as well as to the old who are not too old to learn.   They should be taught the principles strictly and clearly, and they should be informed at the same time of the happy results of applying them to the service.   They should learn how in effect by such knowledge voyages are considerably shortened ; how what may seem dry pursuits and arid studies have direct bearings upon marine duties and marine dangers ; and how by obeying the warning admonitions of a falling barometer, seamen have made preparations to meet storms, and have met them manfully and safely, while others, unheeding or uninformed, have lost ship or life in the tempest.

Particularly should they be instructed in the use of meteorological instruments, in which great improvements have recently been and are now made.   Such instruments should be in their hands, and quickness and facility in reading their indications should be cultivated.   Every school and almost every house, as well as the smallest ship, may now have an aneroid barometer for an outlay of from 50s. to 60s.   These instruments are sufficiently exact to give timely notice of storms or gales, and may be readily fastened, like clocks, on a wall.   There is, too, an excellent and cheap little tractate on barometrical observations and indications, by Mr. Belville, which all may obtain.   It is really wonderful that so simple an instrument as a barometer, and one so replete with momentous warning for every man who traverses the sea, should be so much neglected.   All that has been done by our Department in supplying barometers to fishermen and sailors on our coasts is clear gain, and has been followed by acknowledged benefits.

In our own language we greatly need a good text-book of Oceanic Meteorology, which might be added to Oceanography. The new edition of Maury's 'Meteorology of the Sea' is a reconstruction as well as an enlargement of previous editions, one of which we noticed in this Review ;* but, commendable as it is, it cannot be made a text-book, and for such a purpose it is deficient in some respects, about which we do not now concern ourselves.   What is so much to be desired is the multiplication of ordinary observers, the instilling into all classes of mariners

---

* 'Physical Geography of the Sea—The Atlantic Ocean,' April 1857.

the importance of making some contributions to the general fund of meteorological knowledge.

There would be something not merely very promising to science, but also very much akin to poetry, if we could justify the hope that every ship that sets out on a long voyage would not merely effect the interchange of commodities, but also at the same time be a marine observatory of meteorological phenomena. It is our national boast that all oceans are traversed by our vessels; how much nobler would be the boast that all oceans are traversed by our observers! What moral dignity would there be in the position of men able to brave the tempests of the ocean, not only by their own intrepidity, but with the resources of science, and trained by the acquired knowledge of long years of patient observation to elude their fury, and to escape their destructiveness! Storms will never be less, but men may be progressively more manly. Winds and tempests will never cease to rage, but men may learn calmly to contemplate what once overcame them with terror. The most intractable forces of nature, the hurricanes, that make mere sport of man's boldest buildings and strongest pillars— that lash the seas into fury and make mountains of the waves —may be anticipated in their course, charted in their career, and defeated in their issues. They may rage without ruining, and they may revolve without involving the human race in disaster and death. They may be looked for like the irremediable but half-disarmed evils of human life.

But, in order that this may be anything more than a dream of the future, every navigator must become more or less a scientific observer—the barometer must be his companion and monitor. His pen must be ever at hand, and the log-book must become the record of a multitude of useful observations. By these the humblest mariner may contribute his mite of information, and not a sailor under canvass need despair of giving efficient aid in the grand general advancement. Every naval student should be so taught this science that he may, if opportunity occurs, do something for Oceanic Meteorology; and he may possibly add so materially to our present knowledge of the law of storms, that in time to come it may be said of him, not indeed as it was said of Franklin,

'Eripuit cœlo fulmen, sceptrumque tyrannis,'

yet in a like strain—He disarmed the storm by eluding it, he defeated it by anticipating its approach, and escaping from its fury : thus he stole its wings from the whirlwind, its terrors from the tempest.

ART. III.—1. *Bulletin de la Société de l'Histoire du Protestantisme Français. Documents Historiques inédits et originaux, XVI° XVII° et XVIII° Siècles.* Tomes I.—XIII. Paris: 1852-1864.

2. *Correspondance des Réformateurs dans les Pays de la Langue Française, recueillie et publiée avec d'autres Lettres relatives à la Réforme et des Notes historiques et biographiques.* Par A. L. HERMINJARD. Tome premier. (1512 –1516.) Genève et Paris : 1866.

THE true history of Protestantism in France has remained comparatively unknown until a recent period, for it had been written, for the most part, by men of the opposite party and the victorious creed. But time has, in this, as in many other instances, slowly brought to light the materials on which the judgment of posterity must rest, by publishing the correspondence of the Protestants themselves, and other contemporary documents which attest beyond all doubt the piety and patriotism of the Huguenot leaders and the unparalleled sufferings inflicted on their followers by national intolerance, by ecclesiastical bigotry, and by arbitrary power. The volumes before us consist of these authentic materials, deeply interesting to France, and in some respects yet more deeply interesting to ourselves. They are the result of the labours of a literary society (established in 1852) for the purpose of elucidating the history of Protestantism in France by collecting its scattered materials with care and bringing them into a single publication. For this purpose recourse has been had, not only to the Archives of France and those of the different foreign governments which gave refuge to the Huguenot exiles after the Revocation of the Edict of Nantes, but also to private family papers, to the registers of parishes and the books of notaries, to the records of old parliamentary proceedings—nay, even to inscriptions on tombstones, and extracts from ancient charters and terriers. Taken altogether, we have seldom perused a more interesting mass of original documents. They fully justify the device prefixed by the accomplished editors to each volume, and reflect a clear and steady light over an extensive tract of French history before comparatively dark and neglected. A number of essays, letters, and reviews, for the most part from the well-known pens of the best Protestant writers in France, are interspersed throughout the series, and form a valuable commentary on its contents. These papers have one characteristic in common very honourable to their authors and their faith. Much as French

Protestantism has suffered at the hands of rulers, statesmen, and factions in France, they breathe a spirit of genuine loyalty, and strong devotion to the natal soil. They indulge in no vindictive retrospects, avoid reviving the animosities of the past, and are completely free from illiberality and fanaticism.

We are surprised that this important Society has hitherto attracted so little notice in this country, and that so few English names are to be found in the distinguished list of its supporters. For a very small annual contribution the series of these Bulletins, forming one volume in each year, can be obtained at the Protestant booksellers in Paris, and we hope that the present notice will induce many of our countrymen to support this laudable enterprise.

The work which we have placed second at the head of this article is the first volume of a collection of the correspondence of the French Reformers, which has recently been published at Geneva, under the patronage of a small number of accomplished persons of that city. It consists chiefly of unpublished letters of those who took an active part in the introduction of the Reformed faith into France. These papers, which have been most carefully edited by M. Herminjard, are not at all inferior in interest to the Zurich Letters published by the Parker Society, and they are also a most valuable contribution to the history of Protestant opinions.

Our notice of the contents of these volumes must be limited to a few of the numerous topics which they embrace. They throw a good deal of fresh light on the character of the old Church of France at the period just before the Reformation. In France, as in Germany and in England, that Church had fallen in the esteem of the nation, and was deeply penetrated with elements of corruption. Francis I., on the Field of the Cloth of Gold, spoke openly of appropriating its revenues; and Bayard's exclamation against Julius, ' ce chétif Pape que ' je voudrais tuer,' expressed the thoughts of many of the nobility. The arrogance, the exactions, and the selfishness of the priesthood, and their claims to being above the law, caused jealousy among the higher orders, and the awakened conscience and thought of a generation, enlightened by the revival of letters, rebelled against a series of observances dictated often by avarice and superstition. What especially provoked the inferior classes was the rapacity and sensuality of the clergy, who, with the lessons of the Gospel in their mouths, despoiled the poor of their scanty substance, and, with pretensions to infallibility and sanctity, belied in their lives the name of Churchmen and of Christians. This collection contains a number of sketches by Bernard Palissy, the French Bunyan, of these careless and unfaithful shepherds, but we can only refer our readers to them. We quote, however, the following lines from a curious satirical poem of the time, which we do not remember to have met previously. The Church is supposed to be making complaints of the simony, the profligacy, and the idleness of those who were the stewards of her mysteries:—

> 'Mes ministres qui vivent de la croix,
> Sous faulx semblans me font à grans surcroix,
> Du deshonneur, du mal, et de l'outrage ;
> Ils sont rempliz de venimeux courage.
> Aucuns semblent en leurs habits pollutz
> A gendarmes, et non à clercs salutz,
> Ou à jongleurs, en oyant leurs caquetz.
> Bagues portez, bouquets, et aflicquetz,
> Vos heures sont dictes par grant contraincte.
> D'autres y a qui tiennent femme en caincte
> Avecques eux comme gens mariez,
> Le nom de Dieu jurez à toute actainte.
> Bref, vostre vie est de vices tant taincte,
> Que mon estat par trop dévariez.'

In France, however, as in England, the real Protestant movement commenced with the poorer and humbler ranks of the nation. It is said to have originated at Meaux, but it was most distinctly felt in the south, where probably the traditions of the Albigenses had never been entirely forgotten, and where a colony of the Vaudois had long renounced the Catholic doctrines. It appeared also in the provinces of the north, connected by trade with Holland and England, and it made progress on the western seaboard, especially in the city of La Rochelle, the wealthiest centre of French commerce. The sectaries, like their brethren in England, did not profess a definite creed ; the austere tenets they afterwards embraced were adopted by another generation ; and their religion seems to have been a protest against the evil they saw around, and an endeavour to shape their lives by the Gospel. This was the real secret of their strength. Reviled as these early Reformers were by an incensed priesthood and an ignorant populace, their conduct silenced all accusation ; and wherever they were able to leave their mark, it was one of real moral improvement. Bernard Palissy thus described the change effected in a reformed village :—

'In this wise our Church was first the work of the hands of despised men ; and when the enemy made havoc of it, it had been so blest within a few years, that gambling, dancing, ballad-singing, feasting, and superfluity of bravery and jewels, were no longer to be found among its members. Evil speaking, too, and murder had disappeared, and lawsuits were much fewer than heretofore. At Easter-time bickerings and quarrels were made up ; and we thought only of prayers, psalms, and spiritual songs, not of loose speech and lewd catches. In those times, you would have seen on each Lord's day the guildsmen walking in the meadows and dells, singing psalms and canticles in their companies, and reading and giving knowledge to each other. You might have seen girls and young women in gardens and suchlike places, rejoicing and making holy melody to God ; and even children had been so well brought up, that they had put off a silly look and bore themselves with a staid countenance.'

The Reformation rapidly spread upwards from the inferior to the higher orders. It had its supporters in the palace, especially in the first Margaret of Navarre ; it found its way to the bench of Bishops ; it entered the Parliaments and privileged corporations ; and it met with considerable favour from the nobility. The correspondence of Margaret d'Angoulême (as she is styled in M. Herminjard's collection) with Briçonnet, the Bishop of Lodève and Le Fèvre d'Etaples, and the protest of the University of Paris against the Concordat of Francis I. in the same volume, are most striking proofs of the disposition of the Court, the Church, and the learned bodies to accept with favour the doctrines of the Reformation, and to make the Bible the sole test of religious truth. As yet, however, these opinions were not connected with any party in the State ; they were still essentially religious, unalloyed by corrupt and selfish elements. At the time when our first reforming Parliament was, at the bidding of Henry VIII., suppressing monasteries and denouncing the Pope, the real spirit of Protestantism was purer and more powerful in France than in England, and had a firmer hold on the people. Francis I. hesitated for some years whether he should not encourage the Reformation, at least to a point which would have set free the national Church from the See of Rome ; and had he done so, the whole tenor of French history might have been different. But the fatal marriage of Catherine de Medicis, the terror caused by the Anabaptists of Munster, and the violence of some of the French Reformers—more vehement than their fellows in England—threw the King back upon the Catholic party ; and the influence of the preponderating party in the State, the Court, the Parliaments, and the priesthood, determined finally his resolution. We shall not dwell on the persecutions of his reign, the massacre of the Vaudois of Provence, and the horrible deaths of numerous martyrs, accompanied with every refinement of torture. One of those execrable spectacles is thus described by a contemporary German :—

'I have just seen the burning of two Lutherans. The first was a youth, the son of a cordwainer, a beardless stripling hardly twenty years old. He was brought before his judges, and sentenced to have his tongue cut out and his body burned. Without flinching, he held out his tongue to the executioner, who cut it off and beat his cheeks with it. The mob standing by picked up the tongue and flung it all bleeding and quivering at the victim. When brought to the stake, and being chained to it, he endured with indescribable serenity the insults and shouts of the infuriate crowd. The second martyr was an old man, and though his punishment was milder, I felt even more horror. He had spoken against the monks about the invocation of saints, but had been induced to retract his errors. He was brought to a gibbet, and having repeated his recantation, was half strangled, and cast into the fire. The bystanders thought the sentence too easy, they wished to see him alive in the flames.'

But even in that age many voices were raised in Catholic France against such atrocities. These volumes contain some remarkable letters from different members of the noblesse, who, though evidently of the dominant faith, disapproved of measures of persecution, and honourably declined to profit by them. In spite of torture by fire and steel, the numbers of the Reformers increased, and at the close of the reign of Henry II. they were probably nearly a tenth of the nation, including not a few of the nobility, and a considerable part of the middle classes.*

We find in this collection numerous details of the means devised by the priesthood to arrest the movement, independently of mere secular tyranny. One of the most common was the assumption of powers of a supernatural kind to awe and influence the ignorant populace; and of this there is a curious example in the legend of the Maiden of Vervins, not unlike that of our Nun of Kent. This woman was a miserable epileptic, who was carried about by the clergy of Laon, as a specimen of a Catholic miracle, the pretence being that she was possessed by a devil, who left her at the elevation of the Host and the exorcism of an orthodox bishop :—

---

* The proportion has by some writers been stated as high as *one-sixth ;* but in 1597, when the Edict of Nantes was granted by Henry IV., the Protestants are computed by Sismondi to have amounted to one-eleventh of the whole population of France, then about seventeen millions. In spite of ages of persecution, the addition of Alsace to the French territory has restored the balance, and it is believed that the actual number of Protestants in the empire is still about the same as it was three hundred years ago.

' The process of conjuring was exceedingly tedious, and consisted of strange and absurd colloquies between the exorcist and the demon.   The patient then fell into convulsions, she writhed as if on a burning seat, she sprang up spite of all resistance, she uttered vociferations that echoed over the church and that resembled grunting, barking, and lowing.   But this devilish uproar was soon made to cease ; and as soon as the wafer was placed on her lips she became calm, and completely in repose.   A miracle was then the cry everywhere ; the bells were rung, and processions went through the street to offer up thanks to Heaven, to the great scandal and shame of the Huguenots.'

This series is comparatively silent as to the progress of the Reformation in France during the last three reigns of the House of Valois.   Within this period, as is well known, the Reformers, named thenceforward Huguenots, became a distinct political party, the religious movement being connected to a great extent with secular objects.   It would be idle to say that, at this crisis, they did not fall into many excesses, that their acts, as a whole, were free from censure, and that their policy was unalloyed by some elements of passion and corruption. But the historians have made a great mistake who have represented them as an anti-national faction opposed to the real interests of their country; though no doubt the main cause of the unpopularity of Protestant opinions in France, down to the present day, is the belief that they are at variance with the great principle of national unity and uniformity to which so many of the noblest elements of French society have been sacrificed.   Politically, the Protestant was the right cause ; and in taking up arms in defence of the privileges secured them by a solemn compact, its defenders were not only vindicating justice, but struggling against a foreign influence which would have made France a Spanish dependency.   In that dark crisis when the House of Lorraine was betraying the kingdom to Philip and the Pope, when Catherine de Medicis, base as she was, was trying to escape from their thraldom, and the land was a continual scene of civil war or ominous peace, one figure shines with extraordinary lustre, the purest, we might almost say the greatest, of Frenchmen.   True alike to his faith and the country he loved, and endowed with rare sagacity and penetration, Coligni endeavoured to rescue France from that fatal connexion with Spain and Rome which was to produce such bitter fruit, and, not less grandly and ably than Richelieu, to shape out her natural destiny, as a leading Power on the land and the ocean.   It is characteristic of the execrable faction who rejoiced in shedding his innocent blood, that they invariably designated as a traitor the illustrious and far-seeing patriot who indicated to France her true alliances, and the real sources of her durable greatness. His will shows, in a touching passage, how he resented this calumnious charge, and even from the grave protested against it:——

'The reason why I set this declaration in these presents is, that knowing not the hour when God may call me away, I wish to leave it as a record to my posterity, that they may not bear a note of infamy, as having been disloyal or rebellious. If verily I took up arms, it was not against my Sovereign Lord, but those who by their tyranny compelled those of our religion to defend their lives, which I did with an assured conscience, the rather that I knew it was against the will of the King. I have many letters and documents to prove this.'

It is difficult, indeed, to realise to our minds the intense loyalty of the Reformers to their kings, and their resentment at being stigmatised as rebels. They were in truth obedient even unto death; and we thus may judge of the nature of the wrongs which forced them to abandon a belief associated with their firmest convictions. The following passage is from a Huguenot poem of the date of the middle of the sixteenth century :——

> 'N'aye donc, ô peuple, crainte
> Du supplice qui t'attend,
> Car cette dure contrainte
> Jusque à l'âme ne s'estend :
> Laisse martyrer ta chair,
> Laisse tes membres trancher,
> Laisse toy reduire en cendre,
> Laisse ton cors au bois pendre.
> Car ce grand Dieu vénérable
> Veut qu'on obéisse au roy,
> Ou qu'on s'estime coupable
> Du supplice de sa loy :——
> Puisque ton âme ne peust
> Exécuter ce qu'il veult,
> Ne refuse aucune chose
> De la peine qu'il impose.'

Even when resistance had been determined, it was justified only on the ground of the tyranny of the alien Guises, and not on that of the crimes of the Sovereign.

These volumes contain a complete account of the celebrated interview between the Guises and the Duke of Wurtemburg, in 1562, just before the infamous massacre of Vassy. Its object was to deprive the Huguenots of the aid of the Lutheran Princes of Germany, and to abandon them to the House of Lorraine; and for this purpose the Cardinal undertook to satisfy the Duke that the Lutheran doctrines were not essentially different from the Catholic, but that Calvinism was a damnable heresy. This interview, which has been hardly noticed by historians, with the exception of Michelet, was a curious drama in which the Cardinal exhibited his usual adroitness and skill, and Francis of Guise his wonted duplicity. In reply to the interlocutor of the Duke—the famous Brentius, the friend of Luther—the Cardinal declares that he is ready to give up ' the invocation of saints and the Virgin Mary,' ' that he had gone too far in the sacrifice of the Mass,' and that ' as for the hierarchy, he would wear a black robe as ' readily as a red one '; and he sums up his faith in these singular words :—

'I have read the Confession of Augsburg, I have read also Luther, Melancthon, Brentius, and others ; I entirely approve their doctrines, and I would soon come to an agreement with them about discipline. I will write to you and recognise you as my father in Christ. Ah ! had Beza and the other French ministers been like you ! We then could come to terms, and reconcile the Church. But their case is hopeless, nothing can be done with them.'

Francis of Guise professed himself equally reasonable, said that theology was beyond him, but that if there was not unity in the Church, he was ready to become a Lutheran himself; and, in answer to an earnest remonstrance against the cruelties practised on the Huguenots, delivered himself ' with heavy ' sighs : '—

' " I know well they accuse us of that and other things ; but they do my brother and myself wrong. We will satisfy you on the point before you go." And he added, " They have often tried to slay the Cardinal and myself by shot, steel, and even poison, but we never endeavoured to punish even the guilty." To which the Cardinal added, " I swear to you in the name of God my Creator, and at the peril of my soul, that I am innocent of the blood of any Calvinist." '

The researches of this Society have brought to light a vast quantity of details of interest respecting the massacre of St. Bartholomew, many of which have not been hitherto published. The following letter, written by a Jesuit, while the streets of Paris were running blood, attests the horrible joy of his party :—

' The Admiral has perished miserably on the 24th of August with the whole of the heretic nobility of France. This really may be said without exaggeration. The carnage was enormous; I shuddered at the sight of the river choked with mutilated corpses. We all agree in praising the wisdom and magnanimity of the King, who, having by indulgence and favour fattened, as it were, the heretics like cattle, has caused them to be slaughtered by his soldiers. All the heretic scholars who could be discovered have been massacred and thrown into the stream naked. Ramus, who jumped out of his bedroom from a considerable height, lies exposed on the bank pierced thick with stabs. In a word, there is not one of them, even of their women, who is not slain or wounded. Conrad gave the Admiral the third stab ; at the seventh he fell dead against the chimney of his room. Such was the end of this bad man, who, in life, brought numbers to the verge of destruction, and, in death, dragged many heretic nobles into hell.'

Giovanni Michieli, the Venetian Ambassador, whose knowledge of the secret history of the massacre appears to have been remarkably accurate, shows a touch of humanity in this description :—

' Then was seen what religious animosities could effect. It was horrible to witness in every street atrocities committed on fellow-citizens who had not only given no offence, but were often neighbours or relations of the perpetrators. There was no thought of pity for any one, even though he fell on his knees for mercy, in the most abject attitude of humiliation. It was enough that a man was disliked by another from jealousy or perhaps from a lawsuit—and this happened to several Catholics—on the cry being made that there was " a Huguenot," the victim was at once assassinated. If any one, in the hope of escape, leaped into the river and tried to swim— many unfortunate wretches made the attempt—boats put off at once, and he was drowned. The booty taken was very great, about two millions of livres d'or, many of the wealthiest Huguenots, in fact, having come to Court since the last edict.'

The massacre, as is well known, was repeated in several parts of France, by the orders of the infatuated King and his execrable band of murderous counsellors. We transcribe one of these mandates; it is difficult to imagine how it could have been written :—

' I have already informed you how on Sunday morning the King has done execution on the Huguenots, and the Admiral and the Huguenots in Paris have been slain. The pleasure of His Majesty is that the same shall be done wherever a Huguenot shall be found. Wherefore, if you wish to do the King and Monsieur good service, you will go to Saumur, accompanied by your friends, and kill all the leading Huguenots you can. I have written to M. des Moulins to have you informed. Having done this execution in Saumur, you will go to Angiers, and, with the commandant of the citadel, repeat a similar example. You will receive no other orders than this from the King and Monseigneur.'

This letter of Beza attests the terror and astonishment of the Huguenot party :—

' We are in grief and mourning ; God have mercy upon us ! Such treachery and atrocity were never known. How often I predicted it and gave warning against it! God, a God justly incensed, has permitted it, yet He is our Saviour. Excuse me for writing nothing in detail. We have instituted a fast and extraordinary prayers. The town is filled with fever and pestilence, and is overflowing with unfortunate exiles. They escaped only through the avarice of their enemies, who otherwise spared neither rank nor sex. The King at first charged the Guises with the crime; now he says everything was done by his orders; and these men whom he caused. to be murdered in their beds—these men "of whom the world was not worthy"—he dares accuse these men of conspiracy!'

There are several documents in this collection relating to the well-known tradition that Charles IX. on that fearful night repeatedly fired on his Huguenot subjects. We do not care to examine the tale, but Voltaire expressly informs us that Marshal de Tessé said, that, when young, he had known an old man who had assured him that he had himself loaded the King's harquebuss. Brantôme, too, treats the fact as certain; and this letter from a Huguenot in 1574, two years only after the event, confirms strongly the popular story:—

' A man who had gone in a skiff from Paris to the Faubourg St. Germain, and had witnessed what had been done to the Huguenots in the night, informed Montgomery all he knew on Sunday. The Count gave warning to the vidame of Chartres, and to the noblemen and gentlemen of the religion in the Faubourg; but they, being unable to conceive that the King could consent to such butchery, determined to take boat, and to cross the river, in order to endeavour to see the King, preferring to trust him and not to show mistrust. Others, too, who took it into their heads that the affair was a plot against the King's life, wished to approach him, and tender their loyal services, and even if necessary to die at his feet. But they soon saw about two hundred soldiers of the Royal Guard upon the river, coming towards those who had remained in the Faubourg, and crying out, " Slay, slay every one!" These men fired volleys before the King's eyes, he being at the time at the window of his chamber. It was then perhaps seven o'clock on Sunday morning; and it is said that the King took himself a harquebuss, and exclaimed with an oath, " Let me shoot; they are flying." '

The most important historical questions respecting the massacre of St. Bartholomew are, who were chiefly responsible for it, and whether it had been long premeditated? It is now, we think, pretty well ascertained that the story that it was the result of a scheme, devised by Catherine de Medicis and the Guises so far back as seven years before, and executed at a fitting opportunity, does not rest on a solid foundation. Such a story is not only improbable in the extreme, but is controverted by the facts now known that Catherine, for some time previously, had really wished to support the Huguenots as a make-weight against the House of Lorraine, and that the influence of Coligni with the King was considerable after 1570. A remarkable narrative, published in 1631, and, in the opinion of the editors of this series, deserving especial attention, ascribes the origin of the massacre at least to the jealousy of Catherine and her son Henry, who could not endure the attitude of authority in which Coligni stood towards the King. Having by a hired assassin disabled the Admiral on the 22nd of August, they induced at last their royal puppet to consent to an onslaught upon the Huguenots, which, however, in the event, proved far more terrible than had been contemplated. This narrative rests on a pretended confession made by Henry when King of Poland, and though its genuineness has not been proved, it is well worthy of serious attention. Henry thus describes how Coligni's influence had alienated Charles from his mother and himself :——

'The Admiral had become all-powerful with the King. Without saying one word to me, he began to walk up and down the chamber in a fury. He looked often at me askance, and with an evil eye, putting more than once his hand to his poniard, and so menacingly that I expected every moment that he would collar and stab me. I wished to get away and out of danger, which I did cleverly, for, while he was stalking about, and his back was turned, I hurried to the door, and made my escape with a quick obeisance, much quicker in truth than that on my entry. I went then at once to my mother, and having put together all the reports, the warnings, and the suspicions we had been made aware of, and the time and other circumstances of the interview, we felt convinced that the Admiral had inspired the King with some bad opinion of us.'

The Duke and the Queen, having made up their minds to get rid of Coligni by any means, procured ' Maurevel to slay ' the Admiral, but he proved himself a mere novice.' The intended victim being only wounded, the conspirators, ' now in ' a real alarm,' paid a visit to him, to disarm suspicion, and a scene so striking and lifelike followed, that we quote it at length :——

' This fine stroke having failed so narrowly, we began thinking on our situation towards evening, and, hearing that the King was going to see the Admiral, the Queen and I resolved to accompany him, and to ascertain the condition of the patient. When we reached his chamber, we saw him wounded in bed ; and we, taking the cue from the King, told him all would be well and bade him hope, assuring him too that we would see justice done on those who had brought him to this state, with their aiders, abettors, and accomplices. The Admiral said he wished to speak to the King in private ; and the King having assented at once, the Queen and I were motioned to retire. We fell back to the middle of the chamber, and remained there during this secret conversation. Our suspicions became great, and what increased them was that we found ourselves suddenly surrounded by two hundred gentlemen and captains of the Admiral's party who were in that room and another adjoining. There were others, too, in the hall below; and all these, with sad countenances and unquiet gesture and bearing, were whispering in each other's ears, passing and repassing behind and before us, and, as we thought, with great want of respect, as if they suspected that we had had some part in the wounding of the Admiral. However that may have been, we thought so at least, perhaps imagining more than was intended. We were really terror-stricken at being shut up, as the Queen, my mother, has often admitted to me.'

The fear inspired by the attitude of the Huguenots, and the consciousness of their atrocious guilt, at length caused the conspirators to attempt to win the King to their detestable counsels, and to consent to get rid of the Admiral :—

'As soon as we had reached the closet where the King, my brother, was, she commenced by showing him that the Huguenots were arming against him on account of the Admiral's wounds, that the Admiral had despatched several posts to Germany to procure a levy of ten thousand reitters, and to the Swiss Cantons for ten thousand footmen, and that the French captains of the Huguenots' party had probably departed to raise their musters, the time and place of meeting being already settled. If an army of such force, she continued, was once united with the troops in France, a thing very likely to come to pass, his army would be unable to oppose it, especially as the Huguenots had relations with many towns, communities, and people in the interior of the kingdom and beyond it. He then, being weak in men and money, would have no safety for himself or his realm. And there was another contingency that should be borne in mind; for the Catholics, wearied with their long wars, and harassed with so many calamities, were determined to put an end to them, and if he would not be of their mind, were resolved to elect a captain-general, and to make a league offensive and defensive against the Huguenots, so that he would be surrounded by perils, without authority or real power. Thus France would be divided into two great parties, over whom he would have no control. A danger, however, so great and imminent, such a series of calamities and misfortunes, and the ruin and death of thousands of his subjects, could be averted by a single stroke, and it was only necessary to kill the Admiral, the author and chief of these civil troubles.'

The head of the Huguenots being destroyed, the members could be easily dealt with. The King at first indignantly refused to listen to the advice of the tempters; but at last, if we are to credit the narrative, he rushed headlong into projects of crime more dark and terrible than had been in contemplation.

This sudden change is no doubt singular, but it is consistent with the few facts we really know about Charles IX.

'Though we were seconded by no one, we kept up our spirits, and having firmly insisted on our views, we succeeded at last in carrying our point. A remarkable change, and, as it were, a metamorphosis, came over the King; he took up our side, and fell into our opinions, going much farther and with deadlier purpose; for having before been difficult to persuade, it was now no easy matter to restrain him. He rose, and, telling us to keep silence, he exclaimed furiously and with a tremendous oath, that he was well-minded to slay the Admiral, and not only him but all the Huguenots in France, so that none should remain to charge him with the deed. He bade us then make our preparations, and, rushing out wildly, left us in his cabinet, where we took counsel the entire day, that evening, and a good part of the night, in order to see what was to be done. We made sure of the Provost of the Merchants of the Captains of the Wards, and of other persons whom we thought most bitter against the Huguenots, dividing the two into separate quarters, and telling out individuals to carry out the execution, the Admiral being assigned to M. Besse.'

This narrative, whether genuine or not, is corroborated in some important points by Michieli, who, as we have said, was very well informed:—

'This business, from beginning to end, has been the work of the Queen-Mother, aided by the Duke of Anjou, her son. . . . The Duke of Guise has been accused of the harquebuss-shot, but it was not so. The thing was concocted by the Duke and the Queen. . . . On the evening of Friday, being eager for despatch, the Queen and Anjou went into the King's closet. The Queen opened the matter to the King, pointing out the brilliant opportunity before him, and the certainty of his being able to take vengeance on the rebels, who were now shut up in Paris as in a cage. He would thus wipe out the disgrace of having treated with them, which had been forced on him by violence and terror, and he was not bound to adhere to such a compact. She made him comprehend the artifice of the Admiral's designs, seditious counsels that would lead His Majesty into a war that would prove the ruin of the realm, so long impoverished and overwhelmed by debt. And there was even something worse behind. If the Admiral were not slain, civil war would ensue, for he and his party were resolved on mischief.'

The last years of the unhappy monarch, pursued by the furies of his own conscience, have often been described by historians. We quote this sketch by an eye-witness of his sinister and repulsive aspect:—

'His looks have become dark, and in conversation he does not look the speaker in the face. He hangs down his head, sometimes shuts his eyes, then opens them again, and, as if the effort were painful, shuts them anew with a kind of uneasy suddenness. People fear that he is possessed by the spirit of vengeance ; he was severe, they now think him cruel.   He eats soberly and drinks water only, the same diet as the rest of his brothers.   He craves fatigue at any risk ; remains on horseback twelve hours at a time ; and goes on thus, hunting the same stag two or three days together, stopping only to eat, and resting but an instant at night.   His hands are callous and wrinkled, full of cuts and swellings.   His mood is always for war, it is a fixed idea..   His mother tries in vain to pacify him.'

These volumes are less rich than we had expected in documents on the memorable period between the accession of Henry III. and the settlement of France at the Peace of Vervins.   At that crisis of the destinies of mankind, when Europe was darkened by the shadows of Spanish despotism and Romish bigotry, when the dykes of Holland and the British seas proved the last and only retreat of liberty, and when the dawn of the Reformation seemed sinking in dim and disastrous eclipse, the Huguenots, having definitely become a great political and military party, fought for what was really the national cause, as well as that of the Protestant religion. Had Mayenne and the League triumphed, had the candidate of the Guises been placed on the throne won by Henry of Navarre, France would, undoubtedly, have been absorbed, for a time at least, in the Spanish Monarchy, and the country of Coligni and Sully would have become a satrapy of Philip II. It is idle, therefore, to represent the Huguenots as an unpatriotic faction, and their adversaries as the champions of the nation; such a view, the figment of a Catholic literature, is simply inverting the facts of history.   The Huguenots, however, at the end of the contest, were not more than one-twelfth of the people; and their inferiority in numbers and isolation as a sect have given colour to this charge against them. One of the first acts of Henry IV. was to abjure the faith of his Huguenot supporters, and to embrace that of the mass of his subjects.   In the case of the lover of Gabrielle, who had often shown his indifference to all creeds, conscience probably hardly raised any questions; but, certainly, if there was ever an occasion when expediency becomes the highest law, it was in the instance of this conversion.   The nation, though reconciled to its chief, and hostile to the remains of the League, was, in the mass, sincerely Catholic; and Henry's adherence to the Protestant doctrines would have probably rekindled the long civil war and alienated the great body of his subjects. It was natural, however, that his defection should have been condemned by many of those who had fought for him in the Reformers' ranks, and especially by the Huguenot preachers, who denounced it in passionate and unmeasured language.

The following letter is characteristic of the boldness and licence of these uncompromising men—the true disciples of Knox and Calvin—whose single-mindedness we must respect, though we may think it ill-timed and narrow. The personal sarcasms cannot be mistaken :—

'You, who with a handful of men have won so many trophies and gained so many hearts, who bear the name of great among your titles of honour, must you be alike despised and hated? Among the Kings of Israel Solomon was the wisest and most learned, and nothing could be compared to his glory, as even we see in the New Testament. Yet we know and blush at his disgraceful fall ; how in his old age he became besotted by women, and was led by them into paganism and idolatry. Jehu was the especial servant of God, and was anointed by the Prophet to execute His judgments on Jezebel and the house of Ahab ; nevertheless he fell off and sinned at the end of his reign. Roman history informs us of the first years of Nero, and you know what a monster he became afterwards. Tacitus speaks of Galba as one fit to reign had he not reigned ; that is, he was so esteemed before, not after his advent to empire. These few examples, Sire, taken from many others, may afford you some food for meditation.'

Such appeals doubtless, not to speak of the reproof—conveyed in very different language—of such men as Duplessis Mornay and D'Aubigné, fell lightly on the ear of the Prince, who, as it was said, spent in love the time when he should have been marching against Parma. Henry IV., however, did not fail to do justice to his Huguenot subjects. The Edict of Nantes, indeed, was not an original measure of toleration ; it was a re-enactment, even with restrictions, of privileges conceded many years before ; and, as a compromise, it was deficient, in some respects, in far-sighted statesmanship. Nevertheless the Huguenots esteemed it with justice the Great Charter of their religious rights ; nor was it unworthy of the noble principles bequeathed to France by the illustrious L'Hôpital. It secured, under certain fixed limitations, full freedom of worship to all French Protestants ; made them eligible to any office in the State without imposing any obnoxious test; confirmed their ecclesiastical and political organisation and their possession of certain places of strength ; and even established a separate tribunal in each of the Parliaments to maintain their franchises. A measure so comprehensive and liberal provoked of course opposition in that age ; and singularly enough that opposition was directed not against the most objectionable part of the edict, its leaving the Huguenots their cautionary towns, but against what was its principal merit, its recognition of their religious freedom. Henry IV., however, persisted steadily, and with a courage that does him honour, against the remonstrances of the great bodies of the State, and of many bigoted and ignorant counsellors, and he not only accomplished his object but caused the edict to be observed faithfully. His address to the Parliament of Paris reveals his position and sentiments at this juncture, and illustrates the character of the man—gay, light, and easy, but generous and humane, with great experience in affairs of state, and a true appreciation of the wants of his kingdom :—

' I have come to speak to you, not, like my predecessors, in a royal garb, with sword and robes, nor as a prince who addresses strange ambassadors, but in a purpoint, like the father of a family who wishes to say a word to his children. I entreat you to verify the edict I have caused to be made in favour of the Reformers. What I have done is for the interests of peace ; I have made it abroad, I wish to make it at home. . . . We must put an end to all false rumours ; we must make no distinction between Catholics and Huguenots, but all must be good and loyal Frenchmen. . . . I have for a long time desired to reform the Church, but I cannot do this until peace shall have been made. You cannot convert the Huguenots by force ; and at any rate I am a shepherd-king, and will not shed the blood of my sheep.'

He thus addressed the notables of Toulouse, a town, down to our own times, remarkable for religious animosities :—

' I am surprised you cannot conceal your ill will. You have still too many Spaniards among you. Could any one honestly suppose that men who had exposed their lives, substance, estates, and houses in the defence and preservation of this realm would be unfit for public and honourable offices, like perfidious Leaguers, who deserve to be banished. Those who have moved heaven and earth to destroy this kingdom are, in your opinion, good Frenchmen, and alone worthy and capable of offices ! I am not blind ; I see very plainly ; I wish the Reformers to live in quiet in my kingdom, and to have a right to receive employment from the Crown, not because they are Reformers, but because they are good subjects.'

This interesting record of an interview between the King and Daniel Chamier, one of the most celebrated Huguenot pastors, does honour to Henry's courtesy and good feeling, and shows his endeavour—in which he met with considerable success in his glorious reign—to soften down .the sectarian rancour which was too apparent in both parties :—

' The King took me by the hand, and, having led me to a gallery, asked me if I was soon going away. I replied, as soon as I had received his commands. He said that he wished to make use of my services, not in the way many thought that he gained over his ministers, who were viewed with dislike and called his pensioners. He only asked of me what an honest man might do. He was not, as it was said, ruled by the Jesuits, he ruled them and his ministers too like a king. . . . It was wrong to have called the Pope Antichrist, and to have written letters to strange princes ; it was not well to speak of Frenchmen as Papists; for his part, he would willingly lose an arm could he bring his subjects to agree in religion.' *

The religious animosities of France revived at the death of Henry IV.; and the first years of the reign of Louis XIII. were marked by Huguenot disaffection. It is absurd, however, with many historians, to make the Reformers alone responsible for the period of anarchy and civil war which terminated at the Peace of Alais. They often, indeed, betrayed the vehemence and passion characteristic of their race, and their cause, through their leaders, became identified with the expiring efforts of disorderly feudalism. But the revolts of the Huguenots were really due to their false and anomalous position in the State, to the character of the Government and the times, and to the numerous vexatious infringements, attended with insult and prosecution, that were made upon their chartered privileges. By leaving them in possession of their places of strength, and treating them as apart from the nation, the inevitable result of the Edict of Nantes was to make them a state within the State itself, and to separate them from the mass of their countrymen, with distinct interests, aspirations, and sympathies. The ascendancy of the old faction of the League during the feeble regency of Marie de Médicis provoked naturally their distrust and suspicion; and the perilous situation of Protestantism in Europe—contending against the Romanist reaction, and the enormous power of Austria and Spain, connected with France by a double marriage—inclined them against a Catholic monarchy. They would doubtless, however, have remained quiescent, had it not been for the criminal encouragement the Government gave to violations of their rights, and the series of provocations and wrong they suffered at the hands of the Catholic party. The following catalogue of Huguenot grievances in a petition drawn up in 1621 almost justifies their repeated insurrections :—

'In many places we are not permitted to worship in the manner

---

* The 'Diary of Daniel Chamier (ancestor of the well-known English family of that name), from 1564 to 1621, containing a particular account of his journey to the Court of Henry IV. in 1607, has been published by Mr. Charles Read in a separate volume, which forms part of the series produced by the Société d'Histoire du Protestantisme Français. The 'Memoirs of M. de Bostaquet,' reviewed in a recent number of this Journal, also form part of the same collection.

sanctioned by your edicts. They will not allow us to live or die in peace. In opposition to your edicts, they set priests to lay siege to our sick-beds, and prevent the sufferers from thinking of God by dinning in their ears that they are doomed to perdition. Our enemies, though preferring our graves to our presence, cast stones at those who inter our dead, or unbury those who have been buried and fling the corpses into the common sewers. We are given infamous places for cemeteries; the wills of our testators are set aside, and legacies are frequently invalidated. Our children are taken from us to be baptized; if grown up, they are married or put into employments against the conscientious wishes of their parents, the law of nature and conscience being thus disregarded, and our Christian liberty put under restraint. To sap our churches to their foundations we are denied the means of instructing our children; we are kept out of all honours, offices, and places enjoyed by your subjects; the benefits we should derive from the Chambers of the edict are never obtained within a reasonable time, either on account of vexatious opposition, or of repeated and costly appeals, or because it is impossible to execute their judgments. Our temples are burned; our assemblies attacked; our nobility are removed from your household; their pensions are given to less deserving persons; we are banished from towns, and mobs stirred up against us; in a word, we are persecuted to the death.'

The civil wars of this brief period have scarcely attracted sufficient attention, being, like the wrongs by which they were caused, forgotten in the grand series of events which form the next scenes of French history. The Huguenots displayed great stubbornness and energy: we quote from a contemporary account this sketch of an episode in the siege of La Rochelle, the Londonderry of French Protestantism:—

'More than 15,000 persons died of hunger: M. de Noyres says 23,000. They had not strength enough to dig the pits that contained the dead; when they fell exhausted they could not rise again. Such was their firmness that they would look out for a pit and bier, paying for them whatever price was asked; and, whenever a funeral of their friends took place, those who were most feeble remained in the cemetery, at the side of the new-dug graves, and, having begged their companions to go back, would lie down and at last drop in. The poorer inhabitants, though dying of starvation, never stole the corn of others when it was being brought to the mill. The eloquence of Gaulbert, the minister, wrought in them this endurance; and Guiton, the mayor, was wonderfully obstinate. This man answered a friend, who was pointing him out an honest acquaintance perishing of hunger, "Don't trouble yourself about it, we must all come to this; let them die, but as long as one of us remains to close the gates there will be garrison enough!"'

The energy and ability of Richelieu put an end to the religious wars that had desolated France, and placed the Huguenots in their proper position. He perceived the defects in the Edict of Nantes, deprived the Reformers of their cautionary towns, and interdicted the representative assemblies that gave them a separate political existence. But he guaranteed them a full measure of civil equality and freedom of worship; and his firm, severe, but national administration secured them in the possession of these advantages. The Reformers, no longer isolated as a sect, lost the power and the will to oppose the nation; and, freely admitted into the service of the State, and assured in the exercise of their religion, became contented and peaceful subjects. French Protestantism, during the thirty years that elapsed after the Peace of Alais, adds a brilliant page to the history of France. It is remarkable how large a proportion of the noblest and most distinguished members of the Court of Louis XIV. in the earliest years of his reign were, or had been, members of Protestant families. Even Madame de Maintenon affected to atone by the bigotry of her later years for the errors of her youth. But most of these Huguenot nobles abjured their faith, attracted by the fascinations of the Court, or perhaps indifferent to the cause of dissent when it had ceased to be a point of honour. The great names of La Tremouille and La Rochefoucauld were soon found in the Catholic ranks; and even the Rohans and the Chatillons were seen ultimately among the converts. Some, however, clung to the creed of their fathers; and Schomberg, Guébriant, and Turenne, till manhood, shed lustre alike on France and Protestantism. The Duchesse de la Force, who was incarcerated by Louis XIV. in a dungeon which may still be seen in the Castle of Anger, maintained her faith inviolate, even after her husband had conformed to the mandate of the Court. But the real influence of the Reformers, and the benefits they conferred on the nation, are to be found, not in the records of the great, but in the industrial and general improvement of France during this part of the century. The Huguenots, forgetting their political sympathies, and protected in their religious privileges, betook themselves to the arts of peace; and, by the admission of their detractors, became eminent in the van of progress. Their settlements were enriched by careful husbandry, they increased largely the commerce of the kingdom, and several of the present manufactures of France owe their origin to Huguenot skill and invention. Nor were they deficient in science and letters; their four academies at this period boasted many names of conspicuous merit; and, in the learned professions especially, the Reformers gained very high distinction. As for the moral and social results of this movement, they were such as experience has often verified.   Without becoming indifferent to their faith, the Reformers mitigated some of its asperities, and lived at peace with their Catholic fellow-subjects, united parts of one great community.   Above all, the disaffection vanished which had broken out lately into civil war; the old Huguenot loyalty revived and increased under a just government; and Mazarin, who carried out the policy of his predecessor with scrupulous fairness, could boast that ' his little Huguenot flock was fondly attached to its royal ' shepherd, even if it strayed into bad pastures.'   It was the golden age of French Protestantism, a bright space between two dark eras.

During the early part of the reign of Louis XIV., the number of the French Protestants was not less, probably, than fifteen hundred thousand, and they composed some of the most valuable classes of the nation. The great families of the noblesse had nearly all conformed to the Catholic doctrines, and a considerable portion of the inferior seigneurie had gradually imitated this example. But the Huguenots filled the trading corporations; they had absorbed a large share of the commerce of France; they occupied wealthy and prosperous districts; they had many distinguished intellectual leaders; and everywhere they formed a contented population.   M. Weiss—whose death we regret to notice while commenting on a kindred theme—in his excellent work on the French refugees, has given us an animated and interesting sketch of the state of the Huguenots at this juncture.   Agriculture had made remarkable progress in the provinces, in which they were numerous; and it was owing mainly to their efforts that the slopes of Béarn were thick with corn, that cultivation ran up the Cevennes, that the valleys of Languedoc flowed with wine, and that a thousand farms in Normandy were rich with meadows and gay with orchards.   They traded extensively with the Levant, with Canada, Holland, and the British Islands; and Huguenot captains and Huguenot crews had engrossed much of the profitable commerce between Dieppe, Bordeaux, and London.   Their skill and industry had achieved remarkable results in manufactures; and the silks of Lyons, the serges of Abbeville, the paper of Ambert, and the cloths of Coutances—produced chiefly by Huguenot hands— had become celebrated over the Continent.   As for their intellectual position, it was attested by such names as those of Claude and Basnage—the one the most illustrious reformed preacher, the other the greatest jurist of France—of Conrart, Pelisson, Dacier, and Dubosc, each variously famous in his generation, and of many others less equally known, but eminent at the bar and in the pulpit. Taken altogether, the Huguenots formed a most prosperous and energetic minority in the great mass of the French nation.

That a Sovereign of France should ever have thought of molesting such a body of subjects, in defiance of the laws of his kingdom, and of his own oaths and those of his ancestors, appears at present hardly credible. But France was sinking under a centralised despotism; the institutions and usages of the nation were being forced into a harsh uniformity; and a proud, bigoted, and ignorant king was told by flatterers and interested priests that he could obliterate religious distinctions, and make all Frenchmen of one faith, as easily as he could level differences in taxation. Though he confirmed at first the Huguenots' privileges, Louis XIV. from an early period resolved, as he said, ' to abridge their rights, and gradually ' to fence them round with restrictions.' Thirty years followed of harsh measures and vexatious edicts against the Reformers, the forerunners of a greater catastrophe. Commissions were issued to investigate the titles of the places of worship of the Huguenots, and the inquiries always ended in forfeitures. Their cemeteries were defaced, and their churches despoiled of their bells, ornaments, and other appendages; and it was expressly proclaimed that the royal arms should be erased from such impious edifices. The Huguenots were excluded from all offices of trust, from the upper ranks of the army and navy, and from employment in civil affairs; and, greatly to the annoyance of Colbert, they were banished from the corporate bodies, and forbidden to exercise almost every profession. Then came encroachments on their chartered rights; their tribunals in the Parliaments were closed; they were told to conform or expect no justice; and, like the Jews in the middle ages, they were occasionally forbidden to sue for their debts. At last royal iniquity and folly invaded their homes and broke up their families; and a series of odious ordinances deprived the Protestant parent of his natural authority, allured his children to interested conversions, and bribed them to disobedience and undutifulness. A detestable system of proselytism, too, by threats and corruption, was set on foot; and the influence of a powerful government was brought to bear all over the kingdom to degrade the Reformers and their religion. We quote an account of the deeds of this period, from the pen of a zealous Catholic priest, who played, like his fellows, his part in them:—

' Before revoking the Edict of Nantes, the King had sapped the foundations of Calvinism. He had caused numerous places of worship to be thrown down; had abolished the Chambers of the Edict; had shut out the Huguenots from all higher offices, and from municipal and corporate bodies; had given large pensions to those who abjured; had condemned those who relapsed to death; and had sent missionaries everywhere to preach Catholicism. The way was thus opened to the completion of the good work, the most brilliant feat of an illustrious reign, the masterpiece of power and consummate policy.'

More violent measures were taken with the Reformers between 1683 and 1685. Their children were rudely torn from them on the information of hireling spies; and a host of busy proselytising priests were despatched to preach at them all over the kingdom. The mobs of the towns were stirred up against them; they were openly denounced as heretics and rebels; and lawless invasions of their property were winked at by the official authorities. To Louvois, however, belongs the infamy of having devised the most terrible means of coercing them into a change of religion. The ever-memorable dragonnades were the work of this bold and pitiless minister; and he carried it out with remorseless energy. Dragoon regiments, attended by priests, and usually headed by a bishop and intendant, were marched into the Huguenot districts; the inhabitants were summoned in a body to recant; and troops were quartered upon any recusants, with permission, as was significantly said, to do everything but murder and ravish. What atrocities were committed by this soldiery—how they gave free scope to their cruelty and insolence—how they sacked houses, destroyed villages, and turned whole cantons into desolation—what refined modes of torture they invented, and how they indulged their brutality and lust—is described by Michelet with extraordinary power; and it may be doubted if any persecution has been more indiscriminate and reckless. We see its spirit in this letter of Louvois, for the first time published in this collection:—

'The King has been informed by your letter of the 17th of the obstinacy of the Huguenots of Dieppe. These people having been especially conspicuous in refusing to submit to His Majesty's will, you are to have no clemency whatever towards them; and you may make the quartering of the soldiers upon them as disagreeable and severe as possible. You may increase the number of billets as you please, but without relieving the Huguenots of Rouen; and instead of exacting ten pence and provisions, you may put on each house ten times as much, and allow the troops to do any needful disorder. This is the way you will cure people of the kind, and make an example in the province.'

The documents relating to the dragonnades are so numerous

in this collection, that we scarcely know which to select from them. The following narrative of M. Chambrun, a Huguenot preacher near Avignon, is an average specimen of this persecution. M. Chambrun was very ill and in bed when the dragonnade broke into his town ; and M. de Tessé, the royal commandant, and M. de Cosnac, the Bishop of Valence, at first, as was usually the case, sought to win him over by gentle means :—

' The Count saluted me with much courtesy, asked me how I was, and then placed himself at the head of my bed, with the bishop at the foot. He then told me he took great interest in me ; that he wished to show me particular favour ; that he had not thrown me like my colleagues into prison ; and that to overcome my scruples more easily, he had brought the bishop with him to explain everything. I thanked him for his politeness, but replied that I had a Master in heaven who claimed my obedience.'

Persuasion having been found impracticable, and M. de Chambrun having challenged the bishop to a theological discussion, M. de Tessé suddenly changed his language :—

' He said all that was nothing to the point ; that the King, his master, had resolved to make me a Catholic, and that it was better for me to think upon it and accept the terms that were offered to me. I told him that all I required was a passport, so that I might go to Holland, like other French ministers. After a short time he took his departure, exclaiming that I had too much rhetoric for him, and that it would be well for me to reflect and obey. He had not been away two hours, when he sent forty-two dragoons into my house. These men kept beating drums all night to prevent me sleeping, and to compel me to submit. In a few hours my house was turned upside down. All the the provisions I had were not enough for one of their meals. They broke in the doors to find out if anything had been concealed, and destroyed everything they laid their hands on. My wife resisted them with extraordinary courage ; they insulted and abused her in the foulest language. At night they lit candles all over the house ; yet, bad as all was, it would have been bearable had they not come into my room to stifle me with tobacco-smoke, and kept up drumming throughout the whole night.'

Meantime similar and worse scenes were taking place all over the town :—

' The troops were quartered instantly upon the Reformers, and they had no sooner received their billets than cries were heard in every street. The poor people ran up and down in despair ; here and there a woman was seen at a window crying help for her husband, who was being batooned, or was hung up by his feet over a chimney, or, perhaps was kept with a knife at his throat. Here and there a husband was lamenting his wife, who had miscarried in consequence of blows and other cruelties. Children were screaming everywhere " Help! help! they are killing my father," or " carrying away my mother." But here my hand must lay down the pen. The recollection of these barbarities fills me with such affliction that I cannot go on with the tragic tale.'

Some idea of the dragonnades may be obtained by picturing to ourselves such scenes repeated in every province in France. The efforts of the missionary soldiers were usually crowned with apparent success; and whole towns and settlements of Huguenots were converted by their atrocious arguments. Great was the joy at Versailles and Marly at this example of the providence of God, as Madame de Maintenon piously observed; and Chancellor Le Tellier, when he heard that hardly a Huguenot remained in the kingdom, sang the Nunc Dimittis with senile ecstasy. Yet numerous as were the nominal conversions, many Reformers defied the fiery trial; and, in spite of cruelty and intimidation, refused to abandon the faith of their ancestors. This was the case especially with that sex whose firmness of purpose in matters of conscience has often put that of men to shame; and Huguenot women in thousands of instances gave noble proofs of the martyr's constancy. The wrongs done to many of these victims, how they were torn from their homes and shut up in convents, how they were immured for years in loathsome dungeons, exposed to insults or hypocritical solicitations, would be almost incredible if not attested in hundreds of passages in this series : we quote a striking and horrible example:—

' When these ladies had been committed to their jailer's hands, he flung them into a prison full of mud and filth. He deprived them of their clothes and their linen; and put on them dresses taken from the hospitals, that had been worn by the most diseased patients, and were covered with stains of blood and ulcers. Mademoiselle Ducros was dressed in this manner. The wretch gave them bread that a dog would not eat, and a little water only to drink. He paid them a visit several times a day with warders, who caused them to be stripped, and beat them with extreme cruelty. Besides that, he used sometimes to plunge them into the moat, full of stagnant water and fetid matter, and dragged them out when they had lost all consciousness. They died under torments not surpassed in the annals of paganism.'

One of the most barbarous features of this persecution was the dishonour shown to the remains of those who, at the approach of death, had relapsed, conscience-stricken at the mockery of their conversion. It was a common spectacle in France at this juncture to behold their corpses torn from their graves, or tossed unburied into the common sewers; sights ominous of the yet distant times when brutalised mobs were to violate the tombs of the ancestors and descendants of that persecuting King, and inflict upon his own embalmed remains the outrages which had been offered by his authority to his unoffending subjects.* This series abounds in details of such cases: we select that of M. Paul Chenevix, an eminent member of the Parliament of Metz :—

'When he was dead his body was brought to the jail, and was condemned by the magistrate to be dragged upon a hurdle. The Parliament, shocked at such a treatment of the most aged member of their body, delayed the execution of the sentence for a time; but an order to the contrary came from the Court. The venerable body was then stripped naked and exposed without any covering whatever. It was dragged on a hurdle with every mark of ignominy. The spectators at the sight cried aloud with grief; and when the corpse had been thrown into the sewer, the Reformers rescued it and buried it decently.'

As a general rule, the commands of the King were obeyed with cruel and revolting zeal by all persons in authority in France. The bishops especially were distinguished in these acts of brutality, and vied with each other in making converts and covering their royal master with flattery. The eagle of Meaux, we regret to say, stooped to a flight so unworthy of him; and even the illustrious and gentle Fénélon acquiesced at least in the persecution. There were, however, some honourable exceptions, and this series contains more than one protest of honourable and right-minded Catholics against the folly and crimes of Louis. On the whole, however, the upper classes—the courtiers, officials, and even the noblesse—joined in the outcry against the Reformers, and co-operated in these acts of injustice—a circumstance not to be forgotten, perhaps, in any estimate of the King's conduct. One of the most vexatious trials of the Huguenots was to see renegades from their religion endeavouring to atone for their errors by persecuting with extraordinary severity. The Countess de Marsan was a notable instance :—

'The town of Pons belonged to this aged penitent, who, thinking that tormenting heretics was the best way to obtain pardon for sins, imprisoned and ill-treated those unfortunate persons who refused to

---

* See the curious *Procès Verbal* of the desecration of the Royal tombs in the *ci-devant* Abbaye of St. Denis in 1794. The corpses of Henry IV. and Louis XIII. were found, on opening their coffins, to be scarcely changed; the body of Louis XIV. was dried up to a black mummy; that of Louis XV. was a mass of corruption. All were thrown into the kennel, or scattered to the winds of heaven.

convert themselves to Catholicism. She practised these severities on persons of every age, but she directed her attention towards children particularly, and caused them to be carried off on all sides. Many men and women died after three weeks or a month in her prisons, but others survived and were at length liberated. Some children resisted her with extraordinary fortitude.'

Towards the close of 1685, reports came in from all parts of France that the Reformers had for the most part abjured, though some signs of resistance were visible. The King, ignorant of the truth, and intoxicated by the flattery of the sycophants who compared him to Theodosius and Constantine, was persuaded that a little more rigour would extirpate heresy altogether; and, in an evil hour for his own renown, revoked the salutary and time-honoured edict which, disregarded as it had been of late, was a fundamental law of the monarchy, and a protest against his recent oppression. All Huguenot churches that remained were overthrown; the cemeteries were dismantled and effaced; the Huguenot pastors were ordered to quit the soil of France under pain of death; and the exercise of Calvinism in public was prohibited under severe penalties. The emigration of all Protestants, who were not ministers, was strictly forbidden, the galleys, the halter, or transportation being reserved for those who made the attempt; and bands of soldiers were placed on the frontier to carry the mandate into execution. The trial discriminated and brought out clearly what was weak or vacillating, and firm or unyielding, in the afflicted body of French Protestantism. About one-third of the Huguenots, it is supposed, conformed ultimately to the Catholic doctrines and became absorbed in the mass of the nation, without any seeming religious distinction. Rather more than a third—though many of them had yielded to the storm of the dragonnades—remained in France attached to their faith; and in spite of disabilities and wrongs, maintained the creed of their fathers unchanged, and transmitted it to their existing posterity. The rest, perhaps eighty thousand families, between three or four hundred thousand persons, preferred their religion to the natal soil, and abandoned France when freedom of conscience was denied them within her misgoverned borders. Of these several were arrested and subjected to the terrible punishments denounced against them by the insensate King; but the large majority escaped by degrees in many instances, it is well known, with the aid of Catholic neighbours and friends, who secretly detested his odious tyranny.

The fate of the exiles is a well-known chapter in the history of France and the civilised world.   Some took service in foreign armies, and in a series of bloody contests, from the day of the Boyne to that of Malplaquet, struck down the pride of the House of Bourbon, and avenged themselves on their royal persecutor.   But the mass betook themselves to the pursuits they had followed in the country they had left, and, scattered in colonies in the British Isles, in Holland, Germany, and the American settlements, transferred to distant and alien nations the genius and grace of French industry.   Their factories revived the wasted Palatinate, and repaired the ruin effected by Louvois; they introduced into Prussia and Saxony their manufactures of cloth and silk; the looms of Spitalfields and of Dublin owe their origin to their industrious skill; and, wherever they settled, they formed a population of orderly and well-disposed citizens.   The exiles, too, produced many names distinguished for their public services, their industrial skill, and their private virtues,* such as those of Schomberg, Ruvigny, Romilly, Bouverie, Bosanquet, Hughessen, Martineau, Lefevre, Ouvry, Pigou, Labouchere, and Ligonier.   As for the loss France sustained by their departure, it is best shown in the confidential reports made to Louis after the Peace of Ryswick.   These documents, written by enemies of the Reformers, admit that an extraordinary decline in wealth and prosperity had taken place in the provinces in which the Huguenots had been numerous; and, even to this day, some towns and districts have not recovered from the effects of the emigration.   We quote a passage from this series, referring to the condition of Saumur towards the close of the seventeenth century :—

'The inhabitants of the town of Saumur represent humbly to your Majesty, that your piety has allowed them to destroy the academy and temple of the Pretended Reformers, as they had for several years entreated; but that the French and foreign noblemen's sons who were educated there being now all gone, the merchants from Holland and other countries and nearly all the artisans having disappeared, this town, which was one of the most considerable in the kingdom, has become deserted and without trade, and is decaying from day to day.'

---

* The Camden Society published in 1852 an interesting volume of 'Lists of Foreign Protestants and Aliens resident in England,' 1618—1688, edited by W. Durrant Cooper, Esq., which contains the names of a vast number of these meritorious exiles.   Many of them settled in the city of Norwich, and contributed to the manufacturing prosperity of that place, for England owes the seeds of her greatness as a manufacturing country to the religious persecutions which drove the artisans of France and Flanders to her shores.

The original documents in this series on the Revocation of the Edict of Nantes are less numerous than we might have expected. Those, however, that relate to the cruelties inflicted on the unhappy persons arrested in different attempts to escape are very striking and full of interest. We quote from a contemporary observer a specimen of that ' life in the galleys ' which became the doom of too many men of blameless conduct and high character :—

' People never would believe, were not the fact certain, what refinements of barbarity were practised on these galley-slaves. They were led to the port, coupled with robbers and assassins, with chains on their necks, their hands, and their feet, made a show of to terrify their fellows in religion. The heaviest chains were reserved for them. A red coat and cap was their usual dress, with a coarse shirt and stockings of felt. Their labours on the galleys were frightfully severe. The slaves were bound in pairs on the benches of each vessel, and could not move beyond the length of their chains, each eating and drinking in his own place. They were employed in rowing with the long and heavy oars by which the galleys were set in motion. They had no shelter against the rain and heat or the cold, often so severe at sea, but a thin awning spread over their heads. This was taken off when the vessel was under weigh, as it interfered with her speed. Along the benches ran a gallery, on which the officers walked up and down with a scourge in hand. The unhappy rowers were repeatedly beaten by their overseers. At the hour of Mass, when the Host was elevated, the Huguenot galley-slave was compelled to doff his cap. If he refused, he was stretched on his back naked, and was beaten severely with a rope's-end. His body, when sufficiently mangled and torn, was then washed with salt and vinegar.',

The following is an account of one of the scenes of transportation to the American colonies :—

' You have not, perhaps, yet heard of the new mode of persecution. Our friends are being shipped off to the islands in America, to be there exposed and sold as slaves. I went on board one of the transport ships. I saw eighty young women and others lying down in a pitiable state ; I was horror-stricken, and could not utter a word. In another cabin were nearly a hundred old men in extreme misery ; the tyrant's cruelty had reduced them to despair. They were of all classes and every quality ; no one was spared. The women told me that when they set sail from Marseilles they were two hundred and fifty, men, women, and children, and that eighteen had perished in a fortnight.'

The Revocation of the Edict of Nantes was followed by a series of edicts, extending down to 1724, which, by a cruel and absurd fiction, declared Protestantism extinguished in

France.   The 'Newly Converted,' as the Huguenots were
called, were 'presumed' to be of the national faith, and social
outlawry and civil death were the sentence of the thousands of
recusants whose acts and lives belied the presumption.   The
marriages of the Reformers were invalidated; they were declared incapable of succeeding to property; they were excluded
from employment in the State; and they were treated as a
degraded caste unworthy of the privileges of Frenchmen.
Their religious assemblies, too, were made criminal, and even
their private worship proscribed; their homes were invaded
by an inquisitorial police; and any of their pastors who ventured within the borders of orthodox France were liable to
instant execution and torture.   The galleys or exile were the
penalty of the slightest resistance or complaint; and even the
smallest Huguenot meeting was watched with angry and
jealous suspicion.   Shut out thus from the pale of the State,
and under the ban of persecuting laws, the Reformers during
the eighteenth century became Helots among their fellow-
subjects, and, as is the case with those who suffer injustice
from power, were feared by the Government.   On every occasion when France was at war they were alternately repressed
or conciliated by promises made to be only broken; and when
once they rose up in arms, they were crushed with a
merciless rigour which has made the revolt of the Cevennes a
proverb.   How many unfortunate Huguenot pastors fell the
victims to their zeal for the faith, how many among their flocks
were torn from their homes, and sent to the slave-ship or the
penal settlement, historians, usually on the side of power, have
not as yet, we believe, estimated; but this collection shows
that the number was large.   Yet, even atrocities of this kind
were less intolerable than the degradation of the Reformers in
every social relation.   The French Huguenot, from the cradle
to the grave, was a mark of general scorn and dislike, sneered
at as an unsocial and morose stranger, denounced as a heretic
and a rebel, despised as one of questionable position, and
considered unfit for the rights of Frenchmen from which he
had been iniquitously excluded.   Those who know what, in a
similar state of things, was the condition of the Catholic of
Ireland, during the generation before the Union, will understand the social debasement of the French Huguenot in the
eighteenth century.

The following passage may be quoted from a petition to
Marshal Saxe, who, like Duquesne, was exempted by name
from the disabilities that applied to Protestants—the conqueror
of Fontenoy was felt to be a necessity to the House of

Bourbon—in proof of the state of the Reformers in France about the middle of the last century :—

'Sixty years have been the witnesses of our miseries. Our temples and our ministers proscribed, their flocks wandering and often fugitive, dragoons set upon us as missionaries; ecclesiastics often more cruel than these, who allow us neither to live nor to die without having been constrained to acts which shock our conscience; the jails and galleys overflowing with our martyrs; our marriages dishonoured by hypocrisy or sacrilege; our Bibles burnt by the hangman's hands; our properties confiscated and reduced by fines; such, Sir, are the principal features of our condition. Even if our sufferings have diminished of late, we owe it merely to accidental circumstances. But persecution only slumbers; it is not dead. Our confessors remain in prisons and chains. Some are in the galleys, at the port of Brescou, and others have been immured in the tower of Cutance for ten, twenty, or thirty years. Our marriages are declared invalid and illegal, unless celebrated according to the Romish form, and in marrying we are compelled to make our recantation. Our religious assemblies are treated as seditious, even when our loyalty cannot be questioned; in a word, the old and new laws remain in force, and our enemies only await an opportunity to cause them to be put in execution.'

Another document of the same period gives a sketch of the cruelties practised in 1720 on a party of the Reformers accused untruly of attending a religious meeting :—

'Our prisoners yesterday set off from Montpellier. A company of cavalry, sabre in hand, and one of infantry with fixed bayonets, with six archers, formed the advanced guard. I will call the party neither good nor bad, for some were one and some the other; but each had a collar of iron on his neck, about the length of four fingers, to which a heavy chain was attached, and trailed down from the shoulders to the ground. So, four by four, or in parties of six, they were tied to each other by the neck, and were obliged to keep up the chain in their hands, its weight being really enormous. The prisoners were brought into the citadel in this plight, the garrison turning out, and mocking at them. The rain on that day was very heavy, but it did not prevent them, when they approached Nîmes, from baring their heads and breaking into a psalm. They had been mixed up with robbers and thieves; and indeed three of their women had been chained; two prostitutes, who had been taken up somewhere, being yoked on in the same way. As these good folk had been very ill treated at Montpellier, where they had lain in jail upon wet straw all together, they were now in a state not fit to be seen, all swelled and hardly able to stir.'

And the revolting punishments inflicted on the Huguenot galley-slaves continued in the eighteenth century :—

'You have perhaps heard how, for some time past, they have been more than ever determined to compel us to take off our caps during the Romish service.   Some of us have been tied together and fastened to a bench, to force us to remain bareheaded at Mass ; we have been dragged to the stern where their altars are set up ; in the harbour we have been flogged and condemned to the hardest work.   But nothing was so bad as what took place in October.   The missionaries obtained, or extorted, an order that we should be bastinadoed until we took off our caps at their prayers.'

In spite, however, of persecution, of barbarous edicts, and social ostracism, the numbers of the Reformers increased, and towards the end of the eighteenth century they were not far from a million persons.   That law which enlists the feelings of man on the side of a faith for which he suffers, retained the Reformers in the old ways ; and French Protestantism, after a hundred years of fruitless efforts to root it out, remained deeply implanted in the kingdom.   The ' Church under the Cross,' as it was called, throve under oppression and discouragement ; while that of Fleury, of Tencin, of Dubois, though lapped in splendour, and sustained by power, was sinking into contempt and ruin.   The ministers, at the peril of their lives, watched over ' the congregations of the desert,' to use their simple and pathetic language ; and the Huguenot assemblies met and prayed, in secret and fear, but with not less fervour than when their ancestors blessed the name of the Great Henry in their favoured temples.   A report of 1745 gives us this sketch of one of their gatherings, which, like those of the Scotch Covenanters, kept up the union and spirit of the sect :—

' On this day the Calvinists, or Pretended Reformers, held a public religious assembly, the first that had been seen in this country since the Revocation of the Edict of Nantes.   There were about six or eight thousand people of every age, sex, and quality.   The place of meeting was in a meadow on the banks of the Dordogne, in the parish of Roquette, and diocese of Perigueux, a quarter of a league from the town of Sainte Foy.   Many went to attend this assembly at daybreak, but it was not collected until about eight, and it lasted until two in the afternoon.   Rivoise Yot, a merchant draper, having a loud voice, began with a lecture which lasted nearly two hours ; then came a minister or preacher named Jean de Loire.   He preached, said prayers, and sang psalms.   He baptized two children, published the banns of marriage of eleven couples, and fixed a day for another assembly.   Contributions were given, books were sold and distributed ; and there was a good deal of eating and drinking.'

It would be absurd to suppose that the French Protestants lived contented under this direful tyranny.   They would have been unworthy of their race, and of manhood, had they not keenly felt its injustice.   But they remained quiescent during the century, nor was this simply the result of weakness; there is strong evidence that the old spirit of Huguenot loyalty was never extinguished. This description by a young Catholic officer of a Calvinist assembly in 1757, which he happened to witness to his great annoyance, is a proof of the attachment still felt by the Reformers for the descendants of Henry :—

'After the sermon was over, some verses of the Miserere Mei were chanted which related to the subject of the discourse; and this was followed by a form of prayer in which they prayed for all conditions of men, from the King on his throne to the meanest peasant. But conceive my surprise when the minister prayed by name for the King, the Queen, the Dauphin, and the Dauphiness, and thanked God for Her Royal Highness's delivery. I could not credit my ears, nevertheless it was true. Judge, Sir, how amazed I was. You know in what colours our Huguenots are painted and in what way they speak of their assemblies. I, like many others, had been prejudiced against them, but I see I have been deceived, and that their enemies don't tell the truth.'

The proscription of the Protestant faith in France certainly did not contribute to strengthen the hold of Catholicism or even of Christianity upon the minds of the educated classes. On the contrary, infidelity spread and the authority of the Church declined, precisely during that period when the pious convictions of the Huguenot faith were crushed and extirpated as anti-Christian and heretical. The National Church, relieved from the task of a moral conflict with the Reformers, by degrees lost the true elements of her strength, and declined into lethargy and corruption. A Bossuet appeared to answer a Claude; but the mitred sycophants of Louis XV., who enforced orthodoxy by the galleys and the halter, were, usually, either profligate or ignorant. The place of a Church that had fallen into contempt was usurped by a succession of sceptics, who, destroying all faith in existing usages, proved the heralds of an anarchy of irreligion. Nor was this all; for religion became identified in the thoughts of men with the cruelties perpetrated in its name, and reason and conscience protested against a system allied with tyranny and injustice. 'Your persecution,' said Bayle in 1686, 'will recoil on yourselves and lead to Deism;' and the prediction was fully verified by experience. The ideas which found their highest expression in the writings of Voltaire and Jean-Jacques were antichristian in part and destructive; but this was because the essence of Christianity was confounded with accidents that seemed antichristian; and their strength lay, as has been remarked, in the liberality, the loftiness of thought, and the justice that was mixed up with their errors. So true it is that in human affairs wrong often works out its own penalty, and that the triumph of persecution may become ultimately its avenging Nemesis. Throughout the profligate reign of Louis XV., when the depravity of his Court and the relaxed state of public opinion were tending to the catastrophe which overtook his unfortunate successor, no amelioration took place in the deplorable condition of the King's Protestant subjects. It is a thing almost incredible, and which we were not aware of until we found the evidence of it in these volumes, that little more than one hundred years ago, in the year 1762, a Protestant minister named M. de La Rochette was hanged by sentence of the fanatical Parliament of Toulouse, —the same which had recently perpetrated the judicial murder of the Calas family—for no other offence than that of preaching the Gospel in violation of the law, and that three Protestant gentlemen were beheaded at the same time for the crime of having attempted to rescue their minister. The narrative of this martyrdom is one of the most affecting pages we remember to have read, and the spectacle seems to have produced an effect even on the population of Toulouse, which had assembled to witness it :—

'The prisoners were led to the square of St. George, being the place chosen for extraordinary executions; but the square of La Monnoye was thought more fitting, inasmuch as the space was not so great, and fewer persons could have a view of the martyr. All the avenues were lined by detachments of soldiers; for a rescue was, it is said, feared; and if so it must have been the Catholics who devised such a scheme,—they were grieved at the shedding of innocent blood —for the few Protestants who dwelt in the town had shut themselves up in their houses, in a state of terror, and mourning in private. The windows of the houses that looked into the square were let at a very high rate; wherever the victims made their appearance they were received with lamentation and tears; you would have said that Toulouse had become Protestant. The people asked what was the faith of these men; and when they were heard speaking of Christ and His Passion, there was a general feeling of surprise and affliction. The clergyman of Taur could not stand the sight; he fainted away, and his place was taken by one of his curates. What was most touching was the perfect calmness of La Rochette; his face full of sweetness, of beauty, and of intelligence, his youth, his steadfast and sober words, all this excited profound interest. Besides, there was the additional reflection that he was dying because he would not tell an untruth, that his being a minister was his only crime, that there was no evidence nor even charge against him, that he had only to say a word to save his life, and yet he preferred a cruel death to abjuration.'

The edicts against the Protestants of France continued in force till 1787, and were not unfrequently put into execution. In a letter, written in 1774, Lafayette complains that hundreds of thousands of his countrymen were by law aliens, and deprived of the commonest rights of Frenchmen. Men still living remember the time when the Huguenot pastor who ventured to raise his voice in prayer for his scattered flock was liable to immediate death, and when the Huguenot husband and wife were denounced as living in concubinage and rearing up a family of bastards. The parents of such men of our own day as M. Guizot, Admiral Baudin, and M. Delessert, were excluded by law from the rites of marriage, from the privileges of citizenship, and even from the last indulgence of a tomb in consecrated ground. Even after the accession of Louis XVI. the galleys contained some Huguenot slaves; and not many years before that event, the judicial murders of Calas and La Rochette show that fanaticism had still the power of glutting its vengeance on French Protestantism. By degrees, however, a more kindly feeling grew up towards the persecuted sect; the religious indifference of the age was a security against the oppression of the past; and the awakening intellect of the France of Voltaire confessed and regretted the great crime committed in the preceding century.

The first amelioration in the condition of the Protestants of France was not made until 1787, one of the last free acts of Louis XVI. And it was not until the monarchy was perishing in the revolutionary storm, that the National Assembly redressed the injustice of which his ancestor had been the author, and not only swept away the disabilities to which the sect had remained subject, and raised it to equality with the Catholics, but offered the privilege of French citizenship to the descendants of the exiles of 1685. Since that time, under the various governments which have claimed the allegiance of the French people, the congregations of the Reformers have proved themselves loyal and faithful men; and their churches, protected again by the State, have for the most part retained unchanged the austere simplicity of the ritual and the doctrines of Calvin. At this moment the Protestants in France are stated by themselves to amount to 1,561,000 souls, and in their pursuits and mode of life resemble strongly their Huguenot ancestors. They have given the State some eminent servants, of whom Guizot is the most illustrious; they can show names of eminence in the camp, in art, in letters, and the learned professions; but they abound principally in the middle classes, distinguished by their industry and perseverance, and their strict, yet sincere and fervent, piety.   France, indeed, has never become Protestant; from the days of the Guises to those of Napoleon, Catholicism has been the national faith; yet Protestantism has had a salutary effect on the thoughts, the feelings, and the tendencies of Frenchmen; and even now the Protestant supporters of liberty, of free thought, and constitutional government, comparatively few in number as they are, counteract to a certain extent the evils of a despotic government and an ultramontane clergy.   That France remains in the van of civilisation, that, in the race of the last three centuries, she has not fallen behind like Austria and Spain, may in part be due to the share which Protestantism has had in her destinies.   In our own day, the Protestants of France have acquired, perhaps, rather too much of that sectarian character, which is inseparable from the position of a small minority of persons, differing in opinion on essential points from the nation to which they belong.   But at the head of every good and enlightened enterprise, for the relief of distress, for the spread of knowledge, for the defence of freedom, Protestant names will be found : and amongst these laudable undertakings the attempt of this Society to rescue from oblivion the sufferings and services of their Huguenot forefathers, deserves certainly to be honourably remembered.

ART. IV.—*An Examination of Sir William Hamilton's Philosophy, and of the principal Philosophical Questions discussed in his Writings.* By JOHN STUART MILL. London : 1865.

MR. JOHN STUART MILL'S ' Examination of Sir William ' Hamilton's Philosophy ' has anew turned public attention towards metaphysical studies, and given a powerful impulse to metaphysical thought.   The questions which have for some time past agitated most deeply the speculative mind of the country are there clearly stated and ably discussed ; and there is no volume which the student could more advantageously consult to learn the latest and the highest developments of speculative philosophy.   The opinions of Sir William Hamilton and Professor Mansel are given with such fairness and fullness that we may easily learn and accurately understand the doctrines of the school to which they belong, and of which they are in recent times the most distinguished representatives ; and Mr. Mill, who is certainly one of the greatest masters in the opposing school, gives its teaching in its finest and most defensible forms.

The radical difference between the two schools affects the

nature of all human knowledge. Do we know anything beyond the mind and its modifications? That question has been discussed for more than two thousand years, and we seem to be as far from its solution as ever. The opposing champions have only unhorsed one another. Fifty years ago Dr. Thomas Brown elaborated the idealistic theory with a subtlety and analytic skill which have never been surpassed ; but Sir William Hamilton attacked his system with a logic so resistless, and even so ruthless, that the system crumbled to dust beneath his blows. And on its ruins he reared his own realistic theory so solidly, that it looked as if it could safely defy all assault. But Mr. Mill has now arisen, as if to be the avenger of Brown ; and if he has not demolished the system of Hamilton, he has certainly made most desperate breaches in its walls. All this is very discouraging. It appears as if the truth were never to be found—at least in the directions in which it has hitherto been sought. If it were to be found at all in these tracks of thought, the men we have quoted could not have failed to have found it. It would therefore seem that the only chance of success in this search for truth is to abandon the beaten road and to strike into new paths.

Let us see what are the two prevalent theories in regard to the nature of the mind's knowledge ; for not till we have come to a conclusion regarding them can we decide whether our knowledge be relative or absolute, or give a judgment in regard to the Unconditioned, or solve satisfactorily any of the other problems discussed in the ' Examination.' This inquiry is the primary one, and when it is settled every other will be easy. All philosophers are agreed that Consciousness is the fountain of knowledge, and Mr. Mill and Sir William Hamilton combine in defining consciousness as ' the recognition by the mind or ' ego of its acts and affections.'* But under this apparent agreement there is a wide difference between them. Mr. Mill and the idealists hold that we are conscious of nothing but the mind's own modifications, simply, purely, and apart from every thing else. Sir William Hamilton, on the other hand, holds that in perception consciousness gives as a conjunct fact the existence of me or self as perceiving, and the existence of something different from me as perceived. We are conscious not only of the mental affection, but of its external object or cause.

' We are immediately conscious in perception,' says he, ' of an ego and a non-ego, known together and known in contrast to each other.

* Lectures, vol. i. p. 193 ; *Exam.* p. 108.

This is the fact of the duality of consciousness. It is clear and manifest. When I concentrate my attention on the simplest act of perception, I return from my observation with the most irresistible conviction of two facts, or rather two branches of the same fact, that I am and that something different from me exists. In this act I am conscious of myself as the perceiving subject, and of an external reality as the object perceived; and I am conscious of both existences in the same indivisible moment of intuition.'

The language of all psychologists till very recently involved a belief that thought and consciousness were not identical, but that the one was the object of the other's apprehension. Since the days of Dr. Brown, however, more correct opinions in regard to this matter have begun to gain currency, though the old phraseology is still commonly used, and in many cases the old belief creeps stealthily in and influences our arguments unawares. Whenever we speak of the mind being conscious of its own sensations—of its own ideas—of its own impressions—of its own modifications (and all psychologists ancient and modern use such language), we make consciousness the discerner of what passes within the mind. The mental mood and the consciousness of it are spoken of as different things. But though such language is still used, the opinion in which it originated is now abandoned; and the true nature of consciousness is very accurately described by Brown, the elder Mill, and Hamilton.

'Sensation,' says Dr. Brown,* 'is not the object of consciousness different from itself, but a particular sensation is the consciousness of the moment; as a particular hope, or fear, or grief, or resentment, or simple remembrance, may be the actual consciousness of the next moment.'

'Having a sensation and having a feeling,' says Mr. James Mill,† 'are not two things. The thing is one, the names only are two. I am pricked by a pin. The sensation is one, but I may call it a sensation, or a feeling, or a pain, as I please. Now, when having the sensation, I say, I feel the sensation, I only use a tautological expression; the sensation is not one thing, the feeling another; the sensation is the feeling. When instead of the word feel, I use the word conscious, I do exactly the same thing. I merely use a tautological expression. To say I feel a sensation is merely to say I feel a feeling, which is an impropriety of speech. And to say that I am conscious of a feeling is merely to say that I feel it. To have a feeling is to be conscious, and to be conscious is to have a feeling.'

'Consciousness,' says Hamilton, 'is the fundamental form, the

---

* Lecture XI.
† Quoted by Mr. J. S. Mill, pp. 115–16.

generic condition of all thinking. Consciousness is not to be regarded as aught different from the mental modes or movements themselves. It is not to be viewed as an illuminated place within which objects coming are presented to, and passing beyond are withdrawn from observation; nor is it to be considered even as an observer—the mental modes as phenomena observed. Consciousness is just the movements themselves rising above a certain degree of intensity.'

These quotations carry us very far towards a right understanding of our mental nature. The word Consciousness may almost be regarded as a superfluity in our language. It is improper to say ' I am conscious that I know ; I am conscious ' that I feel,' for that is simply to say, ' I know that I know, ' or I feel that I feel ;' the simple formula ' I know ;' ' I feel,' expresses the whole fact. But here the question urges itself upon us—What do we know ? What do we feel ? Sir William Hamilton says that in perception the mind is conscious both of itself as perceiving, and of the thing perceived. Mr. Mill says that in sensation the mind is conscious simply of its own affections. Now these sentiments both sanction the undoubted truth that all knowledge involves two factors—the subject knowing and the object known. We cannot know without knowing something. We cannot feel without feeling something. But when Mill and Hamilton combine in saying that the mind is conscious of the mind—that the ego knows the ego —that in sentiency we are cognisant of our sensations—they flatly contradict their own previous teaching in regard to the nature of consciousness.

It may be alleged that we must interpret the language of both by their clearly expressed teaching in regard to consciousness; that they merely used the phraseology which has obtained so strong a hold upon philosophical literature, but that neither of them means to affirm that the mind is conscious of its own operations. If it be so, then we ask, Of what, then, is the mind conscious ? When we know, what do we know ? When we feel, what do we feel ? To know nothing, is to have no knowledge : to feel nothing, is to have no feeling. We can find no answer to these questions in the writings of either Brown or Mill. They unwaveringly maintain that we have anyhow no consciousness of the external world ; if then we are conscious neither of the ego nor of the non-ego, neither of the mind perceiving nor of the object perceived, we cannot be conscious at all, for these exhaust all the possibilities of consciousness, unless indeed it be possible to be conscious without being conscious of anything.

Let us state this argument anew.   We cannot be conscious without being conscious of something.   But the objects of consciousness must belong either to the mental or the material world.   The idealistic school declare with one voice that we are not conscious of the material world, and in their explanation of consciousness they demonstrate that we are not conscious of the mental world ; but that we are simply conscient. Conscient of what ?   Of nothing ?   The realistic school maintain that we are conscious both of the mental and material worlds ; but, at the same time, they show equally well as their adversaries that consciousness does not take cognisance of the mind's operations, and thus they annihilate with their right hand one of the hemispheres of knowledge which they had with their left hand put in subjection to the mind.   They may comfort themselves, however, with the thought that the old hemisphere of outness remains to them, whereas their opponents are left in a wide vacuity—knowing, yet knowing nothing.

The truth is, out of the theory of consciousness above explained there has emerged an entirely new idealism—an idealism which does not believe in ideas ; and the modern idealist has now forced upon him one of two alternatives.   He must either admit that we can be conscious without being conscious of anything ; or that we are conscious of our own mental acts and affections, notwithstanding his own repeated protestations to the contrary.   It is certain there are passages in the writings of all the modern idealists which favour the supposition that they often do take refuge in the old and abandoned belief that the mind can be conscious of its own affections. Mr. Mill frequently speaks of us being conscious of our sensations ; and he tells us that Brown held that the object in perception was ' a state of mind identical with the act by which ' we are said to perceive it.' (Examination, p. 161).   Sir William Hamilton, who was himself somewhat infected with idealism, as we shall afterwards see, is still more contradictory of himself on this point.   He expressly declares, that consciousness involves three things.   1. A recognising or knowing subject.   2. A recognised or known modification ; and 3. A recognition or knowledge by the subject of the modification.*

Is the doctrine, then, that we are conscious of our own mental moods defensible ?—is it conceivable ?   We are afraid it is not ; and if we have not greatly misunderstood the writings of the very philosophers whom we have here quoted, it has long ago been abandoned, as open to assault at every

---

* Lecture XI.

point. A mental modification is simply the mind modified ; and therefore when it is affirmed that the mind is conscious of its own modifications, it is affirmed that the mind is conscious of the mind ; and moreover, that the very act of perceiving is identical with the act of being perceived. Subject and object are thus confounded. In the one indivisible state of knowledge, the ego both knows and is known, and the knowing is the being known — two things generally regarded as totally distinct. Does not this doctrine in reality amount to a dividing of the mind from itself—to a doubling of our various mental states, by making them not to constitute our consciousness alone, but to be also the objects of it ? To make such a theory even conceivable, we must, in the language of Hamilton, 'have a ' second consciousness through which we might be conscious ' of the mode in which the first consciousness was possible.' * But Mr. Mill has distinctly repudiated this hypothesis for both Hamilton and himself :—

'From the definition of consciousness,' says he, ' as "the recognition by the mind or ego of it own acts or affections," Sir William Hamilton might be supposed to think (as has actually been thought by many philosophers) that consciousness is not the fact itself of knowing or feeling, but a subsequent operation by which we become aware of that fact. This, however, is not his opinion. By the mind's recognitions of its acts or affections he does not mean anything different from the acts and affections.' (*Exam.* p. 114.)

But no one has better shown the contradictions involved in this opinion than Dr. Brown :—

' To suppose the mind,' says he, ' to exist in two different states in the same moment is a manifest absurdity. . . . There are not sensations, thoughts, passions, and also consciousness. . . . The fallacy of conceiving consciousness to be something different from the feeling which is said to be its object, has arisen in a great measure from using the personal pronoun I, which the conviction of our identity has led us to employ as significant of our permanent self. . . . But when we say, I am conscious of a particular feeling, in the usual paraphrastic phraseology of our language, which has no mode of expressing in a single word the mere existence of a feeling, we are apt, from a prejudice of grammar, to separate the sentient I and the feeling as different—not different, as they really are in this respect, that the feeling is one momentary and changeable state of the permanent substance I, that is capable also of existing, at other moments in other states, but so radically different as to justify our classing the feeling in the relation of an object to that sentient principle which we call I, and an object to it, not in retrospect only, as when the feeling is remembered, or when it is viewed in relation to

---

* Lecture XI.

other remembered feelings, but in the very moment of the primary sensation itself; as if there could truly be two distinct states of the same mind at the same moment, one of which states is to be termed sensation, and the other different state of the same mind to be termed consciousness.' (Lecture XI.)

It is allowed then, on all hands, that sensation is not the object of consciousness, as sensation and consciousness are identical; and this is just another way of expressing the almost self-evident truth that the mind does not take cognisance of its own affections. The modern idealists are therefore driven upon the other alternative; and to save themselves from making shipwreck of their faith, must hold that the mind can be conscious, and yet be conscious of nothing, though consciousness of nothing is certainly synonymous with no consciousness. No doubt it was the difficulty here presented which led the old idealists to separate the idealistic object of our knowledge from the act of knowing it. The Epicureans had their *simulacra rerum;* Descartes had his material images in the brain; Locke and Berkeley had their ideas, conceived as different from the mind, and recognised as different from the mind in knowledge. But the logic which destroyed this theory rendered idealism for ever impossible. And it is strange that Brown, Mill, and Bain, the great master-builders of modern idealism, should have been the men who most effectually undermined the foundations of their own fair fabric.

But it is right we should take their own account of the mental fact involved in consciousness. ' I am conscious of a ' certain feeling,' says Dr. Brown, ' really means no more than ' this, I feel in a certain manner, or in other words, my mind ' exists in that state which constitutes a certain feeling.' This theory of consciousness could not be put more skilfully than it is here. ' I feel in a certain manner.' But can we feel in a certain manner, and yet feel nothing? ' My mind exists in ' that state which constitutes a certain feeling.' True: every mental state is a state of feeling or consciousness; but is feeling possible where nothing is felt; and if the mind does not feel the feeling, what does it feel? Should it be urged that our whole mental life consists in a series of fleeting sensations and ideas, that we cannot tell whence they come nor whither they go; that we do not know whether they have objects or whether they have none, and that therefore we are not warranted to conclude that there is anything but sensations and ideas in the universe; that in these is our whole knowledge. Our answer still is, that we cannot know without knowing something; and as it is demonstrated that we cannot know our mental moods, we can only know—if we know at all—material properties. The alternative before us is knowledge of outness, or no knowledge whatever.

How then are we to escape from these entanglements and contradictions in which the modern idealists have involved themselves by abolishing ideas as distinct entities and yet clinging to idealism? All that we have hitherto said has pointed to one inevitable conclusion—that the mind has no knowledge of its own acts and affections, but only of the external world. Herein it will be found is the true theory of human knowledge; and the theory is very simple and almost self-evident. In all knowledge there is a duality—the mind knowing and the thing known; but the mind always knows and is never known; it is ever the subject of consciousness and never the object of it. Because it is the one it cannot be the other.

We have at length planted our foot on solid land. Taking our premises from the idealists, we have reached the conclusion that we know the outer world, and the outer world only. But in this outer world is included a great deal which is generally and properly reckoned as part of ourselves. There are our bodies with all the myriad sensations which originate in them, and of which we are unceasingly conscious. The mind only knows, and every thing else in the wide universe may be the object of its knowledge—it may be the flow of blood in the vessels of the brain, or the ray which streams from the most distant star. To make this still more certain, let us rapidly analyse the different kinds of knowledge; and first of all sensations.

Our sensations are those forms of consciousness which constitute our knowledge of the sensible properties of matter. When any object of sense is presented to our organs of sense, we have a sensation of it; and in that sensation of it is our knowledge of it. That knowledge is immediate and direct. We have not first a sensation and then a consciousness of that sensation; we have simply a sensation, and thus the sensible object and the sentient mind stand face to face. According to the usual reckoning, there are five special organs of sense; let us now briefly examine the kind of knowledge which each of them gives.

And first, SMELL.—When any odour reaches our nostrils, where the organ of smell is situated, we are said to smell it or to scent it. The sensation we have is our knowledge of the odour, and that knowledge is immediate, and so far as it goes complete. Of course we are not able at first to refer the odour

to its specific source.   We cannot tell whether it is the odour
of a rose or a lily—of a decaying body or a new-mown hay-
field; but that is not the proper function of Smell; it merely
makes us acquainted with the odour, whatever it is, and leaves
us to learn from experience the cause in which it originates.
Of the odour itself, however, though we may be entirely ignorant of its cause, we have at once such a knowledge that
nothing can be otherwise added to it.   Nothing but the smell-
ing of an odour will ever make us understand what that
odour is.

But it is said by the idealists that the sensation which we
have in smell is quite different from the odour which comes
from the rose and penetrates our nostrils.   In one sense it undoubtedly is.   Our knowledge of a rose is not the rose itself;
and our sensational consciousness of its fragrance is not its
fragrance.   But by our organ of smell we feel its fragrance
—immediately, directly—and than that nothing more is possible or even conceivable.   To speak of a sensation in the mind
as the idealists continually do, is, strictly speaking, nonsensi-
cal.·   There can be no such thing as a sensation in the mind.
The mind is sentient when objects of sense are presented to its
organs of sense; it knows them; is conscious of them; but the
mind and its objects can never be transmuted into one another.

TASTE.—When a sapid body is presented to our organ of
taste, which lies along the tongue and palate, we feel, and
feeling we know, the peculiar taste of the body so presented,
though we do not necessarily know the nature of the body
itself.   Taste is the only proper object of this sense; with
that it acquaints us immediately and perfectly, and with nothing
else.

HEARING.—When a sound reaches the ear we hear it.
That is the simplest expression of the fact, and we believe the
most accurate.   It is only after long experience that we learn
to refer the vast variety of sounds which reach us to their different sources; but this is not the office of the sense of hearing
at all.   It simply makes us acquainted with each sound, *per se,*
as it strikes upon our tympanum; and it does this so perfectly
that nothing can afterwards add to our knowledge.   We are
conscious of the sound, and when we say this we do not mean
that we are conscious of what is called the sensation of sound,
for there is no sensation of sound of which we can be conscious; but we are conscious of something external to ourselves which we call sound.   We hear the report of the gun,
the notes of the flute, the chirping of the bird—all things external to us; and such popular expressions are simply true.

We may be told that the vibrations of the air which constitute physical sound must be something quite different from the feeling of sound in the mind. Now here we must protest again that, accurately speaking, there is no such thing as a feeling in the mind ; there is only the mind feeling or hearing, and of course the mind hearing must be quite different from the sound heard. There is no possibility of reducing the duality implied in knowledge into unity—there must ever be the subject knowing and the object known. But in all knowledge we know something that is external to us.

It is a cardinal doctrine of the ideal school that we could never have learned the existence of an external world from the senses of smell, taste, and hearing; and even Sir William Hamilton seems to concede this : ' In hearing, therefore,' says Dr. Brown, ' as in taste and smell, we do not derive from its ' sensations our knowledge of things external, but, in conse- ' quence of our knowledge of things external, we regard these ' feelings as sensations.' ' Our belief of a system of ex- ' ternal things, then, does not, as far as we can judge from ' the nature of the feelings, arise from our sensations of smell, ' more than from any of our internal pleasures or pains.' * Now, if what we have said be true, and the principles of the idealists lead to it, we have in all these sensations a knowledge of what is external to us. The only question is, is it not possible that we may have a sensation of what is external to us, without our knowing that it is so? We sometimes mistake a ringing in the ear for a confused noise heard from a distance, may we not in like manner mistake the external for the internal, and fancy that our knowledge of the outward is a knowledge of the purely inward? Is not the whole ideal philosophy a proof that this mistake, if it be a mistake, is made even by those who have paid most attention to the working of their minds? We frankly confess that we do not believe that this is possible ; and as for the idealists they have been misled more by their speculations than by what they have experienced or can experience. Their appeal is always to the infant, to what it feels and knows. Now we are quite willing to carry our appeal thither too, though we are afraid we shall never get a perfectly final judgment from such a tribunal. We know, however, that the adult cannot smell an odour or hear a sound without an irresistible conviction that the odour or the fragrance comes from without, and we believe that the child of an hour old has the same irresistible conviction too.

* Lecture XX.

It feels something, though of course it cannot tell what that something is. ' It feels something,' such is the simplest form of speech, expressive of the simplest form of consciousness, and in it there is a clear distinction made between the 'It' which feels, and the unknown ' something ' which is felt. But the controversy is set at rest by the principles of the idealists themselves. Mr. Mill, Mr. Bain, and Dr. Brown, and in this they are supported by Sir William Hamilton, all concur in declaring that the mind in consciousness is not conscious of its own affections. If the infant is conscious, and yet not conscious of its own affections, it must be conscious of something else, and consciousness is knowledge.

TOUCH.—The sense of touch is spread in a less or greater degree over the whole body ; and not only over its external surface but over its internal membranes and vessels. We have sensations of this kind from the flow of our blood, the chemical action going on in our stomachs, the motions of our bowels, and the secretions of our glands, as well as from the substances which are constantly pressing against the outer surface of our frame. Extension, figure, solidity, hardness, roughness, and many other qualities of matter are generally said to be the objects of this sense. We have seen, however, that all the other senses which we have yet examined, have only one specific object, and we are inclined to believe that this sense has only one specific object too. By touch we are made acquainted with the palpable. It may be said that this is a mere play upon words, signifying no more than that by touch we know the touchable. But the same may be said of all our other senses, as there must, indeed, be an exact correspondence between the sense and its object. By smell we know only smells ; by taste, tastes ; by hearing, the hearable ; by sight, sights ; and by touch, the touchable. The palpable is quite different from the objects of all the other senses, and it is only through this peculiar sense that we could acquire a knowledge of it. Smell and hearing could never give us a knowledge of the palpable, any more than touch could give us a knowledge of odours and sounds. By the sense of touch our knowledge of the palpable is immediate, and so far as simple palpability goes, perfect. We can never by reasoning, or the assistance of the other senses, improve it ; for each sense has its own province beyond which it cannot pass, and reason can never intrude into the province of the senses, though it may appropriate the knowledge which they furnish, and elaborate it in endless ways.

But how, it will be asked, do we obtain our knowledge of

extension, without which we cannot conceive matter to exist at all ?   We submit that, having a knowledge of the palpable, we have a knowledge of the extended, because palpability includes extension.   We smell perfumes and hear sounds without having the idea of extension forced upon us ; but we cannot touch anything touchable without the rude idea that it occupies space.

But closely connected with this question is the other question —whether our mental sensibilities be not themselves extended ? It is the general belief of the learned that all sensations are felt in the mind, and that the mind is seated in the brain ; but in opposition to this, it is the universal conviction of the unlearned that sensibility is diffused over the whole body ; that when the foot is burned it is the foot which suffers, and not the head ; that when we lift a pen, it is the fingers and not the convolutions of the brain which feel it.   Sir William Hamilton has countenanced this belief by quoting with approbation the old half-paradoxical saying in regard to the mind and its material framework, that it is the whole in every part, and every part in the whole.   And Mr. Lewis, in his very interesting work, ' The Physiology of Common Life,' has endeavoured to prove by a great number of crucial experiments, that consciousness is not confined to the brain, but that it is diffused over the whole nervous system.   We strongly incline to this opinion ; and if it be true, it solves the problem of our idea of extension.   When the mind is conscious of a sensation in the hand and of another in the foot, at the same instant of time, it has a knowledge of extension.   We go farther and say, that when the embryo has sensations in different parts of its body, however dull and indistinct these may be, it has a knowledge of itself as extended.   The very union of the mind with matter, and the diffusion of consciousness along all the living nerves of that matter, implies a knowledge of extension.

Following in the footsteps of Dr. Brown, Mr. Mill has endeavoured to show that the idea of time is the chief element in the idea of extension.   To our mind, the two ideas are totally and altogether dissimilar.   We may measure space by time, we may calculate the number of miles we have walked by the hours occupied in the journey, we may form an estimate of a surface by drawing our fingers along it ; but that which we call extension is *toto cœlo* different from what we call time.   Both ideas are primary, and cannot be explained by each other, or by anything else.   The explanation of the manner in which we acquire our notion of extension given by Mr. Bain in his really great work, ' The Senses and the Intellect,' and which Mr. Mill has quoted with applause, and adopted as his own, assumes a sensational consciousness of certain movements. Now it must be evident to every one that we can have no knowledge of motion unless we have already some knowledge of extended space, as the one implies the other. But in truth, no sensation, muscular or not muscular, can give a knowledge of anything beyond itself, if it be of the sensation alone we are conscious.

Hardness, softness, roughness, smoothness, figure, are all modifications of palpability, and made known to us through the sense of touch. It is only through experience, however, and often only after a series of experiments made with the tactile and prehensile organs, that we learn accurately these qualities of matter just as it is only through experience that we learn to discriminate the flavours of wine or the perfumes of flowers. A knowledge of hardness and softness involves a certain amount of muscular sensation; and our present conceptions of roughness, smoothness, and figure are no doubt founded partly upon vision as well as upon touch. The experiences we derive from both senses become blended together, and form one compound conception.

But we may be told that it has been conceded, even by Dr. Reid, that our sensations of hardness, roughness, and figure are evidently quite different from these properties in bodies themselves.* To this we answer, as we have already done in regard to tastes and odours, that the sensation is certainly different from its object; but that in the touch we have immediate and, so far as it goes, perfect knowledge of the tangible. If the objection implies that our knowledge of the object is not a true knowledge—that it is entirely illusory—then, we ask, what is the proof of this? Have we a more accurate knowledge obtained in any other way? If so, in what does it differ from that of sense, and what is that more excellent way, that so we may follow it? If it has been really discovered that our sensations of hardness, roughness, and figure are not a true knowledge of these properties of matter, this implies that we have reached to a truer knowledge of these things by some other means, and thus been able to correct our old and erroneous impressions. There is no such higher knowledge; no such more excellent way; but the sensations we derive from touch are frequently intertwined with those we derive from vision, and hence there grows up a conception in some respects different from both. Thus we find it difficult to

---

* Inquiry into the Human Mind, chap. v.

form an idea of a rough surface without thinking of the appearance which it presents to the eye, as well as of the impression which it makes on the hand; but the latter is the truer knowledge, as the eye can only tell us of certain varieties of light and shade arising from the inequalities of the surface, with the nature of which we must already have become acquainted by the exercise of our tactile organs. Our sight and our touch work wonderfully to one another, but each has nevertheless its own province, out of which it cannot pass.

SIGHT.—The organ of this sense is the eye; its object is light, but light as it is reflected from bodies in all its manifold gradations of colour. The eyes are not capable of seeing pure light. Isolate an eye in empty but illuminated space, and it would see nothing. Its light would be no better than darkness. But let the same eye receive the same light as it is reflected from wood and field, from tower and town, and it will be filled with visions. By this sense, then, we obtain our knowledge of colours, and in no other way could we obtain it. The blind can have no knowledge of colours. We may endeavour to explain their nature to them as we best can, but at the close of our explanations they will probably think, as a blind man once did, that scarlet must be like the sound of a trumpet.

It is certain that we now derive from sight a vast amount of knowledge beyond what it originally gives us. We learn by a glance of our eye the distance, shape, and magnitude of objects, as well as their colours. Still, after all, it is only their colour which we see; but the various shades of that colour suggest to the mind the distance, figure, and size of the coloured objects. Berkeley has demonstrated this in such a way that it is almost impossible to resist his demonstration. It seems certain, however, that sight gives us some knowledge of extension, as we cannot see colours but as extended, seeing they cannot exist but as extended.

We see no good ground upon which to rest the distinction made by many philosophers, and among others by Hamilton, between the primary and secondary qualities of objects. Odoriferousness is entirely different from hardness, and sonorousness from figure; but all of these are real qualities of matter, and each is immediately known by its appropriate sense. Perhaps, however, the objects of touch and sight, the palpable and the visible, force upon us more powerfully than the objects of the other senses, the idea of outness. We are not only conscious of these objects, but we are vividly conscious of them as external to ourselves. No amount of philosophy will ever bring a man to believe in earnest that the houses and streets, the men and women, whom he sees around him, are but phantasmagoria, or rather shifting moods of his own mind. He sees them, he feels them as entities apart from himself; his consciousness bears the most decisive testimony to the fact; and no arguments will overcome his convictions. The idealist himself is compelled to admit that his native beliefs cry out incessantly against his logic.

We think it will be conceded that the theory of knowing which we have sketched, is simpler than that of either Hamilton or Mill, and that is a presumptive evidence of its truth, for Nature is simple in all her ways. It is also much more in accordance with popular and wide-spread beliefs; and though we are not permitted in philosophy, as in theology, to lay down St. Vincent's rule for our guide (*quod semper, ubique et ab omnibus*); yet it must be admitted that we should not readily conclude that all the world is wrong in regard to the facts of its own consciousness. We smell perfumes, we hear sounds, we see sights, we touch the palpable—so say all the world, and so says the grand old oracle, consciousness, too. A careful investigation of our mental structure bears out the same result. No one now believes, with the older idealists, that the mind discerns only sensations and ideas; that these hang like a pictured curtain between it and externality, and form a kind of shifting panoramic show. And it appears to be more difficult still to believe with the modern idealists, that in consciousness we are simply conscient, without being conscient of anything.

Sir William Hamilton, more emphatically than any other philosopher, makes his appeal to consciousness. To consciousness, therefore let us go, and see how far his system tallies with it. He declares, that in perception we are distinctly conscious of a dualism—of both the mind perceiving, and the object perceived. Now we ask if any one is really conscious of such a dualism. Drunken men are said to see things double; but sober men, never. When we look at a tree, we see the tree, and the tree only—certainly not also our own mind in the act of looking at the tree. There is a duality, but it is only that of the mind perceiving and of the object perceived. But Sir William Hamilton's theory, in common with that of Mill, is further based upon what appears to us the absurdity and contradiction—that the mind in the act of perceiving, perceives itself so perceiving. This is not only contrary to consciousness, but beyond our capabilities of conception.

What can have led so able a reasoner so far astray? Is there no sense in which we can be said to be conscious of ourselves? There is. We are compound beings, made up of body and soul, most intimately blended together. The body is properly regarded as part of ourselves, and of that body we are unceasingly conscious. We cannot for one instant divest ourselves of this self-consciousness; and moreover, this self-consciousness interlaces itself, less or more closely, with every feeling and perception of the mind. The mind—that wondrous principle—so keenly susceptible of all other feelings, can never be conscious of itself, any more than the eyes, ever looking out into the wide world, can ever see themselves; but it is ever-more conscious of the living mantle in which it is clothed. It is even wrong, in some respects, to speak of the body as being aught separate from the soul—of the one being the vesture in which the other is robed — they constitute one being, and that being is conscious of itself.

But there is another circumstance to be taken into account, which is probably partly explanatory of the view held by Hamilton. None of our mental states are entirely simple. Sensations and memories are always less or more mingled toge-ther. It is, perhaps, impossible to have any sensation of the present, without having, at the same moment, some recollection of the past. There is here, then, a kind of double conscious-ness, and the consciousness of such feelings which connect, as it were, the past with the present, and, in the opinion of many, beget the idea of personal identity, may very easily be mis-taken for a consciousness of self. There is, in truth, generally congregated in our mind a miscellaneous crowd of ideas and sensations, which form a kind of background in the picture, when any new sensation presents itself to our attention, and the one as well as the other enter into our consciousness. Here, then, is a dualism, somewhat different from that taught by Sir William Hamilton; but it is a dualism, and we can never have any other.

If Sir William Hamilton has landed himself amid inextri-cable difficulties by maintaining that the mind is conscious of itself, Mr. Mill has environed himself with still greater by teaching that the mind is not conscious of anything beyond itself. First of all, his system is self-destructive, inasmuch as it teaches that the mind takes no cognisance of its own acts or affections; and yet that there is nothing but these of which it can be cognisant. But besides this, his theory makes all those properties purely mental which are generally regarded as purely material. Colour, extension, figure, size, so far as we know these things, become properties of mind, and of mind only. It is rigidly right to speak of our sensations as being green or blue, of our ideas as being round or square; for

greenness and blueness, rotundity and squareness, are nothing
but mental affections.   When a rose meets our eyes, it is not
the rose which is red, but the mind; which is at the same time
figured according to the exact pattern which we erroneously
conceive the rose to possess.   It is very hard to believe this ;
and yet we must believe it, if we adopt this idealism.

But Mr. Mill consistently carries out his theory to an entire
negation of the material world, and this is the legitimate conclusion, as it is the crowning difficulty of the idealistic system.
In this direction he goes much farther than Brown.   Brown
believes in the existence of an external world, though he maintains we are entirely ignorant of its properties.   Mill, following in the track of Berkeley and Hume, maintains that there
is no such thing as an external world—that our belief in matter
is a mere delusion.   He defines matter as ' A Permanent Pos-
' sibility of Sensation.'   ' If I am asked,' says he, ' whether I
' believe in matter, I ask whether the questioner accepts this
' definition of it.   If he does, I believe in matter, and so do
' all Berkeleyans.   In any other sense than this, I do not.'
This is very explicit, if not quite plain.   He believes in matter,
if we agree with him that matter is mind.   (P. 198.)

Matter is ' a permanent possibility of sensation.'   A sensation
is now allowed on all hands to be nothing apart from the mind.
It is simply the mind in one of its moods.   Still it is something.
But a possibility is nothing.   It is a mere abstract word, with
no entity corresponding to it.   And matter is declared to be a
possibility, and nothing more—the shadow of a shade.   This
appears to us simply a roundabout way of declaring it is
nothing.   But it may be said that Mr. Mill means that matter
is nothing but permanently possible sensations.   We do not
think this is Mr. Mill's meaning; but though it were, it does
not mend matters ; for a merely possible sensation is not an
actual sensation, and a sensation which is only possible and not
actual is a nonentity.   The truth is, Mr. Mill's idealism is of
the purest type.   He wishes honestly to teach that there is no
such thing as matter, or even material properties in the universe ; but knowing that the popular belief is against him, he
constructs a theory to account for that belief, and his definition
is a part of his theory.

The question, then, which Mr. Mill sets himself to solve
is this : Seeing there is no such thing as an outer world,
how comes it that all men nevertheless believe that there is an
outer world ?   Mr. Mill has elaborated his answer to this
question with infinite care and skill, and yet we must acknowledge that we have felt the greatest difficulty in understanding

it. This has arisen not from any obscurity in his language, but from the difficulty we have experienced in placing ourselves on his stand-point, and from it looking out on the world. If, therefore, we should in anything misapprehend his meaning, this will be our excuse.

Mr. Mill postulates two things. 1. That the mind is capable of forming expectations, or conceptions of possible conceptions. 2. The laws of association. These taken together, he says, are enough to generate the belief in an external world.

'What is meant,' he asks, 'when we say the object we perceive is external to us, and not a part of ourselves? We mean that there is involved in our perceptions something which exists when we are not thinking of it; which existed before we had ever thought of it, and would exist if we were annihilated. . . . The idea of something which is distinguished from our floating impressions by Perdurability . . . constitutes altogether our idea of external substance. Whoever can assign an origin to this complex conception has accounted for what we mean by the belief in matter.'

Now we must protest that we mean something more than this by our belief in matter. We do not mean simply that 'there is involved in our perceptions something which exists 'when we are not thinking of it;' but that we are cognisant of matter as a thing altogether apart from ourselves. Being thus cognisant of matter, we, of course, believe that it exists altogether independently of our thoughts of it.

'Now all this,' continues Mr. Mill, 'is but the form impressed by the known laws of association upon the conception or notion obtained by experience of contingent sensations, by which are meant sensations that are not in our present consciousness at all, but which in virtue of the laws to which we have learned by experience that our sensations are subject, we know that we should have felt under given supposable circumstances, and under these circumstances might still feel. I see a piece of white paper on a table. I go into a room, and though I have ceased to see it, I am persuaded that the paper is still there. I no longer have the sensations which it gave me, but I believe that when I again place myself in the circumstances in which I had these sensations, that is when I go again into the room I shall again have them, and further that there has been no intervening moment at which this would not have been the case.'

Now what is meant by ' the laws to which we have learned ' by experience that our sensations are subject,' and according to which ' we know we should have felt certain sensations under ' given supposable circumstances?' The principal law of sensation is that it is only when an object of sense is presented to the organs of sense that we can be sentient. To assume that sensations arise like ideas, according to the laws of association, is to assume the whole question at issue. 'I see a piece of 'white paper on a table,' says Mr. Mill. Now he does not here mean that he really sees the white paper, or that there is such a thing as white paper in the universe, but only that he has a certain sensation or group of sensations which he denominates white paper. The white paper exists no farther than it exists in his mind. How then comes it that he is persuaded, as he says he is, that the paper continues to exist on the table though he has ceased to see it? The paper is nothing but his sensation of it; when therefore the sensation vanished, the paper vanished; and how comes it that he should believe it to exist contrary to fact? What law of association will account for this? While he had the paper-sensation he may have had other mental affections—probably some thoughts about the paper—is he equally persuaded that these continue to exist though he no longer thinks them? What law of mind gives perdurability to the one and not to the other? But Mr. Mill further declares that he is persuaded that if he again enters the room he will again see the paper. How should he be so persuaded? Our ideas do not recur in such a fashion; how should our sensations? But in truth, why speak of sensations at all, for, *ex hypothesi,* our sensations are but ideas—both alike being simply affections of mind with no outward objects corresponding to them. But allowing the distinction between sensations and ideas, there is no such uniform experience in our sensational life as to create the persuasion Mr. Mill refers to. We frequently see an article in a room, and when we return we do not see it again, and yet we are not surprised, for we did not expect to see it. We knew it was there once, but we see it is not there now—that is the history of the whole fact.

'The conception I form of the world existing at any moment,' continues Mr. Mill, 'comprises, along with the sensations I am feeling, a countless variety of possibilities of sensation, namely, the whole of those which past observation tells me that I could, under any supposable circumstances, experience at this moment, together with an indefinite and illimitable number of others, which though I do not know that I could, yet it is possible that I might, experience in circumstances not known to me.'

Let all this be granted. Let it be granted that our conception of the world, so far as we can form such a conception, embraces not only our present sensations, but the memory of a myriad former sensations, which having experienced once, we believe we may experience again; all this does not explain the irresistible conviction that the world is something different from ourselves. It is the simple idea of outness, and not the many-sided idea which we have formed of nature, which is to be traced to its source. How that which is a mere series of mental affections, however concatenated, should stand out before us in bold relief, is the mystery to be accounted for, and we apprehend this explanation does not even touch it. The question is, How do we form a conception of the world at all, if the world does not exist?

'There is another important peculiarity,' says Mr. Mill, 'of these certified or guaranteed possibilities of sensations, namely, that they have reference, not to single sensations, but to sensations joined together in groups. When we think of anything as a material substance or body, we either have had, or we think that on some given supposition we should have, not some one sensation, but a great and even indefinite number and variety of sensations, generally belonging to different senses, but so linked together that the presence of one announces the possible presence, at the very same instant, of any or all of the rest.'

Now, it is certainly true that our sensations come to us in groups, and that one sensation very often suggests the recollection of others; but it is as true that no cluster or clusters of mental affections could ever suggest the existence of a material world which did not exist in fact. It is admitted that the idea of outness exists, and the whole question is—how is this idea generated? Outness is, *toto cœlo*, different from Inness (if we may use so barbarous a word); it is its antipodes. There is nothing in the one to suggest the other, any more than there is anything in colour to suggest sound. How can any number of internal sensations, real or contingent, grouped or single, linked by association or not linked, suggest an idea which not only has no true basis, but which is entirely opposed to experience, as Mr. Mill interprets experience? All our experience, *ex hypothesi*, is of the internal, and yet with one consent we believe it is the external. It seems to us that if all our experience is inward, beyond that inward our ideas could not go, any more than the oyster can go out of its shell.

But in truth, according to Mr. Mill's theory, no idea is possible either of an external or of an internal, either of an ego or of a non-ego. He reduces knowledge to an absolute unity. That which knows is identical with that which is known, and the knowing is identical with the being known. Now, the external can be thought only in contrast to the internal; the non-ego only in contrast to the ego; the known only in contrast to the knowing. According to Mr. Mill there is no such contrast; there is only one entity at one instant in the universe,—the passing mental affection. Such a knowledge then is impossible. But further, we apprehend, all knowledge involves a duality, a something which knows and a something which is known; and Mr. Mill denies this duality. He thus renders impossible not only a knowledge of the external world, but all knowledge whatever.

Mr. Mill does not believe in mind any more than in matter. He defines the mind to be ' A Permanent Possibility of ' Feeling.' As feeling includes sensation, mind, according to this theory, includes matter as a part of itself. Mr. Mill does not shrink from this conclusion; he avows it. ' What I call ' outward objects,' he says, ' are possibilities of sensation alone, ' whereas the series I call myself includes along with them, and ' called up by them, all those thoughts, emotions, volitions, and ' permanent possibilities of these, which are generally distinct ' from them and do not occur in groups.' The non-ego is therefore only a portion of the ego. ' The great globe itself ' is simply a province of the mind; and that mind is nothing but a series of feelings, or rather a permanent possibility of these, which is equivalent to a permanent nonentity. Here, however, Mr. Mill confesses that he is confronted with a difficulty which he cannot overcome. The mind's phenomenal life, he tells us, consists not only of present sensations but likewise of memories and expectations, and each of these involves a belief in more than its own present existence. A memory involves a belief in the past, an expectation, a belief in the future.

' If then,' he says, ' we speak of the mind as a series of feelings, we are obliged to conclude the statement by calling it a series of feelings which is aware of itself as past and future, and we are reduced to the alternative of believing that the mind or ego is something different from any series of feelings or possibilities of them, or of accepting the paradox that something which, *ex hypothesi*, is but a series of feelings can be aware of itself as a series.'

Mr. Mill allows this difficulty to be insoluble, but thinks it is the final inexplicability which always comes, and resolves to accept the paradox rather than abandon his theory. It had been wiser if he had renounced his theory and retreated before the absurdity to which it had led him. But the difficulty is even greater than he seems to see. It is as absurd to suppose a feeling conscious of itself as *present*, as either past or future, and thus the difficulty, pointed out by Mr. Mill himself, applies to sensations as well as to expectations and memories.

Such are some of the objections which stand in the way of what Mr. Mill calls ' the Psychological theory of the belief in

' an external world.' The only way to get rid of them is to believe that there really is an outer world, the immediate object of all our knowledge. Man, shut up within the shell of his own consciousness, could never have created such a world for himself. The silkworm has within itself the material out of which to spin its cocoon, but man must have made his world out of nothing.

We have hitherto spoken only of sensations, and have maintained that in every sensation we are immediately conscious of something different from ourselves. But what of memory? it may be asked. When we remember, it may be said, we are not so simply and immediately conscious of an outward object ; we are merely conscious of a present state of mind, accompanied by a belief in something that is past. When such is the case, it may be argued, the doctrine that the mind ever knows and is never known, and in all knowledge knows something different from itself, breaks down. We acknowledge that if the description of memory given above is correct, the doctrine we have hitherto been teaching, signally breaks down here ; but it breaks down in company with the repeated declarations of Brown, Hamilton, and Mill, that the mind cannot be cognisant of its own affections. We further acknowledge that the description we have given of memory is copied from that given by Hamilton, and adopted with applause by Mill ; but we hope to be able to show that Hamilton, in departing from Reid in this particular, and holding that memory gives us a merely representative and not an immediate knowledge of its objects, has in effect abandoned his own system of philosophy, and left it in the hands of the enemy.

' An act of memory,' says Sir William Hamilton, ' is merely a present state of the mind, which we are conscious of, not as absolute but as relative to and representing another state of mind, and accompanied with the belief that the state of mind as now represented has actually been. . . . All that is immediately known in the act of memory is the present mental modification, that is, the representation and concomitant belief. So far is memory from being an immediate knowledge of the past, that it is at best only a mediate knowledge of the past ; while in philosophical propriety it is not a knowledge of the past at all, but a knowledge of the present and a belief of the past. . . . We may doubt, we may deny, that the representation and belief are true.' *

From this passage it is too plain that, so far as memory is concerned, Hamilton was a pure idealist—he admits that the

---

* Lectures, vol. i. pp. 218–19, quoted by Mr. Mill, p. 110.

knowledge which memory gives is representative, and by that admission deals a death-blow to his own system. Mill is quick enough to detect the inconsistency. Sir William Hamilton had argued with great force in regard to perception, that we cannot have a perception without having at the same time a knowledge of the thing perceived. Mr. Mill here turns upon him, and says that if perception involves a knowledge of the thing perceived, belief (as in memory) involves a knowledge of the thing believed. He thus drives him from his doctrine of perception by showing it is inconsistent with his doctrine of memory.

'An act of memory is merely a present state of the mind ' which we are conscious of, &c. . . . All that is immediately ' known in the act of memory is the present mental modifica- ' tion.' So say both Hamilton and Mill. Is it possible then for the mind to know its own present modifications? Am I simply conscious of myself when I remember? We had thought this doctrine was abandoned by everybody since the days of Brown. Is it needful to repeat that, since a mental modifica- tion is just the mind modified, it is absurd to speak of the mind modified being conscious of the mind modified, or of a mental modification being aware of itself? Nor will it do to say that there is simply a present conscious state, for we can- not be conscious without being conscious of something, and the question is, Of what are we conscious? Is it the mental modification, or the thing remembered? When an appeal is made to consciousness on this subject, its answer is decisive. In every act of memory we are distinctly conscious of the thing remembered, we are never conscious of the mind itself. To say that I recollect anything, is to say that I am memorially conscious of it; just as to say that I see anything is to say that I am visually conscious of it. In the one case the object is present to the memory, in the other it is present to the sight. Sense and memory are different; the former gives us a know- ledge of the present, the latter of the past, but in both cases the knowledge is immediate.

Dr. Reid had a true insight into the bearings of this ques- tion.

'Suppose,' says he, 'that once, and once only, I smelled a tube- rose in a certain room where it grew in a pot, and gave a very grateful perfume. Next day I relate what I saw and smelled. When I attend as carefully as I can to what passes in my mind in this case, it appears evident that the very thing I saw yesterday and the fragrance I smelled, are now the immediate objects of my mind when I remember it. . . . Philosophers, indeed, tell me that the immediate object of my memory in this case is not the past sensa- tion, but an idea of it, an image, phantasm, or species of the odour I smelled ; that this idea now exists in my mind or in my sensorium, and the mind contemplating this present idea finds it a representation of what is past. This is the doctrine of the ideal philosophy. . . . Upon the strictest attention, memory appears to me to have things that are past, and not ideas, for its object. . . . In the mean time I beg leave to think with the vulgar, that when I remember the smell of the tuberose, that very sensation which I had yesterday, and which has now no more any existence, is the immediate object of my memory. But though the object of my sensation, memory, and imagination be in this case the same, yet these acts or operations of the mind are as different and as easily distinguishable as smell, taste, and sound.' *

In this passage Dr. Reid has proved himself to have had a far truer vision than Sir William Hamilton in regard to memory. The stone which caused the latter philosopher to stumble appears to have been his difficulty in conceiving how things which confessedly do not exist can be immediately present to the mind. In all perception the object must be existent and present to the senses. But, in memory, the object is not present to the senses, and has often ceased altogether to exist. How can the absent and the non-existent be present to the mind unless by representative images? Now those who put this question forget that sense and memory are essentially distinct faculties, and that whereas the function of the one is to make us acquainted with the present, the function of the other is to make us acquainted with the past. We open our eyes and see a tower ; we turn our back upon it, but remember it ; the tower is as certainly the object of our memory as it was of our sight, and memory is just the mind remembering. To say that we remember not the tower, but a representative image of it, were absurd ; to say that in remembrance we are conscious of such an image, is to say precisely the same thing, though it does not sound so ridiculous ; and the whole belief is a shred of that idealism from which it seems so difficult to shake oneself free.

It is the same with imagination, and indeed with all thinking. We cannot think without thinking of something ; and that something is always *outside* the mind in its act of thinking. There is ever the dualism—the mind thinking, the thing thought of. But anything in the great universe may be the object of thought. We may even transcend the universe of reality, and think of things which never were. We may think not only of the present, but of the past, and recall to memory scenes and circumstances with which we were familiar in our

* Inquiry into the Human Mind, ch. ii. sect. 3.

childhood, and even imagine other scenes and circumstances, perhaps brighter still, which our eyes never witnessed nor our ears heard. But in this last case it may be said there is surely nothing but an image in the mind, of which the very word ' imagination ' is the proof. We can by no means concede this. Of such an image we are utterly unconscious. But our mind recalls the bright and beautiful in the external world, and out of the materials which memory so abundantly supplies builds its castles in the air. The things imagined, and not a mental image, are the object of imagination ; and things imagined are simply things remembered in new combinations. ' Things ' imagined '—in that expression is the whole truth ; it is *things* which are imagined—castles, cities, gardens, golden fruits, crystal fountains—and not mental images. We may be said to have mental images, as we may be said to have sensations, but we are not conscious of the one any more than the other, but only of their objects. The mental image is nothing but the mind imagining, and the mind may imagine anything. It may weave any web for which memory can furnish the weft and the woof. More than this it cannot do, for imagination is nothing but a somewhat loose and very brilliant memory. But what, it may be said, of those things which have no existence at all except in imagination ? What of horned devils, long-haired mermaids, wandering hobgoblins and fiery dragons— these have no objective reality, and therefore they must be purely mental and subjective. The answer is easy. The elements out of which they are formed exist, and the mind only combines them in grotesque shapes. But when the mind thinks of them, it thinks of them as external entities, and it can think of them no otherwise. The mind imagines, but the objects in imagination are always furnished to us in their elementary forms by experience. The mind can no more con-ceive a new quality than it can create a new world. It can merely remember, and all its remembrances are of the external, but it may recall things not exactly as they were, but in new groupings, and this is what we call imagination.

Can the mind, then, in no case, think of itself? Can the mental eye, in no sense, be turned inward ? In a way it can, else a mental philosophy had been impossible. The mind, as we have already repeatedly said, can never be conscious of itself—of its own faculties, acts, or affections ; and this is what constitutes the great difficulty of psychology. But in every act of consciousness, we know what we are conscious of ; and from the contents of consciousness, so to speak, we can infer its capacity. The mind, moreover, can reflect upon all its past experiences, for these can become the objects of its recollection or of its reasoning, and from the things which have been known we can infer the nature and powers of that unknown something which knows.   It perceives the present, we call this sensation ; it recalls the past, we call this memory ; it works up into argument the materials furnished by sense and preserved by memory, and we call this reasoning.   Thus we construct our system of Psychology ; but the fact that we can never make the mind the direct object of its own perception, has been, and ever will be, the great hindrance to our learning its mechanism.

There is still a large group of mental states, which are generally regarded as purely subjective. We refer to those which are not intellectual but emotional—to our feelings, passions and desires.   An analysis of these states, however, will show that they are not exceptions to the universal rule which requires a union of objectivity and subjectivity in order to consciousness ; and that as we cannot know without knowing something, so we cannot feel without feeling something.   The something felt will moreover be found to be different from the mind which feels it.   It is usual to speak of feeling passions, affections, desires ; but such phrases are not more correct than if we were to speak of feeling feelings.   We do not feel feelings : we feel, love, hate, desire—these verbs express the whole mental portion of the fact ; but, of course, there is always a something outside the mind which we feel, love, hate, or desire.   It is usual also to speak of feeling joy, grief, pleasure, pain, &c. These phrases are not more accurate than the others.   Joy, grief, pleasure, pain, are nothing apart from the mind which feels them, just as a sensation is nothing apart from the mind which feels it.   A sensation is simply the mind in a certain mood, and so are joy, grief and all the other emotions.   In the one case, as well as in the other, the mind has an object—the cause and occasion of its mood.   Here a large and inviting field for analysis opens itself up ; but we cannot pursue it further without diverging too widely from our examination of modern idealism.   Let the student of psychology, however, bear in mind the truth taught in common by Mill and Hamilton, that the mind can in no case be conscious of its own acts or affections, and it will serve as a master-key to open doors in mental science which have remained closed for centuries.

We are now, and only now, in a fit position to consider the question discussed by Mr. Mill in the opening chapters of his ' Examination '—the Relativity of Human Knowledge.   Sir William Hamilton laid the first foundation of his future fame by his article on Cousin's ' Philosophy ' in the ' Edinburgh Review '

(1829), in which he strenuously asserted that all our knowledge is relative; and he has reasserted the same opinion in his Discussions and Lectures.   Mr. Mill believes in the relativity of human knowledge too, and so far he has no fault to find with Hamilton; but then he maintains that Hamilton's doctrine of the relativity of knowledge is flatly contradictory of his other doctrine that the primary qualities of matter are known in themselves and immediately, and therefore that either the one or the other must be abandoned. These two doctrines—the immediate intuition of the external world, and the relativity of all knowledge—were those upon which the celebrated Scotch professor put forth his greatest strength, and it is difficult to say with which his reputation is most intimately connected.* Is it possible he exhausted his life in proving contradictories?   Must his disciples now surrender the one thesis to save the other—its alleged antithesis.   It were strange if it were so, and yet stranger things than this have happened in the perplexed history of Mental Philosophy. We apprehend, however, that there is no real contradiction in Sir William Hamilton's teaching on these points, though a few stray expressions may be picked out of his writings to favour the opinion that there is.

Mr. Mill admits that the phrase ' the relativity of human ' knowledge,' may bear many different meanings; and several of these meanings he very carefully discriminates and defines. By most philosophers, he tells us, the phrase is used to indicate that we know and can know nothing of matter beyond the sensations which it produces in us, and that as we have no reason to believe that there is any resemblance between material properties and our mental affections, matter is to us necessarily and altogether unknowable.   In this sense, he says, the doctrine ' is one of great weight and significance, which impresses ' a character on the whole mode of philosophical thinking of ' whoever receives it, and is the key-stone of one of the only two ' possible systems of Metaphysics and Psychology.'   And he may well say so, for this doctrine reduces all our knowledge not only to a relation but to zero.   Yet this is the doctrine which he lays at the door of Sir William Hamilton.   If Sir William acknowledges it as his own, it must be confessed that his philosophy is a contradiction and a blunder.   The passage which Mr. Mill quotes in support of his opinion is taken from one of the Appendices to the ' Discussions on Philosophy.'   Let us see it.

' Our whole knowledge of mind and matter is relative, conditioned —relatively conditioned.   Of things absolutely or in themselves, be they external, be they internal, we know nothing; or know them only as incognisable; and become aware of their incomprehensible existence, only as this is indirectly and accidentally revealed to us through certain qualities related to our faculties of knowledge, and which qualities again we cannot think as unconditioned, irrelative, existent in and of themselves. All that we know is, therefore, phenomenal—phenomenal of the unknown. . . . Nor is this denied, for it has been commonly confessed that as substances we know not what is matter, and are ignorant of what is mind.' *

Now, no one acquainted with the philosophy of Hamilton can have any doubt as to his meaning here. He simply means that we do not know substances, but through their qualities, and yet that we cannot think of these qualities out of relation to those hidden substances in which they adhere. This meaning he only qualifies in a very slight degree when he speaks of our knowing only those ' qualities which are related ' to our faculties of knowledge; ' for, of course, we know only those things which we are capable of knowing. But though the meaning of the passage lies upon its surface, Mr. Mill toils ingeniously to put upon it every possible meaning but the true one. At length he hits upon the true meaning, or something approaching it.

'Perhaps,' says he, ' it may be suspected (and some passages in the longest of our extracts might countenance the idea) that in calling our knowledge relative, Sir William Hamilton was not thinking of the knowledge of qualities, but of substances, of Matter and Mind; and meant that qualities might be cognised absolutely; but that substances being known only through their qualities, the knowledge of substances can only be regarded as relative. But this interpretation of his doctrine is again inadmissible. For the relativity of which he is continually speaking is relativity *to us*, while the relativity which this theory ascribes to substances is relativity to those attributes; and if the attributes are known otherwise than relatively, so must the substance be. Besides, we have seen him asserting the necessary relativity of our knowledge of attributes no less positively than of substances. Speaking of things in themselves, we found him saying that we " become aware of their incomprehensible existence only as this is revealed to us through certain qualities, . . . which qualities again we cannot think as unconditioned, irrelative, existent in and of themselves." There is no reservation here in favour of the Primary Qualities. Whatever in his theory was meant by relativity of knowledge, he intended it of qualities as much as of substances—of primary qualities as much as of secondary.'

From this extract it is evident that Mr. Mill, after getting

* Discussions, p. 643 ; Mill, p. 17.

a glimpse of Sir William Hamilton's meaning, forthwith shuts his eyes, and begins groping about for it as one in the dark. ' The relativity of which Hamilton is continually speaking,' says he, ' is relativity *to us*, while the relativity which this ' theory ascribes to substances is relativity to their attributes.' Now, what Sir William Hamilton continually does say is, that we know substances only through their qualities, and therefore they are known *to us* not absolutely but relatively. ' If the attributes are known otherwise than relatively,' continues Mr. Mill, ' so must the substances.' Is there a necessary sequence here? Is it impossible to know attributes immediately, absolutely, and yet not know so immediately, so absolutely the substances to which they belong? But let us hear the conclusion of Mr. Mill's argument. ' Besides,' says he, ' we have seen him (Hamilton) asserting the necessary ' relativity of our knowledge of attributes no less positively ' than of substances. Speaking of things in themselves, we ' found him saying that we become aware of their incompre- ' hensible existence only as this is revealed to us through ' certain qualities . . . which qualities again we cannot think ' as unconditioned, irrelative, existent in and of themselves.' Now all that Sir William Hamilton means to affirm here is that we cannot think of qualities in and of themselves, or apart from the substances to which they belong. We cannot conceive hardness, for instance, apart from some hard matter, for this plain reason, according to our way of thinking, that hardness is nothing but matter in a hard state. What are the qualities of matter? Are they something different from its substance? We say they are not. They are merely the substance in its different conditions, as sensation and thought are just the mind in its different moods. We cannot, therefore, know qualities without also knowing substances. When we see a round, green object, we see it in that condition which we call greenness and rotundity, but we see *it,* for properties are only modes of substance, and substance must always exist in some mode. It must be admitted that Hamilton has to some degree laid himself open to the criticisms of his adversary by speaking of substances and qualities as if they were different from one another, and as known only in relation to one another; but if it be fully understood that qualities are but modes of substances, and that substances are known only in their different modes, and never absolutely, which means, in no mode at all, the controversy is set at rest. It must be confessed that this is a somewhat lame and impotent conclusion; but it saves the doctrine, infinitely important to all mankind, of immediate knowledge of the outer world.

The doctrine that all knowledge involves a dualism—a mind knowing and matter known—involves the doctrine that all knowledge is and must be relative. Knowledge is a relation, the relation of the knowing and the known. The knowing ego is distinct from the known non-ego, and knowledge is the relation in which they stand to one another. Where there are two factors absolute knowledge is impossible. We know only as we know, and, indeed, only as we are capable of knowing. Our knowledge is limited by the limits of our mind, and is probably in other respects conditioned by it too. But this is very different, as Mr. Mill fully confesses, from saying that we in effect know nothing of the material world, or that our knowledge is at best entirely illusory. It has already been made plain that our knowledge is immediate, and being immediate that it is true.

Mr. Mill has protested with great spirit and force of argument against the doctrine laid down by Mr. Mansel, in his ' Limits of Religious Thought,' that justice, truth, and other moral attributes may be something quite different in Deity from what they are in us. Is it not just as monstrous to suppose that the Deity may know things differently from us, as that He should morally regard them differently? In truth, is it not certain that if He does know things differently, He must regard them differently? Our moral judgments are dependent on our intellectual perceptions ; and if our intellectual perceptions are all illusory, our moral judgments will be so too. Truth with us may be falsehood with God : justice with God may be injustice with us. We are thus driven to the conclusion either that the divine knowledge must be illusory like our own ; or that we, walking in a vain show, are as likely to be deceived in regard to justice and truth as anything else. But the fact is, the divine knowledge is not different from human knowledge ; there is the inevitable relation between the knowing and the known ; but this by no means interferes with the reality of knowledge, though it implies that it is conditioned by the knowing mind.

Mr. Mill has endeavoured to fasten an inconsistency on Sir William Hamilton by showing that immediate knowledge and relative knowledge are irreconcileable and contradictory. We suspect the real inconsistency lies with Mr. Mill, who holds knowledge to be relative, and yet denies the existence of one of the terms necessary to the relation. According to him knowledge is a unity, a conscious state of mind, and nothing more. There is no external world to be known, and no mind to know it. There is only the conscious state—conscious without being conscious of anything, a state without being a state of anything. Besides this conscious state there is nothing else in the universe; it *is* the universe, the absolute, the all in one. To this dizzy height of Hegelianism has Mr. Mill climbed, apparently without being aware of it.

But though Mr. Mill has failed to show that relative knowledge, as understood by Hamilton, is inconsistent with immediate knowledge, it has been shown that the doctrine of a double consciousness, as taught by the Scotch philosopher, is not only destructive of immediate knowledge, but leads inevitably to the doctrine of the absolute. This has been done, not by Mr. Mill, but by Professor Ferrier, in his exquisitely beautiful and subtle ' Institutes of Metaphysics.' He only postulates that along with whatever any intelligence knows, it must, as the ground or condition of its knowledge, have some consciousness of itself (the dualism of Hamilton); and from this he proceeds to prove by a series of propositions, linked together like the propositions of Euclid, that we can have no knowledge of mind *per se*, none of matter *per se*, but that mind and matter in conjunction is the absolute, and is known by us. Nor do we see how we are to resist Professor Ferrier's conclusions if we grant his postulate—and his postulate is simply the double consciousness upon which Sir William Hamilton has built his doctrine of perception. Thus do both Mr. Mill and his opponent, though both earnest preachers of the truth that all knowledge is relative, come by different roads to the same conclusion that knowledge is absolute. There is only one way of escape for them. Let them admit the only possible dualism of mind knowing and matter known, and then there emerges a knowledge which is relative and yet immediate—the knowledge after which Hamilton so strenuously strove, though he did not quite attain to it.

But though we cannot accept of the pure idealism presented to us by Mr. Mill, or of the double consciousness taught by Sir William Hamilton, we must place both disputants in the front rank of modern philosophers. Mr. Mill's ' Examination ' will fully sustain his former great reputation as a clear thinker and most vigorous reasoner, but we suspect he has shown himself more powerful in pulling down than in building up. While he has shattered to pieces many old opinions, we doubt if he has himself built up a system of knowledge which will endure.

ART. V.—*The Albert Nyanza, Great Basin of the Nile, and Explorations of the Nile Sources.* By SAMUEL WHITE BAKER, M.A., F.R.G.S., and Gold Medallist of the Royal Geographical Society. With Maps and Illustrations. 2 vols. 8vo. London: 1866.

THE reader will not have travelled ten pages in the company of Mr. Baker, before he perceives that the last and most successful explorer of the sources of the Nile is a far more accomplished writer than any of the gallant adventurers who have preceded him on the rugged tracks of African discovery. It must be confessed that the number of these works had somewhat abated the edge of the curiosity with which they have been received by the public. To say nothing of missionary travellers whose knowledge of science hardly enabled them to take an observation and whose knowledge of letters appears to be confined to their own hymn-books—to say nothing of adventurers who have contrived to amuse the world with a romance of big baboons and cannibals picked up on the shore of the Gaboon river, it is not always that travellers of the highest character and merit, such as Captain Speke and Captain Grant undoubtedly were, have combined the art of travelling in wild countries with the art of relating what they saw there. Accordingly some of the narratives to which we refer have proved less interesting than might have been expected; and though the world is very well satisfied to be taken to those sources of the Nile which mankind has been in search of since the days of Herodotus, we may be pardoned for wishing to arrive at our destination by a shorter route. But Mr. Baker combines in so remarkable a degree all the qualities of a great traveller, that he has not only made one of the most extraordinary journeys ever recorded by civilised man, but he has given to his account of it an interest not to be surpassed in the pages of romance. Yet the materials of almost all these African expeditions are identical to monotony —village after village of filthy, brutal, and perfidious savages —the tyranny of native chiefs, astonished to find a white man in their power—the frauds of cowardly followers, ever ready to abandon their master in the hour of danger or to plunder him in the hour of confidence—the loathsome and scanty fare, the torrid soil—the drenching rains—the distant and unattainable object rendered valuable only by the difficulty of approaching it —may be repeated to satiety. It must even be acknowledged that the more we know of the interior of Africa, the less do we find in it to reward the stupendous efforts which have been made to arrive there ; and even the mighty mystery of the Nile loses something of its attraction when we have reached the great basins which feed its prodigious stream. Mr. Baker himself, at the close of his labours, when he found himself once more, after years of inconceivable danger and hardship, within reach of civilised man at Gondokoro, appears to have been oppressed by this reflection, and he exclaims, with something of that melancholy which attends the completion of every human achievement,

' We had worked for years in misery, such as I have but faintly described, to overcome the difficulties of this hitherto unconquerable exploration ; we had succeeded—and what was the result ? Not even a letter from home to welcome us if alive ! As I sat beneath a tree and looked down upon the glorious Nile that flowed a few yards beneath my feet, I pondered upon the value of my toil. I had traced the river to its great Albert source, and as the mighty stream glided before me, the mystery that had ever shrouded its origin was dissolved. I no longer looked upon its waters with a feeling approaching to awe, for I knew its home, and had visited its cradle. Had I overrated the importance of the discovery ? and had I wasted some of the best years of my life to obtain a shadow ? I recalled to recollection the practical question of Commoro, the chief of Latooka.—" Suppose you get to the great lake, what will you do with it ? What will be the good of it ? If you find that the large river does flow from it, what then ? " ' (Vol. ii. p. 298.)

The answer to this doubt—the key to this spell which has fascinated so many brave spirits, and which rivets our own attention on these pages—is that it is not the people of Africa but the representative of England, not the savage brutality of the tribes on the White Nile, but the matchless intrepidity of our own countryman, not the most degraded offsets of humanity but the latest pioneer of civilisation, who bears with him our sympathy and commands our admiration. The qualities which everywhere claim respect, shine with tenfold lustre when they are contrasted with everything that is most opposed to them. The native of Central Africa is by some mysterious law of his being sunk considerably below the higher ranks of the brute creation, educated and domesticated by man. He is alike unconscious of a purpose in life, of duty, of affection, of God. The European traveller inflamed to heroism by the resolution to succeed in a great undertaking, strong in his faith in Providence, steeled against all hardships, fearing nothing, daring all things, encounters alone a wilderness of savages, and moved by a lofty conception of the glory of a great action, performs it. Courage and independ-

ence were never more signally displayed.   A private English
gentleman, aided by no public resources, prompted by no
public bodies, starts in the exercise of his own discretion to
attempt the solution of a problem which had baffled ages.   Mr.
Baker's first incentive was the hope of rescuing Messrs. Speke
and Grant from a perilous position, but as he met them at the
outset of his own journey, that motive ceased.   With equal
manliness of spirit they instantly placed at his disposal the
results of their own explorations, and urged him to pursue the
greater task of perfecting what they had well begun.   He had
already devoted several years to the hardiest feats of a great
hunter and a keen shot in the jungles of Ceylon and the highlands of Abyssinia, which had nerved his frame and quickened
his eye.   To these qualifications he added two years of patient
preparation for his great attempt—the acquisition of the power
of scientific observation and the Arabic language—the purchase and adaptation of all the *matériel* necessary for so
protracted a campaign, and the attempt to discipline a numerous band of followers.   To the plots and treachery of
these beings, who repeatedly broke out in open mutiny, and
threatened him more than once with abandonment and death,
he opposed an iron and commanding will, which at last
moulded even these creatures to obey him.   This moral authority was backed by a strength of arm that never failed to
crush the offender by a timely blow and to punish every insult
and infraction of discipline.   Yet in a land where blood is
poured out like water, where inhuman tortures are ruthlessly
inflicted by the strong on the weak, and where every man who
is not a slave himself is seeking to enslave some one else, Mr.
Baker allowed no deed of violence to be committed which he
could prevent, he rescued numberless victims from the lash of
their tormentors, and by a judicious and open-handed liberality, he taught the natives the unknown lesson that an
Englishman is not to be served by slaves, but by the fidelity
of those whom he is ready to reward for their labour.   One
trait remains, and it is the most singular incident in this
remarkable narrative, which gives to the journey of Mr.
Baker an unparalleled interest.   Through these regions where
no white woman had ever been seen, through these tribes where,
woman is degraded by the grossest sensuality to be something
below the beast of burden and the household drudge, he was
accompanied by his wife.   This lady, born of a good Hun-
garian family and married at an early age to the companion
of her adventurous life, possessing, as we infer from her portrait, uncommon personal attractions, and still in the bloom of

youth, not only shared with her husband all the perils of this expedition, but by her quiet imperturbable courage, her tact and activity, contributed most powerfully to its success.   On more than one occasion she said or did the thing that conquered the difficulty.   And, above all, the presence, in the midst of whole races to whom the idea of marriage in our sense of the term is unknown, of the one Wife of the White Man, so ennobled this pair of travellers, and distinguished it so effectually from the marauding columns of ivory traders and man stealers, that even the savages of the White Nile acknowledged her influence.

To sum up in one word the cause of the interest with which this book will be read throughout the world, it consists in the *chivalry* which pervades it.   The breeze which bore the crew of the 'Argo' to the shores of Colchis, the spirit which led the Crusaders to Palestine, the passionate desire to face and surmount unknown dangers, and the proud sense of marching in purity and honour across a world of abject beings, to whom the very sight of civilised man was a revelation, pervade these volumes.   No doubt it may be called knight-errantry to go in quest of such hardships and dangers. But there is little risk that in any age the example will find too many imitators.   Modern civilisation has not, however, extinguished—perhaps it has not even lessened—that gallant spirit.   From the midst of our luxuries and refinements, men are not wanting who will start to encounter any perils and to perform any duty, just as boldly as in harder and in rougher times.   But in addition to the physical strength and courage needed for such exploits, they carry with them a higher sense of the dignity of their mission, and perhaps they are rewarded by a keener enjoyment of success.   These considerations are naturally suggested by Mr. Baker's narrative, for he is himself the very type of modern knighthood—chasing the elephant to his lair, braving the savage, protecting the child and the woman slave, enduring every vicissitude of hunger and thirst, heat and cold, sickness and pain—but withal retaining the simplicity and unpretending tone of a man who thinks it easier to do these things than to present them to the knowledge of the world.   Well is it for England that there are those who go forth in her name, unbidden, to display this strength of character and this nobility of purpose.   They may appeal with confidence to the respect and admiration of their countrymen, and in them they have their reward.   Yet we cannot but reflect with shame and regret that if this is the only country in the world which sends forth men of so much intrepidity and independence, it is also the only country in Europe in which the Sovereign and the State contribute nothing to the honours which are justly due to such exertions.

Mr. Baker's journey commenced in the spring of 1861, for it was then he proceeded to execute his long-cherished design of exploring the sources of the Nile; but he had advanced very little way towards the great object of his ambition before he perceived that a knowledge of Arabic was indispensable to success. He therefore resolved to devote a year to this preliminary acquisition, and to spend that time in examining the Nile tributaries on the right bank of the stream from the junction of the Atbara river to the Blue Nile. It is at this point that the Nile presents the greatest volume of water, for the Atbara is the last tributary which falls into the great stream at a point not less than eleven hundred miles from the sea. An enormous amount of absorption and evaporation of course takes place in the passage of the stream through that dry and rainless region, to which the Nile alone contributes the moisture borne down from the Highlands of Abyssinia and the great nursing lakes of the White Nile. This journey of 1861 does not form the subject of the present volume, and Mr. Baker therefore dismisses it in a few lines; though he promises to give us an account of this expedition in a future publication. But we are at once enabled, by the comparison he has made of the two grand arms of the river, to explain that remarkable phenomenon which so long perplexed mankind— we mean the periodical rising of the Nile, which causes its waters to attain their greatest height and to inundate the plains of Lower Egypt in the months of July and August, when all the other streams of the Northern hemisphere are at their lowest ebb. The vast mass of water which forms the main body of the stream, proceeding from the great lakes discovered by Captain Speke and Mr. Baker, and known as the White Nile, flows perpetually onwards without any sensible variation. The upper waters of the stream being extended in immense lakes or marshes are but slightly affected by the rainy season. The river has, in fact, no banks: there is no water-mark on the stems of trees or along the shore; and nothing indicates any important access or decrease in the quantity of water. The White Nile is the continuous and perennial fountain of the main stream. But the rivers on the eastern bank of the river which were visited by Mr. Baker in 1861 are of an opposite character. They are the great drains of the Abyssinian Highlands—rapid mountain streams—perfectly dry at one time of the year, and swollen into enormous torrents in the rainy season.   Thus the Atbara was perfectly dry when first seen by Mr. Baker—a mere sheet of glaring sand—and it remains in this state for many months in the year, and for a distance of 150 miles from its junction with the Nile.   But the rainy season commences in Abyssinia in the middle of May. From June to the middle of September the storms are terrific; every ravine becomes a raging torrent; the Atbara and the Blue Nile then become huge rivers swollen with the entire drainage of Abyssinia, which they pour into the main Nile in the middle of June.   The Nile itself is already full, though not flooded, at that season of the year, above Khartoum; but the sudden addition of the waters brought down by what we may term these intermittent tributaries at once augments the stream and causes the annual inundation in Lower Egypt. Were it not for the steady volume of the White Nile, Mr. Baker is of opinion that the whole of the Blue Nile and its other tributaries would be absorbed by the Nubian deserts before they could reach the 25th degree of latitude.   It follows, therefore, that although the history of these secondary streams explains the inundation, yet the head-waters of the White Nile are the permanent sources of the river.   The exploration of these sources is thus the grand problem which has now first been solved by Mr. Baker, following to a certain extent upon the track of Speke and Grant, and confirming by actual observation the information which they had collected from the native tribes.*

After this preliminary ramble on the Atbara and the Blue Nile, which lasted about twelve months, Mr. Baker descended

---

* It is amusing to compare the delusions of Bruce, who imagined that he had discovered the principal source of the Nile on a spot called Geesh, which he places in lat. 11° and long. 36° 55′ E., and at an altitude of two miles, with the more accurate accounts of later travellers, though Bruce was undoubtedly a careful and trustworthy observer.   But on the point just mentioned in the text Bruce agrees with Mr. Baker; he says :—' These rains are 'collected by the four great rivers in Abyssinia : all these principal, 'and their tributary streams, would however be absorbed, nor be 'able to pass the burning deserts, or find their way into Egypt, *were* '*it not for the White River,* which rising in a country of almost 'perpetual rain, joins to it a never-failing stream equal to the Nile 'itself.' (*Bruce's Travels*, vol. v. p. 333.)

So too Captain Speke observed when he passed the mouth of the Blue Nile :—' I was never more disappointed than with this river : if ' the White River was cut off from it, its waters would all be absorbed ' before they could reach Lower Egypt.' (*Speke's Journal*, p. 610.)

the latter river to Khartoum and reached that spot (at which the White Nile and the Blue Nile unite) on the 11th June, 1862. Khartoum is the seat of government of the Soudan provinces. It contains 30,000 inhabitants, and about 6,000 Turkish and Egyptian troops; but, above all, it is the principal mart of that rude, inhuman, and brutalising commerce which is carried on between the native tribes of Upper Nile and the scum of Asia and Europe. The nature of this trade, the poverty of the country, the corruption of the Egyptian governors, and the difficulty of communication (for the rapids of the Nile below Khartoum obstruct navigation in that part of its course), are the causes which have in reality shut out mankind from a knowledge of the interior of this country, and which still present the most formidable barrier the traveller has to surmount. Gum-arabic and ivory are the chief articles of export from the Soudan; but this trade would not repay the Egyptians for the occupation of the country, were it not that above all else *the Soudan supplies slaves.* It is this accursed traffic existing in its most odious form which constituted the chief difficulty of Mr. Baker's journey. The trade of the White Nile is kidnapping and murder; yet it is only in some sort of connexion with the traders who frequent the country for their own nefarious purposes, that it is possible to enter it at all. When the traveller has so entered it, he has to encounter the incredulity and hostility of the natives who have never seen any white men except those who come among them to buy ivory and to steal women and children, and he has likewise to brave the jealousy of these traders who regard an English traveller either as a rival or as an antagonist. 'Every one in Khartoum,' says Mr. Baker, 'with ' the exception of a few Europeans, was in favour of the ' slave-trade, and looked with jealous eyes upon a stranger ' venturing within the precincts of their holy land—a land ' sacred to slavery and to every abomination and villany that ' man can commit.' Every house in Khartoum was full of slaves. The Egyptian officers received a portion of their pay in slaves; and they accordingly looked upon the exploration of the White Nile by an English traveller as a dangerous intrusion into their own preserves. Consequently all assistance was refused to Mr. Baker—even boats, and his application for a military escort was rejected at Alexandria. This discouragement only stimulated Mr. Baker's resolution, and at his own cost he engaged three vessels to ascend the Nile to Gondokoro —he hired forty-five armed men for an escort, and forty sailors, besides his own servants—provisions were laid in for four months—twenty-one donkeys, four camels, and four horses, were purchased and embarked—and every arrangement was made which could promote the success and welfare of the expedition.   But alas for the previsions of the ablest and most careful of African travellers!   He is destined to see everything which he may have thought necessary to his comfort, to his safety, and even to his existence, fall away from him in rapid succession; until at length, if it be given him to surmount the inconceivable perils and privations which lie concealed in those frightful deserts between the starting-point and the goal, he must renounce all that he had once relied on for assistance and success—all but his own stout heart and much-enduring frame; and he will return like a shipwrecked sailor or one of the savages of those wilds, bare of everything, starved, fever-stricken, half-naked, with nothing in his hand but the rifle, which has been his chief means of procuring food and of defence.   So it was with Mr. Baker.   Scarcely had he quitted Khartoum on the melancholy voyage of forty-five days through the marshes which divide that place from Gondokoro, when he found that one of his vessels would not sail and broke her yard; that his only European servant, a German carpenter, died, and his best *choush* or native attendant was killed on the bank by a buffalo.   No sooner did he land and begin his march than his men mutinied, betrayed, and forsook him; his horses perished first, then the camels, then the donkeys; the difficulties of transporting baggage being thus increased, much of it was left behind; and at length the expedition was reduced to no more than thirteen persons.   The mutinous spirit of the Khartoum escort broke out already at Gondokoro, for the scoundrels had received five months' wages in advance, that being the custom of the White Nile, and Mr. Baker had no control over them, except that which one European may exact in threatening to flog or shoot the most refractory of nearly one hundred ferocious natives.   It soon became apparent to him that his escort would give him more trouble than the open hostility of the African tribes.

These untoward circumstances were, however, largely compensated by the arrival of Speke and Grant at Gondokoro on the 15th February, 1863—only twelve days after Baker had reached that place, which was to be the real starting point of his explorations.   Not only did this welcome incident relieve him from all anxiety on their account, but the newly arrived travellers proceeded at once to communicate to Mr. Baker the results of their own experience, with written instructions and a rough but accurate map of the country, which proved of the utmost value in enabling him to complete the discoveries they had commenced. This, therefore, may be the most convenient place to point out with precision the share in these discoveries which belongs respectively to each of the two expeditions. Speke and Grant had followed the course of a river which runs out of the Victoria Nyanza at the Ripon Falls, till they were obliged to leave it at the Karuma Falls (lat. 2° 17′). They called this river the Somerset or the Victoria Nile ; and they concluded that it was in fact the Nile. But they were informed by the King of Unyoro (Kamrasi) that this river ran westward for several days' journey from the Karuma Falls until it fell into another great lake, called by the natives Luta N'zigé, from the northern extremity of which the Nile as a navigable river flowed towards the North. This last-mentioned lake Speke and Grant had never seen, though they reported the fact of its existence ; and the question arose whether the river discovered by them was really that river whose unbroken course descends from the Equator to the Mediterranean, or whether it was only a stream flowing from one lake to another. This was the point Mr. Baker undertook to solve.

Speke and Grant had formed an erroneous conception of that vast sheet of water which they term in their Journal ' Little Luta Nzigé.' Upon meeting Baker at Gondokoro, Speke says:—

' Of course I told him how disappointed I had been in not getting a sight of the Little Lake Nzigé. I described how we had seen the Nile bending West where we crossed in Chopi, and then, after walking down the chord of an arc described by the river, had found it again in Madi coming from the West.' (*Speke's Journal,* p. 604.)

And in another place he adopts the opinion of Dr. Murie that ' the Little Lake Nzigé must be *a great backwater to the* ' *Nile,* which the waters of the Nile must have been occupied ' in filling during my residence in Madi ' (p. 611). These are all erroneous conclusions. The river followed by Speke and Grant was not in truth the Nile, but a stream laterally connecting Lake Victoria Nyanza with the second Lake Nzigé : this second Lake, now called the Albert Nyanza, though still unexplored, is certainly of far greater extent than the former sheet of water, and is undoubtedly the principal reservoir of the true Nile. Mr. Baker, and not Captain Speke, is the first European who visited this lake, navigated its waters, and saw from Magungo its northern outlet ; he is therefore the real discoverer of the source of the Nile. This last discovered lake is the *sole reservoir* of the main stream of the Nile, for although the river which Speke traced from the Victoria Lake does eventually flow into the Albert Lake, it adds no appreciable quantity of water to the vast expanse in which the true Nile takes its origin.   This lake is fed by the torrents from the lofty mountains which surround it, and from the enormous fall of rain within its own basin.   Its level is almost 1000 feet above the level of the Tanganika Lake visited by Speke and Burton in their first journey, if the observations made by those travellers are correct; and as water cannot flow uphill, if this fact be true, no communication can exist between these two vast lakes, and the watershed of Equatorial Africa must intervene between them.   It is, however, just to Mr. Baker's illustrious predecessors to add that although we think his discovery has eclipsed their's in importance, yet they were the first to obtain and hand over to him the information which enabled him to direct his own course to the desired end, and if they had not been prevented by the King of Unyoro they would themselves have visited the Albert Nyanza.

The distance from Gondokoro to Magungo, on the Albert Nyanza Lake, near the outlet of the Nile, cannot be more than 200 miles in a straight line, and if it had been possible to march due southward from the starting point, as Mr. Baker originally hoped to do, this expedition might have been accomplished in as many weeks as it took months.   Like the children of Israel on their way from Egypt to Palestine, Mr. Baker was destined to consume a long period of time, all his resources, and very nearly his life, in a long circuit of deserts and mountains before he touched upon his promised land.

The tribe of Africans in possession of the territory immediately to the south of Gondokoro is the Bari tribe.   These people, who were formerly very friendly, have been hunted and murdered by the Khartoumers, until they resent the appearance of every stranger.   They use poisoned arrows, and are now considered the worst population of the White Nile.

‘ The traders' people, in order to terrify them into submission, were in the habit of binding them, hands and feet, and carrying them to the edge of a cliff about thirty feet high, a little beyond the ruins of the old mission-house : beneath this cliff the river boils in a deep eddy ; into this watery grave the victims were remorselessly hurled as food for crocodiles.   It appeared that this punishment was dreaded by the natives more than the bullet or rope, and it was accordingly adopted by the *trading* parties.

‘ Upon my arrival at Gondokoro I was looked upon by all these parties as a spy sent by the British Government. . . . . Gondokoro was a perfect hell.   It is utterly ignored by the Egyptian authorities, although well known to be a colony of cut-throats. . . . . The camps were full of slaves, and the Bari natives assured me that there were large depôts of slaves in the interior belonging to the traders that would be marched to Gondokoro for shipment to the Soudan a few hours after my departure. I was the great stumblingblock to the trade, and my presence at Gondokoro was considered as an unwarrantable intrusion upon a locality sacred to slavery and iniquity.' (Vol. i. p. 92.)

The question was how to convey a numerous expedition across this territory. Symptoms of mutiny were already but too perceptible in the escort. All Gondokoro was interested in preventing an European from penetrating into the interior far enough to reveal the mysteries of the trade of the White Nile; and a conspiracy was soon organised to defeat the expedition. In the following page Mr. Baker gives the result.

'One morning I had returned to the tent after having, as usual, inspected the transport animals, when I observed Mrs. Baker looking extraordinarily pale, and immediately upon my arrival she gave orders for the presence of the vakeel (headman). There was something in her manner, so different to her usual calm, that I was utterly bewildered when I heard her question the vakeel, "Whether the men were willing to march?" Perfectly ready was the reply. "Then order them to strike the tent, and load the animals; we start this moment." The man appeared confused, but not more so than I. Something was evidently on foot, but what I could not conjecture. The vakeel wavered, and to my astonishment I heard the accusation made against him, that, "during the night, the whole of the escort had mutinously conspired to desert me, with my arms and ammunition that were in their hands, and to fire simultaneously at me should I attempt to disarm them." At first this charge was indignantly denied until the boy Saat manfully stepped forward, and declared that the conspiracy was entered into by the whole of the escort, and that both he and Richarn, knowing that mutiny was intended, had listened purposely to the conversation during the night; at daybreak the boy had reported the fact to his mistress. Mutiny, robbery, and murder were thus deliberately determined.

'I immediately ordered an angarep (travelling bedstead) to be placed outside the tent under a large tree; upon this I laid five double-barrelled guns loaded with buck shot, a revolver, and naked sabre as sharp as a razor. A sixth rifle I kept in my hands while I sat upon the angarep, with Richarn and Saat both with doublebarrelled guns behind me. Formerly I had supplied each of my men with a piece of mackintosh waterproof to be tied over the locks of their guns during the march. I now ordered the drum to be beat, and all the men to form in line in marching order, with their locks *tied up in the waterproof.* I requested Mrs. Baker to stand behind me, and to point out any man who should attempt to uncover his locks, when I should give the order to lay down their arms. The act of uncovering the locks would prove his intention, in which event I intended to shoot him immediately, and take my chance with the rest of the conspirators. . . . .

' Upon assembling in line I ordered them immediately to lay down their arms. This, with insolent looks of defiance, they refused to do. "Down with your guns this moment," I shouted, " sons of " dogs ! " And at the sharp click of the locks, as I quickly cocked the rifle that I held in my hands, the cowardly mutineers widened their line and wavered. Some retreated a few paces to the rear ; others sat down, and laid their guns on the ground ; while the remainder slowly dispersed, and sat in twos, or singly, under the various trees about eighty paces distant. Taking advantage of their indecision, I immediately rose and ordered my vakeel and Richarn to disarm them as they were thus scattered. Foreseeing that the time had arrived for actual physical force, the cowards capitulated, agreeing to give up their arms and ammunition if I would give them their written discharge. I disarmed them immediately, and the vakeel having written a discharge for the fifteen men present, I wrote upon each paper the word " mutineer " above my signature. None of them being able to read, and this being written in English, they unconsciously carried the evidence of their own guilt, which I resolved to punish should I ever find them on my return to Khartoum. . . . .

' The boy "Saat" and " Richarn " now assured me that the men had intended to fire at me, but that they were frightened at seeing us thus prepared, but that I must not expect one man of the Dongolowas to be any more faithful than the Jalyns. I ordered the vakeel to hunt up the men, and to bring me their guns, threatening that if they refused I would shoot any man that I found with one of my guns in his hands.

' There was no time for mild measures. I had only Saat (a mere child), and Richarn, upon whom I could depend ; and I resolved with them alone to accompany Mahommed's people to the interior, and to trust to good fortune for a chance of proceeding.' (Vol. i. pp. 122–5.)

All, however, was vain ; the escort dispersed ; and the party was reduced to a very small band of faithful adherents. A plan was formed to make a dash through the Bari tribe on swift dromedaries, but it proved to be impracticable ; and at length nothing remained but to leave Gondokoro on a venture, to march eastward through the mountains of Ellyria to the Latooka country, and to attach the small European party by force or bribery to a band of Turkish traders who were about to march into the interior in search of ivory, although Ibrahim, the chief of the gang, had previously refused to have anything to do with the European travellers. Nothing daunted, however, Mr. and Mrs. Baker started without a guide on this most unpromising adventure.

' I immediately ordered the tent to be struck, the luggage to be arranged, the animals to be collected, and everything to be ready for the march. Richarn and Saat were in high spirits, even my unwilling men were obliged to work, and by 7 P.M. we were all ready. The camels were too heavily loaded, carrying about seven hundred pounds each. The donkeys were also overloaded, but there was no help for it. Mrs. Baker was well mounted on my good old Abyssinian hunter "Tétel," and was carrying several leather bags slung to the pommel, while I was equally loaded on my horse "Filfil;" in fact, we were all carrying as much as we could stow.

'We had neither guide, nor interpreter. Not one native was procurable, all being under the influence of the traders, who had determined to render our advance utterly impossible by preventing the natives from assisting us. All had been threatened, and we, perfectly helpless, commenced the desperate journey in darkness about an hour after sunset.

'"Where shall we go?" said the men, just as the order was given to start. "Who can travel without a guide? No one knows the road." The moon was up, and the mountain of Belignan was distinctly visible about nine miles distant. Knowing that the route lay on the east side of that mountain, I led the way, Mrs. Baker riding by my side, and the British flag following close behind us as a guide for the caravan of heavily laden camels and donkeys. We shook hands warmly with Dr. Murie, who had come to see us off, and thus we started on our march in Central Africa on the 26th of March, 1863.' (Vol. i. pp. 141–2.)

Nothing can be more graphic than the narrative of that forced march, which at length brought the expedition, almost as fugitives, to Ellyria. But they were outmarched by the Turkish party of marauders, and it was only by the consummate tact of Mrs. Baker and the firmness of her husband that, at the most critical moment, they succeeded in gaining over the chief of the Turkish column, and subsequently proceeded with him into the interior. The men who had previously deserted Mr. Baker's camp joined a slave-trading party which was attacked by the Latookas and destroyed. This incident produced a great effect on the mind of the natives.

'No quarter had been given by the Latookas; and upwards of 200 natives, who had joined the slave-hunters in the attack, had also perished with their allies. Mahommed Her had not himself accompanied his people, both he and Bellâal, my late ringleader, having remained in camp; the latter having, fortunately for him, been disabled and placed *hors de combat* by the example I had made during the mutiny. My men were almost green with awe, when I asked them solemnly, "Where were the men who had "deserted from me?" Without answering a word they brought two of my guns and laid them at my feet. They were covered with clotted blood mixed with sand, which had hardened like cement over the locks and various portions of the barrels. My guns were all marked. As I looked at the numbers upon the stocks, I repeated aloud the names of the owners. "Are they all dead?" I asked

"All dead," the men replied. "*Food for the vultures?*" I asked.
"None of the bodies can be recovered," faltered my vakeel. "The
two guns were brought from the spot by some natives who escaped,
and who saw the men fall. They are all killed." "Better for
them had they remained with me and done their duty. The hand
of God is heavy," I replied. My men slunk away abashed, leaving
the gory witnesses of defeat and death upon the ground. I called
Saat and ordered him to give the two guns to Richarn to clean.

'Not only my own men but the whole of Ibrahim's party were of
opinion that I had some mysterious connexion with the disaster that
had befallen my mutineers. All remembered the bitterness of my
prophecy, "The vultures will pick their bones," and this terrible
mishap having occurred so immediately afterwards took a strong
hold upon their superstitious minds. As I passed through the camp
the men would quietly exclaim, "Wah Illahi Hawaga!" (my God!
Master.) To which I simply replied, "Robiné fe!" (there is a
God.) From that moment I observed an extraordinary change in
the manner of both my people and those of Ibrahim, all of whom
now paid us the greatest respect.' (Vol. i. p. 222.)

Although these circumstances diverted Mr. Baker from his
straight course, and even compelled him to make a journey of
nearly fourteen months in a different direction, the result was
not unfavourable to geographical science, and it has contributed
some of the most agreeable chapters to this book. Marching eastward for one hundred miles from Gondokoro, through
Ellyria, our travellers reached the Latooka country, a region
of singular fertility and beauty, abounding in game, and peopled by a remarkably fine race of men, who are distinguished
by a peculiar kind of helmet, composed of feathers and beads
interwoven with their hair. To perfect this elaborate coiffure
requires a period of from eight to ten years.

'The Latookas are a fine, frank, and warlike race. Far from
being the morose set of savages that I had hitherto seen, they were
excessively merry, and always ready for either a laugh or a fight.
The town of Tarrangollé contained about three thousand houses,
and was not only surrounded by iron-wood palisades, but every
house was individually fortified by a little stockaded courtyard.
The cattle were kept in large kraals in various parts of the town,
and were most carefully attended to, fires being lit every night to
protect them from flies; and high platforms, in three tiers, were
erected in many places, upon which sentinels watched both day and
night to give the alarm in case of danger. The cattle are the wealth
of the country, and so rich are the Latookas in oxen, that ten or
twelve thousand head are housed in every large town; thus the
natives are ever on the watch, fearing the attacks of the adjacent
tribes.

'The houses of the Latookas are generally bell-shaped, while
others are precisely like huge candle-extinguishers, about twenty-

five feet high.　The roofs are neatly thatched, at an angle of about 75°, resting upon a circular wall about four feet high ; thus the roof forms a cap descending to within two feet and a half of the ground. The doorway is only two feet and two inches high, thus an entrance must be effected upon all-fours.　The interior is remarkably clean, but dark, as the architects have no idea of windows.' (Vol. i. p. 207.)

Matters went smoothly enough at first, but ere long the brutal Turks began to insult the women of the tribe, and a general attack was threatened, which was only averted by Mr. Baker's foresight in fortifying his camp and by his readiness to defend it.

'It was about 9 o'clock, and the stillness had become almost painful.　There was no cry of a bird ; not even the howl of a hyena : the camels were sleeping ; but every man was wide awake, and the sentries well on the alert.　We were almost listening at the supernatural stillness, if I may so describe the perfect calm, when, suddenly, every one started at the deep and solemn boom of the great war-drum, or nogara !　Three distinct beats, at slow intervals, rang through the apparently deserted town, and echoed loudly from the neighbouring mountain.　It was the signal !　A few minutes elapsed, and like a distant echo from the north the three mournful tones again distinctly sounded.　Was it an echo ?　Impossible.　Now from the south, far distant, but unmistakeable, the same three regular beats came booming through the still night air.　Again and again, from every quarter, spreading far and wide, the signal was responded ; and the whole country echoed those three solemn notes so full of warning.　Once more the great nogara of Tarrangollé sounded the original alarm within a few hundred paces of our quarters.　The whole country was up.

'There was no doubt about the matter.　The Turks well knew those three notes were the war-signal of the Latookas.

'I immediately called Suleiman. It was necessary to act in unison. I ordered him to beat the drum loudly for about five minutes to answer the nogara.　His men were all scattered in several small inclosures.　I called them all out into the open quadrangle ; in the centre of which I placed the baggage, and planted the English ensign in the middle, while the Turks fixed their flag within a few paces.　Posting sentries at each corner of the square, I stationed patrols in the principal street.　In the meantime Mrs. Baker had laid out upon a mat several hundred cartridges of buck-shot, powder-flasks, wadding, and opened several boxes of caps, all of which were neatly arranged for a reserve of ammunition ; while a long row of first-class double guns and rifles lay in readiness.　The boy Saat was full of fight, and immediately strapped on his belt and cartouche-box, and took his stand among the men.

'I ordered the men, in the event of an attack, to immediately set fire to all the huts around the quadrangle ; in which case the sudden rush of a large body of men would be impossible, and the huts being of straw, the town would be quickly in a blaze.

'Everything was in order to resist an attack in five minutes from the sounding of the nogara.' (Vol. i. pp. 231–3.)

These preparations had the desired effect, and Commoro, the Latooka chief, seeing that the strangers were prepared for him, desisted from the threatened attack. But a nearer view even of the best of these African tribes is not encouraging to those who would fain see in them beings above the lowest condition of humanity.

'Although the Latookas were far better than other tribes that I had met, they were sufficiently annoying ; they gave me no credit for real good will, but they attributed my forbearance to weakness. On one occasion Adda, one of the chiefs, came to ask me to join him in attacking a village to procure molotes (iron hoes); he said, " Come " along with me, bring your men and guns, and we will attack a " village near here, and take their molotes and cattle ; you keep the " cattle, and I will have the molotes." I asked him whether the village was in an enemy's country ? " Oh no ! " he replied, " it is " close here ; but the people are rather rebellious, and it will do " them good to kill a few, and to take their molotes.. If you are " afraid, never mind, I will ask the Turks to do it." Thus forbearance on my part was supposed to be caused from weakness, and it was difficult to persuade them that it originated in a feeling of justice. This Adda most coolly proposed that we should plunder one of his own villages that was rather too " liberal " in its views. Nothing is more heartbreaking than to be so thoroughly misunderstood, and the obtuseness of the savages was such, that I never could make them understand the existence of good principle ;—their one idea was " power,"—force that could obtain all—the strong hand that could wrest from the weak. In disgust I frequently noted the feelings of the moment in my journal—a memorandum from which I copy as illustrative of the time. " 1863, 10th April, Latooka : I " wish the black sympathisers in England could see Africa's inmost " heart as I do, much of their sympathy would subside. Human " nature viewed in its crude state as pictured amongst African " savages is quite on a level with that of the brute, and not to be " compared with the noble character of the dog. There is neither " gratitude, pity, love, nor self-denial ; no idea of duty ; no religion ; " but covetousness, ingratitude, selfishness and cruelty. All are " thieves, idle, envious, and ready to plunder and enslave their " weaker neighbours." ' (Vol. i. pp. 240–2.)

Although slavery and the slave trade are the curses of Africa, it deserves to be noted that these abominable practices are indigenous to the soil of Africa, that they have not been taught to the African by the white man, but have ever been the peculiar characteristic of African tribes. The first act of a liberated slave in Africa is to procure a slave for himself. The man who had been kidnapped became a kidnapper, and none of them could be brought to condemn the system when they had ceased themselves to suffer from it.   On the west shore of the White Nile there are tribes even more ferocious than those to the east of Gondokoro.   One of the traders described the Makkarikas as

'Remarkably good people, but possessing a peculiar taste for dogs 'and human flesh.   They accompanied the trading party in their razzias, and invariably ate the bodies of the slain.   The traders complained that they were bad associates, as they insisted upon killing and eating the children which the party wished to secure as slaves: their custom was to catch a child by its ankles, and to dash its head against the ground ; thus killed, they opened the abdomen, extracted the stomach and intestines, and tying the two ankles to the neck, they carried the body by slinging it over the shoulder, and thus returned to camp, where they divided it by quartering, and boiled it in a large pot.   Another man in my own service had been a witness to a horrible act of cannibalism at Gondokoro.

'The traders had arrived with their ivory from the West, together with a great number of slaves ; the porters who carried the ivory being Makkarikas.   One of the slave girls attempted to escape, and her proprietor immediately fired at her with his musket, and she fell wounded ; the ball had struck her in the side.   The girl was remarkably fat, and from the wound, a large lump of yellow fat exuded.   No sooner had she fallen, than the Makkarikas rushed upon her in a crowd, and seizing the fat, they tore it from the wound in handsful, the girl being still alive, while the crowd were quarrelling for the disgusting prize.   Others killed her with a lance, and at once divided her by cutting off the head, and splitting the body with their lances, used as knives, cutting longitudinally from between the legs along the spine to the neck.' (Vol. i. p. 297.)

Mr. Baker's performances in hunting the elephants which abound in the Latooka valley are worthy of a sportsman who had already spent nine years of his life in Ceylon in the pursuit of the noblest and most formidable of animals, and he relates his exploits with extraordinary animation.   But though elephant-hunting is a most exciting amusement, we have so much ground to travel over, in less known regions and under more arduous circumstances, that we must leave the reader to follow the sporting adventures of the author in his own pages. In this respect, as in many others, Mr. Baker's narrative presents a very favourable contrast to the missionary travels of Dr. Livingstone, who is totally insensible to the exploits of the field, and has the bad taste to remark (in his second journey) 'that the proportion of "born butchers" in the 'population must be as great as that of public-house keepers 'to the population of Glasgow.'   Our sympathies are with the sports   n, who risks his life in a running contest with the
ma

fiercest and strongest of the brute creation, and subdues them
by the same qualities which have given to man the empire of
the world.   But the reverend doctor judges these things from
a different point of view.

The object of Mr. Baker was constantly to work round to
the South-west and so regain the Nile valley.   At length a
native of the Obbo country arrived at Latooka, and under his
guidance the party set out on the 2nd of May, 1863, to cross
the chain of mountains which bounds the Latooka valley.
The march was long and difficult, but at last the travellers
reached the Obbo country, peopled by a race of men more
filthy and superstitious than their neighbours.   Here, however,
they were overtaken by the rainy season : the floods were
terrific, the climate detestable ; and not being able to proceed
further south at that time as the rivers were impassable, it was
resolved to return to Latooka once more.   Here both Mr.
Baker's horses died, besides several camels and donkeys.   Mrs.
Baker was attacked by gastric fever, and the small-pox broke
out in the Turkish camp.   At this place, however, Mr.
Baker first got a further clue to the Albert Nyanza, from a
wandering native of a southern tribe who brought cowries from
a place called ' Magungo.'   This spot was described to be
situated on a lake so large that no one knows its limits.   Large
vessels were said to arrive there bringing cowrie-shells and
beads in exchange for ivory.   On this scanty information Mr.
Baker noted in his Journal—

' " His description of distance places Magungo on about the 2° N.
lat.   The lake can be no other than the ' N'Yanza,' which, if the
position of Magungo be correct, extends much farther north than
Speke had supposed.   The ' white men ' must be Arab traders
who bring cowries from Zanzibar.   I shall take the first opportunity
to push for Magungo.   I imagine that country belongs to Kamrasi's
brother, as Wani says the king has a brother who is king of a
powerful country on the west bank of the Nile, but that they are
ever at war with each other." ' (Vol. i. p. 349.)

This faint gleam of light was at length converted into certainty by his subsequent discoveries, and in the month of
March of the following year Mr. Baker reached Magungo
itself on the Albert Nyanza.   But ere this result was accomplished a weary way was to be passed.   The beasts of burden
had all died, down to the last donkey ; their place was supplied
by three oxen (rejoicing in the names of ' Beef,' ' Steak,' and
' Suet '), who were trained to the saddle.   The fevers inci-
dental to the rainy season had become continual : the travellers
were reduced to such a state of weakness that to travel on foot

was impossible; their stock of quinine was exhausted; porters were hard to be procured; and it was not until the month of January 1864 that the march could be renewed.   In the meantime, however, Mr. Baker had acquired increased influence over the people, by the kindness of his wife, and by his own good sense and firmness; and he at length proceeded with one hundred followers from the Turkish party in the direction of Unyoro, the kingdom lying on the east bank of the great lake.   The services of these men were obtained by guaranteeing to their leader Ibrahim 10,000 lbs. of ivory—a pledge which was eventually redeemed more than threefold.   In this manner, after numberless difficulties caused by the necessity of crossing the territories of tribes at war with each other, and all dreading the very name of the great Kamrasi, King of Unyoro, the expedition reached the Somerset River, or Victoria White Nile, on the 22nd of January, and found themselves on the track of Speke and Grant; on the following day they arrived at the Karuma Falls.

'Our course through the noble forest was parallel with the river, that roared beneath us on our right in a succession of rapids and falls between high cliffs covered with groves of bananas and varieties of palms, including the graceful wild date—the certain sign of either marsh or river.   The Victoria Nile or Somerset River was about 150 yards wide; the cliffs on the south side were higher than those upon the north, being about 150 feet above the river. These heights were thronged with natives, who had collected from the numerous villages that ornamented the cliffs situated among groves of plantains; they were armed with spears and shields; the population ran parallel to our line of march, shouting and gesticulating as though daring us to cross the river.

' After a most enjoyable march through the exciting scene of the glorious river crashing over innumerable falls—and in many places ornamented with rocky islands, upon which were villages and plantain groves—we at length approached the Karuma Falls close to the village of Atāda above the ferry.   The heights were crowded with natives, and a canoe was sent across to within parleying distance of our side, as the roar of the rapids prevented our voices from being heard except at a short distance.   Bacheeta now explained, that " *Speke's brother* had arrived from his country to pay Kamrasi a visit, and had brought him valuable presents." . . .

' I ordered all our people to retire, and to conceal themselves among the plantains, that the natives might not be startled by so imposing a force, while Mrs. Baker and I advanced alone to meet Kamrasi's people, who were men of some importance. Upon landing through the high reeds, they immediately recognised the similarity of my beard and general complexion to that of Speke; and their welcome was at once displayed by the most extravagant dancing and gesticulating with lances and shields, as though intending to attack, rushing at me with the points of their lances thrust close to my face, and shouting and singing in great excitement.' (Vol. ii. pp. 33–6.)

Not without difficulty could leave be obtained to cross the river.

' To assure the people of our peaceful intentions, I begged them to take Mrs. Baker and myself ALONE, and to leave the armed party on this side the river until a reply should be received from Kamrasi. At this suggestion the boat immediately returned to the other side.

' The day passed away, and as the sun set we perceived the canoe again paddling across the river : this time it approached direct, and the same people landed that had received the necklaces in the morning.   They said that they had held a conference with the headman, and that they had agreed to receive my wife and myself, but no other person.   I replied, that my servants must accompany us, as we were quite as great personages as Kamrasi, and could not possibly travel without attendants.   To this they demurred ; therefore I dropped the subject, and proposed to load the canoe with all the presents intended for Kamrasi.   There was no objection to this, and I ordered Richarn, Saat, and Ibrahim to get into the canoe to stow away the luggage as it should be handed to them, but on no account to leave the boat.   I had already prepared everything in readiness, and a bundle of rifles tied up in a large blanket, and 500 rounds of ball cartridge, were unconsciously received on board as *presents.*   I had instructed Ibrahim to accompany us as my servant, as he was better than most of the men in the event of a row ; and I had given orders, that in case of a preconcerted signal being given, the whole force should swim the river, supporting themselves and guns upon bundles of papyrus rush.   The men thought us perfectly mad, and declared that we should be murdered immediately when on the other side ; however, they prepared for crossing the river in case of treachery. . . . .

' It was quite dark when we started : the canoe was formed of a large hollow tree, capable of holding twenty people, and the natives paddled us across the rapid current just below the falls.   A large fire was blazing upon the opposite shore, on a level with the river, to guide us to the landing place.   Gliding through a narrow passage in the reeds, we touched the shore and landed upon a slippery rock close to the fire, amidst a crowd of people, who immediately struck up a deafening welcome with horns and flageolets, and marched us up the steep face of the rocky cliff through a dark grove of bananas. Torches led the way, followed by a long pile of spearmen ; then came the noisy band and ourselves—I towing my wife up the precipitous path, while my few attendants followed behind with a number of natives who had volunteered to carry the luggage.' (Vol. ii. pp. 40–2.)

The people of Unyoro who crowded round the strangers the next morning, and were filled with amazement at the long fair hair of that adventurous daughter of the North, who had not feared to place herself in their power, proved to be a far more civilised race than the savages of the Latooka mountains. The women were neatly dressed in short petticoats of bark cloth, for in the kingdom of Kamrasi nudity is considered to be shocking and indecent. The men are good blacksmiths and wire-drawers, and they even make a fine quality of jet black pottery in not inelegant shapes.

Although Kamrasi is a capricious and cowardly potentate, and caused himself to be personated for some time by one of his brothers who assumed his name, he had learned from Speke and Grant the solid advantages of receiving European travellers. Throngs of natives arrived to carry Mr. Baker's luggage *gratis* by the King's orders, and the caravan moved rapidly on through a thickly-peopled and well-cultivated country. The Great Lake was now openly spoken of, and the natives all said that the Lake N'zigé is larger than the Victoria Nyanza. Unfortunately both Mrs. Baker and her husband here fell dreadfully ill from the miasmata of the marsh country along the river.

' " *Feb. 2d.*—Marched five miles. F. carried in a litter, very ill. I fell ill likewise. Halted.

' " *Feb. 3d.*—F. very ill. Carried her four miles and halted.

' " *Feb. 4th.*—F. most seriously ill. Started at 7.30 A.M. she being carried in a litter ; but I also fell ill upon the road, and having been held on my ox by two men for some time, I at length fell in their arms, and was laid under a tree for about five hours : getting better, I rode for two hours, course south. Mountains in view to south and south-east, about ten miles distant. The country, forest interspersed with villages : the Somerset generally parallel to the route. There are no tamarinds in this neighbourhood, nor any other acid fruit ; thus one is sorely pressed in the hours of fever. One of the black women servants, Fadeela, is dying of fever.

' " *Feb. 5th.*—F. (Mrs. Baker) so ill, that even the litter is too much for her. Heaven help us in this country ! The altitude of the river level above the sea at this point is 4,056 feet.

' " *Feb. 6th.*—F. slightly better. Started at 7 A.M. The country the same as usual. Halted at a village after a short march of three miles and a half. Here we are detained for a day while a message is sent to Kamrasi. To-morrow, I believe, we are to arrive at the capital of the tyrant. He sent me a message to-day, that the houses he had prepared for me had been destroyed by fire, and to beg me to wait until he should have completed others. The truth is, he is afraid of our large party, and he delays us in every manner possible, in order to receive daily reports of our behaviour on the road. Latitude by observation at this point, 1° 50' 47" N." ' (Vol. ii. pp. 57–8.)

At length on the 10th of February they reached the capital, where they were received in a dismal swamp, swarming with mosquitoes, cut off by the withdrawal of the canoe, and not without apprehensions of an attack from the treacherous natives. The following extracts give a brief but most expressive picture of the state of the expedition :—

'It rained in torrents, and our hut became so damp from the absorption of the marsh soil, that my feet sank in the muddy floor. I had fever daily at about 3 P.M. and lay perfectly helpless for five or six hours, until the attack passed off; this reduced me to extreme weakness.   My wife suffered quite as acutely.   It was a position of abject misery, which will be better explained by a few rough extracts from my Journal :—

'"*Feb. 16th.*—*All my porters have deserted*, having heard that the lake is so far distant; I have not one man left to carry my luggage.   Should we not be able to cross the Asua river before the flood, we shall be nailed for another year to this abominable country, ill with fever, and without medicine, clothes, or supplies.

'"*Feb. 17th.*—Fever last night; rain, as usual, with mud accompaniment.   One of Kamrasi's headmen, whose tongue I have loosened by presents, tells me that he has been to the lake in ten days to purchase salt, and that a man loaded with salt can return in fifteen days.   God knows the truth! and I am pressed for time, while Kamrasi delays me in the most annoying manner.

'"Kamrasi came to-day; as usual, he wanted all that I had, and insisted upon a present of my sword, watch, and compass, all of which I positively refused.   I told him that he had deceived me by saying that the lake was so distant as six months' journey, as I knew that it was only ten days.   He rudely answered, "Go, if you like; but don't blame me if you can't get back; it is twenty days' march; you may believe it or not, as you choose."   To my question as to the means of procuring porters, he gave no reply, except by asking for my sword, and for my beautiful little Fletcher rifle. . . . .

'"*Feb. 21st.*—This morning Kamrasi was civil enough to allow us to quit the marsh, the mosquito-nest and fever-bed where we have been in durance, and we crossed to the other side of the Kafoor river, and quartered in M'rooli.   I went to see him, and after a long consultation, he promised to send me to the lake to-morrow. . . . .

'"Ibrahim and his men marched this morning on their return to Karuma, leaving me here with my little party of thirteen men."' (Vol. ii. p. 67.)

At length, however, the day of starting arrived and a guide was procured.   Kamrasi himself (or rather the man who personated him) came to take leave of the travellers, or as Mr. Baker puts it, 'to peel the last skin from the onion,' he begging for his watch and his rifle.   Nor was this all; for the savage ended by begging *for his wife.*   The scene must be told in Mr. Baker's own words :—

' In our present weak state another year of Central Africa without quinine appeared to warrant death; it was a race against time, all was untrodden ground before us, and the distance quite uncertain. I trembled for my wife, and weighed the risk of another year in this horrible country should we lose the boats. With the self-sacrificing devotion that she had shown in every trial, she implored me not to think of any risks on her account, but to push forward and discover the lake—that she had determined not to return until she had herself reached the " M'wootan N'zigé."

' I now requested Kamrasi to allow us to take leave, as we had not an hour to lose. In the coolest manner he replied, " I will send you to the lake and to Shooa, as I have promised ; but, *you must leave your wife with me !* "

' At that moment we were surrounded by a great number of natives, and my suspicions of treachery at having been led across the Kafoor river appeared confirmed by this insolent demand. If this were to be the end of the expedition I resolved that it should also be the end of Kamrasi, and, drawing my revolver quietly, I held it within two feet of his chest, and looking at him with undisguised contempt, I told him, that if I touched the trigger, not all his men could save him : and that if he dared to repeat the insult I would shoot him on the spot. At the same time I explained to him that in my country such insolence would entail bloodshed, and that I looked upon him as an ignorant ox who knew no better, and that this excuse alone could save him. My wife, naturally indignant, had risen from her seat, and maddened with the excitement of the moment, she made him a little speech in Arabic (not a word of which he understood), with a countenance almost as amiable as the head of Medusa. Altogether the *mise en scène* utterly astonished him ; the woman Bacheeta, although savage, had appropriated the insult to her mistress, and she also fearlessly let fly at Kamrasi, translating as nearly as she could the complimentary address that " Medusa " had just delivered.

' Whether this little *coup de théâtre* had so impressed Kamrasi with British female independence that he wished to be off his bargain, I cannot say, but with an air of complete astonishment, he said, " Don't be angry! I had no intention of offending you by asking for your wife ; I will give you a wife, if you want one, and I thought you might have no objection to give me yours ; it is my custom to give my visitors pretty wives, and I thought you might exchange. Don't make a fuss about it ; if you don't like it, there's an end of it ; I will never mention it again." This very practical apology I received very sternly, and merely insisted upon starting. He seemed rather confused at having committed himself, and to make amends he called his people and ordered them to carry our loads. His men ordered a number of women who had assembled out of curiosity, to shoulder the luggage and to carry it to the next village where they would be relieved. I assisted my wife upon her ox, and with a very cold adieu to Kamrasi, I turned my back most gladly on M'rooli.' (Vol. ii. p. 77.)

In reality this crowning march from M'rooli to Vacovia on the banks of the Great Lake was not necessarily a very long one. The distance must be under one hundred miles. But it took Mr. Baker eighteen days, and it was interrupted by an accident of a very alarming character. The track lay along the right bank of the Kafoor River to avoid the marshes on the opposite shore, and it became necessary to cross the stream to regain the westerly course.

'The stream was in the centre of a marsh, and although deep, it was so covered with thickly-matted water-grass and other aquatic plants, that a natural floating-bridge was established by a carpet of weeds about two feet thick: upon this waving and unsteady surface the men ran quickly across, sinking merely to the ankles, although beneath the tough vegetation there was deep water. It was equally impossible to ride or to be carried over this treacherous surface; thus I led the way, and begged Mrs. Baker to follow me on foot as quickly as possible, precisely in my track. The river was about eighty yards wide, and I had scarcely completed a fourth of the distance and looked back to see if my wife followed close to me, when I was horrified to see her standing in one spot, and sinking gradually through the weeds, while her face was distorted and perfectly purple. Almost as soon as I perceived her, she fell, as though shot dead. In an instant I was by her side; and with the assistance of eight or ten of my men, who were fortunately close to me, I dragged her like a corpse through the yielding vegetation, and up to our waists we scrambled across to the other side, just keeping her head above the water: to have carried her would have been impossible, as we should all have sunk together through the weeds. I laid her under a tree, and bathed her head and face with water, as for the moment I thought she had fainted; but she lay perfectly insensible as though dead, with teeth and hands firmly clenched, and her eyes open, but fixed. It was a *coup de soleil.*

'Many of the porters had gone on ahead with the baggage; and I started off a man in haste to recall an angarep upon which to carry her, and also for a bag with a change of clothes, as we had dragged her through the river. It was in vain that I rubbed her heart, and the black women rubbed her feet, to endeavour to restore animation. At length the litter came, and after changing her clothes, she was carried mournfully forward as a corpse. Constantly we had to halt and support her head, as a painful rattling in the throat betokened suffocation. At length we reached a village, and halted for the night.

'I laid her carefully in a miserable hut, and watched beside her. I opened her clenched teeth with a small wooden wedge, and inserted a wet rag, upon which I dropped water to moisten her tongue, which was dry as fur. . . . . .

'There was nothing to eat in this spot. My wife had never stirred since she fell by the *coup de soleil,* and merely respired about five times in a minute. It was impossible to remain; the people would have starved. She was laid gently upon her litter, and we started forward on our funeral course. I was ill and broken-hearted, and I followed by her side through the long day's march over wild parklands and streams, with thick forest and deep marshy bottoms; over undulating hills, and through valleys of tall papyrus rushes, which, as we brushed through them on our melancholy way, wavered over the litter like the black plumes of a hearse. We halted at a village, and again the night was passed in watching. I was wet, and coated with mud from the swampy marsh, and shivered with ague; but the cold within was greater than all. No change had taken place; she had never moved. I had plenty of fat, and I made four balls of about half a pound, each of which would burn for three hours. A piece of a broken water-jar formed a lamp, several pieces of rag serving for wicks. So in solitude the still calm night passed away as I sat by her side and watched. In the drawn and distorted features that lay before me I could hardly trace the same face that for years had been my comfort through all the difficulties and dangers of my path. Was she to die? Was so terrible a sacrifice to be the result of my selfish exile?

'Again the night passed away. Once more the march. Though weak and ill, and for two nights without a moment's sleep, I felt no fatigue, but mechanically followed by the side of the litter as though in a dream. The same wild country diversified with marsh and forest. Again we halted. The night came, and I sat by her side in a miserable hut, with the feeble lamp flickering while she lay, as in death. She had never moved a muscle since she fell. My people slept. I was alone, and no sound broke the stillness of the night. The ears ached at the utter silence, till the sudden wild cry of a hyena made me shudder as the horrible thought rushed through my brain, that, should she be buried in this lonely spot, the hyena would . . . disturb her rest.

'The morning was not far distant; it was past four o'clock. I had passed the night in replacing wet cloths upon her head and moistening her lips, as she lay apparently lifeless on her litter. I could do nothing more; in solitude and abject misery in that dark hour, in a country of savage heathens, thousands of miles away from a Christian land, I beseeched an aid above all human, trusting alone to Him.

'The morning broke; my lamp had just burnt out, and, cramped with the night's watching, I rose from my low seat, and seeing that she lay in the same unaltered state, I went to the door of the hut to breathe one gasp of the fresh morning air. I was watching the first red streak that heralded the rising sun, when I was startled by the words, "Thank God," faintly uttered behind me. Suddenly she had awoke from her torpor, and with a heart overflowing I went to her bedside. Her eyes were full of madness! She spoke, but the brain was gone!

'I will not inflict a description of the terrible trial of seven days of brain fever, with its attendant horrors. The rain poured in torrents, and day after day we were forced to travel for want of provisions, not being able to remain in one position. Every now and then we shot a few guinea-fowl, but rarely; there was no game, although the country was most favourable. In the forests we procured wild honey, but the deserted villages contained no supplies, as we were on the frontier of Uganda, and M'tesé's people had plundered the district. For seven nights I had not slept, and although as weak as a reed, I had marched by the side of her litter. Nature could resist no longer. We reached a village one evening; she had been in violent convulsions successively—it was all but over. I laid her down on her litter within a hut; covered her with a Scotch plaid, and I fell upon my mat insensible, worn out with sorrow and fatigue. My men put a new handle to the pickaxe that evening, and sought for a dry spot to dig her grave!' (Vol. ii. pp. 84–9.)

Yet even from this paroxysm of distress, this agony of enterprise, the travellers rallied. They were within reach of the goal of all their efforts. The name of the village was Parkāni. Far to the west rose a range of enormous mountains; but the lake, the long-sought lake, lay *between* those mountains and the expedition. They were within a few hours of the end. By starting early in the morning they would be able to wash in its waters at noon.

'That night I hardly slept. For years I had striven to reach the "sources of the Nile." In my nightly dreams during that arduous voyage I had always failed, but after so much hard work and perseverance the cup was at my very lips, and I was to *drink* at the mysterious fountain before another sun should set—at that great reservoir of Nature that ever since creation had baffled all discovery.

'I had hoped, and prayed, and striven through all kinds of difficulties, in sickness, starvation, and fatigue, to reach that hidden source; and when it had appeared impossible, we had both determined to die upon the road rather than return defeated. Was it possible that it was so near, and that to-morrow we could say, "the work is accomplished?"

'*The* 14*th March.*—The sun had not risen when I was spurring my ox after the guide, who having been promised a double handful of beads on arrival at the lake, had caught the enthusiasm of the moment.' (Vol. ii. pp. 93–4.)

After a delay of eight days at the miserable fishing-village of Vacovia on the lake (lat. 1° 15′ N.), two wretched boats or rather canoes were procured—mere single trees hollowed out. In these a litter was fitted up, and off went the party with four rowers, and a few fowls and fishes on board, to coast along those unknown shores. The waters swarmed with hippopotami and crocodiles, but to avoid delay Mr. Baker repressed his sporting propensities and left them unhurt. Yet even here, the perils of the expedition only assumed new forms.   After the first day the boatmen deserted, the pilot disappeared, and a storm soon sprang up from the south-west which threatened at every instant to swamp these frail barks.   The breakers burst over the canoe, as it tore along before the gale with a large Scotch plaid for a sail ; everything was soaked except the gunpowder which was in canisters ; and although the distance to the shore was not great, it seemed impossible to reach it and uncertain whether they could land on it, if reached.

'On the following morning the lake was calm, and we started early.   The monotony of the voyage was broken by the presence of several fine herds of elephants, consisting entirely of bulls.   I counted fourteen of these grand animals, all with large tusks, bathing together in a small shallow lake beneath the mountains, having a communication with the main lake through a sandy beach : these elephants were only knee deep, and having been bathing they were perfectly clean, and their colossal black forms and large white tusks formed a beautiful picture in the calm lake beneath the lofty cliffs.   It was a scene in harmony with the solitude of the Nile Sources— the wilderness of rocks and forest, the Blue Mountains in the distance, and the great fountain of nature adorned with the mighty beasts of Africa ; the elephants in undisturbed grandeur, and hippopotami disporting their huge forms in the great parent of the Egyptian river.

'I ordered the boatmen to run the canoe ashore, that we might land and enjoy the scene.   We then discovered seven elephants on the shore within about two hundred yards of us in high grass, while the main herd of fourteen splendid bulls bathed majestically in the placid lake, showering cold streams from their trunks over their backs and shoulders.   There was no time to lose, as every hour was important : quitting the shore, we once more paddled along the coast.'   (Vol. ii. p. 123.)

Thus they proceeded for thirteen days coasting the east shore of the lake, which gradually narrowed to a breadth of from fifteen to twenty miles.   The banks were obstructed with an immense growth of papyrus rushes, so thick that a man could walk upon it ; through this they reached ' Magungo,' the spot where the Somerset River falls into the Albert Lake.   At this point the exit of the main stream of the White Nile in a navigable channel from the northern extremity of the lake was distinctly visible, as the natives had announced. More perplexing was the appearance of the Somerset River, which here arrives at the Great Lake in a broad channel of dead water, in singular contrast with the fine flowing stream which rushes down the Ripon Falls, the Karuma Falls, and the Murchison Falls.* To this last-mentioned point, however, Mr. Baker ascended in his canoes. He there saw the river dashing down from a height of 120 feet about twenty miles above Magungo; and from thence (the oxen having been sent round with the guide) the party, exhausted and all but annihilated by fever, slowly made their way along the left bank to the island of Patovan. These observations are important, because, taken in conjunction with what Speke saw of the upper course of the river, which he conceived to be the main stream of the Nile itself, they afford a complete survey of the Somerset River from the point at which it leaves the Victoria Nyanza to that at which it falls into the Albert Nyanza. Mr. Baker sometimes calls this river the Victoria Nile, apparently from a feeling of respect and sympathy for his gallant and unfortunate precursor Captain Speke. We prefer to retain the name Speke himself gave it of the 'River Somerset,' because in fact it is not the Nile at all, but only a stream uniting the two great reservoirs of the main river. The true Nile is the river which flows out of the Albert Nyanza below Magungo.

At this stage of the expedition, though the work was done, the trials and sufferings of the travellers were by no means alleviated. On the contrary, each succeeding month spent in these pestilential marshes, without quinine and with no better remedy than now and then a few sour plums, rendered the attacks of fever more frequent and intense. Animal food was frequently entirely wanting, and they had to live for a fortnight on wild spinach, wild thyme, and wild honey. The only prospect before them was to be buried in these wild regions, uncertain whether even the record of their discoveries would ever reach Europe. Yet at this moment Kamrasi appealed to them to assist him in war against his enemies, and Mr. Baker suddenly roused himself, put on a full-dress High-

---

* When Speke first saw the Victoria branch of the White Nile rushing out of the Victoria Nyanza, he remarked with surprise that the body of water appeared to be as great as that of the Nile itself. This same river had assumed much smaller proportions at the Karuma Falls, and eventually joins the Albert Nyanza with so little energy that it was difficult to perceive the motion of the current. The fact is that in these latitudes, and in the soil of Africa, rivers decrease very rapidly by evaporation and absorption, and if they were not supplied by vast lake basins, they would be dried up altogether before they reach the sea. In fact, as we have already remarked, this tributary, which is the outlet of the Victoria Nyanza, brings no perceptible accession of water to the Albert Nyanza, or to the White Nile.

land suit, with kilt and sporran, which by some inconceivable
chance he had still in his portmanteau, and suddenly appeared
to the eyes of the astonished natives in the heroic garb of a
Scottish chief.   Matters again improved after their return to
Kisoona in Kamrasi's country, but when at length the expected war broke out between that monarch and his neighbours, Mr. Baker terminated the contest by his diplomacy
rather than by his valour—hoisted the British flag, informed
the invaders that the country was under his protection, and
that an attack on it by the neighbouring tribes would be
visited with condign punishment by the Turkish authorities
at Khartoum.   By this time, however, all chance of meeting
the annual fleet of boats at Gondokoro was at an end, and the
party therefore resigned themselves to stay several months in
their quarters and assist the King by their advice in his resistance to his enemies.   At length on the 20th September,
a messenger returned from Gondokoro with reinforcements,
and in November, after a residence of ten months in this
wretched country, the party once more crossed the Karuma
Falls, taking with them so large a quantity of ivory that it
required 700 porters to carry it.   This was the promised recompense to the Turkish escort, which alone secured their
fidelity, and enabled Mr. Baker to effect his return.   The
Bari country was yet to be crossed, and it was not crossed
without a fight, but in this contest, which Mr. Baker describes
as perfect child's play, he disdained to fire a shot; one or two
Baris were killed, but the expedition proceeded unhurt.   Like
the spells of enchantment which the malignant powers in John
Bunyan's immortal tale throw across the path of Christian in
his pilgrimage of Faith, each successive attack decreases in
power as we approach the close of this great initiation, until
perils which to ordinary travellers might appear sufficiently
formidable, pass comparatively unheeded.   At Gondokoro no
boats could be found at that season except the ' diahbech '
which had been engaged for the ivory, and on this vessel the
plague had broken out on her voyage up from Khartoum.
This boat, however, Mr. Baker engaged for the homeward
voyage.   The fumigations he ordered did not dispel the in-
fection ; the men were seized with bleeding of the nose, which
was the first symptom of this terrible malady ; and poor Saat,
a Christian negro boy of fifteen who had served throughout
the expedition with uncommon courage and fidelity, died of the
disorder three days before the boat reached Khartoum.   The
whole story of Saat is most touching, and may well warrant a
hope that even among the debased and forsaken children of

Africa, there is here and there a being with a heart and head
not unworthy of a nobler position in the scale of humanity.
Two more weary months were spent at Khartoum, and when
the voyage could be resumed, it all but terminated fatally at
the passage of the Cataracts.   As it is Mr. Baker's last trial,
he shall relate it himself.

'Many skeletons of wrecked vessels lay upon the rocks in various
places: as we were flying along in full sail before a heavy gale
of wind, descending a cataract, we struck upon a sandbank, fortunately not upon a rock, or we should have gone to pieces like a
glass bottle.   The tremendous force of the stream, running at the
rate of about ten or twelve miles per hour, immediately drove the
vessel broadside upon the bank.   About sixty yards below us was a
ridge of rocks, upon which it appeared certain that we must be
driven should we quit the bank upon which we were stranded. The
reis and crew, as usual in such cases, lost their heads.   I emptied a
large waterproof portmanteau, and tied it together with ropes, so as
to form a life-buoy for my wife and Richarn, neither of whom could
swim : the maps, journals, and observations, I packed in an iron
box, which I fastened with a tow line to the portmanteau.   It
appeared that we were to wind up the expedition with shipwreck,
and thus lose my entire collection of hunting spoils.   Having completed the preparations for escape, I took command of the vessel, and
silenced the chattering crew.

'My first order was to lay out an anchor up stream.   This was
done : the water was shallow, and the great weight of the anchor,
carried on the shoulders of two men, enabled them to resist the
current, and to wade hip-deep about forty yards up the stream upon
the sand-bank.

'Thus secured, I ordered the crew to haul upon the cable.   The
great force of the current bearing upon the broadside of the vessel,
while her head was anchored up stream, bore her gradually round.
All hands were now employed in clearing away the sand, and
deepening a passage : loosening the sand with their hands and feet,
the powerful rapids carried it away.   For five hours we remained
in this position, the boat cracking and half filled with water : however, we stopped the leak caused by the strain upon her timbers,
and having, after much labour, cleared a channel in the narrow
sand-bank, the moment arrived to slip the cable, hoist the sail, and
trust to the heavy gale of wind from the west to clear the rocks, that
lay within a few yards of us to the north.   "Let go !" and, all being
prepared, the sail was loosened, and filling in the strong gale with a
loud report, the head of the vessel swung round with the force of
wind and stream.   Away we flew !—for an instant we grated on
some hard substance : we stood upon the deck, watching the rocks
exactly before us, with the rapids roaring loudly around our boat as
she rushed upon what looked like certain destruction.   Another
moment, and we passed within a few inches of the rocks within the
boiling surf.   Hurrah, we are all right !   We swept by the danger,

and flew along the rapids, hurrying towards old England.' (Vol. ii. p. 346.)

At Berber, the mouth of the Atbara, the party quitted the Nile, crossed the desert to Souakim over the Red Sea, where they found a steamer to convey them to Suez.

The results of Mr. Baker's expedition to geographical science can scarcely be rated too highly, for he has rendered clear and certain what before was doubtful and inaccurate.   Others indeed—as is the case in all human discoveries—had previously contributed to the achievement of exploring the Nile sources, and Mr. Baker has studiously abstained from saying one word to detract from their merit.   But he has had the good fortune to complete the work, and he describes it in the following lines—

'The Nile, cleared of its mystery, resolves itself into comparative simplicity.   The actual basin of the Nile is included between about the 22° and 39° East longitude, and from 3° South to 18° North latitude.   The drainage of that vast area is monopolized by the Egyptian river.   The Victoria and Albert Lakes, the two great equatorial reservoirs, are the recipients of all affluents south of the equator ; the Albert Lake being the grand reservoir in which are concentrated the entire waters from the south, in addition to tributaries from the Blue Mountains, from the north of the equator.   The Albert N'yanza is the great basin of the Nile ; the distinction between that and the Victoria N'yanza is, that the Victoria is a reservoir receiving the eastern affluents, and it becomes a starting point or the most elevated *source* at the point where the river issues from it at the Ripon Falls : the Albert is a reservoir not only receiving the western and southern affluents direct from the Blue Mountains, but it also receives the supply from the Victoria and from the entire equatorial Nile basin.   The Nile, as it issues from the Albert N'yanza, is the *entire* Nile ; prior to its birth from the Albert Lake it is *not* the entire Nile. A glance at the map will at once exemplify the relative value of the two great lakes.   The Victoria gathers all the waters on the eastern side and sheds them into the northern extremity of the Albert : while the latter, from its character and position, is the direct channel of the Nile that receives all waters that belong to the equatorial Nile basin.   Thus the Victoria is the first *source ;* but from the Albert the river issues at once as the great White Nile.

'It is not my intention to claim a higher value for my discovery than is justly due, neither would I diminish in any way the lustre of the achievements of Speke and Grant ; it has ever been my object to confirm and support their discoveries, and to add my voice to the chorus of praise that they have so justly merited.   A great geographical fact has through our joint labours been most thoroughly established by the discovery of the Sources of the Nile.   I lay down upon the map exactly what I saw, and what I gathered from information afforded by the natives most carefully examined.' (Vol. ii. pp. 304–6.)

Some future traveller may carry these researches yet further by navigating the waters of the Albert Nyanza and surveying its shores. It still remains to be ascertained whether that vast expanse of water, which must extend 200 or 300 miles to the south of the equator, is supplied solely by the rains and torrents of its own mountainous basin. But the discoveries of Livingstone, Burton and Speke, Speke and Grant, and Baker, have all concurred to demonstrate the truth of Sir Roderick Murchison's sagacious theory, that the central portion of Africa consists of a great plateau intersected by huge lakes and marshes. The drainage from this vast plateau falls down the southern water-shed to the Tanganika Lake, to the northwest towards the Niger and Lake Tchad; and the Victoria and Albert Lakes are the first of the system of African equatorial lakes which supply the stream of the Nile.

None of the results of Mr. Baker's exploration are more remarkable than the decisive confirmation he has given to the theory propounded by Sir Roderick Murchison in 1852—more than ten years before any European had reached this region—as to the geological conformation of Equatorial Africa. No portion of the globe bears such undoubted marks of the highest antiquity. All the rocks are primitive. This vast plateau, 4,000 feet above the sea, has never been submerged, nor does it appear to have undergone any changes either by volcanic or by aqueous action. And it is probable that the animals and races of man inhabiting this region are as old as any upon the earth. This fact is one of the most curious and important additions made in our time to geological science; and in his Anniversary Address to the Royal Geographical Society, delivered on the 28th of May of the present year, Sir Roderick again referred to the subject in the following terms:—

'On former occasions I have directed your special attention to the striking phenomenon of the long system of water-basins, lakes, and rivers flowing therefrom which prevails in the elevated plateau-ground of Central Africa. Many of these bodies of water lie, so far as we know. in shallow depressions, the edges of which extend into marshy lands. Now, the Albert Nyanza of Baker is a striking contrast to all such lakes; for this enormous body of water, estimated to be about as long as Scotland, is a deep excavation in hard granitic and other crystalline rocks. Looking to the simplicity and antiquity of the geological structure of Central Africa, it is this result of the exploration of Mr. Baker, or this profound excavation in hard rock, which has most interested me, and must, I am sure, interest all my brother geologists as well as physical geographers. For, if this great depression in hard rocks be not due, as I think, either to original conformation or to some of the great movements to which those rocks may have been subjected, how else are we to account for its existence ? I have previously shown, from the absence of all marine deposits of tertiary and detrital age, that Central Africa has not been submerged in any of those geological periods during which we have such visible and clear proofs of great subsidences, elevations, and denudations in other quarters of the globe. Hence we cannot look to the sea as a denuding power in Central Africa. Still more impossible is it to seek in the existence of former glaciers an excavative power ; for here, under the equator, not only can no such phenomena ever have occurred, but even if the application of such a theory were possible it would be set aside by the fact of the entire absence in Central Africa of any of those moraines or transported débris which are the invariable accompaniments of glaciers, or the erratic blocks transported by former icebergs.

'The discoveries, therefore, of Mr. Baker, which show that the deep and vast lake of Albert Nyanza lies in a hollow subtended by hills and mountains of hornblendic gneiss, quartz, and porphyry, is an admirable datum for geologists to rely upon, who, whether looking to the physical geography and outlines of Central Africa, or to its extremely simple geological structure, are fairly enabled to refer this great variation of outline either to the original devious evolutions of great masses of igneous and molten matters, or to some great ancient movements of dislocation. In short, Central Africa presents no existing natural agent which, if it operated for millions of years, could have excavated the hollow in which the great Albert Nyanza lies.'

The results of Mr. Baker's expedition to ethnography, the interests of trade, and the prospects of civilisation are less satisfactory than those we have just indicated, but they are not without importance. He found that the African tribes in the vicinity of Gondoroko, the Latookas and Obbos to the east, the Bari and the Madi to the south on the banks of the Nile, and the reported cannibals to the west, are even more uncivilised, degraded, and ferocious than the natives of the countries visited by Livingstone and by Speke. Their country is so poor that the inhabitants have nothing to offer in exchange for the productions of Europe but ivory and slaves, and the whole value of the ivory brought down to Khartoum in a year hardly exceeds 40,000*l.* But the slave-trade of the White Nile is the true barrier against all commerce and all improvement. As long as that abomination exists, every stranger who sets foot in the country carries with him war, havoc, fear, and hatred. Yet, Mr. Baker argues, nothing would be easier than to suppress this infamous traffic, if the European Powers were in earnest, and if the Egyptian Government were compelled to exert its power for that purpose.   The slave-trade of the Western Coast, with all its horrors, was less detestable, for it had for its principal object the supply of labour to the Western hemisphere, where the African race, in spite of all its sufferings, has risen to a point of civilisation still unknown in its native swamps and deserts.   But the slave-trade of the White Nile is mainly carried on for the purpose of supplying women and children for the basest purposes to Egypt, Arabia, and the East. At the battues of the slave-dealers, when a village is attacked, the men are shot down like game, the women and children are kidnapped and driven off.   But as the gangs of these unfortunate victims of cupidity and lust must all pass down the river, the whole traffic might be paralysed by preventing the departure of vessels from Khartoum for the south except under licence from the Government; by placing military posts at Gondokoro, and by establishing two steam cruisers on the river.   Seven days' march south of Gondokoro, the Nile again becomes navigable, and vessels might ascend direct from that point to the Albert Lake, where they would at once command the trade of the whole extent of its coasts and complete the exploration of its shores.   The tribes on the banks of the White Nile, though barbarous and formidable to a single traveller, have no power to oppose measures taken for this purpose by the Egyptian Government; and indeed their hostility would be disarmed as soon as they found that the object of the stranger was not to burn villages and steal women, but to give them a better price for their ivory and to supply them with cloths and beads from Europe.

These are the practical suggestions with which Mr. Baker concludes his book, and we doubt not that they will one day be acted upon by those who may have the courage and enthusiasm to follow him in his adventurous path.   Meanwhile we are indebted to Mr. Baker himself for one of the most agreeable contributions to the geographical literature of the present day. He has conferred additional lustre on English discovery, which had already contributed so largely in the present century to a more complete knowledge of the habited and uninhabitable portions of the globe.   He has approached nearer than any living man to the solution of that great mystery of the Nile, which has been the wonder of ages.   He has accomplished these great objects by his own sole resources, alone and unaccompanied by any European, except that intrepid lady who is the worthy mate of such a husband; and the record of his travels will be read with interest wherever the English language is spoken.

ART. VI.—1. *Report of the Assistant-Secretary to the Navy on the Attempt to relieve Fort Sumter in* 1861.   New York: 1865.

2. *Reports of the Secretary for the Navy, with Appendices.* Washington: 1861–5.

3. *Diary of the War for Separation.*   Vicksburg: 1862.

4. *Reports on the Fall of New Orleans presented to the Confederate Congress.*   Richmond: 1862.

' To overcome the dangers springing from so formidable an ' insurrection, three results must be obtained. The shores ' of the Seceding States must be effectively blockaded; the ' course of the Mississippi and the whole water-system ' of the West must be mastered; finally, the rebellious ' Government must be driven from Richmond, its chosen ' capital.'   Such were the broad outlines (as traced by the Prince de Joinville's clear pen) of the great task which lay before the forces of the Union at the outbreak of the war five years ago.   Plainly as he pointed out in his ' Campagne ' du Potomac ' the inherent weakness of the Federal military system, and the manifold imperfections of the volunteer armies which it placed in the field, it is not to be supposed that his prevision, or that of any other single observer, reached through the long vista of the chequered struggle to come. Battles, sieges, marches lay before these armies surpassing in interest—even as mere military examples—all that the world has seen since the fall of Napoleon.   Nor are fit chroniclers wanting to them.   Each week seems to add to our knowledge of the campaigns in America.   Grant has issued carefully elaborate reports, excusing or condemning in detail each of his subordinates. Sherman's friends are many, and thoroughly determined not to let their hero's reputation rust.   Lee is himself said to be preparing the history of his great defence of the capital of the late Confederacy.   All over Europe military writers use American strategy for a text, with commentaries as varied as their nationality, knowledge, and candour.

It is manifest, however, that the mass of works thus produced do not cover the whole of the subject.   The important part borne by the American navy in the contest; its absolute performance of the first portion of the task indicated in our opening lines; the powerful share taken by it in the river campaigns which cut the Seceded States in twain; the vast

weight due to its exertions in the final successes of the Federal
Generals, have been but little noticed as compared to the din
and shock of the great battles with which the New World rang.
Yet nothing is more surprising in this great contest—no military, political, or financial success has more completely defied
expectation, prophecy, and precedent—than the work wrought
by this arm of the Union forces ; and wrought by it in the very
process of creation out of actual nonentity.

European journals have not failed to make occasional com-
ments on the Reports of the Secretary of the American Navy.
Yet out of the United States few persons are aware of the
extreme penury of resources with which that officer and his
chief, the new President, had to contend, when the terrible fact
of the unavoidable contest burst upon them. Even in America
the full truth of the difficulties which, in this one department
alone, beset the Cabinet of Lincoln, has only of late been made
known by the publication of documents which, for personal
motives, it had been designed to withhold. An attack upon
the political reputation of Mr. Seward, made some months
after the actual close of the contest, first brought to light
incidentally the full particulars of the failure to relieve Fort
Sumter in April 1861, the papers concerning which had been
once laid before the Senate, but suppressed by that body.
The report of Captain Fox (now Assistant-Secretary of the
Navy), the principal actor in the affair, reveals in vivid
colours the destitute condition of the department at the breaking out of the war, and the shifting nature of the counsels
which prevailed at Washington in the first dread of provoking
actual conflict.   This officer, who had left the navy for private
employment before the era of Secession, was one of many bold
and active spirits who flocked back to the public service of the
Union when its existence was endangered. Events so vast as
to afford a field for the most daring and energetic of the sons
of the North were at hand, and were partly foreseen by the
more clear-sighted of her politicians, though none fathomed
fully their mighty scope and the great results to follow.

On the 9th of January, 1861, the ' Star of the West,' chartered to carry supplies to Fort Sumter, was turned back by
shots from Morris Island, the first hostile missiles of the
civil war, proclaimed by this outrage on the Federal flag.
Captain Fox, being then in New York, and well acquainted
with the approaches to Charleston, lost no time in laying before
certain eminent merchants of strong Union principles his
' views as to the possibility of relieving the garrison, and
' the dishonour which would be justly merited by the Govern-

'ment, unless immediate measures were taken to fulfil
' this sacred duty.' Into the details of his proposal it is not
necessary to enter here. So much effect did his vehemence
and energy exercise on the hearers, that one of them, Mr.
Marshall, undertook to furnish and provision the necessary
vessels forthwith. Whilst these preparations were made, the
authorities at Washington were communicated with; and on
the 6th of February Captain Fox was present at the capital,
summoned by a telegram from General Scott. Next day
his plan was fully discussed in the presence of Mr. Buchanan;
but the simple vacillation of the latter was (as his own
confessions indicate) changed into downright weakness when
news arrived on the following morning that the Seceding
States had actually proceeded to the election of a President of
their own. 'I called upon General Scott,' says Captain Fox,
' and he intimated to me that probably no effort would be made
' to relieve Fort Sumter. He seemed much disappointed and
' astonished; I therefore returned to New York on the 9th
' of February.' Nor can we wonder at the retiring President's hopeless view of the case, when we learn from Mr.
Welles's first Report that the number of seamen officially under
the control of the Navy Department in the first week of March
amounted to *less than* 300 *on home service*, with a propor-
tionately low supply of stores! This weakness was, however,
in the main ostensible only; for even the few incidents already
referred to show what a fund of energy private will could
supply, and what wealth of means private resources could
create when the spirit of the Northern States should be fairly
aroused to grapple with the crisis of their fate.

That crisis was rapidly approaching. The day of com-
promises and expedients ceased with Buchanan; and his successor Mr. Lincoln was no sooner installed in the seat of peril,
when the naval enterprise which had been at first rejected
was again entertained.

'On the 12th of March (continues Captain Fox) I received a
telegram to come to Washington, and I arrived there on the 13th.
Mr. Blair [the Postmaster-General] having been acquainted with
the proposition I presented to General Scott under Mr. Buchanan's
administration, had sent for me to tender the same to Mr. Lincoln. . . .

'Finding there was great opposition to any attempt at relieving
Fort Sumter, and that Mr. Blair alone sustained the President in
his policy of refusing to yield, I judged that my arguments in favour
of the practicability of sending in supplies would be strengthened by
a visit to Charleston and the Fort.'

The visit paid at some personal risk, the adventurer returned to Washington, where his chief difficulties were still the objections made to his scheme by General Scott and other military authorities.   In reply to these, Captain Fox, with a touch of the natural jealousy of the ex-naval officer, ' maintained the ' proposition, and suggested that it was a naval plan, and ' should be decided by naval officers.'

Dismissed by the President with verbal instructions, Captain Fox is again found at New York in consultation with his merchant friends, ' and making preliminary arrangements for ' the voyage.'   At these interviews, no doubt, was laid the foundation of that new naval system to be created through private agency for the public service, which may be considered one of the most remarkable products of the great Civil War.

Undaunted by the withdrawal from the project of his first ally, Mr. Marshall, who thought ' that the people had made up ' their minds to abandon Sumter, and make their stand upon ' Fort Pickens,' Captain Fox pressed his project forward by another visit to the President.   ' Delays which belong to the ' secret history of the time '—in plainer words, the irresolution of the majority of Lincoln's advisers and its effect upon their chief—

' prevented a decision until the afternoon of the 4th of April, when the President sent for me, and said that he had decided to let the expedition go, and that . . . I should best fulfil my duty to my country to make the attempt. The Secretary of the Navy had in commission, in the Atlantic waters of the United States, only the "Powhatan," "Pocahontas," and "Pawnee ;" all these he placed at my disposal, as well as the revenue steamer " Harriet Lane," and directed me to give all the necessary orders.'

In addition to this squadron, Mr. Aspinwall, of New York, offered the large steamer ' Baltic ' to carry the needful provisions and stores.   Three tug-boats were also hired ; but upon the arrival of the ' Powhatan ' (the only steam-vessel of frigate class then available), which was to carry the armed launches and the sailors for manning them, depended the actual execution of the plan of Captain Fox, as he intimates plainly in his account of the failure which ensued.

On the 8th of April the ' Baltic ' sailed from New York, the frigate having left two days before her.   Captain Fox, with the former, made the rendezvous off Charleston before daybreak on the 12th ; and three hours later, the sound of heavy guns told that the attack on Major Anderson was begun. The small party of officers with Captain Fox watched with anxious eyes the engagement, in which they had hoped to take a part; but the weather was rough and their means for landing in the night (the pith of their design) totally inadequate, as were those of the 'Pawnee' and 'Harriet Lane.' A heavy gale along the coast fully accounted for the non-appearance of the tug-boats; but the 'Powhatan' was looked for all day, and through the night signals thrown up. It was not until the next morning—that of the surrender of the fort—that Captain Fox first learnt that the frigate had been carried off to another service by still higher orders than those of the Secretary of the Navy under which he had sailed. The instructions of Mr. Welles to her captain, Mercer (who was to act as senior naval officer), were issued in elaborate detail on the 5th of April, the morning after the President's promise to Fox that the expedition should sail. That in this promise the 'Powhatan' was specifically included does *not* appear; but that both Mr. Welles and Captain Fox *so understood it* is perfectly clear, although this all-important ship (as they considered it) was in reality already secretly engaged by Lincoln for another service!

Whilst Fox had been pressing forward his project for the relief of Sumter, Captain Meigs of the Engineers (since much distinguished for his services as Quartermaster-General) had been not less urgent with the President to attempt the reinforcement of the troops at Fort Pickens, the key of Pensacola Harbour. This port was so weakly garrisoned as to be subject to surprise from Bragg's force on the mainland; and yet of itself it was known to be far more susceptible of defence than Fort Sumter. Whether the merely military view of the question; or the advice of Mr. Seward who favoured this project; or the secret belief of the President that the fall of Fort Sumter was of more political value than the holding it to the Federal cause, prevailed in Lincoln's decision over the arguments of Fox, is not at this time clear. A consolatory letter addressed soon afterwards to the latter by the President concludes its compliments with a remarkable expression, which seems to justify the belief that the failure to relieve and consequent surrender of Anderson were events which his superior foresaw without much reluctance. The paragraph runs thus:—

'For a daring and dangerous enterprise of a similar character, you would, to-day, be the man, of all my acquaintances, whom I would select. You and I both anticipated that the cause of the country would be advanced by making the attempt to provision Fort Sumter, *even if it should fail.*'

Whatever were the cause, the President chose rather to

sacrifice his failing hold on Charleston harbour than give up the fort at Pensacola. So small was the degree of confidence at that time reposed in his own officials, that Mr. Welles remained in complete ignorance of the new design, and was suffered (as we have seen) to issue instructions which secret and imperious orders from his chief set aside. When the 'Powhatan' was ready for sea and about to quit New York, Lieutenant D. D. Porter of the navy and Captain Meigs stepped on board; and the former, producing the President's sign-manual authorising the proceeding, assumed command of the frigate and diverted her course to the Gulf of Mexico.

'It was not,' says Captain (now General) Meigs, in a recently published account, 'without some hesitation that Captain Mercer gave up the ship. The positive order of the President, detaching him and placing Lieutenant Porter in command, overruled the order of the Navy Department. The conflict was the result of the secrecy with which the whole business was conducted, and to that secrecy, in a great measure, was due the relief of Fort Pickens, and the retention of this finest harbour in the South by the United States.'

Besides preserving the control of the harbour of Pensacola (which the Union forces never from that time found difficulty in holding), Porter and his coadjutors were enabled on their way to save the islands of Key West and the Tortugas from yielding to the State authorities of Florida. So rapid and complete was their success, that the first news of it was brought back by Captain Meigs himself, up to the time of whose arrival the destination of the 'Powhatan,' and of the steam-transport 'Atlantic' which had accompanied her, was unknown to any save the President and the officers who executed the design.

The excuse of Lincoln (as made by General Meigs) for keeping Mr. Welles and Captain Fox in ignorance that their project for the relief of Sumter must give way to the operation so brilliantly executed at Fort Pickens, lay in the difference of the local circumstances. The latter place was far more open to assault by escalade from a boating expedition than the former: and the least breath of the true destination of the 'Powhatan' might, if communicated by telegraph to Jefferson Davis, have produced an instant order to Bragg to seize the work, which his superior force could certainly then have done. No such intelligence or orders were transmitted: and Bragg, with whose vacillation and weakness the misfortunes of the Confederate arms are largely identified,* was not of a

---

* Officers lately high in command in the Confederate armies charge this general with not merely wasting the whole fruits of

character to take upon himself the responsibility of commencing active hostilities. His opportunity passed from him when the ' Powhatan ' and her convoy were once allowed to enter boldly in and reinforce the threatened work.

Allowing the truth of all this, and the genuine importance of Pensacola, it is difficult to conceive that the success of Porter could have compensated Mr. Welles and his adviser for the practical abandonment of their counter-project. It is not surprising that in his first Report—that of July 1861—the Secretary of the Navy makes no allusion to an achievement, the conception of which had been kept secret from him; nor that Captain Fox appears to have long harboured a very bitter feeling against Mr. Seward, to whose personal advice he attributed the President's decision. We are not here concerned with the personal or party aspect of the question, but have brought this, the first episode of the naval warfare in America, prominently forward; partly for the light it throws on the political chaos out of which so much energy, valour, and statesmanship was to be born; partly for the picture it affords of the extraordinary want of any ready means by which the Government of the Union could assert its authority. The Congress adjourning without providing any men or material to meet the threatened danger : the fleet so reduced that but one steam-frigate could be found to execute all the designs the President might have for the control of the Seceding ports : a Secretary of the Navy so new to his trust that it was thought necessary to keep from him the knowledge of the orders sent to his own department: a lieutenant sent with secret orders to supersede the post-captain on the deck of his own ship, and at the hour of his departure on an important service : expeditions involving civil war urged on the Government by private citizens, who yet made their aid dependent on the undeclared will of the people; such were some of the strange circumstances which surrounded the Executive of the Great Republic in the day when its power by land and sea seemed rent in twain. Never—if war must come—had a commercial State more need of a navy. Never were the apparent difficulties of creating one greater; for many of the merchant princes of the North inclined (as has been shown in one striking instance) to take a more lukewarm view of the Union cause when its defence seemed to threaten danger to their foreign trade, than

---

the victory of Chickamauga, but with leaving Stuart unsupported on the day of his death before Richmond ; and, above all, with the loss of Wilmington—left unsuccoured by his fatal irresolution.

in the first moments of excitement before the cost was fully counted.

Lincoln, however, was more fortunate in his Cabinet. Neither he nor any of his advisers shrank from the mere magnitude of the duties thronging on them, nor lacked that faith in their cause which should hereafter carry the whole North with it to a triumphant end. Mr. Welles swallowed manfully enough the mortification he had felt, and applied himself with diligence to the vast task before him; whilst Captain Fox was soon to find that the President's expressions of satisfaction with his conduct in the Sumter affair were no mere perfunctory commendations. An Assistant-Secretary of the Navy was one of the first additional offices recommended for the sanction of the new Congress; and on the approval of that body being obtained to this addition to the now important bureau, the appointment was at once conferred on Captain Fox, who held it until the war was brought to a successful end. No better selection could have been made. The happy combination he possessed of cultivated professional knowledge with close experience of the details of the Northern shipping trade, enabled him, in a degree to which perhaps no other man could have attained, to utilise the resources of the latter for the supply of the vast deficiencies existing in the department of which throughout the struggle he held practical charge.

How great these deficiencies were appears sufficiently in the first Report of Mr. Welles, made before the appointment of his energetic and able coadjutor. There is a brevity and frankness about the bare statements in this paper, which contrasts not unfavourably with the more laboured narratives of the work achieved by the department in those which came later. Forty-two ships in commission, with a complement of 7,600 men, formed the active fleet of the United States at the accession of Lincoln; and while thirty of these were absent on foreign stations, four only of the remainder, manned by 280 sailors, constituted the exact force left in the harbours of the States adhering to the Union.

But more serious still was the disaffection among the naval officers, a far larger proportion of whom than in the army sympathised to the full with the objects of Secession. It was found possible at a later time to fill the posts of the 260 who resigned their commissions with volunteers, who, like Captain Fox, had been brought up to the service. But before this could be done, one of the principal naval depôts, the yard at Norfolk, had fallen into hostile hands. In it was a large steam-frigate, the 'Merrimack,' now nearly complete, which the Confederates, on the hasty evacuation of the place, succeeded in saving from the flames when some lesser vessels perished. Possessing thus at least one formidable vessel of war, they forthwith proceeded, with an ingenuity which made up for the limited means at their command, to convert her into such an invincible iron-clad as might hope to defy all the fleets of the North. To the foresight and activity of Captain Fox it was due that this design was foiled in the end, by the counter-measures adopted at his instance.

Before his official appointment as assistant to Mr. Welles, that statesman had in this Report brought the subject of iron-clad vessels before the Houses of Congress ; and a vote of a million and a half of dollars being granted for the purpose of obtaining experimental models, three of those submitted were speedily selected for practical trial. The first of the ships thus ordered was the 'Ironsides'—a steam-sloop armoured through-out with 4½-inch plates, and designed to carry eight of the Dahlgren 11-inch hollow-shot guns, up to that time the heaviest piece known in the navy. The next was the famous invention of Captain Ericsson, the ' Monitor,' the first ship built with a revolving turret. The principles of her construction were (as is universally known) altogether new in the history of naval architecture, and on their general scope it is not need-ful here to dwell. Plated very imperfectly, slow, and danger-ously unseaworthy, inferior even in armament to her successors (her two guns being 11-inch, one of theirs always 15-inch), she yet, by her prompt preparation, and opportune despatch to the Chesapeake, arrived to do the State such service in her single harbour action as few vessels of the longest sea-going history can claim. The ' Galena,' the third model selected, seems to have been a humble and cheap imitation of the ' Moni-tor,' intended for river service, but on trial she proved incapable of facing heavy shore batteries, and therefore of little practical use to the department.

Undeterred by the sneers of the numerous critics, who pro-phesied that the ' Monitor' would never float, or if floating could never venture beyond Sandy Hook, the inventor and his em-ployer with equal eagerness pressed her to completion. Such confidence did Fox and Ericsson inspire in Mr. Welles as the ' Floating Iron Battery ' (her first official name) drew near completion, that the Secretary, before the time of actual test arrived, applied for and obtained, with a little gentle pressure, a special vote from Congress for twenty more iron-clad gunboats, the greater part of which were ordered to be constructed at once on the ' Monitor' principle. This was, however, some months later than the Report we are considering (that of July 1861), which touched only, as has been said, on the question of armoured ships as one for experiment. The additions already made to the strength of the navy in the first four months of Mr. Welles's charge are detailed in it, and comprised, besides 8 steam-sloops sanctioned by the previous Congress, 12 large steamers bought, and 9 more hired from the merchant service, to be fitted for war purposes with from 2 to 9 guns each. Much of the Report is devoted to an apology for the responsibility assumed by the Secretary in making this provision, and in ordering from private yards 23 gunboats of about 500 tons each —measures which are especially justified by a reference to the violence committed at Norfolk on the naval property of the Union, and to the insurrection against the Washington authorities of the people of Baltimore. It is evident that Mr. Welles was yet in some uncertainty as to the support the Cabinet might receive in their vigorous action—an uncertainty at once removed by the prompt approval of the Congress specially summoned to decide whether the Union was to be saved by war.

In the next Report (that of December 1861) it is vain to look for any great progress beyond that shown by returns of expenditure, purchase, and enlistment. With the exception of the disastrous campaign ending at Bull's Run, the autumn of this year was chiefly spent by the North in gathering up her strength by land and sea for that great war which she now saw plainly must be passed through if the Union was to be saved. Critics there were in abundance, at home and abroad, ready to denounce the expenditure as profligate, and the hope of reconquest as visionary. Yet every month added to the majority who supported Congress in their resolution to place the national forces on a thoroughly serviceable footing; and Captain Fox and his superior availed themselves to the full of the grants made for their department. Supplemental estimates for five millions of our money had been submitted in the summer Session, and sanctioned without delay; so that now, in addition to the engaging, by special bounties, a respectable number of seamen, 121 more vessels had been purchased from merchants and converted into transports or vessels of war, in addition to 52 begun or actually completed in the yards, or under special contracts—the greater part by the latter means. Of the old navy the number of vessels brought into service was 76; but one half of these were sailing-vessels, unsuited to the new exigencies of the service. It had already become evident that the proclamation of blockade, without an abundant use of steam-power, would have proved a nullity; while the capture now reported of 153 vessels attempting to break it, proved the wisdom of (we quote from Mr. Welles's fuller description in a later Report) ' the steps which were promptly taken to recall ' our foreign squadrons, and to augment our navy by repair- ' ing and fitting, as expeditiously as possible, every available ' vessel, by rapidly constructing as many steamers as could be ' built at our navy-yards, and by employing, to the extent that ' we could procure materials, engines and machinery, the re- ' sources of the country in adding others from private ship- ' yards.'

The Confederates in the meanwhile had not been idle in their efforts to distract their enemies in the work of cutting off the Seceding States from all efficient aid from abroad.   In hopes of drawing off some part of the blockaders, the Con- federate President had, at the first sound of hostilities, begun to issue letters of marque.   The first privateer which went forth under his authority, the ' Savannah,' fell speedily into the hands of the Federals, and her crew, by an act which now appears one of unjustifiable terrorism, were for some months treated as pirates.   This severity did not prevent her being succeeded speedily by the ' Sumter,' an armed barque, whose captain, Semmes, first set the example of that destruction of Federal property at sea which has done so much to complicate future questions of naval warfare.   The fear of the new Federal steam-fleet soon drove her to take refuge in Gibraltar, where her commander and crew finally abandoned her.   But a more formidable danger to Federal commerce appeared in the ' Nashville,' a large steamer fitted originally for war pur- poses at Charleston.   Having successfully run the blockade in October, she made her way by the West Indies across the Atlantic, and created a burst of indignant outcry in the North by destroying a large trading vessel, the ' Harvey Birch,' just before she ran into Southampton Water.   Hither she was swiftly tracked and thenceforward watched by the ' Tuscarora,' one of the formidable steam-ships brought into Federal service during the nine months past.

On the whole, however, the year 1861 had given but little opportunity to show whether the American navy, under the new conditions, would prove equal to its former reputation. The validity of its blockade, the one work really accomplished, was questioned daily in the foreign press, whose critics— swayed often by national or party prejudice—measured it by the notorious number of escapes rather than by its practical effects upon the South.   Yet as we now look coolly back, it is evident that the marine department of the Union forces had done more during this period of general girding for the strife than the administration of the sister service. It is true that masses of volunteers were accepted for the army and placed in camp: but until Bull's Run had been lost, not the smallest attempt was made to give them consistency and value by a working staff; nor were the efforts of M'Clellan, Halleck, and others for that end honestly seconded, until new and greater disasters taught wisdom to the President and his successive Secretaries for War.

Passing forward another year in our review, we find more conspicuous successes obtained by the energy of Mr. Welles's able assistant than perhaps even he had dreamed of when the mantle of office fell on him in a fortunate hour for the Union. The general result of his energetic exertions, and of the support and confidence he received from the President and Mr. Welles, is best given in the words of the latter's Report of the 4th December, 1862:—

'We have at this time afloat or progressing to rapid completion a naval force consisting of 427 vessels, there having been added to those of the old navy enumerated in my report of July 1861, exclusive of those that were lost, 363 vessels, armed in the aggregate with 1,577 guns, and of the capacity of 240,028 tons.

'The annals of the world do not show so great an increase in so brief a period to the naval power of any country. It affords me satisfaction to state that the acquisitions made to the navy from the commercial marine have proved to be of an excellent character, and though these vessels were not built for war purposes, and consequently have not the strength of war vessels, they have performed all the service that was expected of them.'

Some exceptions may hereafter be made to this broad statement; but the history of the Navy had now become largely the history of the War, and it is necessary to survey its achievements a little more in detail, in order to see how great a share it had already taken in determining the course of events.

Of the important mixed expeditions of the American War, the earliest and one of the most successful was that directed in January 1862, against the vast inner waters of the North Carolina coast, known as Albemarle and Pamlico Sounds. Attempts to blockade these effectually in 1861 had proved the necessity of seizing the possession of points within, in order to avoid the alternative of keeping a squadron to watch each passage between the sandbanks which divide them from the Atlantic. A determined effort to master the Sounds was therefore projected before the close of the year; and on the 13th January, 1862, Flag-officer Goldsborough's squadron of 17 steamers of light draught, carrying altogether 48 guns, appeared off Hatteras Inlet, the chief entrance. Under their convoy came a numerous flotilla of transports with 10,000 soldiers under General Burnside. So narrow and intricate was the channel to be passed that the whole of the troop-ships were not carried in until the 4th of February ; and the following morning found the expedition at last moving slowly against Roanoke Island, which separates the two Sounds, and is the key of both. This was protected by a garrison of 2,500 men, and by a flotilla of seven small gunboats drawn up behind a barricade of piles and sunken vessels. On the 7th, the attacking squadron, under the immediate charge of Commander Rowan, had got within range of the defenders' batteries, and after a five hours' engagement at long range, silenced the latter and drove the covering gunboats off. The troops were landed the same evening ; and their advance next day, though made with all the uncertainty inherent in the attack by recruits of an unknown enemy in a wooded position, soon put Burnside into possession of the feeble works of the Confederates, the chief part of whom, to the number of 2,400, surrendered with their general.

Rowan forced a way for his squadron through the barricade the same day, destroying one of the Confederate gunboats and driving the rest northward across Albemarle Sound. Thither he at once pursued them, and early on the morning of the 10th attacked them in the creek called Pasquotank River, where they had taken refuge under protection of a small shore-battery. The contest was over in a few minutes, the Confederates abandoning and firing their steamers, one only of which was saved by the victors. The conquest of Newbern, Washington, and the minor posts accessible by water from each Sound, followed as a matter of course from these successes of the expedition. The honours devolved chiefly on Burnside, who gained by personal activity, wherever his troops were landed for action, a deserved credit which proved the speedy stepping-stone to that high command where he made such utter shipwreck of his reputation. The navy, however, had shown sufficiently its great importance in the joint operations ; and its officers justified by their confident execution of their orders the care and expenditure by which their service had been already made so superior to that opposed to it.

A squadron, detached by Commodore Dupont from the South Atlantic fleet, about the same time, while reconnoitring the mouth of the Savannah River, was attacked by five small

gunboats under Commodore Tatnall,* but repulsed him after
a short fight, and drove him under cover of his forts.   From
Beaufort as a base Dupont with ease recovered the small Federal
forts on the coast of Florida, and spread terror up the numerous
inlets of the Sea Islands by his light steamers ; and later in the
spring a portion of his command gave General Gillmore in the
siege of Fort Pulaski the same hearty co-operation by service
in the shore-batteries as our own Naval Brigade under the
gallant Peel afforded to the Allied armies in the Crimea.

The greatest success, as a purely naval operation, of the
whole war — the greatest in naval history since Exmouth's
victory at Algiers—was that achieved in the course of this
spring at the mouth of the Mississippi.   Captain Farragut,†
whom Welles had specially selected as fitted by his resolute
character to take charge of the active operations in that quarter,
arrived at the scene of action on the 20th of February.   The
Western Gulf Squadron, hitherto under command of McKean,
had been gradually increased from a few blockading vessels to
a powerful fleet of 6 steam-frigates and 12 large gunboats.
To these a flotilla of 20 bomb-vessels under Porter (raised
to commander's rank for his earlier services) was added by the
18th of March.   But the obstacles to be overcome were of
the most formidable character.   Two strong forts, Jackson on
the west bank, St. Philip on the east, were connected by a
huge boom of rafts and hulks, the approach to which, to be
made against a powerful current, they swept with the fire of
80 guns, and seemed thus to bar wholly the way up the stream.
Above this obstruction a flotilla of gunboats was ready to support the fire of the works ; and iron-clad rams were known to
have been some time in preparation in order to employ in the
coming warfare that use of the blow of the prow disused for so
many centuries, but now revived by the power of steam.

The first attempt of this kind in modern history had been

---

* The same who endeared himself to Englishmen by his prompt
assistance to our wounded in the Peiho disaster.

† An Act passed in December 1861 permitted the President to
select *any captain or commander* for the charge of a fleet with the
title of Flag-officer, and rank equal to that of the old American
commodore.   Farragut's victory and the services of Foote on the
rivers became just pleas for the creation in the following summer of
the grade of rear-admiral, hitherto not admitted in the American
marine.   Four officers were at first thus raised to permanent rank, viz.
Farragut, Foote, Goldsborough and Dupont ; but the President
continued to exercise his right of selection, and those appointed by
him were now styled acting rear-admirals.

already made off one of the mouths of the river by Commodore Hollins of the Confederate service in the previous October, when he had attacked and driven off a blockading squadron with the ram ' Manasses,' a small river-steamer plated rudely with railroad iron. Thus early in the war, however, the means of the Confederates proved unequal to the carrying out their bold designs. The shock of the ram fell partly, as it happened, on a coaling schooner alongside the steamer ' Richmond,' the vessel attacked ; and although the latter was considerably damaged, she was not reduced to a sinking condition, whilst the ram suffered so much in her machinery as to be disabled from continuing the contest. A further attempt on the same occasion to destroy the alarmed blockaders with the fire-barges failed also, the former succeeding in drifting out of the way of the danger. Hollins then drew off without any practical advantage gained beyond the prestige established in favour of the dashing mode of warfare which he has the credit of being the first to revive, and which the fleet of Farragut had to prepare for as one of the most dangerous obstacles to their enterprise.

The navy were from the first designed to bear the labour and reap the honour of the capture of New Orleans unsupported ; although General Butler, with 18,000 men, was despatched to the scene of action. It may be that the fatal example of Pakenham's defeat in his attempt to reach the city by land influenced the arrangements of Welles and Fox. Certain it is that their instructions to Farragut set aside all thought of active use of the troops in the attack. Their simple wording ran (after some preliminary details) thus :—

' When you are completely ready . . . you will proceed up the Mississippi river, and reduce the defences which guard the approaches to New Orleans, when you will appear off that city and take possession of it under the guns of your squadron, and hoist the American flag therein, keeping possession until troops can be sent to you. . . . As you have expressed yourself perfectly satisfied with the force given to you, and as many more powerful vessels will be added before you can commence operations, the department and the country will require of you success.'

Such success might have been all but impossible had the Confederate resistance been as perfectly organised as at the time was believed. A full knowledge of the truth — now easily gained from the official reports laid before the Richmond Congress—shows not only that much was left undone in the way of material preparation on the side of the Confederates, but that their commanders were wanting in the unity, vigour, and activity opposed to them by their formidable assailants.

Farragut's earliest reports refer chiefly to the transport of the needful supplies, and to the steps taken for carrying the larger steamers over the bar.   The difficulties here encountered were greater than had been anticipated, and it was only on the 8th of April that the frigates were completely brought over the obstacle, with the exception of the heaviest, the 'Colorado,' which it was found impossible to tow through the mud-banks, however she was lightened.   The rest had then to be fully armed and coaled ; and in the meanwhile the whole squadron was fitted for the coming conflict, under orders previously prepared by the flag-officer with elaborate care to meet the various contingencies of a battle fought in the contracted space of a river's width.   The mere issuing of instructions was by no means the limit of Farragut's care for his command. Imitating, perhaps unconsciously, the scrupulous anxiety of Nelson before the victory of the Nile, he visited every vessel under his flag, and saw that the commander personally comprehended his own share in the work.   Thus, too, he was enabled (as his detailed report discovers) to utilise such suggestions as the ingenuity of individuals offered.   The first of these was by the engineer of the ' Richmond,' who proposed that the sheet-cables should be stopped up and down the sides in the line of the engines—a plan which was immediately adopted by all the vessels.   Then each commander made his own arrangements for preventing the shot from penetrating the boilers or machinery, by hammocks, coal, bags of ashes, bags of sand, clothes-bags, and, in fact, every device imaginable.   The bulwarks were lined with hammocks by some, by splinter nettings made with ropes by others. Some rubbed their vessels over with mud, to make their ships less visible, and some whitewashed their decks, to make things more visible during the fight, for the actual conflict was · to take place in the night.

Whilst thus consulting in person with his captains, all of whose opinions Farragut declares himself to have heard, that of Commander Porter was listened to with a deference corresponding to his important charge and the reputation he had already gained, rather than to his relative rank.   In his General Order of the 20th of April the flag-officer freely avows this, and declares himself to be about to essay an attack which was a combination of two modes suggested by that able and daring officer.   The forts were at all risks to be run past in the dark, and the troops to be left behind until a sufficient naval force to protect them was in the river above at a point (called the Quarantine) near to which they might be conveyed by a shallow creek which turned the Confederate main works. The latter could then be effectually besieged, whilst the bulk of the joint forces moved up along the stream, prepared to operate further by land or water according to the means of resistance—as yet unknown—which the enemy possessed. This project was in the end not executed in its integrity, because, the forts once passed, opposition practically ceased. The assault was preluded by a bombardment from Porter's heavy mortars. After careful reconnoissance that officer had towed his flotilla within range of the works by the morning of the 18th April, and the work of destruction began by their throwing that day nearly 3,000 large shells about the heads of the garrison.

Those who have wondered at the success obtained at New Orleans need do so no more when they contrast the completeness of the Federal preparations, and the vigour and decision with which Farragut at the proper moment went to work, with the divided counsels and inefficient armaments opposed to them by the Confederates. On the 27th of March, General Duncan, a well-known artillerist, who personally commanded the defences, became aware that the enemy's fleet was crossing the bars. Both he and his superior, General Lovell, had previously anticipated this, and had made urgent and repeated applications for a change of armament at the forts, the guns in which were but old 32 and 42-pounders, justly held to be unfit for repelling the steam fleet which threatened the place; whilst a second line of works nearer to the city mounted but twelve of the former pieces, having been stripped even of the latter 'at the urgent request of the naval authorities,' who wished to use this part of the armament on some gunboats fitting for defence of the creeks. How this most serious mistake of not supplying proper ordnance arose from underrating the imminence of the danger on the river side, appears plainly from General Lovell's Reports. We quote his own words at some length, not only for this end, but to show how early in the war the Confederate naval authorities had turned their attention to the use of iron-clad vessels, of which two large specimens, intended both for ramming and carrying guns in shot-proof batteries, were being prepared at New Orleans. Happily for the success of the Union fleet, the mechanical means which their foes controlled were by no means equal to their powers of conception. This deficiency produced continual delay; whilst the readiness of Fox and Farragut was so far beyond that anticipated by their professional opponents, that the iron-clads (originally designed for the 1st of February) were found unprepared for use when the Federal fleet, three months later, burst its way through to the fated city.

'Immediately (says General Lovell) after I assumed command of the department, finding there were no guns of the heaviest calibre, I applied to Richmond, Pensacola, and other points, for some 10-inch columbiads and sea-coast mortars, which I considered necessary to the defence of the lower river; but none could be spared, the general impression being that New Orleans would not be attacked by the river; and I was therefore compelled to make the best possible defence with the guns at my disposal. Twelve 42-pounders were sent to Forts Jackson and St. Philip, together with a large additional quantity of powder; and being convinced that with the guns of inferior calibre mounted there we could not hinder steamers from passing, unless they could be detained for some time under the fire of the works, I pushed forward rapidly the construction of a raft which offered a complete obstruction to the passage of vessels. The forts had eighty guns that could be brought successively to bear upon the river, were manned by garrisons of well-trained artillerists, affording a double relief to each gun, and commanded by officers who had no superiors in any service. Under these circumstances, although I feared that the high water in the spring, with the accompanying drift, would carry away the raft, yet every confidence was felt that the river would remain closed until such time as the iron-clad steamers could be finished. In March no heavy guns had yet been received, although strenuous applications were made by me to get some from Pensacola, when that place was abandoned. The general impression of all those to whom I applied was, that the largest guns should be placed above New Orleans, not below; although I had notified the department on the 22nd March, that in my judgment the fleet only awaited the arrival of the mortar-vessels to attempt to pass up the river from below.'

The personal exertions of an ordnance-officer, Major Duncan, a relation of the General, did at length procure three 10-inch and three 8-inch columbiad hollow-shot guns and five large mortars, which were mounted just before the bombardment commenced. This was, as before noticed, on the 18th of April; but a week previous to Porter's attack the raft was seriously damaged by a storm accompanied by a flood, which, according to General Duncan's statement, 'parted the chains, scattered ' the schooners, and materially affected the character and ' effectiveness of the raft as an obstruction.'

For six long days did the garrisons of the forts endure the pitiless fire which Porter rained on them. Carefully as the casemates had been constructed, the 13-inch shells inflicted serious damage, and disabled a number of the defenders' guns. The unprotected barracks in the fort were destroyed with all their contents (including the spare clothing most improvidently placed there) within the first twelve hours of this tremendous bombardment. The garrison could make but feeble response, owing to the inferiority of range of most of their pieces ; yet the gunners never flinched, and the enormous expenditure of Federal ammunition determined Farragut to hurry on the endeavour to pass the batteries by main force in the hours of darkness. On the third night, under cover of a furious fire, an expedition of two gun-boats, under Captain Bell, approached the barricade to attempt its destruction by means of petards. ' This duty,' says Admiral Farragut, ' was not thoroughly performed, in consequence of ' the failure to ignite the petards with the galvanic battery.' In fact, no officer of the American services had at that time been trained to the use upon or under water of this powerful engine of destruction.* ' Still,' he continues, ' it was a success, and, ' under the circumstances, a highly meritorious one.' In fact the ' Itasca,' under Lieutenant Caldwell, grappled one of the schooners, which that officer boarded at once, and detached from the chains which had secured her to the barricade which was then laid open. His gunboat was the only one seen by the look-outs of Duncan, who writes :—' A heavy fire was ' opened upon her, which caused her to retire, but not until ' she had partially accomplished her purpose. The raft after ' this could not be regarded as an obstruction.'

The following night the garrison were cheered by the descent from New Orleans of one of the two iron-clad rafts, the ' Louisiana,' mounting sixteen heavy guns. By this time the injuries in their defences were very considerable, and under her almost impregnable cover they had hoped to make the necessary repairs. On conferring, however, with Captain Mitchell, a naval officer who now arrived and assumed charge of all the steamers gathered for the defence, Duncan learnt that her motive power was incomplete, and that so far from taking the offensive against the enemy, his coadjutor was bent on keeping her above the forts until the mechanics had finished their labours. In vain did the General appeal to his

---

* After the war had actually commenced, submarine blasting was being carried on for the improvement of the harbour of New York by a Frenchman, who claimed reward for his work as a patent. General Totten, of the U.S. Engineers, under whom he was employed, entered into correspondence on the subject with Sir John Burgoyne, and then learnt that the so-called secret—the product of Pasley's work on the wreck of the ' Royal George '—had been in regular use thirteen years before by the Royal Engineers at Bermuda.

chief at New Orleans, and the latter to Commodore Whittle, the successor of Hollins and superior of Captain Mitchell. The Commodore's orders were sent indeed to the latter, but with the proviso to execute them only 'if in his judgment it ' was advisable;' and in consequence Mitchell held to his determination of keeping the iron-clad for the present out of fire.   It is fair to say that his view was supported by those of the naval officers under him.   On the other hand, the naval volunteers who chiefly manned the steamers (eight in number, besides the small ram ' Manasses,' and a fire-raft flotilla), which had been prepared for co-operation with the forts, were jealous alike of the interference they had at first met with from the generals, and of that to which they now were subjected when transferred to the rule of their professional brethren.

It is not for us, who inherit the memories of Walcheren, to lean too hardly on the errors which divided the command of the Confederates at this critical time, and kept the real chiefs at New Orleans, twenty miles above the vital point of action. It is enough to say that the fifth day of bombardment and endurance went by in vain correspondence and appeals.   Not only did Mitchell refuse to place the ' Louisiana ' where her battery might be of use, but the only immediate service remaining to be performed—the sending down of fire-ships in the night against Porter's fleet—was left undone, the tugboats allotted for that duty being under repair.   ' This does not ' excuse the neglect,' says Duncan, ' as there were six boats of ' the river fleet available for this service, independent of those ' alluded to, and fire-barges were plentiful.'   More plainly still does General Lovell's Report speak of what occurred that night and during the eventful one which followed :—' The ' river-defence fleet,' he writes, ' proved a failure, for the very ' reasons set forth in my letter to the department of the 15th ' of April.   Unable to govern themselves, and unwilling to be ' governed by others, their almost total want of system, vigi-' lance, and discipline, rendered them useless and helpless, ' when the enemy finally dashed upon them suddenly in a dark ' night.   I regret very much that the department did not ' think it advisable to grant my request to place some competent ' head in charge of these steamers.'

The 23rd of April broke warm and clear.   The garrisons had now given up hope of immediate aid from the steamers, and attempted to repair their pressing damages as they best could under Porter's fire.   Before night the latter slackened perceptibly ; and Duncan, struck by this fact (which he correctly enough, as his letter of that evening proves, ascribed to the

enemy's growing short of ámmunition), and observing movements in the fleet below, once more wrote to Mitchell to urge the
' Louisiana's ' being brought into a position to aid at least by her
battery in the defence.   His request was refused, and when,
somewhat later, he communicated the additional news that his
suspicions were confirmed by the enemy's boats fixing white
flags in the line of their expected advance, he learnt only from
Mitchell's reply that the ' Louisiana ' would be ready *by the
next evening.*   Before that evening had arrived, the luckless
iron-clad was prepared to be blown up by his own orders.
Kept so carefully out of harm's way as she had been, the only
damage inflicted by her was that caused by the explosion to
the garrison she had been built to aid !
    The anxiety suffered by Duncan and his troops during the
early part of the night was enhanced by an increase in the fire
of the bomb-vessels which took place when darkness closed, and
by their ignorance of what the enemy was doing under cover of
Porter's shells ; for, as on the previous night, the promised fire-
rafts were not floated down by the flotilla.   Who it was that
should be charged specially with this omission it is hard to say.
It is clear that Captain Mitchell, though invested nominally
with the whole control of the river defence, was unable to make
his authority felt by the naval volunteers, whose senior officer,
Captain Stevenson, declared officially three days before, in the
name of his force, ' it would not be governed by the regulations
' of the navy or commanded by naval officers.'
    At two o'clock on the morning of the 24th, Farragut gave
his pre-arranged signal——two ordinary red lights, so as not to
excite special notice——and the advance began in two columns.
That on the right, under Captain Bailey (Farragut's second),
was led by the gunboat ' Cayuga,' which bore the flag.   She
was followed by the steam-frigates ' Pensacola ' and ' Missis-
' sippi,' and five other gunboats in succession.   The left
column, the Admiral's own, was similar in formation, but
stronger by a frigate, being led by his fleet-captain in the
gunboat ' Sciota,' which was followed by the ' Hartford ' (the
flag-ship), two other frigates, and five more gunboats.   The
divided counsels of their opponents, the exhaustion of some,
the insubordination of others, the incompleteness of their
defences, were all unknown to the Federals : and how great
was their commander's anxiety as to the issue of his bold
advance, and the prospect of passing the forts with a respectable force, is best shown by his own General Order, sent round
a short time before :——

    ' When, in the opinion of the flag-officer, the propitious time has

arrived, the signal will be made to weigh and advance to the conflict.   If, in his opinion, at the time of arriving at the respective
positions of the different divisions of the fleet, we have the advantage, he will make the signal for close action, No. 8, and abide the
result—conquer or to be conquered—drop anchor or keep under
weigh, as in his opinion is best.'

At half-past three the fleet approached the barrier, the
bomb-vessels having also placed themselves so as to fire freely
on the forts, and being strengthened for the night by the
addition of the sailing corvette ' Portsmouth,' which was towed
up within range of Fort Jackson.   Severely damaged already,
the boom gave way to the rush of the leading gunboats, while
at the same moment the forts opened fire, and one of the most
fearful scenes began which naval annals record :—

' After we had fairly entered into the fight (writes Farragut), the
density of the smoke from guns and fire-rafts, the scenes passing on
board our own ship and around us (for it was as if the artillery of
heaven were playing upon earth), were such that it was impossible
for the flag-officer to see how each vessel was conducting itself, and
he can only judge by the final results and their special reports,
which are herewith enclosed.   But I feel that I can say with truth
that it has rarely been the lot of a commander to be supported by
officers of more indomitable courage or higher professional merit.'

In short, the darkness of the night, the closeness of the
action, and the tremendous calibre of the Federal cannon,
made it hopeless for any officer to do more than control the
movements of a single vessel in the confused uproar which
arose.   The flag-officer's own was soon in danger so imminent
as to task his utmost energies, and we quote from his Report
only that further portion which speaks of her share :—

' I discovered a fire-raft coming down upon us, and in attempting
to avoid it ran the ship on shore ; and the ram " Manasses," which I
had not seen, lay on the opposite of it, and pushed it down upon us.
Our ship was soon on fire half-way up to her tops, but we backed
off, and through the good organization of our fire department, and
the great exertions of Captain Wainwright and his first lieutenant,
officers, and crew, the fire was extinguished.   In the meantime our
battery was never silent, but poured in its missiles of death into
Fort St. Philip, opposite to which we had got by this time, and it
was silenced, with the exception of a gun now and then.'

Silenced perhaps for the minute ; for the gunners at such
times sought shelter in the casemates close by, which had preserved them during the preceding bombardment; yet only to
rush forth at every interval of slackening in the fire of the
frigates, and reply with their feebler pieces to the storm of grape
hurled at them from 9-inch and 11-inch guns.   Their gal-

lantry is not merely testified to by their own commanders. More important witness to it is borne by the detailed Reports of the Federal captains, and especially by those of three gun-boats, the 'Itasca,' 'Kennebec,' and 'Winona,' which became entangled in portions of the barrier after the frigates had gone by, and found the fire of the garrison still so insupportable as to compel them to head down stream, and thus, for safety, to separate themselves from the rest of the fleet.

The forts and boom once passed, with the fire-rafts (of which only one, that which struck the 'Hartford,' did any harm) the squadron of Mitchell had yet to be encountered. These Farragut has estimated at 13 gunboats and two iron-clads, but the truth was, as we now know, far within this. The 'Louisiana' was but a motionless raft, so moored that she could hardly bring her bow-guns to bear, and fired (it was said by the garrison) but twelve shots. The eight gunboats had been but poorly fitted, and some of them mounted but a single large gun, whilst in weight they were no match even for the enemy's smallest vessels. The action, therefore, was of very brief duration, although gallantly undertaken by the Con-federates. Four of their boats had been fitted with iron plates over their bows with the intention of using them as rams, and two of these, the 'Governor Moore' and 'Quitman,' came immediately into collision with the 'Varuna,' which had in the *mêlée* with the forts got ahead of the rest of the Federal fleet. She was in chase of an unarmed steamer, on board of which was General Lovell himself (who had arrived from New Orleans on a visit of inspection just as the firing com-menced), when the 'Governor Moore' attacked her boldly, firing a bow-gun which disabled thirteen of the 'Varuna's' hands, and charging her afterwards on the starboard side. The Federals, however, succeeded in bringing an 8-inch gun to bear on the assailant, and disabling her completely in a few minutes; but the 'Quitman,' which had approached the 'Varuna' on the port side at the same time, now butted at her twice, at the second collision driving in her side. In doing this, however, she swung round, and the Federals, before their vessel sank, sent five of their 8-inch shells into their new enemy, and had the satisfaction of seeing her in flames. Of the rest of the 'defence fleet,' the 'Defiance' was the only one saved under the guns of the fort at daybreak, the others having either been sunk, burnt, or driven ashore, disabled by the overwhelming batteries which the frigates had opened on them. These last had been attacked indeed by the 'Manasses' with a boldness worthy of better success; but her feeble power and small tonnage were found perfectly unavailing to injure the ships through the chain-armour so judiciously prepared. Her encounter with the flag-ship ' Hartford ' has been already mentioned. Passing on whilst the latter was on fire, she charged the ' Brooklyn ' full on the starboard gangway, but with little effect, beyond breaking some of the links of the chain and driving in three planks above waterline. Wedged in between her huge antagonist and the shore, the ram found herself unable to get up speed for a fresh charge, and was glad to drop down stream. She then crossed over to attack the ' Mississippi,' and struck her with a very partial effect, inflicting injuries similar to those of the ' Brooklyn,' and then passing down to the forts, where she lay for a short while.

The gray of early daylight now succeeded to the flashes of the hostile guns which had lighted up the scene ; and Farragut, discovering the completeness of his victory, signalled to discontinue action. His fleet had begun to form and steam slowly upwards when the indomitable little ram was seen singly in pursuit, and preparing to renew her assaults. The Admiral at once signalled the ' Mississippi ' to turn and attack her ; and Captain Smith, aided by the gunboats ' Pinola ' and ' Kineo,' charged her at once. Captain Warly (who, from her first construction, had commanded the ram), seeing the huge bows of the frigate coming straight towards him, steered to avoid the direct shock, and ran his vessel aground, exposing her to the full broadsides of the enemy. From this helpless position he escaped with his crew to the shore, and the once famous ' Manasses ' was fired by the boats of the ' Mississippi,' which had been ordered off to board her. This was the last episode of the battle ; for Farragut, leaving behind him the sheltered forts and the relics of the enemy's flotilla, went upward on his path of conquest. Captain Bailey, still leading in the ' Cayuga,' soon came in sight of a small camp of sharpshooters on the right bank, who, finding their position and line of retreat along the levee under command of the gunboats, surrendered at once. Near this point—the Quarantine—the river is approached by the creek before mentioned, as turning (for shallow boats) the forts and barricade. The flag-officer now made use of it to communicate with Porter and General Butler, and leaving two gunboats to protect the latter's advance from the enemy still left at the forts, proceeded on with the rest of the fleet. The further progress of the Federals occupied all that day and the early part of the 25th, ' owing to the slowness of some of the ' vessels, and want of knowledge of the river ; ' but New Orleans

was finally approached at 10 A.M. on the 26th.   Then came a
ten minutes' contest with the inner works, armed, as we know,
with but a dozen 32-pounders.   The rest of the story of the
conquest—the public thanksgiving ordered by the flag-officer
on board his victorious fleet—the fierce heart-burnings of the
city, which lay helpless under his guns—the unjust obloquy
thrown on General Lovell by the Confederates for not ensuring
its destruction by a useless resistance with his petty garrison of
3,000 men—these things, and, above all, the shame and humiliation which followed on Butler's taking possession, are well
known.   We pass them, therefore, by; citing merely the following paragraph of Farragut's letter, which tells the final history
of the forces of Duncan and Mitchell, and observing that the
surrender of the former was compelled by the violent insubordination of the same volunteer gunners who had obeyed him with
cheerful endurance until their retreat was cut off:—

' On the evening of the 29th, Captain Bailey arrived from below,
with the gratifying intelligence that the forts had surrendered to
Commander Porter, and had delivered up all public property, and
were being paroled; and that the navy had been made to surrender
unconditionally, as they had conducted themselves with bad faith,
burning and sinking their vessels while a flag of truce was flying
and the forts negotiating for their surrender, and the "Louisiana,"
their great iron-clad battery, being blown up alongside of the vessel
where they were negotiating; hence their officers were not paroled,
but sent home to be treated according to the judgment of the
Government.'

With the ' Louisiana ' the Confederates had lost their iron-
clad frigate ' Mississippi,' the most important naval structure
they had undertaken, which was lying unfinished at a wharf
near the city, and was burnt on the approach of Farragut,
whose victory was as complete as any officer commanding
afloat could have desired over a combined land and sea force.
The garrison of Lovell, and all their stores, should perhaps
have been added to the prize; but the Federals were, strangely
enough, not aware that a single ship anchored ten miles above
the city would, at the then height of the river, have completely
commanded the only exit, which, through their ignorance, was
left open for several days.   At the least, however, the success
was almost beyond price to the Union Government from its
moral importance on both sides of the Atlantic.   As to the
material advantage won, it may be best judged of by the
statement of the well-known Confederate writer and partisan
Pollard:—

' The extent of the disaster is not to be disguised.   It was a heavy blow to the Confederacy. It annihilated us in Louisiana; separated us from Texas and Arkansas; diminished our resources and supplies by the loss of one of the greatest grain and cattle countries within the limits of the Confederacy; gave to the enemy the Mississippi River, with all its means of navigation, for a base of operations; and finally led, by plain and irresistible conclusion, to our virtual abandonment of its great and fruitful valley.'

'Treachery' was the cry raised by the indignant South at the loss of its commercial capital : and although such a charge against the Confederate commanders bears no inquiry, the fall of New Orleans and its consequences must, as has been shown, be held due in part to the improvident delays and discordant counsels of the defenders, as well as to the want of appreciation in their chosen Government of the greatness of the danger which threatened the Confederacy at this vital point. Allowing fully for all these, the highest credit must yet be given to the judgment which planned and the vigour which executed this successful stroke. If the language of Mr. Welles seems a little exaggerated when he says, ' It was regarded everywhere, both ' at home and abroad, as the grandest achievement of the war,' no less is it certain that, in calling the capture of New Orleans ' one of the most remarkable triumphs in the whole history of ' naval operations,' he is fully justified, both by the daring with which unknown dangers were faced and the vast importance of the victory gained.

The success of Farragut was marred, as has been seen, by the loss of only a single gunboat; and comment on the battle won by so hastily formed a fleet would be incomplete indeed if it omitted special notice of the fact that the ' Varuna' *was the only one* of Farragut's gunboats ' converted ' from the merchant service, instead of being built expressly for the rougher business of the navy.

'Here let me pause (says Lieutenant Swasey, in a very clear report of the disaster) whilst we reflect upon the unadaptedness of a merchant-built vessel for war purposes, particularly such as the " Varuna " was called to take part in. Had we been built with that strength which all the other vessels possessed, and the need of which becomes more apparent to the mind of the naval officer each day, we would yet be afloat, off the city of New Orleans. Such vessels may perhaps do for the ordinary duties of a blockade, and I think it is yet a question whether they will or not ; but certainly they are not fit to trust lives and property on to engage works of the strongest magnitude.'

New Orleans once secured and handed over to General Butler, Farragut pushed up the Mississippi, and in the course of the next two months the Union flag was hoisted at Bâton

Rouge, Natchez, and every town of importance as high as Vicksburg. This city, strong by its natural position on high bluffs sloping gently landward, and already partly converted into a fortress by entrenchments heavily armed, was now (since the surrender of Memphis on the 6th of June) the only point of importance held by the Confederates on the banks of the great river. It at once, therefore, assumed an importance well warranted by its later history. Summoned on the 18th of May to evacuate the place, General M. L. Smith, who held it, gave a decided refusal; and Farragut found it necessary to await once more the arrival of Porter's flotilla, which was not brought up and reported ready until the 27th of June. On the 28th a general attack took place, Farragut succeeding in taking two of his three frigates and six gunboats above the batteries, but producing no effect on the defences. ' The enemy leave ' their guns for the moment,' says his hasty report, ' but return ' to them as soon as we have passed, and rake us.' About fifty men were killed and wounded on board, and the ' Brooklyn ' frigate, with two gunboats, forced to retreat below the place.

The bombardment continued at intervals, pending an application to General Halleck at Corinth for a corps of his army to aid the fleet, and the result of an experiment (the first of three) made to cut a ship canal through the isthmus opposite Vicksburg, and leave the Federal ships an independent passage. On the 15th of July their possession of the river was suddenly challenged by a large ram, the ' Arkansas,' which the Confederates had been fitting on the Yazoo, a considerable stream entering the Mississippi just above Vicksburg. This new enemy was built, in imitation of those destroyed at New Orleans, with a screw-propeller, and iron-clad sides sloping inwards; and, besides the means of offence offered by her sharp prow, she mounted nine guns. Her plating, however, proved to be weak, and her machinery very defective. Uneasy at the reports of her, Farragut had sent a small river-steamer, the ' Tyler,' to explore the Yazoo, and this probably brought her down incomplete; for she appeared suddenly, on the evening of the 15th, coming into the Mississippi, apparently in chase of the ' Tyler,' and forthwith ran down to take shelter under the guns of Vicksburg. In passing she received and returned the broadsides of Farragut's whole squadron; and several of the heavier shot crashed through her armour, tearing up her unplated deck, damaging her fittings, and killing and wounding some of the crew. But this was not fully known to the Federals, and her escape for the time spread alarm as far as the garrison of Butler at New Orleans. Her history, however, need not be pursued at length. On the first leaving her shelter to co-operate with a Confederate land force in the attack (made 5th of August) on Bâton Rouge, her engines broke hopelessly down when yet five miles from the place, and, drifting to the shore end on, she fell an easy prey to the shells of the ' Essex,' a large iron-plated river-boat, whose commander, W. D. Porter,* had taken charge of the Lower Mississippi on the departure of Farragut. The latter officer, in compliance with orders from Mr. Welles, had abandoned his contest with the Vicksburg works on the 20th of July, and made down stream for New Orleans, whence he proceeded with his squadron to carry on operations along the coast of Texas, where the chief posts were (for the time) recovered to the Union by his detachments in the course of a few weeks. ' All we want,' he wrote on the 15th of October, ' is a few soldiers to hold the places, and we ' will soon have the whole coast. It is a more effectual blockade ' to have the vessels inside instead of outside.' In this simple remark lies the key to the constantly increasing success of the Unionists in restricting their enemies' trade—a success which was complete only when Wilmington fell to Porter and Terry more than two years later in the war.

Second only in importance to the exploits of Farragut's fleet during this remarkable year, were the services rendered on the rivers by the squadrons of the Mississippi and Tennessee. Flag-officer Foote (raised to rear-admiral's rank afterwards with Farragut) directed their operations with extraordinary activity until disabled by the effects of a wound in May. They were continued for the next four months under Captain Davis, who had succeeded to the temporary charge. In October, however, a new flag-officer appeared in the person of Porter, whose services as lieutenant and commander we have already noticed. The constant approval of Farragut, Bailey, and all with whom he served, had fully justified the selection of this officer at the opening of the war for high charge by the President ; and the latter, proud of so fortunate a choice, took occasion now to advance him *per saltum* to the rank of acting rear-admiral, and to the command left vacant by Foote. Much of the uniform though slow success of the Federal armies in the central States depended henceforth on the activity and energy by which Porter showed himself worthy of his unexampled promotion. But the story of his deeds in that quarter, of Foote's, and of Farragut's, when he appeared a second time in the Mississippi

---

* One of the captains under Foote, and not to be confounded with the more famous D. D. Porter.

to co-operate in the fall of Vicksburg, forms so essential a part of the campaigns of General Grant, that we prefer to leave it to those writers who have made the progress of the chief General of the Union their special theme.

The year 1862 and its naval operations have an interest for us even higher than that which belongs to the subjects we have hitherto treated. The world-famous battle of the ' Monitor ' and ' Merrimack ' on the 9th April opened first the way to that practical solution of the proper form of iron-clad steamers which no government as yet has as nearly attained to as that of the United States. It is as well to be fully understood on this matter ; and the Report of Mr. Welles sets forth in the clearest light the importance of the ' Monitor's ' victory, the prescience shown by his practical adviser, Captain Fox, at the outset of the war, and the conditions aimed at in the construction of the original vessels built on the turret principle. The details of the battle —the sudden appearance in Hampton Roads of the ' Merri-' mack,' heavily plated with layers of iron, fitted as a ram, and well armed—her attack and easy destruction of two large wooden ships of war—the dangerous state of the blockading steam-frigates, unfitted to cope with and unable to escape from their antagonist, from whom they were only saved the first day by her dread of the shallows—the unlooked-for arrival (in the middle of that anxious night) of the ' Monitor,' hurried from New York by Captain Fox's exertions to meet and foil the long-threatened design of the Confederates—all these particulars have been so often and so fully given to the world, that we forbear to repeat them. At noon next day the ' Merrimack ' abandoned her attack and retreated to Norfolk, leaving the honours of her discomfiture to her diminutive but invulnerable foe.

' Thus terminated (writes Mr. Welles) the most remarkable naval combat of modern times, perhaps of any age. The fiercest and most formidable naval assault upon the power of the Union which has ever been made by the insurgents was heroically repelled, and a new era was opened in the history of maritime warfare.'

Then, after referring to the numerous vessels of the ' Monitor ' pattern under construction, he continues :—

' Whatever success may attend the large and costly armoured ships of the " Warrior " class, which are being constructed by some of the maritime Powers of Europe for cruising in deep waters, they can scarcely cause alarm here, for we have within the United States few harbours that are accessible to them, and for those few the Government can always be prepared whenever a foreign war is imminent. It has been deemed advisable, however, that we should have a few large-sized armed cruisers of great speed for ocean service, as well as some of the class of smaller vessels for coastwise and defensive operations.

'In the construction of iron-clads of the "Monitor" class, the nautical qualities of the vessel have not been the governing object, for with light draught and heavy armament, high speed is not attainable. But they are adapted to the shallow waters of our coast and harbours, few of which are accessible to vessels of great magnitude. While the larger armoured vessels, with their heavy armament, cannot nearly approach our shores, those of the "Monitor" class can penetrate even the inner waters, rivers, harbours, and bayons of our extended double coast.'

A success so great as that won over the ' Merrimack ' by the first employment of the revolving turret in action, might well cause Mr. Welles and his assistant to press forward the completion of the iron-clad squadron, from which they hoped such further advantage as should throw even the victory at New Orleans—won that same eventful month—into shade. Charleston itself, with the famous Fort Sumter, whose surrender had so bitterly touched the pride of the North, were the prizes intended to be added to the laurels already won by the American navy. The watch which the ' Monitor ' after her victory held in Hampton Roads became no longer needful when her adversary was blown up by Commodore Tatnall's orders to save her from falling into the hands of the Federals on the abandonment of Norfolk in the summer to their army. The Confederates had then no longer any vessel within the Chesapeake waters which their enemy's gunboats could not master, and the ' Monitor ' became available for employment in some new scene. It was not, however, until joined by the ' Passaic,' the first one finished of her consorts, that she prepared to leave Hampton Roads for the Carolina coast. The close of the year had drawn near, and her new commander, Bankhead (for Lieutenant Worden, who had fought her in the spring, was for some months invalided from a wound), was directed to choose his own time and weather for making his way southward.

He started on the 29th December, accompanied, for safety's sake, by a powerful wooden steamer, the ' Rhode Island,' and for the first twenty-four hours had nearly smooth water. On the evening of the 30th a slight gale was encountered, and the vessel soon became nearly unmanageable, pitching heavily, yawing greatly, and making much water round the base of the turret, where the caulking of oakum had become loosened by the motion. After two hours of this the water suddenly (at 8 P.M.) began to gain so fast on the pumps as to show that the shocks had sprung a leak below ; and although every possible assistance was rendered by the ' Rhode Island,' Commander Bankhead was compelled before long to abandon his vessel, which went down soon after, taking with her four officers and twelve men, whom it was impossible to transfer to her tender. The latter had indeed been put to great hazard in saving the rest of the crew from the deck of her unmanageable consort, to come into collision with whose sides or bow would, in the heavy sea-way, have proved instant destruction. Thus were the former detractors of the ' Monitor,' as originally constructed, almost as much justified in their special view as her projectors had been. Great efforts have since been made in America to improve upon the first design as to details, but the immediate result of the disaster was to confirm Mr. Welles in his projected design of leaving to turret ships the operations in shallow waters, and constructing for ocean warfare a few of another class of vessel, a broadside iron-clad of the largest class. His arguments in favour of this opinion are well worthy of the attention of the statesmen of other countries, and are thus very aptly concluded :—

' Each of these vessels must, in order to accomplish its work, present in its construction armour, armament, and propulsion, all the power that the resources of modern invention and mechanical science and art can furnish for attack, resistance, and pursuit. A vessel of this description must, of course, cost a large price. But then a wise statesmanship will not fail to perceive that the possession of even a very few such unconquerable ships must, while vastly augmenting the force and renown of our navy, afford us at the same time an inestimable guarantee of peace with foreign nations; nor, in counting the cost of such floating structures, can we forget that, large as that cost may be, it yet sinks into insignificance in contrast with the expenditures and sacrifices of a single year, or even a month, of foreign war.'

We take this extract from the Secretary's Report for 1863, in which, however, he states that there were no private yards in America fully prepared to build the required vessels, and strongly urges the necessity of Government enlarging its own means for the purpose.

The loss of the ' Monitor' was not suffered to retard the intended attack upon Charleston, and the additional precautions which followed on it enabled her sister vessels to make their way without further accident, from shelter to shelter, as they were separately despatched to join the fleet off that harbour. At the commencement of April 1863, Admiral Dupont had under him the ' Passaic ' and six other of this new class. Some additional strengthening of the central framework had been added to the original design, to enable the chief of the Bureau of Naval Ordnance, Captain Dahlgren, to carry out his favourite design of mounting for sea service his new 15-inch gun throwing a spherical shot of 450 pounds. Greater weight and calibre, this artillerist had long maintained, would avail to give greater accuracy and range, without the wear and uncertainty of rifling; and his theory has since become the favourite one in the American navy, whose large rifled guns on the 'Parrott' (or reinforcing with wrought-iron) system, cannot be considered as successful as their simpler competitors. Each of these seven 'Monitors' carried one of these new gigantic weapons, and one 11-inch in her turret. A smaller vessel, the 'Keokuk,' of the 'Galena' or 'turreted gunboat' pattern, carried one* 11-inch gun only.

Admiral Dupont transferred his flag to the 'Ironsides,' (already described as the first and largest vessel of the three original models selected,) which had been lately sent to aid him in the attack. She arrived just in time to complete the efficiency of the blockade which had been for a few hours put in jeopardy by two small Confederate rams, the 'Chicora' and 'Palmetto State,' which issued from the harbour before daybreak on the 31st January, designing to surprise the Federal squadron. The 'Mercedita,' the first vessel run into by them, was totally disabled and surrendered; but meanwhile the alarm spread so rapidly that the project failed. After engaging and inflicting considerable damage on the 'Keystone State,' the next of the gunboats, the assailants yielded to the resolute advance of Captain Taylor (the senior Federal officer) in his steamship the 'Housatonic,' supported by the 'Quaker City,' 'Memphis,' and 'Augusta,' and returned to the protection of the forts, claiming a success for what was in fact a failure, caused by their small tonnage and slow speed.

Dupont having collected his iron-clad squadron, and issued orders to use their fire solely on Fort Sumter until that work should be reduced, proceeded to the assault at noon on the 7th of April, leaving the rest of his fleet outside. His design was to enter so far into the harbour as to lay his nine vessels round the north-west face of the work; but this a line of obstructions skilfully sunk by the defenders prevented so effectually, that the 'Ironsides' was unable to approach within a thousand yards of the fort, whilst the 'Monitors' lay at from six to eight hundred yards' distance. A tremendous cross-fire was opened on

---

* As stated in the official Return of the chief gunnery officer of Dupont's fleet. Yet she was designed to carry two 11-inch guns in separate turrets.

them from Sumter and the opposite battery at Fort Moultrie before they had reached their positions, and continued until, in obedience to signal, they withdrew from action at 4.30 p.m., having delivered but 139 shot in reply to the vast number which some 70 guns (10-inch hollow shot and 7-inch rifled) had rained upon them. The new experiment of the 'Monitor' system as against strong works had failed decisively; and the 'Keokuk,' which had ventured the nearest, as she was also the weakest of the squadron, was injured beyond repair, and sank at daylight.

'I made signal (reports the disappointed Admiral) to withdraw from action, intending to resume the attack the next morning. During the evening the commanding officers of the iron-clads came on board the flag-ship, and, to my regret, I soon became convinced of the utter impracticability of taking the city of Charleston by the force under my command. No ship had been exposed to the severest fire of the enemy over forty minutes, and yet in that brief period, as the department will perceive by the detailed reports of the commanding officers, five of the iron-clads were wholly or partially disabled; disabled, too (as the obstructions could not be passed), in that which was most essential to our success—I mean in their armament, or power of inflicting injury by their guns. . . . I had hoped that the endurance of the iron-clads would have enabled them to have borne any weight of fire to which they might have been exposed; but when I found that so large a portion of them were wholly or one-half disabled, by less than an hour's engagement, before attempting to remove the obstructions, or testing the power of the torpedoes, I was convinced that persistence in the attack would only result in the loss of the greater portion of the iron-clad fleet, and in leaving many of them inside the harbour to fall into the hands of the enemy.'

This failure of the long-prepared experiment was not suffered to pass unchallenged at Washington. Mr. Welles, before receipt of the official news, had already sent instructions to the Admiral, in case of failure, to make further demonstrations, sufficient to occupy the garrison and prevent their making detachments to the armies in the field. But this measure and the mild terms in which the order was couched were deemed insufficient by the President, and he followed his perusal of the Admiral's first report by taking the matter into his own hands. He plunged, in short, into personal control of the operations with that irregular vigour which had in the previous year proved so fatal to the strategy of M'Clellan. His rights as Commander-in-chief of the Naval Forces had been suddenly laid aside ever since the early expedition to Pensacola, which, as we have seen, was carried out by the actual overthrow of the plans of his secretary.   He now as suddenly assumed them and telegraphed to Dupont : —

'Hold your position inside the bar near Charleston ; or if you shall have left it, return to it and hold it till further orders.   Do not allow the enemy to erect new batteries or defences on Morris Island.   If he has begun it, drive him out.   I do not herein order you to renew the general attack.   That is to depend on your own discretion or a further order.'

The Admiral was not of a character to patiently bear with what seemed to him unmerited censure on the measures he had taken for the safety of his iron-clads, already withdrawn to Port Royal for repairs.   In acknowledging the telegraphic order, and promising every exertion to comply with its provisions, he proceeds in his dispatch to detail fully the dangerous position in which the ' Monitors ' would thereby be placed, adding :—

'I have deemed it proper and due to myself to make these statements, but I trust I need not add that I will obey all orders with the utmost fidelity, even when my judgment is entirely at variance with them ; such as the order to re-occupy the unsafe anchorage for the iron-clads off Morris Island, and an intimation that a renewal of the attack on Charleston may be ordered, which in my judgment would be attended with disastrous results, involving the loss of this coast.'

Finally, with greater wisdom if not greater patriotism than M'Clellan had shown under the like interference, he resigned in the following frank and noble terms the command exercised for the preceding eighteen months with unvarying approbation from his superiors :—

'I know not whether the confidence of the department so often expressed to me has been shaken by the want of success in a single measure which I never advised, though intensely desirous to carry out the department's orders and justify expectations in which I could not share.   I am, however, painfully struck by the tenor and tone of the President's order, which seems to imply a censure, and I have to request that the department will not hesitate to relieve me by an officer who, in its opinion, is more able to execute that service in which I have had the misfortune to fail—the capture of Charleston. No consideration for an individual officer, whatever his loyalty and length of service, should weigh an instant if the cause of his country can be advanced by his removal.'

His resignation was accepted by the President, and Foote (reported to be recovered from his wound) was appointed to succeed him.   This officer, however, falling ill and dying at New York upon his way, the vacancy was finally conferred on Dahlgren, who, with especial view to his powers as an artillerist, had been appointed as second in command. He took over his new charge on the 6th of July; but before handing it to him, Dupont had had the satisfaction of reporting on the most instructive and successful action (according to Mr. Welles's very just view) of the year, and the first in which his successor's famous 15-inch gun was tested against ship-armour.

At Savannah the Confederates had been busy during the spring in the preparation of this, their new substitute for the lost ' Merrimack.' On the hull of a large iron screw-steamer, the ' Fingal,' their engineers had built up a structure which they hoped to make impregnable to the heaviest Dahlgren guns. The vessel had been cut down so as to leave the original hull but two feet above water. A casemate, with the sides and ends sloping at an angle of thirty degrees to the horizon, was erected upon it, so framed as to overlap the sides of the hull six feet and to project over the ends, towards which it was tapered. The sides were protected by timber, running from a point several feet below the water-line to the edge of the deck, forming a heavy, solid overway of wood and armour. The armour, four inches in thickness, was composed of two layers of two-inch rolled iron plates, seven inches wide, the inner of which ran horizontally, and the outer vertically. They were secured to a backing of oak three inches thick, and of pine fifteen inches thick. A pilot-house erected above it in a pyramidal form was similarly cased. Four rifled guns, two of 6-inch calibre and two of 7-inch, were the armament, and the bow terminated in an iron beak, forming a ram. On the 17th of June, with full magazines and a complement of 135 officers and men, this formidable iron-clad descended Warsaw Sound, at that time known to be guarded by two of the ' Monitors ' of the Charleston squadron, the ' Weehawken ' and the ' Nahant.'

There is no doubt now as to the Confederate plan. To make straight for the nearest ' Monitor,' run aboard her and pierce her armour through by the close fire of the rifled guns, was their intention, and from the superior elevation of their portholes (which were guarded by four-inch iron shutters) a decisive advantage at close quarters was expected, while the casing which had been prepared was judged sufficient to keep out any hollow shot fired from a distance at the low velocity which had been remarked as a characteristic of the Dahlgren cannon. The capture of the two hostile vessels was confidently looked for, and as the new ship was calculated to steam ten knots an hour, her transfer to other ports blockaded was designed to follow.

These hopes, however, were destined to a speedy end.   The Federals, having caught sight of their unknown adversary at dawn, steamed with alacrity to meet her.   The ' Weehawken,' having their only pilot on board, led the way ; and when about a quarter of a mile off, opened fire on the ' Atlanta,' (for thus the former ' Fingal ' was now named,) with her two guns alternately.   Three of the first four shots were seen distinctly from the ' Nahant ' to strike the enemy ; and at the fourth a white flag was suddenly run up, and the Confederate colours were hauled down ten minutes after the action had commenced.   The Federals on boarding their prize were scarcely less astonished than their adversaries at the tremendous effect of the fire of the 15-inch gun.   Its first shot had carried in armour and backing, strewn the deck with splinters, prostrated by its concussion about forty men, and wounded fourteen.   The second, aimed higher, had struck the iron plates, which forced the top of the pilot-house, carried it bodily off, wounded the steersman, and left the vessel unmanageable.   The 11-inch shot had done no damage, save to the shutter of one of the portholes, which was struck when opened back and completely shattered.   Never was victory over a confident enemy more decisive and more easily won than this remarkable battle, which at once proved the new Dahlgren gun to be one of the most formidable pieces of ordnance constructed, and put the floating battery or ' Moni-' tor ' into such a foremost position for smooth-water service as even the most sanguine views of its designer, before the days of this weapon, could have never reached.

Notwithstanding the remark made later by a Board of Survey on the imperfect nature of the pine backing used in the ' Atlanta,' which proved both to have little power of resistance and to be extremely dangerous by its splinters to those it was designed to protect, yet there can be no doubt that this roughly built iron-clad would have stood a formidable test from ordnance of the old patterns.   Ignorance, in short, of the true power of their enemy's pieces caused the Confederates to run their new champion into this speedy destruction : but they can hardly be judged over bold, so little do the Federals appear at this time to have known of the exact value of the monster gun.

The victory of the ' Weehawken ' procured her captain, Rodgers,* the rank of commodore ; while Dupont—whose watchfulness had prepared it—left his command with flying colours and

---

* The officer who lately commanded the American squadron during the bombardment of Valparaiso.

the earnest thanks of the department. His views of the strength of Charleston were fully justified by the conduct of his successor. Dahlgren did not repeat the naval attack, and his fleet played but a secondary part in the operations of Gillmore; nor was it until the latter had captured Morris Island that the blockade was made effective by vessels placed in the smooth water near it, and the commerce of the city ceased. Yet so formidable did Sumter, even in its ruins, appear, that so late as the following summer, a fresh attempt to force the 'Monitors' between it and Fort Moultrie was discussed and deliberately rejected by the Admiral and his captains assembled in council of war.

The services of Farragut during the year 1863, including his forcing a passage at tremendous risk and loss past Fort Hudson, the new Confederate fortress in the Mississippi, and his subsequent co-operation in the all-important conquest of Vicksburg, though of themselves gallant and memorable achievements, are yet, like Dahlgren's, of a secondary nature, being bound up with the history of Grant's armies, with which Porter also acted throughout the year.

The spring of 1864, however, found the former Admiral returning from a brief sick leave, and preparing for a new enterprise, more perilous in appearance than the attack on New Orleans, where well-won success had first raised him to fame. Mobile Bay was one of the few refuges remaining to the blockade-runners at this period of the war. The main entrance to it was guarded by Fort Morgan, a bastioned work of great strength armed with 10-inch hollow shot and rifled 32-pounder guns. The channel was narrow at this part, must be entered by daylight, and was thickly beset by such torpedoes as that which had recently, in spite of Dahlgren's precautions, proved fatal to the steam-sloop 'Housatonic' at Charleston, and placed the 'Ironsides' herself in danger. Yet more to be dreaded than fort or torpedo was the ram 'Tennessee,' commanded by Admiral Buchanan, whose courage and ability were well known to Farragut, and of strength and armament beyond any of those which the Confederates had launched. Her description, given with exactness by deserters, spoke of her as built upon the same principles as the 'Atlanta,' but with the casemate large enough to carry six guns, and plated all over with three layers of two-inch iron, by which additional strength the Confederates hoped to save her from the fate of her model. Her speed was slow, and Farragut declared on his arrival that he would not hesitate to encounter her with his larger wooden ships, but for the fear of her taking refuge in such shallow water

as they could not enter. ' Wooden vessels,' he added ' ' can do
' nothing with these iron-clads unless by getting within one
' hundred or two hundred yards, so as to ram them or pour in a
' broadside.'

Four ' Monitors ' being at length supplied him in July, he
prepared to test the strength of his enemies without delay, the
latter being known to be striving hard to add other iron-clads
to the ' Tennessee,' which alone proved ready for action. She
was aided by three gunboats only, when the Federal fleet entered the channel on the 5th of August, in great strength, but
with much uncertainty as to the issue of the attack. The
seven frigates and steam-sloops which carried the principal batteries were not only protected by chains stopped up and down,
but were lashed each to a gunboat on the port side, in order
that if crippled in the narrow channel, they might be towed
out of range of Fort Morgan, which was on the starboard hand.
The ' Monitors ' formed a single line between it and the ships,
engaging the work and absorbing its fire as far as possible.
Thus covered, the wooden vessels in their double column forced
their way up, (the admiral most gallantly taking the lead when
the first ship, the ' Brooklyn,' hesitated at the sudden appearance of a line of buoys), and found themselves in half an hour
above the forts on which their starboard broadsides had poured
such a continuous fire of grape—the missile specially chosen
beforehand by Farragut—as the gunners could hardly endure.
Not one ship was disabled, and but a hundred of their crews
killed and wounded. But the ' Tecumseh,' which led the
' Monitors,' was struck in sight of all by a torpedo, and went
down with her crew. Her fate did not prevent her comrades
from gallantly carrying out the allotted task ; and when the
' Tennessee ' sallied from a side channel higher up to assail the
wooden squadron, the ' Monitors ' strove to take share in the
general assault Farragut directed to be made on her. He had
prepared for this bold movement of Buchanan's by providing
false bows of iron to the frigates to charge the ram more effectually as soon as she drew near ; and having already cast loose
from their respective consorts, they steamed unhesitatingly to
meet her. Then began a contest of a completely new order in
naval tactics, and in which the ram never, as it proved, had a
chance of success. Some of her enemies crowded round her
sufficiently to impede her motion, whilst the larger steamers
strove to run her down in turn. Steering badly, slow in movement, and close pressed on each side, the ' Tennessee' received
in succession the charges of three of her assailants without perceptible damage, ' the only effect being to give her a heavy list,'

and continued to ply her guns for near an hour. The flag-ship 'Hartford,' after charging under the personal direction of the Admiral, (who stood lashed in his main-top) poured a broad side of 9-inch shot at her casemates at a distance of barely ten feet. Two of the 'Monitors' fired their 15-inch guns steadily at her whenever an opening was made; and though one only of their shots damaged the plating of the casemate, another destroyed her steering chains, and her chimney was carried away. The decisive injuries, however, were inflicted by succes-sive damages to the shutters of her gun-ports; and three of them being jammed or made useless by the concentrated fire of the frigates, her reply slackened, until a shell entering one wounded Buchanan dangerously, and caused her immediate surrender. The fall of the forts soon followed, and Mobile, though still protected by a shallow bar above, became harmless against the Union: whilst the victor, whose heroic conduct had won him the personal adoration of his fleet, stood confessed the first seaman of the age. This last achievement obtained for him from the grateful Congress the special rank of Vice-Admiral —a just reward, which placed him on an equal footing with General Grant.

Small as had been the success of the Confederates with their rams, the last brilliant feat of their arms in the war—the cap-ture by Hoke in the spring of 1864 of the forts so long held by the Union forces on Albemarle Sound—was due in great part to the aid of a small vessel of this description, which attacked and drove off the covering gunboats, sinking the boldest of them with a blow of her prow. This first feat of the 'Albemarle' proved, however, to be her last. In the following October she perished by what may beyond question be called the most daring action of the war—the attack on her at night by a steam-launch carrying a torpedo at the bow. Of the gallant volunteers who undertook this work, two only were saved death or capture, the boat being sunk by the effect of their own engine: but one of these was the young commander, Lieutenant Cushing, already four times thanked for conduct before the enemy, whose new exploit might fairly rank with the boldest deeds of the youth of Nelson or Dundonald. His escape forms an episode of the war, so romantic in itself and so well told by the hero, that we prefer transcribing from his simple narrative:—

'A dense mass of water rushed in from the torpedo, filling the launch and completely disabling her. The enemy then continued his fire at fifteen feet range, and demanded our surrender, which I twice refused, ordering the men to save themselves, and removing my own coat and shoes. Springing into the river, I swam, with others, into the middle of the stream, the rebels failing to hit us. The most of our party were captured, some drowned, and only one escaped besides myself, and he in a different direction. Acting-Master's Mate Woodman, of the "Commodore Hull," I met in the water half a mile below the town, and assisted him as best I could, but failed to get him ashore.

'Completely exhausted, I managed to reach the shore, but was too weak to crawl out of the water until just at daylight, when I managed to creep into the swamp, close to the fort. While hiding a few feet from the path, two of the "Albemarle's" officers passed, and I judged from their conversation that the ship was destroyed. Some hours' travelling in the swamp served to bring me out well below the town, when I sent a negro in to gain information and found that the ram was truly sunk. Proceeding through another swamp, I came to a creek and captured a skiff belonging to a picket of the enemy, and with this, by eleven o'clock the next night, had made my way out to the "Valley City."'

No wonder that this feat procured Cushing not merely his step to commander in the volunteer service, but the special thanks of Mr. Welles under his own hand, with the offer from that statesman of a transfer to the regular navy upon the completion of the requisite course of study.

The naval operations of the war, which began by Lieutenant Porter's relief of Pensacola in defiance of Bragg's guns, were fitly closed by Admiral Porter's capture of the defences of Wilmington, the last port of the Confederacy, before the very eyes of the same general. As nothing was here proved of the iron-clads save their general fitness to share in a steady bombardment of forts of inferior armament, and as we are informed from undoubted authority that the Federal success was assured as much by the fatal weakness of the opposing commander (who, though supplied with full means, made no effort to relieve his exhausted garrisons) as by the vast superiority of the fire of the fleet, we do not think it needful to comment on the details.

Long before this affair the efforts of the South by sea had been reduced to what appeared to all the world rather a mere form of revenge than any useful warfare. Failing utterly in the purpose of embroiling the North with any neutral nation, these doings have left a seed of bitterness, such as it will need much wisdom and patience to stay from becoming bitter fruit in the future. From the fall of Wilmington, the advantages of blockade-runners and the mushroom growth of their trade became things of the past. For the rest of the war the Confederate flag only covered what was, after all, (if we except the cruise of the iron-clad 'Stonewall') an ignoble piracy, legalised in default of provision made against it by jurists. The ex-Cabinet of Richmond, which sanctioned this system to the end of their rule, have left as a legacy one of the most difficult problems on international duties ever offered for statesmen to solve. But we are more concerned here to point out the urgent necessity which will arise, in case of England's engaging in a war, for our commerce being more efficiently guarded at sea than by iron-clads of 5,000 tons, or firstrate wooden frigates. A class of swift corvettes, carrying two or three heavy guns, with engines so powerful as to enable them to overhaul any ordinary merchant steamers, will be absolutely indispensable if our trade is to escape ruin, whilst privateering is employed against it. At such a class Mr. Welles and Captain Fox aimed when they ordered the 'Kearsage' and her consorts; but in this particular service alone did their efforts wholly disappoint expectation. The 'Alabama,' 'Sumter,' and 'Florida' (managed certainly with consummate skill under most difficult conditions), roamed unchecked over the ocean. At the close of 1864, the capture of 193 vessels, valued with their cargoes at 13½ millions of dollars, bore testimony to their activity, and to the danger to which, under the new conditions of naval warfare, an unprotected commercial marine is exposed. That these losses were not from expenditure being too narrow, but from the peculiar direction which it had taken under Mr. Welles, is abundantly shown by his Report of that date. The navy which four years before had counted but 76 ships, in and out of commission, and of these about one half sailing vessels, was now increased to a total of 671. Of this number no less than 71 were iron-clads of different classes, 37 of them of formidable strength and carrying heavy Dahlgren guns; and only 112 of the whole were without steam power, being in fact used for transport purposes.

Whether the fleet thus enumerated is, as Americans openly declare, infinitely beyond any that Europe can show in fighting power, is a question we do not here attempt to decide. Our space does not allow us to do more than indicate some of the more important questions connected with the discussion, and raised by even a cursory view of the performances of the Union navy.

The first of these that naturally occurs is the subject of the exact value and use of Monitors. A quotation we have already given from Mr. Welles's original Report upon these vessels shows clearly that it was not in England or France alone that official men mistrusted their ever being fitted for sea service. That they were at first very much disliked by naval officers, and easily disabled in action, the records of the attack on Charleston abundantly prove. On the other hand, it is certain that Mr. Welles and his advisers have since approved of the construction of Monitors, (the ' Puritan,' ' Dictator,' and ' Roanoke '), built specially for sea service—that the navigation of another large one round to the Pacific has been found by no means so dangerous as was anticipated—that the crews of these vessels have not found them unhealthy—and that the Charleston experience has been wonderfully utilised for the improvement of the mechanism of the turret and ports, so that (as is alleged) the same shots which then produced so much disabling effect, might now be easily endured. The value of these assertions no one is more desirous to see practically tested than Captain Fox himself. As we close these remarks it is announced officially that, under the special sanction of Congress, he has undertaken to bring across the Atlantic a large double-turreted vessel, the ' Miantonomah,' for the conviction of the sceptical ship-designers of Europe ;* and in his able hands we may well leave the question for the present.

Closely connected with it is that of the American system of heavy smooth-bore guns ; for such as those which won the fight of Warsaw Sound—and far more the new 20-inch— are evidently too weighty for any broadside vessel now in use. We know the objection which lies to their moderate charges and the consequent low velocity of their projectiles. On the other hand it is clear that this may yet be overcome by even a slight improvement on the present ' Rodman ' method of casting on a cooled bore, or by the use of wrought iron ; whilst even as they exist their 450 lbs. and 990 lbs. balls, fired with only $\frac{1}{8}$th or $\frac{1}{6}$th charges, are missiles so powerful as none but the highest class of iron-clads could endure. Since the result of all late experiments in Europe is to cast great doubt on the possibility of constructing any large rifled guns which can be relied on for more than a few hundred rounds, we cannot but consider it a very grave question whether our artillerists are right in confining their exertions entirely to their improvement, and leaving it to the Americans to complete to perfection the simpler and more enduring piece which has already done such great things

* This vessel is at Spithead at this moment, and she does the greatest credit to the American flag, since it must be confessed that there is not a vessel in the British navy which could destroy her by gunnery, or which she could not destroy. It should be stated, however, that this formidable ship, not having adequate propelling power for a long voyage, was chiefly towed across the Atlantic, as her sister-ship the ' Mohadnock ' was towed round Cape Horn.

in actual practice. But this subject would demand a special article for discussion, and we therefore pass it by. For the same reason we do not enter on that of the torpedo system of defence and assault, to the practical solution of which the American examples serve—although dimly and incompletely— to point the way.

There is one deduction which might be made from a hasty survey of the naval annals of the war, against which we desire to give an earnest warning. Some will say—as some have already said—that the chief thing shown is the possibility of creating, from private resources during actual war, all that a great contest at sea may require without that elaborate preparation and vast expenditure to which in this country we dedicate millions yearly in time of peace. The example of the Great Republic and the precepts of the successful statesmen who have carried her safely to a triumphant re-union, prove, when closely studied, the very contrary. It cost them years of toil and uncertainty and oceans of expenditure before the naval predominance to which the North had full right was completely asserted. No minister has ever more loudly deprecated the relying too much on private shipyards than Mr. Welles, to whose earnest and repeated recommendation it is due that the Congress is even now engaged on the question of determining the site of a grand depôt for the future construction of American iron-clads. We in England, if entering into a struggle for that supremacy of the seas which involves the preservation of our own coasts from danger, and the protection of a vast and wide-spread commerce, must look to meeting not a raw seceding province, but Powers who are ready to attack, and will allow us brief space to prepare. A sufficient fleet must in such event be ready, not waiting the chances of a hurried creation. Be then the shock what it may, we doubt not it would be met by hearts as brave, by heads as cool, and arms as skilful, as those of the seamen whose exploits we have here briefly traced. The jealousies of a day, we trust, will die, while common blood and language will create new ties ; and Englishmen who desire this, will not be slow to recognise as worthy successors of our own great naval chieftains, those names which now fill with pride the hearts of our kinsfolk on the other side of the Atlantic.

ART. VII.—1. *The Natural History, Ancient and Modern, of Precious Stones and Gems, and of Precious Metals.* By C. W. KING, M.A., Fellow of Trinity College, Cambridge. London: 1865.

2. *Handbuch der Edelsteinkunde für Mineralogen, Steinschneider und Juweliere.* Von KARL EMIL KLUGE. Leipsic: 1860.

3. *Gems and Jewels, their History, Geography, Chemistry, and Ana, from the earliest years down to the present time.* By Madame de BARRERA. London: 1860.

4. *Diamonds and Precious Stones, their History, Value and Distinguishing Characteristics, with simple Tests for their Identification.* By HARRY EMMANUEL. London: 1865.

WHAT, we may ask, have been the sources of that fascination which precious stones have from time immemorial exercised over the minds of men? How comes it that in this nineteenth century a little diamond not half the weight of a sixpence will sell for 400*l.*, and as small a ruby for 600*l.* or 700*l.*? Just as in the days of the Triumvirate the opal of Nonias, a stone no bigger than a hazel-nut, was valued at 20,000*l.* of our money (vicies HS.): yet its owner went penniless into exile rather than surrender it to the greed of Marc Antony!

What can thus gift these little bits of stone with such extraordinary value? What sort of passion is it that would seem so little restrained by conscience or by reason? To say that it is mere cupidity is not to explain it. The imagination certainly enhances the pleasure derived from the beauty of a diamond, a ruby, a sapphire, or an emerald; for only an eye trained by custom, or instructed by science, can distinguish these stones from their glass counterfeits. It is not, therefore, this beauty alone that gives them their value. Nor is it their adaptation for practical uses that confers on them this quality; for except in the limited applications of diamond dust, to what useful purpose are these stones applied? Nor is it their mere rarity, else would an ounce of platinum be worth a thousand times more instead of four times less than an ounce of gold, and many a substance in nature would be precious far beyond the diamond. It is not, then, the desire merely to possess what others have not. It is rather the passion for doing what others do, and possessing what it is the fashion to possess, that gives these tiny stones their price. They are pretty objects, and are comparatively rare, and they have the advantage of being almost indestructible, in consequence of their hardness. But what makes them worth many pounds a grain is that they have acquired by tradition a prestige which fashion perpetuates ; a prestige rooted in strange attributes and mystic powers wherewith the fancies of five thousand years have endowed such stones ; a fashion that has been ever pandered to by a harpy host of money-making parasites, and has been fostered by that human weakness which, while endeavouring to associate what is pretty with what is costly in the materials chosen for personal ornament, is apt to attach more importance to their price than to their real beauty, in proportion as cupidity is a passion more common than refinement and taste.

It will be our object to trace some of the sources whence this prestige of the stones accounted precious has sprung ; and after briefly describing such as have attained to this prerogative, to inquire at what periods these became known in the ancient world. By investigating the minerals known by particular names to the Greeks and Romans, we shall have gone over ground not perhaps in itself possessed of other than an archæological interest ; but we shall have prepared the way for a future discussion of the art which these stones so often enshrine, and which makes them the instruments for conveying to us no contemptible part of our heritage in the arts of Greece.

The earliest evidences by which we recognise the action of a human intelligence on our globe, are presented in those singular arrow-heads and axes which come up to us from the fossil world as if on purpose to link the age of man with the long roll of earlier ages through which his planet has passed, and to entwine his history with that of old world animals that till lately were supposed to have passed away ere the reign of our race in nature had begun. Yet even among those weird monuments of early human life we find axes and implements sometimes fashioned out of stones eminently beautiful and obviously chosen for their colour and texture. Such are certain green stone hatchets found in Brittany, formed of a mineral differing from ordinary jade, but related to a translucent variety of zoisite held among the most precious substances in China and throughout the east of Asia. Stone axe-heads of jade are found in New Caledonia ; and the New Zealanders as well as the South African natives also use a fine translucent green serpentine and a jade for personal ornaments, instruments, and weapons. They thus bring a remarkable testimony to the universality of this instinct for the selection and use of coloured stones, by showing that it did not exclusively belong to the archaic period when metal was unknown, but that it at this moment actuates men who are practically living in a stone age of their own, though contemporary with this our period of civilisation.   The Mexicans used to carve into strange and rude forms of men and monsters various green stones, including apparently an augite or green diopsich, occasionally also an amazon-stone felspar, and another stone of rich green mottled with white, probably a jadeite (or zoisite), to which they knew how to impart a most beautiful lustre: while the glory of the Peruvian was the true emerald, astonishing specimens of which must have come to Europe as well as have been distributed over India immediately after the conquest of the New World.

It is perhaps not from caprice that green stones have been especially selected by the various races of men for ornamental materials.   It more probably is due partly to the beauty of their colour, but partly also to the singular toughness (as distinct from mere hardness), and to other useful properties that characterise these minerals.

The belief in the talismanic influences of gems is certainly an extremely ancient one, and presents a phase of the subject which would possess more than a merely antiquarian sort of interest could we trace it to its true sources.   As it is, one can but vaguely surmise what properties possessed by stones first suggested to men's minds the mysterious influences ascribed to them.

A mineral, like heliotrope and blood-stone, splashed with blood-like spots, or a crystal presenting its beautiful clear and polished form beset with facettes symmetrically implanted on it, might seem to bespeak a formative power native in the substance, or a sympathy with human suffering potent to invest the stone with a blood-stained dress, and why not therefore to extend to a beneficent power of healing if only men knew how to avail themselves of such a boon?   So, too, as the crystal is the result of a power competent to fashion the hard material with a spontaneous precision into exact geometrical forms, why should not that power, it might be asked, be able to direct its further growth, nay even (as believed by Theophrastus) its reproduction after its kind?   Boethius de Boot (1609), one of the last of the long list of writers on the dreary subject of the talismanic influences of stones, speaks of precious stones having been formed to be the abode of angels; language in which we may hear the echo of what was said by Arabian writers long before his day, as in this again we have the tradition of older thoughts coming from the distant East, if indeed they be not forms of superstition natural everywhere to the human mind. Throughout the East this belief in mystic powers resident in stones has been always universal: form and system was all that it acquired under the magianism of Persia and of Babylon, but it was with this systematised shape of it that the western nations became acquainted.

A belief in mystic powers animating all nature has a poetical side to it. The fancy of the imaginative East has coloured it with attractive hues; for who has not at some period of life lingered with pleasure in the haunts of Oriental fable, charmed with its tales of those Genii and Efreets that in earlier centuries and in more sombre tints played their part in the religious angelology of Persia and Mesopotamia. It is strange indeed to see this belief in talismans and magic after passing from India and Persia to Greece and Rome, and after playing an essential part in the Gnostic systems of Alexandria, becoming finally transferred into the Christian Church without apparently any inspection of its credentials! Let us not ridicule the poor Arab who has recourse to his blind faith, and possibly indeed to some practical experience in the healing influence of a cold slab of bloodstone when applied to reduce the inflammation and assuage the pain caused by the scorpion's bite; nor think with contempt of the Roman who powdered amber with attar of roses to cure his deafness, or with honey to cure weakness in his eyes,—and the limpid drops of amber, be it remembered, were in one myth the tears a god had wept, even Apollo himself the Sun God, Elector, to whom electrum was sacred. These comparatively harmless forms of credulity were founded probably on as secure a basis of experience as that which makes even Mr. King, the author of the work at the head of this article, believe the wearing an amber necklace to be a certain means of warding off attacks of erysipelas! and they were certainly rational in comparison with the kind of faith exhibited by St. Jerome when we find him gravely writing that the sapphire conciliates to its wearer the condescension of princes, quells his enemies, disperses sorceries, sets free the captive, and even assuages the wrath of God Himself! This was no transient fancy or superstition of an individual writer; rather it formed part of a system handed on from age to age with undiminished vitality, as we may see by perusing the work on stones by Bishop Marbœuf, of Rennes, in the eleventh century, wherein he versified their talismanic influences. Among whole pages of similarly astounding nonsense, he gravely asserts that the heliotrope endows its wearer with the gift of prophecy and immunity from poison, or with proper ceremonies can make him invisible! And even so late as the reign of Elizabeth we find Archbishop Parker presenting to her Highness the Queen's Majesty an agate with an engraving on it of an Androgenous Venus and Cupid, as a prophylactic charm. It seems, to quote from the very appropriate doggrel into which Mr. King has been so good as to translate the Bishop of Rennes' Lapidarium that,

> 'The Agate on the wearer strength bestows,
> With ruddy health his fresh complexion glows;
> Both eloquence and grace are by it given,
> He gains the favour both of earth and heaven.'

This stone was therefore admirably adapted to be the vehicle in a substantial form of the Archbishop's apostolic benediction. With probably a keener sense of what might really constitute the power of a talisman, Runjeet Singh inquired what kind of special spell it was that had made the Koh-i-nur from immemorial time the talisman of Indian sovereignty. 'By what do 'you estimate its value?' asked the Sikh Maharajah of his victim, as the surrendered Koh-i-nur lay on the arm of its new master—'By its good luck,' said Shah Soujah, 'for it hath 'been ever his who hath conquered his enemies.'

The talismanic influence of stones was a belief, no doubt, in some cases linked with the worship of them; but it is impossible to say when or how they first acquired a sacred character. Indeed the line of demarcation between awe and respect for a talisman and the direct worship of the material that embodied it, would depend rather on the degree of barbarism of the fetish-worshipper than on the principle involved in his superstition. The time-honoured and still-subsisting reverence for the Kaaba-stone at Mecca probably originated in the same sentiment that a few years ago made the great meteoric stone that fell at Parnallee in Madras, now in the British Museum, an object of adoration to many thousands of Hindoos. The famous Venus of Cyprus, and the image at Ephesus that fell down from Jupiter, may, in common with the Kaaba and the Parnallee stones, have been meteoric in their origin, and have been seen to fall from the midst of a serene sky to the earth with explosion and fire—as Hephaistos may have fallen on Lemnos.

The Shekinah on the breastplate of the High Priest of the Jews gleamed with a sombre darkness that came over the stones (in one account it was a special stone, the sapphire, that was the sensitive agent of this manifestation) when the anger of the Lord was kindling, but when He was at peace with His people the light of heaven shone brightly on the stones of the sacred vestment. The minute description of the jewels which were to form part of the sacerdotal apparel, in the 28th chapter of

Exodus, indicates the symbolical reverence attached to them even by the Israelites.

A brighter phase in the history of ornamental stones is that in which we see them as the shrines of art, and pre-eminently as the materials on which the Greek loved to lavish all his exquisite powers of expressing form and sentiment; for in the gems he has left us thus adorned, he has transmitted to our time the only unabraded and perfectly fresh illustrations of his art that we possess. Then with an interest not second to this, though invested with very far less of its artistic charm, there comes the application of these beautiful and hard substances to the purposes of signets and seals of various kinds by other nations, during ages that were running their course long before the golden era of Hellenic art had dawned; and we have afterwards later forms of the engraver's work belonging to the centuries which succeeded to the three or four which formed that golden age.

Mr. King, one of the Senior Fellows of Trinity College, Cambridge, has devoted the life and leisure of a fine scholar to the whole of this subject. A treatise, the only one in our language, on Gems in general—that is to say, on hard and more or less precious stones engraved as works of art, was the first volume, which he published in 1860. This was followed in 1864 by a treatise on Gnostic Gems, in which he dealt with some of the more superstitious uses and motives of the works of the gem-engraver. The last of Mr. King's books, published in 1865, is that which stands at the head of this article. It treats of the history of Stones and Metals, and must be looked on as a second and expanded edition of those portions of his treatise on Gems which were devoted to these topics. Never exhaustive of his subject, and hardly ever original in his interpretations of the terms used by Greek or Roman authors, he has nevertheless brought together much curious learning in his book; and if it bears evidence of being the work of a scholar rather than a man of science, it is, on the other hand, the best summary of the mineralogy of antiquity and the middle ages. As regards the modern part of the subject, the German treatise of Kluge is a work of research and erudition, and one is surprised to find that Mr. King's book, published in England in 1865, was apparently written in ignorance of so important a work as Kluge's, printed in 1860. Of the two other works, to which our attention has been directed, that of Madame de Barrera is amusing partly from the sort of matter she has collected in it, but chiefly from the errors with which it teems; while Mr. Emmanuel's book, with several inaccuracies, is still so far better than a mere advertisement that one of the contributors to it has furnished a useful though not very complete list of works and memoirs on the subject of precious stones. It also contains a few interesting references to Chaldee literature, for which Mr. Emmanuel must have placed under contribution the learning of some Rabbi of his race. It is with the ancient lore to which Mr. King's last treatise is chiefly devoted that we have now most to do ; and in taking hereafter a survey of the art of gem-engraving, and of the stones employed for gems, among the nations of antiquity, we shall find him a most valuable, though, perhaps at times, a somewhat too enthusiastic guide.

The materials out of which an account of the knowledge of the ancients in mineralogy is to be built are not very satisfactory. First of all, we have what has come down to us of the mineral substances themselves in the form of gems and ornamental works ; and we have besides what are doubtless imitations in various kinds of glass of the rarer or more valued species of coloured stones. We certainly know minerals and varieties of gems that were never seen in antiquity ; but the ancients, on the other hand, could have known no minerals that are unknown to modern mineralogy, though they undoubtedly obtained precious stones from localities some of which became exhausted so far as their mining art was capable of exhausting them, while others have been lost to our knowledge under the different waves of human circumstance that have swept over the countries from which, in antiquity, minerals were drawn. Thus the conquests of Alexander deepened and strengthened the current of Eastern commerce that, no doubt, even in the dawn of European history was flowing to Europe in the channel of Phœnician enterprise. The concentration of wealth, and the encouragement it gave to the more refined arts in Egypt under the Ptolemies, and in Italy during the Imperial age of Rome, fostered the development of this Oriental commerce, the most important elements of which were doubtless not only the ' ivory, apes, and peacocks ' of earlier times, and the gold and tin of the trans-Indian golden Chersonese (the Malay Peninsula) ; but ebony, the precious stones (sapphires, garnets, &c.) of Ceylon, the diamonds and beryls of Lower India, besides the onyx, the murrhina, and the textile fabrics, both coarse and fine, of India. But the march of Mohammedanism displaced again the barriers within which the tide of Oriental commerce flowed ; perhaps the languid energies of the declining empire had already made its waters stagnant. At any rate, countries that certainly sent many a beautiful mineral into the jewellers' bazaars in Byzantium or Rome receded gradually from the view of Europe, and, strange to say, at this moment we probably know less of the mineral products of the territories that now constitute the Turkish and Persian empires, or even of Africa and of Asia Minor, nay, of Greece and the Levant, than did Theophrastus, the pupil of Aristotle, or King Juba II., the Numidian sovereign contemporary with Augustus.

The only other source of information is to be found in classical authors. There existed, indeed, a special literature on mineralogy in the Greek and Roman libraries. But all that remains to us of it is a treatise of Theophrastus on Stones, the 37th book of Pliny, some notices by Solinus, the author of a geography written probably in the middle of the third century, describing the substances found in the countries he took note of, and a mystic work of rabid magianism, the 'Lithica,' by an author called by the pretended name of Orpheus, generally attributed to the Alexandrian school of Christian philosophy, but by Mr. King supposed to be at least as old as the middle of the second century B.C.

Finally, we have such epithets or allusions to special stones as may be found scattered up and down the poets and the prose literature of the centuries that stretch from Plato to Constantine. Coming down to later times, we may put the encyclopædic compilation of Isidorus Hispalensis (Bishop of Seville from 600 to 635 A.D.) under contribution; or, like Mr. King, we may go to Marbœuf, Bishop of Rennes (1067—1081), Latinised as Marbodus, and study his Latin poem entitled a 'Lapidarium,' from which we have already quoted, in the belief that we may there find really the abridgment, he boasts his work to be, of a 'bulky volume by Evax, King of Arabia, presented ' to Tiberius Cæsar!' Isidorus, however, has but given us a brief summary made from Pliny, together with a few small scraps of knowledge picked up from one or two other treatises now lost. The poem of Bishop Marbœuf is of much the same stamp as that of the pseudo-Orpheus; it is a tissue of marvels, charms, and talismans, which we would commend to the table-turners, rappers, and spiritualists of our time, as a resource when other forms of their 'magorum infanda vanitas' are exhausted.

Theophrastus and Pliny are, therefore, our sole substantial authorities. The Περὶ τῶν λίθων βιβλίον of Theophrastus is a philosophical treatise so far as the subject could be handled philosophically in the absence of all knowledge of the composition of minerals, or of their scientific forms and properties. The great pupil of Aristotle could scarcely write on any subject without showing the result of thought, if not of practical observation, and certainly Mr. King would have done good service if he had employed his scholarship in giving in one of his volumes a good literal translation of this short work, with a few notes' on the corrupt passages with which it unfortunately abounds. This fragmentary work of Theophrastus remained the only treatise on minerals that professed to be philosophical down almost to the age of Linnæus. For all the literature of the subject that has reached our time, if we except one book of Pliny, and a work or two from Persian hands, is little else than one long tissue of talismanic nonsense.

The 37th book of Pliny, on the other hand, the last be it remembered that he wrote, professes to be a summary of what had been written before his time and of the information its learned and laborious author had been able to record in his common-place book. It is a crudely-digested mass of curious but invaluable matter, collected previously to A.D. 77, two years before Pliny lost his life under Vesuvius. He quotes from Theophrastus often word for word, sometimes misquoting or misunderstanding him, and often, there can be no doubt, describing the same kind of stone twice over, first under the title which Greek authors had given to it, and again under the name by which it was known in the Latin world of the age of Titus.

In the origin of the names of the more precious stones our subject assumes a form of very great interest, and one that should be fruitful of some results for the early archæology of minerals. We to this day use with little real change many of the names by which the Greeks spoke of precious stones at least 500 years before the Christian era, however we may have transposed the application of those particular names from one stone to another. Jasper, diamond, sapphire, agate, beryl, are some of these. Yet few of these names are Greek in root or sound though clothed in a Hellenic garb. The Greek, indeed, with an instinct to adopt such words into his language, and with a fine ear and a tongue that played on them with a sort of serious punning as soon as he had adopted them, gave to some of these names, the origin of which was essentially exotic, a Greek meaning and form; often slightly changing the form the better to adapt it to its novel meaning.

Although it may seem hypercritical to seek a root outside the Greek language for so Greek-sounding a term as adamas, ' the indomitable,' the Hebrew word ' achlamah,' derived from ' chalam,' implying, in one of its senses, to be hard, compact, and the Persian name for the diamond, almas, a word said to be foreign in root to the Persian language, suggest the possibility that both the Greek and the Persian terms were originally derived from the Semitic name for a material (probably corundum or massive sapphire), which Phœnician commerce brought from India, or even quarried in its coarser form as the smir (Græcised in form as smyris, our emery), within the basin of the Mediterranean.

The jasper, iaspis, is undoubtedly a word of Semitic origin. It is the Hebrew jashpeh — firm, tough, from jashaf, to be strengthened, a derivation that derives some interest from the fact that nearly all the Semitic (Phœnician) gems we know are engraved on a chloritic green jasper known as jaspis by Greek and Latin lapidaries.

The sapphire, in Greek sappheiros, was the name applied by Greeks and Romans to what we call lapis-lazuli. But it is obviously a word foreign to the Greek tongue. According to the Talmud the tables of the Law were fashioned of sappir. The word is connected with the root from which are derived the Hebrew terms for a book, writing, or engraving. This root is ' safar,' to engrave, but it seems also to have the meaning ' to shine,' and this may be the source of the application of the name sappir to a precious stone.

From these Semitic names we pass to a Persian root. The sard—sardion—sardius, was the favourite stone of the Greek engraver; it was a yellow chalcedony with a dark aspect when looked on but of a fine golden tint when seen through. Pliny, plainly copying from older authorities, tells us it came from near Babylon. It therefore bears a Persian name, zard, yellow.

Mr. King would refer the name hyacinthus ($\dot{v}\acute{a}\kappa\iota\nu\theta o\varsigma$) to the jacut of the Persian, whereof our jacinth is as it were an intermediate form; and thus the myth of the flower that sprang from the blood of Ajax, or, as in another form of the story, of Hyacinthus, is as unsubstantial as the letters AI, AI or Υ pretended to be found upon the flower itself.

The amethyst, again, was a name which in its Greek form ($\tau\grave{o}$ $\dot{a}\mu\acute{e}\theta\upsilon\sigma\tau o\nu$) was capable of translation into the meaning of its being an antidote to the intoxicating influence of wine. Hence a Greek story repeated by Pliny that the wine drank from the amethyst cup was harmless, so far true that such cups must certainly have been very small. But as a gem also it was fondly looked on as an antidote, when worn on the finger, to wine drank from less precious and less moderate cups. Mr. King quotes a pretty stanza from the Anthology on the

signet of Cleopatra—which he has also turned in rhyme—
to show how far the gem fulfilled this promise—

> 'On wineless gem I toper Bacchus reign ;
> Learn stone to drink, or teach me to abstain.'

The emerald, a term at first applied to the beryls or aqua-
marines of India, though afterwards given to other green
stones, came to Europe under its Indian (Sanscrit) name
'marakat,' connected with esmarak, a sea monster, or makara,
the sea. Transferred to Persian and Arabic it became 'zabarjad,'
and in the Greek and Latin smaragdos or zmaragdos, the Greek
recognising probably a Greek root to the word in μαρμαρυγὴ,
a flashing, from μαρμαίρω, to sparkle. In the Hebrew the
term was Baraket. It is observable that maritime subjects, or
any with allusion to water-gods, continually appear in antique
gems engraved on the aquamarine. The root of the name
beryl (ἡ βήρυλλος) is unknown and appears not to have been
the subject of conjecture. The Bdellium of Holy Writ, or
Pedolach, may possibly afford a clue to its source. It is derived
from the Semitic ' badal,' to flow out in drops like a gum, and
was very probably the ancient name for the gum copal found
on the Zanzibar coast, or in other parts of the country gathered
from the living trees. It came apparently to be applied also
to the pearl, perhaps from its drop-like form. Indeed, not
impossibly our word pearl is the same term in another shape.
Its transfer to the stone we know as the beryl would be
one of those shiftings of the applications of words which it is
easier to illustrate by examples than to explain. Mr. King
has drawn attention to a curious etymology of the German
word ' Brille ' (a pair of spectacles), founded on the use of the
beryl as an eyeglass; probably by employing the pieces, often
rather curved in form, that are broken off by the regular clea-
vage from the long prismatic crystals of beryl. The topaz is a
name of which the root may possibly be found in the Sanscrit
term for yellow, ' pita.' This, transferred to the Greek through
a Semitic form, ' patadz,' by transposition of the letters becoming tapadz or topaz, might have been the source of the modern
form of the word.

Such are a few of the more prominent names which suggest
themselves as illustrating this curious philological chapter of
our subject. But it is a chapter capable of being made of
singular interest by a master of the science of language ; for
it would show the intercourse of the East and the West as
evidenced by language, at a time long anterior to all historical
records. Nay, inasmuch as the Oriental words and names that

form the nucleus of Hellenic myths must have preceded the mythology that crystallised round them, we may assume that these relations of archaic intercourse must have existed in times long antecedent to those even of mythic tradition.

We have still to discuss the important section of our subject which deals in the nature and properties of the actual stones that are now and have been in former times accounted precious; but in entering on it we find our path no longer single and straight. It divides at once into two diverging lines, the one leading along the rigid road of modern science, the other into the more obscure but curious tracks of archæology and virtù. One can describe the minerals used as precious stones and gems in the language of the modern mineralogist, or one can speak of them in the phraseology of the modern jeweller, and as they were treated by ancient writers, superficially and without regard to their scientific structure. But as our object is to make as clear as possible what were the stones viewed as precious and as such used by the ancients, and what the names they gave to them, in order on another occasion to go into the history of the art and into the varieties and styles of gem-engraving, we shall treat the subject of precious and quasi-precious stones the rather from this practical and archæological point of view. It will be necessary, however, to follow the stricter path of scientific nomenclature and description up to a certain point, in order that we may afterwards tread on firmer ground among the loose phraseology and inexact definitions of ancient writers and modern jewellers.

This will at once be seen when we observe that colour alone is the property in regard to which the precious stones have been universally classified down to the end of the last century, and still derive their names in the jewellers' shops. Thus, the ancient Egyptians in naming the precious stones they used in their ornaments and inlaid work, called the red jasper and other red stones *khnem* (red, the *red* stone), while the green jasper and the emerald seem to have fallen together under the title *uat* (the *green* stone). The lapis-lazuli, and probably the cyanus or blue glaze and paint of Egypt, were *kheshet* (the *blue* stone); the name of the yellow stone (so rare in Egyptian monuments) seems unknown; but the sard and carnelian had the name of *mat* (the middle or heart of a thing), implying that it occurred in the middle of the rocks in which it was found, as we know it to do in nodules in the heart of trap rocks. Pliny says the sards were found near Babylon enclosed 'like a heart' in other stones when these were broken open, but had failed in his time.

This nomenclature of Egyptian writers accords with the mineralogical systems of later days. The precious stones that Pliny describes are grouped in series of which colour is the distinctive feature; and that the names now employed by the jewellers are very little in advance of this is shown by the ruby, the sapphire, and the Oriental topaz of modern Europe being treated as distinct minerals in their nomenclature, whereas they are one and the same substance differing merely in the accident of colour. So the topaz, the Oriental topaz, the Bohemian or Spanish topaz, are the names given to minerals that have not one mineralogical character in common, except their attribute of a more or less intense yellow or orange hue.

But here we must indicate how it is that modern mineralogy comes to attach so little comparative importance to this attribute of colour. It was not till chemistry, little more than a century ago, had decomposed, and begun to explain the true nature and composition of all the materials of the inorganic and organic worlds, that the mystery was dissipated which had surrounded precious stones from the earliest time, had raised them into talismans, and endowed them with qualities that money could scarcely buy. For when the diamond, the ruby, and the opal severally became in the chemist's eyes simply carbon, alumina, and silica, differing in no respect but in their being crystallised and pure from charcoal, clay, and flint, the mystery of their nature was dissipated and there was no more a dark and magic place in them for the abode of genii. The colours of precious stones were soon found to be in the majority of cases due to minute traces of substances generally foreign to the composition of the mineral, but dissolved as it were in its substance, such as oxides of iron, chrome, or manganese. Thus sapphire and ruby and many other so-called ' oriental ' stones became one and the same mineral, only differently tinged by these colour-giving accidental ingredients. Science, carrying on her inquiries, soon brought all the other physical properties of minerals, and therefore of precious stones, within her domain. Crystallography showed every crystallised substance to have its own peculiar forms, obedient to simple mathematical laws; while optical characters belonging to the crystal structure have also been discovered, so that through the instrumentality of polarised light, the eye of science can discern at a glance the crystal structure and therefore the character of a transparent mineral, even though it be but in a minute fragment. It is thus that the mineralogical characters of a stone need a higher science than the mere eye-knowledge of the dealer in gems, who is almost always grossly ignorant of their real nature, and only knows

enough to enable him to give them names and to convince a
purchaser that the long experience of a trained eye is an infal-
lible authority in fixing on them a jeweller's price.

The actual mineral species employed for personal ornaments
are extremely few, and those on which fashion throws its capricious smile are fewer still.   The more valuable kinds, the really
' precious stones,' are the diamond, the sapphire, the spinel,
the beryl, and the turquoise.   The opal is a variety of the
same chemical substance as quartz-crystal.   But the chrysoberyl and the zircon should be included with the more precious
stones, though out of fashion with the jewellers.   The garnet,
the chrysolite, the tourmaline, dichroite, and different varieties
of quartz, including amethyst, cairngorm stone, and a long
and beautiful array of jaspers and chalcedonies, such as agate,
onyx, sard, plasma, and chrysoprase, may be placed in a list
of stones of the second degree in point of value, if that value
be estimated by rarity and price, and therefore inversely to
the magnitude of the largest specimens.   We propose to take
a rapid survey, in the first place, of these different mineral species, including their coloured varieties, in a scientific order.
We can then discuss them severally in the order of colours,
in conjunction with Pliny's accounts of the stones used in his
day.   It will be only necessary, however, to treat thus separately those mineral species which are distinguished by a somewhat varied colour-suite, and the varieties of which are known
by names more or less equivocal.

The mineral substance that ranks next to the diamond,
whether we estimate it by its hardness, the splendour of its colour
or its rareness in the choicer forms, is that called by the mineralogist corundum.   It is pure crystallised alumina (the oxide of
the now well-known metal aluminium).   To this class belong
the ruby, the sapphire, and other stones of gorgeous colour,
distinguished by the epithet ' oriental' prefixed to the name.
The ruby or red sapphire is the red stone *par excellence* of
jewellery.   Its finest colour is a most rich and lovely crimson,
known as the ' pigeon's blood ' tint, but its scarlet tints are
also beautiful.   It is never a large stone ; for whereas the
sapphire occurs in very considerable masses, a ruby above the
size of three carats is worth more than a diamond of the same
weight.   The yellow variety of corundum is called the 'oriental
' topaz.'   It is of a pale straw-yellow, very rarely exhibiting
the rich orange tint of the true topaz from Brazil, but rather
those of the kinds of that stone from other localities which
rarely if ever possess the colour requisite for an ornamental
jewel.   The oriental emerald is similarly the green variety of

this species, but, like the last stone, it lacks the rich hues of the splendid mineral after which it is named—the true emerald. It is lustrous, but almost universally of an extremely pale hue. There is another green variety called the oriental peridot. This is a pistachio green sapphire, singular rather than beautiful. The oriental aquamarine is a greenish blue sapphire. The blue variety of this mineral is that lovely gem to which the name of sapphire is in common parlance confined. There is one hue of it of a soft pure azure, distinguishable from the commoner kinds by its retaining its fine blue even by candle-light, when an ordinary sapphire looks black. Unlike the ruby, the sapphire occurs in specimens of considerable size. One large and beautiful cut stone was to be seen in the Exhibition of 1862, of which it was related that the noble lady who once had owned it had contented herself with an exact imitation of it for many years, consoled with the sum for which she had sold the original. A splendid suite of sapphires exhibited in the Great Exhibition of 1851, and said now to belong to Miss Burdett Coutts, is among the finest, perhaps as a suite is the finest, in the world.

The 'oriental amethyst' is an amethystine variety often formed by a mixture of ruby and sapphire in the same crystal, part of the stone being one and part the other, the united effect being that of the amethyst. Often, however, the hue is homogeneous. The 'girasol sapphire,' or 'ruby catseye,' is formed from the more opaque kind of stones, which when cut in the boss (or *en cabochon*) form, show a glimmering light in the surface which is rather brighter in its blue, its pink, or its amethyst colour, than is the body of the pale sapphire, ruby, or oriental amethyst, of which it consists. The star-stone, or asteria-sapphire, or ruby, is a similar stone to the last, but exhibiting a six-rayed star corresponding in the direction of the rays with the direction of those planes along which the crystal may be 'cleaved' or easily split (a property of all these crystals). The transparent colourless corundum remains only to be described; it generally has a faint blue tint, but is at times perfectly colourless. It is said to have been sold for the diamond; but this could only have been done fraudulently, as the sapphire never could have been mistaken for the diamond by an eye in the least degree experienced in stones, as its refractive power is less than three-fourths that of the diamond; and is indeed very little, in fact only about one-seventh, higher than that of quartz.

The next species to be described is that comprised in a well-marked mineralogical group termed the spinels. It is, however, only with the transparent and more precious forms of this mineral that we have to do. The name is traced to the Greek σπίνος, connected in its root with σπινθὴρ, a spark. Precious varieties consist essentially of alumina combined with magnesia, and tinted perhaps with iron. Their colour is more limited than in the case of the corundum varieties, but it includes two resplendent stones; namely, the spinel ruby, a scarlet variety of considerable fire and of rich colour; and the balais, or balast ruby, called from one of the most celebrated localities of the spinel in former times, namely Beloochistan or Balastan. The latter is of a delicate and rarely deep rose colour, showing a blue tint when looked through and a redder one when it is looked at. Both of these minerals are termed rubies by the jewellers, and the deeper tinted kinds are sometimes sold for the true ruby. Nearly all the large · and famous stones that pass under the name of rubies belong to this species; such is the ancient ruby in the crown of England, which was presented to Edward the Black Prince by Don Pedro the Cruel, and such the enormous stone, time-honoured in Indian tradition, that accompanied the Koh-i-nur into the possession of Her who is now the Sovereign of India. An orange red variety of the spinel is known by the name of the rubicelle. There are also varieties, the one of a pale Berlin blue and the other of a 'duck blue' containing much green, which are rare and curious rather than beautiful forms of the spinel. It also sometimes occurs with a tint containing more blue than the balais ruby, and approaching the almandine garnet in hue though generally paler; a variety which has received the name of the almandine ruby.

The next mineral to be described is the chrysoberyl, called also by the jewellers the 'oriental chrysolite.' Pliny's stone of this name (chrysoberyllos) is a yellowish beryl. That known to modern mineralogy, when in its greatest beauty, is a stone of almost adamantine lustre and transparence. Indeed, it is more like the diamond in these respects than are the varieties of the sapphire. It is a compound of alumina and the rare oxide glucina, a constituent of the beryl. This stone has usually a peculiar, sometimes a very delicate, greenish yellow or primrose colour: it is then one of the most beautiful of jewels; a lovely specimen, for which Mr. Hertz is said to have received 300 guineas from Mr. Hope, is among the recent acquisitions of the Mineral Department of the British Museum. It occurs also of a yellowish brown hue. In hardness it is very nearly the rival of the sapphire. A green variety from Siberia, called Alexandrite, is of a dull green mixed with a reddish amethyst colour, which latter hue is the only one it exhibits by candle-light. The finer specimens of the transparent and deli-cately-tinted chrysoberyl are from Brazil; the ancients might however have obtained it in its less beautiful varieties from Ceylon. The term cymophane is given by the French to the mineral species of the chrysoberyl, and refers to an appear-ance as of a floating cloud, which is generally, but not always, seen in even the most transparent crystals of chrysoberyl, more particularly in the direction of one plane of the crystal. It is a curious thing thus to see a mist, as it were, lying in a stone which in every other way of looking at it is as limpid as a dew-drop. The more chatoyant kinds forming ' the chryso-' beryl catseye ' are in general only translucent.

The emerald and the beryl are one and the same mineral—a silicate of alumina and glucina, which owes to a small trace of iron its green, blue, pink, or yellow tints, or else to a little chromium the transcendent green which characterises it as the emerald. This beautiful gem is now chiefly obtained from Santa Fé de Bogotà, in New Grenada, a spot which has sup-plied the whole world with emeralds since the conquest of the country by the Spaniards. Siberia furnishes a few stones to our jewellers, and probably the mines in the neighbourhood of Catharinenburg need only enterprise and capital to produce magnificent specimens. Inferior emeralds are obtained in the neighbourhood of Saltzburg, in a mica schist just like that in which they are found in Siberia; and, it may be added also, not to be distinguished from the parent rock in an ancient Egyptian locality, Mount Zabara, worked in the time of the Ptolemies, from which Sir G. Wilkinson obtained several emeralds of pale and poor quality, which are now in the British Museum. The New Grenada emeralds are found in a calcareous rock often charged with bitumeniferous matter. Pegu is also a reputed locality of the emerald.

The beryl, known in jewellery as the aquamarine, is also found in great perfection at Oduntschilon, and Mursinsk, in Siberia. It exhibits every gradation of tint from a pale azure blue to a fine ' mountain green;' a celandine green, or yellow green, are its more usual colours, but these are quite distinct from the pure ' emerald green ' of the true emerald. There is also a pale and pretty orange yellow variety, and many inter-mediate tints again intervene between this yellow and the green. Among other localities of the beryl, one in India, Cangayum in the Deccan, was formerly in much repute. Brazil also has been a rich source of the beryl, and even the Emerald Isle itself might have won its name from the beryls which it has produced from more than one locality; the little blue crystals from the Mourne Mountains vying in colour with those from Siberia.

The zircon, the name of which is derived from 'zerk,' the Arabic word for 'a gem,' is a mineral with a somewhat varied colour-suite. It consists of the mixed oxides of silicon and of the rare element zirconium (silicic and zirconic acids), and is one of the heaviest and most lustrous of gemstones. Sometimes of an unpleasing brownish green colour, termed the jargoon, and very rarely of a deep greenish blue, its colourless variety is the nearest match in brilliancy and refractive energy for the diamond; while the deep orange-tinted red zircon is that transcendent gem the true hyacinth. It is a very heavy stone, and its refractive index is far above that of the sapphire, being about five-sixths that of the diamond; hence its near rivalry of that stone and its always fine lustre.

The tourmaline is a singularly interesting mineral. Its name appears to be in its original form a Cingalese word, 'turamali.' It is a very complex silicate, containing oxide of boron, and often also lithia. Its optical characters are valuable, in consequence of its property of absorbing one of the polarised rays of light, into which it divides every ray that enters the side of its prism-shaped crystal. A slice of that crystal cut parallel to its side becomes in consequence a most useful instrument in the hands of the optical experimentalist. Its colour-suite is very extensive. The finest colour is that of the ruby red variety termed rubellite, or siberite, found in Siberia. Among the varieties of other colours are brown, black, claret, and brownish yellow tints, most of them showing one colour when looked through along the prism and another when seen across it. The green variety called Brazilian emerald is often used as a precious stone: the Catholic bishops of South America use it instead of the amethyst, the episcopal signet-stone of Europe. There is also an indigo blue kind called indicolite; but, like all the rest of the tourmalines excepting the rubellite, it is of a dull and unpleasing hue. Ceylon furnishes brown and yellow varieties, and the latter are the only kinds of tourmaline likely to have penetrated into the Greek or Roman bazaars.

The topaz consists of a fluosilicate mixed with silicate of aluminium. Its Brazilian kind, of a rich orange yellow, when cut forms a very handsome stone. A pale blue kind from Siberia is also a pretty variety, and its colourless crystals, called the *goutte d'eau*, are sometimes mistaken for the diamond by unskilled eyes. The other varieties of the topaz are the pale pink kind, generally produced by heating gently the orange variety, but sometimes also found in nature; the other is the ordinary straw-coloured topaz, a stone with little claim to beauty. Magnificent crystals, forming the finest suite in the world, of a fine sherry-colour, from Siberia, exist in the British Museum; but the light is known to bleach them completely, and they are consequently kept in the dark.

The chrysolite is a pale yellow mineral of which the peridot is a fine pistachio or olive-green variety, composed of a silicate of magnesia; soft for a precious stone, being just under quartz in hardness. Large specimens of the peridot have come from Constantinople, but the rocky home of this mineral is as unknown now as is that of the topazius, the mineral on Pliny's list which it represents. Minute specimens of the yellow kind, called olivine or chrysolite, occur in lavas and basalts, and in some of the masses of meteoric iron that have fallen to the earth from space.

The garnets, like the spinels, form a well-defined mineralogical group, though their composition is more complex. Their more transparent varieties contain similar constituents with the spinels, with, however, the addition of a little iron (chiefly as protoxide) and silica as silicic acid. The precious garnet is thus essentially a silicate of aluminium, magnesium, and iron. The garnets are well-known stones, and can hardly be classed with those we have discussed, if price is to be our guide. They are, however, among the most magnificent of the coloured products of nature's laboratory. The carbuncle is their name in jewellery when cut *en cabochon*, that is to say, of a boss form, usually hollowed out underneath to allow the colour of the stone to be seen. The name garnet is supposed to be derived from granaticus, a pomegranate (from the red colour of the seeds and juice), or else from the term garamanticus, one of its Roman appellations.

The pyrope and Bohemian garnet are names for varieties of a deep blood-red and of fiery character; the almandine (probably a corruption of Pliny's alabandine, though Mr. King thinks it is derived from the almond flower as recalling the pink hue of that blossom) or Syriam garnet (so named from the old capital of Pegu, Syriam), are names given to the kinds which owe to admixtures of blue their very pretty carmine tints. The guarnacino is the Italian name for a brownish red garnet of the colour of tawny port wine, while the hyacinthine garnet and essonite (or cinnamon-stone) are characterised by different tones of orange and yellow mingled with the reds of the other varieties. The finest of these is that with a hyacinthine hue, often called by the jewellers ' hyacinthe la belle,' and still oftener confounded by them with the true hyacinth.

The diamond, it is almost unnecessary to say, consists of crystallised carbon: soft plumbago or pure charcoal are different forms of the same protean element which in the diamond becomes the hardest substance known. The beauty of this gem is due to its very extraordinary reflecting power or lustre, and to its quality of diverting a ray of light from its course to a far greater extent than any other gem. The result is an extraordinary brilliancy in the diamond; but this is independent, to a great degree, of the property of flashing out the colour of the rainbow, which a piece of the heavy glass used to counterfeit the diamond possesses to at least as effective a degree. Our modern supplies of the diamond are drawn almost entirely from Brazil. Borneo sends a few, but India, that supplied the world down to a century ago, no longer furnishes them, or only in very small numbers. The colour-suite of the diamond is rather an extensive one. Brown and a pale brownish-yellow are common colours, a pale pink champagne colour, a fine canary yellow, and a very pale aquamarine or bluish green colour, are also not rarely met with. At Dresden there is a diamond weighing 40 carats of a very fine green colour; and in the collection of the late Mr. Hope was one of $40\frac{1}{4}$ carats of a decided (but rather steel-like) blue. In that same collection were formerly to be found an apricot-coloured diamond of $12\frac{1}{2}$ carats, one of a fine hyacinth red, others with the colours of the Brazilian topaz, the blood-red garnet, the green tourmaline, and one of a lilac colour.

Mr. King has dug out of old books some curious diamond lore. He has found an old engraving of the famous diamond of Charles the Bold, one of the first cut in Europe, by Louis Berquem, and he explodes a story that hitherto confounded it with the Sancy Diamond. He also adds a very curious bit of information which confirms the identification of the Koh-i-nur with the great diamond of Indian tradition, which Tavernier seems to have mistaken for a great diamond which was cut and spoilt at Delhi about 1665. De Boot in 1609 quotes from Monades to the effect that the largest diamond he knew was an Indian one with the weight of $187\frac{1}{2}$ carats. The one Tavernier saw at the Court of Aurungzebe weighed $119\frac{1}{4}$ ratis, which would be about 186 modern English carats, while the Koh-i-nur in 1861 weighed $186\frac{1}{4}$ English carats, corresponding to $187\frac{1}{16}$ Indian carats, a very near approximation to the $187\frac{1}{2}$ of Monades. The great Indian talisman has now been reduced to $102\frac{3}{16}$ carats—to suit the regulation pattern of the modern diamond-cutters, now called ' the brilliant,' a form invented in order to make the most of the lustre with the smallest diminution in weight of octahedral or dodecahedral crystals of diamond. But the art of cutting diamonds is all but extinct in England, and the modern cutters of Amsterdam, and even of Paris, are not what their predecessors were. Their art is one of routine, and they are quite unable to deal with the difficult problem of how to cut a stone so as to preserve its bulk and to develop its splendour, each in the highest degree ; a problem, indeed, which may be said to have never been thoroughly grappled with. Thus the Koh-i-nur had to be reduced to a shape which is only a brilliant in name, for it is far too thin for the true brilliant of the days of Jeffries or of Ralph Potter, the first diamond-cutter Europe has produced, who lived at the beginning of this century. Many a stone is now called Indian, and supposed to be superior to any of the diamonds of Brazil, merely because it was cut when diamond-cutting was more of an art and less of a mechanical process than it is now. No loss in weight, however, can take from the Koh-i-nur its unique prestige. It presents to the eye a much larger surface than before it was cut, and if it lacks the fire and iridescence of smaller diamonds, this is mainly due to its greater size ; for as a stone rises in weight and size above twenty carats it loses proportionally in effect. ·So large a stone as the Koh-i·nur could never be endowed with the splendour of a smaller diamond. Had its old Indian cut and rounded facettes been repolished, it would not have been less beautiful than now. It is now the fifth of the great diamonds of Europe. Before, it was second only in size to the Russian diamond, while it ranked in quality with any diamond among the crown jewels of Europe.

We may now turn to the pages of Theophrastus and Pliny, and inquire how far this and the other stones we have thus far described were known in antiquity, and by what names they were designated. As regards the diamond, the classical scholar will find no difficulty in recalling passages in ancient authors that prove the term adamas to have been used at first in allusion to some very hard metal, sometimes apparently for steel itself, that rarest of substances in early times ; while subsequently it came to be applied, as by Theophrastus, to some precious stone of great hardness. In the age of Augustus the term had come to be technically used for a small precious stone, the *adamas, punctum lapidis, pretiosior auro* of Manilius (iv. 926).

Rings exist of Roman workmanship in which the diamond is set in its original octahedral form unpolished save with its natural somewhat resinous lustre, and there can be little doubt that several of the six varieties enumerated by Pliny under the name, were the true diamonds. Whether the variety first described by Pliny as his Indian adamas was that from Golconda, or whether it was the small sapphire crystal of the Carnatic, remains an unsettled question. He apparently confounded an ' Indian ' adamas, consisting probably, as we have seen, of the colourless and pale sapphire described by some old Greek author when diamonds were scarcely or not at all known, with the true diamond, which in Pliny's time must certainly have come by the direct route from India. So, on the other hand, his ' Arabian ' adamas would probably have been the true Indian stone that found its way into commerce through some other than the ordinary channel. As regards the other varieties of Pliny's adamas, his Æthiopian kind, not larger than a cucumber-seed, was probably also a true diamond, and the description in respect to form, size, and colour correctly represents some sorts of the stone. Possibly it found its way into commerce by the coasting trade up the African coast, having first reached the shores of Zanzibar in that direct trade with India which dared to cross the open sea under the steady breath of the monsoons; or, and this is the more probable conjecture, this name originated in that confusion between Æthiopia and India that even led Alexander to expect he might reach the sources of the Nile in his Indian expedition.

The cenchrea, of the size of a millet-seed, again a characteristic description, Pliny introduces only as a form of the Arabian adamas; while the ' Macedonian ' and ' Cyprian ' varieties are probably taken by the Latin encyclopædist from the same Greek treatise that suggested the first divisions of his Indian adamas, recording the knowledge of a time when that name was applied to the pale little crystals, and perhaps to rolled pebbles of sapphire, supplied partly by India and partly by Grecian localities. His heavy siderites was most likely magnetite, the heaviest and hardest ore of that steel to which, doubtless, the title of adamas was originally vaguely applied. This mineral crystallises in octahedral and dodecahedral forms like those of the diamond. To it Pliny applies this identical name in his description of the magnet in his 36th Book; but *nominis tantum auctoritatem habent,* says Pliny of these kinds of diamond, with good reason.

The agates and jaspers we have not treated among the mineralogical accounts of coloured minerals. They belong to a peculiar chapter of mineralogy, and seem to be more advantageously discussed by themselves.

To gø into the mineralogy of silica, including all the varieties of quartz, chalcedony and opal, would need a more extended field. We may, however, group these innumerable varieties into four divisions, characterised by the one common characteristic that they are silex, or silica (oxide of silicon) in various degrees of purity.

First we have quartz crystal, or crystallised silica, of which the ordinary colourless kind, the amethyst or lilac kind, the 'smoky' quartz and cairngorm stone, as well as the Brazilian kinds with their yellow and orange hues, are the more important varieties. Of these the pale yellow is termed citrine quartz, the more orange 'Bohemian' and 'Spanish 'topaz.' Then we have opal, which is silica in a peculiar physical and chemical condition, not crystalline, perhaps incapable of crystallisation, generally combined with water, and presenting itself with various colours but with a uniform wax-like or resinous appearance. One of its varieties is that most lovely gem the 'noble' or 'precious opal,' in which minute fissures apparently striated with microscopic lines, due it may be to laminæ formed by an incipient crystallisation of quartz, flash out colours of the purest and most brilliant hues. The colour is not due to any colouring matter, but is a consequence of the diffraction of the light produced by these fine lines. The commoner varieties of opal are of various tints of yellow and of brown, and are marked by the characteristic common to all the minerals of the opal kind, a waxy texture and resinous lustre. The fire opal of Mexico is a rich hyacinth red variety of the same stone.

Next to the opal may be put the chalcedonic sorts of silica. Pure chalcedony is a most intimate mixture of silica in the two states of quartz and opal and in variable proportions. It is colourless or of a very pale horn colour; but tinted with small quantities of iron or of other substances, it forms a brilliant and endless variety of sards, agates, and carnelians, plasmas, &c. Mixed with other minerals in a state of mechanical admixture, it forms the equally long catalogue of jaspers; the former we may call the agate chalcedonies, the latter the jasper varieties of chalcedony. We must distinguish certain of each of these groups. Of the agate kind we have the sard, a variety richer probably in quartz than is the more earthy, softer, and more impure, perhaps more opaline carnelian. The sard is translucent, often almost transparent, and presents various red and orange hues. Some are black in aspect but blood red by transmitted light; they represent the various kinds of 'Morio' or mulberry stone of Pliny, and are also in-

cluded in his sardius: they are the sardoine of the French.
Others are red or brown in aspect, but a soft beautiful pale
yellow when looked through. These are the stones on which
the finest remains of ancient art are usually enshrined. The
finest in ancient as in modern times came from India, but the
ancients probably had other sources for the beautiful stones on
which some of the earliest Greek works are engraved.

The prase is the name given by the mineralogist to a dull
but hard green impure translucent quartz, a different kind
from the often beautiful mineral termed prase by the gem collectors, which is the plasma (an Italian corruption of the word
prase or prasina) or green chalcedony of mineralogy. The latter, in its many varieties of colour and translucency, is the
stone so valued by the Romans of Pliny's day, to be recognised probably under several of his names for varieties of
smaragdus, jaspis and prasius. It is found in India and at
Olympus in Asia Minor. The chrysoprase is a kind tinged
with oxide of nickel, of an apple-green. The Silesian locality
of this stone is a modern discovery; but there are gems apparently antique engraved on a stone that cannot be distinguished from chrysoprase.

Agates are mixtures in curious forms of various varieties of
chalcedony. The hardest and finest coloured are those of
India and Uruguay. Softer agates are found in Germany and in
other localities. All these stones have usually been formed by
infiltration of siliceous waters into cavities in trap rocks, and
the layers in the agate mark the successive and often concentric
walls of the cavity as from time to time new deposits were
formed in its interior. When these are cut parallel to the
red, white, or brown layers of successive deposit, and there
are *more than two* of these layers, the stone is called the
sardonyx; when there are *only two* layers it is, in modern
phraseology, the onyx; when one is dark and covered by a
thin white layer, generally ground by the artist till the
under layer is seen through, so as to give this upper white film
a bluish tinge, it is the nicolo (onyculo or choice little onyx),
a favourite stone of the gem-engravers of the Lower Empire.
When the stone is so cut that the layers run across the face of
it—usually dark sard and white layers are those which are
chosen thus to alternate—it becomes the so-called 'tricoloured'
or 'banded agate,' a very favourite stone of the Italo-Greek
engravers. The jasper onyx and jasper agate are varieties in
which one or more of the layers of the agate are formed of a
coloured jasper.

The jaspers, or chalcedonies mechanically mixed with other

minerals, are always opaque, except where they are on the border line that separates them from the agate varieties, when some of them are translucent. The green jasper used in antiquity for the earliest Assyrian cylinders as for the latest Gnostic amulets, is a mixture of the green mineral chlorite with chalcedony. Spotted with red spots it is bloodstone. Heliotrope is a translucent kind of plasma often similarly spotted. There is a fine homogeneous red jasper of a vermilion colour that is found in a breccia in India and also in Egypt, and often used for Roman gems in the later times of the Empire. Besides these there are a pea-green kind, much used for inlaid work in ancient Egypt and occasionally for cylinders in Mesopotamia, a brown jasper, one of a fine yellow tint, and a host of other mottled and otherwise variegated and coloured kinds; but those just enumerated are the most common among the jasper gem-stones of antiquity.

Of all these siliceous minerals we may with some certainty assert the crystallus of the Romans and of Greece to have been quartz crystal. The amethyst also retains the name it bears direct from the Greek tongue, and it is hard to believe that the opalus of Pliny is not the mineral known to us as the precious opal. Although we do not know of any Indian locality for this lovely stone, and Pliny, who describes the precious opal with the vivid language of one who had admired it, mentions India as the locality for the specimens of the finest quality known in his time. The precious opal is so rare a stone that with all our mining enterprise and geological re-search over the far vaster world of modern geography, we know of only two certain localities for it, namely, in Hungary and in Mexico. But the quartz in the trap rocks of the Ghauts above Bombay sometimes shows an iridescence on certain of its crystal planes that seems to be due to. the presence of this kind of opal. It is not impossible therefore that formerly an Indian locality was really known for this stone.

The determination of the names given in antiquity to the varieties of onyx, sardonyx, and agate has called forth a little literature, headed by Köhler; and Mr. King has grappled with the subject with some success, though the exposition of his views is not very lucidly expressed. The onyx of Theo-phrastus was the tricoloured agate; though we believe those with very wavy angular or ribboned strata rarely, if ever, to have been used by the Greeks. Pliny nowhere defines the onyx of his time, though he gives half a dozen of the discordant descriptions of other authors, some of which would point to the onyx as consisting of parallel horizontal layers, like the onyx of our day; others, however, describe a more irregularly marked stone, and the use of the term onychines, as applied to vases and vessels made of such a material, seems to preclude the idea of its being formed of a stone in regular layers. It would appear, in short, and this Mr. King seems to mean, that in one sense the 'onyx' of the Romans was used for a stone lying in regular layers—our nicolo being one variety of it, and an opaque black and white layered stone being another, namely, the Arabian variety—but that in another sense or at another period the word was used for the irregularly marked and eyed agates, an example of which Mr. King recognises in the large tiger's head in the British Museum, from the Townley Collection.

Mr. King is happy in his account of the Vasa Murrhina so far as it goes, but he has not brought out the best point in his explanation of their character. They were like onyx but were not onyx. They came with onyx from the Nerbudda, as related by the author of the Periplus. They were, moreover, 'baked in ovens.' To this day, in the neighbourhood of Broach, nodules of onyx are dug in the dry season from the beds of torrents; they are then of a dark olive green inclining to grey; after being exposed to the sun to dry, they are packed in earthen pots with dry goat's dung, which is set on fire. When removed, after cooling, the stones have changed in colour, often to rich hues of orange and hyacinthine red; and the more ornamental of the mottled onyxes that come from Cambay are those thus artificially beautified. These facts have escaped Mr. King, but in them perhaps we may see the true source of the *Parthis Murrhina cocta focis.* The onyxes of their natural colour are probably the onychines which classical authors contrast, and certainly do not confound as Mr. King seems to do, with these Murrhina.

We may observe that no stones are so porous or so easily coloured by artificial means as the varieties of chalcedony. Sards and onyxes are now imported from Uruguay quite as hard and beautiful as the naturally coloured ones from India, and the jewellers must be reaping a rich harvest from the enormous prices they are in our time charging for ornaments made from this beautiful stone. Many of the opaque varieties of chalcedony, those, namely, which we know as jaspers, are referred by Mr. King to the different sorts of Pliny's achates (the word from which our term agate comes). Some of these belong, however, to the green stones enumerated under other heads by Pliny. The beautiful 'sapphirine,' and, in one or two instances, 'amethystine' chalcedonies, so called from their tints, stones that were very rife among the later Assyrian and Persian cylinders and seals, are included under several of the heads of Pliny's iaspis; indeed, he states them to have been the most valued sorts of jasper, and accordingly of them, as of the prase of modern amateurs (or plasma of modern mineralogy), he makes several varieties.

It might seem very easy for a mineralogist, while making an analysis of Theophrastus and Pliny, to write opposite to each of the several stones they describe a modern name, and so to find a place in their nomenclature for each of the red stones enumerated. It is certainly an easier task in this case than in that of the green stones, but even here we cannot speak with entire certainty. Thus, we cannot say whether Theophrastus knew either the true ruby, or even the spinels. The former is improbable; if he knew the spinel and the balais rubies he certainly confounded them with the garnet, which, in its different varieties, was essentially the ἄνθραξ of Greece, as it was the carbunculus of Pliny. The signification of the two words was the same, the latter being the diminutive of carbo, which, like anthrax, means a live coal. That Roman artists sometimes engraved on the ruby seems tolerably certain. We are not unfamiliar with their works on almandine garnets, but no certain Greek or early Græco-Roman work is recorded on the blood-red garnet. Mr. King adduces a very dubious instance of it, that of the famed Sirius head in the Marlborough Collection; a gem cut into the stone to an extraordinary depth, so that one sees down the very throat of the dog. It is cut with astonishing ability in a transcendent pyrope; but it is without a history. It was described by Natter in 1754, a period suspicious on account of its forgeries in gems, when such a gem could certainly have been cut, and when Natter confesses to having at least copied it. His splendid copy on topaz is in the Hermitage.

Pliny associates with his carbunculus a stone called by a Greek name, lychnis, implying a lit lamp, the anthracites which he takes from Theophrastus, and the sandaresus. The sandaresus is doubtless the stone termed avanturine, a red translucent quartzose stone with little fissures in it, which produce a sort of scintillation. The name is usually derived from the accident which 'peradventure' happened to a Venetian glassblower who upset a pot of glass coloured by copper, and so chanced to form the far more beautiful avanturine glass. This name is more probably, however, of older origin. In the Targum of the pseudo-Jonathan-ben-Uzziel, referred by Mr. Deutsch to the middle of the seventh century, a stone, translated jasper in our version, is called the margniath apanturin, or panther-gem. The step from *apanturin* to *avanturine* is a short one. It is remarkable that Pliny describes a green stone 'like panther eyes.' A green variety, the spangling of which is inferior and only seen in one direction of the stone, is found in large masses in India. It corresponds with the green sandaresus, or sandastros, which Pliny says was from India, of an apple or olive green, and of no value. Mr. King seems to assign another attribution to these names of Pliny's; but for once the mineralogy of Pliny is not at fault. Indeed, the Roman writer also mentions a variety which would not take a polish, and this is no doubt a micaceous schistose stone, of which specimens occur frequently in modern collections very like avanturine, but too soft for use.

The best varieties of Pliny's carbuncles came from India, Carthage, Æthiopia, and Caria, and there were seven other localities for inferior kinds, five of which are taken from the descriptions of the anthrakion of Theophrastus. He says the amethystizontes, the carbuncles tending to an amethyst or violet colour, were the best. These undoubtedly are the almandine garnets, of which we find many carrying good engraved work of the early imperial age. His 'alabandini' were from Orthosia in Caria, and were prepared in the wealthy city of Alabandæ; they were no doubt the 'polygonal and hexagonal' (probably the ordinary rhombic dodecahedron which has the form of a hexagonal prism) kinds of anthrax which Theophrastus called Miletian, from their locality Miletus, in Caria.

Finally, we have to deal with Pliny's lychnis. It was of two kinds; the Indian was the best, the Ionian the next best kind. This latter sort was of two varieties; one with a crimson (purpura), the other with a scarlet (cocco), colour. Pliny derives the name from the ion, a plant which Mr. King calls the pink cyclamen. Pliny also speaks of the lychnis as sometimes called a more languid or paler (*remissior*) carbuncle. This and the divisions into which he groups it would seem to indicate that here we have the true ruby in the Indian lychnis as distinct from the spinels (the spinel, and balais ruby), which we exactly recognise in the Ionian lychnis. These last would probably be found in small specimens in various parts of Asia Minor.

We conclude, then, that Pliny's carbunculus was our garnet, that the favourite sort was our almandine kind; both names as terms for the garnet being in this case probably direct in their descent to our times; but that the Indian lychnis was the name for the ruby, the two sorts of Ionian lychnis comprising our two kinds of red spinel. The Carchedonian and Carian would be garnets often occurring, as coarse and veined garnets now do, of size sufficiently large to form snuffboxes and small vessels. Mr. King describes an antique cup as large as the half of a goose's egg, engraved with the name of its ancient owner, Codrus, and mentions two others possibly also antique. We would only add that the dark kind of Carthaginian garnet is described by Pliny as sometimes showing a star. This is true of some of the deep-coloured carbuncles that come now into the market, when they are cut in the right way to show it. On the other hand, the asteria, or star-stone variety of the ruby or sapphire, is almost invariably confined to the paler tints of those two stones.

The only yellow stones we believe that have come down to us from antiquity are pale citrines, or yellow quartz. Of cinnamon-stone and hyacinthine garnet, perhaps also of the true hyacinth, we have splendid examples among the finest gems of Græco-Roman artists. It is, of course, impossible to affirm that neither Greeks or Romans were acquainted with the more rare of the purely yellow stones of modern jewellery; but the absence in the collections of Europe of any one of these stones other than the citrine with indubitable ancient work on it, goes far to confirm the belief that, at all events, they must have been extremely rare and exceptional. Mr. King quotes a remark from Pliny that the Romans were not fond of the colour yellow, the hue of gold being not in estimation for gems or for other things. And yet the chrysolithus is coupled by Propertius with the emerald in the presents that won the heart of a certain fair Cynthia:—

'quoscunque smaragdos
Quosque dedit flavo lumine chrysolithos.'—II. 16.

What might the stone with this yellow light in it have been?

Pliny says ' Æthiopia sends the hyacinth (our sapphire), *and* ' *the chrysolite,* which has a splendid golden hue *when the light* ' *shines through it (aureo fulgore translucentes)*; the Indian, ' however, are the best.' The stone which this describes exactly, and the only stone that bears out Pliny's further statement, that by contrast it makes gold look like silver, is the hyacinthine garnet, or the transcendent stone of which it is the alter ego, the true hyacinth. It is possible that an Egyptian or Abyssinian locality may have been known in antiquity for the sapphire, the Essonite garnet, and the zircon, just as we now receive them all in the same bags from Ceylon; but the explanation before given of the confusion of Æthiopia in early times with India may well explain the locality here assigned by

Pliny, especially if he was copying from an older author; or the commerce in his own time between India, through Cane, on the Red Sea, with Port Avalites in Abyssinia, might explain it. Mr. King would include with orange yellow or deep honey-coloured stones, the pale Oriental topaz under the chrysolithi. But his ground for doing so is, that Pliny tells of the chryso-lite making gold look pale as silver, and that these were mounted clear without a foil behind them. It is the rarest thing even now to find a yellow sapphire, with its usually so pale a straw yellow, capable of looking other than a very pallid stone when set in gold.

One of the most difficult problems bequeathed to modern mineralogists by Pliny in his 37th book is certainly that of attributing to all the green stones he mentions their corre-sponding modern names. He gives a list of some twelve varieties of smaragdus, a name which would mislead were we to translate it emerald, though our word comes by direct descent from, and applies certainly to, the true and typical smaragdus. Then, with more than his usual mineralogical insight, he classifies the beryl as a kind of smaragdus, with eight varieties which he enumerates.

We will at once select from this formidable catalogue of stones the true emeralds and the beryls. He distinguishes between his first three varieties of emerald—the Scythian, Bactrian, and Egyptian, and the inferior sorts. These three were, in fact, the true emerald; the Scythian coming no doubt from the Siberian locality near Bissersk, to the east of Ekatha-rinenberg; the so-called Bactrian most likely came from a locality unknown to us, to the north or north-east of the Hindoo Coosh, possibly from the Altai, where, in the Tigeretz Mountains beryls are now obtained. It is more probable, how-ever, that their locality may hereafter prove to be within the Chinese frontier. From such a locality a few emeralds are said still occasionally to cross the Himalaya passes, with a pale kind of turquoise, into North-western India. The discovery of the Zabara emerald mines in Egypt, with the houses almost intact in which the workmen formerly lived, establishes Pliny's Egyp-tian locality for the emerald. His beryls would have come from the Cangayum locality in India, and his description of them might have been written yesterday. Of Pliny's other green stones included under the head of Emerald, the medical and the Laconian kind, the first of which is simply the Cyprian sort of Theophrastus, may be assumed to have been malachite, from various localities, or under various guises.

The green iaspis of Pliny was a fine emerald-like stone,

often translucent or transparent. It came from India and from Amisos, and calls to our mind a fine green Indian plasma from the Vendyah Hills. It seems to have been the only iaspis of a green colour, all the other substances included under that name being chalcedonies of a blue or amethyst hue, or, again, of other mixed and variously disposed colours. For the chola, or clora, used in Arabia in conjunction with alabastrites in inlaid architectural ornament, a serpentine marble suggests itself as a probable material; and Mr. King assigns the tanos, with some probability, to the Amazon stone felspar. Of Pliny's inferior green stones, the prasius seems to have been the green jasper of our mineral collections. One kind was spotted with bloodlike spots, our heliotrope or translucent bloodstone, from the neighbourhood of the Nerbudda; the heliotrope of Pliny's Appendix being the opaque bloodstone remarkable for its polish, and probably well adapted for observing solar eclipses by reflection, a purpose to which Pliny says it was applied. Another prasius, also described under the iaspis by Pliny, was a white-veined green jasper, also found in India. The chrysoprasius, of which large cylindri and cymbia (drinking vessels) were made, were from India, and one kind must have had the colour of the very pale oil green or greenish yellow beryl; another was of a rather golden topazius (brownish green) colour. These were most likely the pale yellowish and the deeper green jades, or nephrites, so often used in India as the material for the well-known elegant cups and vases that are among the most beautiful of the products of the native arts and monuments of the untiring industry of the artisans of that country. The Nilion and the molochites close this list. The former was from India; the word in Sanscrit implies a blue or blue green colour; it is the Indian name for the sapphire, and the name of the Nile probably came from it. This mineral was of a poor and dull lustre, and a variety was said to be found in Attica. A bluish green jasper often streaked with white, used for dagger-hilts in India, may possibly be this Nilion; and Mr. King thinks a favourite green jasper in ancient Egypt of a pale pea-green may be the molochites. This, however, was an Egyptian stone, and is found near Thebes, and Pliny would scarcely have called it Arabian.

Of the blue stones the sapphire is the only transparent species habitually employed by the jewellers. The blue diamond is a rare curiosity; so is a greenish blue spinel, and a zircon of a similar tint. The Indicolite, a blue tourmaline, impure in its hue and rarely limpid, is occasionally used. The blue topaz is not deep enough in hue nor rare enough to be a stone of price, and therefore of fashion. The blue beryl was a prized stone in antiquity, the berilhus aëroides of Pliny, and Siberia has produced specimens of it considerable in size and of good colour. It forms a lovely jewel when its colour is of its greatest depth and purity. The only other transparent blue stone calculated for employment in jewellery is the dichroite, or iolite, a mineral more curious than beautiful, from the singular degree to which it exhibits the optical property known as pleochroism, the crystal being blue, yellowish buff, or greyish in colour, according to the direction in which one looks through it. The dichroite is rarely used as a jewel, though it is often met with in parcels of sapphires from the East, and sometimes even passes for that stone. Mr. King brings conclusive, though not novel, arguments to show that the hyacinthus of Pliny was the sapphire of our day. He also allows the Cyprian diamond, at least that which, according to his translation and reading (*aërius color*), an azure hue characterised, to be this stone. But he also includes with these the siderites, distinguished by its high specific gravity and softness from the others; an inconsistency which one can hardly imagine even Pliny to have been guilty of.

There are still two opaque blue stones, and one that is translucent, which remain to be considered. The former are the lapis-lazuli and the turquoise, the last is the sapphirine chalcedony. The sapphirine chalcedony, however, we have already described, and have placed it among the jaspers of Pliny. The callais of Pliny we have also stated to be the blue and more highly appreciated turquoise of modern jewellery, the green variety having been that on which the Romans set the highest value, under the name of callaina.

The turquoise (or Turkish stone) of the vieille roche, so called to distinguish it from a spurious substance made by colouring bone with copper, is a phosphate of alumina tinged with phosphate of copper and phosphate of iron. The finest, or at least the best-known specimens, come from a Persian locality. They occur also in the Sinaitic peninsula, and an Armenian locality is also said to exist. A vast mass of bluish green turquoise in the British Museum found in the Chinese Summer Palace, bespeaks another locality, probably in Tartary, for this stone. The fine suite of turquoises belonging to Lady Wharncliffe was chiefly collected by Lord Wharncliffe in the mountains of Thibet, where the larger specimens were regarded with mystical reverence by the chiefs who wore them. This stone is very liable to lose its colour under the action of alkalies such as are contained in soap, or even by exposure to the light and the action of the air. It is a curious fact that the Mexicans had a turquoise which they used just as the Persians have always done, to ornament objects in clustered masses.

The lapis-lazuli is, without any doubt, the sapphirus of Pliny and of Theophrastus. It is described as an opaque stone with gold spangles in it (of iron pyrites), coming from Media (Bokhara), sometimes tinged with purple (reddish-blue?), sometimes of a rich blue. If we could translate *cum purpurâ* directly as purple, this would exactly describe the lapis-lazuli. Pliny was, in fact, doubtless aware that the artist would produce the deep violet blue of the darker lapis-lazuli by mixing a little of the purpura (moroon red) with the ordinary blue colour of its paler varieties. The word sapphire we have traced to a Semitic source, but it may be doubted whether the Hebrew word really means our sapphire. The tables of the Law were made of sappir; and in Exodus xxiv. 10 it is written, if we translate literally, ' And they saw the God of Israel; and under ' His feet, like the work of pavement of sappir, and like the ' essence of heaven in purity.' This comparison with heaven might apply to either stone, the transparent sapphire or the opaque lapis-lazuli, though the pyrites-studded lapis would at first sight seem the more exact representation of a star-spangled sky and more adapted for an inlaid pavement.

We have now passed in review the more prominent of the stones deemed precious in the modern as well as in the ancient worlds. The Greek, the Egyptian, the Etruscan, and the Roman used coloured stones either as materials for their gems and signets, or, if as ornaments, then only as ancillary to their elaborate and tasteful work in gold. They never cut them with facettes, as the modern practice is; they adhered solely to the use of stones as pebbles, beads, or carved ornaments strung on or set off by gold, a form of the finely coloured jewels too much neglected by modern jewellers, though it has lately been revived by Signor Castellani and his imitators.

It is impossible to treat a subject, scientific in one of its aspects and archæological and involving classical criticism in another, so as to make it interesting to every kind of reader; but the foregoing pages are a necessary introduction to the subject of gem-engraving. We hope to proceed to the discussion of this more generally interesting and somewhat neglected branch of fine art on a future occasion.

Art. VIII.—*Charles Lamb: a Memoir.* By Barry Cornwall. London: 1866.

There is an imaginative and pathetic anachronism in one of the tales of ' Mrs. Leicester's School,' written either by Charles Lamb or his sister, which may well be applied to his own destiny. A little girl is so charmed with the ceremonies and accompaniments of her father's second marriage, and especially by the beauty of the bride, that she sits down at the door of what was her mother's room, and cries with sorrow that her own dear mamma is not here to see how beautiful it all is. So may we lament that Charles Lamb is not here now among us to see with what curious and dutiful interest we honour the memory of a life which passed under the eyes of the last generation utterly unregarded, and how there has been written about his quiet and simple existence at least as much as he wrote at any time on any subject whatever. He would look on our proceedings with pleasure, because he liked the sympathies of mankind ; but his prominent feeling would have been one of intense humorous satisfaction at the oddity of the circumstances, and the contrast between the different ways of the world in its dealings with intellect and genius.

Through the long, monotonous, servile years of his clerkship it probably never came into his head that those masters of his, who were reigning over the distant millions of the East, would soon be utterly extinct and forgotten personages, while his name would be so familiar to the popular literature of his country, that nobody would think of putting ' Mr.' to it; or that, when he parted from their august presence in an ecstasy of gratitude at receiving a pension of two hundred a year, he left no one man in that hive of intellectual industry and political power, not even the philosopher who is now applying with such signal success the stores of his reflection to the practical statesmanship of his time, whose employment would add more lustre to the service of the great Company than his own. But, even if such fancies in some hour of secret self-recognition ever crossed his brain, it must have seemed to him an unimaginable absurdity that posterity should care about those modest, almost austere habits, of his daily life—about the grave calamity that shadowed it—about her who was all-in-all to him, but nothing to any one besides. Yet so it is ; and the story of Charles Lamb and his sister, though known already in its outlines in all literary biography, will be heartily welcomed in a new form by the hand of Mr. Procter, the ' Barry Cornwall ' of his time and its associations.

Charles Lamb might, indeed, have reflected that in one sense this is the common fortune of distinguished humoristic writers. The hopes and fears, the emotions and the caprices, the fancies and the follies of other men are, so to say, the capital of their literary adventure, and they in turn must submit to their own analysis by posterity. The tragedy of the foiled ambition and turbid life of the Dean of St. Patrick's to its catastrophe in mental gloom, and the melodrama of the gay Canon of York, from his vagrant childhood to the dissecting-room at Cambridge, are inexhaustible sources of interest and speculation, and future times may be as curious about Sydney Smith or Theodore Hook or Douglas Jerrold as is the present about the essentially monotonous and uneventful story of Charles Lamb.

It is the lot of Mr. Procter to have outlived nearly all, if not all, that generation of intellects, of which Coleridge was the philosopher, Wordsworth, Leigh Hunt, Shelley, Keats, and himself the poets, Southey the historian, Hazlitt the critic, and Lamb the humorist. Around these now notorious names grouped many men who have not left any distinctive mark on the literature of their time, but whose sympathies sustained, and whose tastes encouraged, the combatants in their long and hard encounter with the social panic the French Revolution left behind it, and with the literary bigotry that associated all novelty of thought and expression with subversive ideas. Of the former we have lately had an example the more in the Diary and Letters of the well-taught and well-tempered Windham, where, in a letter to Mrs. Crewe, he finds his sole consolation for the present state of things in the hope that, ' when he ' meets the Duke of Bedford, the Plumbers, and the Cokes ' in exile and beggary in some town on the Continent, their ' wretchedness, from the greater indulgences which they ' have always required and enjoyed, will be something sharper ' than his own.' The orthodox style and character of Rogers's poems did not prevent Sir Joseph Banks from excluding him, though a Fellow of the Royal Society, from all its social meetings, on account of his supposed liberal opinions; and when to social and political heresies were added the enormities of free thought on ecclesiastical and theological subjects, original or resuscitated forms of diction, wild flights of fancy, and a passionate utterance that might be interpreted into license, the ban was absolute, and all processes of the critical Inquisition legitimate. We, who have come to look on Coleridge as a conservative politician, and on his philosophy as an earnest reconciliation of many tormenting problems with Christian truth—who give to Wordsworth, Shelley, and Keats their unchallenged places on the poetic roll—who can enjoy both the verse and prose of Leigh Hunt, notwithstanding his fantastical conceits and defects of taste, may be permitted to look back on the methods of controversy which were adopted against such men with sorrow and with shame. If, on the one hand, they show the elasticity of real mental power against oppression, they afford painful evidence how much of sheer malice and falsehood will infect and pervert even honest criticism the moment that other than æsthetic considerations guide the pen and affect the judgment. To assume that all the men were habitual drunkards because they met at taverns in days when there were no clubs to go to, and to believe all the women incontinent because Mary Woolstoncraft had vindicated their ' Rights,' was not only permitted, but applauded in the best circles of contemporaneous literature ; and we find the young Byron, himself the victim of a censorship which we should now consider truculent, if not unjust, writing in this strain :—

> ' Yet, let them not to vulgar Wordsworth stoop,
> The meanest object of the lowly group,
> Whose verse, of all but childish prattle void,
> Seems blessed harmony to *Lambe* and Lloyd.'

Here even Lamb's name was not spelt correctly, but the connexion with Lloyd was legitimate, the two young poets having published a volume together in 1797, with some pieces by Coleridge, or, as Lamb expresses it, ' under cover of the ' greater Ajax.' Charles Lamb appears as ' of the India ' House,' both in the title-page and in the dedication to him in 1798 of Lloyd's now forgotten novel ' Edmund Oliver ' (of which the character of the young Coleridge and his enlisting adventure form the main interest)—a designation that now would hardly be assumed by a literary aspirant, but which implies the distinction that the service then conferred on its least important agents.

It was at the age of seventeen that Charles Lamb obtained that post in the Accountant's Office of the East India Company which secured him the decent competence that sufficed for his subsistence, and made literary occupation the luxury, and not the necessity, of his life. The very humbleness and simplicity of his duties accorded with the character of his genius, and was perhaps far more favourable to its development than a more ostentatious career. Next to this good fortune may be estimated his education at Christ's Hospital (of which, in the delightful contradictions of his two Essays, he has given so complete a picture), not only for its special use, but for that friendship which played so important a part in his future life. The intellectual benefit he must have derived from the constant association with so rich and suggestive a mind as that of Coleridge must have been considerable; for, with his lowly origin, rare acquaintances, and uninteresting duties, he might have stagnated into an obscure and even sottish mode of life, redeemed indeed in the estimate of the higher justice by its continual self-sacrifice and noble affection, but lost to the outer world and the benefit of mankind. Besides this, too, the intimacy with Coleridge brought him into the appreciative society which made his own existence and that of his sister as happy as, under the shade of the great sorrow, it could be, and gave him, what is so rare in the circumstances of superior men, habitual intercourse with his equals in intelligence and in position, without taint of the patron or the client, without the requirements of delicacy or the exigencies of gratitude. Who shall say how much of the gentlemanlike repose, the agreeable stand-at-ease of Lamb's Essays, the present contentedness that reigns throughout, making chimney-sweepers pleasant companions, and illness nearly as comfortable as health, was not due to this good connexion with those about him? Who would imagine that the writer had been himself the victim of a domestic calamity of almost fabulous horror; that his reason (having once failed) was only kept stedfast by his own strong will; and that he had never known wealth, nor fame, nor power, nor conjugal happiness, nor the love of children, nor any of those relations with the outer world that naturally make a man satisfied with his own lot and solicitous for that of others?

The story of his great misfortune is now for the first time wholly told. All whom it would afflict are gone, and there is no further ground for reticence. About the end of 1795, three years after he obtained his appointment, his mother was ill and bedridden, his father almost fatuous, and he himself the inmate of the asylum at Hoxton, where, as he wrote to Coleridge, 'his 'head ran upon him, as much almost as on another person who 'was the more immediate cause of my frenzy.' Who this was is unknown; she remains only the 'Alice W.' of his poems, the object of a passion which might have blossomed into happy fruit but for the incidents of the next year. He returned home sane, and the family life went on as usual till the September of 1796. On the 23rd of that month, his sister Mary, who had been for some time ill and moody, was seized just before dinner with a burst of madness. She seized a case-knife lying on the table, pursued a little girl (her apprentice) round the room, hurled about the dinner-forks so as to wound her father in the forehead, and, before Charles could snatch the knife from her hand, she had stabbed her mother to the heart. The sad publicity of a trial was somehow avoided. After the inquest Mary Lamb was removed to an asylum. She rapidly recovered her senses, and the question came what was then to be done. It seems to have been easier then than it now is to obtain the liberty of a dangerous lunatic, for no opposition to her release seems to have been made by the authorities. When becoming sane, Mary said, ' she knew she must go to Bethlehem for life : '. one of her brothers would have it so ; the other would not ' wish it, but would be obliged to go with the stream.'

This one brother, John Lamb, held a clerkship, with a considerable salary, in the South Sea House (the subject of the first of the collected Essays), and seems to have been a hard, dry, selfish man, who cared little for his relations ; but after his mother's terrible death he, too, was in danger from the family disease. ' I fear for his mind,' writes Charles to Coleridge ; ' he ' has taken his ease in the world, and is not fit to struggle with ' difficulties.' But the 'other brother' did not go with the stream. He made up his mind at once what to do, and he did it, his whole life through. To enable him to devote his being entire to his desolate sister, he began by burning the little journal of ' my foolish passion, which I had so long time kept,' and even, under the exaggeration of the first sense of self-devotion, and to wean himself off from the occupations and hopes of a happier past, he got rid of the letters of his best and wisest friends, and of all his own compositions in verse, ' Mention nothing ' of poetry,' he writes ; 'I have destroyed every vestige of ' poor vanities of that kind.' The whole income of the household at that time was, at the most, not more than 180*l.*, 'out of ' which,' he says, ' we can spare 50*l.* or 60*l.* for Mary while ' she stays in an asylum ; if I and my father, and an old maid-' servant, cannot live, and live comfortably, on 130*l.* or 120*l.* ' a year, we ought to burn by slow fires. I almost would, ' so that Mary might not go into an hospital.' The brother and all the other members of the family opposed her discharge, but the solemn undertaking of Charles to act thereafter for life as her protector prevailed. Whenever some irritability or change of manner prognosticated the returning malady, the brother and sister would walk quietly, but often weeping, to Hoxton Asylum, he carrying the strait-jacket, which at that time was the indispensable adjunct of insanity. But even when there he did not leave her entirely. ' When she is not violent, her

' rambling chat is better to me than the sense and sanity of the
' world,' and he rarely went elsewhere for relief or diversion.
' I am afraid there is something of dishonesty in any pleasure
' I take without her.'　　With eloquent pathos indeed does Mr.
Procter write—

' In this constant and uncomplaining endurance, and in his steady
adherence to a great principle of conduct, his life was heroic.　We
read of men giving up all their days to a single object : to religion,
to vengeance, to some overpowering selfish wish ; of daring acts
done to avert death or disgrace, or some oppressing misfortune.
We read mythical tales of friendship ; but we do not recollect any
instance in which a great object has been so unremittingly carried
out throughout a whole life, in defiance of a thousand difficulties,
and of numberless temptations, straining the good resolution to its
utmost, except in the case of our poor clerk of the India House.'

But it may be no extravagance of the theory of compensations
to believe that something besides the satisfaction of accomplished
duty was the result of this devoted life.　Though, in one form of
insanity, structural disease deadens or distorts the perception,
and, extending to the organs of all the faculties, paralyses the intellectual force and reduces the individual to a simple machine,
and, in another, the inefficiency or misdirection of the intellectual force is the sole cause of derangement and produces
disease by the violence of its existence and the want of the habit
of controlling the thoughts and checking the imagination,—there
will always remain a border-land of sanity and madness, in which
the saving power is the abstraction from self— the fixed occupation of the mind in other matters than its own phenomena.
The saddest impression a visitor takes away from an asylum is
the utter lovelessness of its inmates ; and it seems almost as if
the sense of one passionate sympathy might disperse the darkest
of those clouds.　Certain it is that though, just before that
catastrophe, Charles Lamb was placed under control, the precaution was never necessary again, notwithstanding all the
stress of mind caused by the dreadful event and its consequences.
Under the ægis of that intense fraternal love his spirit walked
secure.

In a short essay of his mature years, the ' Sanity of True
Genius ' is nobly vindicated :—

' The true poet dreams being awake : he is not possessed by his
subject, but has dominion over it : he ascends the empyrean heaven
and is not intoxicated : he treads the burning marl without dismay :
he wins his flight without self-loss through realms of chaos and old
night. . . . . Herein the great and little wits are differenced, that if
the latter wander ever so little from nature or actual existence, they
lose themselves and their readers.　Their phantoms are baseless,

their visions night-mares. They do not create, which implies shaping and consistency. Their imaginations are not active, for to be active is to call something into act and force, but passive as men in sick dreams.'

So could Charles Lamb write, looking back, perhaps, in his thoughts even as he wrote, to those distant months in the mental night of Hoxton Asylum, and know himself rescued by his own great wit and great heart, by his humour and his affections.

The only sign of deficient connexion between thought and speech that endured was the hesitation which is said to have added much to the effect of his sayings. For instance: 'Charles,' said Coleridge, 'I think you have heard me preach.' 'I n-n-never 'heard you do anything else;'— or, when Leigh Hunt wondered at Coleridge's religious fervour: 'N-n-never mind what 'Coleridge says—he's full of f-f-fun;'—or, when some one complained of the cold manner of the late King of Hanover, 'It's only natural in the Duke of Cu-Cumber-land.'

The personal reminiscences which give this volume its special charm do not begin before 1817.

'Persons who had been in the habit of traversing Covent Garden at that time (seven-and-forty years ago), might by extending their walk a few yards into Russell Street, have noted a small spare man, clothed in black, who went out every morning and returned every afternoon, as regularly as the hands of the clock moved towards certain hours. You could not mistake him. He was somewhat stiff in his manner, and almost clerical in dress; which indicated much wear. He had a long, melancholy face, with keen penetrating eyes; and he walked with a short, resolute, step, City-wards. He looked no one in the face for more than a moment, yet contrived to see everything as he went on. No one who ever studied the human features could pass him by without recollecting his countenance; it was full of sensibility, and it came upon you like a new thought, which you could not help dwelling upon afterwards; it gave rise to meditation and did you good. This small, half-clerical man, was— Charles Lamb.'

His writings up to that period had been printed in magazines; and though well appreciated by a certain circle of men-of-letters, it was not till their appearance in a collected form in 1818, that they could be said to be known. In fact, as Mr. Procter says, 'they came upon the world by surprise.' His verse, though remarkable for gravity of thought, for the firm simplicity of its diction, and for the avoidance of the magniloquent common-places that so often betray the unpractised writer, was not of a kind to attract attention; and his humour grew with maturer years, as that faculty is wont to do. Even the natures wherein it is strong, often shrink in their youth from its play of contradictions and sudden transitions of ideas, as a violation of that complete unity of thought and life to which the best aspire ; and it is only when that noble hope is beaten down by the difficulties and confusion of circumstances, that the full compensating worth of humour is felt, and its exercise, either in one's own mind or in the minds of others, duly cultivated and esteemed. The ' Farewell to Tobacco ' is an exception to the general character of his verse ; it is a real inspiration of ' the only manly scent '—' Brother of Bac- ' chus, later born,' whose merits a younger poet, under the mask of S. S. C., has lately sung with a humoristic grace * that Lamb would have enjoyed :—

Thou who, when fears attack,
Bidd'st them avaunt, and black
Care, at the horseman's back
   Perching, unseatest ;
Sweet, when the morn is grey,
Sweet, when they've cleared away
Lunch, and at close of day
   Possibly sweetest.

How they who use fuzees
All grow by slow degrees
Brainless as chimpanzees,
   Meagre as lizards :
Go mad, and beat their wives,
Plunge, after shocking lives,
Razors and carving-knives
   Into their gizzards !

I have a liking old
For thee, though manifold
Stories, I know, are told
   Not to thy credit.
How one (or two at most)
Drops make a cat a ghost,
Useless, except to roast,
   Doctors have said it.

Confound such knavish tricks :
Yet know I five or six
Smokers who freely mix
   Still with their neighbours :
Jones (who, I'm glad to say,
Asked leave of Mrs. J.)
Daily absorbs a clay
   After his labours.

But the contributions to Mr. Leigh Hunt's publication, the ' Reflector,' and the Essays on the ' Old Dramatists,' and on the ' Genius of Hogarth,' were worthy precursors of Elia, which designation first appeared in the pages of the ' London ' Magazine,' ' now,' in Mr. Procter's words, ' under the pro- ' tection of that great power called " Oblivion." ' We have here an interesting account of the constitution and character of that periodical, which held a high place in the literature of its time. It began in 1820, and soon numbered among its writers Hazlitt, Lamb, Carlyle, De Quincy, Cary (the trans- lator of Dante), Allan Cunningham, Thomas Hood, George Darley (a writer whose works and remains would be well worth

---

* As a second volume of ' Translations ' from the pen and with the name of Mr. Calverley, has just appeared, there is no longer any secret in the authorship of his most pleasant and scholarly volume of ' Verses and Translations.'

collection and recollection), Elton, and Savage Landor—while Keats, Hartley Coleridge, Montgomery, and Clare appear among the occasional poets, and Mr. Procter, under his pseudonym of 'Barry Cornwall,' was often present, both in prose and verse. These slight sketches of the fraternity make us hope that he may be induced to dive again into the sunny seas of his memory, and give us what, after all, may be only the waifs and strays of literary history, but which should not pass away altogether. He evidently dwells with much pleasure on the personality of Hazlitt, and a companion-volume to this before us, placing the intellectual character and moral nature of that remarkable man in a clear and intelligible light, is a work which perhaps no living man could execute but himself. A name of strange and criminal associations here, too, occurs— Wainwright the poisoner, who is believed to have been the first to apply to his uses the fatal, and still mysterious, properties of strychnine, then quite untraceable by chemical sagacity. Having been transported to Australia for the offence of forging a power-of-attorney, he there ended his days as a popular and skilful portrait-painter, having himself supplied the ideal portraiture for Sir Edward Lytton's hero in the novel of 'Lucretia.' On the death of Mr. John Scott, the editor, the Magazine passed into the hands of Messrs. Taylor and Hessy, who opened a house in Waterloo Place for its publication.

'It was there that the contributors met once a month, over an excellent dinner, given by the firm; and consulted and talked on literary matters together. These meetings were very social; all the guests coming with a determination to please and be pleased. I do not know that many important matters were arranged, for the welfare of the magazine, at these dinners; but the hearts of the contributors were opened, and with the expansion of the heart the intellect widened also. If there had been any shades of jealousy amongst them, they faded away before the light of the friendly carousal; if there was any envy, it died. All the fences and restraints of authorship were cast off, and the natural human being was disclosed.

'Amongst others Charles Lamb came to most of these dinners, always dressed in black (his old snuff-coloured suit having been dismissed for years); always kind and genial; conversational, not talkative, but quick in reply; eating little, and drinking moderately with the rest. Allan Cunningham, a stalwart man, was generally there; very Scotch in aspect, but ready to do a good turn to any one. His talk was not too abundant, although he was a voluminous writer in prose. His songs, not unworthy of being compared with even those of Burns, are (as everybody knows) excellent. His face shone at these festivities. Reynolds came always. His good temper and vivacity were like condiments at the feast. There also came once or twice the Rev. H. F. Cary, the quiet gentleness of whose face almost interfered with its real intelligence. Yet he spoke well and with readiness, on any subject that he chose to discuss. . . . . Cary was entirely without vanity; and he, who had traversed the ghastly regions of the Inferno, interchanged little courtesies on equal terms with workers who had never travelled beyond the papers of "The London Magazine." No one (it is said) who has performed anything great ever looks big upon it.—Thomas Hood was there, almost silent, except when he shot out some irresistible pun, and disturbed the gravity of the company. . . . . Hazlitt attended once or twice; but he was a rather silent guest, rising into emphatic talk only when some political discussion (very rare) stimulated him.—Mr. De Quincy appeared at only one of these dinners. The expression of his face was intelligent, but cramped and somewhat peevish. He was self-involved, and did not add to the cheerfulness of the meeting. I have consulted this gentleman's three essays, of which Charles Lamb is professedly the subject; but I cannot derive from them anything illustrative of my friend Lamb's character.'

Mr. Procter candidly admits the Cockneyism of his friend. He may not have indeed disliked a glimpse of the Lakes, and probably meant what he said, that the day he saw Skiddaw would stand out like a mountain in his life, and that he could live under his shadow for two or three years; but he added sincerely, 'I must have a prospect of seeing Fleet Street at the ' end of that time, or I should mope and pine away.' He said ' the London smoke suited his vision; ' and his Essays are full of contentment with the pleasant place in which his life is cast. When in his comparative wealth he removed to a ' gamboge-coloured house' at Enfield, the country, suburban as it was, weighed heavily on him. 'Let not the lying poets be ' believed who entice men from the cheerful streets.' He could do with the country by the fire and candle-light, but when day returns it becomes intolerable—'he falls into a calenture and ' plunges into St. Giles's.' Perhaps it was not so much the abstract Town that he loved, but his own City, with its story-telling houses and its familiar localities. He would probably have liked Belgravia no better than the green pastures and the ' woolly bedfellows' he had no fancy to ' lie down with:' the streets in which he would set up his tabernacle were all about the Temple where he was born, the Hospital where he was educated, the Salutation-and-Cat-Tavern, in whose little parlour he smoked his Oronooko and heard Coleridge build up his Pantisocracy in lofty talk. ' I gather myself up,' he writes, ' into the old things.' One does not indeed see why he ever left the haunts where he had passed the really happy days of his life—his pure London, and his Wednesday evenings, and his sister's company, when she was well, and his own care of her when she was otherwise, and the frequent play-goings at the time that England had a theatre, and the immense gratification of old books, when the purchase of any one was a serious luxury, to be won by labour and by thrift.

It is this spirit which makes his exposition of past literature so delightful and instructive; there is no antiquarian dilettantism about it. When he kissed an old book, as he often did, it was unwittingly, almost secretly. We have seen an annotated copy of Wither, where some one remarks, ' The beauty of this passage ' is too apparent to need a comment,' and Lamb writes under, ' Then why give it one ?' If the book or passage was not good in itself, Lamb never thought of making it so by his praise. Mr. Procter finds an exception to this rule in Lamb's extreme affection for the Duchess of Newcastle's Life of her Husband. But we cannot admit this; for the serious quaintness of that philosophic and courtly dame has something almost of Lamb's own humour about it, sublimated by the conceit of a supernatural self-importance; and we should have predicted at once that it must be a book after Lamb's own heart, and should have been very happy to have introduced it to him. Nothing can be truer, however, than Mr. Procter's observation that Charles Lamb naturalized and cherished what was in a manner foreign to his age, and brought the wisdom of old times and old writers to bear upon the taste and intellect of the day. The ' dangerous ' figure irony,' as he calls it, was never wielded by more delicate and graceful hands : he may have interrupted grave and plausible discourses with some light jest, not quite irrelevant ; but he would use it tenderly against his friends, as when he told Mr. Cary ' he was a good parson—not, indeed, as good as ' Parson Adams, but perhaps about as good as Doctor Primrose,' and, if ever roughly, only against himself, as when one day he expressed his deep satisfaction at the death of an old woman, ' she has left me thirty pounds a year !' he did not say that it was he himself who had paid her this annuity for many years out of his hard-earned and modest income.

' His jests,' says Mr. Procter, ' were never the mere overflowings of the animal spirits, but were exercises of his mind.'

And again :—

' In reading over these old Essays, some of them affect me with a grave pleasure amounting to pain. I seem to import into them the very feeling with which he wrote them ; his looks and movements are transfigured and communicated to me by the poor art of the printer.

His voice, so sincere and earnest, rings in my ears again. He was no Feignwell. Apart from his jokes, never was a man so real and free from pretence.'

In these two sentences Mr. Procter gives us the intellectual and moral measure of the perfect humorist. In an age and society so meanly furnished with this talent as ours is, we must take what we can get without repining that it is not the best of its kind; we must be thankful when we meet genial spirits with but scanty culture, and we must not dive too deep into the well of pleasantry to look for a goddess at the bottom; but we may show our estimate of something better than our own, by esteeming aright the hero of these reminiscences and the biographer who can so characterise him.

The Prince de Ligne says somewhere that for every good thing a man of real wit utters for the amusement of others, he thinks a dozen for his own pleasure; and it is agreeable to believe that the absence of cynicism which so remarkably distinguishes the writings of Lamb, expresses his habitual condition of mind as well as the gratification and relief he derived from their production. Most justly Mr. Procter describes them as

'Delightfully personal, and when he speaks of himself you cannot hear too much: they are not imitations but adoptions. We find his likings and fears, his fancies (his nature) in all. The words have an import never known before; the syllables have expanded their meaning, like opened flowers; the goodness of others is heightened by his own tenderness; and what is in nature hard and bad is qualified (qualified, not concealed) by the tender light of pity, which always intermingles with his own vision. Gravity and laughter, fact and fiction, are heaped together, leavened in each case by charity and toleration. Lamb's humour, I imagine, often reflected (sometimes, I hope, relieved) the load of pain that always weighed on his own heart.'

So is it with his Letters, of which so many are now public property, and phrases in them already vernacular. It is in these that he pours forth (what he afterwards composed into a charming essay) his feelings at receiving his pension from the East India Company—this was in exact figures, 441*l.* a year during the remainder of his life, and an annuity after his death to his sister. To Wordsworth he writes: ' I came home ' for ever on Tuesday last. The incomprehensibleness of my ' condition overwhelmed me; it was like passing from time to ' eternity.' To Bernard Barton : ' I have scarce steadiness of ' hand to compose a letter. I am free, B. B., free as air. I ' will live another fifty years. . . . Positively the best thing a

' man can have to do is nothing, and next to that perhaps
' good works.' To Miss Hutchinson : ' I would not go back
' to my prison for seven years longer for 10,000*l.* a year.
' . . . My weather-glass stands at a degree or two above CON-
' TENT.' Alas ! in 1829, only four years after this paroxysm
' of delight, he writes : ' I assure you *no* work is more than
' overwork; the mind preys on itself—the most unwholesome
' food. I have ceased to care for almost anything. . . . Home
' I have none. Never did the waters of heaven pour down on a
' forlorner head. What I can do and overdo is to walk. I am
' a sanguinary murderer of time. But the oracle is silent.'
And there he might be seen wandering over all the fields in
the neighbourhood of Enfield, accompanied by, or rather following, a large dog, to whose erratic propensities he became a
slave. The untold usefulness of the habit of mechanical labour
to such a temperament as his became too apparent. His secure
literary success does not seem to have given him any pleasure,
indeed he seems hardly to have believed in it. He asked the
American writer, Mr. Willis (who said he had bought ' Elia ' in
America)—what he gave for it ? ' About seven and sixpence.'
' Permit me then to pay you that,' gravely counting out the
money. ' I never yet wrote anything that would sell. I am
' the publisher's ruin. My last poem will sell—not a copy.
' Have you seen it ? ' Willis had not. ' It's only eighteen
' pence—and I'll give you sixpence towards it.' Nor did the
confidence in his own powers sustain him. He wrote to Southey
a little before this : ' I find genius declines with me, but I
' get clever.' He was worried out of proportion, by being asked
to write in albums and in the pretty glossy illustrated Annuals
that were then so popular. ' If I take the wings of the morn-
' ing and fly to the uttermost parts of the earth—there will
' albums be.' Four years after, in 1833, the Lambs moved
somewhat nearer to their London friends—to Church Street,
Edmonton—his last abode.

The next year Coleridge's health began to decline, and
he died in July, bright and powerful to the last; saying a
few days before his dissolution, ' the scenes of my early life
' have stolen into my mind, like breezes blown from the Spice
' Islands.' Lamb to the end of his life was often heard murmuring to himself, ' Coleridge is dead—is dead ; ' and he said
with solemnity, ' I cannot *think* without an ineffectual refe-
' rence to him.' That Coleridge should thus have possessed
himself of the mind of his friend of fifty years will not be
surprising to any thoughtful man who formed part of the generation in this country to which Coleridge was the paramount

master and interpreter of philosophic truth. No such wide and varied influence over the modes of thought of cultivated men, both in sympathies and in antagonisms, has been given to any writer since his time, although the radiation from the spirit of Thomas Carlyle may bear some comparison with it. When Mr. Mill quoted the ' Lay Sermon ' as an authority of political opinion in a late debate, it must have sounded to more than one of his elder hearers as an echo of his youthful days, when a passage from the ' Aids to Reflection ' was a valuable support on either side of a religious controversy, and when the tyro in metaphysics came down fiercely on his antagonist with the distinctions of the Reason and the Understanding.

Very far short of the many happy years of learned leisure and pleasant converse that Lamb anticipated on his release from his clerkly toil were granted him. In 1833 cough and cramp became his bedfellows; ' we sleep three in a bed,' he wrote. The ' otiosa eternitas ' of his later life, as Mr. Procter expresses it, lapsed into the great deep beyond on the 27th of December, 1839. Mary survived thirteen years, protected by her calamity from fully understanding the magnitude of her loss, and cared-for by all his many friends. Finely does Mr. Procter draw the moral of the tale he has written ; would we could anticipate other such Lives of the Poets and Men-of-letters of our century !

' Charles Lamb was born almost in penury, and he was taught by charity. Even when a boy he was forced to labour for his bread. In the first opening of manhood a terrible calamity fell upon him ; in magnitude fit to form the mystery or centre of an antique drama. He had to dwell, all his days, with a person incurably mad. From poverty he passed at once to unpleasant toil and perpetual fear. These were the sole changes in his fortune. Yet, he gained friends, respect, a position, and great sympathy from all ; showing what one poor unbeneficed man, under grievous misfortune, may do, if he be active and true and constant to the end.'

ART. IX. — *International Policy. Essays on the Foreign Relations of England.* 8vo. London: 1866.

THIS volume is a deplorable proof of the confusion of ideas and the ignorance of principles, in relation to foreign policy and international law, which exist even amongst the educated classes in this country. It contains seven Essays, designed by their authors, some of whom are men filling responsible positions in the University of Oxford, to advocate a more systematic policy in the international relations of mankind, based on a moral, not a political or purely national foundation. So far their object is a laudable one, and we entered upon the perusal of their schemes with curiosity and interest, though the proposition from which they start amounts simply to a truism. But a very short acquaintance with the doctrines which these gentlemen have imported from the school of M. Auguste Comte, destroys all respect for their opinions and all confidence in their conclusions. The morality to which they would subject the international relations of mankind is spurious and fantastical. They are apparently ignorant of the first principles of international law, and of the science of jurisprudence, on which all law is founded. Their knowledge of history is superficial and distorted; and their schemes for the regeneration of political society are governed by sentimental predilections which are paradoxical to absurdity. One of these gentlemen exults in the occupation of Sleswig and Holstein by German troops, on the ground, we suppose, of morality and justice; another would exclude Russia and obliterate Austria from the European system, while he upholds the Turkish Empire, on the ground of its freedom from religious prejudice; another contrasts the piety and morality of the Chinese with the rapacity and bad faith of Christian nations; all recommend the immediate surrender of Gibraltar, as an indispensable sacrifice by the public morality of England to the claims of Spain! To show their superiority to national prejudices, they traduce and defame the conduct of their own country in her relations with other States. In the place of those positive obligations, on which the maintenance of peace and order depends, they would substitute an ill-defined allegiance to the idea of Humanity. In fact their estimate of national rights and duties resolves itself into an application to politics of M. Proudhon's celebrated maxim, ' La Propriété ' c'est le Vol.' It is not our intention to waste any space on a critical examination of these crude and mischievous theories, which will probably find but few readers, and fewer converts. But it is a matter of shame and regret that, at a moment when the affairs of Europe call for wise and cautious consideration, members of the great English University, which ought to be a storehouse of sound knowledge and just principles, should put forth so foolish and discreditable a production.

The moment, indeed, is one, beyond all others in the memory of two generations, when questions such as those which are raised, but not resolved, by these writers, press upon the minds and interests of all European nations. The disorder in the relations of the several States which compose the most civilised portion of the globe is complete. War has broken out in the heart of the Continent of Europe, not only between nations divided from each other by traditional hostility and territorial claims, but between the leading Powers of Germany, which have long been, and ought ever to be, united by common duties immeasurably more important to themselves and the world than the miserable feuds which have bred this quarrel between them. Such a war, as may easily be perceived at the very outset of it, is not a mere civil contest between the rival members of the Germanic Confederation, or a struggle between two great military Powers for a political object. It rends asunder the numerous ties which peace, commerce, and nationality have created throughout that vast portion of central Europe which is peopled and ruled by the German race. It shakes the fabric raised in 1815 at the termination of the great wars of the French Revolution; for the destruction of the union of the German Powers breaks up the very centre and nucleus of the system, and opens a broad and easy path to the ambition, the cupidity, and the separate designs of every neighbouring State. That respect for the general public law of Europe, which had been maintained for half a century, in spite of numerous revolutions and of some partial changes which are inevitable in all human affairs, is lost. The last effort to preserve peace by the good offices of neutral States, and by the temperate authority of a united Conference, failed, and could only fail since no one would have been bound by its decisions. From that moment it became certain that the authority of treaties and the restraint of common obligations are at an end; and even if peace be restored as the result of the prompt and decisive termination of the campaign, it will be long before the relations of the German and the other European Powers will recover their former security.

This great and dreadful change in the condition and the prospects of Continental Europe cannot, in our opinion, be explained or estimated by a mere reference to the incidents which *appear* to have occasioned it. The causes of a struggle, which has brought a million of men into the field, must be sought far beyond the inglorious contest between Prussia and Austria for an illgotten ascendancy in the Duchies of the Elbe, and beyond those passionate aspirations of the Italian people for the liberation of Venetia, which dignify even the imprudences and excesses of their policy by a genuine sentiment of patriotism. It was said the other night in the House of Commons that this was ' a war without a quarrel ; ' and so it is, if it be considered only in relation to the sparks which have lit the conflagration. Down to the outbreak of hostilities in Germany, the question was—for it has ceased to be a question at the present hour—whether the authority of existing public law expressed by treaties is to be maintained, or whether the territories and rights of States are to be abandoned to a lawless scramble? The most extraordinary circumstance in the present situation of the Continent is, that this question has been raised not by the aggressive designs of Russia, not by the military power of France, which has not ceased to recognise the treaties she avowedly detests, but by Prussia, a Power which took an active part in the construction of those treaties, and which risks everything by the subversion of them.

No doubt the work of the Congress of Vienna in 1815 left much to be desired. It too often disposed of nations and provinces on the ground of temporary motives, arising out of dread and hatred of the French Revolution, and not with due regard to their permanent feelings and interests. The work of the Congress was still further perverted in the following years by the reactionary tendencies of the Northern Courts, united to each other by the mystical ties of the Holy Alliance. But Europe owes to the labours of that Congress a general peace of fifty years and a lesson for all time. That lesson, as we read it, is this. Throughout the wars of the French Revolution, from 1792 to 1813, no real union and sincere cooperation existed between the European Powers. Each of the Continental States in turn felt the tremendous force of the military strength of France, guided by the genius of Napoleon ; each of them fell successively at the feet of the great conqueror. England alone maintained a constant enmity to the oppressor of Europe. She laboured in vain for years, and on manifold occasions, to restore to the councils of the Continental States that union which could alone re-establish a solid and lasting peace ; but it was not until the intolerable aggressions of Napoleon had combined all nations in the cause of resistance, that the work of concord was achieved. In other words, a general European interest was established upon the basis of a general treaty, and in spite of the occasional differences and quarrels which have occurred, all the States have till now continued to acknowledge the force and utility of this fundamental compact. France herself, although she regards that compact as one framed in a spirit of hostility to herself, has admitted by her policy that it was more for her advantage to respect that agreement than to violate it; and she judged rightly, for time has enabled her to obtain important modifications in some of its provisions, and she, like all the rest of Europe, has gained incalculably by the general maintenance of order and of peace. The affairs of Europe lay, therefore, as long as this compact lasted, within the grasp of what was fondly regarded as a sort of Amphictyonic Council; and the principle of co-operation has in the end prevailed over temporary dissensions, even when they reached the point of actual war. For it was one of the results of this beneficial arrangement that war itself, as in the Crimean campaign, was strictly limited to its own proper theatre and object; and upon the cessation of hostilities in 1856, the Congress of Paris immediately resumed the authority of the great conclave of Europe, and proceeded to introduce important changes in the maritime laws of the world. The sanction of a public engagement was extended to the principle that States should in future submit their differences to friendly arbitration before having recourse to arms. With what sincerity Prussia and Italy gave their assent to that doctrine the events of the present year show.

On no other basis, then, than some such general concert, can peace and order be restored and maintained. Sooner or later we must revert to that condition of things, though it may well happen that events will take place in the interval which will materially alter the adjustment of the rival forces and render their union hereafter more difficult and more insecure. Indeed it is only by this solemn recognition of a common interest, and by making all the Powers of Europe jointly and severally responsible for the maintenance of their common obligations, that a sanction can be given to public law and authority to public engagements. Those engagements are what the lawyers call contracts of imperfect obligation, because there is no single power competent to enforce them. That power is only to be found in the combined action of the totality, or at least the majority, of the Cabinets of Europe. A State which without provocation assumes the right to pursue its own ends by its own force, without regard to the common interests and engagements of the world, deserves to be regarded as a common enemy; and would be so regarded if the other members of the great commonwealth of nations were not already disunited.

At the present time no such combined action is possible—no genuine alliance exists between any two of the leading Powers—no Minister will venture to affirm that he knows with certainty what are the real intentions of the other governments of Europe, or can place reliance on the assurances of yesterday or the projects of to-morrow. Treaties which have lost the support of those Powers which called them into existence, have lost their vitality; and it is idle to invoke the terms of an engagement when its spirit is departed. This country has of late been accused of too great an indifference to continental affairs, and of having withdrawn her moral support from the stipulations to which she was a party. Yet of all the States in Europe, England is certainly that which carries to the furthest point her respect for the legal and literal interpretation of a treaty; but in several recent and memorable instances she has met with no response from Continental Governments when she has invoked their fidelity to common engagements, and she has recoiled from the Quixotic task of maintaining, single-handed, stipulations which Powers more immediately concerned in them than herself were ready to abandon. We refer more particularly to the efforts made by the English Government to obtain the support of other Powers for the independence of the Free Town of Cracow, when it was annexed by Austria in 1846; for the rights of Switzerland in relation to some parts of Savoy, when that province was ceded to France in 1860; and to the proposal made by England to France and Russia to uphold the Treaty of 1852 for the regulation of the Danish succession. These negotiations were unsuccessful, not however by any default of Great Britain.

It is a melancholy reflection to those who were disposed to place confidence in the formation and stability of a confederacy of nations, governed in their external relations by arbitration and mutual justice, that the present disturbances have broken out within the Germanic Confederation, which was itself a more strictly organised League of the same nature. That body consisted of States united by a common nationality. It succeeded to the traditions of the oldest political institution in Europe—the Holy Roman Empire. It was by its very nature ' a perpetual Confederation for the maintenance of the ex- ' ternal and internal safety of Germany: ' the members of the

Confederation, equal with regard to their rights, equally engaged to maintain the Act which constitutes their Union.   They
expressly promised not to make war against each other upon
any pretext, nor to pursue their differences by force of arms,
but to submit them to the Diet, and to the ultimate sentence
of that body.   These are not only the terms of the Act which
constituted the Bund, they are also the express terms of the
General Treaty of Vienna, to which every other State in
Europe is a party.   What has Prussia done with these engagements?   She has destroyed them by an act of secession more
anti-federal than the ordinances by which the Southern States
of the American Union attempted to resume their independence.
Austria and her allies have, on the contrary, taken up arms
in defence of engagements of the most strict and positive
character.

The decisive step taken by Prussia on the 14th of June,
when in reply to the legal but coercive measures of the Diet
she declared that compact to be at an end, was no more
than the natural termination of the policy she has long pursued.
Indeed, if our limits and our leisure allowed us to look back
to what the Berlin Herodotus called his ' Nine Books of
' Prussian History,' we should find in every page of the annals
of that monarchy, examples of the same aggressive and ambitious spirit, prompting the sovereigns and ministers of Prussia
to similar acts of treachery, bad faith, and violence.   A nation
of which Frederic II. is the hero, may well be said, like his
Scottish biographer, to have deified force and fraud.   The
maxims by which the conduct of that Court has been governed,
since it assumed a place among the greater Powers of Europe,
are so incredibly cynical and immoral, that the authenticity of
the document which contains them has been denied.   But
the acts of the Prussian Government for the last hundred and
fifty years transcend even the language of her rulers.   No
other Government has laid it down as an avowed principle that
self-aggrandisement justifies the breach of every engagement
and the partition or seizure of unoffending neighbours. Prussia
alone, since the fall of Napoleon, has done more than proclaim
these principles, she has given effect to them.

For it is demonstrated by the course of events already
known, as much as if we could trace them to their secret
springs, that Prussia alone has caused this war. Prussia
has taken each successive step to render it inevitable, on
Prussia alone rests the moral guilt of this political crime.
The war began in reality two years ago by the breach of the
Treaty of 1852 and the attack on Denmark.   Her object

in adopting a course of policy, which is now apparently condemned by all the great Powers of Europe and by most of her former Confederates, was not—as was fondly supposed by the credulous enthusiasm of the German people, and even by some of the quidnuncs of the British House of Commons—to liberate the provinces of Sleswig and Holstein from the tyranny of a Danish ruler, but simply and brutally to annex them to her own dominions. This, however, was but the first and smallest step in the scheme of Bismarck. He foresaw that a rupture with Austria was the certain result of the armed intervention in the Duchies whatever course the Cabinet of Vienna might pursue. Had Austria upheld the Treaty of 1852 and opposed the Federal execution in 1864, she might have had our support, but she would have had against her all the rest of Germany with Prussia. Pressed by the fear of war against Germany, and by the insane popular cry of the Germans against Denmark, Austria committed the great fault—the one fatal sacrifice of principle and duty—which can be imputed to her in these transactions. She reluctantly consented to take part in that infamous campaign against a small and gallant monarchy, which had been made only twelve years before the especial subject of a European treaty, signed by Prussia and Austria in conjunction with the other Powers. The result of the war placed not only the Elbe Duchies, but Austria herself, in Bismarck's grasp—for if the Duchies were his spoil, Austria was his accomplice. The joint occupation, the *condominium,* the contested rights of the Diet in these provinces, afforded to Prussia a ready pretext for a quarrel, whenever she pleased to bring it about; and it has been a mere question of convenience and preparation at what moment of the last twelve months it should begin.

For throughout these transactions Prussia *meant* this quarrel. And she meant it for a purpose immeasurably beyond the pretext she avowed. Prussia has not gone to war for the Duchies. Still less to aid the conquest of Venetia by Italy. She went to war because, in the opinion of her daring and unscrupulous Minister, the time is come to strike a great blow for the headship of Germany, to break up the existing Federal system of that country, to destroy and absorb most of the smaller Northern States and territories, and, as an indispensable preliminary, to wrest from Austria that imperial ascendancy in Germany which she had enjoyed for centuries before the name of Prussia had occurred in history, and which she still retains as the perpetual President of the Confederation of the German States. Probably but a few weeks ago, the bare supposition of so bold and violent a project would have been received with intense incredulity in the matter-of-fact, money-making, Europe of this century. The British daily press, with all its numerous correspondents and its high ability, failed to point out the true peril. The diplomatic world, ever eager to rely on temporary expedients, fancied that the storm might blow over. Had the question really been no more than a dispute arising out of the joint occupation of the Duchies, it would have blown over; and indeed it might at once have been settled, as was proposed by Austria, in the most legal and honourable manner by submitting it to the Diet, and by engaging to abide by the Federal award. But Bismarck, like a poisoner who plies his victim with small reiterated doses, had ever in hand some fresh expedient to counteract the diplomatic antidote. He tried every artifice to throw upon his antagonist the apparent responsibility of the rupture. But in vain. Austria committed no mistake in the later portion of these negotiations. She kept her temper; she spoke with unvarying candour, address, and dignity; she maintained her true Federal position in Germany. Nor can she be blamed in any appreciable degree, for attaching conditions to her assent to the proposed Conference, which at once proved that, as regards the other belligerents, that Conference was a mere blind and a sham. Had the Conference met the scene of the rupture would merely have been transferred from Frankfort to Paris—from the Diet, where Austria was surrounded by a majority of the German States, to the Tuileries, where she would have found herself without an ally.

The question, therefore, which has already passed from the control of law to that of force, may be thus stated. Is Germany to remain a composite body of States, possessing equal sovereign rights, but united by a perpetual league for national purposes, Austria, as well as Prussia, being both members of this confederation? Or is the federal system of Germany to be overthrown, the reigning Houses mediatised, and the principle of national unity established by reducing Austria to the condition of a non-German Empire of Slovacks, Czecks, and Magyars, while the King of Prussia assumes the first rank in Germany and one of the first positions in Europe, by subjecting the whole German nation to his sceptre and his sword? The second of these propositions involves one of the greatest revolutions which has occurred in Europe in any age, and one not hastily to be accomplished, even after the great successes of the Prussian army.

The project is based on two certain elements. The ambition of the House of Brandenburg, which has been pursuing this object, by the avowal of Frederic II. himself, ever since it acquired a royal crown; and the incontestable eagerness of a considerable portion of the German people to exchange their petty sovereigns for the common dominion of a great Power. The cry of Italian Unity has reverberated beyond the Alps, and it is in the name of German Unity that Prussia hopes to carry on this contest. There are those among the most advanced Liberals of Germany, who, with a full knowledge of the arbitrary spirit and complete duplicity of Bismarck, think, nevertheless, that he may serve their cause, by bringing about changes which men of legality and good faith could not attempt; and Bismarck may have hoped to throw dust into the eyes of these credulous and unprincipled politicians, and even to convert them into his most active allies. For, on his part, he will not scruple to appeal to the revolutionary element in Germany to lend its aid to an enterprise which is in reality that of military government and arbitrary power. Prussia, however, enters upon this contest without a shred of legal right or political provocation. She has engaged in a difficult enterprise without the open countenance and support of any other Power. One thing alone is wanting to complete the iniquity of her conduct—that she should have purchased the secret connivance of a foreign potentate to abet her revolutionary designs at home.

We, as Englishmen, are cordially desirous to see the steady progress of Germany in the twofold course of freedom and of union—of constitutional government and of national influence in Europe. For we have certainly nothing to apprehend from the increasing power and influence of Germany, when that power is exercised under the control of parliamentary government. It is the irresponsible nature of that power which makes it, at this moment, a curse to the world. But we greatly doubt, and indeed entirely deny, that the formation of a unitarian State in Germany, more or less on the Imperial model, based on democratic institutions and crowned by bayonets, could be regarded as any gain to true freedom. It is, on the contrary, the latest and the worst form that despotism has assumed, for it is despotism disguised in popular sympathies. Such a State would immolate at the feet of a Prussian corporal the noblest elements of German society, and reduce Germany herself to be a bad copy of the French Empire. No result would be more fatal to the cause of liberty in Europe. It is easy to foresee what would be the fate of small and free States, as Holland,

Denmark, Belgium and Switzerland, lying at the mercy of such neighbours as France and Prussia would then be, which despise them for their weakness and hate them for their freedom. One by one the lesser lights would be put out, and England would again find herself the only champion of a free press, and the only free asylum in the Old World.

It is unjust to argue that a Federal Constitution cannot secure to Germany an adequate amount of national representation and force. That may have been the result of the form of the Federal Acts of 1815 and 1820, and they will doubtless now be altered and recast. But the recent struggle in the United States proves that weakness is not necessarily inherent in federal unions. As in North America, so in Germany, we hold that the maintenance of what are called 'state-rights' is an essential condition of freedom and good government in mixed States; and that a revolution which should obliterate these historical distinctions would very shortly consign the whole people of Germany to the uniform despotism of a single ruler. Equality and military glory would become the passion of the people, rather than free institutions and self-government; and the national character of the Germans, which is already degraded to a very low sense of political morality, would sink into absolute servility to the chief who might have the art to gratify their passions or play upon their delusions. No change could, therefore, occur so fatal to the freedom, the virility, and the political education of the German people as that which is offered them at the hands of Bismarck. It may suit the purpose of those depraved politicians who are ever ready to justify violent and illegal actions by suggesting that they are necessary to the triumph of liberal opinions and the progress of mankind, to palliate the iniquitous policy of the Court of Berlin by assuming that the national unity of Germany is to be purchased at this price. But their principle and their anticipations are alike false and unsound. Under this mask of German unity, which has already served as the pretext for so many follies and crimes, the real object is Prussian domination. The scheme of Bismarck is not to confer equal national rights upon the whole population of a great country, but to subdue those independent communities into provinces ruled by the iron sway of the Prussian military system and the Prussian police. The reception given to the Prussian troops in the towns and States they have invaded and seized, within a week from the declaration of war, distinctly proved that the Germans are well aware of the fate in store for them. Resistance was impossible, for everything had been prepared beforehand to overpower it. Hanover,

Saxony, Hesse, Hamburgh, were instantaneously occupied by Prussian troops and placed at the mercy of Prussian commanders. The inhabitants of those States are not passionately devoted to their own petty rulers; many of them, perhaps the majority, would be favourable to the establishment of a true German Empire. But they were not deceived by what M. Bismarck had to offer them. The Prussian troops were everywhere received in sullen silence, for it was well understood that their entry marked the commencement of an epoch of military oppression, far more severe and intolerable than the minor grievances caused by the late governments. In no case, as far as we have been able to ascertain, were they received as liberators or even as friends. In no case could they be mistaken for the harbingers of national independence and free institutions. They mean the extension to the conquered States of the system of insolent oppression which has been successfully maintained in Prussia during the present reign, and they mean nothing else. The *National Verein*, representing the opinions of the most advanced party in Germany, has energetically protested against the means employed by Prussia in support of their own views. The States which have been annexed in the North have yielded to force and intimidation. South of the Maine, the whole of Germany is united against Prussia; and the patriotic party in Wurtemberg, Baden, and Bavaria has distinguished itself by the strongest determination to resist her.

But if the object of Prussia be of questionable value, the modes of attaining it, and its consequences when attained, are still more mischievous and reprehensible. It involves, of course, a total revolution in the political condition of Germany, and a revolution which can only be ratified by sheer military force or by a false appeal to some of the worst passions of the people. It involves the defeat or destruction by Prussia of the armies of Austria and of those States which are acting with her; and the astonishing vigour and success with which the Prussian operations have been conducted, appear already to have attained this result; for there is this peculiarity in the policy of Bismarck that, in order to arrive at the strength and unity of Germany, he directs one half of her fighting power against the other half, a process by which one portion must be destroyed, the other weakened, and the whole therefore notably reduced. And when this point is reached, Germany is fairly warned that she will have to account with France. The Emperor Napoleon has recently expressed his detestation of the Treaties of 1815: Prussia has already torn them in pieces before his eyes. The Emperor has subsequently informed the world that, however contented he might be to leave the balance of Europe unassailed, yet the augmentation of any other State in power or territory will, in his opinion, entitle France to a corresponding acquisition. In fact, Prussia stands in this dilemma—she began the war with no willing allies, relying solely on the valour of her own troops, holding what is notoriously the worst military position in Europe, open to attack on every side, from the frontier of Poland to the frontier of Flanders. If she had been defeated in the plains of Saxony or Silesia, she had nothing to fall back upon between the Elbe and the sea. She would have had to pay the price of defeat; and even if she obtained the doubtful aid of France, she would obtain it at the cost of moral infamy and territorial concessions more degrading to the Court of Berlin than the loss of a dozen Jenas. If, on the contrary, Prussia is successful in her military operations and her political intrigues, and if she places herself by success at the head of a large portion of Germany, united under her own sceptre, then, with one voice the French Government and the French nation would say to Prussia, 'You have altered the fundamental conditions of ' power in Europe. Not content with what you obtained in ' 1815 at our expense, you have now enlarged your dominions ' at the expense of your own confederates. You must give us ' back all that the peace of 1815 took from us.' This is not language to which the German armies and people would listen with indifference, and the ultimate result would be a foreign war far more sanguinary and formidable than that just raging in Bohemia.

Indeed, it deserves to be added, that one of the reasons for which we combat the design of a United German Monarchy is, that we believe it would prove highly unfavourable to the maintenance of peace. The existence of a certain number of small States, too weak to excite apprehension, between the frontiers of Great Powers, by which the neutrality and independence of these small States are guaranteed, is an important security to all Europe. Switzerland and Belgium afford that species of neutral *casing* to the French frontier on its most vulnerable points: and this is the most satisfactory solution of the problem how to dispose of provinces of mixed or contested nationality. The exact line of demarcation between France and Germany has been disputed for a thousand years. Convert each State into a powerful military empire, and the strife will last for a thousand more. But if it be possible to preserve and protect small intermediate States by the authority of public law, the cause of interminable wars may be removed, and it is to this expedient that the peace of the last fifty years is mainly due. Suppose France to take advantage of the divisions of Germany, and to acquire possession of the left bank of the Rhine by conquest or by concession. How long would she hold it unchallenged, when Germany had recovered her strength and union? Or are we to suppose that a people who rose like one man to wrest from the King of Denmark two Duchies connected with his Crown by the most ancient ties and by the most recent engagements, would submit to see Cologne, Coblenz, and Mainz occupied by French garrisons? To raise this question is to prepare the elements of continual or repeated war between the French and German races, and to throw back the civilisation of Europe two hundred years.

However such an example may interfere with the theory of the late Mr. Buckle that human affairs are directed by general causes only, and that the will of individuals has no effect on the result, it must be acknowledged that the events we are now witnessing are distinctly attributable to two persons — a very weak King and a very bold Minister. The statesmen of this age are generally more remarkable for prudence than for enterprise, and for the lesser and more practical qualities of administration than for grandeur and vigour of political conception; just as a country gentleman is a less energetic and conspicuous character than the highwayman who stops him on the road. He, therefore, who greatly and boldly dares, without reference to principles or to consequences, towers into pre-eminence among them; and the gifts of Count Bismarck are of this lofty nature. No living man in Europe has played for stakes so large, except the Emperor of the French, whose successful career will be the eternal apology of hazardous courses and desperate adventurers. When M. Bismarck entered public life about fourteen years ago, it was as an ardent member of the *Kreuz* party—a champion of absolutist opinions and an enemy of the Constitution. To these views he had until lately remained consistent, for his appeal to the doctrine of universal suffrage is but a few weeks old, and not Buckingham or Strafford ever trampled more insolently on the representatives of a people. The principal cause of the differences between the King of Prussia and his Parliament was the military system of the kingdom, the Minister wanting to enlarge and consolidate the standing army. It is now clear that the determination of William I. and his adviser to keep under arms a larger body of regular troops than had served for his predecessors, was not without an object, nor the troops without a use, since they were designed to attack and plunder his neighbours. In King William's recent address to his people, this point is expressly admitted, and it establishes the preconcerted nature of the whole enterprise. The King says:—

> '*In anxious anticipation of what has now taken place*, I have been forced for years to consider it as the first duty of my royal office to prepare Prussia's military resources *for a strong development of force.*'

M. Bismarck did not share the prevailing infatuation of German statesmen and people on the Sleswig-Holstein question. On the contrary, he was wont to describe it as a feverish burst of revolutionary passion, which he, of all men, was disposed to resist: and as late as January 1864 he affected to maintain the principle of the integrity of the Danish Monarchy. War, however, was precipitated by the Diet on the banks of the Eider, and M. Bismarck soon found it expedient to take it into his own hands, to annul the Federal intervention of Hanover and Saxony, to entice Austria into the plot, to repudiate the Treaty of 1852, to crown the Prussian standards with the cheap laurels of Duppel, and to take joint possession of the disputed territory. At the sixth sitting of the London Conference, on the 28th May, 1864, the Prussian Minister expressly demanded on behalf of Prussia and Austria the ' union of the Duchies of ' Sleswig and Holstein in one State, under the sovereignty ' of the Duke of Sonderburg-Augustenburg.' But he accompanied his proposal with a demand for the cession to Prussia of the harbour of Kiel, the canal from the Baltic to the Elbe, and the fortification by Prussia of the strongest points of the country. The Duke of Augustenburg was not base enough to submit to these terms, and the consequence was that Bismarck abandoned, proscribed, and threatened to imprison him. Other candidates were then started—a prince of Hesse, a prince of Oldenburgh: but the real claimant was yet to appear; for it was not until the month of July 1864 that M. Bismarck discovered from the law-officers of the Prussian Crown (there are still it seems 'judges at Berlin' though the Miller is no longer a match for the King) that the true legal title to the Duchies had all the while been vested *in the King of Denmark,* and consequently had been transferred by that sovereign to the victorious Powers by the Treaty of Peace signed at Vienna after the campaign. This discovery M. Bismarck had the audacity to impart to the world, although it condemned *ab initio* every pretext put forward to justify the war. Does he adhere to it now? If so, what has become of the common right of conquest vested in Austria, whose troops have been expelled from Holstein by a superior Prussian force? For if the Treaty of Gastein, which was a mere agreement for the temporary partition of these rights of conquest, be at an end, then the provisions of the Treaty of Peace should resume their force, until they are interrupted by war. The Treaty of Gastein was, however, only another step on this downward path, and it was described by M. Drouyn de Lhuys in the following terms :—

' What are the motives which have guided the two great German Powers ? Was it to confirm the rights of ancient Treaties ? Certainly not. The Treaties of Vienna had established the Danish Monarchy on certain conditions: those conditions have now been overthrown. The Treaty of London was a fresh mark of the solicitude of Europe for the duration and integrity of that monarchy : that Treaty likewise has been torn by two of the Powers that signed it. Was it to recover an alienated inheritance, that Austria and Prussia combined ? Instead of restoring it to the most accredited heir, they have shared it between themselves. Was it in the interest of Germany ? Their Confederates only learned these arrangements of Gastein by the public press. Germany desired an undivided State of Schleswig-Holstein, separated from Denmark, and governed by a Prince of her choice. The candidate is thrust aside, and the Duchies are divided. Was it in the interest of the Duchies themselves ? But that, we were told, required their indissoluble union. Was it to satisfy the population ? The population has never been consulted, and even the Diet of Schleswig-Holstein is not convoked. On what principle then does this Austro-Prussian combination rest ? We can find no base for it but force ; no justification but the mutual convenience of the partitioning Powers. Modern Europe had lost all custom of such practices, and precedents can only be found in the worst ages of history. For violence and conquest pervert the very notion of right and the conscience of nations.'

It is impossible to describe that scandalous transaction in more forcible or becoming language ; and the censure is the more valuable as it proceeds from the pen of a French Minister.

We shall not pursue these details much further. Every part of them is stamped with dishonesty and contradiction. One moment Bismarck engaged in a financial intrigue against Austria; the next he offered her twelve millions for her share of the Duchies. In one of the proposals of 1864, made to implicate Austria in the Danish war, Bismarck agreed to support the Emperor Francis Joseph against Italy, in the event of an attack on Venetia ; in the present year, an alliance with Italy, and a simultaneous attack by the two States on Austria, has been arranged, although such an engagement to aid in foreign war against a confederate is a flagrant violation of the spirit and the letter of the Treaty of Vienna and the Federal Pact. In January of this year, he appealed to Austria to combine with him *against the revolution*, and to crush the feeble agitators who had got up meetings at Frankfort and Altona; in April, he lets loose a proposal for the re-organisation of all Germany by a Radical Parliament, chosen by direct and universal suffrage! These inconsistencies would be ludicrous, if they were not stamped with the mark of guilt. They are indications, not of mere levity, but of a settled purpose to accomplish an object by whatsoever means, fair or foul, true or false, right or wrong.

In spite of Bismarck's manœuvres to throw on Austria the responsibility of taking the first step to hostilities, such has been the prudence and moderation of that Power, that every aggressive movement has been made by Prussia. It was on the 28th February that King William held his first council of war, followed by an attitude of more decided hostility. The armament of Austria had not then commenced. The charges of military preparations brought against her were mere pretences; her preparations barely kept pace with the progress of events. On the 24th March, the Prussian revolutionary proposal for the re-organisation of the Bund was hurled at the Diet. Austria replied that she was not averse to attempt that reform, but that it could only be accomplished at a time of peace, and in a spirit of concord. More recently Bismarck addressed to the Imperial Minister a despatch of unmeasured arrogance and impertinence, in language unknown not only to Courts but to gentlemen. Austria responded by convoking the States of Holstein to deliberate on the affairs of the province, and submitted the whole question to the Diet. Prussia dispersed the States by force, arrested the Austrian commissioner, and stopped one of the Imperial couriers. The troops of Austria evacuated Altona, and marched through Hanover. Still no blow was struck by her, and, at length, Prussia having repudiated the legal authority of the Bund altogether, gave the order to invade the territories of Hanover and Saxony and Hesse, because they had supported the perfectly legal proposition of Austria to call out the whole Federal army. She has since completed the occupation of those countries; hoisted the Black Eagle on the public buildings; assumed the rights of sovereignty; forced their armies to capitulate; and sent their princes into confinement.

No doubt these events afford a signal example of that retributive justice which commonly attends great political crimes. For nearly a century the Partition of Poland has continued to perplex and harass its perpetrators and their descendants. The invasion and annexation of the Duchies of the Elbe, under false and artificial pretences, does not sit lightly on Prussia, or on Austria, which condescended, in a moment of weakness, to join in the act, or on the whole of Germany, which applauded it. That act was deliberately condemned at the time by the judgment of the rest of the civilised world ; and the authors of the offence have now taken upon themselves to avenge it upon one another. But though the mind derives satisfaction from the operation of these laws of eternal justice, which run through the tangled skein of human affairs, and over-rule alike the purposes of the good and of the wicked, the in-direct consequences of such events to private interests, the incalculable losses, the immeasurable woes which rush forth, as from the vials of the Apocalypse, plead to Heaven against their author. Since the termination of the career of Napoleon Bonaparte, what living man has dared to avow and act on the hateful doctrine, that no amount of human suffering should avert the execution of a political design ? Even the nephew of the great conqueror turned aside from the blood-stained field of Solferino and offered peace. Upon King William of Prussia and Bismarck rests, in this age, the first unprovoked and wanton shedding of the innocent blood of their own subjects and countrymen, for no object but their own aggrandisement, arrogance, and ambition.

The rapidity with which the Prussian armies spread over the Northern States of Germany, and completed in a week the bloodless conquest of a flock of undefended princes and king-doms, proves to demonstration that the whole operation had been carefully prepared beforehand. The withdrawal of the Prussian Envoy from Frankfort on the measure of coercion being carried in the Diet was the signal for the execution of a conspiracy and a *coup d'état* against the Federal Constitution, as daring and as determined as the blow of the 2nd December which made Louis Napoleon the master of the Assembly and of France. Indeed, it is to that achievement that M. Bismarck's policy may most fitly be compared in audacity, in secrecy, in promp-titude, and apparently in success. Whatever might be thought of the intentions of the Prussian Government, Europe was not prepared for the astonishing energy with which this design has been carried into effect: still less for the feeble and inadequate resistance which has hitherto been offered to it. It may con-fidently be affirmed that down to the very latest moment, when doubt was possible, the soundest political and military judg-ments in Europe discredited the possibility of such a result.

It was known that the minor German States were unready and ill-prepared to face the perils of a great civil war, and that the storm struck them from the quarter in which they least expected to meet it. But the Austrian army was believed to be the second in Europe. Immense efforts and a vast expenditure had been employed to supply the deficiencies which had proved so fatal to it in the campaign of 1859. The army of the North was placed under the undivided command of Marshal Benedek, an officer of the highest reputation, who had the entire confidence of the troops and the nation. That Austria should not at once assume the offensive was consistent with her habitual caution and with her political position in this quarrel. Her defensive position appeared to be invincible, for her forces were concentrated within the mountainous angle of Bohemia, which has the profile of a colossal fortress. The passes in these mountains, and even the plains of Saxony beyond them, were at her command, though she made no attempt to defend them. Her base rested on a great line of fortresses and strong positions connected by railways : and while Prussia had been compelled to extend her line of operations longitudinally across the whole of Germany, the main Austrian army awaited the attack in a concentrated mass, perpendicular to the line of the enemy. When Bohemia was invaded, the Prussian corps were necessarily separated from each other by a considerable extent of difficult country, and Benedek, holding the concentric position with the power of manœuvring on the inner line, like Napoleon in the campaign of 1814, seemed to be admirably placed to defeat them in succession. Setting apart the skill of the rival commanders, and the arms of the men, the valour of the troops might be taken to be equal : but the Austrians had probably the advantage in numbers, in physical strength, and in experience of war, for except in the Danish campaign of 1864, in which the Prussians had not greatly distinguished themselves, few men in the Prussian ranks could have seen actual warfare. On these substantial grounds the great preponderance of military authority both in France, Russia, and England anticipated the success of the Austrians. The events of the war, down to the time at which we write, have, as is well known, confounded these anticipations. It would be premature to discuss the causes of this unforeseen result, or to speculate on the effects of the reverses hitherto sustained by the Imperial armies in Bohemia. But the most obvious of these causes is the superiority of the fire-arms borne by the Prussian infantry ; and it would seem as if this great crisis in the affairs of Europe turned for the present on the adoption by one of the combatants of a breech-loading gun. To this it may be added that the introduction of arms of precision into modern warfare has rendered a new system of formation and tactics indispensable to the protection of troops from the fire of these formidable weapons. The American war was fought by troops continually entrenching themselves in the field for shelter, and always attacking in light skirmishing order. The heavy columns and close drill of the German armies result in wholesale massacre, when opposed to the rapid fire of the breech-loading rifle. This experiment would seem to be decisive, and it points to a termination of hostilities between forces unequally armed; for the bravest troops in the world cannot bear up against the tremendous odds of a gun which fires at least three shots for one. But if the success of the Prussians in this campaign be chiefly due to this adventitious circumstance, which gives them at this moment an advantage over every other army in Europe, we may be certain that ere long this temporary inequality of arms will cease, and the art of war will adapt itself to these altered conditions.

At the moment at which we are writing it would seem that the first act in this bloody drama is played out. The Austrian army has sustained a defeat at the battle of Sadowa scarcely less decisive than those of Austerlitz and Wagram, and it may be hoped that this dreadful conflict is for the present at an end. It would be ungenerous to insist on the errors of policy and the defects of military organisation which have led to this result, and they are sufficiently obvious. The immediate consequence has been the surrender of Venetia, which appears to have been decided upon before the last Prussian victory; and the reluctant admission by the Court of Vienna of its inability to hold that province is the most important result of the war. We trust that this sacrifice may remove one of the causes which threatened the peace of Europe and may lead to the consolidation of the Italian kingdom. But the future organisation of Germany is still undetermined; and in spite of the prodigious successes the Prussian armies have obtained in the field, and the ascendancy the Court of Berlin has thereby acquired in Europe, the relations of the German States with each other and with the other neighbouring Powers are questions which cannot be solved without the concurrence of the German nation and the other parties to the Treaties of Vienna.

When the treaties which constitute the fundamental compact of Europe are denounced by one great Power and broken by another; when the legitimate alliances of States

for avowed objects are dissolved, and countermined by clandestine associations of conspirators against the peace of the
world; when these Governments recoil from publicity, defraud
their own subjects of all control over their affairs, and complete
the destruction of liberty by schemes of war, we can entertain
no hope that a re-settlement of Europe will be speedily or
easily accomplished, or that when it is accomplished it will
bear the mark of wisdom, justice, and permanence. It will
still be the law imposed by conquerors on the conquered. It
will still be conceived in the spirit of mutual distrust. Far from
disarming the enormous military establishments of Europe,
it will increase them. It will inflame the military spirit of
another generation, and perhaps re-open an indefinite series
of recurring wars. The crowning trait in the policy of Bismarck is to attack the revolutionary influence of France in
Europe by acts more revolutionary than her own; as a traveller sets fire to the leeward side of the prairie or the forest
to escape from a conflagration threatening him to windward.
But this is a race in which the Imperial power of France will
not long be left behind.

We hold it to be no reproach to the Parliament and the
statesmen of England that they have not been swift or eager to
express opinions on the tremendous military operations now
taking place in central Europe; and that, committing themselves to no partial view on either side, they have studied rather
to maintain a neutral and impassive attitude in so great a
quarrel. For in its details the political interests of this
country are not at present concerned. Whether Germany be
divided into two or three States, or into many; whether her
national government be federative or single; whether the chief
seat of power be in the north, or in the south, or in the
centre, are matters of which the Germans are the sole judges.
We have ceased to have any territorial connexion with that
country, and we have entirely relinquished the obsolete theories
which pledged us, for the sake of a disputed province or a
reigning House, to take an active part in the affairs of the Continent. England, moreover, has nothing to envy or to dread
in the aggrandisement of Prussia, or in the successes of the
army which fought by her own side at Waterloo.

But it would be a mistake to imagine that because we now
require our Ministers to abstain from restless interference and
unsolicited advice in these disputes, we are insensible to the
great general interests which bind this country to the continent
of Europe. The withdrawal or diminution of the moral influence of England from the affairs of the Continent would be

an abdication of that lofty and glorious position which the freeest State in the world has held for centuries; and would be not less injurious to the interests of mankind than to our own honour. We cannot with impunity see the weak trampled on by the strong, when by holding out a hand it is in our power to help them. This very war is an example of the service which would have been rendered to all Europe, if two years ago a British fleet in the Belt and the Sound had resolutely announced that Denmark 'was not alone' in her hour of danger, and had saved the Duchies from a Prussian invasion. We cannot see the fabric of European treaties swept away, and the balance of power between European States overthrown, without remembering that there are points we may have to defend, and there are principles we can never abandon.

The first condition of the foreign policy this country desires to practise is a close and honest understanding with France, because we are convinced that we have more common interests with the French than with any other people, and that the combined power of the two great Western States is irresistible when it is exerted for the same public objects. And this alliance has further the advantage that, as long as it lasts, it can never be used to oppress or injure other nations, since one Government acts as a check upon the other. We believe and hope that the Emperor Napoleon sets on this connexion a high value, and that, whatever his views may be in reference to other States, he will not willingly engage in a course which would lead to the greatest of all calamities—a rupture with England. For that is a quarrel in which both parties have literally everything to lose, and, from each other, nothing to gain. But having ourselves no objects to conceal and no desires to gratify, except a very cordial wish for the restoration and maintenance of peace, we have a right to claim from other Cabinets a frankness equal to our own. The cession of Savoy and Nice to France by Piedmont in exchange for the acquisition of Lombardy, was a matter of no territorial importance to this country; but we had reason to complain that the transaction was wrapped in mystery and even in denial, and to require that the rights of Switzerland, affected by the transfer, should be respected. It was the disappointment justly felt by this country on these points which gave rise to a temporary coolness between the two governments, and greatly modified the feelings of Lord Palmerston towards the French Emperor. Events are possibly tending to the acquisition by France of a certain extent of territory on the left bank of the Rhine. Such an accession of a territory would, in our opinion, be a very doubtful benefit to the French

Empire, for the population would be disaffected and the resentment of the Germans implacable. But England has no interest in the matter, beyond the desire that provinces should not be bartered and chaffered by the sole right of conquest. We readily make to the alliance of France the sacrifice of many old prejudices and jealousies; but we have a right to expect that her policy should be controlled by a reasonable deference to the real interests and security of Great Britain, when they are at stake. In justice to the Emperor Napoleon it must be said that the views of the British Cabinet have frequently had great weight with him—that he has more than once yielded his own intentions to them, as in acknowledging the unity of Italy—and that we have no reason to impute to him any but the most friendly sentiments towards this country.

Foreign nations, which are still apt to form very superficial and inaccurate notions of the opinions and policy of this country, have adopted the belief that England is enervated by her prosperity, and emasculated by the selfish doctrines of the Manchester school. The Emperor Nicholas acted upon that conviction in 1853, and the Crimean war, the defeat of Russia, and the miserable termination of his own reign and life, were the results of the delusion. For it is a delusion to suppose that this country is either less powerful than of old, or less energetic in the use of her power, though she may be more prudent in the application of it. Events may happen—possibly they may soon happen—which would rouse the people of England with irresistible force, and suddenly change this apparent listlessness into a new display of conscious power and determined will. We do not intend to interfere in the internal affairs of foreign nations: we do not conceive that the interests or the dignity of England are affected by fancied consequences arising out of a modification of territorial possessions on the continent; but if the great principle of the independence of nations were attacked, if advantage were taken of the present disordered state of affairs to establish any paramount authority by force of arms over the rights and liberties of other States, we are satisfied that the support of England would not be wanting to the cause of right and justice, which is not always strong enough to protect itself without her assistance. If that time comes, the voice of England will be heard to recommend institutions framed in a more liberal spirit, more unrestricted commercial intercourse, more enlarged religious toleration, a nicer regard to the sensitive distinctions of national feeling, and a more intimate connexion between the common interests of neighbouring countries. Dark as is this day, we are not without hopes that the storm will sweep away much that is worthless and antiquated; that it will contribute in the end to the progress of nations; and that when peace is permanently restored, it may be no longer an armed peace, scarcely less oppressive to mankind than war, but a peace established upon a firmer basis of national content, of mutual confidence, and of public law.

We have witnessed with the deepest concern the fall of the Liberal Administration, which had presided for seven years over the destinies of the British Empire; and this regret is heightened by the transfer, at this momentous crisis in Europe, of the direction of foreign affairs from tried to untried hands. In the Earl of Clarendon, the country possessed a Foreign Minister of complete experience, of consummate address, of indefatigable activity, and of the highest influence abroad. His successor is no doubt the ablest member of the new Government and one of the most promising statesmen of England—inferior to none in power of work and in enlightened liberal views—but the experience derived from a long and intimate acquaintance with men and things abroad, and the personal influence abroad which that experience confers, cannot but be wanting to Lord Stanley. In times such as these, a change in the Foreign Office, when its duties have been so ably discharged, is a serious loss and evil to the country. But this and all minor consequences are included in the general catastrophe which has just broken up the Administration and transferred the Government of the country to a Ministry and a party avowedly not possessing a majority in the House of Commons or the confidence of the country.

We shall not here discuss the causes which have brought about this untoward event. Recrimination on the past is useless; and the future course of action of the Liberal party has yet to be determined. But we may be permitted to remark that nothing has occurred which was not foreseen and predicted by ourselves twelve months ago. It was argued by this Journal in July 1865 (pp. 288–290), that 'the progress of Parliamentary ' Reform had been checked, not so much by the resistance of ' the Tory Opposition, as by the want of uniformity and agree- ' ment among the Liberal Members of the House of Commons ' as to the shape the new Reform Bill should assume:' that ' whenever the Liberal party is united, and resolved as one man ' to carry a Reform Bill, the Bill will be carried; but that ' until that time be come, the preparation of the measure is ' incomplete:' and that ' nothing could be more fatal to the true ' Liberal interests of the country than the belief that Ministers

' are prepared to force on measures for which the country is
' not prepared.' The experiment has now been tried, and we
are not consoled for the overthrow of a Liberal Administration
and a certain period of Tory rule, by the assurance that the
party to which we have the honour to belong will be trium-
phantly restored to office by a great increase of popular agita-
tion and radical ascendancy.

For we assert with unabated confidence that the majority of
the House of Commons and of the country is, at this moment,
WHIG. The majority is not in favour of radical changes in
the Constitution, for even the Reform Bill of the late Government, which well deserved to be regarded as a measure of con-
ciliation, did not obtain efficient support in the House of
Commons. The majority is certainly not in favour of Tory
principles or Tory government, for it is only by borrowing Whig
principles that the Tories can hope to govern. The opinion of
the country, almost without reference to the old distinctions
of party, is in favour of a liberal and progressive policy—a
cordial sympathy with the cause of freedom and national rights
abroad, without abetting war and revolution—a desire to extend the electoral franchise at home, without throwing preponderating power into the hands of the democracy. Yet by
an extraordinary concourse of events, the present Ministers of
the Crown are taken from the party which has no claim to
represent these opinions; and the leader of the old and renowned party, identified with these moderate and liberal principles for two centuries, falls from office at a moment when
its policy is indisputably in the ascendant! Such is the result
of the division, which, be it from one side or from the other,
has paralysed the majority and disunited the Liberal party.
The evil will probably not be of long duration; but whenever
it comes to an end, the lesson to be learnt from these events is
that extreme measures are fatal to the combination by which
a Liberal Administration can alone be supported, and tend to
defeat their object by throwing a considerable proportion of
public opinion and political influence into the opposite scale.
We therefore, in conclusion, humbly tender our advice to the
future leaders of the Liberal party, whether in or out of office,
to avoid the ' madness of extremes,' and to adhere to that wise
and temperate mean course which can alone give strength to
the Government and security to the country.

No. CCLIV. will be published in October.

THE

EDINBURGH REVIEW,

OCTOBER, 1866.

No. CCLIV.

ART. I.—1. *The History of the Sepoy War.* Vol. I. By
JOHN W. KAYE, Esq. London : 1864.
2. *Notes on the Revolt in the North-Western Provinces of
India.* By CHARLES RAIKES, Judge of the Sudder Court
at Agra, late Civil Commissioner with Sir Colin Campbell.
London : 1858.

IT was for some months our intention to await the publication
of the second volume, at least, of this important and deeply
interesting work, the first part of which Mr. Kaye has written
with so much vigour and ability, before we proceeded to pass
our judgment upon its merits. And we were confirmed in
this resolution, which accords with our usual practice, by the
consideration that we had previously gone over much of the
ground traversed hitherto by Mr. Kaye; and had not only
devoted a whole article to the expression of our opinion upon
the policy and character of Lord Dalhousie, but had also
found occasion, in reviewing the recent advancement of British
India in material prosperity, to state briefly the conclusion
to which we had come, ' that the mutiny of 1857 was in no
' manner or degree the consequence and retribution of civil
' misgovernment. It was the ferocious outbreak of a pam-
' pered and blindly trusted soldiery, not the insurrection of an
' oppressed and indignant people.' And there we might have
been content to let the matter rest for a while—however serious
we felt it to be—if we had found that there was any prospect
of the completion, or even the continuation, of the ' History of
' the Sepoy War' within a short period. But being disappointed
in this hope, and adverting to the strength and earnestness
with which Mr. Kaye has urged an opinion directly at
variance with our own—as if it were a point of indisputable

certainty—and that, too, in a work so ably and popularly written, and so universally read, as to carry erroneous impressions on the subject into the minds of thousands, we feel bound to do justice, without further delay, both to the Government and to the people of India, by stating explicitly the grounds on which the opposite conviction is founded. The point at issue between us and Mr. Kaye is a highly practical one, because it is clear that the terrible events of 1857–8 ought to teach us essentially different lessons for the guidance of our future conduct, according as we are satisfied, after the careful investigation which such a question demands, that those events were the results either of a military mutiny or of a popular rebellion.

Mr. Kaye has devoted much time and labour to trace back the outbreak to causes lying deep in the more recent policy of our Indian Government towards native princes of every class, and in our fiscal treatment of certain members of our own agricultural community. He speaks of ' manifold causes.' We, on the contrary, believe that an influence so powerful as to be rightly regarded as the main—almost, indeed, the sole—motive of the insurrection is to be found much nearer the surface, and is, in truth, so simple as to admit of being defined in a very few lines. Mr. Kaye, in short, regards the rising as a rebellion of the people of India; to us it appears to have been merely a military mutiny, of which a few who wished to shake off our rule, and a few of those who loved license and plunder— both classes together utterly insignificant, in point of numbers, when compared with the subject millions,—took advantage to further their respective ends.

In maintaining the former opinion, Mr. Kaye, we regret to say, has made himself, to a great extent, the mouthpiece of a party small in numbers and smaller in ability, Englishmen too —for the verdict of thoughtful foreigners has been very different—who regard the onward march of their country in India as one great crime; who can see in each acquisition of territory nothing but the result of an unscrupulous and short-sighted greediness; and who maintain that to assume that the people of India are better governed and more happy under British dominion than when ruled by their native princes, if it be not a mere figment to cloak ambition, is, at the best, but the dictate of national vanity, without the slightest root in reality.

We lament that Mr. Kaye should have been impelled— by honest convictions, we have no doubt—to lend the credit of his. high reputation to abet those party-writers who

have not scrupled to brand Lord Dalhousie as ' the very
' worst and basest of rulers,' and have even expressed
' sincere regret ' that that great statesman ' could not have
' lived a few years more to witness the definitive downfall of
' his once great reputation ; ' ' to feel his labours nullified and
' his plans annihilated by wholesale revision and reversal, his
' titles and dignities tarnished and vulgarised, his wealth
' turned into a shame and a reproach, every memory em-
' bittered, and every thought of posterity poisoned by the
' unanimous censure of two nations.' Mr. Kaye, it gives us
pleasure to record, writes in a very different spirit. He has
given Lord Dalhousie full credit for the entire singleness
and purity of his motives. He has said generously, but not
more than justly, while deprecating his policy :—

' At the bottom of this great error were benign intentions.
Dalhousie and his lieutenants had a strong and steadfast faith in the
wisdom and benevolence of their measures, and strove alike for the
glory of the English nation and the welfare of the Indian people.
There was something grand, and even good, in the errors of such a
man ; for there was no taint of baseness in them, no sign of anything
sordid or self-seeking. He had given himself up to the public service resolute to do a great work, and he rejoiced with a noble pride
in the thought that he left behind him a mightier empire than he
had found ; that he had brought new countries and strange nations
under the sway of the British sceptre, and sown the seeds of a great
civilisation. To do this he had made unstinting sacrifice of leisure,
ease, comfort, health, and the dear love of wedded life ; and he
carried home with him, in a shattered frame and a torn heart, in the
wreck of a manhood at its very prime, mortal wounds nobly received
in a great and heroic encounter.'

Again, speaking of the inevitable antagonism of the British
Government to the superstitious and idolatrous abominations of
the people, Mr. Kaye observes :—

' From love of this kind (of " truth above error "), from the
assured conviction that it was equally humane and politic to substitute the strength and justice of British administration for what
he regarded as the effete tyrannies of the East, had emanated the
annexations which had distinguished his rule ; and as he desired, for
the good of the people, to extend the territorial rule of Great Britain,
so he was eager also to extend her moral rule, and to make those
people subject to the powers of light rather than of darkness ; and
so he strove mightily to extend among them the blessings of
European civilisation.'

Strange that one thus capable of appreciating the motives
and aims of Lord Dalhousie should speak elsewhere of that
great statesman, and of those who shared his views, as if they

were actuated by the vulgar greed of mere territorial aggrandisement!

In return for his support, the more rabid of the assailants of Lord Dalhousie have taken offence at Mr. Kaye's candour, and denounce him as a half-hearted comrade, wanting in courage to follow out his conclusions to their logical consequences; meaning thereby his refusal to ascribe the meanest and basest motives to every one who dares to differ from them in regard to the policy and character of the British Government in India. Towards those who presume to hold that the mutiny of the Bengal army was not the rebellion of the people of India their language is, if possible, still more unmeasured and contemptuous.

We have said that distinguished foreigners have arrived at very different conclusions in respect both to the character of the Government of British India and to the causes of the mutiny. We cannot cite higher or more impartial authorities than MM. de Tocqueville and de Montalembert. The former has compressed his opinion into a single sentence, as vigorous as it is profound. 'Je crois,' he observes, speaking of the mutiny, 'que les horribles évènements de l'Inde ne sont en 'aucune façon un soulèvement contre l'oppression; c'est une 'révolte de la barbarie contre l'orgueil.' M. de Montalembert, after stating, 'sans hésiter, que la Compagnie des Indes 'Orientales est de toutes les dominations connues dans l'his- 'toire des colonies du monde ancien et moderne, celle qui a fait 'les plus grandes choses avec les plus petits moyens, et celle 'qui, dans un espace de temps égal, a fait le moins de mal et 'le plus de bien aux peuples soumis à ses lois,' proceeds to ob- serve, with reference to the mutiny, 'Ainsi j'explique un fait de 'la plus haute importance, et qui suffit à lui seul pour absoudre 'la domination anglaise. Depuis bientôt dix-huit mois que 'dure l'insurrection, elle est restée purement militaire; *la* '*population civile n'y a pris aucune part sérieuse.** Sauf dans 'quelques rares localités, elle a refusé tout concours aux in- 'surgés, malgré les occasions, les tentatives nombreuses que 'lui offraient les désastres partiels des Anglais et le nombre 'si restreint de leurs troupes. Loin de là; on sait que c'est 'encore maintenant au concours des princes indiens et d'auxili- 'aires empruntés à des races différentes de celles qui composent 'l'armée du Bengale que l'Angleterre doit d'avoir pu lutter 'victorieusement contre les insurgés. La révolte a été exclu- 'sivement l'œuvre des Cipayes enrégimentés de la Compagnie.' And almost in the words of M. de Tocqueville he calls the in-

---

* The italics are M. de Montalembert's.

surrection ' une lutte engagée entre la civilisation et la barbarie.'
With these opinions that of Sir John Lawrence, reviewing
with the pen of his secretary, in a despatch to the Supreme
Government, the trial of the ci-devant Emperor of Delhi, entirely concurs.   The secretary writes :—

' Nothing has transpired on this trial or on any other occasion to
show that he (the Emperor) was engaged in a previous conspiracy
to excite a mutiny in the Bengal army.   Indeed, it is Sir John
Lawrence's very decided impression that this mutiny had its origin
in the army itself; that it is not attributable to any external or
antecedent conspiracy whatever, although it was afterwards taken
advantage of by disaffected persons to compass their own ends ; and
that the proximate cause was the cartridge affair, and nothing else.'

That was, no doubt, the match that fired the train.   The
questions at issue between Mr. Kaye and ourselves are, what
was the combustible matter which that train primarily exploded?   Was the gathering together of that matter the result of
a wide-spread and long-concerted conspiracy, embracing many
and powerful native princes, landholders of every class, and
especially those who had been newly adjudged liable to pay
revenue, as well as great numbers of the general community,
particularly those of the Moslem faith ?   Or was, as we affirm,
the explosion limited, in the first instance, to the ranks of the
Sepoy army, from which the conflagration spread when the first
outbreak seemed to promise success, to the disaffected of every
grade, to the rabble of the large bazaars, to the convicts whom
they let loose, to the Goojurs, and other half-reclaimed tribes
of freebooters; and, lastly, to a considerable number of ambitious
or fanatic Mahomedans, who deemed that the happy opportunity had come, through the internecine strife of two bodies
of infidels, for the re-establishment of their ancient and only
legitimate dominion ?

Now, without building upon the high authorities whose
opinions we have cited, and to whom it would be easy to make
large additions, we are satisfied that we shall be able to prove,
by an abundance of the strongest evidence converging upon the
point at issue, the fallacy of the former and the soundness of
the latter theory.   But we are bound to make one admission.
We do not doubt that Brahminical influence had been for some
time at work, poisoning the minds of the Sepoys, and indoc-
trinating them with an undoubting conviction which their most
trusted and best-loved English officers were unable to eradicate,
that their chief rulers, both in India and in England, entertained
a deliberate design to destroy their caste, to subvert their religion, and to compel them to become Christians.   It must

seem scarcely credible to those who have no practical acquaintance with the people of India, that any men could be
so absurd as to fear that they might be made Christians against
their will, either by fraud or violence.   But there is nothing
strange in such an apprehension to those who know what the
faith of ignorant Hindoos, such as our Sepoys were, really is.
It is absolutely devoid of the slightest spiritual essence.   It is
a thing composed exclusively of 'meats, and drinks, and divers
' washings and carnal ordinances.' It is certain, indeed, that as
respects what we mean by religion, not a Hindoo in the whole
Sepoy army could have given an intelligible account of what
he believed; but it is equally certain that there was not a man
in its ranks who could not have told what his caste was, what
privileges it conferred, what observances were essential to its
due maintenance, and how it might be endangered or lost.

This state of things being premised, it will be seen that one
half of the fear of the Sepoys was reasonable.   It was absurd,
of course, to suppose that the Government could make them
Christians whether they would or not; but it was not absurd to
believe that the Government, if so minded, might entrap them
into some act of ceremonial uncleanness which would deprive
them of their caste, and thus render them outcasts from Hin-
dooism.

By whatever means the impression had been infused into
their minds, the great bulk of the Hindoo Sepoys sincerely
believed that such a pitfall had been dug before their feet, and
that it was the one great aim of the British Government to
push them headlong into it.   They were firmly persuaded that
Lord Canning and General Anson, both newly arrived, had
been commanded by the Queen, and had pledged themselves to
her, to make all the natives of India Christians.   This, with
the vast majority, was the sole cause of the mutiny.   Upon
some minds the effect of this delusion was mere terror, but it
stung fiercer natures to frenzy; and hence, we are persuaded,
resulted such acts of murderous cruelty as were actually perpetrated by Sepoys, and not—as probably most of them were
—by ruffians from the bazaars and jails.   Thus the few committed the crimes for which the whole body of each mutinying
regiment was necessarily and justly held responsible.   But
there were some, no doubt, who were actuated in part, at least,
if not altogether, by ambition.   They knew—for the Sepoys,
in their frequent changes of quarters, became acquainted with
every station in the country—that there were but two British
regiments between Calcutta and Agra, a distance of 800 miles;
and they were, consequently, persuaded that they were masters

of the situation.   Why, then, should they submit to be the ill-paid tools of the Feringee, when they might be colonels and generals, or even governors and princes themselves?

Together with a few Hindoos, chiefly Mahrattas, the great majority of those who joined the insurrection under the influence of ambition were Mahomedans. At the same time, we are satisfied that the professors of that faith were not, as many have supposed, the contrivers, the instigators, or the leaders of the outbreak. As to a deliberate plot, indeed, we do not believe that beyond the injection into the minds of the Sepoys of the delusions to which we have referred, there was any plot at all. As regards the part taken by Mahomedans, it is certain that the first overt acts of mutiny at Barrackpore were committed by Hindoos; that the single Sepoy, 'faithful found ' among the faithless,' who risked his own life to save the lives of his English officers, when Mungul Pandy fired the first mutinous shot, was a Mahomedan; and Mr. Kaye records that ' the inquiries into the state of the 34th Regiment at Barrack-' pore,' at the same period, ' had resulted in the belief that the ' Mahomedan and Sikh soldiers were true to their salt, but ' that the Hindoos generally of that corps were not to be ' trusted.' That the first, as a body, should have remained faithful, with such a tempting bait before them, in their view of the crisis, as the probable recovery of their ascendancy, is more than could be expected of human nature in general, certainly of Mahomedan nature. Many yielded to the temptation, and flung themselves, heart and soul, into the conflict. Many, no doubt, but by no means—as the ill-informed and credulous in general, and especially the Calcutta alarmists, believed—the whole body of the Moslem of India. The great bulk of the population of that creed remained throughout the crisis passive and neutral. Not a few, we are happy and proud to know, were faithful to the salt of the Government which they had served, or under whose rule they and their fathers had enjoyed a large measure of civil and complete religious liberty, together with the peace and prosperity flowing from those sources. There is, indeed, no greater or more mischievous delusion in regard to India than the vulgar error of supposing that all Mahomedans are bigots and fanatics. Beyond question there are many such among them; just as many as—it may be, perhaps, more than—there were Christians of a like character in Europe when the Inquisition murdered its thousands, and when Henri IV. and William of Nassau fell by the hands of assassins, from which our own Elizabeth scarcely escaped. But neither did then more than a few in Europe, nor do now more than a few in India, act up to even what they believed and believe to be the treacherous and bloody dictates of their respective religions.   And millions, probably, in both instances, had not and have not any practical belief in the obligations of such a creed as their fanatical co-religionists accepted and endeavoured to render universal and effective.   There are lukewarm and indifferent Mahomedans, there are sceptics and unbelievers among those who are numbered with Mahomedans, just as there are the same classes of characters among those who ' profess and ' call themselves Christians.'   Millions prefer their ease, their safety, and their immediate worldly interests to their religion, even with Mahomedan ascendancy superadded ; and we rejoice in the knowledge that while the faith of Islam, as interpreted by bigots, is held to enjoin the extermination of infidels, there were not a few among the Mahomedans of India whose conduct during the mutiny was governed rather by their natural sense of right, or by a feeling of gratitude and affection towards individual Christians, than by the Koran, or by intensified glosses put upon its dogmas by fanatics.   For the Koran does not enjoin the destruction of ' men of the book,' as Christians are.   At any rate, whatever the motives, this much is certain, that from the outbreak to the suppression of the mutiny, and from one end of India to the other, thousands upon thousands of Mahomedans, high and low, rich and poor, princes and servants, soldiers and civilians, not only refrained from lifting a finger against the British Government, or any Christian individual, but rendered active and most useful service—at the hazard often of their lives and fortunes—to both it and them.   It would fill pages to enumerate, even in the baldest manner, instances in substantiation of this position.   Let these suffice.   Of native princes, the Nawab of Rampore, a Mahomedan of the Mahomedans, a descendant of the gallant Fyz Mahomed, (who struggled so bravely, though in vain, against the British force with which Warren Hastings abetted the cruel tyranny of the Nawab of Oude,) and the Begum of Bhopal, whose subjects are also Rohillas, Affghans by descent, and perhaps the most warlike tribe in Hindostan, were not merely faithful but signally helpful.   The Newab of Tonk, son of the celebrated Ameer Khan, a formidable leader in the Pindaree war, who probably rules over more Mahomedan fanatics than any prince in India, stood by the British Government with exemplary firmness. Salar Jung, the Prime Minister of the Nizam, not only kept down the turbulent and bigoted population of the Mahomedan city of Hyderabad, but when he was informed that a fanatic was preaching in a mosque the duty of a crusade against the

Christians, went in person with his bodyguard to the spot, arrested the preacher in the midst of his harangue, and sent him to cool his zeal in jail.   A Mahomedan Rissaldar (a native major) of our Irregular Cavalry, who was happily spending his furlough in his native village, within a few miles of Delhi, received and treated with the utmost hospitality and kindness many, both male and female, of the Christian fugitives from that city; fed, clothed, protected, and finally convoyed them in safety to the British garrison at Agra.   Upon that gallant and faithful soldier we are happy to record that Lord Canning conferred the village in which he did the good deed, in fee simple, free of revenue, to him and his heirs for ever.   Again, when the Commissioner of Patna called upon the civil officers of the several districts under his authority to leave their respective stations, and to seek refuge at Patna, a Mahomedan gentleman took charge of the beautiful district of Sarun from the magistrate and collector—of the treasury, the jail, the records, and of all the public and private property necessarily abandoned—maintained the most perfect order and security during the absence of that functionary, and restored everything intact to him on his return.   Recently, in recommending a retired Mahomedan native officer for a grant of land in the Punjab, the Lieutenant-Governor stated that in addition to his own services his two brothers had fought gallantly on our side at Cabul and at Delhi; that his nephew had killed with his own hand at Kalabagh the ringleader of the mutineers of the 9th Irregular Cavalry, a Mahomedan also; and that his son, also in the service, had saved the life of a British officer in the outbreak at Goorgaira in 1857.   Again, Ram Pershad Dooby, a Hindoo, was executed lately for the murder in 1857 of Meer Sabit Ali, a Mahomedan Tehsildar (collector of land revenue) at Bijeragoghur, on the border of Bundelcund, and the officer reporting on the case observes: ' The slaughter ' of the Tehsildar was a deliberate premeditated deed.   He ' remained, like many others at that period, boldly and loyally ' at his post, though he must have known the risk he was ' running.'   We will only add, that we have the highest authority for affirming that fully two-thirds of the native troops sent down from the Punjab who aided so materially in the recapture of Delhi were Mahomedans; and that the instances of fidelity to their Christian masters and mistresses, in peril of their lives, on the part of Mahomedan domestic servants, were numerous and signal.

Nevertheless, the press of Calcutta, of whose ' odieuses ex- ' citations ' to cruel acts of revenge M. de Montalembert speaks in just terms of scorn and disgust, raised a frantic clamour against every Mahomedan, when Mr. Samuells, appointed Commissioner of Patna at a very critical moment, took with him as an assistant Moonshee Ameer Ali, a Mahomedan gentleman of great ability and influence, and a large land-owner in the province.   No language was deemed too strong to denounce the rashness of the Commissioner, the imbe-cility of the Government, and the certain treachery of the Mahomedan assistant.   Notwithstanding these predictions, however, that gentleman furnished another instance of Ma-homedan trustworthiness, and rendered very useful service to the Commissioner and the Government.   Very recent events have afforded a still stronger confirmation of our argument. Certain Wahabee Mahomedans, resident at Patna, have been convicted of treason against the British Government, the overt act of which was the supplying money to foment and support the war carried on against us by sympathising fanatics harboured in the wild hills upon our north-western frontier.   Here, no doubt, was Mahomedan bigotry engaged in active and practical intrigue against our rule.   But the officer of police in the Punjab who gave the first information of the conspiracy, and who, when his original charge was dismissed by the English magistrate before whom he laid it, for want of sufficient evidence, sent his son to the scene of action to obtain fuller and more certain proofs of the designs and acts of the traitors, was also a Mahomedan.   Why should the treason of the one, rather than the fidelity of the other, be accepted as the universal type of the class?

It is a remarkable fact that when the four regiments which mutinied at Cawnpore proceeded to elect their colonels, three of them chose Hindoos (we know not who was the elect of the fourth), and that one of the three was a corps of cavalry, of whom the great majority were Mahomedans.

Fully admitting, then, that the prejudices and passions of the Sepoys had been worked upon by enemies of the British Government, whether Brahmins or others, and believing that Mr. Kaye is quite justified in his conviction that railways and telegraphs, and the rapid progress of English education and consequent enlightenment, had raised the fears and kindled the animosities of the sacerdotal class which had long thriven upon the ignorance and delusions of the mass of the people, we pro-ceed to examine what may be called the civil causes to which that gentleman attributes the series of events under our con-sideration, premising that we cannot understand why, with his convictions, he did not follow the example of Lord Clarendon, and call his work the ' History of the Great Indian Rebellion,' rather than the ' History of the Sepoy War.'

The first and chief of the causes alleged by Mr. Kaye is the policy of Lord Dalhousie in refusing to recognise the ceremony of adoption, when exercised by childless Hindoo princes, as conveying to the adopted son the right to succeed, without the sanction of the British Government, which he held that it was free to give or to withhold, to the sovereignty of the adopting father—this doctrine being practically carried out in the cases of Sattara, Nagpore, and Jhansi.

And, secondly, Mr. Kaye attributes the outbreak to what are called Resumption operations—namely, the investigation of the titles of persons claiming to hold lands under grants from former sovereigns or competent local authorities, free from the payment of revenue to the State, and the compelling of those who failed to substantiate those claims to bear their proportionate share of the public burdens. This grievance, it may be remarked, is of far older date than the Administration of Lord Dalhousie; and had, in fact, been consummated throughout Bengal, Behar, and the North-Western Provinces, before he set foot in India.

But what if the causes so largely elaborated produced no effects — or none, at least, in any degree commensurate with their alleged potency? Are they to be regarded as causes nevertheless? What if the native princes, so malcontent in regard to the past, and so suspicious of our designs in the future, declined to rise in arms against the oppressive British Government, and left the Sepoys to fight out their own battle, some of them even giving effectual assistance towards their discomfiture? What if the landholders, who had been adjudged liable to pay revenue long wrongfully withheld, refused to make common cause with the mutineers, and remained quietly at home ploughing their newly-assessed fields? Are we still bound to believe that the alleged wrongs of these classes were two of the principal provocatives of the insurrection; that the Bengal Sepoys, not one in ten thousand of whom ever heard the name of Sattara, sympathised so intensely with the injustice done to an obscure Mahratta boy, by refusing to allow him to be transformed into a Rajah, (the Mahrattas having been for more than a century the dreaded scourges of North-Western India, and having plundered and murdered up to the very gates of Calcutta,) that they rose in arms to avenge and redress it; and that the people of Nagpore, within whose broad bounds, as Sir John Malcolm wrote in 1805, ' there are not more Mahrattas, in

' proportion to the original inhabitants of the soil, than there are
' European inhabitants in proportion to the natives of Bengal
' and Behar,' were so enamoured of the rule of that false and
cruel race that they were ready to shed their blood to perpetuate it ?

But let us apply the simple test of fact to Mr. Kaye's theory.
Hindoo princes and chiefs were alone affected, or in any danger of being affected, by what is called Lord Dalhousie's policy
in respect to annexation, consequent on the refusal of permission to adopt a successor.   The sovereign princes of India professing the Hindoo faith range themselves in three great classes
—the Rajpoots, the Mahrattas, and the Sikhs, for the latter
are Hindoo Puritans.   Not a leading individual of any one of
these classes, not one known to history or possessed of any
real power for good or evil, if we except the wild Ranee of
Jhansi, took advantage of the mutiny of the Sepoys to rise in
arms against the British Government.   Several of them, and
especially the Sikh Rajahs of Puttialla, Jheend, and Nabha,
rendered us very valuable assistance at the most critical
moment of the struggle.   Nor is there the slightest shadow of
proof—there is not, to our knowledge, the least suspicion—that
any one of the princes in question had tampered with the Sepoys
before they broke out.   There are suspicions—still far short of
proofs--that the Nana busied himself, during the months which
preceded the mutiny, in travelling from station to station in
the north-west; when he had opportunities, no doubt, if
such were his object, of playing upon the credulity of the
Sepoys in regard to our designs on their religion and caste.
Some one must have given currency and emphasis to those lies,
and why not the Nana, a Brahmin, and a deeply-disappointed
man, as well as another ?   We shall show in the sequel that
he had no real grievance ; but as there are bodies so diseased
that a scratched finger will fester into a gangrene, so even a
groundless sense of wrong was sufficient to goad to frenzy passions so fierce and malignant as those which events proved the
Nana to be cursed with.

As respects chiefs of minor rank and power, we have before
us a carefully compiled list of all those who took part, or were
suspected of taking part, in the insurrection throughout the
North-Western Provinces.   The great majority of them are
so petty and obscure that if the mutiny had not occurred
their very names or titles would never have been heard more
than a few miles from their respective homes.   But of those
who made themselves prominent, and were so distinguished
either by treachery or atrocity as to be deemed to deserve

capital punishment, and who suffered accordingly, three were Mahomedans and two Hindoos; and three others, who richly deserved the same fate, and escaped by fortunate accidents—the Nawabs of Feruckabad, Banda, and Nujebabad—were all, as their titles indicate, Mahomedans. Surely, none but the most heated partisans of a theory could detect in such results as these the disquieting and alienating effect of Lord Dalhousie's policy upon the minds of Hindoo princes.

Here, we regret to say, we must pause to notice two instances in which his vehement desire to make out a case against that policy has betrayed Mr. Kaye into taking up positions the falseness of which nothing short of the strongest foregone conclusions could have prevented him from seeing. In the first case, however—the question of succession by adoption—he evidently had misgivings. ' It is,' he says, ' with the question ' of adoption only in its political aspects that I have to do in this ' place.' But he does not, on that account, abstain from letting his readers know—not one in a hundred of whom has the faintest conception of the distinction between the religious and the political aspects of the question—that ' LAPSE is a dreadful and an ' appalling word, for it pursues the victim beyond the grave ; ' its significance in his eyes is nothing short of eternal condem- ' nation. The son, says the great Hindoo lawgiver, " delivers ' " his father from the hell called Put." There are, he tells ' us, different kinds of sons ; there is the son begotten ; the ' son given ; the son by adoption ; and other filial varieties. ' It is the duty of the son to perform the funeral obsequies of ' the father. If they be not performed, it is believed that there ' is no resurrection to eternal bliss.' All this is quite true, but it has not the slightest bearing upon the question which, as Mr. Kaye admits, is alone at issue, otherwise than 'ad invidiam.' No one dreamed of preventing the Rajah of Sattara, or the Maharajah of Nagpore, or his widow, from adopting a son to perform his funeral obsequies and to inherit his private property. But it is not necessary, to qualify an adopted son to perform those rites, that he should be a reigning prince ; and the succession to that position, in right of the adoption, was all that the Government refused to bestow, in any of the cases referred to, on the boy adopted.

In the same spirit, Mr. Kaye allows it to be inferred from his manner of treating the subject—though he is too discreet to say so broadly—that in his judgment the British Government acted unjustly towards the Nana Sahib in refusing to grant him a part at least, if not the whole, of his adoptive father's pension of 80,000*l.* per annum ; and that, consequently,

it was but natural that he should be bitterly hostile to those
who had thus wronged him. He manifests this bias by devoting
twelve pages to what he truly terms ' the story of the Peishwa,'
while he can spare but a few lines for the grounds on which
the claim was rejected. He omits to mention that Sir John
Malcolm, who promised the pension, states in his letter of the
19th of June, 1818, as his reason for making it so large that
Lord Hastings hesitated to sanction it, that if the fugitive
Peishwa had not been thus induced to surrender, ' the least that
' would have occurred would have been the necessity of our
' bringing into the field armies which would have cost more than
' the value of the life pension granted to Bajee Rao. . . . I
' therefore fixed his pension at one lac more than that enjoyed by
' Amreet Rao, as considering it only temporary, being for his
' life, and including all his family and future dependents, with
' whom he had not made separate terms.' But he does not forget
to state that the Nana replied ' with not unreasonable indigna-
' tion ' to the argument that he was too wealthy to stand in
need of pecuniary assistance from the State ; and he winds up
the narrative with the tart remark that ' the Court of Directors
' of the East India Company were hard as a rock, and by no
' means to be moved to compassion.' The truth is, that there
was not the shadow of a claim, on the score of justice, for the
continuance of this enormous pension beyond the original life-
grantee ; and it certainly requires some effort to get up a sentiment of ' compassion ' on behalf of an applicant for such
support from the public purse, whom Mr. Kaye admits to have
inherited 300,000*l.*, and who probably possessed much more.
    We may remark in passing that Mr. Kaye and Mr. Urqu-
hart between them appear to have misled Mr. Trevelyan, in
his striking narrative of the Massacre of Cawnpore, into confounding this denial of a pension with a refusal to sanction an
adoption.
    As regards the second head, it is not quite so easy to show
that Mr. Kaye had no solid grounds for his assumptions, but
only so because the persons whom he alleges that the fiscal
measures of our Government had tended to make rebels are
too numerous, too widely scattered throughout our provinces,
and, for the most part, too humble in station, to be capable of
being identified in the ranks either of the disaffected or of the
loyal. But the remarkable freedom of one province, where the
class in question is certainly the largest and most influential,
from any treasonable action on the part of its members will go
far to prove that the alleged wrongs of that class had not
stung them so poignantly as to impel them into rebellion.

Behar is the beautiful and fertile province that lies between Bengal Proper and the Province of Benares. Patna is its capital, and it comprises five districts—Behar, Patna, Shahabad, Sarun, and Tirhoot. The aggregate population of these exceeds seven millions, and the land revenue is 886,816*l*. The number of tenures held free of revenue within its limits was so large at one time that no less than 250,000*l*. per annum, at a low estimate, has been added to the public rent-rolls of the five districts by the results of investigations which proved the bulk of those exemptions to be invalid. Here then, if anywhere, it might reasonably have been expected that there would be an open manifestation of that disaffection which, according to Mr. Kaye, our fiscal measures had done so much to provoke. If such were the feelings of the many who had been adjudged liable to pay land revenue, and had been compelled to bear, in that respect, their fair share of the public burdens, they had abundant opportunities of displaying them. The people are a warlike race, very different from their southern neighbours, the effeminate Bengalees. In former days they furnished very many and still not a few Sepoys to our army. There was but one English regiment—the 10th Foot—quartered at Dinapore, the cantonment of Patna,—in the whole province, and not another within 400 miles to the south-east, and an equal distance to the north-west. The single corps at Dinapore was fully occupied in watching three regiments of Native Infantry, also stationed there, which eventually broke out into mutiny, and in keeping in check the city of Patna, with its 284,000 inhabitants, among whom were not a few fanatic Mahomedans, including Wahabees, who had shortly before remonstrated vehemently against the injustice and insult of permitting Christian missionaries to preach in their streets. Every other court of justice, jail, and treasury in the province was exclusively in native keeping, under the superintendence of a score or two of English civil servants. And these the Commissioner, from an ill-judged but, no doubt, a benevolent regard for their personal safety, (for what was passing at Lucknow and Cawnpore was well known both to natives and Europeans, but best known, certainly, to the former,) had ordered to abandon their respective districts and to take refuge at Patna. The officers of two districts— Sarun and Tirhoot—obeyed this order implicitly, and quitted their posts. We have already had occasion to tell how a Mahomedan gentleman took charge of the former, thus deserted by all the English officials, maintained strict order, and security to life and property, both public and private, during their absence, and restored to them the district, in full integrity, on their return.

A detachment of mutinous troopers, who attempted to plunder Mozufferpore, the capital of Tirhoot, were driven out of it by a small body of native local militia (who appear to have behaved extremely well), and by the townsfolk, who failed to appreciate that mode of deliverance from the fiscal rapacity of their English rulers, and both town and station were held by them in trust until the English officers resumed their functions.* In neither of these instances—Sarun and Tirhoot —embracing an area little short of 10,000 square miles, full of landholders who had recently been subjected to novel assessment, was there a single corporal's guard of English soldiers to keep down the thousands whom Mr. Kaye represents as ripe and ready for revolt. Why then, in the name of ordinary common-place cause and effect, did they not rise in arms? Why, on the contrary, were they so illogical in their disaffection that they gave—of their own accord, and when left perfectly free to follow their own will—cordial assistance to the Government of whom not an English representative remained among them, by maintaining order and protecting property? Is it not probable that they did not do the one, and that they did do the other, because their feelings towards that Government were exactly the reverse of what Mr. Kaye has represented them to be?

---

* 'Here we had no troubles whatever,' writes an indigo planter of this district, in a letter now before us, 'nor do I believe there was the slightest shadow of disaffection on the part of either high or low among the natives of Tirhoot. . . . We travelled about the country just as in the quietest times. From the first, the jail guards, or Nujeebs, were suspected; fears were entertained for the treasure in the Collectorate, which was all under their custody, and a resalah (squadron) of Irregular Cavalry was brought down from poor Major Holmes' regiment, at Sugowli, to keep them in check, and be in some measure a protection to the town. These men, *custodes custodium*, were the only body who proved false to their salt in Tirhoot. On the night when the station was deserted and all the officials had left under orders of the Commissioner, they robbed the dâk (letter mail) and carried off some guns and horses from the Collector's residence, and afterwards tried to induce the jail guard to join them in looting the treasury and bazaar, but unsuccessfully. The rich mahajuns in the town had sufficient influence to preserve the fidelity of the Nujeebs, and after a day spent in futile attempts to bring them over to their side, the Irregulars rode off and were no more heard of. It was said at the time, true or not I have no means of ascertaining, that the bazaar people pelted them with mud as they left.'

There were outbreaks at Arrah and Gyah, the capitals respectively of the districts of Shahabad and Behar. That which occurred at Arrah was very serious, because the three regiments of native infantry which broke loose from Patna, and were allowed, through gross mismanagement, to march away from that station with arms and ammunition and altogether unscathed, formed a nucleus around whom not only the mob of the bazaars and the convicts whom they released rallied in force; but because a Zemindar of high caste, nominally of large landed property, and certainly of much influence over his tenants and clansmen—Kooer Singh by name, so widely known during the mutiny—threw himself and all the means that he could command into the cause of the mutineers, and stood shoulder to shoulder with them against the Government.

Here, then, Mr. Kaye and those who hold with him may say is a case of genuine rebellion, headed by a man of old family and high station, who had much to lose in case of failure, and who could have been driven to such a desperate venture only by intolerable wrongs.

The first answer to this argument—as far as it is general—is that in Shahabad, as without a single exception throughout the Bengal Presidency, there was not even the most partial insurrection of the people until Sepoys had risen in mutiny, or had marched in from places where they had mutinied; and this, be it observed, although there was not in one place out of twenty a single British soldier to protect the British authorities, if even a few scores of native malcontents, out of the millions among whom they were dwelling in confidence, had desired to destroy them. We repeat it advisedly, and we challenge contradiction—for this is the test of truth in the controversy between Mr. Kaye and ourselves—that in no single instance throughout Bengal, Behar, and the North-Western Provinces, did any class of the people, however lawless and turbulent in their habits, rise in rebellion against their un-armed and unprotected rulers until the bad example had been set and hopes of plunder and license excited by the temporarily successful mutiny of the Sepoys. In some cases, no doubt, stations were plundered after they had been abandoned by the civil authorities; but the rabble of a town may have a taste for booty so easily gotten without being very desperate or deliberate rebels.

Under such circumstances—and such only—all law and all fear of retribution having been placed in abeyance by the murder or expulsion of the English authorities, the classes whom we have already described raised their heads and reigned paramount for the time being.   But the scenes of violence and rapine which these ruffians enacted were no more like a rebellion of the people of India than the riots in London in 1780, or those at Bristol or Nottingham in our own day, resembled a rebellion of the people of England.   They were just such risings of the dangerous classes as would assuredly carry terror through any large city in Europe, from which magistrates, soldiers, and police had been suddenly and entirely withdrawn, with no immediate prospect of their return, and where—as is generally the case in India—those who had houses to defend and property to lose had neither the self-reliance nor the confidence in each other essential to the prompt organisation of any effectual resistance.   The instant impulse of the insurgents in every case to break open the jails, and to fraternise in the work of havoc with the convicts whom they let loose, affords the truest indication of the classes to which these so-called rebels against the British Government belonged.

But, to return to the particular instance of Arrah, the case of Kooer Singh requires explanation.   It cannot be given better than in the words of a letter now lying before us from Mr. Herwald Wake, the gallant gentleman who so well defended the little house at Arrah, fortified for the nonce by Mr. Boyle.   As magistrate of the district, Mr. Wake had the best opportunities of knowing both the antecedents and the character of Kooer Singh.   He writes :—

'You are quite right in supposing that Kooer Singh had always been in high favour with the authorities, and had been, and, indeed, up to the last was, a personal friend of many of them.   The reason of his turning rebel was, in my opinion, a simple one.   It was his only chance, and on the expulsion of the British depended whether he was to retain his large possessions and his position as undoubtedly the chief person in Shahabad, or he and his family end their days as beggars.   His expenditure had always been reckless, and he had been universally preyed upon by Brahmins ; he was overwhelmed with debt and perfectly insolvent.'

Mr. Wake proceeds to state that the Government, two or three years before the mutiny, had broken through all general rules, in the hope of saving Kooer Singh from ruin, by placing his property in trust and under protection from the ordinary processes of the courts of law ; but these attempts having failed, through his continued extravagance :—

'He was once more at the mercy of his creditors.   Add to this that he was a bigoted Hindoo; always the tool of his priests; that he was a proud, ignorant, thorough-bred Rajpoot; and that, in the event of the success of the rebels, the Rajpoots would have been the masters of the whole of Behar, and Kooer Singh their undoubted chief, and it is not difficult to understand his conduct.'

Again :—

' He was hopelessly involved, therefore it was clearly his interest to aid in any movement which would sweep away all courts and records, and place him, the most powerful man in Behar, in a position which would make the mahajuns (the money-lenders) too glad to give him a receipt in full.'

Mr. Wake adds :—

' Kooer Singh had no grievance against the Government ; none of his land had been resumed.'

History assures us that such a state of hopeless ruin as that to which Kooer Singh had brought his affairs has proved amply sufficient to make rebels from the days of the Roman first depicted as ' alieni appetens, profusus sui,' to those of the old Rajpoot chief of Shahabad, without the superaddition of any of the special provocatives to insurrection laid at the door of the Government of India by Mr. Kaye.

With respect to the general state of feeling in his district and in the province, Mr. Wake writes :—

' With the exception of Kooer Singh and his relations, no land-holder of any importance in Behar took any part in the disturbances; on the contrary, they were with us, some affording valuable assistance. As regards Chuprah, Shahabad, and Tirhoot, I speak *with certainty* on this point; about Gyah (the capital of Behar) I am almost sure. In my district nothing took place that was not easily put a stop to by myself and forty or fifty Sikhs, and in no instance did I meet with armed resistance. The Rajahs (there are several large landholders of this rank in the province) everywhere gave us what assistance we wanted, lending us men for supplementary police, elephants, &c., &c.; and in the expedition against Rhotas, a large Zemindar of both Behar and Shahabad (I am ashamed to say I have forgotten his name) furnished a contingent of 200 matchlock men, and remained with us, making himself useful, for a month.'

The case of Gyah, the capital of the district of Behar, is a somewhat complicated one, and requires to be stated in detail. When the local authorities received, on the 31st of July, the orders of the Commissioner above adverted to to abandon the station and retire to Patna, Gyah was perfectly quiet. But the order was regarded as peremptory, and all obeyed it in the first instance. Within three hours, however, of this evacuation, Mr. Alonzo Money, the magistrate and collector, feeling ashamed of having obeyed an order which obliged him to leave more than 80,000*l.* in his treasury, and some 700 criminals in the jail, at the absolute disposal of 120 Nujeebs (a very humble sort of local militia), determined to return to his post; and he was supported in this spirited resolution by Mr. Hollings, an officer of the opium department.   He found everything as he had left it, and the Nujeebs professing loyalty.   These two brave Englishmen were at first the sole representatives of the British Government.   But two days afterwards a detachment of eighty men of her Majesty's 64th marched in from Calcutta, and on the third day information was received that Kooer Singh was advancing upon them from Shahabad, and other bodies of mutineers from the opposite direction.   In this aspect of affairs Mr. Money took counsel with the commanding officer of the detachment, and they came to the conclusion that as the Nujeebs were but little to be relied on, and the Europeans were far too few to defend all that required defence, it was their duty to carry off the treasure before the station was beleaguered.   This step was taken on the 3rd of August. But the removal of the rupees was too severe a trial for the fidelity of the Nujeebs, who up to that time may have thought that they were guarding the treasury for their own benefit, or for that of their expected compatriots.   So they mutinied, let loose the prisoners from the jail, and together pursued and attacked the detachment.   In his report of th 5th of August, Mr. Money spoke of 'the night attack made 'by the Gyah prisoners and the Nujeebs.   I say the Nujeebs, 'for we were fired into; and the prisoners have no muskets.' The attack was repulsed, with some loss to the assailants, and on the 7th idem Mr. Money wrote again, 'The town of Gyah is 'still safe, and likely to continue so.   I got news this morning; 'the prisoners dispersed almost immediately.'   During all this time there was no insurrection of the people, though, in the absence of all authority, there was anarchy, riot, and robbery. There were several petty risings in the interior of the district, for purposes of plunder or private revenge, but nothing of the nature of combined action against the Government.*   Meanwhile, Mr. Money carried the treasure safely down to Calcutta; and on the 16th of August (within a fortnight of the final evacuation, and with no conflict in the interim), the civil autho-

---

* In many places, especially in the North-Western Provinces, old feuds about boundaries or what not broke out, as soon as the repressive power of the magistrate fell into abeyance, and numerous scores of long standing were paid off by fierce tribes or individuals, and many a faction-fight took place, which had not the slightest relation to political disaffection.

vinced of their good feeling towards us, and their pleasure in seeing the English in the ascendancy. The only classes who regretted it were those who had been gainers by a state of lawlessness, and who were prevented by the restoration of order from enjoying property which, in our absence, they had seized on.' 'To the best of my knowledge,' he adds, ' there never was a desire on the part of the agricultural or mercantile classes to combine with the native army in a common war with the white race ; but, on the contrary, had not the very opposite opinion existed, it is impossible that order could have been at once restored, as soon as our troops prevailed over the mutineers.'

In another quarter, the northern corner of Rohilcund, Mr. Shakespear, the magistrate and collector of Bijnore, an officer of great spirit and energy, whose reports are before us, not only mentions the pitched battles that were fought in that district between those whom he calls ' the loyal Hindoos ' and the Mahomedan insurgents, but names several persons of the latter creed—men of station—who remained faithful throughout the struggle to him and to the British Government. Such instances, indeed, of Mahomedan fidelity were by no means rare in the North-west. Mr. Raikes states :—

' Major Mackenzie, of the 8th Irregular Cavalry, told me that his Ressildar, Mahomed Nizam, when a mile or two out of Bareilly (where almost all the English had just before been murdered), in the retreat to Nyna Tal, was told by the Major to go back and look after his three motherless boys, who were left in the lines of the mutineers. The old man answered, "Give me your hand;" then, looking up to heaven with tears in his eyes, "I will go on with you, and do my duty." '

These are the people, specimens of the millions inhabiting the North-Western Provinces, whom Mr. Kaye has represented as so thoroughly malcontent, because (1) the Talookdars had been partially set aside in the settlement of the land revenue, because (2) the holders of invalid rent-free tenures had been compelled to bear their share of the public burdens, and because (3) much land had been sold, under decrees of our civil courts, in liquidation of the debts of its owners, that the disaffection, thus engendered, contributed largely to the causes of the outbreak of 1857. He cites Mr. William Edwards, the magistrate and collector of Budaonin Rohilcund at the date of the mutiny, in support of this opinion; and quotes from his narrative of ' Personal Adventures during the Indian Rebellion,' an assertion that the measures of the Indian Government had been such as ' to convert into bitter enemies those whom sound ' policy would have made the friends and supporters of the ' State.' Mr. Kaye, when he leant upon this broken reed, could not have been aware that Sir Henry Harington—a judge of the Sudder Court at the time when Mr. Edwards made the allegation in question—stated in the Legislative Council of the Supreme Government, of which he subsequently became a member, that that gentleman had been officially called on by the court to substantiate these charges, and had failed to make them good.   As respects the transfer of ancestral estates from landholders of old family to capitalists of yesterday, Mr. Kaye cannot be ignorant that this is a course of things which has been going on in every land where society is progressive, from time immemorial; that it is a natural process which no Government could arrest, or ought to arrest if it could; and that it was by no means the first instance of the kind in our own country when

> ' Helmsley, once proud Buckingham's delight,
>   Slid to a Scrivener and a City Knight,'

though former events of a like nature had found no poet to commemorate them.

We now proceed to redeem our pledge to consider specially the cases of the two provinces—the one known as the Southern Mahratta country, the other that of Oude—where, if anywhere, events occurred bearing a resemblance to a general rebellion of the people.   The former was the cradle of the Mahratta race, whose chiefs, signally bold and astute, following in the steps of the great Sevajee, had succeeded in wresting supreme dominion out of the hands of the Mahomedans before we came to the front as competitors for the empire of India.   There, consequently, it cannot be doubted that the recollection of recent greatness, the mortification of defeat and subjection, and a natural craving to recover lost power, combined to inspire many of Mahratta blood with a desire to renew the struggle on the first favourable opportunity.   There, too, the Nana, the adopted son of the last of the Peishwas (whose seat of government was in the province), had numerous and devoted followers; and it seems certain that his agents had been active and successful both in propagating general disaffection and in tampering with one regiment at least (the 27th) of Bombay Sepoys.   That corps rose in mutiny, murdering three of its officers. But this outbreak was not followed by any general insurrection.   The principal chiefs, of whom there are many in that tract of country, the descendants of the great feudatories of the Mahratta empire, whose possessions were spared to them on the fall of the Peishwa, were apparently unwilling to risk life and their goodly domains on so desperate a cast of the die.   On the other hand, there is no question that the remarkable promptitude and courage with which the Government of Lord Elphinstone confronted the emergency, although the flower of the European troops attached to the Presidency had been generously dispatched to Bengal on the first summons of Lord Canning, conduced most materially to repress the natural tendencies of all classes of the Mahratta population.   Colonel Le Grand Jacob, a distinguished officer, was placed in charge of the province with large powers both political and judicial, and with all the military means at the command of the Government ; all the native troops employed in the province, with the grave exception above stated, remained true to their salt ; and although disaffection, doubtless, existed for some time in a smouldering state, it did not burst into flame.   So late in the day, indeed, as May 1858, the petty chief of Nurgoond broke out and murdered Mr. Manson, the political agent.   But he met with no effectual support from his countrymen ; was soon captured and executed ; and this, with the rising in arms of three or four small landholders, and the mutiny of the 27th Native Infantry, were the only overt acts of hostility to the Government worthy of notice which occurred in that quarter.

The state of Oude in 1857–8 more nearly resembled a rebellion of the people than any of the events referred to in the foregoing pages, or of those which took place in other parts of India.   Unquestionably the malcontent Talookdars did rebel.   But those of them who took up arms against the Government were by no means the whole of that powerful class.   Many remained neutral, while some took an active and resolute part in protecting British officers driven from their stations.   Hurdeo Buksh sheltered Mr. Probyn and other fugitives from Futtyghur, and Durbijah Singh saved and sent forward, to join the force advancing under General Havelock, the four sole survivors of the massacre of Cawnpore.   But the rebellious Talookdars, who had undoubtedly been injured by the measures of the Government, (whether necessarily, in doing justice to others better deserving, or otherwise, we cannot now stop to inquire) could have done no serious mischief if they had not been backed in their quarrel by a large body of the warlike yeomen and peasantry of the province.   In a misapprehension of the motives which impelled these classes to take the field against the British Government lies the fallacy of the assumption that the agricultural population of Oude followed the Talookdars into rebellion, as the Highlanders of 1745 followed their chieftains.   This mistake is a very strange one, when we consider,

on the one hand, what manner of men very many of the
Talookdars were, especially in their relations to the yeomanry
of the province ; and, on the other, that he who runs may
read, in the patent circumstances of the case, that motives of
the strongest that can sway the human mind, wide as the
poles apart from sympathy with the Talookdars in their grievances, were in full operation upon those who are assumed to
have followed the great landholders with the blind devotion of
feudal vassals.   What reason the rural—identical with the
military—population of Oude, and especially the more influential middle-classes of that body, had to love the Talookdars, let
Sir William Sleeman, the British Resident at the Court of the
King of Oude, as quoted by Mr. Kaye, give evidence :—

'The Talookdars, he says, in his diary, keep the country in a
perpetual state of disturbance, and render life, property, and industry
everywhere insecure.   Whenever they quarrel with each other, or
with the local authorities of the Government, from whatever cause,
they take to indiscriminate plunder and murder over all lands not
held by men of the same class ; no road, town, village, or hamlet, is
secure from their merciless attacks ; robbery and murder become
their diversion, their sport, and they think no more of taking the
lives of men, women, and children who never offended them, than
those of deer and wild hogs.   They not only rob and murder, but
seize, confine, and torture all whom they lay hands on and suppose to
have money or credit, till they ransom themselves with all they
have or can beg or borrow.   Hardly a day has passed since I left
Lucknow in which I have not had abundant proof of numerous
atrocities of this kind committed by landholders within the district
through which I was passing, year by year, up to the present
day.'

And again :—

'It is worthy of remark that these great landholders, who have
recently acquired their possessions by the plunder and the murder of
their weaker neighbours, and who continue their system of plunder
in order to acquire the means to maintain their gangs and to add to
their possessions, are those who are most favoured at court.'

We may add that other records show that when these
'Barons,' as it is now the fashion to call such ruffians, could
not extort more in ransom from their victims, they raised the
funds that they required by the compendious process of selling
them, by the hundred, into slavery.

If the village Zemindars had so warm an affection for these
cruel tyrants that they were led by this sentiment to come fiercely
forward to risk life and limb to vindicate their rights, and to re-
establish them in the possession of all the broad acres which they
had acquired by force or fraud from those very men, or their

immediate predecessors, they must be very unlike any other human beings on the face of the earth.

In truth, however, the real cause of the vehement hostility manifested by the yeomen peasantry of Oude is much more consistent with the ordinary impulses of human nature. It may be told in very few words. The Sepoys, who had originally provoked the internecine strife which was raging within the walls of Lucknow, were the fathers, brothers, or sons of the men who now rushed to their rescue, and who sided with the Talookdars, not because they sympathised with their special grievances, not because they had any quarrel with the British Government other than that of the Sepoys, least of all because they had any attachment to the ousted dynasty that had so long and so grievously misgoverned their land; but simply because, being a warlike race, they saw that their earnest co-operation afforded the only chance of saving their brothers and cousins, the husbands of their sisters and the brothers of their wives, from being crushed by the Feringees. The Talookdars, no doubt had some personal followers, but the bulk of the rural population sided with them only as having a common enemy; not as rebels, in any ordinary sense of the term, but as being the compatriots of the mutinous Sepoys. If the Talookdars had rebelled on their own account, and not as the allies of the Sepoys, who were fighting with halters round their necks, they would have had no aid from the great body of the rural population, the fighting men of Oude.

Having thus, we trust, demonstrated by a process little short of exhaustion that civil grievances. had nothing to do with the origin of the insurrection, a few instances will serve to illustrate the reality of the terrors that operated so violently upon the minds of the Sepoys as absolutely to dominate their reason, their long experience of the justice and tolerant spirit of the Government, and the respect and affection which many of them undoubtedly felt for their English officers. Whatever may have been the wilful fraud and guilt of those who concocted and first propagated the lies about cow's fat and pig's fat, bone-dust mixed with flour, and the flesh of pigs and cows thrown into wells for the purpose of destroying the caste of those who might drink the water, it is beyond question that ninety-nine, at least, out of every hundred Sepoys sincerely believed these tales, and suffered torments under the delusion. This being so, the operation of such terrors upon minds so ignorant and prejudiced as those of the Sepoys is abundantly sufficient to account for all the effects produced upon their conduct, without calling in a tittle of aid from the hypothesis of sympathy on their part with the unrecognised adoptees of Mahratta princes, or with landholders, long exempt, compelled to pay revenue. If either or both of these classes had risen against the British Government, with grievances a hundred times as great as they were alleged to suffer, but at a moment when the Sepoys had no fears about the safety of their caste, they would not only have refused to make common cause with such malcontents, but would have shot them down without mercy at the ordinary word of command. Those who actually followed the Sepoys to the field were, with few exceptions, of a very different character from those alleged to have had such good cause for being our deadly enemies.

At page 592–3 of Mr. Kaye's work will be found an extract from a letter written by Sir Henry Lawrence to Lord Canning on the 9th of May, 1857 :—

'I had a conversation,' he says, 'with a Jemadar of the Oude artillery for more than an hour, and was startled by the dogged persistence of the man, a Brahmin of about forty years of age, of excellent character, in the belief that for ten years past Government had been engaged in measures for the forcible, or rather fraudulent, conversion of all the natives. . . . He often repeated, "I tell you " what everybody says;" but when I replied, fools and traitors may say so, but honest and sensible men cannot think so, he would not say that he himself did not believe, but said, "I tell you they are all " like sheep; the leading one tumbles down and all the rest roll " over him." '

At page 553, Mr. Kaye tells, on the authority of Lieutenant Martineau, that a non-commissioned officer, detached for rifle-practice at Umballa, having been 'publicly taunted by a ' Soubahdar ' (a native captain) of his own regiment (the 36th), then forming the escort of the Commander-in-Chief,'

'With having become a Christian, cried like a child when he told it to the lieutenant, said that he was an outcast, and that the men of his regiment had refused to eat with him.' The men of the detachments, Mr. Kaye proceeds, 'had written letters to their distant comrades, and received no answers; and now they asked, not without a great show of reason, "If a Soubahdar in the Commander-in-" Chief's camp, and on duty as his personal escort, can taunt us " with loss of caste, what sort of reception shall we meet on our " return to our own corps? No reward that Government can " offer us is any equivalent for being regarded as outcasts by our " own comrades." '

In the extraordinary manifesto issued at Cawnpore by the Nana on the 7th of July, 1857, proclaiming how, as the result of a conspiracy between the Governor-General and his Council, Queen Victoria, and the English merchants of Calcutta,

' 35,000 Europeans had been dispatched to Hindostan to make
' all the natives Christians,' but had got on their way no further than Egypt, where they had been destroyed by the Pasha,
acting under the ' Firmàn of the Sultan of Roum,' so that not
' even a single European escaped,' there is not the most distant hint at any other grievance or ground of quarrel with the
Government than this alleged intention of compulsory and
wholesale conversion. Of the authenticity of this proclamation
there is no doubt. We have the highest authority for stating
that ' a copy of it was found on the person of an influential
' native, captured by us in the neighbourhood of Agra,' shortly
after the date that it bears. And it is equally certain that
those who drafted it were not likely to make a mistake as to
the key-note proper to be struck for the purpose of inflaming
the passions of the ignorant through their fears.

But the most remarkable illustration of the extraordinary
hallucination under which the Sepoys laboured remains to be
told, and we tell it in the words of Colonel (now Major-
General) W. Maule Ramsay, who was in command of the
Gwalior Contingent at the period of the mutiny. Speaking of
the arguments urged upon him by a Soubahdar (a native
captain) of that corps, shortly before the actual outbreak, he
says :——

' I remember well the old man entreating me to get the Governor-
General recalled, saying that if he remained the whole army would
mutiny. I said : Why, what has the Lord Sahib done to make the
army mutiny? The Government is the best friend the army has.
The old man, with tears running down his cheeks, told me that
Lord Canning had come out pledged to the Queen of England to
make all the army Christians, and had undertaken to have all the
native officers to dinner at Government House before he left. I
laughed at the idea, and endeavoured to prove to him that the
Government had always protected the religion of the Hindoos and
Mahomedans. The old Soubahdar was just as positive he was right,
and enumerated the advantages of the Company's service, telling me
he was perfectly aware that the King of Delhi would neither grant
pensions after long service, nor give a pension to the widows and
orphans of soldiers killed on service, nor have hospitals for the sick,
nor remit their money for them, &c., &c. I said when the Government attempts to force the native army to become Christians I will
tender my resignation, and will let you know ; until I do that your
religion is quite safe. He rose up to take his departure, saying he
should never again have such masters, but that unless Lord Canning
was removed the army *must* go, and he must join his comrades.
I saw him repeatedly afterwards, but he was always of the same
opinion.'

General Ramsay adds :—

‘When the 1st Cavalry mutinied, a native officer escorted Captain Burlton and two other officers into the Agra fort. He came to pay me a visit, and I endeavoured to persuade him to remain with us, telling him that a large European force was close to Calcutta. He said he knew he was quitting the best service in the world, repeating nearly all the Soubahdar had said about the advantages of it ; “But, “ sir,” he said, “ you know all our feelings, you know how we hate “ the Hindoos, and how they detest us, but in this it is (quoting a “ Hindustani proverb) two riders in one saddle. We are unanimous ; “ does not this show it is the work of the Almighty ? ”   And so saying, he went back and cast in his lot with the mutineers.’

It is very remarkable, that well knowing all this, and much more to the same purport, having written pages to narrate how often, and with how much violence, at different periods and in many parts of India, Sepoys had mutinied under the exclusive impulses of their own grievances or their own fears ; and having quoted from Sir Henry Lawrence's Essays, ‘ What the Eu-‘ ropean officers *have* repeatedly done, may surely be expected ‘ from natives ; we shall be unwise to wait for such occasion ; ‘ *come it will, unless anticipated ;* a Clive may not then be at ‘ hand :’ adding, ‘ the emphatic italics are Lawrence's :’—it is remarkable, we say, that having himself placed on record all these facts and opinions, Mr. Kaye should insist upon calling in the aid of other, and, to speak in the mildest terms, petty and trivial causes to account for the terrible outbreak which deluged India with the blood, first, of the stranger, and then, in far larger quantities, of her own children.

We believe that it will not be found difficult to trace this inconsistency to its source. The author who aspires to write what is called a philosophical history is exposed to a great snare. He must on no account permit his mind to run in the wheel-ruts, and he feels bound to regard with suspicion any solution of social problems which has been accepted as suffi-cient by the common herd of mankind. He is, consequently, in constant temptation to cast about for occult and recondite motives of action which have not suggested themselves to ordi-nary minds. It is evident that just in proportion to the power of the imagination, and to the ingenuity of such a writer, is the danger that he will first mislead himself, and then his readers. Mr. Kaye has not escaped this snare ; and the pro-cess by which he deludes himself is very curious. He first paints a fancy scene, and then builds on the pasteboard as if it were granite. For example, he is speaking of the mysterious rumours of disasters about to befall the British Government, which, he tells us, preceded the outbreak, and of the general disaffection of the people, which led them to welcome joyfully such shadows as the coming events cast before them:—

'All along the line of road,' he says, 'from town to town, from village to village, were thousands to whom the feet of those who brought the glad tidings were beautiful and welcome. The British magistrate, returning from his evening ride, was perhaps met on the road near the bazaar by a venerable native on an ambling pony —a native respectable of aspect, with white beard and white garments, who salaamed to the English gentleman as he passed, and went on his way freighted with intelligence refreshing to the souls of those to whom it was to be communicated, to be used with judgment and sent on with despatch. This was but one of the many costumes worn by the messenger of evil. In whatever shape he passed there was nothing outwardly to distinguish him. Next morning there was a sensation in the bazaar, and a vague excitement in the Sepoy lines.'

Now all this ingenious word-painting has not the slightest real groundwork. Mr. Kaye guards himself with a 'perhaps,' but who saw the old gentleman with the white beard, or detected personified rumour in any of his other 'many costumes?' To ninety-nine, at least, out of every hundred of the dealers in any given bazaar, 'the feet' of a new customer with a few rupees in his girdle would have been far more 'beautiful and 'welcome' than those of any conspirator against the Government under whose protection they and their fathers had bought and sold for long years in peace and safety. There is not a tittle of evidence that the people in general had any premonitory intimation of the intended rising of the Sepoys, if, indeed, the Sepoys themselves had any long-premeditated intention to rise. It is well known that after the mutineers had marched out of Meerut on the road to Delhi, they halted within twenty-five miles of the former station to debate whether they should not turn round and make for Bareilly. So little was there of any preconcerted plan. And it is believed by some well qualified to form an opinion, that if they had been briskly pursued by the Carabineers they would have laid down their arms. In several instances—at Mozufferpore, Dacca, and Chittagong, for example—the townspeople drove out the mutineers. Many hundreds, probably thousands, of the Sepoys were robbed and murdered by the villagers as they were straggling to their homes from Delhi or Cawnpore with their ill-gotten booty. With the exception of the vilest rabble, who followed them as the jackal follows the tiger, and who lived, in a great measure, by plundering the plunderers, there was no sympathy between the mutineers and the people.

Every man who had intelligence enough to look beyond the passing hour, and who had the smallest property to lose, was well aware what the consequences of the ascendancy of his armed fellow-countrymen must be.   If they had no special affection for their English rulers, they felt in their heart of hearts that the domination of the white man was immeasurably preferable to anarchy and unbridled rapine.   And they well knew that such tribulations would assuredly and speedily follow the victory of the Sepoys.

We fear it may be thought that we have dwelt at unnecessary and tedious length upon this much-disputed question of mutiny or rebellion.   But, in truth, it is of far greater importance than all other questions connected, directly or indirectly, with the events of 1857, put together, that the people of England should be able to come to a certain conclusion whether the people of India, as a body, or any considerable portion of that body, were inimical to the British Government on that occasion, in such a sense that they either committed, or attempted or desired to commit, overt acts of deadly hostility against it; or whether our danger—our whole real danger—sprang from the large and highly-trained native army, and the extreme numerical disproportion of that army to the English force stationed in India at the time of the outbreak.   We think that we have brought together a mass of evidence which it is impossible to reconcile with the hypothesis of general disaffection, of such a character as to be fairly synonymous with rebellion; and that we have proved, on the contrary, that almost our only enemy—certainly our only formidable enemy—was the Frankenstein of our own creation, whom we had nursed up into such perilous dimensions, unchecked by any adequate counter-balancing power, that nothing but the signal courage and tenacity of our race enabled us to come conquerors out of the struggle for life or death against such fearful odds and disadvantages.

If, then, these propositions have been demonstrated, what is the logical corollary ?   Not, certainly, that we should cherish a chronic distrust of the whole native population, and especially of the Mahomedans, and allow ourselves to believe that they are only biding their time to rise and slay us.   Not, as certainly, that we should write books or pamphlets (which thousands of the natives nowadays can read and understand as well as we do), to denounce the British Government as atrociously perfidious and unjust, and the statesmen delegated by England to exercise supreme power in India as ' the worst and basest of ' rulers.'   But, surely, if the premises which we have endeavoured to establish be true, the one great lesson to be learned from the fearful perils through which God has carried us safely is this: that whilst we are bound to use our most earnest and sustained endeavours to win from the more intelligent and the best-disposed of our subject millions—if we cannot hope for their affections—the confidence, the respect, and the conviction of self-interest involved in the stability of our rule, we should, at the same time, most carefully guard ourselves against a repetition of the grievous mistake of establishing an enormous native army, which we have found by sad experience that it is indispensable to watch and keep in check by a British force so large, that it puts the severest strain alike on the finances of India, and on the population of Great Britain, to maintain it in the necessary strength and efficiency.

Where, then, is the escape from this dilemma? We have read of machines of vast power, but yet so heavy and unwieldy that they could hardly give motion to their own bulk, still less communicate force to other bodies. Our power in India is in danger of being crippled by its own weight. We are told that we must maintain a very large native force. It is certain that we cannot safely do so unless we keep up, at the same time, a body of English troops, upon which we may depend as fully competent to control that force at all times, and to destroy it if it rise against us. But the cost of this double necessity is ruining us; it is, at the least, exhausting the means of rendering our Government ten times more beneficent than with all our efforts we can now make it. It is the old case 'propter vitam, vivendi perdere causas.' We spend so much in guarding our field that we have not the wherewithal left for its proper and creditable cultivation.

But before we fold our arms in hopelessness, let us consider if it be not possible to cut the knot of the difficulty. Is it absolutely certain that the safety of our dominion is involved in our keeping on foot a native army of 135,000 men? Can we feel sure of their loyalty at the moment of our greatest peril? At such a crisis, should we not be safer with half of them, if only we had at hand a comparatively small body of English soldiers? 'The more troops we had,' says Mr. Raikes with reference to Agra in 1857, 'save our one weak European 'regiment and battery, the greater our danger.' Not to press the argument too far, is it not possible, is it not probable, that our dominion would be quite as secure if defended by 75,000 native troops, and 50,000 English soldiers as it is now under the protection of 135,000 of the former and 70,000 of the latter, the Government saving the difference between the cost of maintaining the larger and the smaller body, or—what is better—investing that sum in railroads and their feeders, in works of irrigation and navigable canals.

That which has happened once may happen again. We have crushed with extreme difficulty, and at a vast expense of blood and treasure, a simultaneous uprising of an enormous native army, making use for our destruction of the weapons that we had put into their hands and of the skill and discipline which we had taught them. But during the century of our tenure of power it has never been imperilled for a moment by any insurrection of the people. There have been petty outbreaks, no doubt, but they have occasioned no anxiety, and have been repressed without difficulty. And we may safely assure ourselves that such risings will be less frequent and less formidable as every year passes by. The history of all lands and of all times should teach us how soon and how thoroughly, under a strong and just Government, and with circumstances otherwise tolerably favourable, even an excitable and warlike population settles down to the pursuits of peaceful industry and forgets the use of arms, and what the Roman historian called 'certaminis gaudia.' The Jâts who defended Bhurtpore against Lord Combermere, in 1826, nine-tenths of whom had never heard a shot fired in anger, were as different from those who, trained to arms from their youth, manned the same walls against Lord Lake in 1805, as the present farmers of Huntingdonshire from Cromwell's Ironsides. Compare the Britons who fought against the Romans with those who fled before the Saxons; the Highlanders of 1745 with their living great-grandchildren. We know how little that petty portion of the population which was most hostile achieved against us, apart from the Sepoys, in 1857--8. They have since been disarmed, and lost, therefore, a great part of the power for mischief which they previously possessed. Surely, then, we do not need a large native army to keep them down, and then 70,000 British troops 'custodire ipsos custodes.' Yet simply because the latter cost us, man for man, twice as much as the native soldier, we are continually sending home regiments and batteries of Europeans, or reducing their numerical strength, whilst our native army, though certainly much smaller than it was before the mutiny, is maintained in formidable force.

Taking the average of the whole country, there are, probably, no people in the world so docile, so addicted to the pursuits of industry, and, consequently, so easily governed, as the natives of India. There are wild races on its extreme north-western and its north-eastern frontiers who have given us trouble in times past, and may give us trouble again; but as long as we keep out of their fastnesses they are almost powerless for mischief, and even if we march into their hills to seek them they are antagonists utterly contemptible to soldiers who have confronted Russians and Frenchmen. Our only real enemies on such occasions are malaria, snow, and the difficulty of forwarding supplies—enemies to be overcome not by force of arms, but by the foresight and general resources of the civil administration. We have one or two savage tribes, such as the Bheels and the Sontals, in the jungles within our own borders, but it has not been found impracticable to win their confidence and to humanise them; and when they occasionally break out they are no match, in thousands, for a few hundreds of their own kinsmen, trained and led by English officers. For the rest, we cannot imagine any insurrection of the people which a body of well-organised police, acting promptly, on the first manifestation of danger to the public peace, could not easily suppress. Indeed, such a force, with just discipline enough to ensure combined action and mutual support in actual conflict, but not drilled into soldiers, appears to us to be the very instrument best fitted to maintain our authority over our own subjects, at the same time that it involves the least danger to our rule; for the police of one district has no relations with the police of any other district, except, to a very limited extent, with its immediate neighbours. The policeman of Patna knows no more of the policeman of Meerut than he does of the policeman of Berlin or Madrid. The two have no means of making common cause for any object. The native soldiery, on the contrary, though less homogeneous than before the mutiny, are in a far greater degree a united body, very many of them born in the same province, sprung from the same clan, members of the same caste, fraternising in camps and cantonments, or meeting on the line of march in the frequent changes of quarters. The Sepoy at Calcutta has brothers or cousins in the regiments at Agra, or even Peshawur, and the system of cheap postage renders intercommunication easy and frequent. And these men, unlike the police, are sedulously drilled into the highest state of discipline and efficiency.

Yet, strange as it must appear, it is nevertheless true that for one word that is said in deprecation of a too large native army a hundred voices are raised to insist upon the danger of what is called, for the purpose of evoking prejudice, a military police; as if it were not in our own power to fix the point to which organisation and drill should be carried, and no further; as if there were not more latent and possible mischief

in a single regiment of thoroughly disciplined and armed soldiers than in ten times their number of rough-and-ready
policemen.   Even in Parliament, when Lord Cranborne
brought forward, with so much ability, the last Indian budget,
the same cuckoo note was raised by those who ought to have
known better.   But 'there are some men,' as Dr. Johnson said,
' who would have cried fire in the deluge.'

An event which took place at Bareilly, the capital of Rohilcund, in 1816, affords the aptest illustration and proof of the utter
impotence of an undisciplined multitude, however individually
brave and well armed, and with all the fervour of fanaticism
superadded, to bear down the defences or to resist the onset
of a very small body of regular troops, led with ordinary courage and judgment.   On the occasion in question, resistance to
a novel house-tax had been inflamed by accidental bloodshed
into vehement religious excitement, under the influence of which
some 5,000 to 6,000 Rohillas (some accounts say more than
twice as many), brave and reckless to a proverb, and well provided with matchlocks, swords and spears, had risen in violent
insurrection.   The only troops at hand to resist them were
about 270 men of the 27th Native Infantry, with two guns,
and 150 of a provincial battalion—a wretched sort of local
militia—together with a regiment of Irregular Horse.   Let the
historian (H. H. Wilson) tell the result of the conflict:—

' Their first attack was made upon the Sepoys.   Being formed in
a square (we have been assured by an officer who took part in the
engagement that the Sepoys were drawn up in a triangle, from
want of numbers to form a square), the troops repulsed every charge,
though the assailants fought with fury, some of them making their
way into the square, where they were cut down or bayoneted.   On
his side, Captain Cunningham's horse charged the masses of the
multitude, and threw them into confusion.   Repulsed in their forward movements, they took up their ground in a grove defended by
a low wall, but were driven out of it by the troops, who pursued
them into the old town and set fire to the huts in which they had
taken shelter.   This put an end to the conflict.   The insurgents
dispersed, leaving between three and four hundred dead, and a
greater number wounded and taken prisoners.   The loss of the
troops was inconsiderable—twenty-one killed, sixty-two wounded.'

Bearing in mind that the Rohillas have, perhaps, the highest
reputation for courage among the martial tribes of India (as
they have proved in a hundred conflicts with ourselves and
others), that they were in 1816 well provided with arms, and
accustomed to their use, and that, since the mutiny, they have
been, as we believe, pretty effectually disarmed, there ought to
be no insuperable difficulty in coming to the conclusion that

we do not require our present complement of 135,000 native troops to assist, say, 40,000 English soldiers and a well-organised police in suppressing any possible insurrection of our subjects, at a period when railways afford us the altogether novel advantage of the means of rapidly concentrating our forces on any point of rising danger.

There is another consideration, the importance of which, in its bearing upon the question under discussion, to which we earnestly invite the attention of the authorities, can hardly be overestimated. We have spoken only of the railways. It has been objected that they might easily be broken up by insurgents, at the very moment of need. The same may be said of the electric telegraph, which, nevertheless, was worked long enough in 1857, when it flashed the intelligence of the mutiny at Meerut to Lahore, to be the means of preserving many invaluable lives, and to cooperate largely with other causes in saving the Punjab from being crippled at the very commencement of the struggle. As regards the railways, however, it must be borne in mind that they could be destroyed only in close proximity to the actual scene of insurrection, and that, at the worst, they would serve to convey troops from distant stations to within a few marches of the field of action. But we possess other advantages over the races subject to our rule in India which, being absolutely in our own hands, could not be turned against us. At no period of history were science and mechanical ingenuity so actively and successfully engaged in turning to practical account the resources of nature and art; and no field, we believe, is now so assiduously cultivated as that which bears fruit in the invention or improvement of engines and munitions of war. Whatever of evil may result from this undeniable tendency of the age, this much is certain, that it gives an irresistible advantage to the soldiers of wealthy and civilised nations in conflict with those who, from whatever cause, are unable to provide themselves with weapons of equally destructive power. The introduction of rifled or otherwise improved artillery, throwing explosive projectiles with the greatest accuracy to distances till recently deemed fabulous; of breech-loading or repeating rifles, by the use of which a handful of men may maintain a fire equal to that of a battalion armed as in old times; of the field telegraph; and of other inventions—yearly improved and extended—gives to those who alone, from their wealth and knowledge, can command such resources a superiority in war over rude and uncivilised peoples greater, perhaps, than the possession and use of gunpowder afforded in

the middle ages.   Mere numbers will be of no avail against
troops armed and equipped in the manner which we have indicated.   We have seen how much 'the needle gun'—however aided by other causes of superiority—has effected for
Prussia in a conflict with a people of equal military reputation.   From this instance we may form some estimate
as to what would be the effects of breech-loaders, and of
artillery and projectiles of the latest and most approved
invention, employed against Asiatics who could not possibly
possess themselves of similar weapons.   The use of these
improved arms would of course be confined to British troops.
It would be rash to place them in the hands of natives, by
whom they might be turned against ourselves.   But then
how absurd a thing it would be to maintain an enormous native
army, which we should be compelled to arm in a comparatively
inefficient manner !   The true policy is to have a smaller force,
perfectly trustworthy, and rendered invincible by the superiority of its arms.

Be it observed, too, that this argument tells with tenfold
force against those who—if their opinions are to be inferred
from their conduct—differ from us in seeing no danger in the
maintenance of 135,000 disciplined native troops, whom they
hold to be indispensably required to protect our Government
against insurrections of the people.   But if that be the quarter
from which danger to our Indian Empire really threatens,
where or how are the supposed insurgents, the Ryots of the
plains, or the artisans of the large cities, the Bheels, or the
Sontals, or even the wild tribes on our frontiers, to obtain
weapons wherewith to face Armstrong guns and breech-
loading rifles of the newest construction?

The classes throughout India who might once have been
dangerous learnt a lesson in 1857 in respect to the power of
England and the immeasurable superiority of the British soldier
which they are not likely to forget for one or two generations;
by which time, unless we wilfully keep it alive, the military spirit
of the people will, for the most part, have died out.   What we
deprecate is a course of conduct which at once feeds that spirit
in a proportion of the population needlessly large, and compels
us to drain the labour-market of England of the young men
whom its industries can very ill spare, in order to keep in
check a large native force which India would be better without.

There is no danger that could assail us from external foes
without affording us ample time to strengthen our hands
to meet it.   The native princes within the Peninsula are
altogether powerless for serious aggression; and reducing

our own force, we might well demand that they should disband
a corresponding number of their own troops.   With ordinary
watchfulness on our part, no one of them could collect the
means of harming us, and all experience has shown that they
are incapable of combining for such a purpose.   Our only
neighbour who has a real army is strong only in his native
mountains.   The last campaign in Oude has dissipated whatever
notion previously existed that the troops of Nipal could give us
any trouble on the plains.   And while we believe the invasion
of India by Russia to be the most hollow of bugbears, it is
certain that long before any army could march from the steppes
of the Sea of Aral through the defiles of Affghanistan and
debouch upon the Punjab, troops might be sent from England
which, combined with what could be spared from the ordinary
garrison of India, would form a force abundantly capable of
dealing with the invaders.

This is an Imperial even more than it is an Indian question.
Year by year, as the minds of our labouring classes are enlarged,
either by education or by a wider intercourse with their kind,
they are becoming less and less 'adscripti glebæ;' the attractions of America or Australia grow stronger; the master finds
it necessary to court the man, not the man the master; and the
difficulties of raising recruits for the army are from these causes
greatly increased.   The reduction by one-third of the amount
of European force now maintained in India would be a very
sensible relief to England.   But this cannot, we freely admit,
be safely done as long as we persist in keeping up our
native army at its present strength.   And in order to bring
about a state of opinion in this country which would permit an
adequate reduction of that army, it is indispensable that the
public mind should be thoroughly disabused of the mischievous
error that the terrible events which sickened or maddened every
English heart in 1857 were the work of an insurgent people,
goaded into rebellion by long years of misgovernment, and that
an overwhelming military force is required to guard against
fresh outbreaks of the same nature.   We have endeavoured to
show the real origin and character of the insurrection of 1857,
and to prove from the experience of the past where, and
where alone, serious danger to our rule lies in the future.
Danger for danger, it is far less hazardous to trust the population, than to lean on the broken reed of a native soldiery.   We
shall profit, if we are wise, by the counsel which the late Rajah
of Puttiala, our faithful ally, and himself a Sikh, addressed to
Mr. Raikes:—

    ' Wait, sir, till this excitement of victory, this surfeit of plunder, be over; wait till you mass large bodies of Sikhs in your cantonments; and then remember that I warned you of the danger.'

Mr. Raikes proceeds:—

'This conversation made the greater impression on me, as comprising the views of Brigadier Chamberlain,* who a few days before had said to me: "The Sepoys have waited a hundred years to "mutiny; the Sikhs, if subject to like temptations, will not wait "ten."

He also had received from the Rajah of Jheend (a Sikh) a similar warning.

Since the foregoing paper was sent to the press we have seen a letter from Sir John Lawrence on the subject of the mutiny, dated so recently as the 18th of April last. The opinions to which he has given the stamp of his high authority, corroborated by those of the chiefs and people whom, as he states, he has consulted, are so entirely in accordance with the views which we have expressed—being couched, indeed, almost in identical language—that we feel that we should do less than justice to the very important truths which we have felt it our duty to enforce if we held back this opportune communication from our readers:—

'As regards the mutiny, I am fully convinced not only that it arose in the native army, but that it did not extend to the people of the country to any great extent, except where they were the relatives and connexions of the native soldiers. As the Sepoys were destroyed or dispersed, all the people, save and except those who had committed themselves by acts of atrocity, speedily settled down. In the greater part of the Delhi territory there was scarcely a shot fired after the recapture of the city. This is the universal testimony of the chiefs and people whom I have consulted, as well as my own observation. In the upper part of the Gangetic Doab many of the Sepoys, on their way to their homes, were waylaid by the countryfolk, plundered, and murdered. Hindostan, and indeed all India, are full of predatory races, who for ages have been robbers and plunderers, and who seized on the opportunity of the mutiny to return to their old ways. The Goojur, the Mehwatee, the Mena, the Boondela, and so forth, rejoice over the good old days of plunder and rapine, and naturally took to the ways of their forefather.'

---

* Now Sir Neville Chamberlain, K.C.B. and K.S.I., an officer of great distinction, and with equal knowledge of the military classes of North-Western India.

ART. II.—*Causeries d'un   Curieux: Variétés d'Histoire et d'Art ;   Tireés d'un   Cabinet d'Autographes et de Dessins.* Par F. FEUILLET DE CONCHES.   Tomes Premier et Second, 1862 ; Tome Troisième, 1864 : Paris.

THE title of this book is untranslatable.   There is no English equivalent for *causerie,* which is something less formal, continuous, and pretentious than ' conversation,'— something more intellectual, refined, and cultivated than ' talk.' An earnest preoccupied man may converse; an over-excited or coarse-minded man may talk ; but neither the one nor the other can *causer* in the precise French acceptation of the word.   Boswell says, ' Though his (Johnson's) usual phrase for ' conversation was " talk," yet he made a distinction ; for ' when he once told me that he dined the day before at a ' friend's house, with " a very pretty company," and I asked him ' if there was good conversation, he answered, " No, Sir, we ' had " talk " but no conversation; there was nothing dis- ' cussed." '   On another occasion, however, when he said there had been good ' talk,' Boswell rejoined, ' Yes, Sir, you tossed ' and gored several persons.'   Positiveness, loudness, love of argument, and eagerness for display, are fatal to *causerie;* which we take to consist in the easy, careless, unforced flow and interchange of remarks, fancies, feelings, or thoughts,—the results of reading, observation, or reflection; begun without defined object or formed purpose, and continuing its course like Wordsworth's river which ' windeth at its own sweet will,' or Burns's verses when he trusted to the inspiration of ac- cident—

> ' And how the subject-theme may gang,
>   Let time and chance determine ;
> Perhaps it may turn out a sang,
>   Perhaps turn out a sermon.'

In strictness, therefore, perhaps the title of *causeries* should only be given to such a book as we should call ' Table-Talk.' But we are not disposed to quarrel with M. Sainte-Beuve for giving it to his valuable collection of familiar essays, critical and biographical, the justly celebrated ' Causeries du Lundi ; ' still less to find fault with M. Feuillet de Conches for be- stowing it on a book which, without any extraordinary stretch of fancy, we can imagine to have grown out of conversations with persons of congenial pursuits,—the scene varying between the library, the picture-gallery, the museum, and the collec- tor's cabinet.   Each freely and frankly communicates the discoveries he has made or the information he has collected ; the *pièce justificative,* or illustrative document, in the shape of an autograph letter, manuscript, engraving, or portrait, is produced or appealed to ; then come inquiry, comment, amicable difference, and discussion ; till materials are accumulated for a book rivalling the ' Curiosities of Literature ' in erudition, and far surpassing it in accuracy, penetration, and suggestiveness. Indeed, we have rarely met with one which opens so many fruitful fields of inquiry, supplies so many important topics of speculation, or brings the critical faculty so pleasantly and profitably into play.

The tendency and utility of such a work are so obvious, that there was little need of the apologetic preface of sixty pages, addressed to the celebrated advocate and jurisconsult, M. Chaix d'Est-Ange. Considering how chronicles, journals, correspondence, household-books, news-letters, broad sheets, loose scraps of every kind, have been ransacked and turned to account by recent writers of note,—the literary world in general, and historians in particular, would seem to be sufficiently awake already to the value of well-authenticated details and contemporary evidence, however homely and minute. M. Philarête Chasles might safely have been left unanswered when he exclaimed, ' What care I about the patience or scrupu- ' lousness of a former frequenter of the Alexandrian library ' who should have saved for me, in twenty-five volumes folio, ' the *billets-doux* of Cleopatra and the bills of her washer- ' woman and jeweller.' Twenty-five volumes in folio would be a large order, but can it be doubted that Cleopatra's bills, to say nothing of her *billets-doux,* would help to throw light on the habits and manners of the lady, the country, and the time ? Can M. Philarête Chasles have forgotten the philosophic reflection of Pascal that, if Cleopatra's nose had been shorter, the whole face of the world might have been changed ? Minute personal details have been rightly treasured by biographers ; and we feel grateful to Mr. Forster for printing the bill of Goldsmith's tailor, Mr. Filby of Water Lane, although it does not specify the charge for the famous peach-coloured coat which provoked the sarcasm of Johnson.

At the same time we are not sorry that M. Feuillet de Conches has been seduced into a vindication of his plan ; for, if superfluous, his preface is the opposite of commonplace or dull. It comprises a brief and rapid but masterly appreciation of the leading French memoirs ; and after illustrating by instances the advantages of biographical details and private letters in estimating books as well as men, it proceeds to give proofs of the serious liability incurred by authors who are content with secondhand authority.

'When we write a book, it is our reflection, our reason, that speak; we express only our ideas, sometimes only the hypocrisy of our ideas. When we write letters, we more commonly express our sentiments and our passions. Read, for example, the elegant pages in which Sallust raises altars to poverty, proclaims the ineffable sweetness and the eminent dignity of the Stoic moralists, stigmatises with burning declamation, with virtuous anger, the corruption of Rome, the extortion in the provinces. Is it after reading this that we shall recognise this Sallust, the corrupter of the domestic hearth, the bloodstained tribune, the slave of Cæsar, the impudent extortioner, whose famous museum-gardens were built with the gold and the tears of Numidia? Incredible power of abstraction! prodigious miracle of taste and art! This man, branded with infamy, talks of virtue like Cato; pen in hand he becomes virtuous.

'Shall we believe also in the disinterestedness of Seneca, in his philosophy, his austerity, his clemency, by reading nothing but his moral treatises, from which morals seem to flow rather than words. Read his life, and you will avert your looks. Alongside of some real public and private virtues, what shameful weaknesses! What infamy and crime! He knew how to die: he did not know how to live.'

When Seneca wrote his treatise in praise of poverty, he had some millions sterling out at usurious interest; and it was the pointed saying of South, that when he (Seneca) recommended people to throw away their money, it was with the view of picking it up himself.

Amongst moderns there is the familiar tale of Rousseau, invoking parental care for infancy and sending his own children to a foundling hospital; and the less known contrast between the published sentimentalism and the private conduct of Saint Pierre, the author of 'Paul and Virginia,' who has been handed down to posterity, upon the not quite unimpeachable testimony of his wife, as a man of desolating egotism, violent against the feeble, mendacious with the powerful. 'I 'have gathered from the mouth of an intimate friend of this 'worthy woman,' adds M. Feuillet de Conches, 'the most 'startling anecdotes of this pretended good man.'

Fortunately for poor humanity, there is a compensating process or principle simultaneously at work, by aid of which the private characters of authors neutralise the repelling impressions of their works. The Count Joseph de Maistre proclaimed the hangman the keystone of the social edifice. He deliberately laid down that, in the study of philosophy, contempt for Locke is the beginning of wisdom; that the Essay on

the Human Understanding ' is most assuredly, deny it who
' may, all that the absolute want of genius and style can produce
' most wearisome ; ' that Bacon is a charlatan ; that the *De Aug-
mentis* is ' perfectly null and contemptible ;' and the *Novum Or-
ganon* ' simply worthy of Bedlam.'   No writer of anything like
equal eminence has given expression to so startling an amount
of prejudice, illiberality, and insulting arrogance in his books ;
whilst his familiar letters teem with proofs of a kindly and
loving nature, of candour, liberality, and Christian virtues.

We are also told to be on our guard against drawing too
broad an inference from some one memorable passage or action
with which a name has been inextricably and disadvantageously
mixed up.   ' If there are certain cries of the heart which
' paint the entire man and betray the secrets of his soul, he
' may let drop ill-considered words in an emergency which
' are in contradiction to his real sentiments, to his whole
' life.'   Or, to adopt the language of Bruyère, ' Je ne sais s'il
' est permis de juger des hommes par une faute qui est unique,
' et si un besoin extrême, ou une violent passion, ou un
' premier mouvement, tirent à conséquence.'   Thus, we are not
to believe Barnave a Robespierre because, when the death of
Foulon was announced amidst the indignant murmurs in the Constituent Assembly, he exclaimed, ' *Le sang qui coule, est-il donc
' si pur qu'on ne puisse en repandre quelques gouttes?* ' He lived
to make ample reparation for this outrage.   Nor will it be forgotten that the Vicomte de Bonald was honest, firm, and highminded, although, hurried away by intolerance, he impatiently
replied to those who objected to making sacrilege a capital
crime, ' *Eh bien! les coupables iront devant leur juge naturel!*'

In order to inculcate the value of documents, M. Feuillet
de Conches has unsparingly exposed celebrated authors who
have proceeded on the *mon histoire est finie* principle ; and he
relates an anecdote which will be new to most readers.   M. de
Lamartine meeting M. Alexander Dumas soon after the publication of the History of the Girondins, inquired anxiously
of the famous romance-writer if he had read it.   ' *Oui ; c'est
superbe!   C'est de l'histoire élevée à la hauteur du roman.*'

A friend calling on Archbishop Usher found him busily
engaged in placing his choicest books and manuscripts under
lock and key, a precaution which he explained by mentioning
that he expected a party of bibliophiles and collectors to
dinner.   ' What most of all and still afflicts me,' complains
Evelyn, ' those letters and papers of the Queen of Scots,
' originals and written with her own hand, which I furnished to
' Dr. Burnet, are pretended to have been lost at the presse.

' The rest I lent to his countryman, the late Duke of Lauder-
' dale, who never returned them; so as by this tretchery my
' collection being broken, I bestowed the remainder on a
' worthy and curious friend of mine, *who is not likely to trust a*
' *Scot with anything he values.*'

A Scot is not always on the safe side in these matters. Sir
Walter, after mentioning the sepulchral vase of silver sent him
from Athens by Lord Byron, says that there was a letter sent
with this vase more valuable than the gift itself. ' I left it
' naturally in the urn with the bones, but it is now missing.
' As the theft was not of a nature to be practised by a mere
' domestic, I am compelled to suspect the inhospitality of some
' individual of higher station; most gratuitously exercised, cer-
' tainly, since, after what I have said, no one will choose to
' boast of possessing this literary curiosity.'

With such tendencies abroad, M. Feuillet de Conches is
quite right in warning collectors against the predatory habits
of their associates; although, when he comes to particulars,
his own personal grievances may turn out more imaginary than
real:

' We need not go out of France in search of such adventures.
Woe to the too confiding collector who forgets that of King Can-
daules; another Gyges might nefariously cut his throat after robbing
him of his treasure! The lords of the literary world know full
well how to cajole them at need, these poor collectors. One while
they publish their autographs, in spite of the owners; one while
they borrow what they never return, or they do not even deign to
cite their names whilst making use of their treasures.

' " Sicut canis ad Nilum, bibens et fugiens." Thus Lord
Brougham, to whom, through the channel of an illustrious academician, I had lent letters of the eighteenth century for his notices,
published at Paris, of Voltaire and Rousseau, has profited by my
communications, and has not indicated the source, so that, without
falling into the grasp of the law, I should not even have the right
to reprint what belongs to me.'

No such consequences could ensue, had Lord Brougham
withheld the required acknowledgment; and in the preface to
' Lives of Men of Letters of the Time of George III.,' edition
of 1855, we find, ' Besides the letters of Voltaire, communicated
' by Mr. Stanford, and which were given in the former editions,
' there are some of his, and one of Helvetius, now inserted,
' which had been given in the French edition, having been
' kindly communicated by M. Feuillet, a gentleman of great
' respectability.'

Another story, well authenticated by references, relates
to the Mallebranche correspondence, purchased at the Millon

sale by a collector, and lent to a *grand philosophe* (not named) who forthwith made arrangements for publishing the letters and refused to return the originals.

' Philosophy, I presume, has privileges which simplify the domestic economy of property, and are denied to vulgar simplicity. " Oh, physics! preserve me from metaphysics," exclaimed the great Newton every morning of his life. The poor collector would not give in. He appealed to the authority of the worthy and loyal academician (the witness of the loan). Vain effort! A common friend, the author of the excellent edition of Pascal after the originals, was not more fortunate. Plato hugged his prize, *his* by right divine.

' Comply with the conditions, objected M. F . . . ., or restore. He who has bought and paid is the lawful owner. To print in spite of him in the *Journal des Savans*, would be the violation of his right; for after all, if he brought an action against you, what right could you allege? " *My right*," replied the philosopher, with a vivacity which had at least the merit of frankness, " *My passion is my right.*" '

Taking for granted, then, the value of original documents and evidences of all sorts, as well as the rights of property in them, to be established by the preface, we proceed to the main body of the work, which opens with an attempt to ascertain what are the oldest manuscripts and likenesses, painted or carved, that are proved by history or tradition to have once existed; how far down they can be traced, and when they were destroyed or lost sight of. The sacred archives come first, and questions arise, what became of the tables which Moses deposited in an ark? or of the copies of the law which the successive kings of Israel were directed to write out? or of the title-deeds which, like that of Hanameel's field, ' were put in ' earthen vessels that they might continue many days '? The wars of the Jews, their eventual subjugation and dispersion, with the repeated spoliation or destruction of the holy buildings in which their archives were deposited, sufficiently account for the disappearance of the originals at an early period; including the original of the Septuagint version of the Bible, made 277 B.C.), from a copy, for which, according to Josephus, an enormous sum was paid by Ptolemy.

The persecutions of the early Christians, and their scattered state, will equally account for the rapid disappearance of the autographs or originals of the Gospels, the Acts, the Epistles, and the Apocalypse. There is not so much as an authenticated scrap of the handwriting of any of the Fathers of the Church. The Greek copy of the Evangelists, known as the Codex Alexandrinus, in the British Museum, is assigned to the beginning of the fifth century, and the tradition attributing it to St. Thecla, one of St. Paul's virgin converts, is apocryphal at best. The pretended autograph of the Gospel according to St. Mark is still shown at Venice in a dilapidated, fragmentary, and utterly illegible state. Such as it is, it was brought with great ceremony from a convent in Aquileia in 1420, and is held to be nothing more than a devotional compilation for the use of the nuns. The autograph of autographs (priceless as the seamless coat), could it be recovered, is the letter of our Saviour to Abgar, Prince of Edessa, promising to send a disciple to cure his leprosy and teach his people the true faith. An Armenian historian of the fourth century, who gives the text of the prince's application and the reply, says that Abgar, after having been baptised by the Apostle Thaddeus, wrote to Tiberius to confirm the miraculous life and death of Christ. St. John of Damascus relates the same incident with modifications. Procopius, in the time of Justinian, mentions this holy letter, then augmented by a postscript promising the city of Edessa that it should never fall into the hands of enemies; and in 940 A.D. the Roman emperor got possession of it; that is, he procured from Edessa a document in Greek which was there treasured as the original. He had it magnificently framed in gold and jewels, which probably caused its destruction; for it disappeared for good and all during the revolution of 1185, when the people of Constantinople rose and plundered the imperial palace.

Copies have been preserved; the oldest extant being one in the Escurial, made by a monk in 1435; and the authenticity of the epistle was first questioned by a celebrated philologist of the fifteenth century, Laurentius Valla, who went so far as to deny the existence of Abgar. The controversy was learnedly and conscientiously revived by an ecclesiastical historian of repute in the last century. 'But,' remarks M. Feuillet de Conches, 'knowledge and good faith are not criticism.' So, spite of this testimony, the epistle in question has been long since relegated to the company of the counterfeits, with the text of the sentence pronounced by Pontius Pilate, with the letters of Christ which fell from heaven after his ascension, with the letters of the Virgin and the verses of the Sibyls, with the letters of the Devil (of which facsimiles have been published by Collin de Plancy), with the letter of the same Pontius Pilate on the life of Jesus Christ, and finally that of Publius Lentulus, which gives, from life, the portrait of the Messiah.

The letter of Lentulus opens a subject of the deepest and most reverential interest; but it has been so fully and admirably treated by Lady Eastlake that a bare outline of the main argument may suffice in this place.* This famous document purports to be a Report from a Roman proconsul to the senate, describing from actual observation the form, features, voice, bearing, look and manner of the Messiah,—the pure and open brow, the rich wine-coloured (*vinei coloris*) hair parted in the middle and falling on the shoulders, the clear blue eyes, the regular features with their grave yet sweet expression; painting, in short, so far as words can paint, the very *beau idéal* popularly received of the mortal attributes of the Divine Founder of our faith. It has been confidently alleged that this letter was extracted by Eutropius from the archives of the senate; that several Fathers of the Church made mention of it; and that portraits were painted after it by the command of Constantine the Great. To all this, the decisive reply is, that there was no proconsul named Lentulus in Judæa at the period; that no trace of the letter is discoverable in Eutropius; that none of the Fathers (including St. Augustine, who speaks of pretended portraits of Christ) make mention of it; and that the earliest notice of it occurs in the fifteenth century, when the famous preacher, Père Olivier Maillard, produced it in macaronic French.

Not content with these strong grounds for incredulity, M. Feuillet de Conches maintains that it would not be difficult to arrive at the source of the forgery, to pick out word by word the elements in the different traditional portraits in writing which lie scattered amongst the Fathers or the Greek ecclesiastical writers. He proceeds to proof, and a valuable piece of criticism is the result; from which we shall simply borrow an episodical passage or two on the startling doubt which long vexed and divided the Fathers, namely, whether the Divine Essence was reflected in the beauty of the outward and visible form, or hidden, for the wisest and best of purposes, under a mean and unattractive exterior.

The New Testament gave no help to either side. The Old Testament inflamed the controversy by an apparent diversity. ' Thou art fairer than the children of men,' is the inspired language of the Psalmist. ' He hath no form nor comeliness,' is the similarly inspired prophecy of Isaiah. The holy disputants, as was their wont, declined any rational explanation or reconciliation of the texts; and as no reference was made to

* ' The History of our Lord as Exemplified in Works of Art, &c. ' Commenced by the late Mrs. Jameson. Continued and completed ' by Lady Eastlake. London : 1864.' We refer to the introduction.

the authority of Lentulus, the fair inference is that none of
them had ever heard of him.   St. Justin declared positively
for ugliness : ' By appearing under an abject and humi-
' liating exterior, our Saviour did but add to what the mystery
' of the redemption offers of sublime and touching.'   Tertullian was strong for the same theory : ' Ne aspectu quidem
' honestus.'   ' Nec humanæ honestatis fuit corpus ejus.'   ' Si
' inglorius, si ignobilis, si inhonorabilis, meus erit Christus.'
The pagans, accustomed to deify beauty, saw their advantage
and struck in.   ' Your Christ is ugly,' exclaimed Celsus with
true Epicurean logic, ' then he is not God.'   The three great
divines of the Western Church, St. Ambrose, St. Jerome, and
St. Augustin, stoutly held out for beauty, and the opposite
opinion, discredited in Europe, was eventually confined to the
Manichæans and some doctors of the East.

It may be collected from these disputes that no certain
image or representation of the form and features of Christ has
been handed down by tradition.   There is also much weight in
the remark, that the most ancient effigies are stamped with a
Greek or Roman character, both in physiognomy and costume,
without any trace of the Arabian or Israelite type.   Thus,
before the Byzantine style fixed *à la grecque* the face and costume of Jesus, the paintings of the Roman catacombs gave him
a Roman face, and clothed him with the toga and the pallium.
Dating from these productions, there have been two principal
types—the type of the Western Church and the type of the
Eastern ; varied to infinity by degrees of civilisation, by race,
by manners, and by clime.   ' The Greeks,' says Photius, ' think
' that He became man after their image ; the Romans, that He
' had the features of a Roman ; the Indians, that of an Indian ;
' the Ethiopians make him a black.'   Black Virgins, we need
hardly repeat, were painted and carved in ebony according to
the received tradition, and still abound in Catholic countries.

The extent to which some of the great painters have travestied
sacred subjects is familiar to all students of art ; and the liberties
taken by a ruder school are amusing by their mingled absurdity
and singularity :

' In some of his pictures Rembrandt made Abraham a burgess of
his time, and the Messiah a burgomaster of Saardam.   In the old
paintings representing the fall of Adam and Eve, it is not uncommon to find the forbidden fruit varying with the country or
province.   In Normandy and Picardy it is the classic apple, one of
the riches of the country ; in Burgundy and Champagne, the bunch
of grapes ; in Provence and Portugal, the fig and the orange ; whilst
in America it is the guava.   The guide to the paintings of Mount

Athos prescribes the fig. The fig-tree is under the protection of a Greek saint, Theodora, named the fig-eater. In Greece, then, it is generally the fig which is adopted on account of the sweetness and abundance of the fruit. In Italy it is sometimes the fig, sometimes the orange, according to the province or caprice.'

The Venerable Bede, not content with giving the names and ages of the Magi or wise men of the Epiphany, enters into minute details of their personal appearance and their respective gifts. Thus, Melchior, a white-haired sage, offers the gold; Gaspar, beardless and fresh-coloured, the frankincense; and Balthasar, dark and full-bearded, the myrrh. Bede followed the tradition of his age, the seventh century. But what did Cardinal Mazarin follow, or direct to be followed, when he ordered for his gallery an unbroken series of portraits of the Popes, beginning with St. Peter. A similar series has been reproduced in mosaic at Rome, and may also be seen in the schools of theology at the Seminary of St. Sulpice; the portraits being about on a par with those of the early Kings of France, beginning with Pharamond, at Versailles, or those of the Kings of Scotland at Holyrood, which (as Sir Walter Scott relates) elicited an acute criticism from a Persian ambassador. Addressing the housekeeper, who was doing the honours, he asked, ' You paint them yourself? ' and on her modest profession of inability, he continued, ' You no able ? ' you try, and you paint better.'

The establishment of the National Portrait Gallery under the auspices of Earl Stanhope and the discriminating superintendence of Mr. Scharf, and the Exhibition at South Kensington, have enabled us to take stock, as it were, of our possessions in this line of art, and to determine with tolerable certainty which of our earliest portraits may be accepted as authentic, i. e., as paintings from the life. The oldest known in our time was the portrait of Edward III. in St. Stephen's Chapel, Westminster. This was destroyed by fire in 1834, but careful copies were fortunately taken from it for the Society of Antiquaries in 1812. The oldest extant of recognised authenticity is the portrait of Richard III. in Windsor Castle, where, however, there is a portrait of Edward IV. which good judges (including Mr. Scharf) are inclined to think genuine. They are not so sure of her Majesty's portrait of Henry IV., although some put faith in it, relying on the features and costume. The earliest of the genuine pictures in the National Portrait Gallery is a Richard III., next in quality and equal in genuineness to the one at Windsor. The second earliest in that collection is a Cardinal Wolsey. The earliest at South Kensington are the portraits of Sir John Donne by Memling (No. 18) and Edward Grimston by Petrus Christus (No. 17); both by artists of considerable distinction in the history of art.

We can abandon with comparative indifference any small remains of faith we may have cherished in the traditional likenesses of barbaric kings or popes, but it is a very different matter when we are required to believe that no trustworthy images of the heroes, statesmen, poets, orators, and philosophers of classical antiquity have descended to us; that the busts of Alexander, Cæsar, Pompey, Hannibal, Pericles, Homer, Virgil, Horace, Demosthenes, Cicero, Plato, Socrates, and Aristotle, with a host of others which we have been wont to admire or venerate, are apocryphal. The *primâ facie* argument is rather favourable to many of them. Fame is more lasting than brass, *ære perennius*, but brass, bronze, and marble are lasting enough to have endured to our time, and retain a faithful reflex of form and features, of character and mind. We know that the ancients were never tired of multiplying statues of their great men, and that the highest genius was employed on the greatest : Phidias, on Pericles, Socrates, and Alcibiades; Praxiteles, on Demosthenes; Lysippus, on Alexander and Aristotle, and so on. Alexander issued a decree reserving the right of reproducing his image to three artists : Apelles, for painting; Pyrgoteles, for stone engraving; Lysippus, for statuary in bronze. The more statues, the more honour, and the number erected to the popular favourites was immense. Unluckily they were knocked down as eagerly as they had been set up when the tide turned. No sooner had the news of the battle of Pharsalia reached the capital, than all Pompey's statues were thrown down and mutilated. Augustus began his reign by destroying all the busts and images of the assassins of Cæsar. At the same time he set about forming a collection of the triumphal statues of the great men who had contributed to the power of Rome ; and the imperial city at that time boasted many private galleries rich with the spoils of Greece. If Mummius burnt Corinth with most of its inestimable treasures of art—that same Mummius who gave the well-known caution to the carriers of what he saved—Sylla thanked the gods for having granted him two signal favours : the friendship of Metellus Pius, and the good fortune of having taken Athens without destroying it.

But independently of the risks of removal, and the increased difficulty of identification, the accumulation of all the finest productions of art in one place, and that place the capital of the world which ambition or sedition periodically converted into a battle-field, was one main cause of their being wholly lost, or of their descending in an unsatisfactory condition to posterity. *Furor arma ministrat:* anything or everything, sacred or profane, becomes a weapon in a deadly conflict when the blood is up. 'I expect little aid from their hand,' said Front de Bœuf, alluding to the stone images in his chapel, 'unless we 'were to hurl them from the battlements on the heads of the 'villains. There is a huge lumbering Saint Christopher yonder, 'sufficient to bear a whole company to the earth.' The Roman warriors thought and acted like the rude Norman baron. When Titus Flavius Sabinus, the brother of Vespasian, was besieged in the burning capitol by the troops of Vitellius, he repaired breaches and formed barricades with the statues of the Temple of Jupiter. Fire and earthquake co-operated with civil war and barbaric conquest to complete the work of devastation; whatever was left unbroken or distinguishable lay buried under heaps of ruin; and when the superincumbent mass of rubbish was cleared away after the lapse of ages, the grand difficulty arose of appropriating the proper names to the best preserved images, and of duly assorting the arms, legs, heads and noses of the mutilated.

This difficulty was aggravated by a known practice of the ancients, which may have suggested to Sir Roger de Coverley the notion of transforming by a few touches of the brush the sign of 'The Knight's Head,' set up in his honour, into 'The 'Saracen's Head!' When the Rhodians decreed the honour of a statue to a general, he was desired to choose which he liked amongst the existing votive statues, and the dedication was altered by the insertion of his name. The prevalence and antiquity of this method of substitution are proved by Plato's proposed law for compelling the statuary to form each statue out of a single block; and instances abound of the change of heads from vanity, caprice, or accident. A striking passage in Statius charges Cæsar with the incredible folly of cutting off the head of an equestrian statue of Alexander by Lysippus, and replacing it by a gilded effigy of himself. Tacitus states that Tiberius decapitated a statue of Augustus to make room for his own head; and the gods of Greece, including the Jupiter Olympus of Phidias, were similarly treated by Caligula with a view to his own deification. There is a statue of Pompey at Rome reputed to be the very one at whose base, 'which all the 'time ran blood, great Cæsar fell.' But, objects M. Feuillet de Conches, we must have recourse to some anecdote, suspicious as ingenious, to be persuaded that the head, very badly restored, is really the original head. Rome is full of antiquity-mongers, who will supply any number of consuls' or emperors' heads and noses to order.

Napoleon was a great admirer of Hannibal, and one day, during a visit to the Louvre, he stopped before the bust which bears the name of his hero, and inquired of M. Visconti, the distinguished antiquary, whether it was authentic. ' It is possible,' was the reply; ' the Romans erected his statue in ' three public places of a city within the bounds of which, alone ' among the enemies of Rome, he had cast a javelin. Caracalla, ' who ranked him among the great captains, also raised several ' statues to him; but all this is much posterior to Hannibal.' ' This effigy,' rejoined Napoleon, ' has nothing African about ' it. Besides, Hannibal was blind of one eye, and this is not. ' Are there any medals of the time confirmatory of this bust?' ' There are medals, also long posterior.' ' Then it has been ' done *après coup*. I do not believe in it.'

Although the inference from the eye may not be deemed conclusive by connoisseurs, that drawn from the want of contemporary medals carries weight. When medals and gems fail, the deficiency is not unfrequently supplied by inscriptions or books. The fine bust of Cicero at the Vatican is authenticated by a passage in Livy as well as by medals. There are no well-authenticated busts, medals, or gems of Virgil or Horace; although the biographers of Virgil do not hesitate to describe him as tall and dark, with long, flowing hair, whilst the personal peculiarities of Horace may be collected from his writings. The best bust of Plato is apocryphal, which is probably the reason why Mr. Grote's last great work, ' Plato ' and the other Companions of Socrates,' appears without a frontispiece.

This range of subjects is inexhaustible; and our immediate object is simply to skim the cream of a semi-classical, semi-artistic *causerie*. We will now suppose the conversation turning on some other singularities of classical antiquity, which throw light on its intellectual or secret history, and suggest parallels or contrasts with modern life and manners.

We can hardly persuade ourselves that we are not listening to the story of an English or French collector, when we are told of Libanius of Antioch hearing that an Iliad and an Odyssey of prodigious antiquity were about to be sold at Athens, and commissioning a friend to purchase them. On receipt of the coveted treasures, he sends a fine copy of the Iliad, more recent but correct, in acknowledgment of the friend's services. He next learns that a copy of the Odyssey which seemed contemporary with Homer, is for sale, and purchases it.

But he is so ill-advised as to lend it, and as it is not returned, we find him complaining and lamenting, very much like Evelyn when he denounced the carelessness or dishonesty of the two Scot borrowers, or the French gentleman who was done out of the Malebranche's letters by the philosopher. Why, asks M. Feuillet de Conches, did he not act like the Faculty of Paris who held out against Louis XII., all absolute as he was, and refused to lend him an Arabian manuscript without a deposit of a hundred gold pieces, and would not abate a livre on seeing the royal treasurer forced to sell a part of his own plate to make up half of the security?

The greatest private collection of autographs at Rome is said to have been that of Mucianus, the friend of Pliny the Elder. He especially rejoiced in the possession of the reputed letter of Sarpedon to Priam, which he had discovered in a temple whilst he was governor of Lycia. Among other celebrated autographs in which the Greek and Roman collectors put faith, may be named the letters of Artaxerxes and Democritus to Hypocrates, the correspondence of Alexander and Aristotle, the letter of Zenobia to Aurelian in the handwriting of Longinus, and the letters of Titus to Josephus, testifying to the trust-worthiness of his history of the Jews. It might safely be taken for granted, without evidence of the fact, that the autographs of Livy, Cicero, Horace, Virgil, &c. &c., were as eagerly sought after and as highly prized in ancient times as those of the corresponding celebrities in our own. But we are not left to conjecture. Pliny speaks of having seen autographs of Cicero and Virgil. Quintilian mentions manuscripts of Cicero, Virgil, Augustus and Cato the Censor, *apropos* of certain differences and singularities of orthography which the copyists had not preserved. Cicero refers to an autograph of Ennius for the same purpose. Aulus Gellius had seen a manuscript of the Georgics, corrected by the author, as well as a manuscript of the second book of the Æneïd which passed for the original, or at least came from the house and the family of Virgil. The first known use of the word autograph is in Suetonius, *Literæ Augusti Autographæ.*

A great variety of materials were employed for writing by the Romans, besides the waxed tablets, without which no Roman of condition ever went abroad. For epistolary corre-spondence they used a fine papyrus called Augustan; the second quality was called Livian; the third, Claudian. They had also (adds M. Feuillet de Conches) ' great eagle paper ' like ourselves. Curious points of analogy abound in this por-tion of his book. The ancients had ingenious cyphers for their secret dispatches, and sent private orders to their commanders or ambassadors which could not be opened, so as to be legible, without a peculiar contrivance or the key. Cæsar's usual method was to write by agreement the fourth letter of the alphabet for the first; for example, D for A, and so on, varying the arrangement occasionally. The Romans had also short-hand writers, a chosen number of whom were employed by Cicero to take down a speech of Cato. Martial and Ausonius bear testimony to the surprising skill of some of them. We find emperors and consuls scribbling on monuments, and as careless of profaning or defacing them as modern travellers or bagmen. M. Letroune found the names of Hadrian, Marcus Aurelius, and Lucius Verus, inscribed on the statue of Memnon at Thebes. He might also have copied from it, had he thought fit, ' *Pierre Giroux le grand vainqueur, grenadier de* ' *la deuxième demi-brigade, division Desaix, passait par Thèbes,* ' *le 7 Messidor, An VII, pour se rendre aux cataractes du Nil.*'

The conceit of compressing the greatest quantities of writing into a given space was carried to excess by the Romans. Cicero speaks of the entire Iliad having been written on just so much skin or parchment as was contained in a nutshell—*in nuce inclusam.* This *tour de force* was rivalled by the poet, mentioned by Pliny, who contrived to inclose a distich in letters of gold within the husk of a grain of corn, an exploit which may pair off with that of the Frenchman who wrote the four canonical prayers on his nail. M. Feuillet de Conches has discovered a marked analogy between the French bureaucracy and the Roman scribes, who formed a corporation of which Horace was a member. They had gradually grown into considerable importance, and must not be confounded with the copyists, masters and journeymen, who answered to our printers and booksellers. The Sosii were the Murrays and Longmans of the Augustan age of Rome. The patricians were not ashamed to compete with them in this peculiar line of business. The house of Atticus is described as an immense establishment in which skilful workmen, mostly slaves, were busied in copying, pressing, and binding for the book-market. One amongst them, named Tiron, highly commended by Cicero, turned out copies that took rank like Elzevirs.

Women were much employed as copyists, and occasionally as scribes or secretaries. We have heard, prior to the abolition of serfdom, of white slaves in Russia embarked in commerce or eminent in art, vainly offering enormous sums for enfranchisement; and cases of the same kind were of frequent occurrence in Greece and Rome. An actor was prepared to give a sum equivalent to seven or eight thousand pounds sterling for his liberty.   One Canisius Sabrinus (mentioned by Seneca) a man of enormous wealth who wished to shine as a diner-out in spite of his natural dulness, procured a dozen slaves who were made to learn by heart select passages from the popular poets and instructed how to prompt him when he broke down or had nothing to say.   As the required duty implied memory and tact, the slaves are said to have cost him, on the average, a hundred thousand sesterces (about 800*l.*) apiece.

Mural and monumental inscriptions apart, the oldest specimens of Roman writing extant are those discovered in Pompeii and Herculanum.   Next in order of antiquity to these stand a Terence of the fourth century and a Virgil of the fifth, both on parchment, now in the Vatican.   How happens it that, out of the multitude of manuscripts in general circulation for several centuries later, not a single known original, and hardly one perfect copy, of an eminent classic author has survived the dark ages ?   The best solution will be found in the never-ceasing war waged against learning and knowledge, by bigotry and ignorance, from the decline of civilisation to its revival or new birth.   ' The Romans,' says Disraeli the elder, ' burnt the books ' of the Jews, of the Christians, and of the philosophers ; the ' Jews burnt the books of the Christians and the Pagans ; the ' Christians burnt the books of the Pagans and the Jews.' Take, for instance, the fate of Livy, of whom we have only thirty-five books, and those incomplete, out of one hundred and forty.   Independently of the long chapter of accidents common to all, he was honoured by the senseless enmity of Caligula, who ordered his works, along with those of Virgil and Homer, to be cast out of all the libraries.   Livy was afterwards treated much in the same fashion by Gregory the Great, who placed him in the *Index.*   This same Pope (says Disraeli) ordered that the library of the Palatine Apollo, a treasury of literature formed by successive emperors, should be committed to the flames. He issued this order under the notion of confining the attention of the clergy to the Holy Scriptures.   From that time all ancient learning which was not sanctioned by the authority of the Church has been emphatically distinguished as *profane* in opposition to *sacred*.   This pope is said to have burnt the works of Varro, the learned Roman, that Saint Austin might escape from the charge of plagiarism, being deeply indebted to Varro for much of his great work, ' The City of ' God:'

This is not the only irreparable loss that has been attributed to plagiarism.   Cicero's treatise *De Gloriâ* was extant in the fourteenth century and in the possession of Petrarch, who lent it, and it was lost. Two centuries later it was traced to a convent library, from which it had disappeared under circumstances justifying a suspicion that the guardian of the library, Pierre Alegonius, had destroyed it to conceal the fraudulent use made of the contents for his treatise *De Exsilio,* many pages of which (to borrow a simile from the Critic) lie upon the surface, like lumps of marl on a barren moor, encumbering what they cannot fertilise. Leonard Aretin, believing himself the sole possessor of a manuscript of Procopius on the War of the Goths, translated it into Latin, and passed for the author, until another copy turned up. The *Causeur* relates a similar anecdote of Augustin Barbosa, Bishop of Ugento, who printed a treatise *De Officio Episcoporum.* His cook had brought home a fish wrapped in a leaf of Latin manuscript. The prelate had the curiosity to read the fragment. Struck with the subject, he ran to the market, and ransacked the stalls till he had discovered the book from which the leaf had been torn. It was the treatise *De Officiis,* which, adding very little of his own, he published among his works ' to the greater glory of God.' This was a bolder stroke for fame than that of an Irish bishop, still living, who incorporated a brother divine's sermon in his Charge. Plagiarism, however, was not esteemed so heinous an offence as it is at present, and our actual stores of thought and knowledge have been enriched by it. Thus, Sulpicius Severus, the Christian Sallust, is believed to have copied his account of the capture of Jerusalem from the lost books of Tacitus.

How little comparative value was attached for some time after the revival of letters to the classic masterpieces, may be inferred from the confession of Petrarch, that he had seen several in his youth of which all trace had subsequently been lost; among others, the Second Decade of Livy. Its fate was curious, although not perhaps singular. The tutor of a Marquis de Ronville, playing at tennis near Saumur, found that his racket was made with a leaf of old parchment containing a fragment of this Decade. He hurried to the racket-maker to save the remains: all had passed into rackets.

Tacitus had a better chance than Livy; for his imperial namesake, after supplying all the public libraries with his works, ordered ten fresh copies to be executed annually; yet thirty books were lost, and the manuscript of what are saved escaped by a miracle; a single copy in a state of rapid decomposition having been discovered in a convent in Westphalia.

We have lingered with pleasure over this classical *causerie,* which is just such as may be supposed going on at Earl

Stanhope's, Dean Milman's, Mr. Gladstone's, or Mr. Grote's, when the late Sir George Lewis and Lord Macaulay were alive to join in it. *Decies repetita placebit ;* and although many of the details may not be new to the accomplished bibliophile—to the Duc d'Aumale or M. Van der Weyer—we are not afraid of falling under the sarcasm levelled in Gil Blas at the pedant who solemnly narrated that the Athenian children cried when they were whipped; ' a fact of which, but for his vast and select ' erudition, we should have remained ignorant.'

We shall pass more rapidly over the chapters devoted to China. But although the gloss of novelty has been taken off by recent travellers, there is still a good deal left in the Celestial Empire for the philosophical inquirer to glean and speculate upon. The respect paid by the Chinese to paper or parchment on which written or printed characters have been impressed, contrasts strikingly with the European mode of thinking, ancient and modern. Martial's friend, Statius, tells him that his book has all the air of paper in which Egyptian pepper and Byzantian anchovies are to be packed; and the same vein of pleasantry may be traced in a letter from Hume to Robertson: ' I forgot to tell you that two days ago I was in the House of ' Commons, where an English gentleman came to me and told ' me he had lately sent to a grocer's shop for a pound of raisins ' which he received wrapped up in a paper that he showed me. ' How would you have turned pale at the sight ! It was a leaf of ' your History, and the very character of Queen Elizabeth which ' you had laboured so finely, little thinking it would soon come ' to so disgraceful an end.' After stating that the publisher, Millar, had come to him for information to trace out the theft, he adds : ' In vain did I remonstrate that this was, sooner or later, ' the fate of all authors *serius, ocyus, sors exitura.* He will not be ' satisfied and begs me to keep my jokes for another occasion.'

To the Chinese, who regard the art of speaking to the eyes by marks or signs as a gift from on high, handwriting and printing, means for the reproduction of thoughts, are sacred. The trade of ink-making is esteemed honourable for the same reason. Hence in China a scrap of printed paper or writing is never wittingly trodden under foot or used as a wrapper: it is carefully picked up ; and in the vestibule of each house is a perfuming-pan destined to receive and burn all waste papers of the kind. ' Tea and other objects of commerce,' adds M. Feuillet de Conches, ' are always packed in blank paper.' Thus, too, pocket-handkerchiefs being in China an object of show and luxury, every great dignitary is followed by a valet, who, on visits of ceremony, carries his spitting-box and presents him with small pieces of paper every time he wishes to blow his nose. These pieces of paper are blank, never printed or written.

The same veneration for writing was professed by a Christian saint, François d'Assise, who flourished in the thirteenth century. If his eye fell on any scrap of writing in his walks, he scrupulously picked it up, for fear of treading on the name of the Lord or any passage treating of things sacred. When one of his disciples inquired of him why he picked up with equal care the writings of pagans, he replied, 'My son, it is with the ' letters of these writings that we form the most glorious name ' of God.'

A religious respect for the staff of life, bread, is not confined to the Chinese. We are told of a janissary dropping out of a procession at Aleppo, and dismounting to remove a piece of bread, lest it should be profaned by the horses' hoofs. During the great fire of London, popularly attributed to the Catholics, a member of the Portuguese Embassy was apprehended on a charge of throwing fireballs into houses. On examination it was proved that he had simply picked up a piece of bread, and placed it on the ledge of a window; an act which he explained by stating that, according to a feeling prevalent among his countrymen, to have left it on the pavement would have been a sin. To return to the Chinese : it stands to reason that they attach the highest value to the handwriting of their rulers and worthies—in other words, to autographs. Even fac-similes are held in high esteem, and the interiors of temples are adorned with them, posted like advertising bills against the walls. The great pagoda of Canton boasts no other decoration ; neither does the great temple of Confucius at Pekin. By some fatality no manuscript from the actual hand of this philosopher has been preserved. All his autographs have disappeared, although autographs are extant of the two preceding centuries.

The use of red ink is reserved to the emperors, so that it would be neither easy nor safe to counterfeit their autographs, which are carefully deposited in the state archives when the immediate purpose has been served. The signature of the Mongol emperors consisted merely of the impress of the forefinger and thumb. The first-class mandarins claimed the privilege of authenticating documents in the same manner. The Dalar-Lama made his mark with the entire palm. Writing, however, was part of the imperial education. Kang the Third, contemporary with Louis Quatorze, rivalled the Grand Monarque in the importance which he attached to his matutinal condition and preparations. It was his wont, at his *lever*, to circulate among his courtiers a bulletin written with his own hand, in

his own red ink, containing words to this effect: ' I am well ! '
One of these papers has been sold for forty pounds in the
autograph market of Pekin; and the price sounds far from
exorbitant.

In the competitive examinations of China—in which, by the
way, they were as much in advance of Europeans as in the first
rude invention of printing and gunpowder—the handwriting
carries as many marks as the composition; and in the case of
aspirants to the Academy of Pekin, it is the Emperor in person
who examines the papers, counts the strokes of the letters, and
verifies their agreement and form. ' One is always sure, there-
' fore,' concludes M. Feuillet de Conches, ' when one has to
' do with a *Han-Lin*, or academician, to have to do with a
' scholar, a distinguished man of letters, and one skilled in the
' caligraphy of his country.'

With a reasonable distrust of their school of painting, the
Chinese have never formed a picture-gallery, although in the
strictly imitative arts they never were excelled, not even by
the grapes of Zeuxis, the curtain of Parrhasius, or the door at
Greenwich Hospital.   Their grand stumbling block is perspec-
tive, in which their most formidable rivals are the Pre-Ra-
phaelites.   ' Their style,' remarks M. Feuillet de Conches,
' talent apart, is that of Cimabue and Giotto, abandoned by
' Massaccio, resumed by Fra Angelico da Fiesole, and, an age
' later, by Holbein himself in some of his portraits.'

The next, the third part, of these *Causeries*, starts with the
aphorism that all collections are useful, although some may be
more useful than others.   Just so, we have heard it plausibly
maintained that all wine is good, although some is better
than another, and all women handsome, although some are
handsomer than others.   Yet we are quite willing to concede
the utility, provided the disproportioned trouble and expense
in some instances are conceded in return; as in forming collections of postage-stamps, of advertisements, of ropes with which
celebrated criminals have been hanged, or of bills of fare or
menus of the best tables, with which a friend of ours, well
placed in diplomacy, has filled an album of several volumes.
A startling variety are enumerated by M. Feuillet de Conches,
illustrated by anecdotes, and setting consecutive description at
defiance; but his pages are so rich in materials that quoting
from them at random is like dipping into the kettle of
Camacho: something tempting and racy is almost certain to
come up.   Thus, *apropos* of Frederic the Great's collection of
snuff-boxes (containing more than 1,500) he describes a snuff-
box of Talleyrand and its use.   It was double, two snuff-boxes

joined together by a common bottom. The one was politely offered to his acquaintance; the other, never to be profaned by the finger and thumb of a third person, was reserved for himself. Here we recognise the diplomatist, so eternally on his guard, that when a lady requested his autograph, he wrote his name on the very top of the sheet of paper handed to him.

The principal collector of ropes is declared to be an Englishman, and a member of the Humane Society, who died about seventeen years ago. To each rope was attached a memoir of the subject or sufferer; and in most instances the last dying speech and confession was annexed, proving, it is added, the perfection to which, by dint of practice, the eloquence of the drop has arrived in the United Kingdom. 'Can it be, as is ' asserted on the authority of an English writer, whose name I ' forget, that in England the masters were wont to practise ' their pupils in this kind of composition, so that every good ' Englishman on entering into the world had his peroration ' ready *en cas* of the accident of the gallows?' Is there anything that a Frenchman, lettered or unlettered, will not believe of an Englishman,—not at all out of ill-nature or ill-will, but out of sheer ignorance? In the month of January 1866, a French journal described the English aristocracy as habitually risking their *centaine de guinées* on the result of a cockfight; and M. Feuillet de Conches reproduces, without questioning, the statement of Diderot that, in a secluded quarter of St. James's Park, there was a pond in which the female sex had the exclusive privilege of drowning themselves. So well-informed a writer might surely have learned that the English occupy only the third or fourth rank in the statistics of suicide, and that the Prussians stand first.

The collection of ropes begins with Sir Thomas Blount, who was executed in the reign of Henry IV. It contains instruments which, according to the notes annexed, had served in executions when the culprit or martyr was hung between two dogs, or with a dog tied to his feet. There, too, was the silken cord which Lord Ferrers begged hard to substitute for the hempen one—as great a curiosity as the sword which Baalam wished for to punish his ass; and with it might have been appropriately ticketed one of the willow twigs, the received makeshifts in Ireland; so received, in fact, *temp.* Elizabeth, that a rebel with a rope round his neck claimed the privilege of the twig. Bowstrings, which had done signal duty in the East, abounded; and one rope professed to be the very rope with which Lord Bacon's friend tried whether death by suffocation was agreeable or not. The practical conclusion, contrary to

the theoretical one of some recent essayists on the abolition
of capital punishment, was in the negative.　An appropriate
inscription to be placed over the door of a collection of this
kind might be taken from the *Trödelhexe's* speech in the *Wal-
purgisnacht,* or from a well-known passage in *Tam o' Shanter.*

Light is thrown on manners by collections, common in
France, of *billets de naissance, de mariage,* and *de mort* or
d'enterrement.　Those in use towards the middle of the last
century were adorned with emblems, like valentines; and artistic skill of a high order was frequently employed upon them.
An account of the *billet d'enterrement* of the Duke de Lavan-
guyon, a masterpiece of the kind, may be read in the Literary
Correspondence of Grimm.　The same fashion partially prevailed in England; and the card of invitation to the funeral of
Sir Joshua Reynolds, engraved by Bartolozzi, would fetch a
high price.　A plentiful harvest was offered to collectors of a
gloomy and reflective turn by the violation of the graves at
St. Denis in 1793.　One of them, Ledon, *physicien* (conjuror)
by profession, contrived to abstract fragments of the tombs
sufficient to construct a sarcophagus for the rest of his acquisitions, consisting of bones, crowns, sceptres, shrouds, and other
relics and emblems of defunct kings and queens.　The bodies
were mostly in different stages of decomposition; but a few
were perfectly preserved and had a complete look of life.
Henry IV. looked as if he had just fallen asleep, and his
fresh appearance led to an incident, related by a bystander,
which seems to have escaped M. Feuillet de Conches:—

'A soldier who was present, moved by a martial enthusiasm at
the moment of the opening of the coffin, threw himself on the body
of the conqueror of the League, and after a long silence of admiration, he drew his sabre, cut off a long lock (*mèche*) of his beard,
which was still fresh, exclaiming at the same time in energetic and
truly military terms: "And I too am a French soldier.　Henceforward I will have no other moustache."　Placing this precious
lock on his upper lip: "Now I am sure of conquering the enemies
of France, and I march to victory."　So saying he withdrew.'*

The Grand Monarque, also, was found in perfect preservation, and his exact proportions were carefully measured and

* Description Historique et Chronologique des Monumens de
Sculpture réunis au Musée des Monumens Français.　Par Alexandre
Lenoir, Fondateur et Administrateur de ce Musée; augmentée d'une
Dissertation sur la Barbe et les Costumes de chaque Siècle, du
procès-verbal des Exhumations de Saint-Denis et d'un Traité de la
Peinture sur Verre, par le même auteur.　Sixième édition, Paris,
an X de la République (1802).

calculated before he was broken up. His height was under five feet eight; and this result supplied Lord Macaulay with the text of one of his most ornate and characteristic passages. Turenne, who, as well as Du Guesclin, had received the royal honour of a burial at St. Denis, was also torn from his tomb, and was on the point of being flung into a newly dug pit with the rest, when a *savant*, struck by his high state of preservation, claimed the body for the National Academy of Anatomy. It remained there till September 1800, when the First Consul, ashamed of the indignity to which the military glory of France was thus exposed, caused it to be removed with becoming solemnity and deposited in the Church of the Invalides.

Stranger still, and yet better fitted to point a moral, was the destiny of Richelieu, whose body was torn from the grave in the church of the Sorbonne and rudely trampled under foot, after the head had been cut off and exhibited to the bystanders, amongst whom was Lenoir. A grocer got possession of it, and kept it as a curiosity till he married, when, to calm his wife's fears, he sold it to M. Armez *père*, who offered it to the Duc de Richelieu, Minister for Foreign Affairs under the Restoration. The offer remained unacknowledged, and the head devolved on M. Armez *fils*. At a sitting of the Historical Committee of Arts and Monuments, on the 13th June, 1846, attention was called to the circumstance, and the president, M. de Montalembert, supported by the committee, attempted to repair the profanation. Their exertions proved vain, and were renewed with no better result in 1855. 'We accuse no one,' observes M. Feuillet, ' still the fact is undeniable that this terrible head, the ' personification of the absolute monarchy killing the aristocratic ' monarchy, is wandering upon the earth like a spectre that has ' straggled out of the domain of the dead.' During the same popular phrensy in 1793, the fine marble statue of the Cardinal at the Château de Melleraye was decapitated, and—' to ' what base uses we may return, Horatio'—the head was used as a balance-weight for a roasting-jack by a zealous republican of the district.

Not content with emptying the tombs, the heroes and heroines of the Reign of Terror danced among them. Over the entrance to a cemetery was a scroll: *Bal du Zephyr;* and once on a time the patronesses stood at the doors distributing copies of the ' Rights of Man,' bound in human skin supplied to the binder by the executioner. M. Villenave possessed one of these copies. What would not an English collector give for one? What would not the drum made out of Ziska's skin fetch

at Christie's, should it accidentally turn up?   Mathematicians
will be glad to hear that there is a joint of Galileo's back-bone
in the Museum of Padua, surreptitiously abstracted by the
physician entrusted with the transfer of the relics to the Santa
Cruce at Florence in 1737.

The worshippers of the Goddess of Reason were anticipated
in their taste for horrors by the fine ladies, the *belles marquises*,
of the early part of the reign of Louis XV.   If we may trust
the Marquis d'Argenson, their favourite object of contemplation was a death's head.   They adorned it with ribbons, lighted
it up with coloured lamps, and remained in mute meditation
before it for half-an-hour before the promenade or the play.
The queen Maria Leczinska had one which she called *la belle
mignonne,* and pretended to be the skull of Ninon de Lenclos.
One may suppose, without any lack of charity, that there was
nothing very elevating or purifying in the train of meditation
which the skull of Ninon de Lenclos would inspire.   Yet Queen
Maria Leczinska passed for virtuous, and was guilty of nothing
worse than folly, or a shade of hypocrisy, in sanctioning such a
fashion by her example.

A collector of walking-sticks, M. Henri de Meer, a Dutchman, attracted attention to his collection by going mad and
dying with a walking-stick in each hand; feeble imitator of
Dr. Morrison, who breathed his last grasping a box of his own
pills and calling loudly for more.   But the collections which
afford most aid to history, and most scope to speculation, are
those of wigs, hats, caps, and head-dresses.   The vacillating
and erratic tendency of national taste, the march of mind, the
progress of events, may be traced by them.   A war, a peace, a
new play, a scientific invention, a public disaster, an actor, a
beauty, a hero, a charlatan, anything or anybody that made a
noise, originated a headdress and gave a name to it.   There
was the *perruque à la Ramilies* or *à la Villeroy,* by way of
set-off to the cravat *à la Steinkirk,* emblematic of the battle in
which the star of William paled before that of Luxembourg.
' The jewellers,' says Macaulay, ' devised Steinkirk buckles :
' the perfumers sold Steinkirk powder.   But the name of the
' field of battle was peculiarly given to a new species of collar.
' Lace neckcloths were then worn by men of fashion; and it
' had been usual to arrange them with great care.   But at the
' terrible moment when the brigade of Bourbonnais was flying
' before the onset of the allies, there was no time for foppery ;
' and the finest gentlemen of the court came spurring to the
' front of the line of battle with their rich cravats in disorder.
' It therefore became a fashion among the beauties of Paris to

' wear round their necks kerchiefs of the finest lace studiously
' disarranged, and these kerchiefs were called Steinkirks.'

During the exultation caused by the naval combats of the
' Juno ' and the ' Belle Poule,' the French ladies went about
with mimic frigates on their heads.   There are individual memories associated with this class of articles which have a painful
yet irresistible attraction.   We cannot avert our eyes from the
wig of Queen Margaret, the faithless and fascinating wife of
Henry IV., of whom it is recorded that she had her pages
clipped to hide under their fair tresses the black locks which
nature had bestowed upon her.   Still less can we refuse the
evidence of the ' True Report ' of the last moments of Mary
Queen of Scots, which sets forth that, when the executioner
lifted the head by the hair to show it to the bystanders with
the exclamation of ' God Save the Queen,' it suddenly dropped
from his hands.   The hair was false ; the head had been shaved
in front and at the back, leaving a few grey hairs on the sides.*

The author of ' Waverley ' remarks that the vanity of personal
appearance may be found clinging to the soldier who leads a
forlorn hope, and the criminal who ascends the scaffold.   The
minutest details of Mary's dress at her execution were carefully
studied.   According to one account, ' her kirtle was of figured
' black satin, and her petticoat-skirts of crimson velvet, her
' shoes of Spanish leather ; a pair of green silk garters ; her
' nether stockings worsted, and coloured watchet (pale blue)
' clouded with silver, and edged on the tops with silver, and
' next her legs a pair of Jersey hose.   She wore also drawers
' of white fustian.'   This account is adopted by Miss Strickland
on the authority of Burleigh's reporter.   She adds that the
details coincide with those communicated by Chateauneuf, also
from the notes of an eye-witness, which is true with the exception of the stockings.   Chateauneuf's eye-witness declares these
to have been silk, and the garters he describes as *deux belles
escharpes sans ouvrage.*

The stockings and garters are preserved in a collection that
has been laid open to the *Causeur,* and he reminds us, in
reference to the large stock of garters comprised in it, that
this compromising ligature was not formerly what it is now, a
secret or concealed article of dress.   Women wore drawers,
otherwise called *chausses,* fastened to the *bas de chausses*
(which for shortness we call *bas*) or stockings.   The garter,
fastened beneath the knee by a rich clasp or buckle, was the

---

* The authority is Chateauneuf, the French ambassador.   See
' Lettres de Marie Stuart,' &c. &c.   Par A. Teulet.   Paris : 1859.

connecting band between the drawers and stockings. There was, consequently, no reason for its not being exposed to view. 'This,' he continues, 'explains why in riding dress 'ladies wore stockings richly worked and garters set with 'jewels; how a Duchess of Orleans (whose garters were inven-'toried) could venture during her widowhood to have tears and 'thoughts (*pensées*) enamelled on them; how Edward III. could 'found his great order of the Garter without degrading it by 'avowing its origin.' But what was its origin? Surely an antiquarian of M. Feuillet de Conches's attainments and calibre must know that the old story of the Countess of Salisbury has been given up on all sides, and that the utmost exertions of his learned brethren to solve the mystery have proved vain; although it by no means follows that the actual garter dropped by the Countess may not be found duly labelled in the collection of his friend.*

We must return to the inexhaustible subject of wigs and hair-dressing, if only to point out that the new fashion (set by the Parisian *demi monde*) of yellow or golden hair, with a tinge of red or auburn, is simply the revival of one which began under more respectable auspices towards the commencement of the reign of Louis XIV. The two queens, Anne and Maria Theresa, dowager and regnante, the seductive heroine of the Fronde, the Duchess de Longueville, and the two first favourites, Mesdames De la Vallière and De Fontanges, were *blondes;* so, for all the aspiring beauties whom nature had made a shade too dark there was no alternative but to wear a wig or dye. The men fell into the custom, as may be learnt from Molière, who makes the Misanthrope exclaim to Celimène—

> 'Vous êtes-vous rendue, avec tout le beau monde,
> Au mérite éclatant de sa perruque blonde.'

The assumption of the perruque by Jean Baptiste, the son of Racine, secretary of embassy in Holland, is regularly discussed between him and his mother-in-law: 'Your father deeply 'regrets the necessity which you say you are under of wearing 'a wig. He leaves the decision to the ambassador. When 'your father is in better health he will order M. Marguery to 'make you such a one as you require. Madame la Comtesse

---

* All the various theories of the origin of the Order are investigated and declared unsatisfactory by Mr. Beltz. See 'Memorials 'of the Order of the Garter,' &c. By G. F. Beltz, Lancaster Herald : 1841. Ladies invited to the feasts of St. George wore the garter round the arm.

' de Gramont is very sorry for you that you should lose the
' attraction which your hair gave you.'

The entry in Pepys's Diary for May 11, 1667, runs thus :—

'My wife being dressed this day in fair hair, did make me so mad
that I spoke not one word to her, though I was ready to burst with
anger. After that Creed and I into the Park and walked, a most
pleasant evening, and so took coach, and took up my wife, and in my
way home discovered my trouble to my wife for her white locks,
swearing several times, which I pray God may forgive me for, and
bending my fist, that I would not endure it.'

They renewed the discussion the next day, Sunday, and
came to an understanding that she should give up her white
locks, on his agreeing to give up keeping company with one
Mrs. Knipp, of whom there is frequent and rather compromising
mention in the Diary.

There was no concealment or fear of detection on the part of
either sex. The false hair was put off and on by the women
like a bonnet or a cap; and a court lady would have felt little
abashed at an accident such as recently happened to a fair
equestrian, who had the misfortune to drop the whole of her
back hair or *chignon* in Rotten Row.

The fashion of powdering the hair with gold dust, which has
recently found votaries both at London and Paris, was commenced by Poppæa the wife of Nero, and copied by Lucius
Verus (the adopted son of Aurelius), who was extravagantly
vain of his hair. Authorities are not wanting to prove that
the golden and auburn tints which we admire in the portraits of Titian, Tintoret, and Paul Veronese, were produced
by a tincture in vogue at Venice in the sixteenth century.[*]
The collections show that other shades of colour, especially
brown and black, have had their day; and it is a disputed
question in connoisseurship whether the highest degree of beauty
has not been attained by the *brunettes.* Red or carroty
(which is the correcter translation of *roux* or *rousse*) has been
at a discount in all ages. It was thought ominous of evil by
the ancients, and typical of villainy during many ages of the
Christian era. 'Judas-coloured hair' is the spiteful reproach

---

[*] We are indebted to M. Feuillet de Conches for a very elegant
volume, entitled 'Les Femmes Blondes,' in which he has collected
with his usual learning and gaiety all the Italian authorities on the
most approved methods of turning the colour of the hair. The
Venetian ladies applied vinegar and water to their heads, and then
sat in the sun, with a rim or shade of straw to protect them from
sun-stroke. This book, which is a bibliographical curiosity, was
published last year in Paris.

of Pope. '*Aussi, dans tout notre musée de coiffure, pas un
' cheveu roux ardent, couleur de carotte.*'

The reason why Racine put off ordering his son's wig is
obvious enough, when we find that the price of one of the
fashionable colour was a thousand French crowns. The gentleman whom Sydney Smith, in reference to the length and re-
dundancy of his curls, accused of growing hair for sale, might
have driven a profitable trade at that time. Down to the period
immediately preceding the French Revolution, which introduced crops *à la Brutus*, the wigs commonly worn by English
gentlemen in the streets cost from thirty to forty guineas; and
Rogers, appealing to Luttrell in our hearing, thus described a
mode of theft as practised in London within their common
memory. The operator was a small boy in a butcher's tray on
the shoulders of a tall man; and when the wig was adroitly
twitched off, the bewildered owner looked round for it in vain;
an accomplice confused and impeded under the pretence of
assisting him, and the tray-bearer made off.

Fine hair was a frequent resource in want, and a far higher
class were occasionally tempted to recur to it than the heroine
of a repulsive episode of *Les Misérables*. Mrs. Howard,
afterwards Countess of Suffolk, the favourite of George II., is an
example. In her earlier and domestic days, when her husband
was English Minister at Hanover, they were in want of money
to give an indispensable dinner or entertainment of some sort,
and to supply the deficiency she magnanimously sacrificed her
hair. Large allowance should be made for the frailties of a
woman who thus understood and practised the self-denying
duties of a wife.

Of course there were not wanting censors and puritans to
denounce wigs and cosmetics, as vehemently as Prynne denounced the unloveliness of love-looks. An Abbé de Vessets
published a treatise against *Le Luxe de Coiffures* in 1694,
containing a chapter headed, *Mariage : une fille coëffée à la
mode n'est digne de recevoir ce sacrement.* Another Abbé is the
author of a book on *L'Abus des Nudités de Gorge.* The name
of the first member of the priesthood who adopted the peruke to
the scandal of the lay public, has been preserved. It was the
Abbé de la Rovière, a courtier of Gaston of Orleans, and he
afterwards became Bishop of Langres. How modes of thinking,
even on sacerdotal subjects, vary with time and country!
When the cadet of a noble family, who had been a Captain of
Dragoons, was made a bishop by George III., he nearly went
down on his knees to his Majesty to be permitted to dispense
with the wig; and the king remained inexorable. The rise

and fall of Kant's wig are thought to indicate not only the fitful changes of the curiosity-market, but the rise and fall of his philosophy. It (the wig) fetched thirty thousand florins at his death. At one of the subsequent fairs at Leipzig it was sold for twelve thousand dollars, a fall of from fifteen to twenty per cent. 'The system of Kant was going down. Can the 'same be said of the philosophy of J. J. Rousseau, whose 'shoes (*sabots*), sold at the same fair, were given for ten dollars?' M. Feuillet de Conches has had in his hand a pair of the spectacles brought from Venice in the seventeenth century, which (he adds) became so much the fashion that the *élégantes* never took them off, not even in bed. The glasses were double the size of those now in use. He has, also, examined a packet of the toothpicks, imported into France by Antonio Perez, which popularised the habit rendered memorable by Coligny, who was never seen without a tooth-pick between his teeth. After the massacre of Saint Bartholomew, his body was exposed with the eternal tooth-pick in his mouth ; but we are not aware that it has been preserved.

A collection of buttons was exhibited at the University of Ghent in 1845, for the benefit of the poor, and proved a valuable contribution to the history of manners and art. They were not only of all shapes and sizes, in polished steel, in silver and gold, and set with the costliest jewels ; but an entire series were painted in miniature by the first artists of the period—the first years of Louis XVI. There were portraits of celebrated beauties, with copies of ancient statues and scenes taken from ancient mythology. Klingstet made double buttons with a spring, containing two surfaces, and each a *chef-d'œuvre* in its way. Honoré Fragonard, a decorator of note, painted for a gay marquis a set of buttons *à la Watteau*, which have been preserved. Another man of rank wore a set of small watches, without, it is slidy added, becoming more famous for punctuality. Equal extravagance was indulged about the same time in waistcoats, which, although the material was more perishable, afforded wider scope for luxury and design. An exquisite of the first water was then an improving study for both the sempstress or embroiderer and the scene-painter. One might be seen with the amours of Mars and Venus on his stomach, and another with a cavalry review. 'We are assured,' says a writer in the *Mémoires Secrets*, 'that an enthusiast has ordered a dozen waist-'coats representing scenes from the popular plays, so that his 'wardrobe may become a theatrical repertory and some day 'serve for tapestry.' After the assembly of the Notables, there were *gilets aux Notables*, copied from the print described by

Bachaumont: ' The king is in the middle, on his throne : in the ' left hand he holds a scroll on which are these words, *L'age* ' *d'or ;* but by a very offensive oversight it is so placed that he ' seems to be rummaging his pockets with his right hand.' A little later, the guillotine grew into fashion for ornaments, especially for brooches and pins.

The same vaunted collection, which re-opens so many curious chapters of social annals, is described as particularly rich in gloves. M. Feuillet de Conches boasts of having himself contributed the identical pair of gloves which Anne of Austria sent to Spain to the Duc d'Arcos, with a letter of business ending with this P.S. : ' Monsieur LeDuc et Compère, I send ' herewith a pair of gloves which will serve as a pattern for ' the dozen which I request you to have forwarded to me.' These gloves are of coarse leather ; and surprise is expressed that they could be worn by a woman who, it was feared at Madrid, was too delicate to be able to sleep in Holland sheets. Alongside of them are placed the gloves which Antonio Perez, Spanish ex-ambassador, sent to Lady Knolles with a letter saying : ' These gloves, Madam, are made of the skin of a dog, ' the animal most praised for its fidelity. Deign to allow me ' this praise, with a place in your good graces. And if I can ' be of no other use, my skin at least might serve to make ' gloves.' He was so pleased with this conceit, that in a letter to Lady Rich he repeats and improves upon it :—

'I have endured such affliction at not having ready at hand the dogskin gloves desired by your ladyship, that I have resolved to sacrifice myself for your service, and to strip off a little skin from the most delicate part of myself, if indeed any delicate skin can be found on a thing so rustic as my person. . . . The gloves are of dogskin, Madame ; and yet they are of mine, for I hold myself a dog, and entreat your Ladyship to hold me for such, as well on account of my faith as my passion. The skinned dog (*perro decollado*) of your Ladyship, ANTON. PEREZ.'

The most curious collection of *chaussures* (boots, shoes, and slippers) is stated to be in the possession of an Englishman, Mr. Roach Smith. Besides specimens of every successive age, beginning with the boots of a bishop in 721 A.D., he has several to which an historic or romantic interest is attached ; e.g. the shoes of most of the beauties of Charles II.'s court, including the Duchess of Cleveland, the Countess of Muskerry, and la belle Hamilton (afterwards Comtesse de Grammont), with those of Miss Jennings and Miss Stewart (the original of the Britannia on the guinea), stolen, according to the labels, by Rochester and Killigrew.

There is an entire compartment devoted to some of the shoes crowned by the *Société des Petits Pieds*, over which the member with the smallest foot presided till she was displaced by a competitor; a Cinderella-like slipper being kept to test the qualifications of the candidates. If Pauline Buonaparte (Princess Borghese) had competed, she would have been hailed president for life by acclamation. Her feet, besides their smallness and exquisite shape, were plump (*potelés*) and rosy like those of a child; and she was by no means chary in exhibiting them. On ceremonial occasions, a page entered with a cushion of crimson velvet, on which she placed her foot, whilst he knelt and drew off the stocking, with the favoured circle looking on. Her remark on sitting for a nearly nude figure to Canova is well known.

The *Curieux* relates a trait of enthusiasm on the part of a milord which we suspect will prove new to his countrymen. A Scotch earl, Lord Fife, gave Madame Vestris a thousand guineas to allow a cast to be taken of her leg, which was superb. The earl died, and this cherished leg was sold for half-a-crown! The moral reflection is conveyed in a line from Lamartine:

. ' J'ai pesé dans ma main la cendre des héros.'

This leg should have been sent to the fair at Leipsic along with Kant's wig. The Germans are, or were, the people for answering to an extraordinary call on sensibility or sentiment. When Sontag was in the height of her celebrity at Berlin, a party of her military admirers bribed her maid to give them one of her cast-off slippers, had it set as a cup, and toasted her in it till it was worn out. There is another story that a party of students rushed into her hotel whilst her carriage was driving off, and made prey of a wine-glass not quite empty, out of which she had just been drinking. This was put up to auction on the spot, and fetched seventeen dollars. A pair of shoes has been preserved with extravagantly high heels painted by Watteau to represent a flock or sheepfold (*bergerie*) of Loves. The Duchess de Berry had a shoe that once belonged to Louis XIV., of dark velvet, embroidered with *fleurs-de-lis*, and adorned with a battlepiece painted by Parrocel.

' *Puisque nous causons*, let us pause a little to speak of the ' history of flowers, of the flowers that Marie Antoinette loved ' so well, that she so largely contributed to multiply and em-' bellish.' We willingly pause to record the plausible claim put in for the invention of what is commonly called the English system of gardening, by a Frenchman, in the time of

Louis Quatorze. It was the poet Du Fresnoy, we are assured, who first ventured on substituting the picturesque variety of the landscape-painter for the rectilinear style of the architects, and was made comptroller of the royal gardens in recognition of his merit. But nature and simplicity were sadly out of keeping with the artificial grandeur of Versailles. The genius of Du Fresnoy was chilled or rebuked by his royal patron, and the reform planned by him stopped short. 'His system re-' turned to us,' says the *Curieux*, 'in the following age, with ' the British stamp on it, as so many products of French ' imagination return to us.' Girardin created Ermenonville; M. Boutin, Tivoli; M. de la Borde, Mereville; the poet-painter Watelet, Moulin-Joli. The Prince de Ligne did his best to correct the stiffness of his paternal alleys and flower-beds. Then, in 1774, came Marie Antoinette, who, under the direction of Bernard de Jussieu and a clever gardener, con-verted Trianon into a charming parterre, where the system of the English painter, William Kent, and his rival, Browne (the inventor Du Fresnoy was altogether forgotten) was more fol-lowed than the severe harmony of Le Nostre and De la Quintenie.

Kent died in 1748; and Browne achieved his highest dis-tinction by laying out the grounds of Blenheim, where he com-mitted a solecism which elicited a cutting sarcasm on his illustrious employer, the great Duke of Marlborough. A mag-nificent bridge over a streamlet provoked the epigram:

'The lofty arch his high ambition shows,
The stream an emblem of his bounty flows.'

Our neighbours were in no hurry to reclaim their property in the invention, if it can be so termed; and we suspect that the resumption simply formed part of the Anglomania that came over them about the time when Marie Antoinette began amusing herself with the creation of *Le Petit Trianon*. Her fondness for flowers led to one of those revolutions in head-dresses of which specimens may be multiplied to weariness. When flowers got common, the court ladies took first to fruit, and afterwards to vegetables. Chaplets of artificial radishes and carrots were in vogue. Madame de Matignon appeared one day, *à la jardinière*, in a headdress of brown linen striped with blue, ornamented by the artist hand of Léonard with a head of brocoli and an artichoke.

The bare list of collections visited by the *Curieux* would fill many pages. But his master-passion is for autographs; and he is constantly digressing to expatiate on their value and their charm; on the best methods of utilising, and the sacred duty of preserving, them. Indeed, he is a veritable Chinese in his reverence for written paper; and he would cordially assent to the second branch of the *rouè* maxim, *Write not, Burn not,* without regarding, probably without suspecting, the consummate profligacy that lurked in it. Yet in his highly interesting dissertation on the *Cassette aux Poulets* of Fouquet, he incidentally demonstrates the imprudence, to use no stronger term, of giving a permanent form to any shade of forbidden feeling, or any passing burst of irritability, disappointment, or caprice. The one may make an enemy or unmake a friend; the other may destroy a reputation. Trifles light as air, once committed to paper, have often led to complications in which peace, fortune, and happiness have been wrecked.

Fouquet, the prince of financiers, was not less renowned for gallantry than for liberality and wealth. His downfall was owing to his indiscreet rivalry with his royal master both in magnificence and love. The first step after his arrest was the seizure of his papers, including the casket in which he kept those notes and letters of female friends and applicants which pass under the denomination of *poulets*. The opening of this casket was dreaded like that of another Pandora's box, without Hope at the bottom. What varied evils, what scandalous disclosures, what revelations of broken fortunes and fallen or falling virtue, might come forth! The King himself opened the casket, and its contents were read by only two persons besides himself, the Queen and Tellier (the royal confessor). All sorts of stories were afloat, and Madame de Molteville remarks that few persons about the Court were exempt from the charge of having sacrificed to the golden calf; that the fable of Danäe was fully borne out, and that, since, by extraordinary ill-luck, Fouquet kept all the letters addressed to him, things were read which did great harm to very many persons. Rumour and malice added, coloured, or invented. A pretended letter from Madame Scarron (afterwards Madame de Maintenon), was handed about, containing this passage:—

'J'ai toujours fuy le vice, et naturellement je hais le péché; mais je vous avoue que je hais encore davantage la pauvreté. J'ai reçu de vous dix mille écus; si vous voulez encore en apporter dix mille dans deux jours, je verrai ce que j'aurai à faire.'

Another version of the letter commences differently, and ends: '*Je ne vous deffends pas d'espérer.*' The *Curieux* indignantly denounces this letter as a fabrication, and justifies his incredulity by a passage in the *Souvenirs* of Madame de Caylas: 'I remember to have heard that Madame Scarron, being one

' day obliged to go to speak to M. Fouquet, she thought fit
' to go so negligently dressed that her friends were ashamed
' to take her there. Everybody knows what M. Fouquet
' was, and his weakness for women, and how the vainest and
' the best placed sought to please him.' The uncharitable
might put an opposite interpretation on this neglected dress;
and the best defence for Madame Scarron is the continued
respect in which she was held by the Court and her private
marriage to the King. There is no hatred like religious
hatred, and this very marriage became a fresh topic for calumny
in the hands of those who had suffered from the persecutions
encouraged by her bigotry. ' In 1835, at the French Hospital
' in London,' says the *Curieux*, ' I found, in the possession of
' an old female inmate, an English libel against Madame de
' Maintenon, entitled, *The French King's Wedding, or the*
' *Royal Frolic ; being a pleasant account of the intrigues, comical*
' *courtship, catterwauling, and surprising marriage ceremonies*
' *of Louis XIV. with Madame de Maintenon, with a Comical*
' *Song, sung to His Majesty :* 1708. The old Protestant ob-
' stinately refused to cede me the book, which she read and
' re-read with pleasure, although she found difficulty in under-
' standing it.'

Another lady whom the *Curieux* deems unjustly calumniated
was the Marquise du Plessis-Bellière, accused of having assisted
Fouquet in his designs on Madame de la Vallière on the
strength of what is termed a hideous apocryphal letter amongst
the papers of Conrart. The Marquise was a friend of Fouquet and rendered him important political services, whether
she was paid for them or not. The reputation of another great
lady, the Princess of Monaco (*née* de Grammont), who was
also compromised by the correspondence, is abandoned as not
worth defending ; and in this instance at least a sound discretion has been exercised. Leaving her husband to the solitary
enjoyment of his miniature sovereignty, she lived a gay life at
the French Court, where she was renowned for the rapid succession of her lovers, every one of whom was regularly hung in
effigy by the Prince in the avenue of his palace at Monaco,
with a label round the neck. The number became startling ;
strangers came from far and near to admire the spectacle ; and
the circumstance at length came to the ears of the Grand
Monarque. He tried at first to interfere with a high hand,
but finding his threats vain, and the scandal on the increase,
he was fain to conciliate the Prince by a promise that a strict
guard should henceforth be kept on the Princess ; whereupon
the effigies were removed.

Another letter to Fouquet, which no virtuous woman could have written, endorsed *Lettre d'une Inconnue* by Conrart, was by turns attributed to Madame Scarron and Madame de Sévigné in the *Memoires sur la Bastille*, and finally given to Madame de Sévigné by the rest of the scandalous chronicles in circulation. Her known and avowed letters go far to refute the calumny. 'With him' (Fouquet), she writes to Bussy, ' I have always the same precautions and the same fears, which ' notably retard the progress he would willingly make. I ' believe he will be tired at last of always recommencing use- ' lessly the same thing.'

The following passage is copied *verbatim et literatim* from an autograph letter of hers to Ménage in the possession of the *Curieux* :—

'Je vous remercie, mon cher monsieur, de toutes vos nouuelles. Il y en a deux ou trois dans vostre lettre que ie ne sauois point. Pour celles de M. Fouquet, ie nentends parler dautre chose. Je pense que vous saues bien le deplesir que iay eü dauoir esté trouuée dans le nombre de celles qui luy ont escrit. Il est vray que ce nestait ny la galanterie, ni linterest que mauoient obligée dauoir vn commerce avec luy. Lon voit clairement que ce nestait que pour les affaires de M. de la Trousse ; mais cela nempesche pas que ie naye esté fort touchée de voir quil les avoit mises dans la cassette de ses poulets, et de me voir nommée parmy celles qui nont pas eü des sentimens si purs que moy. Dans cette occasion iay besoin que mes amis instruisent ceux qui ne le sont pas. Je vous croy asses genereux pour vouloir en dire ce que Mᵉ. de la Fayette vous en aprendra, et iay receu tant dautres marques de vostre amitié que je ne fais nulle facon de vous coniurer de me donner encore celle-cy.'

Bussy-Rabutin who, like Fouquet, had failed to touch his charming cousin's heart, quarrelled with her, and took an ungenerous revenge in his *Histoire Amoureuse des Gaules.* But he soon grew ashamed of his conduct, and did his best to compensate for the wrong by (to use his own language) ' siding with ' her loudly against the people who sought to confound her with ' the mistresses of the minister.' To be well-armed for the campaign, he saw Tellier, and was assured by him that ' the ' letters of Madame de Sévigné were the letters of a friend who ' had a great deal of wit, and that they had amused the King ' more than the insipid tenderness of the other letters, but that ' the surintendant had *mal apropos* mixed love with friendship.' Tellier, it is justly added, was not the man to palliate evil if there was any, for it was he of whom the Comte Grammont said, on seeing him go out from a private conference with the

King, ' He looks like a polecat that has just been killing
' chickens and is licking his blood-stained muzzle.'

Both Madame de Sévigné and Madame de Maintenon are
in high favour with the *Curieux*, having both contributed
largely to his collection of autographs; and he insists on
throwing the entire responsibility of the revocation of the
Edict of Nantes and other arbitrary measures suggested or
sanctioned by Madame de Maintenon, on the King.   The in-
grained absolutism and egotism of Louis XIV., he contends,
were at their acme from his earliest years.   In the public
library of St. Petersburgh, under the glass covering of a
collection of autographs, may be seen one of the copybooks in
which his Majesty practised writing as a child.   Instead of
' Evil communications corrupt good manners,' or ' Virtue is its
' own reward,' the copy set for him was this : ' *Les rois font
' tout ce qu'ils veulent.*'

The best mode that could be hit upon for teaching history
to Louis XV. was that recommended by St. Simon to Fleury,
the royal preceptor, afterwards cardinal and minister.   It was
to hang a gallery with historical portraits and sketches, to
make this the place of reception for the children of the nobility
who came to pay their respects to their young sovereign, to
have them tutored beforehand and accompanied by preceptors,
who were to lead the conversation to prominent events or characters, and so draw him on to make inquiries and pick up
information.

More than half (300 pages) of the third volume of the
Causeries is devoted to Montaigne, who is held in high favour,
despite of two peculiarities which might have been expected to
lower him in the opinion of a collector of autographs.   He was
an infrequent and careless correspondent, and he expressed a
thorough contempt for all who wrote letters with a view to
publication or literary fame.   He excepts none, not even
Cicero and Pliny the Younger, of whom he says :—

' This surpasses all meanness of heart in persons of their rank,
to have wished to derive glory from egotism and prattle, to the
point of employing for this purpose their private letters to their
friends ; so that, some having missed the time for being sent, they
have notwithstanding published them with this worthy excuse that
they were unwilling to lose their pains. . . .   Does it become two
Roman consuls, sovereign magistrates of the imperial State of the
world, to occupy their leisure in arranging and dressing up a fine
missive, to draw from it the reputation of understanding well the
language of their nurse ?   What could a schoolmaster, who gained
his livelihood by it, do worse ? '

What would Montaigne have said had he lived to be told of the miserable subterfuge of Pope, who surreptitiously caused his letters to be published, and then denounced the publication as a theft ; or of the anxious care taken by Horace Walpole to transmit corrected copies of epistolary gossip to posterity ? Be their motives what they might, we are indebted to them for compositions which the world would not willingly let die.

Throwing over Pliny, somewhat unceremoniously and unnecessarily, M. Feuillet de Conches takes up the cudgels for Cicero, who, he vows, did not write his letters to his familiars —*ad familiares*—for any eyes but theirs ; and the proof is that when Atticus applied to him for copies, with a view to a complete collection, he had none. Montaigne, too, it is retorted, printed some of his own letters ; and his mode of speaking of them and his method of epistolary composition, are strongly marked by self-complacency :—

'On this subject of letters, I wish to say this one word, that it is a work in which my friends hold that I am capable of something ; and I should more willingly have chosen this form of publishing my whims, had I had anyone to address (*si j'eusse eu à qui parler*). I needed, what I have had at other times, a certain commerce that attracted, sustained, and excited me. If all the paper was in existence that I have ever blotted for the ladies, when my hand was truly carried away by my passion, there would haply be found some page worthy to be communicated to idle youth misled by this madness.'

After saying that he writes very fast, and very badly, trusting to the indulgence of the great personages with whom he corresponds to excuse blots and erasures, he continues :—

'The letters which cost me most are those that are worth least ; from the moment that I flag, it is a sign that I am no longer in the vein. I readily begin without plan ; the first sometimes produces the second. . . .

'As I had rather compose two letters than close and fold one, I always resign this duty to another ; so that, when the substance is finished, I would willingly charge some one with the duty of adjusting those long harangues, offers, and prayers, that we place at the end, and wish that some new custom would deliver us from them.'

His wish has been granted, and our formal conclusions are now speedily dispatched. His habit of beginning without a plan recalls Rousseau's *beau idéal* of a loveletter, which (he maintains) should be begun without the writer knowing what he is going to say, and end without his knowing what he has said. The letter of a celebrated Frenchwoman to her husband is a model of conciseness. ' *Je commence, parce que je n'ai rien* ' *à faire : je finis, parce que je n'ai rien à dire.*'—T. A. V.

The increased facility of communication has encouraged brevity and haste ; we dash off a dozen letters in an hour instead of devoting half a morning to the production of one ; and literary people are more remarkable than others for carelessness in this respect,—probably on the principle avowed by Madame de Stäel : ' Since I have aimed openly at celebrity ' by my books, I have left off paying any attention to my ' letters.'

The literary public are indebted to M. Feuillet de Conches for a valuable collection of letters in which the place of honour is assigned to Montaigne ;* and his familiarity with the style and hand-writing of this, the quaintest and most original of essayists, led to his being called in to decide an amusing and instructive controversy. An autograph letter of Montaigne belonging to the Countess Boni de Castellain was put up to auction in 1834, and the agent of M. de Pixérécourt, having received an unlimited commission, gave 700 francs for it to the extreme disgust of his employer; who, on the chance of getting rid of his bargain, started what at first sounded like a plausible objection to its authenticity. The autograph was a Report, dated February 16, 1588, to Maréchal de Matignon of what befell the writer and his party in an encounter with a troop of Leaguers, and contains this sentence : ' Nous n'osions cependant passer outre ' pour l'incertitude de la sûreté de nos persones, de quoi nous ' devions estre esclercis sur nos *passepors.*' The doubt arose from the word *passepors,* which, it was contended, was more modern. The reply was that, besides being used in another letter of Montaigne's and in one from the Cardinal de Lorraine of anterior date, it actually occurs eight times in the *Ordonnance d'Institution des Postes* framed under Louis XI. in 1464. An autograph, however, like Cæsar's wife, cannot endure suspicion: to be once discredited is enough; and the letter which cost 700 francs was subsequently thought dear at thirty. The word passport, it may be remembered, is introduced by Shakspeare in Henry V.'s speech before the battle of Agincourt : ' Let him depart: his passport shall be made.' But it appears from ' The Sentimental Journey,' published in 1768, that passports were not then in general use for travelling in time of peace : ' I had left London (says Yorick) with so much precipitation ' that it never entered my mind that we were at war with

---

* Lettres Inédites de Michel de Montaigne et de quelques autres Personnages pour servir à l'Histoire du Seizième Siècle.

' France; and had reached Dover, and looked through the hills
' beyond Boulogne, before the idea presented itself; and with
' this in its train, that there was no getting there without a
' passport.' He contrived, we need hardly add, to reach Paris
without one.

' I have no drill sergeant to arrange my productions, but
' chance. I put together my reveries as they present themselves.
' Sometimes they throng in crowds, sometimes they drag along
' in single file. I wish people to see my natural and ordinary
' pace, irregular as it may be; I let myself alone as I find
' myself.' This passage from Montaigne is chosen by M.
Feuillet de Conches for the motto of his Fourth Book, entitled
Voyage où Il vous Plaira; a book, if possible, more miscellaneous than the rest. In the first chapter he analyses the nature
of the interest we take in the personal qualities of authors, and
strengthens his theory by the authority of Addison, in the
' Spectator,' who begins by drawing a portrait of himself, which,
although verging on caricature, has preserved two or three of
the genuine and strongly marked features of the original. If
not quite so taciturn as his literary double, Addison used to
say of himself that, with respect to intellectual wealth, he could
draw bills for a thousand pounds, though he had not a guinea
in his pocket. It was said of Corneille *qu'il avait tout son esprit
en génie;* and he pleads guilty to the impeachment :—

> ' J'ai la plume féconde et la bouche stérile,
> Bon galant au théâtre et fort mauvais en ville ;
> Et l'on peut rarement m'écouter sans ennui,
> Que si je me produis par la bouche d'autrui.'

According to an autograph note written by the Abbé
d'Olivet for Voltaire and verified by the *Curieux,* there was
another peculiarity in which the author of the *Cid* resembled
another English writer of genius. Pope says in one of his
letters that he had been three weeks waiting for his imagination; and his habit was to take instant advantage of it when
it came ; rising frequently in the middle of the night to fix a
thought, an image, or a rhyme. The fitfulness of Corneille's
inspirations is thus illustrated in the note. One day whilst
Molière was dressing, two men of letters dropped in and spoke
with high praise of a tragedy by Corneille played the night
before for the first time. Molière listened without uttering a
word. When he was dressed, he began, ' Well, gentlemen, so
' you believe that Corneille is the author of what you have heard?
' Learn that there is a little demon who has conceived a friend-
' ship for him, and who has the wit of a demon. When he sees

' Corneille seating himself at his desk to bite his nails and try to
' make verses, he approaches and dictates four, eight, ten, some-
' times twenty verses in succession, which are superior to any-
' thing that a mere man can make.   After which the little
' demon, who is as mischievous as a demon, withdraws some paces
' off, saying "Let us see how the rogue will get on without help."
' Corneille then makes the ten, twenty, thirty following verses ;
' amongst which there are none but very ordinary, or even there
' are some very bad.   The next day the same game is recom-
' menced between the demon and Corneille.   The whole piece is
' composed in this manner.   Beware, gentlemen, of confounding
' the two authors.   The one is a man, but the other is far more
' than a man.'

    This differs somewhat from the fine criticism of St. Evre-
mond : ' That which is not excellent in him (Corneille) seems
' bad, less from being bad than from not having the perfection
' which he had managed to reach in other things.   *He* preferred
' *Rodogune* to all his pieces ; the public, *Cinna.*'   The note
' concludes : ' This is what I have heard related by the late
' Baron, our Roscius, who was present when Molière said it.
' I can also certify that M. de Mancroix, canon of Rheims, who
' died in 1708 at the age of ninety, told me that the audience
' at the theatre rose when Corneille entered, as for the Prince
' de Condé ; and this he has told me more than once.'

    Inferring from the popular interest in the personality of
authors, that the public may wish to know something of his own
habits and character, the *Curieux* indulges in a chapter of reminiscences, which, branching off in all directions, embrace incidents
which we little expected to find among them.   Thus, in giving
an account of the *Pension Savouré*, at which he was brought
up, he relates, on the authority of a schoolfellow, Admiral
Baudin, that in the month of March 1796, a little pale man
with long black hair alighted from a shabby yellow *coupé* at
the door of the seminary, and requested to see the Citizen
Savouré.   On his appearing, the little man said, ' I am General
' Bonaparte.   I have searched all Paris for an establishment
' uniting with the tradition of the old and good studies of
' the university that of religious instruction, now forgotten
' everywhere, and I have found but yours.   I have a young
' brother whose education unhappily bears traces of the troubled
' and disorderly times in which we have been living.   I come
' to beg you to admit him among your pupils, and to make a
' man of him.   I am named general-in-chief of the army in
' Italy, and I am on the point of quitting Paris to take the
' command.   If during my absence you would have the good-

' ness to send me every ten days a bulletin of the progress and
' conduct of my brother, occupied as I may be with the affairs
' of my army, I shall always find time to answer you.'

The nomination of the future autocrat to the army of Italy
had not been publicly announced, and he was best known by the
13th Vendémiaire, an exploit little calculated to conciliate those
who, like M. Savouré, disliked the Convention and its acts.
He replied drily, after accepting the charge, 'It is well under-
' stood, General, that here religious instruction is the primary
' base of education.' 'Eh, Monsieur,' rejoined Bonaparte, ' it
' is for that that I came.' Some days afterwards he brought
his brother Jérome, who continued in the academy for three
years. Napoleon came to see him on the conclusion of the Italian
campaign, and kept a watchful eye on his progress till the expedition to Egypt, when the duty of personal superintendence
was transferred to Barras, with whom M. Savouré found it
impossible to get on. Once or twice a week one of the Director's
aides-de-camp came for Jerome, and carried him off to the
theatre or some more objectionable place of amusement. He
was brought back exhausted and dissipated, idle himself and
the cause of idleness in others. At length the preceptor took
the bold step of writing to the temporary guardian in these
terms. ' Citizen Director, when General Bonaparte entrusted
' me with the education of his young brother, it was his desire
' that I should make a cultivated and able man of him. Now,
' it is my duty to tell you that nothing is more contrary to this
' end than constant association with your *aides-de-camp*. Have
' the goodness, therefore, to leave me entirely master of young
' Jerome's education, or remove him from my house.' Jerome
was removed immediately; but always spoke of his old master
in terms honourable to both.

Cuddie Headrigg says of Lady Margaret Bellenden, ' My
' leddy dinna like to be contradicted; as I ken naebody does if
' they can help themselves.' The *Curieux* does not like to be
interrupted; ' not,' he adds,·' out of pride, but because inter-
' ruption staggers and troubles his thoughts, and puts him out
' in his interrogations.' He has often been heard to exclaim, like
M. de Fontenelle, ' My children, if we were to speak but four
' at once! what would you have? The *Curieux* has his nerves;
' you have yours.' This grievance would be comparatively
little felt in England, where conversation is more elliptical, and
the best talker is liable to be voted a bore if he habitually
transgresses Swift's rule (strongly recommended by Sydney
Smith), of not occupying more than half a minute without a
break; it being free to all to get as many half minutes as they

can.   The well-known incident of the Frenchman watching his
opportunity to strike in, and murmuring *S'il crache, il est perdu*,
could hardly have occurred in this country ; at least not since
the two most eminent of recent English historians have been
taken from us.

If there is no precise reason why *causeries* of this kind
should stop anywhere, they must clearly stop somewhere, and
M. Feuillet de Conches's readers are not like the audience in
' The Critic,' who (according to Mr. Sneer) were perfectly indifferent how the actors got off the stage so long as they
did get off.   The *Curieux*, therefore, despite of his dislike to
interruption, introduces a *Deus ex machinâ* in the shape of his
publisher, ' *le fidèle* Henri Plon,' exclaiming, ' *Ah, Mon Dieu,*
' *est-il possible !*   So you are still rummaging among the ashes
' of antiquity.   You are still lingering among the frosts of the
' North ; you are still at Aulnay with Huet ; at Caen with
' M. de Malherbe, in Burgundy with Rabutin.   Are you
' not also going to run off to London, to Florence, to Mantua,
' to Venice ?   And my third volume ?   And then your photo-
' graph, which my subscribers insist upon.'   The bare mention
of the photograph provokes a diatribe against this new and
popular substitute for the miniature and engraving.   ' Photo-
' graphy,' replies the *Curieux*, 'is my aversion ; if it reproduces
' monuments and chalk or pencil drawings to admiration, it has
' infirmities and intolerable falsehoods for living nature.   It can
' make nothing of distances, and does not see true.   It falsifies
' features.   It falsifies colours.   In a word, it is the antipodes
' of art ; it is the slave of an instrument and has all the defects
' of one.   When Daniel du Moustier painted people, he made
' them better-looking than they were, giving as his reason,
' " They are such fools that they believe themselves to be what I
' make them, and pay more."   But there are sitters more stingy
' than foolish, and if photography was dear, no one would submit
' to it ; for it makes uglier than nature. It has been popularised
' by cheapness.'

And so he runs on, till he has fairly run himself out, and is
content to conclude in right earnest.   We are content to conclude along with him, although by no means suffering from
wearisomeness or satiety.   It was Bubb Doddington, we believe, who first laid down the maxim, ' When you have made a
' favourable impression, go away !'   By analogous reasoning,
the point at which we always prefer terminating a review is
when, to the best of our belief, we have conveyed a fair and
favourable impression of the author and the book.

ART. III. — 1. *Les Métaux precieux.* Par M. ROSWAG. Paris : 1865.

2. *Etat de la question de l'uniformité des Poids et Mesures.* Par M. NAHUYS. Utrecht : 1865.

3. *Production der edlen Metälle.* VON SOETBEER. Berlin : 1865.

4. *Revue Contemporaine.* Articles on International Coinage, by M. DE PARIEU : published in 1858, 1860, 1861, and 1865. Paris.

5. *Eighth Report of the International Association for obtaining a uniform decimal system of measures, weights, and coins.* London : 1865.

6. *Decimal Coinage.* By FREDERIC HENDRIKS. London : 1866.

7. *Rapport adressé à S.M. l'Empereur par M. le Ministre des Finances sur un Projet de Loi relatif à la Convention Monétaire passée entre la France, la Belgique, l'Italie et la Suisse. 14th Avril,* 1866.

CHANGES have been effected since the year 1860 in the monetary legislation of several foreign countries, and especially of the Western States of continental Europe, which deserve a more careful attention than they have yet received from British political economists, who have for the last century taken so prominent a part in the progress of monetary science. These changes, which have been accompanied by a movement in public opinion, and by a vast deal of discussion on the altered condition of the currency of the world, affect many important interests in a manner which we shall now endeavour to explain, with the aid of a careful examination of the works of foreign writers on this subject, and of the debates which have taken place this very year in the parliamentary assemblies of France, Italy, Belgium, and Switzerland.

The leading points we wish to explain relate, first, to the internal legislative modifications of the currency in these countries, which have resulted from the vast importations of Californian and Australian gold ; secondly, to certain international arrangements which have been engrafted on these legislative measures, and have actually constituted in Europe what may be termed a *Münz verein*, or monetary union, having France for its centre ; and lastly, to the feasibility of a more extended application of the same principle to the great monetary systems of the world, and more particularly to that of Great Britain, as one of the chief producers, consumers, and distributors of the precious metals.

It is well known that the proportion which had existed between the production of gold and of silver since the discovery of the New World, has been largely disturbed by the working of the auriferous deposits of California and Australia. M. Soetbeer, a modest and intelligent economist of Hamburgh, has collected a multitude of curious returns on this subject, from which we extract the two following statements:—

In 1800, the value of the gold produced stood to that of the silver in the proportion of 28 to 72 upon a total of 10,813,400*l.*

In 1863, the value of the gold produced stood to that of the silver in the proportion of 67 to 33 upon a total amounting to 38,444,813*l.*

This new proportion, eminently favourable to the greater diffusion of gold, has existed from 1849 to the present time, with slight variations; and, in the last fifteen years, the quantity of gold thrown into circulation amounts to 340 millions sterling *more* than would have been produced under the proportions of the previous metallurgical production. The effect of this great change in the relative production of gold and silver has certainly not been confined to a reduction in the price of gilding or in other applications of gold to manufactures. It has also brought about a complete perturbation in the monetary system of those States which had made both metals a legal tender, including the United States, France, Spain, &c. Gold having become more common than silver, has been substituted for that metal as the habitual instrument of exchange; and as, on the other hand, the East has absorbed all the silver thus set at liberty in exchange for the silk, the tea, and the other Eastern commodities we import into Europe, the double standard has become in fact purely nominal, and gold is now the principal current money of all these countries. But as silver is an indispensable part of the monetary system to effect minor payments in small change, the circulating medium has been rapidly deranged in the countries in which the double standard still nominally exists.* Great Britain, being

---

* One of the reasons for which the French cling to the use of the double standard, in spite of the rapid disappearance of silver and the enormous increase of gold in their circulation, is that the silver standard is connected with the French decimal system of weights. The French franc is a *weight*, representing in silver five grammes, and may be used for the purpose of weighing a letter or any other article. This circumstance connects it with the whole metrical sys-

exempt by reason of her own gold and paper currency from the inconvenience which has thus been felt elsewhere, may regard these circumstances with indifference. Yet there have been times when this country too has suffered from similar embarrassments, arising not from any excess in the production of gold, but from other causes affecting the price of silver, and the Acts of Parliament of 1773 and 1816 successively established our gold coinage as the sole standard of the currency, and reduced the coinage of silver to its true character of mere tokens or counters for change, to borrow an expression used by Lord Liverpool in the House of Lords in 1816. By the Act 56 Geo. 3. c. 68, which regulated the new silver coinage, the pound troy of silver was coined into 66s. instead of 62s., and the difference of 4s. retained as a seignorage (amounting to six per cent.); so that bullion must rise so much above the Mint price, before coin could be brought on a par with it.[*] In other words, to prevent the silver being melted in case of rise of value, the silver for which the gold sovereign may be exchanged would not in reality purchase the quantity of gold contained in the sovereign; but the inconvenience which might have arisen from this debasement of the intrinsic value of the shilling, was provided against by restricting to forty shillings the use of silver as a legal tender. The change in the proportion of the production of the precious metals could only have affected the monetary system of Great Britain, if the price of silver in bars had become equal to the price of our silver coin; but the profit on silver in bars has never reached that which is artificially bestowed upon the silver coinage by the Act of 1816. The nature and effect of this operation is described in the following terms in the Report of the French Minister of Finance to the Emperor:—

' Ces Commissions ont appelé l'attention du Gouvernement sur le procédé adopté par divers États pour conserver l'argent en concurrence avec l'or, dans la circulation monétaire. Ce procédé consiste à établir, entre l'or et l'argent monnayé, un écart de valeur monétaire moins considérable que celui qui est le résultat de leur valeur commerciale; l'argent ainsi rehaussé est émis sous la forme de

---

tem. This argument may have its value in the mathematical or theoretical view of the subject, but it appears to us to be of no practical importance, and the utility of applying coins to be measures of weight is diminished by the fact that their own weight is liable to be diminished by detrition, and is therefore not strictly accurate.

[*] See Mr. Wellesley Pole's excellent speech, delivered May 30, 1816, on the introduction of the Silver Coinage Bill. (*Parliamentary Debates*, xxxiv. p. 946.)

monnaie d'appoint, dont le concours est limité de manière à en pou-
voir remplacer, dans les grands payements, soit l'or, soit les monnaies
d'argent supérieures.   Le système de monnaies d'appoint en argent
à cours limité et avec une proportion d'alliage suffisante pour ne
pas permettre de les exporter avec profit, a été depuis un demi-siècle
pratiqué avec un grand succès en Angleterre, et étendu plus tard
aux États Unis, au Portugal, à la Suisse, et à l'Italie.'   (*Rapport,
&c.*, p. 3.)

The States which have suffered from this disturbance of
their monetary system, caused by the excess of gold, have not,
as yet, thought it expedient to adopt the entire principle of our
own currency ; they have imitated it partially, but none of them
has altogether abandoned the double standard.   The United
States of America, by an Act of Congress of 1853, reduced
the weight of the half-dollar in silver from $206\frac{1}{4}$ grains to 192
grains, and that of the quarter-dollar from $103\frac{1}{8}$ to 96.   The
Continental States of Europe, whose numeration is based upon
the franc, found themselves in a position of greater difficulty.
For the United States, whose monetary unit is represented to
be in gold and silver by the dollar (equal to rather more than
one-fifth of the English pound), supplied the wants of the community in small change by a somewhat depreciated coinage of
half-dollars and quarter-dollars, corresponding to our florins
and shillings, whilst the dollar itself, the basis of numeration
and of value, remained unaltered.   But in the countries in
which the monetary unit is extremely low in value, as the
French *franc*, less than our shilling, and the Spanish *real*, of a
still lower denomination, it was impossible to issue an abundant
supply of small silver coin, without some modification of the
intrinsic value of the piece of money on which the whole currency and numeration of the country is based.   This difficulty
seems at present to have prevented Spain from taking any
measures in this direction ; and it has long been a subject of
hesitation and discussion in France, and in the three countries
adjacent to France, which, from political traditions or mercantile convenience, have adopted the French monetary system,
established in a part of Italy and in Belgium under Napoleon I.,
and more recently introduced into the rest of Italy and into
Switzerland.

Some writers in these countries have boldly recommended
the complete, or all but complete, adoption of the British
system.   M. de Parieu, a Vice-President of the French
Council d'Etat, defended this course with great ability and
firmness in several articles published by the ' Revue Contem-
' poraine,' between the years 1858 and 1865 ; and M. Levasseur

took nearly the same view in his ' Recherches sur la Question ' de l'Or,' which were published in 1858, in opposition to the arguments of M. Michel Chevalier, who maintained, at that time, that in conformity with the French Law of An XI, gold should cease to be in France a legal tender.

Of the four States which have adopted the franc as the basis of their currency—and it may here be added that the Grand Duchy. of Luxemburg has followed their example— Switzerland was the first to modify in practice the intrinsic value of the silver coins in use. This innovation was made by the Federal Law of the 31st January, 1860, and as Switzerland had only adopted the French system in 1850, the novelty of the experiment seemed to embolden her to complete it. Her immediate object was, however, to prevent her small silver coinage from flowing out of the country, and for this purpose she imitated the example of the United States of America ; but as she could not preserve her unity of value in the silver franc, as the Americans had done in their dollar, the Swiss Government took the five-franc piece as the standard silver coin, and resolved that the smaller coins of two francs, one franc, and fifty centimes, should be struck below the standard ; thus, while the five-franc piece continued to be struck of $\frac{900}{1000}$ths of fineness, the minor coinage was reduced to $\frac{800}{1000}$ths.

Italy adopted the same course as Switzerland by the Law of the 24th August, 1862, but she did not proceed so far in the depreciation of the standard of small coin ; she reduced it only to $\frac{835}{1000}$ths, or about the intrinsic value of our shillings minted under the regulations of 1816, and of the half-dollars and quarter-dollars now struck in the United States.

France hesitated at first to follow the example of her neighbours, but by the law of the 25th May, 1864, she too adopted the principle of the Italian coinage, and reduced her standard to $\frac{835}{1000}$ths, but only for the small pieces of fifty centimes and twenty centimes.

Belgium was still more undecided, although M. Nothomb had advised her, as early as the year 1861, to follow the example of Switzerland, and had even pointed out, with singular perspicacity, that this measure would lay the foundation of a common monetary system between France, Belgium, Switzerland, and perhaps Italy. The Belgian Government, however, took the highly judicious step of proposing that a monetary conference should be held between the States whose currency is based on the franc. This conference was held in Paris in the months of November and December 1865, and led to a Convention between the Four States, which is now before us. The Commissioners of France, Belgium, Italy, and Switzerland agreed to adopt the standard already introduced by the Italian Mint in the coinage of silver small pieces; and Switzerland engaged so far to modify the system she had adopted in 1860 as to withdraw from circulation in a few years the coins she had issued at $\frac{800}{1000}$ths. These conditions having since been ratified by the respective legislatures of the four contracting States, the uniform result of the monetary arrangements of these countries may be stated in the following terms :—

They retain the double standard of gold and silver, represented by gold coins of 20 francs, 10 francs, and 5 francs, of the former weight and value, and likewise by the silver five-franc piece of $\frac{900}{1000}$ths of fineness.

They depreciate or lower the silver coins of 2 francs, 1 franc, 50 cents., and 20 cents., to be struck hereafter to $\frac{835}{1000}$ths instead of $\frac{900}{1000}$ths of fineness.

Waiving the difference in the denomination and the value of the coins affected, and the substitution of a lowering by alloy instead of a lowering by weight, this system is identical in principle with that of the United States; and it secures to the contracting States the maintenance of a permanent supply of small silver coin, even if gold were hereafter to become more abundant in relation to silver than it is at present. These are in fact the same advantages we have ourselves derived from the British Act of Parliament of 1816; but in the countries associated by this Convention, these advantages are combined with the retention of the double standard, on the basis of the proportion of 1 to 15½, which was adopted by the French Law of the 7th Germinal, An XI, as the legal relation of gold to silver.

The most important innovation introduced by the Monetary Convention, which was signed in Paris on the 23rd December, 1865, by the representatives of France, Belgium, Switzerland, and Italy,* is the principle of establishing a legal and official system of monetary union upon mutual concessions in the currency of four countries in which the metallic circulation had previously been imperfectly assimilated. The proceedings of the Monetary Conference, which have been printed in Belgium in the appendix to the Bill brought in to give effect

---

* The Commissioners were M. de Parieu and M. Pelouze for France; M. Fortamps and M. Kreglinger for Belgium; MM. Artam and Pratolongo for Italy; MM. Kern and Feer Hergez for Switzerland.

to the terms of the Convention of the 23rd December, show that the Commissioners of the four States adopted with eagerness and enthusiasm a plan designed to extend the circulation of the gold and silver coinage of their respective nations over the whole territory of the Four States, on equal terms, without reference to the Mint in which they were struck, or the effigy they bore. Their intention was that from Antwerp to Brindisi travellers should pay their way in the same coin, without any of the risk or inconvenience of national exchanges, and that this coin should have precisely the same value over this wide extent of European territory, whether it bore the effigy of free Helvetia, the head of Victor Emmanuel or of Napoleon III., or of the two successive Kings of Belgium.

M. Michel Chevalier, a well-known French economist, whose name can never be mentioned on this side of the Channel without respect, as he was one of the chief promoters of the French Commercial Treaty, proposed to the Commission on weights, measures, and coin, which sat in London in 1862, a monetary alliance between Great Britain and France, in the shape of a gold coinage, bearing on one side the effigy of Queen Victoria, and on the obverse that of Napoleon III. In making this suggestion, M. Chevalier renounced the predilection he had previously expressed in favour of an exclusive silver standard, on the ground that the recent discoveries of gold had made the value of that metal subject to far more depreciation and fluctuation than silver, and that permanence of value is a condition of the first importance to the standard of currency.

The negotiators of the Convention of the 23rd December took a still broader view of the principles of monetary union. Their object was that the gold and silver coinage of the four countries should be identically the same in weight, size, and value, though each country should issue money stamped with its own distinctive emblems, and even though the name of the coin should not in all cases be the same, inasmuch as the Italians prefer to retain the familiar appellation of *lira* for that which the other three nations call a *franc*. The first Article of the Convention is expressed in the following terms:
—' Belgium, France, Italy, and Switzerland constitute a ' Union in relation to the weight, standard, dimensions, and ' value of their coined money of gold and silver.' The design of the Conference, and more especially of its President, M. de Parieu, who was, we believe, the author of the draft which was adopted after sundry amendments, was to establish this unity of coinage in essentials, leaving to each State as much liberty and

independence in the detail of the coinage as were not incompatible with the general scope of the project.

The four contracting States did not go so far as to make it compulsory on their respective subjects or citizens to receive gold and silver coins minted abroad. But the treasuries of the four States bound themselves to receive these monies, without distinction, in payment of the public dues ; and although they are not yet made strictly legal tenders between man and man in each of the countries respectively, it is hoped and anticipated that use and public convenience will speedily remove all difficulty on this score. Indeed, practically the gold napoleon and the silver five-franc piece, wherever struck, have long been received, indiscriminately, in the ordinary transactions of life, throughout the countries where the decimal monetary system of France prevails, and even in Spain and a great part of Germany.

The amount of small coin of the depreciated standard to be struck by each State is fixed by the Convention at six francs per head of the population; and as we have in the last fifty years struck about 16,000,000*l.* in shillings, for the use of the United Kingdom and a portion of our own colonies, the proportion of six francs per head is not immoderate.

No change has been introduced in the legislative provisions respecting the lower coinage, which consists in France and Italy of an alloy of copper, and of nickel in Belgium and Switzerland.

The parties to the Convention of the 23rd December agreed to leave it open to any other State to join the Union on the same terms. No express addition has yet been made to it; but the Pontifical Government promulgated an Edict on the 16th June, 1866, by which it virtually adopts the system of the Monetary Union, with the exception that the Pope reserves the right of striking and issuing certain coins, which are not included in the terms of the Convention, viz., a piece of 2 lire and 50 cents., which does not exist in France, and a piece of 25 cents., which is substituted at Rome for the piece of 20 cents. adopted by the Union. This Pontifical Edict has, however, the merit of laying down with precision, in its first Article, the fundamental doctrine of the value of the franc in gold, on which the whole superstructure of the Convention rests. It states, ' The new monetary unit of the Pontifical States is ' founded on the value of 5 grammes of silver and 0·32258 of ' gold, both at a standard of $\frac{900}{1000}$ths, and it takes the name of ' the *Lira Pontificia*.' It is not improbable that some of the States, contiguous to the countries already included in this

Convention, will gradually adopt the same system, and this without the intervention of the causes which, under the First French Empire, extended the monetary system of France far beyond the present boundaries of that country; for many of the territories which were then annexed to France by the conquests of Napoleon, have never entirely lost, or discarded, the use of the French monetary system; and the sense of mutual convenience in personal intercourse and in commercial transactions might easily revive it.

Having thus shown in what manner 68,000,000 of the inhabitants of the continent of Europe have solved the difficulty of reducing their monetary circulation to a common standard, by this remarkable Convention, which subjects their respective gold and silver coinage to certain fixed and uniform rules, and even determines the relative proportion of their issues of small coin, we shall now proceed to consider the scheme of a more extended union, which has been mooted by several writers, and discussed in the French press, as one of the ulterior results of the Convention of the 23rd December. It is certain that some progress has been made, since the commencement of the present century, in drawing nearer together the monetary systems of the world. Several States which still retain their own distinct unit of value, and which have not adopted the French metrical system, have nevertheless proceeded so far as to divide their dollars, florins, drachmas, &c. on the decimal scale, which is a step in the right direction, and a great convenience in calculation. This has been done in Sweden, Turkey, Portugal, Austria, Greece, the Netherlands, and Spain,—countries including 211,000,000 of inhabitants. To these Mexico may be added since the French occupation; and the relation of the rupee of India to the English sovereign also affords facilities for decimal arithmetic. The monetary Convention which was concluded in 1857, between Austria and the German States, brought under one system 70,000,000 of inhabitants, whose coins and units of value are distinct, but have been rendered mutually convertible by a simple process : thus the three leading coins of Germany, the Prussian thaler, the Austrian florin, and the South German florin, are represented by the following equations :—

4 Prussian thalers = 6 Austrian florins = 7 S. German florins.

The French Convention with Belgium, Italy, and Switzerland, which has just been more fully described, is another important addition to the principle of uniformity, since it has linked together 68,000,000 of souls, by the use of the same coinage, extending from Brest to Constanz, and from Antwerp to Tarentum, under the terms of the Convention of the 23rd December, published in England by M. Hendriks, in the pamphlet cited at the head of this article. The same principle has, to a certain extent, been acted upon by the British Government in the proclamations of February 3, 1866, giving to sovereigns minted in Australia legal currency in this country. The result of all these changes has been to diminish the innumerable variations of money, which previously existed in the world ; to reduce them to five or six leading denominations; and to render the public more sensible of the advantages and convenience which would arise from a further introduction of the principle of a uniform coinage, or of a coinage which could be converted and interchanged by the application of fixed and uniform principles. These views have been ably expressed upon a recent occasion by M. Louvet, a member of the French legislative body, in a report drawn up by him on June 13, 1866. The tendency of modern civilisation, with its lines of railway extending over and across the frontiers of many States, and its lines of telegraph* bringing into direct communication countries lying at the opposite extremities of Europe, and even of the globe, is to create great common interests, irrespective of national and local differences. And it is obvious that all the operations of trade, and the exchange of money, would be greatly facilitated by the reduction of the representatives of weight, quantity, and value to a common form, or by the adoption of some principles which would make the conversion of different signs of value more easy and accurate.

Our own country has hitherto stood aloof from any of these combinations, and we are separated from the rest of Europe and America by the duo-decimal system of numeration, and by the high value of our unit,† the pound, almost as much as by

---

* The necessity of establishing a common tarif for the transmission of telegraphic despatches through different countries, has not been without effect upon the question of international coinage and numeration. Thus the Telegraphic Convention which was signed at Paris, on the 17th May, 1865, between France and almost all the States of Continental Europe, adopts the franc as the monetary basis of international tarifs for telegraphic messages. The 30th Article of this treaty adds that the tarif of messages between any two points in the dominions of the contracting States, is to be so adjusted, that the charge on every despatch of twenty words is always to be some multiple of the half-franc.

† It deserves observation that as we proceed from Portugal, at the south-western extremity of Europe, where the monetary unit is

the sea which surrounds these islands. And we do not anticipate that any change will speedily or easily be effected in habits so deeply rooted amongst a commercial people. But it is by no means impossible to bring our coinage and our basis of numeration into a closer and more constant connexion with the leading systems of the European continent and of India, without any important change in its present denomination and value. The practical method which has been suggested to effect this object is as follows:—

The English sovereign contains 123·274 grains troy weight, with $\frac{1}{12}$th alloy, or in other words, 113·002 grains of fine gold, representing 7·322 French grammes. The French twenty-franc piece, added to the French five-franc piece (in gold), contains 7·258 grammes of fine gold, exclusive of $\frac{1}{10}$th of alloy. Hence the difference between an English sovereign and twenty-five francs in French gold is 64 milligrammes.

If these 64 milligrammes (or about $4\frac{1}{4}$ grains troy) were subtracted from the sovereign, which would thus be reduced 0·825 per cent. in value, and if the proportion of alloy in our gold coinage were raised from $\frac{1}{12}$th to $\frac{1}{10}$th, the sovereign would be worth a little less, but it would weigh a little more than it does at present:* it would therefore be more dissimilar than it now is to the French napoleon, but it would be precisely equivalent to 25 francs in French gold, and would in fact be a 25-franc piece. It would obviously be a great convenience to travellers in both countries respectively, and in all the countries which have adopted the monetary system of France, to carry with them in their own coinage definite representatives of value, which would be independent of the variations of the exchange and the exactions of money-changers; and the same benefit would accrue, on a much larger scale, in the financial and commercial relations of this country with foreign nations. If such a common basis of numeration and coinage were in existence, it would not be difficult for the Governments of France and England to agree upon certain uniform principles of coinage, and to give legal currency respectively to these foreign coins, which would then represent distinct forms of value, based on

---

$\frac{1}{4000}$ of the sovereign, through Spain, France, South Germany, North Germany, Russia in the north-east, and England in the north-west, the value of the coin which serves as the base of numeration, increases continually, being least in the south and highest in the north.

* A pound troy at the standard of $\frac{11}{12}$ths of fine gold gives 46*l.* 14*s.* 6*d.*; and at the standard of $\frac{9}{10}$ths of fineness it would give only 46*l.* 5*s.* 6*d.* in coin.

the same standard : thus, the napoleon would be in England a 16-shilling piece, and the French Government, in conjunction with its monetary allies, would doubtless not only accept the English sovereign as a twenty-five-franc piece, but would probably strike twenty-five-franc pieces of its own, which would be identical with the English sovereign.

On the other hand, it would be easy for the British Government to issue gold pieces of two florins, or four shillings' value, representing two-tenths of a pound, which would correspond to the five-franc pieces of the Franco-Belge and Helvetico-Italian Union, and would thus become a practical link of union between the two circulations, whilst they would offer a means of accord with those large European and American populations which use the Spanish piastre or dollar. The five-franc piece, whether in gold or in silver, may be regarded as the most familiar unit of monetary circulation in France and in the countries allied with her, and it is not inaccurately described by M. de Parieu, in one of his articles in the ' Revue Contemporaine,' as the dollar or crown piece of both hemispheres.*
The colonial and commercial interests of this country are by no means confined to our connexion with the continent of Europe. It is perhaps of still greater importance to ourselves to consider, in the adjustment of our monetary system, the relation it bears to the coinage of our neighbours, our dependents, and our customers in other parts of the globe. The units of value which at present play the most important part in the intercourse of the world are the pound, the American and Spanish dollar, the rupee, and the franc, and all these coins stand, by a fortunate coincidence, in relations to each other which may be represented by multiples of the number five. Thus, the British sovereign is equal to about five dollars of four shillings each ; to ten rupees ; and to twenty-five francs. If it were possible to correct the slight variation which exists in these proportions, by adopting a coinage in America, India, and Europe, based on a uniform principle, under the different denominations familiar to each country, the most arduous part of the question of monetary union would be solved. An English four-shilling piece, the fifth of a pound, might thus

---

* M. Dumas, a Senator of France, went so far as to declare in his report on the Monetary Convention, that the legislature of France had erred by adopting too low a unit of value in the currency, and that the more enlightened disposition of the present times is to correct this error by substituting the five-franc piece for it, or the quintuple of the franc itself.

represent the dollar, current in America and in several of our own colonies; it would also represent two Indian rupees, and five European francs—conditions which would give it currency in all parts of the world. The five-shilling piece, on the contrary, which has been abandoned as a cumbrous and inconvenient coin, has the disadvantage of not being readily convertible into any system of foreign coinage. The recent introduction of five-franc pieces in gold has been attended in France with great convenience to the public, and we think that the British half sovereign is a piece of too high a value to serve as the lowest gold coin in our circulation. These gold five-franc pieces at first appeared to be rather too small, especially to a community which were previously accustomed to the heavy silver crowns which they have superseded. But use has removed this objection in France, and would speedily have the same effect in this country, though it has been remarked that northern nations prefer the use of coins heavier than those of the south. Thus, in the French monetary conference of 1865, Italy insisted on the reduction of the smaller pieces of silver to 20 centimes, against the wish of Belgium and Switzerland.

On this basis, the monetary circulation of British and Australian gold might be extended to 68,000,000 of inhabitants of continental Europe, and it might be possible, as we have indicated, to include India and America in the same arrangement. This point being once attained, time would probably adjust the silver coinage of these respective countries to the same system.

The future effect of this combination of a gold circulation between Great Britain and the Western Continental Union, would probably be further extended by the fact, that, as Germany and the Low Countries have no gold circulation of their own, they necessarily use a large quantity of the French gold coinage. The German Commercial Congress which met at Frankfort in 1865, expressed a hope that Germany might strike and issue gold pieces of the value of 20 francs, of the French standard and pattern, and that these coins should be made a legal tender in Germany,—a measure which would give legal currency to the French napoleon, or its equivalent, throughout central Europe. M. Soetbeer, of Hamburgh, is a decided partisan of this scheme, and it is also supported by the ' Boersen halle' of Hamburgh, of the 17th July, 1866. Probably one of the first results of the unification of Germany will be to give an increased impulse to her monetary union; but with a view to her international relations the extension of the area of that inconvenient coin the Prussian three-shilling thaler is to be deprecated, as it bears no regular analogy to the other monetary systems of Europe.

The result, therefore, of an understanding between England and France on this subject would probably be to give their coinage an universal acceptance in all the principal States of this hemisphere, except perhaps in Russia, where the conditions of the circulation are peculiar, from her vast extent, and from her own large metallic productiveness.

The great objection which may fairly be urged against the adoption of a scheme that threatens to modify, in however slight a degree, the established and intrinsic value of the English sovereign, is sufficiently obvious. The National Debt is a liability represented nominally by a given number of pounds sterling, equivalent to a fixed and determined weight in gold. The interest of the debt is paid in sovereigns of the same value. All private debts, mortgages, and contracts are expressed in the same terms; and to reduce the value of the coin in which they may be paid, is to take from the creditor and give to the debtor a sum equal to the amount of the difference. If the gold coin of England were brought into conformity with the gold coin of the Continent, the loss would be, as we have seen, 64 milligrammes of fine gold on each sovereign, or 0·825 per cent. in weight, and about two pence in value.

But this difficulty, formidable as it undoubtedly appears to be, is one which has been met and surmounted by other States of as high credit and probity as our own; and there appear to be two ways of dealing with it. The first is simply to reduce the intrinsic value of the sovereign to this extent, without taking account of the debts and liabilities contracted before the conversion, and this is the course advocated by M. Hendriks in his pamphlet. It is the course which was taken by the Dutch Government in 1839, when it reduced the Dutch florin from 9·613 grammes of fine silver to 9·450 grammes, diminishing the coin by about 163 milligrammes, representing *two* per cent. of the original weight, on the principle, as we presume, that what was lost by each member of the community in one capacity was gained in another, and therefore that the process of conversion did, upon the whole, compensate itself.

Mr. Hendriks remarks in his pamphlet:—

'In considering the question of a re-adjustment of the Mint Exchange or measure between coin and bullion, it must be observed that there is satisfactory historical precedent for such a course. We have remarked that the ratio of 3*l.* 17*s.* 10½*d.* per ounce is empirical. It may even turn out on inquiry that the alteration to 3*l.* 17*s.* 1½*d.*

international standard fineness would be less empirical, and nearer to the real present ratio of gold, as measured by silver in the open market for bullion.   The English standard until 1816 was a silver one, with the collateral alternative standard of gold coins in a fixed proportion settled by royal proclamations and Mint indentures according to the then assumed ratio of gold to silver.   Here we have ample precedent for re-adjustment, and the gold discoveries of the last fifteen years appear to call for something of the kind being again considered.   The 3*l*. 17*s*. 10½*d*. per ounce was originally authorised by Charles II.   But the government of William and Mary increased it to a larger amount of gold coin per ounce of bullion.   This, however, as shown by Sir Isaac Newton and others, was an over-estimation of gold, and made the coined guinea (for pounds were not then in existence) equal to 21*s*. 6*d*. instead of to its normal 21*s*. in silver.   Silver coins could not, in this state of things, remain in circulation ; they were melted (just as the French 5-franc pieces have been of late years), and the government of George I. (A.D. 1717) again changed to the ratio which has since prevailed.'

But, secondly, if the British legislature were resolved to effect this change in the current coin of the realm, without the slightest deviation from those strict principles to which it has honourably adhered from the reign of Queen Elizabeth, and without so much as the appearance of any abasement in the currency, then an allowance must be made in the payment of all existing debts, so as to render the amount paid in the new coinage exactly equivalent to the engagements contracted in the old one.   This state of things would be productive of temporary but short-lived inconvenience, and it would be exactly analogous (though in the inverse sense), to what took place in France, when the franc was substituted for the old French livre at the beginning of the present century.   The franc was worth one livre three deniers, and the livre was worth 99 centimes : there was therefore a difference of one per cent. between the two coins.   To meet this difficulty, the Government published, on the 26th Vendémiaire An VIII, an official table of equivalents, and all payments and accounts were subjected to this process of conversion, according to the established scale, until after a certain lapse of time the old livre had fallen into disuse.   So too, the Pope has recently published official tables for the reduction of the Roman scudo into Pontifical *lire*.

This suggestion has found adherents both in England and in France, and the practical inconvenience attending it is, perhaps, less than may be imagined.   In England it has been associated with a further proposal for what is called the decimalisation of a pound, on the pound and mil scheme.   To us it appears that these plans deserve and require very careful consideration. We should hail with great satisfaction the adoption of a complete and careful plan for the introduction of the decimal system, in the numeration, and in the coins, weights, and measures of this country, because we are satisfied that this system, in its integrity is of incalculable advantage to science, to trade, and to all the operations of daily life. But before the British Government and legislature can be asked to sanction any change in the old-established habits of the people, which must always be productive of temporary inconvenience, they must be well assured that the change is to be made *once for all;* and that it is so contrived as to embrace all the *desiderata* of a new and improved currency. It would unquestionably be a useful work to enable us to assimilate our coinage, under its principal existing denominations, with that of foreign countries, so, at least, as to render our money convertible into its precise equivalents and to give it currency abroad. But this is only one portion of the reforms we should be glad to effect in our monetary system ; and whenever the British Government is sufficiently enlightened and sufficiently supported by public opinion to undertake the adjustment of these questions, we trust that a modification of our coinage would not only bring us into closer relations with the monetary system of the Continent, but would also establish our own coinage and numeration on the basis of the decimal system. The two things are distinct, and one of them might be effected without the other ; but having regard to the serious temporary inconvenience of any modification in the representatives of value, it is highly expedient that if any such change should be attempted it should be complete.

One of the chief inducements, however, to make an effort to assimilate the gold currency of this country with that of Western Europe, in the manner we have pointed out, is the minuteness of the change required to effect that object. We are separated from the monetary system of France, Italy, Belgium, and Switzerland by a very narrow line of division, and, as we have shown, the double standard still retained in some of those countries, and even our own duo-decimal system of numeration, present no serious obstacles to the desired result. To establish a theoretical conformity between the monetary systems of different nations may be impossible ; but there is a point of contact between them which may be employed to bring about their practical union.

It is not unworthy of the attention of the financiers and economists of England to note the important changes which are taking place in foreign countries, with a view to render the means of exchange more simple and universal; for these changes are one of the progressive signs of the age. Even in the United States, the House of Representatives has recently manifested a disposition to entertain proposals calculated to bring their monetary system into a closer connexion with that of Europe. Whatever the difficulties may be, it is not impossible for the common interest of mankind to surmount them; and no common interest is more obvious than that of establishing a similarity or identity between those different representatives of value, which may be described as the very language of trade; for to use the words of Landgrave Philip of Hesse at the beginning of the 16th century—

> 'Hätten wir alle einen Glauben,
> Gott und Gerechtigkeit vor Augen,
> Ein Gewicht, Maass, Münz und Geld,
> Dann stünde es besser in dieser Welt.'

Which may be rendered—

> 'Had all men but a single creed,
> Faithful to God and just in deed,
> One weight, one measure, coin, and gold,
> 'Twere better for all an hundredfold.'

ART. IV.—*Histoire de Jules César.* Par NAPOLEON III. 2 vols. 8vo. Paris: 1865–66.

THE two volumes of the Emperor Napoleon III.'s ' History ' of Cæsar ' have been already so long before the world— they have excited so widely the interest and attention of educated men—they have been made so much the occasion of sarcasm, of banter, of violent philippic, of sardonic criticism— they have been also so ably dealt with, with a more just and honourable purpose, by judges of a different order, to whom the study of Cæsar himself was a higher object than the study of a modern potentate's mode of dealing with him—that little seems left for the ordinary reviewer to say on the subject of them.   We can do little more than repeat, and combine, what others have observed before us.   If there is anything about which it is next to impossible to be original, it is a book which from the circumstances of its authorship has lain on every table, and been commented on in every journal, from the day of its appearance until now.   We have little, either of information or entertainment, to promise our readers; but that little shall be said, at all events, with the best exercise of our impartial judgment—impartial, both as to the book, and, what is more rare, as to the author.

We have to deal, be it observed, with no unpractised writer. The collection of the works of Louis Napoleon was already a pretty voluminous one, before the present important addition was made to it. Many of us were more or less familiar with him as a writer, before Fate and his own strong resolution made him the master of the leading country of Europe. Successful, in the common sense, as a literary workman, he certainly has not been. He lacks altogether the graces of a popular author. He is quite incapable of interesting the reader by mere charm of manner, or through such sympathy of sentiment as masters of the art are able to excite. His style is not only meagre but harsh and grating: test it by reading aloud, and this quality becomes very obvious. He seems to have at once little ear for beauty of cadence, and little appreciation of neatness of diction. No Frenchman can possibly be otherwise than epigrammatic; but he is less so, and less successful when he is so, than any other distinguished French political or historical writer of our day. In this respect he is more felicitous in the turn of his occasional letters or addresses, than in his more elaborate and finished compositions. In these, generally speaking, there is a simplicity about his mode of stating or commenting on facts which verges on commonplace. And the ordinary reader, of a mind refined into overfastidiousness by modern cultivation, is apt to set the matter down as mere commonplace accordingly, and to discover in it occasion for nothing but weariness. But he will often find himself mistaken. Louis Napoleon does not, in point of fact, write for minds such as these. His thoughts, though he gives them in all honesty to the world in general, are in reality, perhaps unconsciously, addressed to sectaries and enthusiasts. We say deliberately enthusiasts, because—strange as it may appear to material Englishmen, who are familiar with the enthusiasm of loyalty, nationality, liberty, but cannot at all realise the enthusiasm which clings to a mere name as a political reality—the 'culte' of the dead Napoleon was for many years a substantial fanaticism in France. Men, who were neither fools nor dreamers, persuaded themselves that the regeneration of the country was to be effected, not by remodelling her institutions, not by extending personal and political freedom, not by educating her people, but by carrying out the first Emperor's 'ideas;' whatever that obscure phrase might mean. Look, accordingly, at the 'Idées Napoleoniennes' as they are collected in the three-volume edition of Louis Napoleon's works (1848). At first sight, the scattered essays so entitled will probably appear to contain rather a dry résumé of the first·Emperor's views, or those attributed to him, on a very wide range of subjects, almost always too general, and often too trivial, to be attractive to a practical man. The inference first drawn will rather be that great as he was on the throne as well as in the camp, he does not shine as an 'ideologist.' But read a little more attentively, and, as far as you can, borrow the eyes of men of very different training and mental cultivation from yourself: men, the angles of whose understanding have not been rounded off by over polish: and you will find that many of these propositions, almost unmeaning in your eyes, have in reality oracular truth and oracular force when addressed to minds prepared to receive them. It is the old story of the Koran of Mahomet; it conveys to you no ideas at all; but in it uncounted millions have really found, or persuaded themselves that they found, ideas which have subdued in their day a large part of the world, and which are as yet so far from decrepit that they are even now extending their moral and material conquest over many a dark corner of the earth in the Malay isles, and in the recesses of Western Africa.

In this respect, the present Emperor may to a certain extent be also compared to a writer to whom he has indeed very·little analogy, except in the circumstance of the influence exercised by his thoughts over many minds, and yet over none except minds of the sectarian order: we mean Joseph Mazzini. To one who is not already imbued with ' Mazzinianism,' the effort to read even a few pages of the great patriot's compositions is— if we may be allowed to speak from our own experience—a most wearisome exertion. Line seems to succeed line, and page to follow page, without imparting any definite notions at all: there seems to be no thought, no argument, no attempt to grapple with a difficulty or to make out a case: nothing but wire-drawn sentiment, repeating itself in maudlin language. Such, we say, is the effect produced by Mazzini on us—the effect produced by him on the world is a very different matter. And so, ' Napoleonic ideas ' may be to many of us a mere bottle of smoke—but Napoleonism, somehow, is a tremendous fact; a great·creation of modern times, the ultimate contest of which with the other opposing tendencies of the age has yet to be fought and decided, and may perhaps prove the Battle of Armageddon of distant political prophecy.

That the avowed object of the writer is not to establish historical truth, but to establish the great political doctrine of the future, is amply proved by reference to a single passage of the Preface, in which the moral of the whole work is briefly summed up in words which we may call (in the present state and prospects of Europe and America) of terrible significance. No man can say, can even approximate to a conjecture, how much of the destiny of himself, or of his children, is involved in those few suggestive sentences.

'What precedes is enough to show the object which I propose myself in writing this history. That object is to prove that when Providence raises up such men as Cæsar, Charlemagne, Napoleon, it is in order to point out to the nations the road which they have to follow, to stamp with the signet of their genius a new era, and to accomplish in a few years the work of many ages. Happy the nations who understand them and follow them! Woe to those who misconceive them and oppose them! They do as the Jews—they crucify their Messiah: they are both blind and guilty; blind, for they do not perceive how powerless are their efforts to suspend the definitive triumph of good; guilty, for they do but retard progress, by impeding its promptness and rapidity.' (Preface, p. vi.)

The first object of the author is therefore (as usual with his countrymen when they turn historians) to establish a political theory of the necessitarian class: most Frenchmen (whether they admit it or not) being by the turn of their genius disciples of Comte. The second object, very second in the present instance, is to do so by means of the investigation of a particular chapter in history. Here, to say at once what it would be mere idle politeness to envelope in circumlocution, the 'History of Cæsar' is altogether unsuccessful. As a record of the series of events in the foreign and domestic annals of Rome which preceded, and led to, the civil war (political significance apart) it is unsatisfactory to the last degree. The author seems to have really approached his task without any preparation for it beyond a superficial knowledge of a few classical authors, and of the modern compilations on the subject which were popular in ordinary education fifty years ago. He does not even exhibit the appearance of knowing that such further qualifications could exist, or could be required. With the school of sceptical but close inquirers into early Roman history which began with Niebuhr and ended (for the present) with Lewis, he does not seem to have formed the slightest familiarity. Nor is he at all more acquainted with the concentrated light which German investigation, conducted by writers such as Mommsen, has thrown on the whole subject of inner Roman domestic life and outer policy. It is no part of his business to raise or discuss doubts on the authenticity of a tradition, or a narrative, or a document.* He scarcely shows himself aware that they are disputed. In short, and to put the case as plainly as possible, he seems to believe that, in order to be capable of forming his own favourite political deductions, which are the true essence of all history, a student needs no more acquaintance with facts than might have been acquired at school with the help of ordinary school-books.

It is needless to say more on this subject; for public opinion seems already to have pronounced its verdict. No one will read the History of Cæsar to acquire whàt is usually meant by historical knowledge, except in one subdivision only.

The treatment of that subdivision forms a curious contrast to the execution of the rest of the work. The author displays, as an author, those characteristics by which he has made so powerful an impression on the European mind, for the last seventeen years, as a statesman; *Quicquid vult, id valdè vult.* Long before he became a ruler, even, perhaps, before his long and persistent dream of becoming one had dawned on him, he was an engineer officer by profession, and a strategist by favourite study. How intense his preoccupation was in regard to these subjects is known, not only to his intimates, but those who are at all familiar with his scattered writings. To a mind possessed with such inclinations as these, it may well be believed that the desire to trace step by step the military history of the great Roman captain, with all the advantages which executive power could place at his disposal, must have been a very predominant motive in the choice of a subject. And it is impossible not to notice at once, both in the different spirit which here animates the writer and the different value of the execution, the relief which he feels in approaching it. He delights to draw out his hero from the dull details (to one like him) of the Comitia and the Senate, into the open fields, with the warlike but

---

* Not even in the most fundamental instance of all for his purpose —the authenticity of the 'Commentaries' which he uses. We have little doubt that the safest course is to rely on it; but the opposite belief requires notice, at least from any conscientious historian of Cæsar. Arnold was not a very accurate or deep scholar on such subjects, but he had a breadth of thought, and habit of judging on the general aspect of things, which was apt to render his views clear where men with minds more deeply involved in particulars see faintly. He was curiously sceptical on this head. 'The more we ' read them,' he says, 'the less can we persuade ourselves to consider ' Cæsar as their author' (History of Rome, vol. i. p. 257). We are not sure, however, whether in this passage he means the whole work, or the 'De Bello Civili' only.

capricious Gaul for his enemy, the staunch legionary, with pickaxe and javelin, for his agent, and around him the mountains, rivers, marshes, defiles, existing now as they existed then, and giving out their buried stores of ancient relics to guide the research, and reward the conjectures, of the ablest explorers of France, with an imperial antiquary at their head. Both these main divisions of his work are animated, no doubt, by the same intense spirit of personality. That he had his visions of continuing certain traditions of empire we all know; but those visions embraced also certain other traditions of military glory. Half his aspirations were fulfilled in abundant measure; the other half (to the extreme relief of mankind) the Fates ' dispersed in empty air.' But they are evidently dear to his remembrance.

In reading these volumes, therefore, which have, as has been said, little enough of the attractions of style, or eloquence, or imagination, to prevent us from diverging from the study of their contents to meditation on their author, we are inevitably led to impersonate him to ourselves in several distinct characters. He is here before us as the steady, pertinacious dreamer of dreams to come true; he who proposed to himself, and executed, the task of acting out on the great stage the drama of which the first Napoleon only performed the prelude. The hero of that drama is the great monarch, ruling, not through the people, but by and with the people, and ready at any moment to appeal from all opposition by the so-called liberal and cultivated classes to that fundamental power of all from which he derives his origin and his strength. But the author is before us also in that very rare character of a philosophical statesman, who may be driven indeed, as others are, to govern by shifts and expedients calculated to meet present emergencies, but whose mind is always in the future; who directs his course, in the main, by an estimate of the strength of opposing forces, not as they are to the superficial observer, but as certain signs show that they will be. We meet with him, lastly, as the military archæologist, on ground chosen by himself and which he has thoroughly investigated, discussing, temperately and ably, questions minute and uninteresting except to the few, but inviting much intellectual subtlety; and deciding them in general, so far as we are able to judge, with much acuteness, and a remarkable freedom from prepossessions and crotchets. But all the rest of the work—all that does not bear, directly, on its great political purpose, or that is not contained in the special chapters on the Gaulish campaigns—is mere rough cement, holding together materials of some value, but quite unconnected with each other;

mere 'padding,' to use a more obvious phrase out of the modern literary dictionary.

The leading principle on which rest the foundations of Cæsarism, or Napoleonism, whichever name may be applied to it, is of course the doctrine of Necessity; the assumption of a law, according to which, when public events have reached a certain turning point in their natural course, they can only proceed thenceforth in a previously ascertained direction. That absolute power begets aristocracy, the latter democracy, and democracy by corruption engenders tyranny, was the old pre-Comtian formula of ages gone by. And we do not know that political wisdom, although it has invented many fine-sounding phrases to adorn the same series of propositions, has in reality proceeded much farther :—

' Thus,' says the author, speaking of the last days of the Republic, ' everything was struck with decay. Brutal force gave power, and corruption place. The Empire no longer belonged to the Senate, but to the commanders of the armies ; the armies no longer belonged to the Republic, but to the chiefs who conducted them to victory. Numerous elements of dissolution disorganised society ; the venality of judges, the traffic in elections, the arbitrary proceedings of the Senate, the tyranny of wealth, which oppressed the poor by usury and braved the law with impunity. Rome was divided between two well-marked lines of opinion : one side, seeing no safety except in the past, attached themselves to abuses, through fear lest the displacement of a single stone should make the whole edifice crumble. The other wanted to consolidate that edifice by making the base larger and the summit less unsteady. The first rested its cause on the institutions of Sylla ; the other had taken the name of Marius as the symbol of its hopes.' (Vol. i. p. 282.)

After doing ample justice to the motives and purity of character of some, at least, of the leaders of the ' Parliamentary ' party, the Imperial positivist proceeds :—

' And nevertheless, the cause maintained by men such as these was condemned to perish, like everything else which has lasted its time. With all their virtues, they were only an additional obstacle to the regular march of civilisation, because they did not possess those qualities which are most essential in time of revolution, the just appreciation of the wants of the moment and the problems of the future. . . . But their influence was so considerable, and ideas consecrated by time have such an empire over the spirits of men, that they would even yet have prevented the success of the *popular* cause, if Cæsar, by placing himself at its head, had not given it new lustre and irresistible force.' (Vol. i. p. 307.)

' Never is the period of decline of a society more plainly indicated than when the law becomes the machine of war for the use of the different parties, instead of remaining the honest expression of the general requirements. Every man who had arrived at power in Rome rendered himself guilty to-day of what he had condemned yesterday, and made the institutions of his country serve the passion of the moment. At one time it is the Consul Metellus (A.U.C. 697) who delays the nomination of the Quæstors in order to prevent that of the judges, with the view of protecting his relative Clodius against a judicial accusation. At another we find Milo and Sextius, under pretext of reprisals against the same consul, opposing all imaginable obstacles to the convocation of the Comitia. Then again, the Senate (A.U.C. 698) endeavours to delay the choice of judges, in order to prevent Clodius from being named Ædile. The ancient usage of consulting the auspices had become, in the eyes of all, a mere political manœuvre. None of the great personages whom the momentary favour of the people or the Senate brought into prominence preserved the true sentiment of right. Cicero, who sees the whole Republic in himself, and who attacks as monstrous everything done against him and without him, declares all the acts of the Tribunate of Clodius "illegal." Cato, on the contrary, défends, from personal interest, the same acts, because the pretensions of Cicero wound his pride, and tend to invalidate the commission which he had received from Clodius. Caius Cato violates the law by revealing the Sibylline oracle. On all sides recourse is had to illegal means, which vary according to the temperament of the actor. Some, like Milo, Sextius, Clodius, put themselves openly at the head of armed bands: others act with timidity and dissimulation, like Cicero, who, one day, after a first unsuccessful attempt, carries off by stealth from the Capitol the brazen plate on which the law for his proscription was engraved. Singular error, to suppose that history may be effaced by causing some marks of the past to disappear.' (Vol. ii. p. 376.)

And, consistently enough, following the same line of thought to its conclusions, he makes every additional usurpation on the part of the military chiefs whose increasing ascendancy was ruining the Republic, an additional proof of the inadequacy of the Republic to meet the exigencies of the times :—

'It was every day more and more evident (A.U.C. 702), in the eyes of all men of sense, that the institutions of the Republic were becoming unequal to the maintenance of order within, perhaps of peace without. The Senate could no longer meet ; the Comitia no longer be held ; the judges no longer pronounce a sentence, except under the protection of a military force. It became necessary *therefore* to place the state at the discretion of a general, and to abdicate all authority in his favour. Thus, while popular instinct, *which is seldom in the wrong,* saw the safety of the commonwealth in the elevation of a single man to power, the aristocratic party, on the contrary, saw no danger, except in this general inclination towards the single man. On this account Cato had himself inscribed among the candidates for the consulship for the year 703, signalising Pompey and Cæsar as equally dangerous, and declaring that he only aspired to the highest magistracy in order to repress their ambitious designs. This competition, opposed to the spirit of the time and to the popular instincts which were engaged in the contest, had not a chance of success; and the candidateship of Cato was set aside without diffi-culty.'   (Vol. ii. p. 449.)

Now, to say the truth, at the expense of being thought very wanting in profundity, the ordinary allegation that the institu-tions of Rome were ' effete,' and required to be destroyed and created afresh, at the particular period when Cæsar con-descended to undertake that task, has long appeared to us an instance of the practice of reading history backwards, and assuming (in the infinite variety of human circumstances) that the event which happened was precisely the only event which could happen.   It is usually laid down in a manner which is a perfect specimen of reasoning in a circle. The institutions of Rome were rotten, therefore they fell ; they fell, therefore they were rotten.   On what grounds do we pro-nounce them thus obsolete?   Certainly not that of age.   The old Roman polity was, in truth, remarkably short-lived.   The period of development of the old aristocratic commonwealth scarcely outlasted three centuries, from the end of the Samnite war, when Rome became absolute mistress of Italy, to the time of the Gracchi, or, if you will, of Marius and Sylla. And that period was not at all of a stationary character: it was one of perpetual change and reconstruction of internal elements.   The revolution commenced by the Gracchi threw a mass of power, till then wielded by the aristocracy, into the hand of the city populace.   But then, as if providentially to counterbalance this tendency, came the changes effected by the Social Wars, which in the end balanced that new power by the introduction of whole races of free Italians to the suffrage. Such great alterations could not take place without trying the strength of the old system to the utmost ; but there is nothing, in our judgment, except the event, which we must protest against as a false criterion, to prove that, guided by more honest and more reverential hands, the machine was not elastic enough to outlast the pressure, and might not have continued to perform its functions with renewed energy.   We must not be seduced, in this matter, by the commonplaces of poets and rhetoricians about the contests of the venal forum, and enor-mous fortunes, and foreign conquest, and the lust of gold. Where a living public spirit exists, a commonwealth may endure all these, assimilate their good results, and to a certain extent reject their evil.   It will never do for us Britons—with a foreign empire more than equalling that of Rome, and foreign commercial relations greatly exceeding hers, and private fortunes elaborated every day out of our common resources to which that of Crassus was poverty, with bribery rampant, luxury to which that of Lucullus was simplicity, and social vices equalling at least those of the Suburra,—to acquiesce in the servile doctrine that the institutions under which those vast changes have been effected, and which have hitherto borne the strain of them, have become 'effete,' and stand in need of a manipulation by an inspired autocrat. And whether we are flattered or alarmed by the comparison, no two communities have ever exhibited more striking analogies in their development of public life than those of republican Rome and constitutional England.

We may, in fact, illustrate our meaning still further, by comparing the course of events in both countries, at a period in their respective destinies by no means dissimilar. After all allowance made for the comparative size of the theatres on which the performances took place, the last days of the Stuart monarchy, in England, exhibited a crisis similar in many respects to that which agitated the Roman Republic from the Syllan 'restoration' to the establishment of Cæsarean power. The old division of the English nation into the popular and aristocratic parties still remained, but in the course of events these had assumed shapes so new and so distorted, that the Whigs and Tories retained little more than a traditional resemblance, maintained by hereditary obstinacy, to the Roundheads and Royalists of old times; just as the partisans of Pompey and Cæsar did to those of Marius and Sylla.* And party warfare, while keeping clear of absolute civil war, had degenerated into excesses so utterly unscrupulous that civil war itself seemed tolerable in comparison. The life, property, honour, of every man engaged in politics were held by him absolutely at the mercy of the antagonist faction, whenever it obtained temporary power. Consequently, every struggle for power was also a struggle for existence, and ambition became only another word for the spirit of self-defence. The Whigs shed noble and innocent blood by wholesale in the matter of

---

* It may be worth the notice of those who register coincidences, that the period assigned by the Emperor for the duration of the popular struggle against the Roman Senate—sixty-three years, from the time of the Gracchi to the Consulate of Crassus and Pompey, A.U.C. 684 (vol. i. p. 275)—exactly agrees with that between the accession of Charles I. and the English revolution (1625–88).

the Popish plot. The King's friends, when uppermost, sent to the gallows as a conspirator every leading antagonist who did not escape their clutches; and punished rebellious outbreaks—such as those of Monmouth and of the Covenanters—in such a manner that the revenge bore a proportion to the provocation never perhaps surpassed in political history, except in Jamaica in 1865. And yet all, or almost all, was done, just as in the parallel instance of decaying Rome, under colour of law. The old tenacious respect for forms and legal observance prevailed throughout the struggle.

'The evidence now produced for the crown,' says Macaulay, 'was at least as worthy of credit as the evidence on which the noblest blood of England had lately been shed by the opposition. The treatment which an accused Whig had now to expect from judges, advocates, sheriffs, juries and spectators, was no worse than the treatment which had lately been thought good enough by the Whigs for an accused Papist.'

Even when Lord Rochester said (in his private letters to his wife) that 'things are now reduced to that extremity on all ' sides, that a man dares not turn his back for fear of being ' hanged, an ill accident to be avoided by all prudent persons,' the sufferers had the consolation that they were duly executed with all the constitutional forms. As Hallam says, there were, under Charles II., ' no means of chastising political ' delinquencies, except through the regular tribunals of justice, ' and through the verdict of a jury.' The consequence was— in striking analogy with what was passing at Rome in the time of Milo and Clodius—that every politician's hope, not only of victory but of life, lay in securing the jury in his favour. And, in the metropolis at least, for some years, the question which party should prevail, or rather be able to show its face in public, depended on the election of the sheriffs, whose duty to their cause it was to pack the juries. Now, if a clever Cæsarist were to pronounce that the parliamentary constitution of England, thus turned by parties into a mere cover for mutual violence, had become ' effete' in 1688, he would be able to show quite as valid an array of arguments and probabilities in favour of his assertion, as he who were to predicate the same of the Roman Republic in A.U.C. 700, or of French political freedom in 1848. And the same fate-appointed consequence would have been ready at his hands—namely, that a Cæsar was needed to replace the worn-out system by a new one. And nothing would have been easier, had Providence so willed it, than the career of an English Cæsar in 1688. The bulk of all parties, tired of what seemed an insoluble problem, would have thrown themselves at his feet. But it did not please Providence to send us a Cæsar. It sent us a Dutchman, incapable of a Cæsar's designs or a Cæsar's crimes.* It sent us a preserver, highminded, indeed, able, and resolute, but phlegmatic and sickly, whose personal ambition, such as he had, lay in quite another direction, whose sense of honour and justice would have restrained him from revolutionary projects had he been otherwise inclined to them, and who would no more have dreamt of making himself Emperor among us than Pope. The general result was that, instead of the establishment of a magnificent despotism, nothing happened among us more exciting than the rise out of political anarchy of a Whig aristocracy, which, with continually increasing reinforcement from the popular power, has managed to patch up our effete institutions, and kept them going for a century and three quarters. And for our own parts, believing the changes in states to be by no means accountable on absolute laws of Positivism, but subject to many a bias of accident and opportunity, we are aware of no reason why the institutions of Rome also might not have undergone a similar process of petty and gradual reconstruction, had Fate denied her the blessing of a Cæsar, and given her something approaching the feebler type of an Orange or a Washington. To sum up the subject in words which may, perhaps, possess an approximation to common sense, instead of savouring of the mystic and oracular : there are, no doubt, crises in the history of free states when they can only be saved through the energy or influence of a few, or even of a single man. But it depends very greatly on the character of the deliverer himself, whether he shall complete his task by the reconstruction of society on the old basis, or shall destroy society, and render himself the absolute master of a new one. The courtier, who worships success in a ' Cæsar,' is a public enemy of a vulgar type. The timid, or fastidious, or cynical politician, who extols him simply for the energy which he displays in trampling down opposition, is considerably worse. But worst of all is the fatalist philosopher, who preaches that the usurper is a necessity.

---

* It is a singular instance of preoccupation by a single idea, that Louis Napoleon, in his ' Historical Fragments' (comparing 1688 with 1830), turns William III. himself into a ' Cæsar.' The Stuarts, he says, reigned by fomenting personal ambitions : ' Guillaume, au ' contraire, mettait sous ses pieds tous les obstacles, et faisait con- ' courir toutes les opinions diverses comme tous les individus opposés ' à un seul but, l'intérêt du pays.' (*Œuvres de Louis Napoleon*, vol. ii. p. 102.)

That the master of events, on his road to supreme power, is justified in employing to the utmost extent the ordinary methods of corruption and intrigue which the abuses of the constitution place at his disposal, is evident from the following passage, descriptive of Cæsar's conduct after he had succeeded in establishing the first triumvirate :—

'Without changing the fundamental laws of the Republic, Cæsar had obtained a great result. He had substituted for anarchy an energetic power, mastering at once the Senate and the Comitia. By effecting an understanding between the three most important citizens, he had merged mere personal rivalries in a moral authority which had permitted him to establish laws favourable to the prosperity of the Empire. But it was essential that his departure should not draw with it the fall of the edifice so laboriously raised. He was not ignorant of the number or power of his enemies ; he knew that if he abandoned to them the Forum and the Curia, not only they would annul all his acts, but would go so far as to deprive him of his command. . . . Against such hostility as this it was necessary to do a difficult thing—to contrive to manage the elections. The Roman Constitution brought forward every year new candidates for public office. It was indispensable to have partisans among the two consuls, the eight prætors, and the ten tribunes named in the Comitia.' (Vol. i. pp. 401–2.)

The character and designs of the friends and supporters of Cæsarism, destined to abet the Cæsar of the day in his successful attack on the institutions of his country, form always a ticklish subject for the panegyrist to deal with. The Catiline, Clodius, Curio of all times—those desperados who prepare the way for a *coup d'état*, and those who abet it in execution— are generally somewhat sinister figures in history, whom one would willingly keep in the shade as far as possible. On the whole, we think the Imperial writer has dealt judiciously with this portion of his subject. Without ignoring these untoward partisans of his hero, he has contrived not to make them too prominent, and, amidst due reprobation for their excesses, to insinuate the gentle apology that the evils of the time left them no other course, and Cæsar no better allies.

'In epochs of transition, when it is necessary to choose between a glorious past and an unknown future, audacious and unscrupulous men alone put themselves forward ; the others, more timid and more enslaved by prejudices, keep in the shade, and form an obstacle to the movement which is drawing society in a new direction. It is always a great evil for a country which is a prey to agitators, when the party of *les honnêtes gens,* or of "the good," as Cicero calls them, does not embrace the new ideas, in order to direct and moderate them. Hence profound divisions. On the one hand, worthless men are apt to become masters of the good or evil passions of the multitude ; on the other, honourable people, either standing aside or placing themselves in opposition, impede all progress, and arouse, by their obstinate resistance, a legitimate impatience, or even mischievous violence. This opposition has the double inconvenience of leaving the field open to those who belong to an inferior type, and at the same time of maintaining doubts in the mind of that floating mass which judges parties much more by the character of the men engaged in them than by the value of the ideas which they represent.

' What then passed at Rome offers a striking example of these truths. Was it not reasonable, in truth, to hesitate before preferring to the faction which had at its head such illustrious personages as Hortensius, Catulus, Marcellus, Lucullus, and Cato, that which counted as its supporters men such as Gabinius, Manilius, Catiline, Vatinius, and Clodius ? What more legitimate, in the eyes of the descendants of the ancient families, than this resistance to all change, and this disposition to consider all reform as an utopia and a sacrilege? . . . And yet the cause, defended by such men, was doomed to perish, like everything else which has had its time. Notwithstanding their virtues, they were only an additional obstacle to the regular march of civilisation ; because they were deficient in those qualities which are the most essential in times of revolution, the power to appreciate justly the necessities of the moment and the problems of the future.' (Vol. i. pp. 306–7.)

It would certainly be difficult, under cover of a chapter of ancient history, to adumbrate more distinctly both the character of the events which have placed later Cæsars on the seat of empire, and the apology for them. In another passage the experience of modern crises is called in even more boldly to vouch for the favourite interpretation of ancient ones :—

' In civil troubles every class of society guesses, as if by instinct, the cause which answers to its aspirations, and feels itself drawn towards it by a secret affinity. Men born in the superior classes, or raised to the same level by honours and wealth, are always attracted towards aristocratic causes ; while those who are kept by fortune in the inferior ranks remain firm supporters of the popular cause. Thus, at the return from Elba, most of the generals of Napoleon, gorged with wealth like the lieutenants of Cæsar, marched openly against the Emperor ; but in the army, all up to the rank of colonel said, after the example of the Roman centurion, showing their weapons, " These will place him on the throne." ' (Vol. ii. p. 495.)

When, however, the Emperor points out the personal shortcomings and weaknesses of the aristocratic or constitutional party, during its long struggle with the popular chief—when he represents it as sometimes rushing violently into the employment of gold and corruption, at other times carrying on what he calls ' a little war of sarcasm and chicane '—he is, we must admit, supported by the opinions of writers less devoted to partisanship than himself.

' Except Quintus Catulus (says Mommsen), who with honourable pertinacity continued to occupy his unenviable post as defender of a beaten party until his death (A.U.C. 694), there is no chief to be named belonging to the highest rank of the nobility, who represented the interests of the aristocracy with courage and steadfastness. Even their ablest and most admired members, such as Quintus Metellus Pius and Lucius Lucullus, substantially abdicated, and withdrew themselves, as far as they could do so with decency, to their villas, to forget as far as possible the forum and the senate amidst their aviaries and fishponds. This naturally applied still more to the younger generation of the aristocracy, which either sank entirely in luxury and literature or turned to the rising sun.'

So again, speaking of the terror caused to the aristocratic party by the meeting of the Triumvirs at Lucca, A.U.C. 698, Mommsen says :—

' It was now time for the aristocracy to make their high enterprise good, and to carry on the war as boldly as they had begun it. But there is no more melancholy spectacle than that of cowardly men who have been so unlucky as to take a courageous resolution. Nothing had been foreseen. It did not seem to have occurred to anyone that Cæsar might possibly put himself in a posture of defence, that Pompey and Crassus might once more coalesce. This seems incredible ; but it becomes comprehensible when we examine the individuals who then led the party of the defenders of the constitution. . . . They had taken up arms but to lay them down again, as soon as the adversary only rattled his sheath. The mere intelligence of the conferences between the Triumvirs at Lucca was enough to break down every thought of a serious opposition, and to bring back the mass of timid people, that is to say, the enormous majority of the Senate, into that position of subjects which they had abandoned in an unlucky moment. . . . Thus the corporation performed public penance. Individual leaders came in secret, one after another, frightened to death at their own rashness, to make their peace and promise unlimited obedience.' (*Geschichte Roms*, vol. iii.)

Unfortunately this is all too true ; and true of other times, and feuds, besides those of the last days of the great Republic. It has been the uniform misfortune of those arrayed against the overmastering popular party, whether that party assumes the colours of democracy or of Cæsarism, sometimes to exaggerate its strength, more frequently to undervalue it, but always to miscalculate it. Hence the shouts of triumph with which the partisans of the higher classes invariably greet the success of any temporary measure or manœuvre which defeats for a time the combinations of their opponents, as if it were an indication of a real change in public feeling. Hence the tremor of suspense with which, the first burst of exultation over, they watch the effect of their own achievement on the temper of the defeated; like the little pugilist, in Statius, after he has managed to plant a hit on the body of his gigantic adversary: 'eventuque impalluit 'ipse secundo.'   Hence the unworthy haste with which, as soon as convinced that the other side are seriously in earnest, they are apt to abandon their cause as lost, and take refuge in protests that their meaning has been misunderstood, that they have been all along the true friends of the popular cause, and have only differed from their excellent friends opposite as to the best means of supporting it.   Such phenomena will reproduce themselves in each successive struggle of the few against the many, whichever party may happen for the time to be in the right, and whether the object of the struggle is to oppose the slightest extension of popular rights, or to keep out an armed 'child and champion of democracy' at the door.   But to judge of the justice, or expediency, of a cause from the qualities displayed by its partisans or opponents is a weakness unworthy of a true historian.

Generally speaking, however, it will be found that the new biographer of Cæsar judges fairly and temperately of the leading members of the Roman 'parliamentary faction' which set itself in opposition to his hero.   He is lenient even to Pompey himself, to whom he applies the expressive phrase, 'qu'il n'avoit 'pas le courage de ses opinions.'   On one point, and we may almost say on one only, we find him going seriously beyond those boundaries of self-restraint which he has imposed on himself in general, when dealing with those leading men engaged in the great Roman struggle who most excite his political antipathies.   This is in his treatment of Cicero.   We are not going on the present occasion to enter on the still vexed question of the judgment to be passed by us moderns on the moral character of the great orator.   It seems to be disputed at the present day with almost all the partisanship of his own period; and the reason is plain enough.   It was a character made up of many noble qualities and many weaknesses.   Cicero is a frail man, not the impersonation of an idea; compared with Cato, for instance, he is like a personage of Shakspeare as against one of Corneille.   Every critic, therefore, according as he is favourably disposed towards one or the other of the two great causes which the Emperor's volumes bring once more into the lists, as they have been brought so many times before, finds it easy, with the help of a very little party prejudice, to paint his Cicero with a bolder dash of black or white according to his mind. But, whatever else may be said of Cicero, of his political conduct, his political language, his philosophy, his rhetoric, his effusions to his familiar friends, they all stood in the clearest and most recognised contrast to the career of the great soldier-sovereign. His deep attachment to the institutions of his country; his clinging even to the merest forms and shreds of legality; his aversion from the decision of the sword, and love of the wordy contests of the pen or the tongue; his persevering faith that the Republic, in the hands of 'good men,' would ultimately right herself, and that what was really wanted was not the brutal violence of the soldier, nor the equally brutal impulses of the mob, but the union of those imagined 'good men,' and the discarding of private ambitions and jealousies; his genuine and intense adoration, at which none but those who are incapable of it can in their hearts mock, of the τὸ κάλον, the great principle of life, and right, and symmetry, pervading the actions of men no less than the laws of nature; his conviction that

> ' There is on earth a yet diviner thing,
> Veiled though it be, than Senate or than King ; '

all these were in his lifetime impediments in the way of advancing autocracy, and remain, after two thousand years, standing rebukes to it. Men can afford, no doubt, to be 'catholic' and charitable in their judgments of most of the departed heroes of antiquity; but Cicero and Cæsar are the representatives (so Fate has willed it) of political and social predilections which are as active in our day as they were in their own, and no man can really love both Cicero and Cæsar. It is no matter of surprise, therefore, if the nephew of Napoleon cannot see his way to be just, much less generous, towards him who was at Rome what poor Léon Faucher once called himself to us at Paris, ' la der-' nière expression du système parlementaire.' Instances of this almost petty ill-will towards the memory of the orator may be traced in every page of the political portion of this history; we will content ourselves with pointing out one or two.

When, on the imminent danger of invasion by Cæsar (A.U.C. 705) the Senate assigned to its principal leaders their several military commands in Italy, ' Cicero,' says the Emperor, ' *always prudent,* chose Campania, as being farthest removed ' from the theatre of war.' (Vol. ii. p. 510.) There is really no foundation at all for this pointed sneer, except the general notion that the orator had no military fervour. No ancient author suggests it. Cicero himself simply says that Campania was assigned to him, not that he chose it. But Campania was by no means removed from danger : it was very likely to become the seat of military operations, as it generally had been in Italian wars, owing to its central situation, its open character, and its wealth.   Dr. Merivale gives as the reason of his acquiescence in this appointment, with more apparent justice, that ' he was extremely unwilling to leave the imme-' diate neighbourhood of Rome, where he conceived that his ' real sphere of usefulness lay.'

A little before, we find Cicero—without the slightest foundation that we can discover—dragged in as a sort of accessary before the fact, to a supposed project of assassination against Clodius. ' Chaque jour voyait une émeute dans les rues. ' Milon jurait de tuer Clodius, et Cicéron avouait plus tard que ' la victime et le bras qui le devait frapper étaient désignés ' d'avance.' (Vol. ii. p. 367.)   This is literally true, no doubt, but so partially stated as entirely to misrepresent Cicero's meaning.   The orator has been recounting to Atticus a desperate attack made by Clodius on the house of Milo, ' quæ ' erat in Germalo ; ' with an attempt to burn and rob it, which was frustrated by some armed partisans of the owner.   The two party chiefs therefore defied each other, and each placed himself at the head of an armed force.   Milo challenged Clodius to meet him in the Forum.   A state of open war existed between them.   In this condition of things, Cicero says, ' I think if Clodius shows himself in the street, Milo will ' kill him.'   It is needless to point out how different this picture is from that of Clodius as a ' victim,' whose murder, and murderer, were ' already resolved upon.'

In another passage, we find the writer dexterously appropriating a passage from Dio Cassius—who is evidently giving, not his own sentiments or those of historians in general, but Cæsar's own account of the affair—to show the exalted superiority of character manifested in Cæsar's dealings with his wordy antagonist at the time of the first Triumvirate :—

'Cæsar endured with difficulty the attacks of Cicero.   But, superior to resentments, as men are who are guided by great political views, he temporised gently with everything which could have an ascendant over the public mind, and the word of Cicero was a power.   Dio Cassius thus explains the conduct of Cæsar : " He " wounded Cicero neither by his words nor his actions.   He said that " men often launch, on purpose, vain sarcasms against those who are " above them, in order to drive them into disputes, with the hope of " appearing to have some likeness to them, and of being placed in the " same rank, if they succeed in getting themselves abused in return. " Cæsar, therefore, judged that he ought to enter the lists against no " one.   Such was his rule of conduct against those who insulted

" him ; and as he at that time saw plainly that Cicero's object was
" less to offend him than to provoke him to the utterance of some
" injurious retort, and thus to satisfy his desire to be regarded as
" Cæsar's equal, he gave himself no concern at what the orator said,
" and even allowed Cicero to outrage him in words, and to praise
" himself, entirely at his ease. Nevertheless, Cæsar was far from
" despising Cicero, but, naturally gentle, he did not suffer his temper
" to be easily provoked. He had often to punish, as was unavoid-
" able in the midst of such great affairs as those in which he was
" engaged, but he never gave way to passion." ' (*Dio Cassius,*
xxxviii. xi.—vol. i. p. 399.)

Surely the parts played by Cæsar and Cicero respectively,
in the struggle of the first Triumvirate, are too well known to
be thus artificially dealt with. If Cicero was a mere puppet,
Cæsar would seem to have taken extraordinary pains to de-
molish him. The profligate Clodius was bent on the destruction of Cicero as his personal enemy. Cæsar, who, as has been
truly said, counted on the services of Clodius, contrived his
adoption into a plebeian family whereby he was qualified to be
elected tribune. His election to the tribuneship was well
known to be the signal for the persecution of Cicero. Cæsar—
who had brought that election about—was so well aware
of this, that he endeavoured, whether from motives of kindness or policy, to rescue Cicero from the impending danger
by inducing him to accept some inferior and dependent post
out of the city—an acceptance which would of course have
been equivalent to a complete victory over the orator without
the unpopularity of a direct attack ; and which Cicero had the
courage to decline. Cicero was thus driven into banishment,
by all but the immediate act of Cæsar himself. This was not
treating him as a mere contemptible enemy. That Cæsar was
capable of great generosity, no less from nature than policy,
all the world knows : to suppose him incapable of resentment
for offences against his interest, or against his pride, is to suppose him what neither he nor any other man ever was, and
what his occasional conduct towards individual enemies, however exceptional, plainly disproves. There are occasions,
says Thiers, in his ' History of the Republic,' speaking of the
passage of arms between the first Napoleon and Siéyès, at
Gohier's dinner, just before the 18th Brumaire, on which,
' dans les hommes de la plus grande supériorité, l'orgueil l'em-
' porte sur la politique. Si, du reste, il en était autrement, ils
' n'auraient plus cette hauteur qui les rend propres à dominer
' les hommes.'

The curious interpretation of the Catilinarian events (in
which, however, the Emperor is by no means alone among

modern historians) by which Catiline is made a *grand homme incompris*, Cicero an outrageous violator of the law, Cæsar a superior being calmly rebuking the revolutionary fervour of the first and the reactionary excesses of the second,* have been too often commented upon by critics to need farther criticism here.   But the passage is accompanied by a brief lecture, in which is conveyed a remarkable axiom of modern political morality :—

'One may *legitimately* violate *legality* when, society being at the point of ruin, a heroic remedy is indispensable to save it, and when the government, sustained by the mass of the nation, makes itself the representative of the general interests and desires. But, on the contrary, when, in a country divided by factions, the Government only represents one of them, then, if it has to suppress a plot, it ought most scrupulously to observe the law in doing so ; for at such times every extra-legal measure appears inspired, not by the general interest, but by a narrow instinct of self-preservation ; and the majority of the public, indifferent or hostile, is always disposed to sympathise with the accused, whoever he may be, and to blame the severity of the repression.'

This certainly solves the question of the lawfulness of the employment of 'martial law,' of which we have heard so much lately, in the most compendious manner.   If proclaimed by a sovereign representative of the people in order to save society, it is 'legitimate.'   If proclaimed by a constitutional, that is, a party government, it is illegitimate ; for such a government represents nothing but the party which has brought it into power.

We believe we may leave Cicero safely to the charitable consideration of the after world, notwithstanding all that the lovers of success may have to urge against him.   But we will cite one little testimony in his favour, even more for the sake of the writer, John Henry Newman, than of the subject :—

'On the whole, antiquity may be challenged to produce an individual more virtuous, more perfectly amiable, than Cicero. None interest more in their life, none excite more painful emotions in their death.   Others, it is true, may be found of loftier and more heroic character, who awe and subdue the mind by the grandeur of their views, or the intensity of their exertions ; but Cicero engages our affections by the integrity of his public conduct, the correctness

* Those who are tempted to dismiss the obscure question of Cæsar's complicity in the conspiracy of Catiline with the curt observation of the 'Histoire,' that 'il est facile de se convaincre que 'César n'était pas un conspirateur,' had better read the brief and judicial summary of Mommsen, by no means an enemy to Cæsar.

of his private life, the generosity, placability, and kindness of his heart, the playfulness of his temper, the warmth of his domestic attachments. . . . Want of firmness has been repeatedly mentioned as his principal failing ; and insincerity is the natural attendant on a timid and irresolute mind.   On the other hand, it must not be forgotten that openness and candour are rare qualities in a statesman at all times, and while the duplicity of weakness is despised, the insincerity of a powerful but crafty mind, though incomparably more odious, is too commonly regarded with feelings of indulgence.' (*Encyc. Metropolitana.*)

We have already said that the merely historical and introductory part of the work, wherein Cæsar himself is but indirectly concerned, may be safely passed over by the conscientious reader.   One extract only we intend to make from it ; because this, also, touches closely on some subjects of interest at the present day.   It is a passage in which, exactly following the footsteps of his uncle in the ' Memorial de Ste. Hélène,' he passes in review the particular qualifications of Rome to be the natural metropolis of Italy.

' The geographical position of Rome did not contribute less to the rapid increase of its power.   Situated in the middle of the only large fertile plain of Italy (Latium), and on the banks of the only important river of central Italy, which connected it with the sea, it was capable of becoming at the same time agricultural and maritime ; conditions at that time indispensable for the capital of a new empire.   The rich districts which occupied the shores of the Mediterranean were destined to fall easily under its dominion ; and as to the mountain countries which surrounded it, Rome had the means of becoming their mistress by occupying gradually the outlets of all their valleys.   Thus the City of the Seven Hills, favoured alike by its natural position and by its political constitution, bore within itself the seeds of its future greatness.'   (Vol. i. p. 62.)

To pass from the first to the second volume of this singular work is to migrate, at once, from the realm of pamphlet to that of grave history.   We should rather say, from the second to the third ' book ; ' for the second volume affords an instance of very inartificial workmanship, tending to the least possible result.   For some reason which the author has not explained, he has devoted his third book, separately and exclusively, to Cæsar's Gaulish campaigns.   These are recounted with a view solely to their military and topographical details, and without any connexion whatever with the contemporary political chronicle of Rome.   Then, in the fourth book, we are taken to Rome again, and brought back to the same point of time, A.U.C. 696, at which the Gaulish campaigns began.   To use the writer's own account of this curious distribution of his work (at the commencement of book iv.) :—

' In the preceding book we have reproduced, following the Commentaries, the narrative of the Gaulish wars, endeavouring to elucidate doubtful questions, and to fix the spots which were the theatre of so many battles.   It will now be not without interest for us to repeat the leading features of the eight campaigns of the Roman proconsul, avoiding all merely technical details.   We shall at the same time examine what passed during this period on the banks of the Tiber, and the events which brought about the Civil War.'

The result is that the whole story of the Gaulish wars is told twice over ; once minutely, by itself, and once in a summary connected with other events.   A master of historical narrative would certainly have avoided such a recapitulation.   We can imagine the result of the application of such a method to modern events, by supposing that a historian of the French revolution were to devote a chapter to Napoleon's campaigns in Italy, and then a separate chapter to the same campaigns again in connexion with what was passing at the same time at Paris under the Directory.   But however liable the process may be to this kind of criticism, the consequences are, no doubt, in some respects advantageous to the reader.   For the whole of the third book might be extracted bodily from the rest of the work, and printed separately as a running commentary on the books ' De Bello Gallico ; ' and so, we have little doubt, it will be; and it will retain its value for future archæologists and topographers, when the speculations even of an Emperor on political commonplaces have ceased to excite more than a languid interest.   And in the meantime it is most refreshing even for us readers of the present day, to find ourselves relieved for a space from the perpetual ring of modern newspaper oratory which runs as an accompaniment through the rest of the volumes, and find ourselves alone with the great military genius of antiquity, explained and adapted to our present knowledge by one whose tastes and education have made the task a labour of love, and whose position has placed in his power the means of thoroughly executing it.

The author himself reminds us that he is not the first sovereign who employed his authority as head of the Government to collect materials for illustrating this part of the Commentaries :—

'Charles V.,' he says in the preface to this volume, 'who professed a lively admiration for Cæsar, left a copy of the Commentaries full of marginal notes by his own hand.   It was at his instigation that the viceroy of Sicily, Ferdinand Gonzaga, sent a scientific mission to France to study the campaigns of Cæsar on the spot.   The forty plans which were made by this mission (among which is that of Alesia) were published in 1575 in the edition of Jacopo Strada.'

Following the example of Charles V., with all the additional appliances at the service of modern explorers, Napoleon has not only studied, personally, for some years past, the sites of some of the most remarkable passages of the Gaulish war, but has despatched officers of his staff in all directions, to make themselves more thoroughly masters of the topography than his own leisure enabled him to do. Their labours are amply acknowledged in various passages of the notes, and are embodied in the very valuable 'Atlas' which accompanies the second volume; a model of neatness of execution, as well as severe simplicity of design.

If this division of the work does not present very agreeable reading to the literary lounger—the subject is untoward, and it cannot be said that the author possesses the special talent of making a dry topic entertaining—it furnishes most valuable materials for the serious student of antiquity. We can, however, scarcely include in this commendation the sketch of Gaulish geography and ethnology with which this third book commences. As we have said respecting former parts of the wcrk, it is singularly uncritical, and might quite as well have been compiled by Rollin or by Goldsmith, for any use which is made in it of modern scientific inquiry. We find our old friends the Druids, without any notice whatever of the shrewd doubts lately cast on the authenticity of their mysterious renown, re-established in all their old dignity, such as the first legendary accounts received by the Romans make them, ' expound- ' ing the movements of the stars, the greatness of the universe, ' the laws of nature, and the omnipotence of the Almighty ' Gods.' We have the ordinary statements respecting the polity, military and social customs, of the Gauls—confused, and in part almost unintelligible, as they are—laid before us without any attempt at discrimination. But we have them made subservient, in one remarkable passage, to the purpose of instilling into the mind certain peculiarly Napoleonic ideas respecting the causes of the strength and weakness of States :—

' The Emperor Napoleon I. said with justice, " The principal " cause of the weakness of Gaul lay in the spirit of insulation and " locality which characterised its population. At this period the " Gauls had nothing of the spirit of a nation, or even of a province ; " the spirit which governed them was that of a city. It is the same " spirit which, in later ages, has forged the chains of Italy. Nothing " is more opposed to the national spirit, to general ideas of freedom, " than the special spirit of the family or the township. From this

" division into small fractions and parties it resulted also that the
" Gauls had no *standing army*, regularly maintained and exercised,
" and consequently no military art or science.   Every nation which
" were to lose sight of the importance of keeping regular troops per-
" petually on foot, and were to place its confidence in hasty levies
" or national armies, would undergo the lot of the Gauls, without
" having the glory of opposing the same resistance to the invader ;
" for this was the effect of the barbarism of those times, and of the
" state of the soil, covered with forests and marshes, and destitute
" of roads, which rendered it difficult of conquest and easy of
" defence." '   (Vol. ii. p. 43.)

This was, no doubt, very much in the first Napoleon's line of
thinking; but we are rather surprised at finding a man of so
far more comprehensive a mental education as the present
Emperor, seeming to express his concurrence in it.   A nation
divided against itself falls, not because it is so divided, but
because its division renders it incapable of maintaining a
standing army !

The conjectural estimate given by the author of the population of the Gauls at the time of Cæsar's invasion is curious at
all events, and, abridged, stands as follows.   He makes the
ordinary assumption of one fighting man to four persons.   Now
the great levy of A.U.C. 697 gave 296,000 combatants (Belgæ).
That of A.U.C. 702 (campaign of Alesia) 281,000.   Deduct
from the latter 80,000 for the number who may probably have
served in *both* the levies.   The actual levies may be taken to
represent from three-fifths to one-fifth of the actual fighting
population ; the proportion varying according to distance from
the theatre of action and other circumstances.   Calculations
founded on these assumptions give 1,087,200 as the fighting
population comprised in the tribes associated on these two occasions.   Add 92,000 Helvetians, and 625,000 for the tribes
which took no part in the two great levies, estimated according to the comparative extent of their territory.   Total,
1,804,200 men of fighting age, equal to 7,216,800 inhabitants
for the whole of Gaul exclusive of the Roman province, assuming the usual proportion of non-combatants as three to one.
In corroboration of this assumption, the Emperor adduces
the rough estimate of Diodorus Siculus, that the population of
each of the nations of Gaul varied from 200,000 to 50,000
' men.'   Reading men as ' souls,' in modern phraseology, and
adopting Tacitus's number of sixty-four Gaulish nations or
tribes, this would give a not very dissimilar number, or
about eight millions, for the whole population a century after
the time of Cæsar, if Diodorus used the statistics of his own

day. Dureau de la Malle ('Economie Politique des Romains,' as cited by Dr. Merivale) gives Gaul ten millions and a half in the fourth century. Dr. Merivale himself will not allow it more than six millions in the time of Cæsar, inclusive of the Province ('Romans under the Empire,' chap. v.). Mommsen's estimate, if he meant to carry out with regard to Gaul in general the principles of calculation which he has applied to the country of the Belgæ, would be a good deal higher. On the one hand, it may be observed that neither of these calculations seems to make any account of the slaves, of whom some at least of the Gaulish tribes seem to have possessed a considerable number. On the other hand, it must be owned that a relative population of thirty or forty to the English square mile (that is, within the limits of ancient Gaul, not modern France,) seems quite considerable enough for a pastoral country, with scanty agriculture, and interspersed with vast tracts of marsh and forest. These abounded everywhere, but in the northern parts especially they seem to have been preserved with care, as forming a tolerably effective boundary between hostile tribes, and places of refuge in time of war. (See the accounts of the Morini and Menapii, Bell. Gall. books 3 & 6, vol. ii. p. 17.) There were in every independent state principal towns, says the Emperor, called by Cæsar indifferently 'urbs' or 'oppidum.' He does not appear to have entered at all into the refinements of modern antiquaries on this subject. Only two or three places in Gaul (Avaricum, Gergovia, Alesia) have in Cæsar the title of urbs.* But, adds the Emperor, the name oppidum was given by preference to places of difficult access and carefully fortified, situated on heights or in marshes; and he seriously quotes (with that peculiar simplicity, in matters of etymology, which everywhere characterises him) the wise conjecture of Paul Diaconus, 'oppidum dictum quòd ibi homines opes suas conferant.' (Vol. ii. p. 29.)

For the elaborate details of the topography of the eight glorious campaigns, we must needs refer the reader to the work itself. The narrative of the attempted Helvetian emigration, and Cæsar's pursuit and destruction of the migrating force—in itself one of the most singular passages in military history, and one of the least intelligible without such a lecture on the text as these pages afford us—seems to us most masterly. (Vol. ii. pp. 45–73.) So does that of the campaign of Paris,

---

* According to a writer in the Mém. de l'Acad. des Sciences, quoted by Dr. Merivale, 'History of the Romans,' ch. v.

A.U.C. 702, in which Labienus was relieved by Cæsar; and that of the final struggle before Alesia. The site of every place of note mentioned by Cæsar has been explored with the utmost care, and is in every important instance identified: whether to the exclusion of all future antiquarian doubt, we cannot undertake to say : but it seems difficult to shake the pillars of the Emperor's construction. Bibracte (Mont Beuvray, near Autun), Gergovia (six kilomètres south of Clermont in Auvergne), the much-contested Alesia (Alise Sainte-Reine, in the Côte d'Or), and many other famous scenes of Cæsar's operations, have not only been conjecturally fixed from the written evidence, but the conjectures verified by the most careful and extensive works executed by engineers, revealing the sites of Gaulish oppida and Roman entrenchments; so as to carry home conviction, if all is accurately reported, to the most incredulous, and, every now and then, to bring the explorer into startling proximity with the object of his researches. At Alesia a fragment of antiquity of no ordinary interest was thus brought to light. Of the largest of the four Roman infantry camps before Alesia, ' the vestiges of the *remblais* ' (the moved earth, brought to fill up excavations) ' are visible at this day, ' over the greatest part of the area, because the plough has never ' passed over the soil. This is the only example known of traces ' still apparent of a camp of Cæsar.' At Uxellodunum (Puy d'Issolu) the explorations made revealed not only arms and utensils of the Gaulish defenders of the citadel, but charred relics of that very fire, which, according to Hirtius (in the eighth book ' de Bello Gallico ') consumed certain covered galleries erected by the Romans in the course of their siege operations.

All this portion of the work is truly worthy of an author who was a laborious student and an active writer before he became a sovereign, and whose zeal impels him at once to erect a durable monument to the memory of his favourite historical hero, and to furnish a solid contribution to the local memorials of that country of which he is himself creating the modern history. Nor will the reader fail to detect, in these laborious chapters, the traces of those peculiar characteristics which have displayed themselves in so many of his more notorious achievements : patience and resolution, and an eye always steadily directed towards its main object.*

---

* It is very remarkable in how many instances the process of identification has conducted the inquirers to some obscure site, still known by the name of the ancient place of which they were in search. Gergovia is so called to this day : Bibracte,

The general account of ' Britain in the time of Cæsar ' is disappointing, for the same reason as that of Gaul. The author either has not taken the pains, or has purposely neglected, to add anything of consequence to the meagre text of Cæsar himself.   He passes by, with that complete indifference which we have noted on other occasions, all the corrections, and additions, which modern ingenuity has made to its scanty contents. Now, considering that Cæsar spent only a few days in the island, that is to say in one corner of it, and that during that time he was continually occupied in fortifying, fighting, and negotiating—while, for all he says about Britain in general, he can have had no knowledge beyond hearsay—it is only in the utter absence of better authorities that we rely on him at all.   Cæsar says that all the trees common in Gaul were found in Britain, *præter fagum et abietem*—except the beech (*hêtre*, as the writer translates it) and fir.   It might surely have been worth his while to inquire—before simply reproducing this often-contested and many-ways interpreted passage—whether the primæval beech woods of the Chilterns, composed of a tree which has given name to a county town and to other places in abundance, do not tell a very different story.   It is surely much more probable that Cæsar was misinformed, than that great forests had been already produced, before the arrival of the Saxons, from a tree imported by the Romans.   A little caution in looking beyond the letter of ordinary writers would have in like manner guarded him from asserting (not on the authority of Cæsar, who is not in fault here) that pearls were found in the ' Scottish sea : ' the Romans may have thought so, but we—familiar with the wealth of Scottish mountain streams, so singularly rediscovered of late years—ought to know better. So again, when he tells us that the Britons ' obtained from ' Gaul their implements of amber ' he is probably, in common with his misinformed classical guides, confounding with real amber the so-called ' jet ' of our Eastern cliffs.*   So idle a

Alesia, Uxellodunum (Puy d'Issolu), all furnish remarkable instances.   In truth, names of spots marked by strong natural features (as is the case with these) seem almost indelible in countries where no sweeping change of nationality has taken place.   It is, however, with difficulty that we can admit that Genabos—*inclyta* Genabos, the great seat of the Roman traders who penetrated into independent Gaul, hitherto, we believe, unanimously fixed at Orleans—is to be found in the out-of-the-way town of Gien.   But the reasons given are very strong.

    * ' We ourselves,' says Mr. Scott Surtees, in his pamphlet, ' Julius ' Cæsar : did he cross the Channel ? ' of which we shall speak presently,

traveller's tale as that recounted to Cæsar, no doubt, by some
imaginative pedlar or skipper, that the Britons ' would not eat
' hares, fowls, or geese, from superstitious motives, but bred
' them for their amusement,' if worth repeating at all, was
scarcely worth telling as a solemn truth; although it cannot be
denied that their descendants deal in a similar way with foxes.
It is odd, too, that one so well acquainted not merely with our
language but with our country, should inform us that the
Forest of Anderida ' extended over the counties of Sussex and
' Kent in the district now termed Wealds' (vol. ii. p. 550).

The Emperor's detailed explanation of those passages of the
Commentaries which concern the topography of Cæsar's two
invasions of Britain have, as might be anticipated, met with
very close, and not very friendly, criticism, on the part especially of our insular antiquaries. It would be impossible for
us to devote sufficient space to the thorough investigation of
the questions raised in this controversy. Suffice it for us to
point out, briefly, one or two leading points of inquiry.

1. The Emperor endeavours to establish that Cæsar on both
occasions (A.U.C. 696 and 700) embarked at Boulogne. Wissant,
Calais, Etaples, and Mardyke, have been suggested by others.
We have seen a good deal of hostile observation directed against
this passage of the ' Histoire; ' some being apparently of
opinion that the writer's main reason for maintaining the theory
was that his uncle, the first Napoleon, had maintained it before
(Précis des Guerres de César); had, moreover, done the same
harbour the honour of making it the rendezvous of his flotilla
for the invasion of England eighteen hundred years afterwards; and had even constructed flat-bottomed boats for the
purpose, ' almost of the same dimensions as those employed by
' Cæsar ' (vol. ii. p. 171). The parallelism is thought suspicious; but as the writer justly observes, ' notwithstanding the
' difference of times and of the art of war, the nautical and
' practical conditions of the problem had not changed; ' and on
the whole—admitting what may be urged to the contrary from
the ambiguity of the name ' Gesoriacum,' and the vagueness of
the passage of Strabo relied upon by the partisans of Boulogne
—our own opinion is that on a question on which certainty is

' when young, have searched for and sometimes found amber on the
' beach at Cromer,' that is, the jet aforesaid. We cite this as a curious
instance of the enormous leaps which the seven-leagued boots of an
antiquary are able to make. Strabo (a century or so after Cæsar) is
supposed to say that the Britons possessed utensils of amber. Jet is
found on the coast of Norfolk. Therefore, Cæsar landed in Norfolk.

unattainable, the author has fairly and industriously made out his own case as the most probable.*

2. To pass to the second, and by far the most interesting, of these debateable issues ; namely, the point at which Cæsar disembarked in his two expeditions (for this, also, was probably the same on both occasions). This the Emperor fixes where the received opinion of former days fixed it with little scepticism, namely, on the beach of Deal and Walmer. Many of our readers are probably conversant with the minute and interesting discussion which has been raised on this subject by some English antiquaries, who have recently started (or rather renewed) the conjecture that the place of disembarkation was to the west, instead of to the north, of Dover ; and probably near Hythe, immediately under the site of that picturesque old Roman castle of Lymne, which still frowns over the Marsh. The Emperor does ample justice to the acuteness and industry of Mr. Lewin, the latest and most learned supporter of this view. But his reasons to the contrary are powerfully urged ; and we admit again (without entering on a discussion which would require an article of itself to do it justice), that here also we hold with the foreign against the English authority. It is singular that the question should mainly turn on points of such very minute investigation as the set of the tides in the Straits of Dover on the 26th of August, B.C. 55 ; and the exact meaning of the Latin phrase ' post diem quartum ; '

---

* We adopt this view, not without having had regard both to the serious doubts raised by former writers of weight, and also to the somewhat arrogant and noisy criticism directed against this part of the ' Histoire ' by a portion of the English press. The argument for ' Wissant ' derived from the similarity between its name and ' Ictius,' has no effect on us, who cannot but suppose that ' Wissant ' is simply either ' Whitesand ' or ' Westsand '—the first point, or near it, at which the Teutonic local nomenclature meets one journeying eastward along the coast of the Channel. Our friend Mr. Surtees is particularly imaginative on the unlucky ' Portus Ictius.' ' Is not ' this the port of the Ictii ? Ictis was clearly situated in the German ' Ocean—one of the ἰκτερίδες, or Glessariæ, where amber is engendered, ' over against Britain. Now turn to our dictionaries : Latin, glessum, ' or glæsum, amber ; French, ictère, jaundice ; Greek, ἰκτερίας, yellow.' The British amber, or jet—if that is what Mr. Surtees is thinking of —being all the while black. Anyone who is curious enough to trace questions to their original will find that all we know about British amber is contained in one short and very obscure passage in Strabo, and that it is a very hazardous conjecture that the substance mentioned by him, Lyncurion, was either amber or jet.

whether it is to be read inclusive, or exclusive, of the day of disembarkation.

We proceed to the third point; on which we are not able to arrive at our Imperial antiquary's conclusions.   After effecting his landing in the second expedition (A.U.C. 700), and capturing the British 'oppidum' on the Kentish Stour, and repulsing the attack of Cassivelaunus on his entrenchments, Cæsar crossed the Thames in pursuit of the British prince. His army forded the river at a point—

'where the landing-place opposite was defended by a palisade of sharp stakes, in front of which other stakes, driven into the bed of the river, remained hidden under the water.'

'Unfortunately, it is impossible to fix with precision the point at which Cæsar crossed the Thames. Of this we have been convinced by the researches of every kind which have been executed by the two officers, Messieurs Stoffel and Hamelin. They were assured by all the Thames boatmen that there are, at this time, eight or nine places where the river is fordable. The most favourable is at Sunbury. At Kingston, where General de Goeler fixes the passage, there is no reason for supposing that a ford ever existed. The same thing must be said of Coway Stakes. At Halliford, notwithstanding the termination of the name, the inhabitants have preserved no tradition relative to an ancient ford. The only thing which appears to us evident is that the Roman army did not cross anywhere below Teddington. It is known that this village, of which the name is derived from "Tide-end-town," marks in point of fact the last point of the Thames at which the tide is felt. It would be impossible to believe that Cæsar exposed himself to the risk of being surprised, during his passage, by the swelling of the water.' (Vol. ii. p. 191.)

We are surprised that Messrs. Stoffel and Hamelin—whom, we should imagine, the nature of their questions must have transformed, in the eyes of the Thames boatmen, into a pair of very suspicious Gallic invaders—should have brought back only the materials for a note so full of careless assertion as this. We pass over the singular simplicity (often observable in these pages) with which a cockney myth, such as we conceive the popular derivation of Teddington to be, is transformed into a serious piece of archæology. But it is curious that it did not strike a brace of able engineer officers, that the Thames has been entirely changed in character since Cæsar's time by the erection of locks.   Then, and for sixteen hundred years afterwards, it must have been, comparatively, a rapid and shallow stream down to where it met the tide, and even lower.   Now, it is a succession (speaking again comparatively) of ponds, kept at a certain height by the locks; and, especially in the neighbourhood of these locks, quite altered in level and depth.

The ford which the French officers found at Sunbury, for example, is caused by the lock immediately above it. ' Remove
' the weir,' it has been truly said, ' and Cæsar's ford at Sun-
' bury would be swept away in a twelvemonth by the scour of
' the river.' And the tide itself in all probability (in the
absence of these modern obstructions) rose considerably higher
than ' Tide-end-town.' The whole subject has been examined
with so much assiduity by Dr. Guest in a lecture delivered
recently at the Royal Institution, that we shall without scruple
borrow from his researches (the substance of them is printed in
the ' Athenæum ' of July 28 last).

With regard to Coway, with its mythical ' stakes,' which in
old times were generally supposed to settle the question, there
is in reality not much to be said. The supposed place of passage there is finely situated in the vast and beautiful meadow
immediately west of Walton Bridge, and certainly suggests to
the eye a probable spot for the movements of a disciplined
army endeavouring to cross the ford, and a host of warlike
half-savages attempting to resist them. But the river is, now-
a-days at least, narrow, rapid, and deep ; and the evidence is
trifling. Bede saw the stakes, or rather his informant, one
Nothelm, a London priest. And so did Camden. But Daines
Barrington, the antiquary, a century ago, in a very unusual fit
of common-sense, pointed out a serious objection to the theory
founded on them. The stakes—as seen by the old describers,
and as described to Barrington by a fisherman who had been
employed by some neighbouring Vandal to take up some of the
few of them which remained—were disposed in two rows *across*
the river ; those mentioned by Cæsar, *parallel* with the course
of the river. If this be so, the theory falls to the ground. Dr.
Guest has framed another, which has at least the merit of ingenuity :—

' I think,' says Dr. Guest, ' the stakes formed part of what may
be called a fortified ford, and were distributed so as to stop all transit
over the river, except along a narrow passage, which would bring
the passenger directly under the command of the watch stationed on
the northern bank to guard the ford and to receive the toll.'

This sounds so plausible that one would be glad to embrace
it ; but the difficulty is that no one, so far as we are aware, in
any part of the world, ever saw or at least described a ' fortified
' ford ' such as our antiquary has here evolved from the depths
of his own consciousness.

On the whole, however, the old guess has a nearer semblance
of truth than those which have succeeded it ; and Coway ranks

higher in the competition than Sunbury.   We will leave Dr. Guest to indicate for himself the most obvious canon of interpretation, the simplicity of which is attractive to us, in spite of Messrs. Stoffel and Hamelin.

'There is one means of arriving at a conclusion on this much-vexed question which has hitherto been neglected,—I mean the topography of the Thames valley. When we find a village or hamlet on the banks of a stream bearing a name which ends in the word *ford*, we may infer with certainty that, *at the time the name was given*, there was a ford in the neighbourhood of such village or hamlet. Such names are frequent on the upper Thames, *e.g.*, Oxford, Shillingford, Wallingford, Moulsford, &c., and even in the forest-district round Marlow we have Hurlyford ; but from Hurlyford to the sea, a distance of nearly 100 miles from the sea, taking into account the windings of the river, there is but one place on the banks of the Thames which bears a name ending in the word *ford*.   This single solitary place is Halliford, at the Coway stakes.   Cæsar says there was but one ford on the Thames — meaning, of course, the lower Thames, with which alone he was acquainted ; and we give the name of " ford " to only one place on its banks.   Our topography is in perfect agreement with his statement ; and, to my mind, this coincidence is almost decisive of the question.'

If the critic still remains unsatisfied, one additional fact may be left for his consideration, to which the Emperor, rather negligently, does not advert.   ' Cæsar's passage was made in the ' height of summer, and the season was remarkable for its ' drought : " eo anno frumentum in Galliâ propter siccitates ' " angustiùs provenerat." ' (Merivale, ' History of the Romans,' ch. x.)   We find even at Rome, Cicero complaining of the unusual heat.   The Thames, therefore, may after all have appeared less of a difficulty to Cæsar than it has to his commentators.

But we must not dally too long with a subject so tempting to a few old-world inquirers, and so little attractive, we fear, to the generality of our readers.

The Emperor does not think it necessary to go out of his way to pass moral judgments on the acts of Cæsar in achieving and maintaining his grand conquest ; for which we are by no means disposed to quarrel with him.   History conveys its own moral even the more impressively from not being accompanied with a perpetual running commentary of praise and blame.   He does not, however, shrink from signalising honestly, if not quite adequately, some of those great atrocities, exceeding even the ordinary limits of Roman severity towards obstinate opponents, by which the great chieftain of Rome showed how easily that lenity, which is commonly represented as the leading trait in his character, could be eclipsed not only by the policy of the hour but by the spirit of revenge. Thus his barbarity in cutting off the right hands of the ' heroic defenders of Uxellodunum ' is pointed out as ' an unpardonable act of cruelty, even if it had ' appeared necessary.' Of Cæsar's treatment of the Veneti— whose senators he put to death, and sold the commonalty for slaves—the author only says that ' this cruel chastisement has ' been made the subject of just reproach; nevertheless this ' great man so often gave proofs of his clemency towards the ' conquered, that he must have yielded to very powerful ' political reasons before ordering an execution so contrary to ' his habits and character.' (Vol. ii. p. 129.) Elsewhere, he quotes on the same subject the judgment of his uncle :—

' The Veneti,' says the latter, ' had not *revolted;* they had indeed given hostages. and promised to keep the peace; but they were in possession of all their freedom and all their rights. They had given Cæsar occasion to make war upon them, but not to violate the law of nations in their case, and to abuse his victory in so atrocious a manner. This conduct was not just; it was still less politic. Means like these never attain their object; they exasperate and revolt nations. The punishment of some chiefs is all that justice and policy allow.'

This passage, quoted by the nephew without comment, seems to us a marked specimen of the usual logic of conquerors. In the first place, as others have observed, Cæsar *did* attain his object: the Veneti were crushed; they never troubled Rome again. If massacre is justified where it succeeds in inspiring durable terror, this one was undoubtedly so. But no one can really see his way to the right conclusion in such matters who cannot disembarrass his mind entirely of this fatal confusion between ' policy' and 'justice,' and recognise the difficult truth that where considerations of right and wrong are once involved, considerations of policy cease in the eyes of the judge, *quà* moralist, to have any weight at all. In the next place— assuming Napoleon's own distinction, that the Veneti were not ' rebels,' but free people who had broken a treaty—what right could Cæsar have acquired to punish ' some of the chiefs,' any more than to exterminate the nation ?

The subject is thus summed up in the fourth book. After pointing out, with much clearness and force, both the merits of Cæsar's general policy of clement moderation in Gaul, and also those of his special policy in conciliating and strengthening the more powerful tribes, in order to render them the allies of Rome in keeping the peace among the others, the writer proceeds :—

' We may pardon Cæsar some acts of cruel vindictiveness, when we remember how little familiar his age was with sentiments of humanity, and how much a victorious general must have been hurt at witnessing the constant revolts against his authority of those whose oath of loyalty he had received, and whom he had crowned with honours.'

Constant revolts! One cannot but ask, with some perplexity, what constitutes a ' revolter,' and what a defender of his country? But even in the same way was the first Napoleon wont to complain, in the most touching terms, of the cruel injustice done to his motives by Spanish guerillas and Tyrolese sharpshooters; and to speak of the ungrateful return made to him by the princes of Europe whom he had excepted from his system of absorption; and even such a bitter sense of ingratitude does Prussia now experience from the unthankful conduct of the governments of Denmark, Hanover, Saxony, and Bavaria.

And, after all, there remains a strong residuum of personal motive to be detracted from the heroic composition even of the most magnanimous of conquerors. There can be little doubt that Cæsar went to Gaul, much as British conquerors have gone to India, to do the state service, but at the same time to make his own fortune in the most ignoble sense of the word. Such was the rule with Roman proconsuls in general. Some pillaged provinces of treasures and works of art. Others, like Brutus (who is of course duly held up to reprobation in these pages), accommodated their subjects with loans at usurious interest. Gaul had no treasures, and no security to offer for loans. But it had an inexhaustible fund of human material for slaves, to be obtained at the cost only of the blood of Roman legionaries. The prisoners, or a large proportion of them, constituted the commander-in-chief's share of the prize-money. For eight years Cæsar must have afforded the slave-markets of Italy their most regular and valuable supply, both in respect of quality and quantity :—

' If we are to believe Appian, Cæsar had made presents to Curio to the amount of more than 1,500 talents. And at the same time he was buying at quite as high a price the consul Æmilius Paulus, without asking anything of him in return except neutrality. It is difficult to understand how Cæsar, while paying his army, was able to make such sacrifices and to incur so many other expenses. To augment, by his largesses, the number of his partisans at Rome; to build theatres and other public monuments in the Narbonensis, and a magnificent villa near Aricia in Italy; to send rich presents to distant cities; such were his outgoings (about A.U.C. 704). How was he to find means for them by extracting the required funds from a province exhausted by eight years of war? The immensity of his resources admits, however, of explanation. Independently of the tributes paid by the conquered, which amounted, for Gaul, to forty million sesterces a year (more than seven and a half million francs, 300,000*l.*), the sale of the prisoners to Roman merchants produced enormous sums. Cicero informs us that he obtained himself twelve million sesterces (say 100,000*l.*) from the purchase-money of the captives sold after the unimportant siege of Pindenissus. If we suppose their number to have reached 12,000, this represents 1,000 sesterces (about 8*l.*) per head. Now, notwithstanding the generosity of Cæsar, who often restored his captives to the conquered tribes, or gave them away to his soldiers (as he did after the siege of Alesia), it may be admitted that 500,000 Gauls, Germans, and Britons were probably sold as slaves during the eight years of the Gaulish wars, which may have produced 500 million sesterces, or about ninety-five million francs. In reality, therefore, Roman money, furnished by the slave-dealers, formed the greatest part of the booty. Just as now, when in hostilities with distant countries European nations appropriate the produce of foreign customs to repay themselves the expenses of the war, it is, in fact, European money which makes the advances.' (Vol. ii. p. 484.)

This candid passage certainly throws light on the enormous vicissitudes of poverty and wealth which Cæsar's biographers indicate, and which have so puzzled their modern critics. In this matter Cæsar was neither better nor worse than the other leading statesmen of his day, with a few honourable exceptions only. If the great Julius was a slave-dealer, the virtuous Brutus was an usurer. 'Lucri bonus est odor ex re quâlibet' was the motto of men who stand higher in the catalogue of fame than Vespasian.

These are base realities; but they are not altogether inappropriate to our exit from that temple of false hero-worship in which the author of the 'Histoire' has sought to detain us. We have already stated, as fairly as is in our power, the real merits of the work as a contribution to political philosophy, such as they appear to us, although to a certain extent obscured by its literary deficiencies as well as by its imperfection of moral purpose. Of one merit, however, we have not as yet spoken; and it appears to us a great one: it is the gracefulness and simple dignity with which an author so highly placed has descended into the arena of ordinary literature. This may seem slight praise, but it is not so: it must be exceedingly difficult, for one thus circumstanced, to avoid at once the air of assumption and that of pretentious humility, and liberate himself altogether from that sort of constraint in which self-consciousness would naturally envelope him; but the task has been performed with perfect success. And we believe the reason to be, that characters which have certain elements of real greatness are little troubled with self-consciousness.

But, after all, the greatest pleasure which we have ourselves derived from the exercise of a reviewer's duty, in this instance, has been through the invitation which our task pressed on us to go once more for ourselves over that enchanted classical ground which the work occupies, and in the best company—that of the original authorities whom the references compel us to consult, or whom the text suggests. Many of our readers may have seen a pretty contrivance commonly exhibited on the Continent in favourite spots for hunters of the picturesque—we have noticed such at the Falls of Schaffhausen and the castle of Heidelberg—rooms fitted with glazed windows of different colours, through which in turn you take your peep at the ruin or the waterfall, until you close your inspection by looking, by way of comparison, through a pane of colourless glass. Such, we have often thought, is the effect produced on our intellectual eye by contemplating historical events through the colouring of one modern authority after another. And when we have interested or entertained ourselves for a while with gazing on the last convulsions of Republican Rome, through the violet medium of Napoleon III., or the democratic rose-colour of Arnold, or the sober tint of Mommsen, it is indeed an inexpressible relief to come to the colourless glass at last—to return to our ancient guides, who represent to us the scene as it really appeared to them and their contemporaries, not indeed free from prejudice and preoccupations of their own, but free, at all events, from what they could not have—the tendency to work up pictures for the eyes of another generation, brought up in theories derived from the extended experience of a world twenty centuries older.

ART. V.—*Felix Holt, the Radical.* By GEORGE ELIOT. 3 vols. post 8vo. London : 1866.

' FELIX HOLT ' has some of the defects of ordinary novels, but ordinary novels have none of the merits of ' Felix Holt.' The great writer who, like Madame Dudevant, adopts the ungraceful disguise of a masculine pseudonym, has, after an excursion into a foreign country and a distant age, happily returned to her own region of provincial English life, in full possession of her former vigour, of her dramatic fidelity to nature, and of her unrivalled humour. Few readers have any knowledge of a state of society which is apparently described from early recollection, aided by local tradition, but a creative imagination spontaneously produces real and living beings. Some of the inhabitants of Treby Magna and its neighbourhood are eccentric and even grotesque, but their language and their modes of thought are so natural and credible that the personages of the story seem to have a real existence. Some justly celebrated humourists produce all their effects by the more or less delicate use of caricature. Wilful exaggeration of oddities may be a legitimate comic method, but an engrained organic absurdity furnishes deeper and more lasting amusement. Mrs. Holt is not less illogical than Mrs. Nickleby, but she is not meant merely to be laughed at. The puzzled and unwilling submission of a commonplace and conceited old woman to a son who has grown out of her comprehension, is not a mere exercise of playful ingenuity, but an illustration of human experience. George Eliot takes almost excessive pleasure in recording the muddle-headed processes of dull and uneducated understandings, but she always enters into the characters which she reproduces, instead of contemplating them as subjects of farce or satire from without. The intelligent reader is conscious that if nature and circumstances had left his mind a blank, he would have thought and talked like the collier at Sproxton, even if he had not ' been obliged to give his wife a black eye, ' to hinder her from going to the preaching.' Miss Austen was as fond as her more ambitious and powerful successor of incoherent talkers, but, as all her characters occupied the same level of cultivation, she contented herself with studying various forms of intellectual imbecility. Searching deeper into the strata of society, George Eliot finds in the absence or narrowness of education a sufficient explanation of sluggish understandings and of inconsecutive arguments. With scarcely an exception her untaught or half-taught personages set logic at defiance. Her zeal for the elevation of the humbler classes is the more laudable because she has an extraordinary relish for the picturesque results of satisfied ignorance. In her fictions she always recurs by preference to the pre-scientific days, in which conscientious moral agriculturists had not yet learned the duty of extirpating flowering weeds.

In the difficult enterprise of a historical novel George Eliot has been less completely successful. In preparing to write 'Romola,' she had either read too much about Florence, or had remembered too much of what she read. The admirable development of two or three principal characters in the book is provokingly overlaid by a profusion of irrelevant learning. The judicious student, conscious of the limits of human memory, resents the assumption that he is bound to care for the minute details of Florentine life and history in the fifteenth century. It is possible that Bartolommeo Scala may have sat in his garden at the Porta di Ponte with a loose mantle over his tunic and with his 'too stately silk lucco thrown aside,' but it was not worth while to devote half a dozen pages to an ironical analysis of his little scholastic squabble with the more celebrated Politian. '" That loud-barking hound of the Lord," ' said Francesco Cei, the popular poet, " is not in Florence ' " just now. He has taken Piero de Medici's hint to carry ' " his railing prophecies on a journey for a while." ' It is necessary to explain in a note that Savonarola and the Dominicans were facetiously described as *Domini canes*, and perhaps the information is less valueless than the dialogue which proceeds to explain that a standard with a red eagle, a green dragon, and a red lily was the gonfalon of the Guelf party. Severe study is the worst possible preparation for the production of an imaginative work. The novelist and the poet ought to speak out of the fulness of the heart, as George Eliot reveals without effort the odd mysteries of custom and character which grow up in some remote Midland village. The exquisite inaccuracy of Shakspeare and of Scott belongs to the essence of historical fiction. Hector may quote Aristotle, and the contemporaries of Cœur de Lion may be sons of the companions of the Conqueror, without disturbing the illusion so harshly as when a tiresome extract from an obsolete Florentine chronicle is inserted in the dialogue of a novel. Notwithstanding drawbacks which are by some tastes regarded as attractions, 'Romola' is a wonderful performance. The whole force of the writer's dramatic genius has been concentrated on the character of Tito. The conventional villain of romance is coarse in texture by the side of the easy, good-natured, and graceful Greek adventurer, whose selfishness, untainted with malignity, passes gradually through meanness into treachery and crime.   The morbid pathology of symptoms which to a less subtle observer would indicate perfect moral health, is painful in proportion to the accuracy of the demonstration.   Under the influence of fear, as in the careless pursuit of pleasure, Tito illustrates with undeviating consistency a theory which corresponds with the theological doctrine of original sin, except that it is not universally applicable.   That an ignoble nature is incurable appears to be one of George Eliot's most habitual convictions ; and she delights to dwell on the sufferings of women under unworthy masculine supremacy. The heroic elevation of Romola herself supplies almost too glaring a contrast to the pliant smoothness of her husband. Her gloomy history may suggest the thought which is expressed by Mrs. Transome in 'Felix Holt,' 'I would not lose the ' misery of being a woman, now I see what can be the baseness ' of a man.'   The character of Savonarola is almost as remarkable a specimen of psychological analysis as the more difficult study of Tito, but nine-tenths of the personages of the story are merely figures in a pageant ; and the best proof that indigenous humour degenerates in a foreign soil is furnished by the flashy and tiresome prattle of Nello the comic barber. The last feverish struggles of Florence for republican liberty, and the half-willing martyrdom of Savonarola, retain their historical and dramatic interest after the lapse of centuries ; but lively mannerism and the ready use of familiar allusions, although they are the necessary vehicles of social gaiety, are by their nature ephemeral and perishable.   No bookish knowledge can supply the homely associations which are indispensable to humorous fiction.   One sentence of Tommy Trounsem's in ' Felix Holt ' is well worth all the pages which are allotted to the Florentine Figaro.   Scott had forgotten all the dates and the particulars of Philip de Comines's history when he reproduced with admirable fidelity the central figure of Louis XI. His imitators in England, in Germany, and above all in Italy, uniformly fall into the error of exhibiting antiquarian knowledge.   George Eliot, though far superior in genius to Manzoni, has not altogether avoided the minute pedantry which disfigures the 'Promessi Sposi.'   Her brilliant experiment ought to satisfy roving ambition, for, like Wordsworth, whom she resembles in few of her qualities, she leads but an artificial life in an unfamiliar atmosphere.

> ' Then back to Earth, the dear green Earth.
>   Whole ages here if I should roam,
> The world, for my remarks and me,
> Would ne'er a whit the wiser be ;
>   I've left my heart at home.'

In Loamshire, and at Treby Magna, there are no gorgeous processions, watched by spectators with historical names, requiring each a paragraph of description; but the sporting rector in his velveteen shooting jacket, the pompous butler in the steward's room at the manor, the retired London tradesman who tells his admiring neighbours in the country stories about Mr. Pitt, require no long explanation to make them intelligible and pleasant. The preliminary chapter, which describes a day's journey on a coach, has never been excelled as a sketch of the varieties of English town and country scenery.

George Eliot's power of constructing a fable is not equal to her skill in delineating character. Her shorter tales, as ' Silas Marner,' and the ' Scenes of Clerical Life ' have more unity and rapidity of movement than the ' Mill on the Floss,' or ' Felix Holt ;' yet the celebrated public-house conversation in ' Silas Marner ' has scarcely any connexion with the principal story. A subtle perception of motives and peculiarities perhaps tends to interrupt the continuous flow of narrative. Scott said that a favourite character, like Dugald Dalgetty, ran away with him, and in the most humorous of fictions, the story of Tristram Shandy never makes the smallest progress. By far the best part of ' Adam Bede ' consists in the proverb-like sayings of Mrs. Poyser, who has little or nothing to do with the plot. It is not surprising that a writer who has the power of drawing a typical portrait in a few strokes, is tempted to imitate the copious irregularity of Nature, instead of adhering with severe accuracy to a preconceived design. Some of the episodes of ' Felix Holt,' after a laboured commencement, end in nothing; and the legal complication which forms the framework of the story is arbitrarily disregarded in the final solution. The doubtful title to the Transome estate, although it is the subject of significant allusion in the introductory chapter, and of incessant anxiety and uncertainty through the entire course of the narrative, exercises no eventual influence on the fortunes of the principal personages. One of the triumphs of English jurisprudence consists in the mixed feeling of curiosity and awe with which it has impressed authors and more especially authoresses of fiction. The law supplies to modern novels the place of that supernatural machinery which was once thought indispensable in epic composition. Like the gods of Olympus, or the Destiny of later times, some entail or settlement operates in its relentless course, impenetrable, inexorable, and sovereignly unjust. The father of Mrs. Browning's Aurora Leigh was prevented by the will of a remote ancestor from leaving not only his landed estate but his large accumulations of personalty to his only child. George Eliot is perhaps a better lawyer than Mrs. Browning, but she appears to be almost equally incapable of understanding that perpetuities are among the few anomalies which are unknown to the law of England. ' I saw ' clear enough,' says Tommy Trounsem, the poaching bill-sticker, 'as, if the law hadn't been again' me, the Trounsem ' estate 'ud ha' been mine.' Some such vague notion that the law is opposed to the right which it constitutes, underlies many ingenious fictions. The settlement of the Transome estates was made ' a hundred years ago by John Justus Transome, ' entailing them, while in his possession, on his son Thomas and ' his heirs male, with remainder to the Bycliffes in fee.' Thomas had ' without the knowledge of his father, the tenant in pos- ' session, sold his own and his descendants' rights to a lawyer- ' cousin, named Durfey. Therefore the title of the Durfey ' Transomes, in spite of that old Durfey's tricks to show the ' contrary, depended solely on the purchase of the " base fee " ' thus created by Thomas Transome; and the Bycliffes were ' the " remainder-men," who might fairly oust the Durfey ' Transomes, if the issue of the prodigal Thomas went clean ' out of existence, and ceased to represent a right which he had ' bargained away.' Base fees and remainder-men produce a salutary feeling of respect, but the anxieties which disturbed the peaceful enjoyment of Transome Park might have been dis-sipated by careful examination of the title. Esther Lyon or Bycliffe, represented as the rightful claimant of the property, was the daughter of a Bycliffe who died as a young man in 1811 or 1812. The settlement of 1729 could only take effect for twenty-one years beyond a life in being; and consequently, even if Maurice Bycliffe, the father of Esther, was the imme-diate successor of the original remainder-man, the effect of the limitation must have expired long before 1832. During the progress of the story, on the death of Tommy Trounsem, the last descendant of Thomas Transome, Esther's claim is sup-posed to accrue. In the learned language of some former Attorney-General, 'Upon the decease of Thomas Transome, ' otherwise Trounsem, we are of opinion that the right in ' remainder of the Bycliffe family will arise, which right would ' not be barred by any statute of limitation.' On the same principle an entail might tie up property for centuries, while an intermediate tenancy descended from generation to genera-tion. The power of Thomas Transome when he was only heir in tail to cut off his own issue by a sale which was inoperative against the Bycliffes, is another illustration of Tommy's propo-sition that ' you'd better not be meddlin' wi' things belonging

' to the law, else you'll be catched up in a big wheel, and fly
' to bits.' The puzzle is additionally complicated by the
threatened treachery of the family solicitor, who has the secret
of Esther's birth and of Tommy Trounsem's pedigree. As
Mr. Jermyn had contrived to charge the estate with annuities
and mortgages in his own favour to the amount of 3,000*l.* a
year, he might have been trusted to abstain from invalidating
his own security.

The alarm which may have been caused by the description
on the title-page of Felix Holt as a Radical is relieved by the
discovery that he is neither a popular speaker nor primarily a
politician, but a social reformer. The determination of a clever
and well-educated son of a tradesman to pass through life as a
member of the working class is justly regarded by his neighbours as a crotchet, although the authoress admires his choice
and the heroine rewards it with her heart and hand. Sympathy is perhaps less subtle than satirical intuition, for
Felix Holt, though his conversation is manly, sensible, and
thoughtful, is a less masterly portrait than Tito Melema. The
virtue of wearing a cap instead of a hat, and of dispensing
with a neckcloth, is rather ostentatious than sublime. If a
man who has the power of earning a comfortable income by
the exercise of his knowledge and ability, prefers a handicraft
and weekly wages, his asceticism is as unprofitable as if it were
practised in a Trappist cell, and it involves the non-monastic
disadvantage of enforcing useless hardships on the modern
saint's wife and children. By a happy instinct George Eliot
passes over the sordid incidents which constitute the real sting
of poverty. Felix Holt converses in the tone of a gentleman
and philosopher with cultivated associates, and although he
earns a bare livelihood as a journeyman watchmaker, his time
seems to be always at his own disposal. When his mother
teazes him with her twaddle, he answers her with a joke about
' the Ciceronian antiphrasis ; ' and except as a teacher or missionary, he seems to have no social relations with his fellow-
workmen or nominal equals. He says, indeed, that he has
the stomach of a rhinoceros, so that he can live on porridge,
and he even boasts that he is not a mouse to distinguish between a wax and a tallow-candle ; but an artisan who can
amuse himself with Ciceronian figures of speech, resembles a
workman as a shepherd at the opera or in Sèvres china is like
a common farm servant. In one of her novels George Eliot
compares a feeling of moral repugnance to the dislike of a
refined temperament for a coarse odour or a flaring light ; yet

Felix Holt's contempt for the wax-taper which was necessary to Esther's comfort is represented as a proof of superiority.

If unusual schemes of life are generally fantastic mistakes, self-sacrificing devotion to the supposed good of the community is not the less a respectable rule of conduct. Esther Lyon, cultivating in a humble sphere the tastes of a fine lady, is at first shocked or startled by Felix's paradoxical bluntness, and she has always felt a kindly contempt for the pious orthodoxy of the Independent Minister whom she believes to be her father. If the nature of women is truly delineated by writers of their own sex, an overbearing spirit and a kind of masculine roughness are the qualities which above all others ensure success in love. In ordinary practice reproof and contradiction will be sparingly employed by the judicious suitor; but in novels the incivility of the hero rarely fails of its desired effect. A sensible woman might indeed extract a kind of compliment from the reproof which she has earned by some little burst of nonsense. When Felix Holt reproached Esther for real or affected frivolity, ' she resented his speech, but dis-' liked it less than many Felix had addressed to her.' ' You ' have enough understanding,' he said, ' to make it wicked that ' you should add one more to the women who hinder men's ' lives from having any nobleness in them.' In her anger, slightly modified by a sense of gratification, Esther attempts in vain a pretty and natural diversion.

' " What is my horrible guilt," she said, rising and standing, as she was wont, with one foot on the fender, and looking at the fire. If it had been any one but Felix who was near her, it might have occurred to her that this attitude showed her to advantage; but she had only a mortified sense that he was quite indifferent to what others praised her for. " Why do you read this mawkish stuff on a Sunday, for example?" he said, snatching up Réné, and running his eyes over the pages. . . . " You have no reason but idle fancy and selfish inclination for shirking your father's teaching, and giving your soul up to trifles." " You are kind enough to say so: but I am not aware that I ever confided my reasons to you." " Why, what worth calling a reason could make any mortal hang over this trash? Idiotic immorality dressed up to look fine, with a little bit of doctrine tacked to it, like a hare's foot on a dish, to make believe the mess is not cat's flesh. Look here: ' Est ce ma faute, si je trouve partout des bornes, si ce qui est fini n'a pour moi aucune valeur?' Yes, sir, distinctly your fault, because you're an ass. Your dunce, who can't do his sum, always has a taste for the infinite. Sir, do you know what a rhomboid is? Oh no, I don't believe these things with limits. ' Cependant, j'aime la monotonie des sentimens de la vie, et si j'avais encore la folie de croire au bonheur——' " " O pray, Mr. Holt, don't go on reading with that dreadful accent;

it sets one's teeth on edge." Esther, smarting helplessly under the previous lashes, was relieved by this diversion of criticism. " There it is," said Felix, throwing the book on the table, and getting up to walk about. " You are only happy when you can spy a tag or tassel loose to turn the tables, and get rid of any judgment that must carry your author after it." '

A lovers' quarrel before the conscious beginning of love has never been recorded with more delicate insight.   The vigorous and eager *secutor*, with reason and conviction on his side, finds himself constantly hampered by a cast of the net on the part of his fugitive adversary.   An argument which includes a French quotation cannot be more effectively parried, than by a complaint that that dreadful accent sets one's teeth on edge. The loose tag or tassel serves for a moment the purpose of turning the tables, but after all the victory remains with the champion of the rightful cause.   The number of women ' who ' hinder men's lives from having any nobleness in them ' would be incalculable, if potential nobleness were not almost propor- tionally rare.   Men, however, have generally some employ- ment, if it is only selling tape or drawing pleadings, beyond the limits of home.   Too many women cultivate with super- fluous care their own original narrowness, by shutting them- selves up in a circle of family interests which is but a wider form of selfish isolation.   Esther Lyon, like the ordinary reader of her history, fails wholly to understand the principle on which Felix has resolved to belong to the working classes ; but after some hesitation, and with a temporary disposition to favour a rival lover, she yields to the logic of personal attach- ment, and allows his life to be shaped according to his own ideal of nobleness.

Mr. Lyon, the simple-minded Independent Minister, is one of the most agreeable characters in the book ; and yet it is a commonplace contrivance to make a modern preacher talk in the long-winded sentences of the seventeenth century.   His involuntary contempt for the tradesmen of his congregation, and his preference of the secular reformer Felix Holt to orthodox ' church members,' relieve Mr. Lyon from the impu- tation of weak and excessive softness.   There is a pleasant fallacy in his argument that Wellington and Brougham may be introduced into sermons as properly as Rabshakeh and Balaam ; but one of his eccentric proceedings is improbable in itself, and it makes the story run capriciously off on a siding. Mr. Lyon takes advantage of a warm acknowledgment for a trifling service which he had rendered to the Tory candidate for the county, to ask Mr. Debarry to induce his uncle the

rector of Treby Magna to engage in a public discussion on
Church-government and the theory of an Establishment. The
Reverend Augustus Debarry, in defiance of all probability,
accepts the challenge, not for himself but for his curate ; and
after general expectation has been excited in the town, the
curate takes fright, Mr. Lyon is disappointed, and the whole
digression ends in nothing. It seems as if the writer had
changed her intention at the last moment, on the ground that
an ecclesiastical controversy would be an incumbrance on the
plot ; and it would have been better to pull down the scaffold-
ing when the project of the building was abandoned. Some
such abortive experiments seem to have been tried during the
development of organic life by natural selection ; but art
compensates for its inability to copy the multiplicity of Nature
by deliberate attention to unity. Mr. Lyon's desire for a public
debate is not inconceivable, but a sensible aristocratic rector
would never have indulged his fancy. If the proposal and the
subsequent failure were worth describing at all, they ought to
have formed a separate sketch in a magazine, and not an
episode or excrescence in a novel.

For the purposes of the story Mr. Lyon's time is better
employed in receiving the confidence of Mrs. Holt on the self-
denying honesty of her son. The old contrast between lofty
impulses and selfish prudence is as well illustrated by Felix
Holt and his mother as by Don Quixote and Sancho Panza ;
but, with a happy sense of the fitness of things, George Eliot
makes her hero fight with vulgar considerations of questionable profit, and not with imaginary giants. The late Mr. Holt
had left to his family the gainful secret of three specifics, which
had acquired much popularity in the neighbourhood. Having
learned enough of medicine to ascertain that Holt's Pills,
Holt's Elixir, and Holt's Cancer Cure were mere impostures,
Felix made up his mind to discontinue the sale. His mother
was naturally shocked at a decision which deprived her of her
livelihood. Her husband, as she informed Mr. Lyon, ' had a
' wonderful gift in prayer, as the old members well know, if
' any one likes to ask them not believing my words ; and he
' believed himself that the receipt for the Cancer Cure, which
' I've sent out in bottles till this very last April before Sep-
' tember as now is, and have bottles standing by me—he be-
' lieved it was sent in answer to prayer ; and nobody can
' deny it, for he prayed most regular, and read out of the
' green-baize Bible.' The profane Felix has told his mother
that she had better never open her Bible, ' for it's as bad
' poison to me as the pills are to half the people as swallow

' 'em.' Like several of George Eliot's favourite female characters, Mrs. Holt is profoundly impressed with her own
moral and religious excellence. Mr. Lyon mildly remarks
that Felix ought not to be judged rashly.

'"Many eminent servants of God have been led by ways as
strange." "Then I'm sorry for their mothers, that's all, Mr. Lyon,
and all the more if they'd been well spoken women. For not my
biggest enemy, whether it's he or she, if they'll speak the truth, can
turn round and say I've deserved this trouble. And when everybody
gets their due, and people's doings are spoken of on the house-tops,
as the Bible says they will be, it'll be known what I've gone through
with those medicines—the pounding, and the pouring, and the letting
stand, and the weighing—up early and down late—there's nobody
knows yet but One that's worthy to know; and the pasting o' the
printed labels right side upward."'

Such touches as the green-baize Bible, and the merit of letting
the medicine stand, and of pasting the labels right side upward
are only given by the hand of genius.

The story has the defect of running in two parallel lines
with only an occasional and arbitrary connexion. Mrs. Transome and her son know nothing of the world of Independent
Ministers, and, if they had heard that the son of a quack-
medicine vendor had voluntarily become a journeyman watchmaker, they would scarcely have appreciated so imperceptible
a declension in the remoter portion of the social scale. Except
in a single interview in matters connected with the election,
Felix Holt never speaks to Harold Transome, and to Mrs.
Transome his existence is probably unknown. The heroine
indeed turns out, as in many other novels, to be the heiress of
the estate, and for a time she wavers between the admirer
whom she expects to dispossess, and the stern ascetic who
requires her to take a non-celibate vow of poverty; yet it is
evident that either half of the story would have stood by itself,
if Esther Lyon had not been employed as a link between the
Minister's little house in Malthouse Yard and the stately
park with the bad title. At the beginning of the book the
docile reader thinks that he is to be exclusively perplexed and
interested by the fortunes of the Transome family, and by the
results of their past misdeeds. Mr. Sampson, the coachman,
is supposed in the introductory chapter to amuse his pas-
sengers with a vague account of the Transome baronets, summing up his narrative with the luminous remark that

'"There had been ins and outs in times gone by, so that you
couldn't look into it straight backward." At this Mr. Sampson
(everybody in North Loamshire knew Sampson's coach) would

screw his features into a primary expression of entire neutrality, and appear to aim his whip at a particular spot on the horse's flank.'

At the opening of the story, Mrs. Transome, who has long administered the affairs of her paralytic husband, awaits the arrival of her son Harold from Smyrna, where, before the recent death of his elder brother, he had made a fortune in trade.   The disappointment of the proud and energetic mother when she finds that her son intends to assume the exclusive control of the estate is described with admirable intuition into character, and with less perfect apprehension of the legal relations of the parties.   The good-natured selfishness of Harold, his contempt for the business capacities of women, his cleverness, and the obtuseness of his perception, are so elaborately delineated, that some disappointment arises when, in the course of the story, he subsides into comparative insignificance.   Mrs. Transome wishes to retain the management of the estate, not merely from a love of authority, but because she has placed herself in the power of Mr. Jermyn, the fraudulent family solicitor.   Her son, however, supersedes her without even perceiving that she is dissatisfied, and he inflicts an additional shock by announcing his intention of standing for the county as a Radical, although he might easily have been returned on the hereditary Tory principles of her family.   The necessity of employing Jermyn as agent for the election postpones the impending rupture and the consequent disclosures, and the contest forms a considerable part of the action of the story; but the paradoxical radicalism of Harold Transome leads to as abortive a result or absence of result as Mr. Lyon's projected discussion on Established Churches.   Felix Holt is convicted of riot and manslaughter at the election, on evidence which would satisfy any juryman who was not in the secret of the novel; and Harold Transome scarcely troubles himself about a defeat which leaves him at liberty to quarrel with Jermyn.   By filing a bill against the dishonest agent he produces an explosion, which might have been avoided if Harold and the author of his fictitious being had remembered that his father was alive. As long as old Mr. Transome ostensibly owned the estate of which he was tenant in possession, his resolute and active wife might have defied her son's unwelcome intrusion.   Even if Mrs. Transome had over-estimated the privileges and power of the stronger sex, Mr. Jermyn, having a common interest in supporting her administration of affairs, would not have failed to dispute the pretensions of an encroaching remainder-man. The part of the mystery which concerns the title to the estate disappoints expectation; for, although Mrs. Transome and

Jermyn had resorted to questionable methods of resisting an action of ejectment twenty years before, the Bycliffe claim had been at that time invalid, as Tommy Trounsem was still alive. Jermyn seems to have concealed from his client the strong point of her case, and to have aided her in an unintelligible plot for imprisoning Bycliffe by mistake for a total stranger. It is difficult to comprehend how a charge of forgery, whether true or false, could have divested Bycliffe's unfounded or premature claim. Bycliffe died in prison, and it was believed that his family was extinct, until half the personages in the story discovered by a cluster of simultaneous accidents that Esther Lyon was his daughter and heiress. An early intrigue between Mrs. Transome and Mr. Jermyn introduces a gratuitous and disagreeable complication. Near the close of the story Harold strikes Jermyn over the face in public, and in a scuffle which ensues Jermyn tells him 'in a grating voice, " *I am your father.*" ' The episode is equally purposeless and painful, for Jermyn disappears, Harold proposes on the same day to Esther, and ' he heard from her lips that she loved some ' one else, and that she resigned all claim to the Transome ' estates.' If Mr. Sampson had not been superseded by the railway, he might have remarked more impressively than ever, that ' there had been ins and outs in time gone by, and ' that you couldn't look into it straight backward.' Harold Transome must have looked forward with grave anxiety to the termination of twenty years from the death of Tommy Trounsem. An estate held under a verbal resignation of her rights by a woman may involve many alarming ins and outs.

Harold Transome's radical doctrines are not so amusing as the external and temporary conversion of his uncle Mr. Lingon, the Tory parson of the parish. On the night of Harold's return, over a second bottle of port, Mr. Lingon was not indisposed to persuade himself that Toryism was extinct, and that Whiggery was a ridiculous monstrosity. The next day he was less satisfied with his own arguments, but his nephew relieved his scruples, by informing him that he was a Radical only in rooting out abuses.

' " That's the word I wanted, my lad," said the Vicar, slapping Harold's knee. " That's a spool to wind a speech on. Abuses is the very word, and if anybody shows himself offended, he'll put the cap on for himself." '

When he is left to himself he reflects that—

' " It's a little awkward, but a clergyman must keep peace in a family. Confound it! I'm not bound to love Toryism better than my own flesh and blood, and the manor I shoot over. That's a heathenish, Brutus-like sort of thing, as if Providence couldn't take care of the country without my quarrelling with my own sister's son." '

Mr. Lyon's scholastic phraseology expresses more elevated sentiments, but the old-fashioned clerical gentleman is perhaps a pleasanter object of contemplation. It is right that office, and especially clerical office, should imply corresponding duties, nor indeed is it improbable that in some future generation property itself may be regarded as the salary of a public function. From an age long anterior to the Reformation till a time within living memory, a benefice was by a large portion of the clergy and of the laity regarded as a life-estate, burdened with certain definite payments in the form of ceremonial observances, as well as by a general understanding that the clergy ought to lead tolerably decorous lives. An incumbent of good income was a smaller kind of country squire, who was generally resident, unless he happened to be a pluralist. It never entered into his mind, or into the imagination of his parishioners, that he had undertaken to be a rural missionary, or to visit from house to house. His modern successor, like himself, conforms to the public opinion of his time, not without some good results, and not with unmixed moral gain to himself. The English clergy of former times were entirely exempt from a desire to aggrandise the Church, inasmuch as they valued their position as gentlemen far more highly than any privileges of the priesthood. They were also exceptionally free from the sacerdotal propensity to work on the feelings of women, because in the ordinary intercourse of society, on the bench of magistrates, and in the management of local business, they had their fair share of nfluence with men. George Eliot, who perhaps inclines to Mr. Lyon's revolutionary doctrines on church establishments, always dwells with affectionate minuteness on the peculiarities of the old-fashioned parson. In ' Felix Holt ' there are two well-born specimens of the class, Mr. Debarry being somewhat more refined than his neighbour. Mr. Lingon's electioneering speech in support of his nephew is a model of bucolic rhetoric It is not surprising that the Tory farmers in the neighbourhood were heartily amused by their favourite parson's transparent assumption of a new-fangled creed.

'"Come, now, you'll say I used to be a Tory, and some of you, whose faces I know as well as I know the head of my own crabstick, will say that's why I'm a good fellow. But now, I'll tell you something else ; it's for that very reason—that I used to be a Tory and am a good fellow—that I go along with my nephew here, who is a thorough-going Liberal. For will anybody here come forward and

say, " A good fellow has no need to tack about and change his road."
No, there's not one of you such a Tom Noddy. What's good for one
time is bad for another. If anyone contradicts that, ask him to
eat pickled pork when he's thirsty, and to bathe in the Lapp
there when the spikes of ice are shooting. And that's the reason
why the men who are the best Liberals now are the very men who
used to be the best Tories. There is not a nastier horse than your
horse that'll jib and back, and turn round, when there is but one
road for him to go, and that's the road before him. And my nephew
here—he comes of a Tory breed, you know. I'll answer for the
Lingons. In the old Tory times there was never a pup belonging
to a Lingon but would howl if a Whig came near him. The Lingon
blood is good rich old Tory blood, and that's why, when the right
time comes, it throws up a Liberal cream. There's plenty of Radical
scum. I say, beware of the scum and look out for the cream. . . .
Harold Transome will do you credit. If anybody says the Radicals
are a set of sneaks; Brummagem halfpennies; scamps who want to
play at pitch and toss with the property of the country; you can
say, " Look at the Member for North Loamshire." And mind what
you'll hear him say; he'll go in for making everything right—
Poor laws, and Charities, and Church—he wants to reform 'em all.
Perhaps you say, " There's that Parson Lingon talking about
Church reform—why he belongs to the Church himself—he wants
reforming too." Well, well, wait a bit, and you'll hear by and by
that old Parson Lingon is reformed; shoots no more; cracks his
joke no more; has drunk his last bottle; the dogs, the old pointers,
'll be sorry, but you'll hear that the Parson at Little Treby is a new
man.—That's what Church reform is sure to come to before long. So
now here are some more nuts for you, lads, and I leave you to listen
to your candidate.—There he is—give him a good hurray. Wave
your hats, and I'll begin—Hurray!"'

The farmers were quite right in giving the parson a 'friendly
hurray' before he began.

' " Let's hear what Old Jack will say for himself," was the predominant feeling among them; " he'll have something funny to say,
I'll bet a penny."'

If the North Loamshire election fails to assist the progress
of the story, it displays the writer's extraordinary knowledge of
out-of-the-way modes of English thought, and her dramatic
faculty of giving life to the most insignificant character. The
address of a Radical agent to the colliers of Sproxton, assembled
for their Sunday drinking, is exactly adapted to the peculiar
minds of the audience. One of the colliers had heard that it
was the time to get beer for nothing, and his companion sagely
infers, ' That's sin the Reform—that's brought the 'lections
' and the drink into these parts; for afore that it was all kep
' up the Lord knows where.' Eloquence, however, even when

seasoned with beer, is an enjoyment too purely intellectual for the Midland collier mind.

' " Let's have our pipes then," said Old Sleck, " I'm pretty well tired o' this." " So am I," said Dredge, " it's wriggling work, like following a stoat : it makes a man dry. I'd as leef hear preaching, ony there's nought to be got by 't. I shouldn't know which end I stood on if it wasn't for the tickets and the treatin'." '

The best and wisest inhabitant of Treby on the whole displays the smallest amount of common sense. Felix Holt, who had been endeavouring to persuade the colliers to send their children to school, is indignant at the attempt of his own party to employ his sluggish disciples for purposes of riot. On the election day he takes command of a riot, for the sole purpose of leading the rioters out of mischief, and from the same motive he trips up and accidentally kills a constable who attempts to interfere with the proceedings. He is more fortunate than he deserves in obtaining a pardon on the application of the magistrates headed by the Tory and Radical candidates ; but the story was coming to an end ; Esther had, after some wavering, determined to refuse Harold Transome; and Felix was required to accept the hand which had long awaited his condescension. It is impossible to judge, from any summary of the plot, of the abundance of thought and humour which more than compensate for any complications or improbabilities in the story. Mrs. Transome's old attendant, with her cynical philosophy of life, forms a life-like and remarkable portrait, although her character is only indicated in one or two short conversations with her mistress ; and the farmers and tradesmen who visit the butler at the Manor are each distinguished by some natural and recognisable peculiarity. Less original writers identify their minor characters by some trite or cant saying, but George Eliot always denotes the intellectual or moral differences of the dullest and most commonplace of mankind by some little idiosyncrasy of language or of thought. If ' Felix Holt ' has none of the tragic depth of ' Romola,' it is a truer picture of life, and the changes which have occurred since the date of the story almost give the book a historical value.

ART. VI.—1. *Das Leben Jesu : für das deutsche Volk bearbeitet.* Von D. F. STRAUSS.   Leipzig : 1864.

2. *Dr. D. F. STRAUSS'S ' New Life of Jesus : '* the authorised English Edition.   2 vols.   London : 1865.

3. *Histoire des Origines du Christianisme; Livre deuxième :* *'Les Apôtres.'*   Par ERNEST RENAN.   Paris : 1866.

4. *' Ecce Homo:' a Survey of the Life and Work of Jesus Christ.* Fifth Edition, with a new Preface.   London : 1866.

IT was said a great many centuries ago, and in a book of very high authority, that one result of the coming of Christ into the world would be ' that the thoughts of many hearts should ' be revealed.'   And though such a result is not without its parallels and analogies in other cases, there is no other case in which either the disclosures of men's characters have been so searching and profound, or in which the effect has been so certainly repeated whenever a fresh interest has been awakened in the person and history of the great Teacher.   The consequence is, that no epochs are better adapted for taking a review of the state of religious opinion than those in which popular attention has been strongly fixed upon the ' Life of Christ.' With other religious questions it is possible to fence and play, and act a part, whether in defence or opposition, as the case may be ; feeling all the time, with the mediæval disputant, how easy it might be to shift one's ground and take up the brief for the other side.   But this question is too closely intertwined with men's personal feelings and hopes for that.   It is no matter of gladiatorial display.   It is a matter of life and death. And, therefore, interesting as it may always be, even at times when men are following each other like a flock of sheep along some narrow path of dogma, to try and understand the meaning of the dogma which unlocks the history of their period, that interest culminates at times when the life of Jesus is in question—when men are thoroughly alive, and thoroughly in earnest ; when reserve and reticence are broken through ; and when the books, reviews, and pamphlets of any one year may easily offer (as it were, in section) a complete conspectus of all the main lines of contemporary thought.

Such a period, there can be no doubt, is our own.   Never since the time of the Reformation—never, one might almost say, since the time of the Apostles—has a more earnest attention been paid to the life of Jesus than at the present moment. There have been controversies without number as to His nature,

confusions without end as to His doctrine, conflicts interminable about His Church, but to the present generation (strange
to say) seems to have been bequeathed the task of arranging
in an intelligible form the facts of His purely human history.
The reason probably is, that never before have systems of
belief foreign, yet analogous, to Christianity been so clearly
understood, or so much vigorous intelligence been diverted
from policy and war to a critical handling of classical, and still
more of Oriental, modes of thought. Thus the desire of understanding the origin of Christianity, and the means of gratifying
that desire, seem to have presented themselves simultaneously :
and the impatience of mankind will bear no compromise, and
take no refusal, until theologians have fairly girded themselves
to the task of presenting the human life of Jesus in some
strictly historical shape.

The difficulty of this task is probably least understood by
those who most loudly make the demand. Were an invasion
of England to shatter at one blow the framework of the State,
to destroy the metropolis, and involve in common ruin the civil
and ecclesiastical institutions of the country, it is not likely
that for the next thirty or forty years, at least, much literary
activity would be displayed, or any work be bequeathed to
posterity except writings intended for an immediate practical
purpose. But if by chance some fragment or offshoot of the
National Church had vigour enough to outlive the catastrophe,
its first energies would be devoted to collecting the memorials
of its earlier and more tranquil days, and especially to forming
into a sort of canon for future reference all the writings which
a hasty criticism could select as the genuine relics of its first
founders. In fact, no course at such a time could be more consonant to sound sense and simple fidelity. But the crisis which
we have supposed was far exceeded in severity by that fearful
crash which ruined the Jewish State, destroyed the Temple,
and scattered the population of Judæa, not very long after the
first preaching of the Gospel. For the small geographical scale
of Palestine—a country about as large as Wales—rendered
the calamity more intense by concentrating it in that narrow
area, and the furious passions that blazed out at the revolt
would not for a long time cool down to the temperature of
literary composition. Moreover, in this case, the inhabitants
of the country were sown broadcast over the world. Every
slave-market in three continents was full of them. And although
it is true that these outcasts would find synagogues and settled
communities of Jews wherever they went, still, the blow
having crushed the political and religious hopes of all alike —

with the sole exception of the Christian sect — it is likely that the only efforts of the pen which would be left from this epoch would be, on the one hand, Jewish and Christian collections of existing traditions, with occasional reflective attempts to find a key to the terrible events of the past; and, on the other, fugitive pieces of a hortatory or polemical character. Now this is exactly what we do find. The Mishna and the New Testament are the collection of traditions, written or otherwise. Josephus' History at Rome, St. John's Gospel at Ephesus, and probably the fourth Book of Esdras in the far East, are works of reflection, searches for the key to the past. And the remains of apostolical fathers and of Judæognostic heretics are specimens of pieces inspired by a special purpose, and singularly barren of any important historical materials. When we add to all this the fact, that just at this period of the world, amid the slow but sure advance of universal decrepitude and decay, the most singular rage had seized mankind for pseudonymous composition, we have said enough to indicate that the historian of those times must walk warily, and be prepared to forego too hasty generalisations, and that the demand for a prompt and unimpeachable account of all that Jesus and His Apostles did and said is made in profound ignorance of the real conditions of the problem.

Still, men are always to be found, armed with more or less of learning and critical acumen, who will be prepared straightway to give an answer to the most impossible questions. To them patience seems no scientific virtue at all. And when they have lit upon some plausible solution of their problem, open at a hundred points to fatal assaults, disdaining to hold it as a mere hypothesis rough-hewn for after rectification, they must needs impose it upon the world as the one and only possible key to the whole question. In a word, they dogmatise. And strongly as both of them would repudiate the charge, we are sorry to be obliged to fix upon M. Renan as well as upon Herr Strauss this odious imputation of *dogmatism.* If it is dogmatism to found one's whole argument upon an *ipse dixit,* if it is dogmatism to state boldly as an axiom what is so far from being self-evident that it is denied by the whole opposing party, and if it is dogmatism to select for this axiom the very point which, clothed in other words, is the proposition to be proved, then MM. Renan and Strauss are dogmatists. For while the very point in dispute is, whether Jesus was a superhuman personage or not, both of these writers lay it down as the first postulate in their argument that no superhuman hypothesis is admissible. Their argument therefore

becomes neither more nor less than a vicious circle.   The
Gospels are untrustworthy, because they record miracles ; and
no miracles are credible, because the books that record them
are untrustworthy.*   It is wonderful that men of so much
ability should be guilty of such false logic, and should at this
time of day be beguiled by the threadbare sophism of Hume,
of which Strauss thinks so highly as to say : ' Hume's treat-
' ment of miracles is so universally convincing, that by it the
' matter may be considered as virtually settled.' (P. 148.) Yet
Hume's celebrated argument is a mere *petitio principii.*   All
experience [i. e. for the most part, testimony of others], being
against miracles, it is more likely that testimony should be false
than that miracles should be true.   Which is the same thing as
saying, ' All experience being against Atlantic cables, it is far
' more likely that Messrs. Glasse and Field are playing upon our
' credulity than that the cable should be laid.'   The reply of
course is, But the cable *is* laid, for we have the results in our
hands : and your argument from ' experience ' is good for
nothing, for unless it carefully keeps the experience of Messrs.
Glasse and Field out of sight, it is inconclusive ; and if it
does, it amounts to saying, ' The experience of all, *except those*
' *who have had the experience*, is against Atlantic telegraphs.'
Just so the Christian apologist may reply : ' Your argument
' against miracles is futile : for not only are results in our
' hands, which cannot be otherwise accounted for, but the " ex-
' perience " you appeal to begins by excluding the experience
' of Matthew, Mark, Luke, and John, and then of course the
' desired conclusion follows of itself.'†

---

* Compare, for instance, the following passages :—(1.) ' So long as
' the Gospels are regarded as historical sources, in the strict sense
' of the word, so long a historical view of the life of Jesus is impos-
' sible ' (*Strauss*, p. 40) ; for ' historical enquiry refuses absolutely
' to recognise anywhere any such thing ' as a miracle.   (P. 146.)
(2.) ' In the person and work of Jesus nothing supernatural hap-
' pened ; . . . for thus much we can soon discover about our
' Gospels, that neither all nor any of them display such historical
' trustworthiness as to compel our reason to the acceptance of a
' miracle.' (P. xv.)
  Similarly M. Renan :—(1.) ' The first twelve chapters of Acts are
' a tissue of miracles. Now, an absolute rule of criticism is, to allow
' no place in historical narration to miracles.' (P. xliii.).   (2.) ' Show
' me a specimen of these things, and I will admit them. . . . . The
' *onus probandi* in science rests with those who allege a fact.' (P. xlv.)
  † The subject of Miracles has recently been handled with extraordinary acuteness and force of reasoning by the Rev. Mr. Mozley,

It is quite clear, therefore, that if these books of MM. Strauss and Renan are to receive that estimation which is, in some respects, justly due to them, they must be taken apart from the ridiculous premiss on which they are professedly based, and judged with as little reference to it as possible. The childish simplicity must be forgiven of such passages as these : ' By miracles like that of feeding the multitudes, &c., ' *natural science* would be rased to its foundations ' (*Strauss,* p. 39)—(that it would be much put out by a *super*-natural event we should quite expect) ; and ' if Jesus had not become ' transformed by legend, He would be an *unique phenomenon* ' in history ' (*Renan, Vie de J.,* p. xlvi.)—(which is precisely, what Christians maintain Him to have been). The prerogative of the Almighty to address men through the senses, if it should seem good to Him to do so, must be dogmatically re-affirmed (for one piece of dogmatism is just as good as another) ; and these works must be studied, not for their arbitrary marshalling of texts in parody of the simple and noble delineation of Christ's life in the Gospels, but for their valuable aid towards realising the *human side* in His being, who was (under every hypothesis) ' very man ' ; and especially for their meritorious contributions towards setting it in an intelligible framework, and pointing out those nearer links of connexion with previous and subsequent history which alone were wanting to substantiate the Christology of the Church. For it must be remembered, the Catholic doctrine has ever affirmed that Christ was a link *in* history, not out of it : a link heated to whiteness, it may be, and imparting that heat, but a link of precisely the same materials, and occurring in the same historical order, as the rest—' perfect man,' and coming ' in the ' fulness of times.' And therefore, when writers, such as those in question, take much pains to display the preparation of the world for Christianity, and the strangely inflammable state of the materials which it enkindled, they may perhaps do so with no more kindly intention than to suggest how little wonderful was the conflagration that ensued ; but they are nevertheless unconsciously doing the Church's work. It is not their affirmations, but their negations which she repudiates. And she can well afford to receive, with full acknowledgments, all that they bring ; for the convictions by which Christians lay hold

---

in his Bampton Lectures for last year. We know of nothing more able or more eloquent in our theological literature, and we would especially point out the Fourth Discourse, in which the writer proves that a belief in the possibility of miracles is identical with, and inseparable from, a belief in a personal God.

of the Divine side of the question, and put themselves into personal relationship with Christ, are of another order altogether, and are but little affected by negative criticism.

The fact is, that in disentangling profound and intricate problems, everything depends on the quarter from which they are approached. The solar system, so long as it was viewed from the earth as a centre, was an inextricable web of confusion ; but directly a standing-point for the imagination was found in the sun, everything fell at once into its right place. In so complex and subtle a question as that of the truth of Christianity, this is still more surely the secret of success. The question is one which addresses neither the reason alone, nor the imagination alone, nor the conscience alone. It is, in its essence, an ethical question. But, making pretensions to stand upon the solid ground of historical fact, it is inevitably mixed up with matters of a secondary interest—points of criticism, various readings, and other documentary questions—and becomes subject to the demands of the imagination, that its origin and history be presented in a readily conceivable form. But it makes all the difference in the world whether a man begin by entangling himself amid petty critical details, or by determining at all costs to satisfy the imagination,—or whether he begin by grasping the central object of the whole system by an ethical process, and then endeavour to arrange, in the best way that circumstances admit, the intellectual and pictorial details. Christianity itself makes no pretensions to be understood by either of the former methods. It is no fault of the Gospel if men will persist in approaching it from the wrong quarter, and make confusion worse confounded in the attempt. For it emphatically claims to be, not a revelation to philosophers, but to babes ; and no words can more distinctly point out the right clue than its own :—' If any man will do ' His will, he shall know of the doctrine, whether it be of God, ' or whether I speak of myself.'

Now, it is precisely this clue which both MM. Strauss and Renan have entirely missed, and which the author of ' Ecce Homo ' has, with admirable judgment and surprising success, taken up. Strauss's ' New Life of Jesus ' is not indeed so purely a dry intellectual feat as the original work, which in 1835 startled the world by its audacious attempt to sift the Gospels into a heap of barren rubbish. Fired by the rapid popularity of M. Renan's Galilæan idyll, and stung by the persistent refusal of the educated classes to acknowledge themselves brought over to his views, he now appeals to ' the ' German people,' works up his sifted particles afresh into a concrete but lifeless figure—that could never have converted anybody, much less the world—and ends by arranging in little heaps of (so-called) legendary matter the large proportion of the Gospel narrative, which is rejected as fictitious because it is miraculous. Thus Strauss, too, like Renan, finds himself compelled, in the earnest prosecution of his studies, to draw sensibly nearer towards Christianity. The Christ of his later work is a far more real and tangible personage than the faintly-sketched and misty figure that floated as a possible residuum of fact amid the hallucinations, myths, and forgeries of which the former book was full. Here we have the whole of Part I., comprising no less than 150 closely-printed pages, devoted to the real and historical Jesus of Nazareth, as the author conceives him to have actually lived and died. And though an equal space, it is true, is given to a critical introduction of very high interest, and a far larger number of pages to an elaborate classification of no less than twelve groups of myths, arranged in their respective imaginary layers, yet the concessions made in these 150 pages are so important, and the reality of Christ's earthly history as described by the Evangelists is, in its main features, so candidly confessed, that we seem to have here restored to us almost all that was worth contending for.

Jesus of Nazareth, then—according to Herr Strauss's latest and most advanced criticism of his human history—was a Galilæan peasant of the lower orders, himself a carpenter and the son of a carpenter, and quite devoid of any education except such as he would gather for himself from an assiduous study of the Old Testament, and from observation of the curiously-mingled society around him.

' Neither in the substance nor in the method of Jesus' teaching is there anything which—always bearing in mind his inward endowments—we cannot explain by supposing a careful study of the Old Testament and a free social intercourse with learned people, especially with the disciples of the three leading schools [Pharisees, Sadducees, Essenes] : while, on the other hand, his originality, freshness, and freedom from every trace of school-pedantry, (such as stamps so unmistakeably even the spiritual Apostle of the Gentiles,) render it probable that his development was still more independent of extrinsic aid even than that. And to this no circumstances could be more favourable than those of his Galilæan home. The inhabitants of that region, it is well known, were — especially in the Northern parts—much mixed up with the heathen; as is plainly confessed in the epithet " Galilee of the Gentiles " (Matt. iv. 15, following Isaiah viii. 23). And since the province was, yet farther, cut off by the whole breadth of Samaria from the proudly orthodox

Judæa, its natives were looked down upon as of little worth, and not regarded as Jews in the strict sense of the word. Yet these very untoward circumstances might contribute all the better to the formation of a free religious character.' (P. 194.)

Indeed the circumstances in question were themselves—as Strauss takes great pains to make us understand—the fruits of a long preparation in antecedent history.

'I know not whether any supernatural origin that men may ascribe to Christianity can really do it more honour, than is done by history—in proving how it is the ripe fruit of all the best growths in every branch of the human family. Never would Christianity (we may safely say) have become the religion of the West as well as of the East—nay, have remained in the end more peculiarly a Western faith—if it had not, from the very first, breathed a Western as well as an Eastern, a Græco-Roman as well as a Jewish spirit. Israel must first be brayed in the mortar, the Jewish people must first by repeated captivities be scattered among the heathen, that so the irrigating streams of foreign thought might be conducted by many a channel upon the mother soil, ere it could be fecundated so far as to produce from its bosom such a harvest as Christianity. And above all, a marriage of the East and the West must take place by the conquests of the great Macedonian hero, and a bride-bed (as it were) be laid in Alexandria, before any such appearance as that of Christianity could be thought of. Had there been no Alexander for a forerunner, Christ could not have come. This may sound a hard saying for theological ears. But directly we become convinced that even the Hero has a divine mission, it loses all its offensiveness. . . . Thus we see, as it were, two converging lines, each lengthening itself by inner forces of its own, yet each destined at last to meet in that one point which should become the birthplace of the new religion. And would we express in one short formula the law of these two apparently opposing yet really co-operating forces, we may put it thus : Judæa, in all the stages of its history, sought God ; Greece sought man.' (P. 167.)

No one who remembers Mr. Gladstone's eloquent expansion of this thought, in his late farewell speech at Edinburgh, needs to be reminded that all this is thoroughly Christian and even Churchman-like. Nay, to deny it would be downright heresy. For it is taught in every Catechism and Manual of Church History; it is stated in plain terms by the deepest thinkers of antiquity ; and it is itself the direct fulfilment of many a noble passage of Hebrew prophecy, which shrinks not from giving a divine mission to a Cyrus, a Melchizedek, a Jethro, a Job, a Hazael, a Nebuchadnezzar, and looks forward gladly to the day when ' Israel shall be the third with Egypt and with ' Assyria: whom the Lord shall bless, saying, Blessed be

' Egypt my people, and Assyria the work of my hands, and
' Israel my inheritance.' (Isaiah xix. 24.)

With the exception of these few facts, however, in the early
life of Jesus, Strauss finds nothing very trustworthy until we
arrive at his baptism by John. At this point his real history
begins. That he was baptised by John, and remained with
him for a short time, there can be no reasonable doubt. But
John, like the hermit Banus at a later period, to judge from
the descriptions of both given by Josephus, was a sort of independent Essene, whose rigorous asceticism and rugged re-
proachful method of address soon became distasteful to one of
so cheerful and social, of so courteous and merciful, a temper
as Jesus. Still the aim of both was the same, though their
methods were different. ' Repent ye, for the kingdom of
' heaven is at hand; ' this was the voice which resounded in
the wilderness among the crowds of excited and expectant
Jews. And it meant (says Strauss) nothing more or less than
this: that the Messiah was about to appear, but that his appearing would bring good only to those whose *hearts* were preparing for his coming; while to the rest he would be like a
winnowing fan, separating the chaff for the burning (p. 189).

Now all this, again, is precisely what the Church has always taught. And if she has chosen to clothe her statement
of it in words culled from Isaiah and Malachi, we really do not
see how it makes any difference in the facts. The facts remain—so far as we can understand—uncontested : that John
the Baptist was, in plain words, a forerunner of the Messiah ;
that, unlike all his contemporaries, he was inspired with the
idea that the true preparation for him was, not the purchasing
of daggers or the broadening of phylacteries, but the conversion
of the heart ; and that while he was thus foremost among the
files of the Jewish prophets, still he was less clear in his assurance that Jesus was that Messiah, and more open to offence
at his new methods of procedure, than the least of those who
had actually attached themselves to his person. Add to all
this—what seems likewise allowed—that he actually foretold
what soon after came to pass: viz. that those who rejected
the Messiah would be utterly and fearfully destroyed, while
the remnant that accepted him would form the germ of a great
future organisation, subject in some way to his sovereignty ;
and we really do not know what Churchmen could ask for
more from Mr. Strauss.

The next scene acknowledged to belong to the genuine history of Jesus is his Galilæan ministry; the duration of which
could not have been more than a few years, for even Tacitus

(Annals, xv. 44) places his crucifixion under Pontius Pilate, whose procuratorship ended A.D. 36. During these few years, and with the means at his command which have been already described, it somehow or other came to pass that this Galilæan carpenter made such an impression on his contemporaries, that they almost unanimously hoped, or feared, he was the Messiah; that they came to attribute to him the most astonishing miracles: that, so far from being brought to their senses by his crucifixion, they got it into their heads that he was risen from the dead, and had conversed, walked, and eaten with several of those who had known him best before; nay, that on subsequent reflection they felt nothing could possibly account for his greatness short of some theory which made him positively divine,—a theory for which they found no precedent or authority whatever in Judaism, but were obliged to shape it by the help of Alexandrian Platonism, whose line of thought converged exactly at the right moment upon that precise spot. Yet we are constantly reminded, it was with the most consummate wisdom and genius (to say the least) that Jesus managed to produce these results. The Messiah of the popular imagination was no Man of Sorrows meekly riding on an ass; but a warrior, a good hater of the Romans, a zealot like Judas the Gaulonite. He was to be no ' Son of Man,' but a ' Son of God,'—a human hero, that is, like David and Solomon of old; armed with God's fury and God's arrows against the heathen, who had run up such a score of vengeance in captivities, taxations, and oppressions of all sorts upon Jehovah's favourites, that it was a perfect marvel—under which none but a cold-blooded Sadducee could sit still—that the crack of doom was delayed so intolerably long. Amid such an atmosphere as this it was that Jesus had to work; and out of this red-hot seething mass of Jewish fanaticism, by a—we must not say ' divine: ' let us say—*skilful* blow, to forge the Christian Church. Let us see how he went to work.

' It is the life of a wandering teacher that the Evangelists with one consent attribute to Jesus. Capernaum, the home of his favourite disciples, was indeed his frequent resort: but for the most part he traversed the country attended by a company of trusted disciples and of women who provided for the wants of the society out of their own resources.' (P. 243.) ' That Jesus as a teacher made an overpowering, and upon sympathising souls an ineffaceable, impression, is not only told us by the Evangelists, but is ratified by the historical results. He was no Rabbi. He taught not as the Scribes. With logical artifices he had nothing to do; but only with the word that smites conviction by its own intrinsic truth. Hence in his Gospels that rich collection of sentences or maxims, of terse and pregnant sayings which, apart from their religious worth, are for their clear spiritual insight and for their straight unerring aim so beyond all pride. "Render unto Cæsar the things that be Cæsar's," &c.,—these are imperishable sayings; because in them truths, that experience is ever ratifying afresh, are clothed in a form which is at the same time precisely expressive and also universally intelligible.' (P. 253.) 'The consciousness of a Prophetic mission arose in him before that of his Messiahship. Or rather we may well conceive that Jesus, while himself clear upon the point, chose in speaking to others an expression [Son of man] which was not yet in vogue as a title for the Messiah. Thus he avoided imposing upon his disciples and the people a mere authoritative belief in his Messiahship, but allowed it to grow up spontaneously from within. . . . The more so, as he found reason to fear that by giving himself out at once for the Messiah he should wake up all those political hopes, which bore a sense diametrically opposite to that in which alone he would consent to be Messiah.' (P. 227.) 'Meanwhile, however much Jesus might decline any corporeal miracles, do them he must—according to the ideas of that time—whether he would or no. So soon as ever he was held to be a Prophet, at once he was credited with miraculous powers : and no sooner was he credited with them, than they were sure to appear in reality. It were strange if, among the crowds that approached to touch his garments wherever he came, none found a cure or an alleviation of his disease from an excited imagination or from a strong sensuo-spiritual impression. And the cure was then attributed to the wonder-working power of Jesus.' (P. 265.)

For ourselves, we are content with such admissions as these from the greatest living master of the modern destructive criticism. No one in his senses, who is not the victim of some preconceived idea, can possibly go so far as this, and not soon be compelled to go a good deal farther. He may not indeed be able to embrace—until, at least, he understands their real meaning—the barbarisms that have been bequeathed to us by the scholastic philosophy. He may disdain to pronounce aright the Shibboleth of a mere Latin orthodoxy, entangled in dry legalisms, stupefied with forensic fictions, and catholic in nothing but the name. He may not picture heaven and earth to his imagination as they once were pictured, or conceive of Christian miracles in the childish way which M. Renan supposes to be the only one the Church allows, viz. as ' special interventions, like ' that of a clock-maker putting his finger in, to remedy the defects ' of his wheels.' (*Apôtres*, p. xlvii.) He may have seen, in short, that the lessons of the Bible and of Theology are learnt, like all other really effective lessons, in an order which is educational rather than philosophical ; and that the true order of thought reverses the order of the lesson-book. But that very enfranchisement of his mind from the preconceptions of the nursery renders him less willing to be bound by the mere dogmas of the lecture-room. And unless he is content meekly to stop short just where Strauss has drawn the line, at a conception of ' a mere individual genius, designed (when fuel enough ' has been collected) to apply the enkindling spark ' (p. 167); or immures his thought within some Hegelian pantheism, that (like the witch of Endor) conjures up gods out of the earth, instead of bringing down God from heaven; he will not be warned off from the yet farther and deeper inquiry, ' *who* then ' designed ' all these converging lines ? and *whence* came that clear unerring mind, that pure and guileless spirit, which, in Christ the ' corner-stone,' completed all, gave a meaning to all, and by the master-stroke of a few years' work in long-prepared Galilee created Christendom ?

These are the points which it really concerns us to know. And they are points upon which the bewildered philosophy of MM. Strauss and Renan has absolutely no answer to give. For they cannot surely mean to tell us that Christ is only the ultimate development of forces latent in the mushroom and the sponge: that he is the product of an unconscious series, pushing outwards towards consciousness and rationality ; a series calculated by no pre-existing Mind, a product brooded over by no life-giving spirit. Why, the very sponge and the mushroom, the icthyosaurus and the plants of the coalmeasures, the light of the nebulæ and the serial law itself, all reveal a Reason human in quality, but ante-human in time, and super-human in degree, and presenting not the slightest indications of development or change of any sort. Now this all-embracing and changeless Reason is what Theology means by God: and the arrangements by which, at crossing-places in their orbits, man's world is met and illumined by phenomena belonging to another zone, and moving in another plane, are what she terms Miracles. And knowing, as we do, nothing whatever about God, except what He pleases to reveal to us,—and impotent as our imagination is (by the very laws of its nature) to project any sane conception of God upon its mirror, except under a personal form,—when we find a point in history at which a Person stands, who ' shines out as a ' thoroughly and intrinsically lovely nature, who needed only ' to unfold himself from himself, to grow to greater con- ' sciousness of himself, greater confidence in himself, with no ' need for change of aim, no need of self-correction ' (*Strauss,* p. 208); and when we know, from nineteen centuries' experience, how the spirit of this single Person has poured through all the veins of human society a fresh and vital force, given hope to publicans and sinners of all time, redeemed men's souls from the swine-troughs of sense, and shown for once the highest ideal of man clothed in actual flesh and blood,— we challenge anyone to produce a more rational theory about this Person than that which has obtained currency in the Christian Church ; or to point out any bar which a mature and philosophical conception of God presents against regarding this unique Person as an incarnation of the Divine Reason upon earth.   For all that is required to be conceded, in order to stamp this conception with perfect credibility, is that Pantheism be false and Theism true : in other words, that the distinction between moral good and moral evil be held a real one ; and that the convergence of all the lines of history to produce a human conductor of heaven's light and life to earth has been the work of a conscious Reason, and not of a mere blind force which explains nothing, but rather begs humbly for explanation itself.

How then do these writers manage to escape a—to them— wholly undesired conclusion ? They have invented two devices, two loopholes, the most extraordinary and unscientific (as it appears to us), that ever were proclaimed in the name of science as breaches in the fortress of religion.   And these loopholes they labour, by every manœuvre in their power, incessantly to enlarge.   Reason having tried her utmost against Christianity in vain, the assault is now to be attempted through the imagination.   And while the ridicule is unsparing which, in his earlier work, Strauss heaped on the worn-out methods of the rationalists, we may safely predict that the time is not far distant when the same measure will be as deservedly meted out to himself, and to M. Renan, who is mainly responsible for the second of the two remarkable arguments we are about to describe.

Everyone is perfectly aware that by the laws of our imagination, every scene which is impressed upon the retina of our eye, every sound which is carried through the nerves of the ear, receives a colour, shape and meaning, from the living and personal qualities of the recipient.   It is impossible that it should be otherwise.   A living human brain is not like a dead sheet of paper, which passively receives and helplessly retains everything that may happen to be marked upon it.   It is only by a process of selection and grouping, in accordance with habits and qualities given by education and nature, that coherent images are formed and sane conceptions engendered. If anyone doubt this, let him only watch the spontaneous

effort of his mind, when some object presents itself in the dusk
or in the distance, to mould it into an intelligible shape, and he
will catch himself (as it were) in the very act of conception.
The colour, the outline, the motion, the top part, the bottom
part, will be spontaneously selected for attention; and some
person previously known, some hobgoblin previously believed
in, some animal thought likely to be there, will be created out
of the impressions given, and be projected without a moment's
delay upon the imagination.   Now this, which in its proper
proportions is a scientific truth, is seized upon by Mr. Strauss,
exaggerated into the most enormous and grotesque extravagance, and then employed as an engine to overthrow the truth
of Christianity.   The Jewish mind (he says) in the first century was full of Old Testament ideas.   The Prophets and the
Mosaic law had so far educated the nation, that they had supplied them with a whole series of types and forms of thought.
So that when Jesus of Nazareth appeared, and especially after
his abrupt and violent death, the events of those few pregnant
years threw themselves into the shapes for which Judaism had
prepared men's minds, but which in fact had no reality, and
for which this preparation had been quite fortuitous.   Need we
point out, once more, the strange discovery which Strauss here
makes of his essential, though unconscious orthodoxy?   The
slightest violence done to the surface of the philosopher reveals
the doctor of divinity within.   For every word of this, so far
as it is affirmative and not negative, is precisely the doctrine of
the Catholic Church from the beginning.   It is the denials
only that she denies.   It is the negations which she thinks are
difficult to prove.   Nor has Strauss succeeded in proving them,
unless, as before, Hegelianism be allowed to have blotted out a
conscious God from history.   All he has done is, to caricature
the old church theory by a ludicrous exaggeration; and to
conjecture, among the Jews at that time, such an inflamed condition of the function above described, as to transcend all like-
lihood and all nature, and to generate Christendom out of
a nation of lunatics.   For what mental condition short of
lunacy could have argued, as Strauss supposes the Apostles to
have argued, ' The Old Testament represents Christ as doing
' such and such things; therefore, although we neither heard
' nor saw anything of the sort, he did them.'
    ' But,' replies Strauss, ' we have no notion how the Apostles
' argued or what they said; for all our accounts are at second
' hand.   Mark and Luke are confessedly so; and Matthew is
' a translated and expanded work, on the basis of Matthew's
' genuine collection of discourses; while John is a wholly ficti-

' tious gospel, due to some one well versed in the Alexandrian
' philosophy about the middle of the second century.'   Now,
without entering into all the perplexed detail of gospel criticism,
let the reader simply recollect the following facts, and he will be
in a position to judge whether we can depend upon the New
Testament or not.   Irenæus and Tertullian were two writers in
the last quarter of the second century ; the former had spent his
youth among the churches of Asia Minor, and had migrated
among the Christians of Gaul ; the latter was a presbyter in the
Latin Church of North Africa.   Both were strong tradition-
alists ; and both distinctly appeal to the four canonical gospels
by name.   But would churches so widely remote as those of
Smyrna, Carthage, and Lyons, with one accord receive as
Scripture four books which were only a few years old ?   And
besides, Irenæus had been in his youth a companion of Poly-
carp, the disciple of St. John.   Is it credible that St. John's
Gospel could have been received by him if it had been never
heard of till A.D. 150 ?   Moreover, about A.D. 150, Celsus
quotes both the synoptical gospels and St. John, and says, ' all
' this I have taken out of your own Scriptures.'   About the
same date, Theophilus and Tatian both constructed a Harmony
of the Four Gospels ; and ten years earlier still, Justin
Martyr speaks of gospels written by the Apostles and their
companions ; meaning, there can surely be little question, the
four as we now have them.   Twenty years before that, Poly-
carp uses St. Matthew, and quotes the First Epistle of St.
John, which is allowed on all hands to be (under any supposition) by the same author as the Gospel.   And about the same
period, Papias, a bishop in Asia Minor, who tells us he took
particular pains to collect oral information from survivors who
had known the Apostles, describes how Matthew wrote originally in Hebrew, and how Mark drew his materials from St.
Peter.   The passage is but a fragment preserved in Eusebius,
so that no sound argument against St. John can be drawn
e silentio, any more than against St. Paul or St. Luke.   Thus
we are brought down to about A.D. 100, without a trace of any
conciliar action, or of any controversy on the subject which
cannot easily be explained.   The Church emerges from the
first century with the sacred book of the four Gospels in her
hand.   The very earliest apocryphal gospels only attempt to
fill up the blanks in their narrative, and never give a competing
account.   The most ancient of all was held by Jerome, who
translated it, to be the Hebrew original of St. Matthew.   The
Montanists, in their wildest hatred of St. John's Gospel, could
only attribute it to his contemporary Cerinthus.   And every

recent discovery, such as the missing end of the Clementine
Homilies (containing a quotation from St. John), and the
original Greek of Barnabas (giving St. Matthew's Gospel the
honourable title of 'Scripture'), only tends to corroborate the
proof, that we have in the four Gospels the primitive records of
Christianity, and a trustworthy means for understanding what
the mind and the preaching of the Apostles really was.* And
if so, we repeat, the supposition that the healthiest, simplest,
and sanest form of religion the world has ever seen, should
have taken its rise from such a hotbed of fatuity and insanity
as Strauss would have us believe, appears to us to make greater
demands by far upon our credulity than the hypothesis it is
invented to supersede; and to be fitly suspended upon the
following sentence, written for a very different purpose :—
' There are things which do not, indeed, like miracles, contra-
' vene the laws of nature, but which contradict historical proba-
' bility ; that is, are easier to conceive of as imaginary than as
' true.' (*Strauss*, p. 402.)

The second loophole by which these writers, and especially
M. Renan, endeavour to escape from the necessity of believing
the testimony of the Evangelists, belongs to the same class of
arguments. The object, in both cases alike, is to maintain the
Pantheistic as against the Theistic view of history; and to
elude the recognition of what Theology (in its popular language) calls 'the finger of God' in Christianity, by showing
that it can be accounted for by causes which are well within
the narrow horizon of our own experience. Little indeed
would be gained by success. For a god Pan, who developed
himself in such a blundering and ridiculous way as is here
supposed, would quickly set people thinking whether he were
a god at all ; or did not need some better interpreters, at least,
who would credit him with an honest walk and conversation
along the highroad of Nature and Health, instead of tracking
his cloven footsteps among the devious by-ways of disease.
It would be an ill exchange, if we were to give up the supernatural Christ for an infra-natural one ; and, to retort Hume's
argument upon himself, it is far more consonant to probability
that philosophers should err, than that the world should have
been regenerated by myth-bewildered fishermen and hysterical
Magdalens, while God was (as it were) asleep, and suffered
disease and error to steal a march upon Him, for the endless
benefit of the human race.

---

* This argument is well drawn out in Tischendorf's pamphlet,
' Wann wurden unsere Evangelien verfasst ? '

Yet such is, in plain words, the theory of M. Renan.
'The formation of Christendom,' says he, 'is the greatest
'event in the religious history of the world.' But only a few
pages farther on we read,

'The glory of the Resurrection belongs then to Mary Magdalene.
Next to Jesus, it is she who has done the most for the founding of
Christendom. The shadow created by the delicate senses of the
Magdalen hovers still above the world. Queen and patron of idealists, she above all others has known how to make her dream a
reality and to impose on all men the sacred vision of her impassioned
soul. Her grand affirmation of the woman's heart, "He is risen!"
has been the basis of the world's faith. Get thee gone then, impotent Reason! Presume not to apply thy cold analysis to this
master-work of idealism and of love. If Philosophy gives up the
attempt to console this poor race of men, betrayed by fate, let madness approach and put her hand to the task. Where is the sage
who has ever given such joy to the world, as the possessed woman—
Mary of Magdala?' (*Apôtres*, p. 13.)

If we had not the page lying open before us, it would seem
positively incredible that a man of such mental and moral
qualities as M. Renan possesses, should be so far the victim
of a foregone conclusion as to think this a rational explanation
of the literary and historical phenomena of our Lord's Resurrection. Yet after an interval of three years for reflection, this
expansion of the hint given in his earlier volume, this revived
embodiment of the long-buried calumny of Celsus,[*]—still
seems to this almost-Christian, who, unlike his own Magdalen,
loves yet cannot believe in Christ, worth putting down on
paper as a sufficient solution of the problem! In Strauss, a
person of colder and more masculine temperament, we are prepared for anything. The dissecting knife is for ever in his
hands. And he cannot even put together again 'for the
'German people' the *disjecta membra* of their Christ, without
perpetually flourishing his favourite weapon, and making a
surgical demonstration of every member in detail. The consequence is, they will not believe that a Christ so put together
can be alive. M. Renan, on the other hand, presents to his
countrymen a thoroughly living and to them, it seems, conceivable Christ. But, alas!—we hope we shall be pardoned,
for it cannot be otherwise expressed—his Jesus is a French
mesmerist, and his Magdalens and Maries may be met with any
day, in all their gushing and sentimental beauty, kneeling in
Notre Dame, or walking on pilgrimage to the wonder-working
Lady of La Salette. No wonder that such a 'fifth Gospel'

---

[*] Cf. Origen c. Celsum, ii. 55.

of sentiment and hallucination should meet with little acceptance on this more prosaic side of the Channel! No wonder that a drama, in which figures take their part that have assuredly never lived in the flesh, but only in French prints or in the waxwork of a convent chapel, should be rejected with disdain by the practical and sober Englishman! No wonder that, in spite of the fascination of its style, the candour and lucidity of its argumentation, and the extreme interest and value of its historical sketches——especially from the twelfth chapter onwards, where the victory of Christianity over Paganism is described—— this second volume must be condemned as a greater theological failure even than the first; to be pardoned only for its important admissions of the genuineness of St. John's Gospel, of St. Luke's two books, and of the seven main Epistles of St. Paul, and for its heartfelt sympathy for all that is freest and noblest in the Christian ideas.

It is with feelings of great relief, therefore, that we turn from Strauss and Renan and open the now celebrated work of our own countryman, whoever he may be——the author of ' Ecce Homo.' There are few, probably, of our readers who are not already well acquainted with the book. For not only has it passed through five or six editions, but it has been reviewed in every periodical, been canvassed in every social circle, and been carried by the angry waves of controversy into unnumbered nooks and corners, whither in calmer weather it would assuredly have never found its way. The controversy, indeed, which it has occasioned, is quite as curious and interesting a phenomenon as the book itself, and highly instructive as to the present state of English theological opinion. Nor could we desire any plainer corroboration of the statement laid down at the beginning of this article, than is given by the exhibition that reviewers, quarterly or otherwise, seem to have been compelled to make of their true selves in presence of this graphic and admirable ' Survey of the Person and ' Work of Jesus Christ.' But on this subject we shall have more to say by and by. At present we wish simply to draw attention to the salient features of the work, and to show sufficient cause for our judgment that it is, without any exception, the most important contribution towards a restoration of belief that our own generation has seen.

Had not the grave closed over the once speaking eye and toiling brain of Robertson of Brighton, there is little doubt that this anonymous book would have been ascribed to him. For the calm and even march of its sentences and the balanced self-control of its bearing, even amid the hottest fire of controversy, does not wholly conceal the martial ardour which glows within; and there are many passages which reveal the scorn of a manly soul for Pharisaism whether of the first or of the nineteenth century, and which indicate abundant vigour to chastise it. There is, too, the same unflinching determination to push through all the cloud of skirmishing polemics, and to arrive at the heart of the ques-· tion; the same stern resolve to crush the shell of dogma and release the vital ⁎germ of truth; the same earnest loyalty to Christ, and even to his Church,—which gave to Robertson such wonderful power, and have spread his fragmentary ' Sermons ' wherever the English language is spoken. Perhaps our countrymen are, in theology as well as in other things, sus- picious of an over-completeness. And therefore the fragmen- tary condition and tentative attitude of ' Ecce Homo,' too, may have contributed to its wide influence. At any rate, we hold ourselves justified in saying that in this book—incomplete, un- dramatic, and not very critical, as it confessedly is—we have the English ' Life of Jesus,' thoroughly adapted to, and characteristic of, the country whence it sprang; and not only worthy of comparison with the more scientific and more his- trionic works which have proceeded from Germany and France, but distinctly taking the lead of them in point of successful handling of the question.

That question is: What was the origin of Christianity? Was it human or divine? Was Jesus Christ a great genius, or the Son of God? Now, in the solution of this question, everything depends—as we said before—on the avenue by which it is approached. Germany has chosen to approach it by the Reason; and entangled at the very outset in an infinite multitude of knotty critical details, has never been able to advance one step; till Strauss, with his rash sword of ' the ' Mythical hypothesis,' at length hewed the whole subject into pieces, and left it incoherent and useless for all the practical wants of men. France, on the other hand, has approached it on the side of the Imagination; and shrinking from the infinite- simal detail of critical labour, has—perhaps with over-haste— grasped at results, and arranged those results by the aid of a totally fallacious canon, viz. that beauty of form is some guarantee for truth of fact. It was reserved for England to make her approaches on the Moral side, and to show how, seizing the clue laid down by the Founder of Christianity himself, it was possible to advance at once into the very centre of the labyrinth, to grasp there at one view, not indeed all the details, but the broad grouping of those details and their relative importance to the question and to each other, and from thence, with the tranquil vigour which such a position always inspires, to proceed at leisure and with perfect security to the gradual unravelling of the interesting matters that surround the main question in dispute.   Thus ' Ecce Homo ' could hardly hope to escape the charge of being an incomplete work. Its incompleteness is its glory.   It is not so much a new work as a new method.   And a new method is what mankind have long been groaning for : not a mere negative method, such as Strauss thinks good enough, but a positive one which shall lead to a rational tranquillity, and show them how to ride at anchor through the storms of modern doubt and disbelief.

Accordingly the author of this book—seizing his clue— plunges at once *in medias res.*   His critical introduction occupies twelve lines ; or rather, is no introduction at all, for it occurs at the beginning of chapter v.   Whereas Strauss's ' Einleitung ' fills no less than 162 pages of closely-packed German type ; and Renan's ' Critique des documents originaux ' demands 64 octavo pages.   For this he makes no apology. It is part of his method, which he trusts his readers and reviewers will have wit enough to understand, to take these questions last, instead of first ; and therefore to delay them till the appearance of the second volume.   He acknowledges that. ' What is now published is a fragment.   No theological ' questions whatever are here discussed.   Christ, as the creator ' of modern theology and religion, will form the subject of ' another volume.'   And accordingly,

'In defining the position which Christ assumed, we have not entered into controvertible matter. We have not rested upon single passages, nor drawn from the fourth Gospel. To deny that Christ did undertake to found and to legislate for a new theocratic society, and that he did claim the office of Judge of mankind, is indeed possible, but only to those who altogether deny the credibility of the extant biographies of Christ. If those biographies be admitted to be generally trustworthy, then Christ undertook to be what we have described ; if not, then of course this, but also every other, account of him falls to the ground. . . . . The account we have of these miracles may be exaggerated ; it is possible that in some special cases stories have been related which have no foundation whatever; but, on the whole, miracles play so important a part in Christ's scheme, that any theory which would represent them as entirely due to the imagination of his followers, or of a later age, destroys the credibility of the documents, not partially but wholly, and leaves Christ as mythical a personage as Hercules. Now the present treatise aims to show that the Christ of the Gospels is not mythical, by showing that the character these biographies portray is in all its large features strikingly consistent, and at the same time so peculiar as to be altogether beyond the reach of invention both by individual genius and still more by what is called the " consciousness of an age." Now if the character depicted in the Gospels is in the main real and historical, they must be generally trustworthy, and, if so, the responsibility of miracles is fixed on Christ. In this case the reality of the miracles themselves depends in a great degree on the opinion we form of Christ's veracity, and this opinion must arise gradually from the careful examination of his whole life.' (*Ecce Homo*, p. 41.)

In these last words we have the key to the whole book. The author's plan is here distinctly revealed. It is not his intention to begin by discussing miracles or the trustworthiness of the Gospels in detail, and so to hew his way (like a traveller through the tangled growths of a South American forest) to a conviction about Christ. Such a course seems to him, as it does to us, and as experience has abundantly proved it to be, impossible. He chooses the reverse course. Postulating only, in the broadest sense, the general trustworthiness of the only record we possess, he is prepared to evoke from that record, fairly and sensibly handled, a moral conviction of the purity and grandeur of Christ's character, such as shall rise like daylight upon the scene and flood the crannies and the crevices of groping criticism with heathful sunbeams. And nobly has he fulfilled his purpose. Limiting the area of his investigation strictly to the Ministry of Christ, he describes in the first five chapters the object and ideal of that ministry as it existed in Christ's own mind ; and proceeds in his remaining chapters to show how that ideal became actually realised in historical fact by the consummate practical wisdom of that same incomparable mind. Chapter vi. opens thus :—

' The first step in our investigation is now taken. We have considered the Christian Church in its idea, that is to say, as it existed in the mind of its founder and before it was realised. Our task will now become more historical and will deal with the actual establishments of the new Theocracy. . . The founder's plan was simply this, to renew in a form adapted to the new time that divine Society of which the Old Testament contains the history. The essential features of that ancient Theocracy were: (1) The Divine Call and Election of Abraham ; (2) the Divine Legislation given to the nation through Moses ; (3) the personal relation and responsibility of every individual member of the Theocracy to its Invisible King. As the new Theocracy was to be the counterpart of the old, it was to be expected that these three features would be reflected in it.' (P. 52.)

Yet—strange, at first sight, to say—while the first of these three features occupies our author during the four succeeding chapters, and the second during the thirteen chapters that follow, just when our attention and interest are raised to the highest pitch, and we are preparing ourselves for a full discussion of the third and most decisive question of all—the book abruptly closes. The *nature* of Christ's sovereignty and of his personal relations to the Church has never received any discussion at all; though the *fact* of his making royal claims has been often incidentally touched upon. How is this? Has the author forgotten his plan? Or rather, have we not, in this abrupt fracture, the intrinsic quality, not only of the fragment which is now in our hands, but also of the whole work in its future completeness, revealed? It appears to us beyond all reasonable doubt, that the alarms and lamentations which have so loudly resounded from the orthodox side over this book are wholly ill-timed and uncalled for. Everything indicates that he has not rashly taken pen in hand, before having made up his own mind. Everything points to the conclusion, that 'the inquiry which proved serviceable to ' himself' proved so by convincing him that the faith of his childhood was a reasonable one, and that the homage he had once paid to Christ need not on farther investigation of his claims be withdrawn. We need only call attention to such passages as the following :—

'We have found Christ undertaking . . . to occupy a personal relation of Judge and Master to every man, such as in the earlier Theocracy had been occupied *by Jehovah himself* without representation.' (P. 52.) 'Within the whole creation of God *nothing more elevated or more attractive* has yet been found than he.' (P. 52.) 'This enthusiasm, then, was shown to men in its most consummate form in Jesus Christ. From him it flows as from a fountain. How it was kindled in him who knows? The abysmal deeps of personality hide this secret. *It was the will of God to beget no second son like him.*' (P. 321.) 'What comfort Christ gave men . . . by offering to them new views of the Power by which the world is governed, by *his own triumph over death*, and by his revelation of eternity, will be the subject of another treatise.' (P. 323.) 'The achievement of Christ, in founding by his single will and power a structure so durable and so universal, is like no other achievement which history records. . . . If *in the works of Nature* we can trace the indications of calculation, of a struggle with difficulties, of precaution, of ingenuity, then in Christ's work it may be that the same indications occur. . . . Who can describe that which unites men? Who has entered into the formation of speech which is the symbol of their union? Who can describe exhaustively the origin of Civil Society? He who can do these things can explain the origin of the Christian Church. For others it must be enough to say, " The Holy " Ghost fell on them that believed." No man saw the building of the New Jerusalem, the workmen crowded together, the unfinished walls and unpaved streets; no man heard the clink of trowel and pickaxe; *it descended out of heaven from God.'* (P. 330.)

With this striking passage our author concludes the present instalment of his work. He has endeavoured to show, and we think he has succeeded in showing, that taking the life of Jesus only in its broadest features, in the mass and not in detail, in those general outlines which must be allowed to belong to it, if we are supposed to know anything about it at all, nothing more is required than a fearless mental freedom and an unclouded moral appreciation, in order to arrive at a profound and tranquil conviction that he is our souls' rightful Lord and King, and—as we cannot hesitate to add by anticipation—in some true sense ' Divine.' And in following him step by step in this truly charitable work at a time of doubt like our own, we pity —far more even than the robbed and half-dead traveller— the supercilious passer-by who sees no need of the oil or wine, has no heart to praise, no intelligence to understand, the saving efforts,—nay, spurns the very flask beneath his priestly feet because there is something suspicious about its shape. Yet what has the author done? He has simply translated the dead formulæ of orthodoxy into the living language of modern thought and of men of the world. That is to say, he has presented Christianity in the only shape in which men will receive it at the present day, and in which alone it can effect the redemption and conversion of their souls. He has dared to call charity the ' enthusiasm of humanity;' he has dared to describe the regenerating mission of the Christian Church as ' the improvement of morality;' he has ventured to change the salvation of souls into their ' restoration to moral health;' to speak of the Holy Spirit as ' the Spirit of Holiness,' and of the sacramental means of grace as ' sacred rites,' ' essential condi-' tions of membership,' symbols of that ' intense personal devo-' tion, that habitual feeding on the character of Christ,' without which ' the health of the soul' cannot be regained; and all this he has done with imperfections, with occasional (though very slight) exaggerations, and with a few (though very glaring) defects of good taste. Yet when all has been said, what are these crimes—if crimes they be—compared to the merit of having penned the following noble passage :—

' We ought to be just as tolerant of an imperfect creed as we are of an imperfect practice. Everything which can be urged in excuse for the latter may also be pleaded for the former. If the way to Christian action is beset by corrupt habits and misleading passions, the path to Christian truth is overgrown with prejudices and strewn with fallen theories and rotting systems which hide it from our view. It is quite as hard to think rightly as it is to act rightly, or even to feel rightly. And as all allow that an error is a less culpable thing than a crime or a vicious passion, it is monstrous that it should be more severely punished; it is monstrous that Christ who was called the friend of publicans and sinners, should be represented as the pitiless enemy of seekers after truth.' (P. 72.)

Cannot the unpardonable sin of certain contemptuous expressions about 'little-minded and vexatious prohibitions,' ' spasmodic efforts to kindle feeling,' 'a hollow, poor, and sickly ' Christianity,' be forgiven for the sake of so truly evangelical a passage as this :—

' Justice is often but a form of pedantry, mercy mere easiness of temper, courage a mere firmness of physical constitution ; but if these virtues are genuine, then they indicate not goodness merely but goodness considerably developed. We want a test which shall admit all who have it in them to be good whether their good qualities be trained or no. Such a test is found in Faith. He who, when goodness is impressively put before him, exhibits an instinctive loyalty to it, starts forward to take its side, trusts himself to it, such a man has faith, and the root of the matter is in such a man. He may have habits of vice, but the loyal and faithful instinct in him will place him above many that practise virtue. He may be rude in thought and character, but he will unconsciously gravitate towards what is right. Other virtues can scarcely thrive without a fine natural organisation and a happy training. But the most neglected and ungifted of men may make a beginning with faith.' (P. 66.)

And yet once more, might not an occasional rebuke of Churchmen's besetting sins be atoned for by such a noble conception of the Christian Church as this :—

' However impossible it may seem, this speculation of a commonwealth developed from first principles *has* been realised on a grand scale. It stands in history among other states ; it subsists in the midst of other states, connected with them and yet distinct. Though so refined and philosophic in its constitution, it has not less vigour than the states which are founded on the relations of family, or language, or the convenience of self-defence and trade. Not less vigour, and certainly far more vitality. It has already long outlasted all the states which were existing at the time of its foundation ; it numbers far more citizens than any of the states which it has seen spring up near it. It subsists without the help of costly armaments ; resting on no accidental aid or physical support, but on an inherent immortality, it defied the enmity of ancient civilisation, the brutality of mediæval barbarism, and under the present universal empire of public opinion it is so secure that even those parts of it seem indestructible which deserve to die.' (P. 325.)

But no; nothing, it appears, can atone, in the judgment of dogmatists, for not arriving at dogma in the authorised way. Health is nothing. The nostrum is everything. And, like Molière's physician, these doctors would rather see the patient die *selon les régles* than recover by a process that outraged all that was customary. Unless this author will consent, not only in his future volume and at a more mature stage of his argument, but now, on the spot, and at the word of command,— whether or not it ruin his plan, and threaten *vivendi causâ vivendi perdere causas,*—to utter the recognised formulæ of orthodoxy, he shall not be allowed to pass muster. Not the mispronounced word, but the unpronounced word, is to be his condemnation. Hew him down! 'The Lord will know his ' own.' We do not exaggerate. We repeat, and are prepared to prove, that the way in which this book has been in certain quarters reviewed, reflects the deepest disgrace on the writers, and displays, in a shape which it would be superfluous to carica- ture, the almost hopeless senility of modern ' orthodoxy.' We are unwilling to drop for a moment the usual periphrases of courtesy ; but indignation compels us to pronounce the words, that the two main offenders against the first principles of fair- play and Christian toleration are the ' Quarterly Review' and Mr. Spurgeon. Will it be believed, that a supercilious critic who complains of ' ignorance' should be ignorant that St. John i. 17 does not contain the words of the Baptist? that one who charges others with ' defiance of elementary principles ' which are familiar to children and peasants,' should state that ' a church of which the ultimate object was the improvement of ' morality [the equivalent in ' Ecce Homo ' for the ' saving of ' men's souls '] would not be Christian but infidel '? And that this staunch *malleus hæreticorum* should himself fall into the fol- lowing deadly heresy, ' The doctrine that He who was perfect ' God and perfect man could admit the idea of taking wrongful ' courses, that He could entertain the Temptation for a moment ' if it arose . . . is only consistent with some of the lower grades ' of Socinianism'?* And yet once more, is it credible that ' The ' Sword and Trowel,' edited by Mr. Spurgeon, to represent (we may presume) Dissenting principles of freedom and toleration, should in one breath describe the writer as ' no blasphemer of ' the Lord Jesus, but a warm admirer of the self-denying love ' of the Man of Sorrows,' as ' not denying miracles, nor im- ' pugning even the Deity of Christ,' as ' clearly seeing that ' Christ's kingdom is spiritual . . ., and its principles in the

---

* Quart. Rev.; April, 1866.

' highest degree promotive of freedom, philanthropy, brother-
' hood ,and progress,' and then turn round upon him with the
most vulgar vituperation : ' if this treatise be the production of
' a minister of any denomination of Evangelical Christians, he
' ought,. if he has even half as much honesty as any ordinary
' thief, to resign his position at once ' ? *

For such a reception as this, in such quarters, we do not
think the author of ' Ecce Homo ' could have been prepared ;
nor yet for the singular inability of a great Roman Catholic
writer in ' The Month ' to perceive that ' to exhibit some sides
' of Christianity and not others,' † which he holds to be ' the
' main fault of the author,' is precisely an essential part of his
plan.   To have his noble and truthful work characterised by
a philanthropical earl as ' the most pestilential work that was
' ever vomited out of the jaws of hell,' must have cost him far
less surprise and far less pain.   Nor has he met with better
usage at the hands of the opposite party.   The critics who
have exercised their ingenuity on ' Ecce Homo ' in the ' West-
' minster Review ' and in ' Fraser's Magazine,' are evidently not
men who would be alarmed at any want of orthodoxy ; but we
must be permitted to say that they have entirely failed to
apprehend the scope of the work, and that their objections
apply to that which the author of it certainly never intended
his book to be.   But whether received with vituperation or
with misunderstanding, whether pertinaciously censured as if
complete when it proclaims itself incessantly to be ' a fragment,'
whether scorned by unbelievers, rejected by believers, or
neglected by men of the world,—the author may at least take
comfort from the reflection, which every day's experience
must make more clear, that he is at least understood by
those for whose especial benefit he has been labouring, has
kindled faith afresh in many a wavering soul, and inspired with
that love of Christ which saves and redeems men, many a
heart that could find no beauty in dead formulæ and no rest in
barren ' Evidences.'   From such thoughts he may well draw
lessons of thankful tranquillity and content, and find courage to
prosecute his fruitful studies in peace.   For ' no greater subject
' can in our own day employ any man's noblest energies than
' preservation or renewal of the truth of God,—not fettered
' overmuch by the human accidents of our ancestors in the
' faith, yet with reverential tenderness even for these.' ‡

---

* Sword and Trowel ; January, 1866.
† The Month ; June, 1866.
‡ Williams' 'Rational Godliness,' p. 404.

Art. VII.—*History of England, from the Fall of Wolsey to the Death of Elizabeth.* By James Anthony Froude, M. A., late Fellow of Exeter College, Oxford. Reign of Elizabeth. Vols. III., IV. London : 1866.

Two more volumes of Mr. Froude's copious history invite the study of the learned, and the enlightened curiosity of that large class of readers to whom the annals of their own country, presented under new aspects and enriched with fresh materials, are ever an object of lively interest. In former numbers of this Journal* we followed Mr. Froude through the eight preceding volumes of his work ; and while we endeavoured to do justice to his remarkable merits, we did not shrink from the unwelcome task of pointing out, in the interests of truth, some of his faults as an historian. It was mainly, however, in his treatment of the reign of Henry VIII., and his paradoxical conception of the character of that monarch, that we found ourselves at issue with him. When his judgment ceased to be perverted by the idolatrous worship of that equivocal hero of his own creation, his views became more consistent with the received opinions of history ; and if he was less original, he approached more nearly, as we venture to think, to the higher aim of historical research—severe and simple truth.

The peculiar merit of Mr. Froude's work is its wealth of unpublished manuscripts ; and the reign of Elizabeth is remarkably illustrated by the correspondence of the Spanish ambassadors, and other agents of the Court of Spain, which have been preserved in the Archives at Simancas. The extraordinary interest of such illustrations is apparent in every page of these volumes : they give novelty to the narrative, and variety to the well-known incidents of the time ; and they bring in aid of historical evidence, the contemporary opinions of society upon current events. The discovery of such treasures is apt to seduce the historian into an undue estimate of their historical value, and to lead him to prefer their version of facts to more common-place conclusions founded upon published documents. The reader, perhaps, is also prepared to receive too readily, as decisive, the testimony of witnesses so original and unexpected. But we must be on our guard against these natural prepossessions. The authority of manuscripts is not to be accepted as superior to that of printed documents : they may be more interesting, by reason of their novelty, but they are not more trustworthy ; and they need

* Edin. Rev., July 1858 ; and January 1864.

a scrutiny even more careful, as they have not been exposed to the criticism of other writers.

It may be safely affirmed that recent researches into the unpublished state papers of different countries have generally served to confirm rather than to disturb our previous convictions as to the events and characters of history. They have made most valuable additions to our stock of knowledge: they have filled up its broad outlines with an infinite variety of picturesque details and suggestive illustrations: they have multiplied proofs in corroboration of facts and traditions already received; but they have rarely overthrown the evidence presented by printed records, accessible to all the world. Mr. Rawdon Brown, in the preface to his interesting 'Calendar of 'Venetian State Papers,' thus aptly estimates the value of such documents:—

'Nor must we expect that the revelations of unpublished MSS. will make black and white change places in our estimate of character, and suddenly alter the notions we have formed of the great actors in the drama of history. With respect to characters, as well as facts, it is rather by minute and repeated touches that the force and colour of truth are to be restored, than by substituting a new picture for an old one.' *

Regarded in this point of view, the Simancas papers are singularly interesting. Philip II. of Spain, as consort of the late Queen Mary, was closely connected with England and with Elizabeth; and as the most zealous Catholic prince in Europe, he was deeply concerned in a country which had again renounced the ancient faith, and was still agitated by the religious and political discords of the Reformation. His ambassadors watched narrowly the stirring events of the time; and their opportunities of observation were peculiarly favourable. As representing a sovereign allied by marriage to the Queen, they were admitted to confidential intercourse with the court, and conversed freely with Elizabeth and her councillors; as ministers of a Catholic prince, they were the friends and advisers of Mary Queen of Scots, of the Catholic peers, and of the leaders of that restless and disaffected party who were ever plotting to overthrow their Protestant Queen and restore the old religion. All the secrets of Catholic malcontents and conspirators were confided to them; and too often they were themselves the contrivers of treason. All their busy doings— everything they saw or heard,—their hopes, fears, and conjectures, were fully reported to Philip. Intriguers and gossips as they were, there was no lack of materials for their despatches;

* Rawdon Brown's Pref. to Calendar of Venetian State Papers, p. xciv.

and De Silva, the first ambassador with whom we become acquainted in these volumes, was an accomplished gentleman and a clever letter-writer. He could report his conversations with Queen Elizabeth or Cecil with a dramatic spirit scarcely inferior to that of our own distinguished diplomatist, Sir Hamilton Seymour; and the curiosity of his royal master gave constant encouragement to his facile pen. And now, after the lapse of three hundred years, all that was written for the secret information of Philip is revealed to the present generation, and throws a flood of unexpected light upon a critical period in English history.

The Simancas papers, however, full and instructive as they are, form but a small part of the manuscript evidence which Mr. Froude has embraced in his researches. He has also ransacked the records in London, at Edinburgh, at Hatfield, and at Paris. With so large a mass of new materials, his history naturally assumes an original character. Where the narrative differs little, if at all, from that of other historians, the authorities are not the same; and as he prefers his own recent discoveries to more familiar documents, and cites them at great length, his work possesses at once the charms and the blemishes of contemporary memoirs. The reign of Elizabeth is so hackneyed a theme in English and foreign literature, that it is refreshing to read the ' oft-told tale ' in the very language of the actors themselves. But if too much prominence be given to such authorities, the higher philosophy of history is in danger of being lost in a multiplicity of secondary events; while the historian, whose guidance we seek in a concise and comprehensive narrative, is found to rival the memoir-writer in fulness of detail, and consequently in voluminousness. Into this latter fault, at least, we fear that Mr. Froude is liable to be beguiled. The two volumes just issued embrace no more than six years and a half of the reign of Queen Elizabeth, beginning in February 1567, and ending in August 1573. As this reign continued for thirty years after the last of these dates, we might look forward to not less, perhaps, than ten more volumes, if the remaining years of the Queen's life were treated with equal prolixity. If the history of England is to be written throughout at such length, may the Lord have mercy on our children, and send them readable abridgments!

With these introductory remarks, we will now follow Mr. Froude through these interesting volumes, inviting special notice to the more striking revelations of his new witnesses, and touching, with friendly criticism, upon such of his conclusions as we may not be prepared to accept.

The eighth volume of this work concluded, as our readers may remember, with the murder of Darnley, in which crime no pains were spared to prove, with crushing force, the complicity of Mary Stuart. The narrative is here continued, and Scotland occupies the larger portion of the present volumes. Her celebrated Queen is still the heroine of the tale, but every shred of romance, with which her character has hitherto been veiled, has been ruthlessly torn away. From various causes, no other Queen in history has occasioned so zealous and long-continued a controversy as Mary Stuart. She was beautiful, brave, and unfortunate. She was the hope of one party,—the dread and abhorrence of another. She was accused of crimes which her friends indignantly denied, and her enemies reiterated ; and her adventures, her sufferings, and her wrongs have been illustrated by history, poetry, and romance. Some writers have boldly undertaken to vindicate her reputation from all stain, while others have chosen to dwell upon her attractions and accomplishments as a woman, and her cruel misfortunes as a Queen, rather than upon the dark and evil mysteries of her life. Her ablest champions were Chalmers, Whitaker, and the elder Tytler, to whom we must add the late Professor Aytoun, who, in his spirited poem of ' Bothwell,' was able to shield his heroine with fair poetic license. A modern French author, M. Wiesener, has recently produced an elaborate volume in her defence; and Prince Labanoff was moved by the same sentimental interest to publish a valuable collection of all the letters known to exist from her pen. But our greatest historians, Robertson, Hume, Laing, Hallam, and Sharon Turner, have been persuaded of her guilt ; and even the Catholic Lingard, though inclining to her side, has scarcely ventured to acquit her. Among contemporary writers, the learned and judicious historian of Scotland, Mr. Fraser Tytler, reluctantly declines her defence,* and the eminent French historian, M. Mignet, with the aid of the most recent authorities, including the Simancas papers,† gives sober and dispassionate judgment against her memory.‡

---

* See Hist. of Scot., vol. vii. pp. 109, 121, 122, 140, 268, &c.

† The list of these authorities, as given in his preface, is sufficiently long, but is by no means exhaustive. M. Mignet has not, we believe, visited Simancas himself, as Mr. Froude has done ; and he therefore only quotes those documents of which copies had been made for the French Government.

‡ Histoire de Marie Stuart, vol. i. p. 261, 263, 281, and App. G., vol. ii. p. 51, &c.

The case was but too clear before Mr. Froude approached it; but, if he has added few direct proofs to those already accumulated, he has found confirmation of them in the adverse opinions of contemporary observers. All this evidence, direct and indirect, he uses not with the calm temper of a judge, but with the fierceness of a bitter advocate. Her guilt is the great argument of this history. If Mary was guilty of the murder of her husband, he maintains that Elizabeth and her ministers were justified in their treatment of her; if she was innocent, they must stand condemned. Hence his merciless severity against Mary, whom he brands throughout these volumes with opprobrious names, which he is never weary of reiterating. The issue raised by him is not, however, to be so accepted until he is able to show that the Queen of England and her ministers were entitled to judge an independent Queen, or that their treatment of Mary was founded upon their convictions of her guilt. She may have been guilty, as we believe her to have been; but we are not, on that account, prepared to defend the conduct of Elizabeth.

The whole of Mary's conduct after the murder of Darnley tended to confirm suspicions as to her own participation in that monstrous crime. On the following morning, Paris, Bothwell's French page and one of the gang of assassins—

'went to the apartments of the Queen, where Bothwell followed him directly after. Mary Stuart had slept soundly, but was by this time stirring. The windows were still closed. The room was already hung with black, and lighted with candles. She herself was breakfasting in bed, eating composedly, as Paris observed, a new-laid egg. She did not notice or speak to him, for Bothwell came close behind, and talked in a low voice with her behind the curtain.' (*Reign of Elizabeth*, vol. iii. p. 5.)

She declared that ' whoever had taken the enterprise in ' hand, it had been aimed as well at herself as at the King, ' since the providence of God only prevented her from sleeping ' in the house which was destroyed.' Yet the intended assassination, of which she had no suspicion herself, was known several days before both in London and in Paris. This coincidence, however, must not be pressed too far. No one doubts that the murder had been deliberately planned by Bothwell and his confederates; but, unless the Queen had been an accomplice, she was the very person from whom the plot would have been most carefully concealed.*

---

* In his extreme eagerness to fix upon Mary the guilt of the murder, Mr. Froude sometimes even contradicts himself. Thus he

But the most damning evidence to her prejudice was her scandalous intimacy with the murderer Bothwell, and her determination to protect him from justice.   This part of her conduct has already been condemned by all candid writers; but Mr. Froude places before us more distinctly the state of public opinion in Scotland and elsewhere, upon these events :—

'Midnight cries,' he says, 'were heard in the wynds and alleys of Edinburgh, crying for vengeance upon the Queen and Bothwell. Each day, as it broke, showed the walls pasted with "bills," in which their names were linked together in an infamous union of crime ; and bold as they were, they were startled at the passionate instinct with which their double guilt had been divined.'   (Vol. iii. p. 8.)

The nobles were too familiar with deeds of blood to be much moved by the recent murder, and many were accomplices in the crime; but the people, already touched by the moral influence of the Reformation, cried furiously for justice.   Their feeling against the Queen was shared by higher personages. Her ambassador at Paris wrote to her, ' Yea, she herself was ' greatly and wrongously calamnit to be motive principal of the ' whole, and all done by her order.'   ' He could but say that, ' rather than that vengeance were not taken, it were better in ' this world had she lost life and all.'   The Spanish ambassador at the Scottish court—a Catholic, and a friend of the Queen—suspected her guilt ; and Queen Elizabeth, while willing to believe her innocent, addressed her in these remarkable words :—

'I cannot but tell you what all the world is thinking.   Men say that instead of seizing the murderers, you are looking through your fingers while they escape ; that you will not punish those who have done you so great a service, as though the thing would never have taken place, had not the doers of it been assured of impunity. . . . I exhort, I advise, I implore you deeply to consider of the matter—at once, if it be the nearest friend you have, to lay your hands upon the man who has been guilty of the crime—to let no

---

stated in chap. x. (vol. ii. p. 351), that Morton required ' the ' Queen's hand for a warrant' before he would join the conspiracy for the murder of Darnley.   Bothwell promised that he would produce it, ' *but it never came.*'   In chap. xiii. (vol. iii. p. 28), he says, ' Morton was invited to join, and had only suspended his consent till ' assured under the Queen's hand of her approval.   There were other ' writings also, which were afterwards destroyed.'   The fact is, that no such writing was ever known to exist at all.   So, too, there is no evidence for the assumption that Darnley's illness previous to the murder was caused by poison, yet Mr. Froude believes it.

interest, no persuasion, keep you from proving to everyone that you
are a noble princess and a loyal wife.' (Vol. iii. p. 23.)

Even Catherine de Medicis and the King of France told her,
' that if she did not exert herself to discover and punish the
' assassin she would cover herself with infamy.'

But Mary Stuart turned a deaf ear to these righteous counsels : she was passionately in love with Bothwell, and, far from
avenging the death of Darnley, she was preparing to marry
his assassin.   He was already married, indeed, but this slight
obstacle was to be removed by a divorce, sought on the ground
of his own adultery.   Bothwell was, at length, called to take
part in a mock trial ; but, instead of being placed in custody,
he rode gallantly from Holyrood on the murdered Darnley's
horse, and was cheered by the smiles of Mary Stuart, who
nodded a farewell from her window.   By trickery and force, it
had been contrived that no prosecutor should be forthcoming ;
and he was pronounced not guilty.

Meanwhile, the intended marriage was whispered about
among the people, and everywhere denounced as monstrous
and unholy.   But there was no hesitation either in Mary or
Bothwell.   A packed Parliament confirmed the ' purgation ' of
the latter ; and, in order to conciliate the Protestants, the Queen
now formally recognised the Reformation.   It was not the first
time that a divorce, sought for the sake of another marriage,
had favoured the Protestant religion.   The next thing to be
done was to secure the support of the nobles ; and Bothwell,
having invited the primate and four bishops, and several noblemen—including the Earls of Argyll, Huntly, Sutherland, and
Eglinton—to supper, surprised them over their wine into sign-
ing a bond, by which they engaged to resist all slanders against
their host, and to promote his marriage with the Queen.

But so scandalous a marriage could not be contracted without
embarrassments ; and, to avoid all further obstacles, a forcible
abduction of the Queen was planned.   Her advocates have
naturally endeavoured to lay all the blame of this outrage upon
Bothwell ; but her own letters betray her.   In them she concerted with her lover the whole scheme of their elopement ; and
whatever there appears ambiguous was arranged between them
by their emissary the Earl of Huntly, Bothwell's brother-in-law.
She enjoined him to ' make himself sure of the lords, and free to
' marry.'   She acquainted him that Huntly had great misgivings, ' because there are many here, and among them the
' Earl of Sutherland, who would rather die than suffer me to
' be carried away, they conducting me.'   She therefore charged
him to be ' the more circumspect and to have the more power.

' We had yesterday more than 300 horse. . . . For the honour
' of God, be accompanied rather of more than less, for that
' is the principal of my care.'   Huntly tried to dissuade her
from the enterprise; but she told him that, if Bothwell did
not withdraw from it, ' no persuasion, nor death itself, should
' make her fail of her promise.'*   Again, in her conduct at the
time of the abduction her collusion was transparent. ' She said
' she would have no blood shed; her people were outnumbered,
' and, rather than any of them should lose their lives, she would
' go wherever the Earl of Bothwell wished.' She went quietly
away with him, and, the day after the iniquitous divorce had
been obtained, she announced her approaching marriage by
proclamation.   In another week they were married; and, to
gain favour with the Protestants, the ceremony was performed
according to the Calvinist service.

The sequel of these infamous nuptials is well known.   The
lords revolted; Bothwell fled; and the Queen being imprisoned in Lochleven Castle, was forced to abdicate in favour of
her infant son; while the Earl of Murray, her half-brother,
was appointed regent.   Then followed Mary's romantic escape
from Lochleven; the defeat of her army at Langside; and her
fatal flight across the Solway into England.   Mr. Froude's
narrative of these events differs so little from other histories,
that we need not dwell upon them.   But he brings out into
stronger relief the popular abhorrence of Mary Stuart's conduct,
as well as the resources, the courage, and the energy of her
character.   While she was in captivity, Sir James Balfour
placed in the hands of the confederate lords a silver casket
which the Queen had given to Bothwell, and which contained
her own letters to himself, some love sonnets, and the documents which afforded proofs that in the murder of Darnley he
had been acting with the sanction of the Queen and half her
council.   Morton, Huntly, Lethington, Argyll, and others had
been in the plot; and as these disclosures affected them no less
than Mary Stuart, the contents of the casket were tampered
with; but everything prejudicial to the Queen was brought

---

* Hist. of Eliz., vol. iii. pp. 59–63, 117 *et seq.* These letters are from
the celebrated silver casket, the authenticity of which Mr. Froude
fully believes.   Mr. Fraser Tytler does not place so much reliance
upon them, the originals having long since disappeared; and the
copies being garbled. (Hist. of Scotland, vol. vii. p. 257.) M. Mignet, however, in an elaborate note (G. vol. i.), gives numerous proofs
that they are genuine, which his opponent, M. Wiesener, has vainly
attempted to rebut.

forward against her,—a circumstance which cannot but throw some discredit upon such evidence.

The Presbyterians already detested her as a Papist, and were shocked by her crimes ; their ministers denounced her from their pulpits with fiery wrath. John Knox, Craig, and other popular preachers demanded that she should be put to death, for which righteous judgment they found ample warrant in Scripture. It would seem that Mr. Froude is of the same opinion. ' Unhappily,' he says, ' the hands which would have ' executed this high act of justice were themselves impure ;'* and again he blames Elizabeth for not remaining neutral in the contest, when she would have been ' delivered for ever ' from the rival who had troubled her peace from the hour of ' her accession, and while she lived would never cease to trouble ' her.' † He feels no pity for the Queen in her worst misfortunes. In his eyes, as well as in those of her enemies, she was ' a ' trapped wild cat,' who might be slain without compunction. We cannot bring ourselves to believe that the spirit in which he treats this erring and unhappy Queen will command the sympathy of his readers, or even their sense of rigorous justice. In a lawless age, in a half-civilised country, and surrounded by savage and treacherous nobles, who were guilty of every crime, she alone is singled out for vengeance. Who in that age was blameless ? Darnley had murdered David Rizzio under Mary Stuart's eyes, with revolting outrage and dishonour to herself. The first nobles of the realm had been concerned in the murder of Darnley. The two first regents who governed the realm in the name of her son were assassinated by the contrivance of their enemies, and the third was suspected to have been poisoned. Nor were the characters of other royal ladies of her time unstained. The sinister rumours concerning the death of Leicester's wife, to make way for his marriage with Elizabeth, and her devoted intimacy with the man on whom so foul a suspicion rested, cannot be forgotten. Nor can we fail to recall the infamous and blood-stained memory of Catherine de Medicis, and the Massacre of St. Bartholomew. In Italy murders were a part of the state policy of the Borgias and Medicis, and even of Popes. The history of Europe, at this period, abounds in assassinations, judicial murders, cruel imprisonments, and other hateful deeds of violence and fraud. We condemn them and their guilty authors, while we deplore the low moral standard of the age of which they are the reproach. But is it consistent with the calm equity of history to brand Mary Stuart, above all others,

---

* Hist. of Eliz., vol. iii. p. 126. † Ibid., p. 130.

as a murderess, and to justify every wrong committed against her by her enemies? Mr. Froude could find justification or excuses for the selfish cruelties and lust of Henry VIII.: he cannot spare one word of pity for a beautiful and gifted woman, whose sins were visited with bitter retribution. God forbid that history should ever condone crimes; but surely a gentler temper towards Mary Stuart would have been at least as impartial in the historian; while a more generous and manly treatment of a woman's sufferings would have found a readier response in the heart of his readers.

With so strong a bias against the character of Mary, Mr. Froude is not likely to be tempted into a romantic treatment of her personal adventures; but he is unable to ignore those spirited and graceful qualities which have won for her so general an interest. Let us visit her at Lochleven:—

'The curtain rises for a moment over the interior of Mary Stuart's prison-house. When the first rage had passed away, she had used the arms of which nothing could deprive her; she had flung over her gaolers the spell of that singular fascination which none who came in contact failed entirely to feel. She had charmed even the Lady of Lochleven, to whose gentle qualities romance has been unjust; and "by one means or another she had won the favour and good "will of the most part of the house, as well men as women, whereby "she had means to have intelligence, and was in some towardness to "have escaped."' *

Her escape was at length effected; and here we have a picture of her spirit and energy:—

'Off shot the troop—off and away into the darkness. Eleven months had passed since Mary Stuart had been in the saddle, but confinement had not relaxed the sinews which no fatigue could tire. Neither strength nor spirit failed her now. Straight through the night they galloped on, and drew bridle first at Queen's Ferry. Claud Hamilton, with fresh horses, was on the other side of the Forth, and they sprang to their saddles again. A halt was allowed them at Lord Seton's house at Long Niddry, but the Queen required no rest. While the men were stretching their aching legs, Mary Stuart was writing letters at her table. She wrote a despatch to the Cardinal of Lorraine, and sent a messenger off with it to Paris. She sent Ricarton to collect a party of the Hepburns and recover Dunbar, bidding him, after the castle was secured, go on to Bothwell, and tell him that she was free. Two hours were spent in this way, and then to horse again. Soon after sunrise she was at Hamilton among her friends.' (Vol. iii. p. 213.)

---

* Hist. of Eliz., vol. iii. p. 157; Throgmorton to Elizabeth, MSS. Scotland.

She was soon at the head of an army ; but it was routed at Langside, and she was again a fugitive :—

'The country had risen, and all the roads were beset. Peasants, as she struggled along the bye-lanes, cut at her with their reaping-hooks. The highway was occupied by Murray's horse. Harassed —for once terrified—for she knew what would be her fate if she fell again into the hands of the Confederates—she turned south, and with six followers, those who had been with her on the hill, and Livingston, George Douglas, and the foundling page, who had con-trived to rejoin her, she made for Galloway. There, in the country of Lord Herries, she would be safe for a week or two at least, and the sea would be open to her if she wished to leave Scotland. By cross paths, by woods and moors, she went, as if death was behind her—ninety-two miles without alighting from her horse. Many a wild gallop she had had already for her life. She had ridden by moonlight from Holyrood to Dunbar, after the murder of Rizzio ; she had gone in a night from Lochleven to Hamilton ; but this, fated to be her last adventure of this kind, was the most desperate of all. Then she had clear hope before her ; now there was nothing but darkness and uncertainty. At night she slept on the bare ground ; for food she had oatmeal and buttermilk. On the third day after the battle, she reached Dundrennan Abbey on the Solway.' (Vol. iii. p. 228.)

Is it surprising that so high a spirit and such adventures should have raised Mary Stuart, despite her crimes, into a heroine of romance ?

We must now leave her, for awhile, in her misfortunes, and turn to the great Queen who was to become the arbiter of her destinies. As Mr. Froude delights to paint Mary Stuart in the darkest colours, so he endeavours to portray the Queen of England in the most favourable light. Whatever her conduct, the best construction is put upon her motives. Thus, her treatment of Mary is represented as kind and sisterly—generous and merciful. That she offered her good advice we have already seen ; and when Mary was imprisoned and deposed by her own subjects, Elizabeth espoused her cause as one common to all princes : she could not tolerate rebellion against a crowned head. 'The head cannot be subject to the foot,' she said, ' and ' we cannot recognise in them (the lords) any right to call their ' sovereign to account.' Her feelings are thus described by Mr. Froude :—

'Elizabeth's behaviour at this crisis was more creditable to her heart than to her understanding. . . . She forgot her interest ; and her affection and her artifices vanished in resentment and pity. Her indignation as a sovereign was even less than her sorrow for a suffering sister. She did not hide from herself the Queen of Scots' faults, but she did not believe in the extent of them ; they seemed as nothing beside the magnitude of her calamities, and she was prepared to encounter the worst political consequences rather than stand by and see her sacrificed.' (Vol. iii. p. 131.)

She threatened the confederate lords with her vengeance if they proceeded to extremities against their queen; and when Mary's execution was discussed amongst them, ' each post from ' England brought fiercer threats from Elizabeth, which all the ' warnings of her council could not prevent her from sending. ' It might have been almost supposed that, with refined in- ' genuity, she was choosing the means most likely to bring ' about the catastrophe which she most affected to dread.' * The lords naturally resented her interference, and sternly went their own way. Whatever her motives, friendship in such a shape was not a little dangerous to its object, and Cecil did not scruple to tell her that ' the malice of the world would ' say that she had used severity to the lords to urge them to ' rid away the Queen.' †   When Mary was deposed, Elizabeth threatened to restore her to her throne by force, and intrigued with her friends in Scotland against the Regent:—

'So,' says Mr. Froude, ' were sown the seeds of those miserable feuds which for five years harassed the hearths and homes of Scotland—which made for ever impossible that more temperate spirit which but for this might have softened the rigours of Calvinism— which caused the eventual ruin of the person whose interests Elizabeth was intending to serve, by tempting her to take refuge in the dominions of a sovereign who was so persistently pretending to be her friend.' (Vol. iii. p. 169.)

Such was Elizabeth's friendship to Mary, while she remained in Scotland; and even Mr. Froude appears to be not wholly without misgivings as to its sincerity. What was her friendship, when Mary, ruined and desolate, fled to her dominions for protection? Mary craved permission to be admitted to her presence, but was refused; she had come to seek comfort from her royal friend and sister, and found herself a prisoner; she had merely fled from one prison to another. ' A guard of two ' hundred men was sent from Berwick to Carlisle Castle,—men ' so faithful that if there was any attempt at flight, Elizabeth ' expressed a fear that they would make short work of their ' charge.' ‡   Mary's flight into England was, no doubt, embarrassing; and Mr. Froude says that ' in the golden era of the ' Plantagenets, such a difficulty would have been disposed of ' more swiftly and more effectively;' but now, in a more scrupulous age, ' the beautiful and interesting sufferer was mani-

* Hist. of Eliz., vol. iii. p. 137.   † Ibid., p. 151.   ‡ Ibid., p. 239.

' festly a dangerous animal which had run into a trap, difficult
' to keep, yet not to be allowed to go abroad, till her teeth were
' drawn, and her claws pared to the quick.' Elizabeth still
affected friendship, but she readily accepted the harsh counsels
of her ministers. She wrote affectionate letters, she continued
her intermeddling policy in Scotland, but she held her prisoner
safe, and was taking measures to destroy her reputation and
influence.

' Oh, Madam,' she wrote, ' there is not a creature living who more
longs to hear your justification than myself; not one who would
lend more willing ear to any answer which will clear your honour.
. . . On the word of a prince, I promise you that neither your subjects, nor any advice I may receive from my own councillors, shall
move me to ask anything of you which may endanger you or touch
your honour.' (Vol. iii. p. 248.)

Most people will think such professions as insincere and insidious as the rest of Elizabeth's conduct; but Mr. Froude
regards her as ' in reality Mary's best friend, who was fighting
' for her against all her own ministers, and, guilty or innocent,
' wished only to give her a fresh chance upon the throne which
' she had forfeited.' We fear, however, that her friendship was
about equal to her generosity. Mary, who had fled without
her wardrobe, complained to the Queen that she was even
without a change of linen; her necessities were nobly relieved
by ' a couple of torn shifts, two pieces of black velvet, and two
' pair of shoes.'

The rags of Elizabeth's friendship were not more worthy of
gratitude. While she made a show of supporting Mary in
Scotland, with high words and menaces, she was betraying her
into submission, and casting toils around her. She had no
right to meddle between Mary and her subjects: she had no
claim to dictate to a neighbouring and friendly State; yet she
assumed to judge of Mary's guilt or innocence, and beguiled
the unhappy captive, by terms of pretended sympathy, into
compliance with her treacherous advice. She promised that if
Mary could acquit herself of the charges made against her, she
should be restored. Mary declined with queenly dignity to be
thus put upon her trial :—

' I came,' said she, ' to recover my honour, and to obtain help to
chastise my false accusers—not to answer those charges against me
as if I were their equal, but myself to accuse them in your presence.
. . . Madam, I am no equal of theirs, and would sooner die than
so, by act of mine, declare myself.' (Vol. iii. p. 255.)

In vain Lord Herries protested, on her behalf, that Elizabeth
' had no right to constitute herself a judge between the sove-

' reign and subjects of a foreign realm. She replied that she
' would not quarrel for the name of judge, but on the reality she
' intended to insist.' No less vainly did he entreat that she
might be permitted to leave England. Elizabeth was resolved
to hold her fast, and to degrade her.

' As to her going to France,' she said, ' I will not lower myself in
the eyes of my fellow-sovereigns by acting like a fool. The King,
her husband, when she was in that country, gave her the style and
arms of this realm. I am not anxious for a repetition of that affair.
I can defend my own right. But I will not, of my own accord, do
a thing which may be turned to my own hurt.' (Vol. iii. p. 261.)

According to Mr. Froude, ' she wished only that so much
' evidence should be brought forward as would justify the
' Lords in their rebellion, and would justify Elizabeth also in
' restoring the Queen with a character slightly clouded—to be
' maintained under her own protectorate, and with her hands so
' bound as to incapacitate her from further mischief.' * ' She
' told De Silva that the Queen of Scots should be restored, but
' restored without power, and her acquittal should be so contrived
' that a shadow of guilt should be allowed still to remain.' † But
Mary herself naturally treated her professions as hypocrisy;
and Cecil wrote ' that it was not meant, if the Queen of Scots
' was found guilty of the murder, to restore her to Scotland,
' however her friends might brag to the contrary.' ‡ At all
events, the unfortunate rival was to be made an instrument of
Elizabeth's ambition and love of intrigue. If she would not
be put upon her trial, before a tribunal which had no pretence
to jurisdiction, the lords were to be charged with rebellion, and
in their own defence were to bring accusations against their
sovereign, which she might answer or not, as she thought fit.
It was a cunning device; but the Queen's jurisdiction was
equally wanting; and her purpose was no less dishonest than
cruel. She intended Murray ' to utter all he could to the
' Queen of Scots' dishonour; to cause her to come in disdain
' with the whole subjects of the realm, that she might be the
' more unable to attempt anything to her disadvantage;' § while
to persuade Mary to appear, she was pretending that if she
could clear herself she should be restored to her kingdom.

After protracted negotiations, intrigues, and vacillation,
Elizabeth completed her subtle scheme. In October 1568,
a commission was opened at York, in which Elizabeth was
represented by the Earl of Sussex, Sir Ralph Sadler, and the

---

* Hist. of Eliz. vol. iii. p. 262.   † Ibid., p. 271.
‡ Ibid., p. 276.   § Ibid., p. 289.

Duke of Norfolk, Scotland by the Regent Murray in person and other commissioners, and Mary Stuart by Lord Herries, Boyd, Livingston, Cockburn, and her chief adviser John Leslie, Bishop of Ross.   All these parties were playing a cross game : Elizabeth was intent upon obtaining evidence of Mary's guilt, without sacrificing her entirely to the Regent; the Duke of Norfolk was forwarding his own design of a marriage with the fugitive Queen ; Murray, distrusting Elizabeth, was fearful of exposing himself to the vengeance of his own sovereign, in case of her restoration ; and Mary was hoping that partly by the aid of Elizabeth, and partly by intrigues with her own friends, and a compromise with her enemies, she might be restored to liberty and power.

The confederate lords were accused of rebellion ; and in reply, Murray defended them on the ground of Bothwell's crimes and the Queen's marriage, without accusing her of being concerned in the murder.   But while he withheld this public accusation, he showed the Commissioners, in private, the proofs which he was able to offer.   ' To this point,' says Mr. Froude, ' Elizabeth ' had brought it ; she had spun refinement within refinement, ' artifice within artifice.   The Queen of Scots was to be accused ' and not accused, acquitted and not acquitted, restored and ' not restored.'   Suddenly, however, she heard of Norfolk's projected marriage, and at once cancelled the York Commission, and summoned all the parties to Westminster.

Here she assembled a council of Peers, before whom the proceedings were resumed.   The Bishop of Ross entered a ' protestation that while ready to treat for an arrangement, ' he was submitting to no form of judgment, nor would admit ' any judge or judges whatever to have authority over his sove- ' reign.'   Murray now openly accused Mary of having been the contriver of her husband's murder, but without producing the proofs ; and the Bishop of Ross contended on her behalf, that she was now insidiously put upon her trial, contrary to the engagements of the Queen of England.   If she were to reply at all, it could only be in person, before the Queen herself and the Peers.   Another attempt was now made to stop the case and arrange a compromise ; but the Queen was resolved that the proofs should not be withheld.   The Bishop of Ross pro- tested, and declared the conference at an end ; but Murray, when called upon to justify his accusations, produced the fatal casket and other evidence.   In this manner, the Queen of Scots had been betrayed into proceedings by which she found herself put upon her trial, in a court having no pretence to jurisdiction over her ; and the proofs of her guilt were now in the hands of the sovereign whose enmity she had too much reason to dread. She was tried in her absence, and in a form which put it out of her power to rebut the adverse evidence, without acknowledging the usurped jurisdiction of the Court.

Mr. Froude is pleased to affirm that ' Elizabeth had not meant ' to deceive ; but a vacillating purpose and shifting humour had ' been as effective as the most deliberate treachery.' * That she showed vacillation in contriving the means of ruining Mary Stuart may be admitted ; but as to the object itself there was throughout an inflexible resolution. She now artfully advised her victim to abandon her defence and throw herself upon her forbearance, which would have been no less than a confession of guilt. This snare was avoided ; she was afraid of being ' entrapped and allured ;' but Mary was disgraced in the eyes of the peers and privy council ; and, as she had refused to offer a defence, there was still an excuse for continuing her imprisonment. On the other hand, Murray had been tricked by false promises into the production of evidence of his sister's guilt, but failed in obtaining a confirmation of her deposition, or an acknowledgment of his own title as regent. Elizabeth had been false, fickle, and treacherous to all parties ; she had betrayed them all alike for her own selfish and tortuous ends. Mr. Froude finds traces of a ' weak and unreasoning tenderness,' and even of ' generosity,' in her conduct, where others see hypocrisy and hardness of heart.

We are unable to accept his judgment upon these events, or to acquit Queen Elizabeth of injustice and perfidy. The flight of Mary into England had been prompted by her own strong professions of friendship, and her pretended indignation against those who had dethroned her ; and to reward her confidence with imprisonment, and reduce her by insidious devices to the degraded position of a criminal, needs a better excuse than vacillation to redeem her conduct from imputations of treachery. However embarrassing Mary's flight into England may have been, it was the clear duty of Elizabeth to have left her free ; and the artful scheme of assuming a jurisdiction over her, which had no warrant in international law, was a monstrous usurpation of power. Her conduct was no less impolitic than unjust ; and however much reason there may have been for apprehending Mary's intrigues with France or Spain, her unjust imprisonment in England was the cause of the greater part of the troubles of Elizabeth's reign. Mr. Froude has laboured heavily to vindicate or excuse her ; but

---

* Hist. of Eliz., vol. iii. p. 350.

we think he has laboured in vain; and that M. Mignet's sterner estimate of her conduct is more consistent with historic truth. Speaking of this period, he says :—

'As for Mary Stuart, she remained a prisoner in England. Elizabeth not only did not assist her against her subjects, as she had promised, but did not even restore her liberty, of which she ought never to have deprived her. Without respect for the rules of justice and the rights of hospitality, as well as for the prerogatives of crowns, she was not afraid to imprison a suppliant and to bring to judgment a queen. She had not been sensible either of the trust of the fugitive, or of the prayers of the relative, or of the affliction of the woman, or of the honour of the sovereign. Mary Stuart, on her side, had no longer any reserve to maintain towards Elizabeth. Arrested with perfidy, defamed with hatred, imprisoned with injustice, she was justified in attempting everything to gain her freedom. She did not fail to do so.' *

More serious difficulties were about to disturb Elizabeth's reign than the torture of a defenceless woman, and officious intermeddling in the affairs of a friendly State; and they were due, in great measure, to her treatment of Mary, and to her insincerity and vacillation in dealing with her own subjects and with foreign sovereigns. The Reformation was so recent that religion was still one of the chief causes of embarrassment in England, as in several other States. The Catholics had been put down; but they hoped for the restoration of their faith in another reign, if not in this. They had looked forward to the succession of Mary Stuart; and her hard treatment by the Queen now led them to espouse her cause, and to precipitate their plans for overthrowing the Reformation, and with it the Queen herself—the chief Protestant sovereign of Europe. The aid of the kings of France and Spain, as great Catholic Powers, was naturally relied on; and hence arose a succession of intrigues and rebellions which distracted Elizabeth's reign for eighteen years.

In August 1568, the Spanish ambassador, De Silva, was replaced at the Court of London by Don Guerau de Espes. The one was a high-bred and accomplished gentleman, averse to intrigue, and without fanaticism : the other was at once a conspirator and a fanatic.

'On Don Guerau had descended the dropped mantle of De Quadra. Inferior to his prototype in natural genius for conspiracy, inferior to him in intellectual appreciation of the instruments with which he was working—he was nevertheless in hatred of heresy, in unscrupulousness, in tenacity of purpose, and absolute carelessness of personal

---

* Histoire de Marie Stuart, 3rd ed., vol. ii. p. 63.

risk to himself, as fit an instrument as Philip could have found to communicate with the Catholics, and to form a party among them ready for any purpose for which the King of Spain might desire to use them.' (*Hist. of Eliz.*, vol. iii. p. 328.)

He at once became the centre of intrigues and conspiracies, into all the secrets of which we are admitted by the Simancas archives and other state papers of the time. Mr. Froude has entered into them with elaborate and instructive detail; he has traced out all the agents in the dark plots by which Elizabeth's throne and life were threatened; and he has introduced us to the inner councils of the Queen and her advisers, by whom these plots were countermined.

Two conspiracies, to which Don Guerau was a party, were speedily set on foot; and in both the foremost place was assigned to Mary Stuart. The northern lords were projecting a Catholic insurrection, the dethronement of Elizabeth, the crowning of Mary Stuart, and her marriage with Don John of Austria. The Duke of Norfolk and his adherents merely sought the overthrow of Cecil, and the marriage of Norfolk to Mary, who was to become a member of the Church of England. While these plots were being hatched, Elizabeth's conduct to Spain and France was so false and treacherous that she narrowly escaped a war with both. She had encouraged and protected English privateers who preyed upon the commerce of Spain; ships laden with Spanish treasure were seized in the ports of Plymouth and Southampton, and appropriated by the Queen; and outrages were committed upon the persons and property of Spanish merchants resident in England. Redress was withheld by cunning subterfuges and falsehood. A policy no less provoking was pursued towards France. While the Queen professed herself neutral in the civil war raging between the King and the Huguenots, she was aiding the Prince of Condé at Rochelle with money and ammunition; and English privateers sailing under Condé's flag seized French ships, and openly sold their prizes at Plymouth and Dover. The remonstrances of the French ambassador were met with transparent evasions.

Happily, the jealousies of France and Spain prevented them from making common cause against England; and Elizabeth continued her deceptions without the cost of a foreign war. But conspiracies at home were naturally fomented by so impolitic an irritation of the Catholic Powers. Elizabeth might have taken the lead of the Protestant cause in Europe. She might have aided the Huguenots in France and the Netherlands, and have conciliated the Reformers of all denominations in England

and Scotland.   Such a policy might have been hazardous, but while generous and noble in itself, it would have secured a hearty support to her throne against the intrigues of the Catholics ; and who can say what an impulse it would have given to Protestantism in Europe !   The mean and pitiful course pursued by her, so far from effectually supporting the Protestant cause abroad, merely encouraged the Huguenots in an ineffectual resistance, while it provoked the Catholics throughout Europe, and won no Protestant sympathy in England.

Such being her relations with foreign Powers, she was exposed to the treasons of her own subjects encouraged by their ambassadors.   The Duke of Norfolk, feeble, hesitating, and timid, had separated himself from the northern lords in pursuit of his own personal objects ; but he had been so far tempted into treason as to seek assistance in his plot from the Duke of Alva ; and when Elizabeth peremptorily forbade his projected marriage with Mary, he was nearly driven into revolt.   But his courage failed him ; he allowed himself to be arrested, and was imprisoned in the Tower.   There he renounced his alliance with Mary, and, after some time, obtained the Queen's forgiveness.

But the Earls of Northumberland and Westmoreland, and their confederates in the North, were more earnest in their conspiracy, and were encouraged by the strong Catholic sympathies of the northern counties, and by promises of support from Alva in Flanders.   All their measures were concerted with the Queen of Scots and Don Guerau ; and in November 1569, the counties of Northumberland, Durham, and Yorkshire were in arms against the Queen. But the South was true and loyal ; the rebels were foiled in their attempt to rescue Mary Stuart ; they received no aid from Alva ; and the Queen's forces soon drove the leaders across the border into Scotland.   Northumberland was taken prisoner by the Regent, greatly to the disgust of the Scottish people, and lodged in Lochleven Castle ; and Elizabeth, not content with the most cruel punishments inflicted upon the rebels whom she had in her power, demanded the extradition of the earls by the Scottish government. Wholesale executions were carried out, in which the Queen showed herself as intent upon lucre as upon vengeance. Numbers of those who had no lands were to be hung by martial law on the parish green or market-place ; and the servants of the principal insurgents were to be executed near their masters' houses ; and ' the bodies were not to be removed, but ' to remain till they fell to pieces where they hung.'   Those who had lands were to be formally tried, in order that the

Queen might be assured of the escheats; and if judgment was not given for the Crown, the prisoners were to be remitted to the tender mercies of the Star Chamber. Elizabeth, ' to ' whom,' says Mr. Froude, ' nothing naturally was more dis-' tasteful than cruelty (!) when Sussex's arrangements (for ' these executions) were made known to her, was only impatient ' that they should be carried out;' and on the 11th January she wrote that ' she somewhat marvelled that she had as yet heard ' nothing from Sussex of any execution done by martial law ' as was appointed; and she required him, if the same was not ' already done, to proceed thereto with all the expedition he ' might, and to certify her of his doings therein.'

While these executions were proceeding, the Queen was trying to force the Regent to surrender Northumberland, and was offering bribes for the treacherous capture of Westmoreland. Murray did not venture to comply with her demands; he had already roused a bitter feeling by the imprisonment of Northumberland; and while he was still holding out against Elizabeth's persistent claims, he was himself struck down by the hand of the assassin Bothwellhaugh.

The Regent Murray is one of Mr. Froude's favourite characters, and deserves a large share of his panegyrics. That he was the enemy of Mary Queen of Scots, and had driven her from her kingdom, would alone have been a sufficient claim to his favour; but Murray had many eminent qualities which, in evil times, commend him to our respect. If it be exaggerated praise to affirm with Mr. Froude that ' when the verdict of plain ' human sense can get itself pronounced, the " good Regent " ' will take his place among the best and greatest men who have ' ever lived,' * we cannot but admire his moral superiority over the ruffians by whom he was surrounded. They were without any sense of religion or justice; he was an earnest Protestant, yet above the narrow intolerance of the fanatics of his own age and country; and he honestly desired that Scotland should be quietly governed and her deadly factions quelled. His greatest embarrassments had been due to Elizabeth's meddling and inconstant policy, and his chief errors to her dictation.

The second of Mr. Froude's new volumes opens with some observations on the influence of the Reformation upon the character of the people in England and in Scotland, which

---

* Hist. of Eliz., vol. iii. p. 581. Mignet's estimate of Murray's character is less favourable; but he does justice to his eminent qualities. (Histoire de Marie Stuart, vol. ii. p. 116.)

will help us to understand some of the political problems of
Elizabeth's reign.   Three-quarters of the peers, he tells us,
and half the gentlemen were disaffected; and they had the
goodwill and encouragement of France and Spain, whom she
had insulted and provoked : yet the northern rebellion had
miserably failed.   It was, indeed, a rash and ill-concerted rising,
and was readily put down by the strong arm of the executive
government; yet if the Catholic body were as numerous and as
disaffected as they are represented to have been, it is singular
that the northern earls met with so little support.   Doubtless
it was one thing to conspire for the restoration of the ancient
faith, and another to rebel against their lawful sovereign ; but
much was due to the characteristics of the two religions.

'Catholicism in England was still to appearance large and imposing, but its strength was the strength of age, which, when it is
bowed or broken, cannot lift itself again.   Protestantism, on the
other hand, was exuberant in the freshness of youth. . . . The
Catholic rested upon order and tradition, stately in his habits of
thought, mechanical and regular in his mode of action.   His party
depended on its leaders, and the leaders looked for guidance to the
Pope and the European Princes.   The Protestant was self-dependent,
confident, careless of life, believing in the future not the past, irre-
pressible by authority, eager to grapple with his adversary where-
ever he could find him, and rushing into piracy, metaphorical or
literal, when regular warfare was denied him.'   (Vol. iv. p. 4.)

With such supporters of her throne, Elizabeth was able to
defy Catholic disaffection and foreign intrigues.

The influence of the Reformation upon the character of
the people, was far more striking in Scotland than in England.

'Elsewhere the plebeian elements of nations had risen to power
through the arts and industries which make men rich—the commons
of Scotland were sons of their religion.   While the nobles were
splitting into factions, chasing their small ambitions, taking securi-
ties for their fortunes or entangling themselves in political intrigues,
the tradesmen, the mechanics, the poor tillers of the soil, had sprung
suddenly into consciousness, with spiritual convictions for which
they were prepared to live and die.   The fear of God in them left
no room for the fear of any other thing ; and in the very fierce intolerance which Knox had poured into their veins, they had become a force in the state.   The poor clay which, a generation earlier,
the baron would have trodden into slime, had been heated red-hot
in the furnace of a new faith.' *

In this faith there was, indeed, a large leaven of bigotry and

------

* Hist. of Eliz., vol. iv. p. 24 ; see also another instructive passage upon the influence of John Knox, p. 456.

fanaticism; but we can never fail to recognise its elevating influence upon the moral character of the Scottish people, nor to admire their resolute independence and indomitable love of liberty. It was one of the faults of the late Mr. Buckle that in his historical review of the people of this country, he dwelt with too much contempt upon their fanaticism, and appreciated too lightly the virtues by which it was accompanied, and the political and social results of an earnest, if narrow, creed.

Religion was still the chief moving cause of the political events of this time. During the northern rebellion, many Catholic gentlemen had scrupled to take arms against the Queen, who had not been excommunicated by the head of their Church; and in order to assist the Catholic cause in England, and if possible to unite Spain and France in a crusade against a Protestant Queen, Pope Pius V., in February, 1570, framed a bull of excommunication against Elizabeth, in which he absolved her subjects from their allegiance, and forbade them to recognise her any longer as their sovereign. As this missive had not the sanction of Philip II., it was confided to the Cardinal of Lorraine, to be issued at the first convenient opportunity. Meanwhile, Elizabeth was resolved upon punishing the rebel lords who had taken refuge in Scotland; and as they were not given up to her, Lord Sussex was commanded to make a raid across the border, which he did in such a fashion that he destroyed " ninety strong castles, houses, and dwelling- ' places, with three hundred towns and villages.' And while executing this outrage upon a friendly State, Elizabeth was increasing the dissensions of that unhappy country by constant intrigues with its various factions. She still refused to recognise the infant James; she still pretended to contemplate the restoration of Mary Stuart; she seemed to favour both religions; she offered her support to any party which would assist in executing the law against the English rebels; she was changing her course from day to day; she was deceiving friends and enemies, until she was assured by Sussex that ' she must ' decide quickly, or she would lose both parties.'

Still she was able to betray and trifle with all who trusted her. She had provoked and insulted France and Spain, but they had shrunk from making war upon her; she had outraged Scotland, but was able to defy its resentment. France threatened to send troops to assist her Scottish ally, but the threat was not carried out. Again an English army crossed the border, and this time it descended upon the Hamiltons, the main supporters of the Queen of Scots, whose restoration Elizabeth pretended to have in view.

Mary's party and the Catholics were furious at this hostile movement; and on the 15th of May, while the army was still in Scotland, the bull of excommunication was found nailed against the Bishop of London's door. Appearing at such a time, it seemed as if France had resolved to carry out her threat, and that a Catholic crusade was about to explode against England. In Elizabeth's councils there was now a serious division of opinion. Lord Arundel, Leicester, and other councillors who favoured Mary Queen of Scots, proposed to avert war by the release of Mary Stuart, an accommodation of affairs in Scotland, and the recall of the army from that country. Cecil was for open defiance of France and the Catholics, and exclaimed 'that the Queen had no friends but 'the Protestants, and if she yielded, she would lose them all.' The stern Lord Keeper Bacon condemned Arundel and his friends 'as secret servants of the Queen of Scots,' and said—

'After what you have done and are doing in Scotland, you cannot now turn back; courage alone is safety—courage and persistence. Go on as you have begun, and there will be soon no Queen's party, no French party, no Catholic party to trouble that country more. English influence will be supreme there, and religion, the Protestant religion, will be established beyond reach of harm from end to end of Britain.' (Vol. iv. p. 63.)

Elizabeth, as usual, was undecided, but she at once recalled her troops to Berwick and renewed negotiations with Mary Stuart. So far the Catholic party had prevailed; and while Elizabeth was doubting and vacillating, she was surrounded by conspirators. Arundel was plotting her overthrow, and Don Guerau was planning a Catholic insurrection the instant Mary Stuart was set at liberty, to be aided by a Spanish army from Flanders. But again Elizabeth changed her course, and while pretending to negotiate with Mary Stuart, she assured the Scottish lords 'that in no wise they should shrink or yield; 'and whatever the Queen of Scots or her friends might say to 'the contrary, they might assure themselves of the support of 'England.'*

It were tedious to follow Elizabeth through all her windings; her fickleness and falsehood exceed belief. She had hitherto prevented the appointment of another Regent to succeed Murray: at length she signified her assent to the nomination of the Earl of Lennox; but, at the same time, repeated her intimation that she was bent on treating with Mary Stuart. No wonder that Randolph, her minister at the Scottish Court,

---

* Hist. of Eliz., vol. iv. p. 71.

declared that she would soon not 'have a friend in Scotland to
' serve her turn.' She had forfeited the confidence of all
parties, whom she had alternately injured, insulted, and betrayed. A third foray was soon made across the border.
Dumfries Castle was blown up, and 'not a stone house left
' standing in Galloway capable of giving shelter to armed men.'
Assuredly Scotland owed little gratitude for Elizabeth's goodwill.

Meanwhile the Papal bull had encouraged a religious reaction in favour of the ancient faith, and sustained the hopes
of the disaffected. Mr. Froude here reverts to the religious
condition of England in such a manner as to call for remark.
He says truly that ' the Catholic spirit was naturally strongest
' where the people were least exposed to contact with strangers.
' In the Midland and Northern Counties, where the feudal
' traditions lingered, the habits were unaltered and the super-
' stitions undispelled;' while the new faith was readily embraced by the merchants and traders of the towns and seaports.
We will not contest his views as to ' the quieter, purer, nobler'
form of Puritanism; but we must take exception to his unjust treatment of the Church of England. The Church, he
says—

'was a latitudinarian experiment, a contrivance to enable men of
opposing creeds to live together without shedding each other's blood.
. . . In itself it pleased no party or section. To the heated contro-
versialist, its chief merit was its chief defect.'

And again, it was the extreme reformers or Puritans—
' who formed the noble element in the Church of England. It was they
who had been its martyrs; they who, in their scorn of the world, in
their passionate desire to consecrate themselves in life and death to the
Almighty, were able to rival in self-devotion the Catholic saints. . .
It would have fared ill with England had there been no hotter blood
there than filtered in the sluggish veins of the officials of the Establishment. There needed an enthusiasm fiercer far to encounter the
revival of Catholic fanaticism; and if the young Puritans, in the
heat and glow of their convictions, snapped their traces and flung
off their harness, it was they, after all, who saved the Church which
attempted to disown them, and with the Church saved also the stolid
mediocrity to which the fates then and ever committed and commit
the government of it.' (Vol. iv. pp. 107–115.)

An English churchman may afford to smile at the irreverent
sneer of this last passage, and to ask where are the Puritan names
which can be arrayed against the illustrious line of worthies
who have adorned the Church of England?* But he is bound

---

* Mr. Froude has introduced into his fourth volume an elaborate panegyric of Thomas Cartwright; but by how many living

to protest against Mr. Froude's view of the latitudinarian scheme of his Church.   Doubtless, it was designed to be comprehensive : in an age of heated controversy, it was intended to avoid needless offence to tender consciences ; it was contrived so as to sink narrow points of difference among Christians in a broad ground of agreement and reconciliation ; it favoured moderation and discouraged fanaticism.   The scheme was at once pious, rational, and statesmanlike.   That it was not entirely successful is to be ascribed rather to the spirit of intolerance which was permitted to deface it, than to its own inherent defects.   And notwithstanding the errors of kings, bishops, and statesmen, the Church so far prevailed over all other religious communions, that within a century after Elizabeth's reign it comprised at least nine-tenths of the people of England. The Catholics had been nearly rooted out of the land, and the Puritan non-conformists were but an inconsiderable sect.[*] When, in our own time, the articles and formularies of the Church of England have been subjected to the closest judicial scrutiny, the keenest legal intellects of the present age have been struck by the extraordinary skill and wisdom with which the groundwork of the English Church was laid.

Apart from differences of doctrine and ceremonial, Catholics were repelled from communion with the Reformed Church by their faithfulness to the papal supremacy ; and many who had submitted to outward conformity were encouraged by the papal bull to discontinue their attendance at the parish church, and to resume their own forms of worship.   The Pope had further absolved them from allegiance to an heretical prince ; and their faith thus naturally led them to disaffection, if not to active treason.   To restore their religion was a sacred duty ; and the overthrow of the Queen was but a necessary means to that end, sanctified by the head of their Church.   Elizabeth was surrounded by traitors : they sat at her council ; they plotted in the House of Peers ; they were betraying her, and scheming against her life, as ambassadors from friendly Powers ; and the rallying point of their treasons was Mary Queen of Scots.

Englishmen would the works of Cartwright now be known if they were not rescued from oblivion by his controversy with so great a man as Hooker ?   But the name of Hooker does not yet occur in Mr. Froude's pages.

* In 1696, out of 2,599,786 freeholders in England and Wales, there were only 13,856 Roman Catholics, and 108,676 Protestant non-conformists. (*Census Report on Religious Worship*, 1851, pp. c. ci.)

To avert the perils by which the Queen was beset at home and abroad, Cecil was sent to Chatsworth to treat personally with Mary Stuart, and Walsingham was despatched to Paris to secure a closer alliance with France.   As regards Mary, we cannot believe that more was intended than to beguile her, by false hopes, from her intrigues with France and Spain, and with the Catholic nobles.   Whatever the purpose, Mr. Froude is ever ready for her execution :—

'There she lay, deserving, if crime could deserve, the highest gallows on which ever murderer swung, yet guarded by the mystic sanctity of her birth-claim to the crown. . . . What to do with her at present, and till the times were ripe for the sharp remedy of the axe, might well try the strongest intelligence.' (Vol. iv. p. 118.)

With France, Walsingham's negotiations took a turn sufficiently ridiculous.   The Court and the Huguenots had lately brought their civil war to a close, and the government were now free for any enterprise which ambition might prompt them to undertake.   Taking the Catholic side, they might espouse the cause of Mary Stuart, and marry her to the Duke of Anjou ; or siding with the Protestants, they might enter into an alliance with England and the Prince of Orange, and drive out Alva and the Spaniards from the Netherlands.   It was a great occasion for adroit diplomacy ; but the negotiations, instead of being directed by high statesmanship, were rendered at once absurd and revolting by the coquetry, indecision, and falsehoods of Elizabeth.   The Duke of Anjou had been spoken of as a suitor of Mary Stuart ; and it was suggested that by marrying him herself, she could disappoint her rival, and secure the support of France against all her enemies.   The idea was not a bad one ; and even Cecil favoured it ; but Anjou was a boy of twenty, and Elizabeth a mature spinster of thirty-seven.   State marriages, however, are not always governed by domestic considerations, and this objection might have been submitted to on either side ; but Elizabeth was already known as a false and silly coquette.   She had befooled many suitors ; five years before she had declined an alliance with Anjou's elder brother Charles, King of France ; lately she had renewed her diplomatic flirtations with the Archduke Charles ; and could anyone regard her present overtures otherwise than as a cunning pleasantry ?   La Mothe the French ambassador, and Catherine de Medicis, at first believed that she merely designed to separate France from Mary Stuart, and to foment jealousies between France and Spain ; and this was probably Elizabeth's real purpose, while her feminine vanity and caprice were gratified by a new matrimonial project.

But Cecil was in earnest. He was persuaded that his mistress's marriage was necessary for the security of her throne; and he believed that this alliance with the French royal family would frustrate treasons at home and combinations abroad. So soon as the French Court could bring themselves to believe in the seriousness of the scheme, negotiations were actively commenced. The governments of the two countries were in earnest; but the parties more immediately concerned were not quite assured of married bliss. The Queen expressed to La Mothe her fear that her suitor's—

'affections must have been already centered in some fairer quarter. She was herself an old woman, and but for the hope of children would be ashamed to think of marriage. . . . French princes had a bad name for conjugal fidelity . . .; and she would not like to find herself the wife of a man who might respect her as a Queen, but would not love her as a woman.'*

The youthful lover, on the other hand, appears not to have shrunk from the ripe charms of his mistress; but he was horrified by tales of her profligacy. If he married a woman of infamous character, his own honour would be touched. Possessed by this fear, he raved against the match, until his mother, fearful of wholly losing the prize, actually wrote to La Mothe, in her own hand, inquiring if Elizabeth would accept his younger brother, the Duke d'Alençon, who was only sixteen, and was amenable to reason! La Mothe, however, assured her that the stories against Elizabeth were unfounded scandals, that her court was pure, and that she enjoyed the respect of all her subjects. Anjou was satisfied, and became eager for the marriage; while Walsingham wrote cleverly from Paris that the Queen-mother was resolved to provide for her son in Scotland, if not in England; and ' of all impending perils that would be ' the greatest.'

That the marriage was politic in itself was proved by the consternation with which its announcement was received by Mary Stuart, by the Catholic conspirators, and by Spain. Negotiations and intrigues became more rife than ever; and the correspondence to which we are here introduced, reveals the extraordinary activity and address of Mary and her agents, of the Spanish Ambassador, of Alva, and of the Catholic nobles, in conspiring against the throne, and even the life of Elizabeth. The Duke of Norfolk was prevailed upon to solicit in his own name, and in the names of forty other nobles, the invasion of his country by a Spanish army, to overturn the Protestant

* Despatch from La Mothe, January 23, 1571.

faith and dynasty, while he, professing himself a convert to the Roman faith, continued, in outward observance, a Protestant, the better to deceive the government as to his designs.*

While these plots were thickening, and the negotiations for the French marriage were proceeding, Elizabeth found herself constrained, by an exhausted exchequer, to call another parliament, after an intermission of five years. The occasion was seized upon by the conspirators, and their plot well-nigh exploded. The nobles brought up their retainers in great numbers, and it was arranged that they should surprise the Queen and Cecil, and make them prisoners, and that Mary Stuart should at the same time be rescued from her prison-house; but the plot failed through the irresolution and cowardice of Norfolk. This parliament was chiefly memorable for its Puritan majority, and for the independent spirit with which it asserted its own privileges against the Crown. Its most important measure was that requiring subscription to the Thirty-nine Articles. It is difficult to repress a smile when we find that the subsidy, for which this parliament had been assembled, amounted to no more than 100,000*l.*—a sum, at that time, adequate to hold France and Spain at bay, to over-awe Scotland, and to quell rebellions in Ireland.

While parliament was still sitting, Cecil found means to discover the dangerous conspiracy which was at work, and to detect the secret correspondence with the Continent. It was evident that Spain was preparing to assist the English rebels, and the alliance with France became all the more urgent. But Elizabeth was trifling with the marriage, as had been at first suspected; and at length Anjou himself, happily for the Queen's credit, threw up the affair in disgust. Negotiations, however, were continued with a view to an alliance between England and France for the liberation of the Netherlands. At this very time Philip II. was discussing with his council, at Madrid, the best means of promoting a Catholic revolution in England. It was resolved that the assassination of Elizabeth should first be attempted; and this enterprise was entrusted to one Chapin Vitelli. Mr. Froude, who dwells perpetually on the horrors of Darnley's murder, discusses this project with philosophical equanimity, and employs the very same arguments which we directed against himself a few pages back.

'Assassination,' he says, 'in that passionate sixteenth century was not peculiar to creed or nation. Catholics profess abhorrence of the murder of Beton in Scotland. Protestants retort with effect

---

* Hist. of Eliz., vol. iv. pp. 149–174, 203–223.

by pointing to the Regent Murray, the Prince of Orange, and the black butchery of St. Bartholomew. But both Protestants and Catholics might well drop their mutual reproaches; their sin was the sin of their age, the natural refuge of men who were driven desperate by difficulties which fair means would not clear away for them.' (Vol. iv. p. 251.)

Don Guerau was urging that the blow should be struck without delay. 'The Catholics were three to one, and were all 'prepared.' *

But Cecil, ever watchful, was penetrating, by fair means and foul, deep into all the secrets of the conspiracy. At length, by artful snares, and by the torture of servants and accomplices, the whole of the wide-spread plot was brought to light. Norfolk was again arrested. 'He fell upon his knees when the 'warrant was brought to him, and cried for mercy like a 'poltroon.' Far nobler was the bearing of Mary Stuart. When she was told that her 'practices against the Queen of the 'realm did deserve a sharper dealing, as time would shortly 'make clear to all the world,' she replied with haughty defiance 'that she had come to England as a free Princess, relying 'upon promises which had been repeatedly made to her, and 'instead of friendship and hospitality, she had found a prison. '. . . She was a free Princess, the Queen of England's equal, 'and was answerable neither to her, nor to any other person.' †
Her chief agent, the Bishop of Ross, was less brave, and confessed everything that concerned his royal mistress, the Spanish ambassador, and the nobles.

Don Guerau being summoned before the council, was told that his practices had been discovered, and that he must depart the realm. The villany of this envoy was almost without a parallel: for three years he had been plotting against the throne and life of the sovereign to whom he was accredited; and now that he was dismissed, he hired two bravos to assassinate Cecil, and lingered on the road, hoping to hear that the foul deed was done. Elizabeth had committed many wrongs against Spain, which would have justified war with England; but that the Spanish King and his ambassador should seek vengeance in the murder of the English Queen and her first minister, is a reproach even to such an age. The coward treachery failed; and Elizabeth had now to deal with her enemies at home.

---

* This Spanish plot is also described by Mr. Motley, in his 'Rise 'of the Dutch Republic,' vol. ii. p. 285.
† Hist. of Eliz., vol. iv. p. 296.

Mary Stuart's part in the conspiracy was visited upon her by the publication of Buchanan's ' Detectio,' in which all the ' doings of Mary Queen of Scots, touching the murder of her ' husband, and her conspiracy, adultery, and pretended mar- ' riage with the Earl of Bothwell,' were exposed.   The casket letters, which had not hitherto been made public, were appended to the work in French and Latin ; and copies were circulated throughout Europe.   At the same time, the Queen threatened ' that if Mary gave any more trouble, the difficulties about her ' would be promptly ended.'

Norfolk was put upon his trial for high treason ; and the unfortunate noble, who had been timid and irresolute as a con- spirator and pitiful as a captive, bore himself bravely before his peers in Westminster Hall.   According to the barbarous fashion of that time, he was denied the aid of counsel, and was at once prisoner, witness, and advocate in his own cause. No trial so conducted can be approved as fair ; but the weak man had allowed himself to be drawn into treason, and the verdict of guilty against him cannot be pronounced unjust. Elizabeth, in pity for his weakness, and in consideration for his rank, would gladly have spared his life ; and he lingered in prison until, some months afterwards, the Commons insisted upon his execution.   The same parliament also sought the life of Mary Queen of Scots; but the time was not yet come when she was to be released from her long imprisonment by the axe of the executioner.

During these critical events, the project of the French mar- riage had been revived ; and as Anjou recoiled from the honour proposed for him, his boy-brother Alençon was seriously pro- posed as his substitute.   The importance of a close alliance with France was now more apparent than ever.   The enmity and hateful plots of Spain had been exposed, while the Court of France was not only eager for a connexion with England, but was also, for a brief interval, friendly to the Huguenot cause.   An effective treaty between England and France might have caused a momentous change in the relations of the two faiths, and in the course of history.   Mr. Froude even goes so far as to say that ' France and England linked together ' by a stronger tie than words, would have freed the Nether- ' lands from Spain.   The Catholic States of Germany could have ' been swept into the stream of the Reformation, and Europe ' might have escaped the thirty years' war, and the Revolution ' of '89.'   If we hesitate to accept so vast an historical specu- lation, we recognise too fully the force of the sword upon the faith of nations, to doubt that a Protestant crusade undertaken by France and England against Spain would have given a strong impulse to the Reformation in Europe, which had been checked and subdued by the temporal power; millions would have been added to the Protestant faith; and in an age when religion was at the very root of politics, who can venture to divine the results of such a change? With more certainty we may conjecture that if France had thoroughly committed herself to the Huguenot cause by a war with Spain, she would have escaped the horrors of St. Bartholomew.

This treaty, however critical, was associated with the marriage of an elderly lady and a boy; and the lady was fickle and insincere. The highest interests of nations were at stake; but this preposterous marriage marred the policy of the ablest English statesmen. In the words of Mr. Froude—

'Elizabeth would give no answer about Alençon. . . . The same in everything—with Norfolk, with the Queen of Scots, with Scotland, with her marriage, with the terms of the alliance—she could decide on nothing. From a mixture of motives, some honourable to her, some merely weak, some rising from the twist in her mental constitution, she hesitated to adopt, and she would not reject, the means which were pressed upon her for preserving her throne, and she laid, with flapping sails, drifting in the gale.'

But to the habitual indecision of the Queen, were now added the silly inconstancies of the woman. One day 'she would ' not marry a boy with a pock-spoilt face;' another, she desired him to come and see her that ' she might try if she ' could like him.' Her ministers were embarrassed by her ' continual dalliance and doubtfulness;' and the French Court was outraged by her insincerity. While affecting to be anxious for the French alliance she was treating, or pretending to treat, with Alva for betraying Flushing into his power. The suspicions of the French Court were confirmed; and these idle and deceptive negotiations were suddenly terminated by the massacre of St. Bartholomew.

When Catherine de Medicis was convinced of Elizabeth's double-dealing, she turned against the Huguenots, whose battles she had been prepared to fight, and threw herself into the arms of the bigoted faction who thirsted for their blood. Her zeal was quickened by jealousy of Coligny's influence over the King. The assassination of the Admiral alone was first attempted; and then the infamous Catherine, under the pretence of a Huguenot rising, wrung from the weak young King his assent to the destruction of their leaders. The bloody work was commenced by the royal guard; and even the King's own guests were murdered in his sight.

' The retinues of the King of Navarre and the Prince had been lodged in the palace at Charles' particular desire. Their names were called over, and as they descended unarmed into the quadrangle, they were hewn in pieces. There, in heaps, they fell below the royal window, under the eyes of the miserable King, who was forced forward between his mother and his brother, that he might be seen as the accomplice of the massacre.'

The mob, more earnest Catholics and not less savage than the court, were soon maddened by the shedding of Huguenot blood, and revelled in a general massacre. Nor were these atrocities confined to Paris; it was pretended that the Huguenots would take up arms; and orders were given to exterminate them in Lyons, Orleans, Rouen, and other towns. These massacres were as savage as those revolutionary butcheries which disgraced France more than two centuries later. The first began with the court—the latter with the people; the frenzy which animated the former was religious; the madness which inspired the latter was political; but both alike illustrate the hideous excesses into which an excitable people may be betrayed by wicked leaders and the dominion of extravagant ideas.

There were rejoicings at Rome; and ' Philip, when the news ' reached him, is said to have laughed for the first and only time ' in his life; ' * but in England there was a general cry of horror and indignation. From many pulpits the preachers demanded ' blood for blood; ' and the bishops besought the Queen that the Catholic priests and gentlemen who were in prison for refusing the oath of allegiance should be immediately put to death! A new direction was at once given to English policy. Elizabeth was estranged from France, and renewed friendly relations with Spain; the English Catholics were neglected by Alva; and the Queen was still at peace with Europe, and mistress of her own rebellious subjects. It is impossible to read Mr. Froude's pages without being impressed with the extraordinary influence of England in the councils of Europe. Notwithstanding the weakness, vacillation, and insincerity of the Queen, all countries courted her alliance, and shrank from resenting the wrongs which they suffered at her hands.

At length, also, a more decided policy was forced upon Elizabeth in the affairs of Scotland. At first it was proposed that Mary Stuart should be given up to the Scots, and by them tried and executed. The terms of this arrangement

---

* For a fuller account of Philip's grim merriment, see Motley's ' Rise of the Dutch Republic,' vol. ii. p. 333.

could not be agreed upon; but her cause was utterly ruined. The French massacres had aroused so strong a feeling of disgust in Scotland, that all parties renounced any remaining sympathy with France, and were ready to 'join with England 'in some straighter league.' The blood-stained nobles might not have been deeply moved; but 'a middle class, made strong 'by faith in God, was stepping forward into energy and self-'reliance; and in worldly strength as well as spiritual power, 'they were making good their place in the commonwealth.'* Such men as these were fired by a sacred indignation against so foul a massacre of their brethren in the Protestant faith; and their preachers gave noble utterance to the popular wrath. John Knox, whose life was fast ebbing away, rallied his strength to preach before a Convention of the Estates, at which the French ambassador was present.

'Turning to him, as a Hebrew prophet might have turned, he said, "Go, tell your king that sentence has gone out against him—that God's vengeance shall never depart from him or his house—that his name shall remain an execration to the posterities to come, and that none that shall come of his loins shall enjoy that kingdom unless he repent."' (Vol. iv. p. 443.)

While the Scots were possessed by such feelings as these, the sacrifice of Mary Stuart's cause naturally offered the means of reconciliation between Elizabeth and the King's party in Scotland. The Regent Lennox had already fallen a victim to the violence of Mary's friends; at this very time the Earl of Mar was carried off, not without suspicions of poison; and it fell to his successor, the Earl of Morton, to continue the negotiations with England. He was resolved that Mary Stuart's party should be effectually crushed, and for this end he sought the aid of England. Money was his most pressing want, and this, with her accustomed parsimony, Elizabeth long continued to withhold by contemptible tricks unworthy of a queen. It was wrung from her at last: she was obliged to recognise the King, without further shifting and equivocation, and to promise armed assistance if required. The effect of her recognition of the young King was decisive upon the Scottish factions. Nearly all the leaders of the Queen's party at once swore allegiance to her son, and accepted Morton as Regent. What miseries would have been spared to Scotland, if Elizabeth had yielded earlier to the obvious necessity of acknowledging the *de facto* King! Edinburgh Castle was now the only stronghold of Mary Stuart's few remaining friends, held by Grange, Mait-

---

* Hist. of Eliz., vol. iv. p. 441.

land, and other leaders on her behalf.   They would soon have surrendered; but they received secret aid from France; and, after the doubtful policy of Elizabeth, they did not believe that she could be induced to interfere in the struggle.   Nor were they without warrant for their doubts.   Having promised assistance to the Regent, she began to fear that her own influence would be weakened by the utter ruin of Mary's cause, and she grudged the expense of sending an army across the border: but, at last, she was brought to reason by the adroit persistence of her clever envoy Killigrew.   An English force was sent from Berwick to aid the Regent in the reduction of the castle, which was soon obliged to surrender; and with it fell the last hopes of Mary Stuart in Scotland.

Elizabeth had little cause for pride in the part she had played throughout these troubles.   She had been arbitrary, meddling, officious, and unjust to all parties.   It was not for her to espouse the cause of any faction.   The Queen had been deposed, and she ought at once to have acknowledged the young King.   Mary fled to her for protection.   She was not at liberty to judge her—that was the office of her own subjects; still less was she justified in consigning the fugitive to a prison.   Her affected interest in her cause merely served to keep alive the dissensions of her distracted country.

Throughout his narrative Mr. Froude has done his best to save Elizabeth's character, at the expense of her weakness and indecision; but he now gives up her defence in the following bitter but too truthful words:—

'To this it had come at last; and the shuffling, and the falsehood, and the broken promises had been thrown away.   A few plain words would have sufficed to annihilate the hopes of the party of the Queen of Scots, which Elizabeth herself had created and had kept alive by her uncertainty.   She had encouraged them to take arms; she had led them to believe that in her heart she was on the Queen of Scots' side; and in the end, after the Regent had been murdered, and her true friends brought to the edge of ruin, after having brought her own throne in danger, and imperilled the very Reformation itself, her diplomacy broke down, and she was obliged to trample out the sparks with her own feet, which she and only she had kindled.' (Vol. iv. p. 465.)

Here, with the exception of a chapter upon Ireland, into which we do not propose to follow him, Mr. Froude's volumes are brought to a close.   From an original history we necessarily gather many new impressions; but we are unable to affirm that our general judgment of the events and characters of this period has been modified by the perusal of this work.   The greater detail, however, into which it enters presents a picture of them on a larger scale. Mr. Froude has laboured hard to paint Elizabeth in more attractive colours than she generally wears; but it is the old face after all. He endeavours to shade her moral obliquities under her irresolution of purpose; and, assuredly, he has succeeded in presenting that aspect of her character in a most striking light. But we are still able to discern, no less clearly, the other faults of her disposition. She was at once fickle and obstinate; she was cold, vain, niggardly, false, and treacherous; and, if we find her weaker than we believed her to be, she appears not more amiable, but only less wise. As for Mary Stuart, if hard words could lower our estimate of her character, she would have fallen low indeed: but the historian's rancour against this unhappy queen has failed to obscure her womanly graces, her high courage, and her rare talents and accomplishments. Nor are we able to lose all pity for her wrongs and misfortunes, though she was stained with all the duplicity and guilt of the House of Lorraine, from which she sprang.

Cecil shows himself to great advantage, as the shrewd, sagacious, and active statesman; and we are enabled to estimate the difficulties which encompassed him—an intractable Queen, a divided and intriguing council, a discontented nobility, an unsettled Church, a people distracted by political and religious dissensions, and the Catholic Powers ever plotting his ruin. That so great a man should have been unable to exercise a more salutary control over Elizabeth is mainly to be ascribed to the influence of other councillors, especially of Leicester, in whose base and cunning counsels may probably be found no little excuse for her vacillation. The Lord Keeper Bacon is just as rough, honest, and fearless as we took him to be. The Regent Murray rises to a higher place in history than has usually been assigned to him—superior to the factions of his country, and pious without fanaticism. Several of the secondary figures, such as Walsingham, Throgmorton, Sussex, Knollys, Drury, and Killigrew, also make a favourable impression upon the reader. In the difficult positions assigned to them they displayed courage and diplomatic sagacity, with a straightforward purpose, which puts to shame the mistress whom they served. And lastly, we are introduced to Alva, not as the cruel bigot with whom we are too familiar, but as a cool and far-seeing statesman, offering moderate counsels to Philip, and not to be betrayed into political indiscretions by an undue zeal for the Catholic cause.

We must now reluctantly take leave of Mr. Froude, whose

volumes will afford an intellectual treat to every class of readers. However familiar they may be with the reign of Elizabeth, they will find it presented to them from new points of view; the characters are drawn at full length, and may be judged by their own words. We read the minutes and marginal notes of statesmen; the despatches of ambassadors; the debates of the council board, and the conversations of the Queen and her ministers. We have before us an animated representation of the time. It is not so much a picture as an historical play, in which the actors perform their several parts with a reality and truthfulness which the most graphic descriptions fail to convey. For the present, the curtain has dropped upon a stirring act; and we await, with deep interest, its rising for another.

ART. VIII.—1. *Antique Gems: their Origin, Uses, and Value as Interpreters of Ancient History, and as illustrative of Ancient Art; with Hints to Gem Collectors.* By the Rev. C. W. KING, Fellow of Trinity College, Cambridge. London: 1860.

2. *Pyrgoteles: Die edlen Steine der Alten im Bereiche der Natur und der bildenden Kunst, mit Berücksichtigung der Schmuck- und Siegelringe insbesonders der Griechen und Römer.* Dr. JOHANN HEINRICH KRAUSE. Halle: 1865.

A RECENT article in this Journal* was devoted to a survey of the minerals that have been invested with different degrees of intrinsic value, and have served for the purposes of ornament among various races of mankind. While seeking to trace the history of precious stones from this point of view, we endeavoured in particular to identify those among them which have been described and alluded to in classical authors.

Our purpose now is to perform a similar office by the art which these imperishable materials have been the means of handing down to us in the form of Gems; and though we might easily fall into the error of exaggerating the importance of this subject as a department of archæology or of æsthetics, archæologists and students of art seem in our day, or at least in our country, to have gone to the other extreme, and to have somewhat undervalued the works of the gem-engraver. By the word ' Gem' we understand, not alone the precious material of the stone, but the combination of that material with a work

---

* Edin. Rev. No. 253, p. 228.

of art either cut in intaglio into the hard and grainless texture of the mineral, or standing in relief as a cameo upon it. The shell-cameos with which Italy now floods the world were almost, if not entirely, unknown to the Greek or Roman artist of ancient times; for the Greek and the Roman artist sought in the sard or onyx a material at once imperishable and beautiful, and of a texture to receive, with difficulty indeed, but not with rough resistance, the incisions of an adamantine tool. The soft shell-cameo needs no such tool, but possesses no such imperishability. It came into vogue during the cinque-cento period, but was then only rarely used, and is chiefly known in the works of a few artists, who availed themselves of this very soft material to engrave in a microscopic manner a multitude of figures within the oval of a small cypræa shell. The vast number of cameos now worked in Italy, on the West Indian Strombus shell, and on the *Cassis rufa* of the West Coast of Africa, are a commerce of this century.

No doubt, the extension of this commerce has tended to demoralise the cameo-engraver in pietra-dura, as well as to spoil the demand for the far more expensive and far more noble works of the lapidary-artist. Of other causes that have also been at work to produce this decay of a beautiful art, we shall have more to say when we sketch the history of that art; for they are causes which influenced both its branches, and have left the world as destitute of great engravers in intaglio as it is of artists in cameo-cutting.

For above two thousand years before our era, intaglio engraving subserved important purposes. The intaglio design, cut in a hard stone, was employed as the seal and signature of its owner. But side by side with this use of a particular art, the scope of art in general, and especially of those branches of it which are allied to sculpture, gradually came to extend beyond the office of historically recording the deeds of Egyptian and Asiatic kings and empires, or figuring their divinities; for, borne upwards by the cunning hands, and guided by the sensitive perceptions, of the Greek race, art passed out of this phase into one in which it dealt more lovingly with nature. Beautiful form and godlike grace began then to conquer the severity of sentiment of the elder artists; and progressing with this freer growth of the arts in general, those of sculpture, of die-sinking, and of gem-engraving entered upon their finest period. To the age that had seen the Parthenon finished, and was daily handling the money coined by the Cyzicene confederacy of Dorian towns, or by Elis, Clazomenæ, and other states of Greece, a few lovely Greek gems must be referred;

and the claims of such gems to admiration as works of art were not only recognised by contemporary eyes, but made them objects to be collected so soon afterwards as collectors arose to gather them. The fine state of many Greek coins existing in European cabinets must, in some cases at least, be attributable to their having been preserved for their beauty. It is hardly likely, however, that, before the days of Alexander the Great, collections of coins and gems began to be made, but it is highly probable that soon afterwards they would have been so.

The first dactylotheca we hear of is that made by Mithradates, and brought to Rome among the spoils of that splendid king, who united to the taste and education of a Greek gentleman the trained eye for jewellery of a Shah-Jehan. This dactylotheca probably included, besides great numbers of mounted or unmounted gems, gold and other rings and precious stones. But Pliny, while mentioning this collection, tells also of one made by Scaurus, the extravagantly magnificent stepson of Sulla, who probably acquired the tastes of a collector in the East, and, by bringing them to Rome, inoculated therewith the wealthy patricians of the capital. During the Augustan era these tastes were gratified by many a luxurious Roman; and conspicuous among such gem-collectors was Mæcenas, who rivalled Cardinal Antonelli himself as a connoisseur of gems and precious stones. Rome was then the centre of gravitation for all that was precious and portable in that wide world that stretched from the gold and tin-bearing sands of the trans-Indian Chersonese to the steep seaboard of the Celtiberian Mountains. The tastes as well as the arts of Greece became Roman by adoption, yet withal retained something of an exotic character. Would we see the Greek gemengraver and his works at home, we must transport our minds to the rich towns of Sicily and Magna Grecia, or visit in fancy some of the Greek colonies along the coast. Indeed, we may almost see again, in all the activity of living art, Panticapæum, the city of that famous Pontine sovereign, half Sultan, half Tyrannos, whose dactylotheca Pliny tells of. To do so, we have only to make a pilgrimage to that imperial palace of art, the Hermitage at St. Petersburg, and linger for a few hours in the room where lie the golden filagree ornaments, the gems, the vases, and the other marvels that have been exhumed from the tombs of Kertch. At Kertch, as in every spot where Greek was spoken, this art was in its home, and thrived so long as Greek nationalities retained vitality. In Rome, indeed, Greek art was domiciled and became a fashion, but was never really at home; and then, as luxury sapped the character and culture grew less refined, the objects sought after by the wealthy became debased, and vulgar ostentation, such as in the exhibition of vast masses of plate, took the place of the artistic fashions of earlier times.　Thus the taste for gems and the encouragement of Greek artists, so rife in the days of Augustus or of Hadrian, had waned before the commencement of the lower empire; and the gem-engraver's art, in common with the rest, sank with the taste it had gratified, and on which it had been fed.

But to be under eclipse is not necessarily to have become extinct, and gems, usually in cameo work of a flat kind on pretty onyxes, are not rare, which, by their Greek inscriptions and the style of the designs, may be recognised as evidently Byzantine.　The subjects they represent are usually the sainted personages of the Oriental Church.　Between these, the character of which remained stereotyped through centuries, and Italian works of the later middle age, the differences of style are not very marked; indeed, the amphibious ecclesiasticism of Venice may be said to have bridged the gulf that separated the East and West—at least so far as ecclesiastical art was concerned.

Among the many examples of mediæval works preserved in collections, we may mention a cameo paste of Italian work of the fourteenth century, in the British Museum, having for its subject the Seven Sleepers.　The material is the reddish-brown kind of opaque glass on which the gold was cemented in ecclesiastical mosaic work—a material that often seems to have been thus employed for the paste in which casts of such gems were taken.　In Moscow, in the Cathedral Treasury on the Kremlin, may be seen some large and beautiful onyxes and sardonyxes cut in cameo, in the Byzantine manner of the fourteenth century.

To the tenth century belong other works of undoubted genuineness, cut in intaglio on rock crystal.　Two of these rare relics are also to be seen in Mr. Franks' department in the British Museum: one is a large slab of quartz crystal, long preserved in the Abbey of Vasor, on the Meuse, representing the history of Susannah and the Elders, wrought in unpolished intaglio, in a series of small tableaux exquisitely drawn, by order, it is recorded, of Lothaire, King of France: its age is, therefore, the latter half of the tenth century.　The other is a large thick mass of the same hard and clear material, in the general lentil-form of the Vesica piscis.　It represents the Crucifixion, and is probably Carlovingian, or possibly Anglo-Saxon work of the same century.　The engraving is again in intaglio, apparently roughly scraped into the stone along the lines of a somewhat careful drawing.

The existence of gems during those centuries is sufficient to prove that the art of gem-engraving had not been lost in either of its branches. The cutting of signets had, however, evidently ceased to be the chief purpose for which it was employed, the sigils of those periods having been engraved almost invariably in metal. But the energy of Lorenzo de' Medici, in the fifteenth century, gave a new impulse to the half-lost art. He collected lapidaries in Florence, he brought together ancient gems for their study, and left behind him a school of gem-engravers that produced, during the cinque-cento period, those enormous numbers, more particularly of fine cameos, but also of beautiful intaglios, in which we recognise a finish and an execution able to vie with the handiwork of the best age of imperial Rome.

In design, indeed, the works of this period will generally be felt to betray a certain mannerism and a pseudo-classical feeling reflected from the character of the age that produced them. And this impression is enhanced by the sympathy of that age for the works belonging to the revival of Roman art under the Antonines—works vigorous in their handling, but florid in design ; loaded with accessories, and evincing a great contrast with those that grew under the thoughts and hands of Grecian artists, always so simple and graceful, so gently moulded, and so tenderly finished. The seventeenth century had, too, its considerable artists ; but the vigour that came down from the cinque-cento period was waning, and by the beginning of the eighteenth century was dead. Some may regret the artificial character of the classical revival of the renaissance; but at least it was so far genuine that the artist went to school among the relics of classical times, and then set about producing works of his own—inspired, indeed, by classical originals, but not mere slavish copies from them. The gem-engravers of the eighteenth century inherited the mechanical part of their craft, which had then become more perfect, perhaps, than any known to Greek or Roman artists; but they used this unrivalled power of execution, not to hand on a vigorous art, healthily repro-ducing such artistic energy as the age may have possessed : they sat down simply to copy, even to forge, the finest gems wrought by the artists of Greece or of Augustan Rome. The very names of real and imaginary Greek artists were counterfeited to give a colour to the deception, and to increase the ignoble gains derived from it. Anyone who has made gems a study must have noticed, among the public and private collections of Europe, reiterated cases of a particular subject treated in repetition, not with the slight variation which the antique artist always allowed himself when he copied, whether from a painting, a statue, or a bas-relief, but in a spirit of intentional and servile copying, whereby the subject has been several times repeated, so as often to leave even the skilful critic at a loss to declare which, among many, was the original.

While the great and wealthy were, during the last century, vieing with one another in collecting gems, it was no wonder that the market should be supplied with them, even though 'antique' works had to be manufactured to order—a process all the more easy in proportion as the detection of the fraud was difficult; for, in fact, it was next to impossible to detect what was genuine among so many counterfeits, in an age so thoroughly uncritical. The wheel of Sirletti at one time, and that of Riga at another, and indeed of a host of most skilful artists at all times in the last century, were busy in producing such counterfeits: copies of a gem being repeatedly made by the same artist, and distributed to eager collectors or to the hungry agents who supplied them. The respectability of Natter and of the Pichlers has been supposed proof to the charge of having knowingly contributed to the confusion; but it is certain that many exquisite quasi-antique gems passed from their ateliers, and in particular from that of Natter, into the market, and passed current for what they were not. It is true that, in the latter part of the century, some of those artists, like Marchant, aspired to doing original work, and that a few of Riga's heads are almost Greek in character and finish. But in general these attempts at original design were not successful; and we must remember how statuesque is the design adapted for a gem, and how dependent the growth of a gem-engraver's art must ever be on the progress of sculpture. Hence, an age in which the latter art is in a sort of abeyance is not one in which the art of gem-cutting may be expected to flourish. Some of the earlier artists in the century had even made the mistake of taking elaborate pictorial compositions as the subjects of their design; but another cause also came in to interfere with the progress of this branch of art.

By a natural law of reaction, an age of collecting is succeeded by an age of fastidiousness and criticism. Moreover, in the first quarter of this century scholarship was already becoming more sceptical, and classical archæology was at the same time growing into a closer alliance with scholarship; whence a touchstone more sensitive and more sure than any to which they had yet been submitted began to be applied to gems. Under the scrutiny of these finer tests, the collections of the previous generations have been resolved into their many heterogeneous elements.

When we analyse an average collection of gems formed in the last century, they may be more or less easily distributed into certain general groups. First there are the laboriously-finished but inflexible works of the Archaic-Greek style ; then come the quaint, exaggerated, and incompletely-finished figures on Etruscan scarabæi. About such there could be little or no hesitation ; nor can the critic doubt the age of the rude and half-barbarous gems turned out by the more degenerate artists of the middle empire, although, strange to say, it is not always easy to discriminate between the work of rude archaism and that of barbarous decrepitude. Again, the simple attributes of the pure Greek gem of Greece proper and her eastern colonies can be generally recognised ; while the more voluptuous but elegant art of Magna Græcia and Sicily, like that of the early empire and of the age of Hadrian, presents in its finer productions characteristics sufficiently distinguishable by the experienced eye. In short, whatever was most and least perfect in antique art usually asserts itself in characters easily read. But difficulties in abundance arise so soon as we come to deal with gems of an intermediate character. It is when a gem might have been the work of the more ordinary artist belonging to the Italo-Grecian or to Imperial Roman times, or might again have been an imitation of such work by a modern or even a cinque-cento hand, that we feel uncertainty as to its age.

The direct copies made in the last century from antique gems of the highest class may sometimes puzzle the critic ; but an eye trained in the recognition of the different mechanical conditions of polish and of surface, in the peculiar application of the tools at different epochs, and in the nature, form, and quality of the stone itself, is not often foiled in the endeavour to find satisfactory evidence as to whether a gem was worked two thousand or one hundred years ago. Allowing, however, for exceptions on which even experts must differ, the majority of the gems in a collection may be generally discriminated and grouped as antiques of various ages and races, or as modern works belonging to one of the three centuries succeeding the renaissance. These modern works usually form a large proportion of the collections of the last century. Of cameos, by far the greatest number belong to the cinque-cento period. Among the Greeks, the cameo seems to have been a rare form of gem, for it was used, not as a signet, but as an ornament.   To the Greek period some of the noblest remains of cameo work may have to be attributed if, as we believe Mr. Newton deems to be not improbable, the beautiful Borghese Tazza at Naples, and the world-famous glass cameo vase in the British Museum— the Portland vase—should prove to be of Ptolemaic date. With the Romans, cameos became more common, especially at a time when the rarest products of India were attracted to the capital of the world, and large and beautiful specimens of onyx and sardonyx were brought from Indian hills and river-beds into the studios of the gem-engraver.   Then, in that luxurious age—the age of Hadrian and of the Antonines—these poly-chrome works came into fashion, and the several varicoloured layers of the sardonyx gave half the effect of a painting and more than the effect of a mosaic to the cameos into which they were converted.   Large and complicated groups were to be seen, such as those which still survive in the world-famous cameos of Paris and Vienna and the Hague, worked in the character of low ' bas-reliefs, ' in which the wreath or the paludamentum worn by an Emperor may be carved in one layer of the stone, the hair in another, and the flesh in a third chosen for its marble whiteness, while the whole is backed by a ground composed of a dark sard-like stratum of the stone. A large cameo in the Marlborough Collection, measuring 8 inches by 6 inches, has no less than four such layers.   We have seen that this taste lingered on in the ecclesiastical forms of Byzantine art to the very dawn of the renaissance ; and the wonderfully beautiful works in cameo of the sixteenth century were really the result of a rejuvenescence of a venerable art, that through long ages had retained a sluggish but genuine vitality.   Some of the most splendid works of Græco-Roman art are to be found in the phaleræ or ornaments of the coat of mail, often cut from fine blocks of chalcedony into cameos in high relief.   Of such, perhaps the noblest existing specimen is a huge Medusa's head in the Blenheim Collection, which must have stood like a boss on the breastplate of an Emperor and glared with something of the severe majesty of the Gorgon herself on all who looked at it.   But however salient the relief of the ancient cameo, where the material was monochrome, or however the artist might riot in the fantastic use of the different coloured layers of the sardonyx, in a relief that was in that case generally low, this kind of work was never undercut, or was so only in rare and peculiar instances.   The more modern forms of cameo are, on the other hand, constantly undercut, apparently with the intention of increasing the effect of the relief by the aid of the shadow thrown by a projecting part of the design.

An amusing anecdote is told apropos of the infallibility of collectors almost within our own age, and is said to have given gem-collecting a severe shock in this country. A little cameo had been purchased by Payne Knight. It represented, in the form of a fragment, a profile head of Flora, in very high relief, on a pretty and not very antique-looking sardonyx. Cut with the grace and skill of a considerable artist, it represented the goddess with roses in her hair; and these are left in a red layer of the stone, elsewhere cut away. Proud of his acquisition, and of the antique characteristics which Payne Knight would fain recognise in it, here at least that collector thought he might boast of possessing a cameo irrefragably Greek; and for once throw back at Thorwaldsen his cynical saying—' Sunt gemmæ, sunt virgines.' But, alas! the ' Greek ' artist came forward to claim his own! ' Remove the setting,' said Pistrucci, ' and you will see the artist's name—the name ' of Pistrucci.' The anecdote does not go on to relate whether this clever engraver had put red roses (and double roses, too!) in the hair of Flora as a joke. He could hardly have seriously put them there as an antique attribute. Nor would any artist who really knew what antique art was, and wished to imitate it, have left the nose in a profile portrait undercut in complete relief! Strange to say, this incident seems rather to have increased the general mistrust of gems than to have thrown doubt on the discrimination possessed by some of those who collected them.

The artist who cut this cameo, and whose daughters have with some success pursued his art, deserves a passing tribute. By domicile an Englishman, he was one of the last as well as ablest of modern gem-cutters. His delineation is always beautiful, often finely classical, and his finish in execution is worthy of a Pichler.

It was during the last century that the greater number of the collections, as well public as private, now known in Europe were formed. It is true that two or three private gem-cabinets had been made in an earlier century, and portions at least of some of the great public collections of Europe had their origin in still earlier ages.

Lord Arundel, the great collector of artistic works in the reign of Charles I., brought together a valuable series of gems peculiarly rich in small ancient cameos, and famous also for that magnificent work of the cinque-cento period, the Marriage of Cupid and Psyche—perhaps the most exquisite cameo in the world. Of the same age was Praun, a wealthy burgher of Nuremberg in Nuremberg's palmy days, whose name has been familiar to the gem-student on account of the fine collection—so rich in subjects, and in the varieties of the stones they were engraved upon—which some years ago was bought from his descendants by Madame Mertens-Schaffhausen, and was recently the property of the Rev. Gregory Rhodes. Much described by German archæologists, this was the collection which Mr. King chose for the chief illustration of his work on Gems. It was offered to the British Museum, at perhaps an inopportune time, for 1,000 guineas; but the offer was declined, and the collection, together with Madame Mertens-Schaffhausen's additions to it, in all some 1,800 gems, is now dispersed.

Portions of the dactylotheca of Lorenzo de' Medici are still among the treasures of the Uffizi Palace at Florence; while Vienna and Paris, like the Vatican, inherited heirlooms of ancient gems, the history of which is in many cases obscure or entirely lost. Some of these would seem to have been spoils from the days of the Crusades—the less valued remains, it may be, of choice and antique ornaments from Byzantine treasure-chambers shorn of their golden mountings; others, again—and they include certain of these last-mentioned—were relics of the past, preserved in the shrines and sacristies of religious houses, through the ages when art was ecclesiastical, by monks who classed such gems amongst their valuables. Sometimes they were held venerable from the distance of the age when they were dedicated, or were esteemed for their association with a precious material in which, as now on the golden altar-plates of San Ambrosio at Milan, they were enshrined; or again, the engraved subjects which they bore gave them a sanctity in pious eyes, that saw in the representations of a pagan myth or heathen god themes drawn from the traditions of Christian hagiology. Mr. King, in his 'Antique Gems,' records some extraordinary illustrations of these interpretations. Isis and Horus passed for representations of the Virgin and the Child; a muse holding a mask was held to be Herodias with the Baptist's head; the head of the Olympian Jove was held to be that of St. John, and the enthroned figure of Jove with his bird was the seated form of that evangelist with his symbolic eagle. The innumerable heads of Jupiter Serapis were received as portraits of so august a Person as Christ Himself, and gave the type to the later representations of Him; while, however, these differed widely from the traditionary similitudes of Him in old Christian frescoes in Egypt, or in the Christian glass and other relics in the catacombs of Rome.

Among the public collections of Europe it would be difficult to select one that in all respects stands before the rest. Florence would perhaps carry off the palm for its equally fine examples of cameos and intaglios. Paris, like Vienna, is rich in the former, and contains the Bigarris Collection, formed in the reign of Henri Quatre, afterwards incorporated with the purchases and acquisitions of Louis XIV., the gems of Gualdi, Lanthier, and De Morceaux, and with those bought by King Louis's uncle, Gaston of Orleans. Since the Duc de Luynes' collections have been given to the public, perhaps the French collections may rival Florence in intaglios also. Berlin is especially conspicuous for a magnificent collection of intaglios, in variety of subject the richest, as it is, thanks to the scholar-like labours of Professor Toelken, the best catalogued in Europe. This Berlin Collection consists for the most part of that formed by Baron Stosch in the last century, and purchased by Frederic the Great for 30,000 ducats. With a few gems that had previously been brought together by members of his house, and with purchases made from time to time, the number of gems and pastes have risen to as many as 5,000. At Naples there is a beautiful collection, admirably exhibited; while the Hague contains many fine gems, including the Hemstershuys Collection, famous as having been that which awakened Goethe's admiration for this form of art. It had been formed by Natter's advice and aid, and contains several works by his hand. The collection of St. Petersburg is a very extensive one, comprising the renowned Orleans gems, together with a portion of the Strozzi Collection from Florence, and other collections purchased at various times.

In our own country, we have in the British Museum the national collection, which, it is reported, will shortly be arranged and exhibited to great advantage. It comprises the private collections of Townley, Payne Knight, Hamilton, and Cracherode; and the unrivalled series of cylinders and stamps brought to light by Mr. Layard, besides many well-chosen additions which have been made to it by purchase from time to time. Quite recently a considerable number of gems have been acquired from Signor Castellani, including the St. Angelo Collection from Naples. The anxiety, perhaps extreme, to buy nothing but what was genuine and antique beyond dispute, has interfered in former times with the increase of the national cabinet of gems; but it is nevertheless a rich collection, more particularly of intaglios, and is gradually rising into a position by the side of the older and larger collections of the continent.

Among the private gem-cabinets formed by the taste of the wealthy in the last century and a half in our own country, the following deserve to be particularised :—

First on the list comes that formed by George third Duke of Marlborough—the 'Magnificent' duke, to whom Blenheim also owes its gallery of pictures—the chief adorner of that splendid palace, as the present duke may fairly be called its restorer and illustrator. The Blenheim gems consist in part of the collection of Lord Arundel before alluded to ; one of the few now remaining undispersed that were formed before the great age of forgeries. It came into the hands of Lord Charles Spencer, the brother of the third duke, through his wife, Lady Mary Beauclerk ; having passed to her from her great-aunt, Lady Betty Germaine, the second wife of Sir John Germaine. Sir John had received them under the will of his first wife, the divorced from Henry seventh Duke of Norfolk, the great-grandson of the Lord Arundel who formed the collection. To the Arundel gems the 'Magnificent' duke added the collection of Lord Bessborough, formed when he was Lord Duncannon, which Natter had catalogued, and some of which Worlidge etched. To these were added by purchase many very valuable gems, and the whole now amounts to some eight hundred. It is a collection so choice in regard both to the intaglios and cameos forming it, that it may fairly assert a claim to rank even with the great national collections.

The Devonshire Collection is another of the great English cabinets of gems. It has acquired a deserved celebrity for the fantastic but pretty mountings in which the late duke had the choicest gems of the series set, when they were fashioned into the personal ornaments that formed the unique parure of the late Lady Granville. They were worn by her at the coronation of the Emperor Alexander II., in the Cathedral of the Assumption, on the Moscow Kremlin. Mr. King has given in his treatise a short account of some of the more remarkable gems in this parure.

No doubt, other scarcely less splendid inheritances of gems are to be found in the mansions of the English nobility. The Earl of Home possesses a portion of the collection that once belonged to a Duke of Montague ; and Castle Howard must contain the gems collected by the Lord Carlisle of that past generation in which Worlidge etched the finest gems he could procure for the exercise of his art.

The choice collection of Dr. Nott, and the vast one formed by Mr. Herz, have been dispersed ; while those of Mr. Gregory Rhodes, of Mr. King, and of Mr. Bale, may be said to be still

forming. These three have been made with much discrimination ; Mr. Bale's, though small is extremely choice, as well
for the beauty of the stones as for the Greek work embodied
in them, while Mr. Rhodes' Collection has been formed with
much instinctive taste for art, and contains some very fine
gems.
   In France, the collection of the Duc de Luynes has now become the property of the nation, by a munificent donation from
that accomplished nobleman ; and that of the Duc de Blacas,
said to contain the best of the Strozzi and of the Schillerscheim
gems, has just lost the noble owner who did so much to form
it.   M. Fould and Baron Roger are among other collectors
who have brought taste and wealth to forming cabinets of gems
in Paris; and if in our own country, the formation of such
cabinets has ceased to be the pleasure of the wealthy and has
become confined to a few gentlemen of refined tastes but not
princely means, in France, at least, it still has the advantage of
being prosecuted by men who possess both.
   Mr. King's book on ' Antique Gems ' is a valuable addition
to our literature, as being really the only work on the subject
in the English language.   With the charm of a sort of art-
miscellany, we may open it where we will and are sure to find
pleasant reading, though it has nothing of the accuracy and
nothing of the dryness of such a book as a German scholar
would have written.   The second section—on the styles of art
and the tests of antiquity—is, so far as it goes into these two
subjects, almost as good as it can be.   A part of this section
treats of the tools in use in antiquity—a subject of great difficulty, but on which Mr. King has not thrown much new light.
Yet one would think that by means of the microscope, and
by a knowledge of the manner of cutting by tools now in use,
we ought to be able to say whether the work bequeathed to
us by any particular age in antiquity was wrought by similar
instruments.
   The modern engraver uses chiefly two sorts of tools—the drill,
a blunt little point or button of various forms, with which he
drills holes downwards into the stone ; and the wheel, a minute
disc, varying also much in size and form, on the end of a fine
wire, which cuts by means of its periphery as the drill does by
the whole of its front surface.   Both rotate rapidly, and are
fed with oil and diamond or emery dust, which, bedding itself
in the soft iron or copper material of which the tool is made,
produces an adamantine cutting or grinding surface.   The
artist having drawn his design on the stone with a fine point,
now brings the stone into contact with the revolving tool, and

cuts into the hard substance, first sinking hollows with his drills, and then cutting the finer lines with his various sorts of wheels. He continually examines the work by taking impressions of it on soft wax, and so controls his progress. Lacking the power of correcting a too deep incision, or erasing a line that has wandered even a hair's-breadth beyond its intended course, the gem-engraver needs a marvellous skill and delicacy of hand and eye; and all the more so as he is so little aided by that instinct which in other arts—such as those of the musician and the painter—gives to the hand an unconscious sympathy with the eye and the mind of the artist.

Let us now turn to the workshop of the antique gem-cutter. Pliny tells us of the *terebrarum fervor* and the *ferrum retunsum* used for these; also of the fine splinters of adamas, *adamantis parvæ crustæ,* mounted in iron, and used actually to scrape lines into the stone. We have also a passage in that work of Fronto, so curiously recovered from the wreck of ancient books, wherein (writing in the age of the Antonines) he speaks of the cœlum and marculus, the engraving tool and little mallet, whereby they grave the little gems, probably here meaning cameos (*gemmulas exsculpunt*), as distinguished from the cold chisel and sledge-hammer by which large stones are broken up. These passages really seem to contain all we know from the literature of antiquity about the gem-engraver's tools, and they accord remarkably with what we see now in the mechanical treatment of the works the ancients have left to us. If we read for the splinter of adamas, small sharp splinters of hard minerals like sapphire or emery, formed sometimes perhaps of the actual pin-points of diamond, sometimes of somewhat larger splinters of those other minerals, we may satisfactorily account for the fine grooving by sharp artistic lines which certainly is constantly met with in Greek work, and was held by Natter and is held by Mr. King to characterise it, even in times when we must remember the diamond would have been unknown. The drill seems to have been the one weapon of the early Etruscan workman, though he must have known a way of using it as a traversing tool much like the wheel, if we may judge by the appearance presented more particularly by the 'Etruscan border' when seen in the microscope. Later he must have used the splinter. The great question, however, is as to the date of introduction of the wheel, and on this Mr. King quotes Pietramari, an engraver at Rome, with whom he seems to concur in placing the date in the reign of Domitian—that is to say, just at the beginning of the revival of the art under Hadrian — and no doubt in that case this revival may have been accelerated or even produced by it. Natter, however, while giving the Greek all the prerogative due to his masterly use of the splinter, denies that he was ignorant of the use of a wheel, though he seems to allow that some gems were produced by the former only. Natter's authority, however, would carry more weight had he lived in a more critical age, and were we consequently sure that his conclusions were drawn from veritably Greek gems. Still, the microscope seems to confirm his view, by showing continually that rounded form at the ends of the longitudinal section of the incised lines which characterises the work of the wheel. We may illustrate this point by reference to a gem, the pedigree as well as the Greek character of which are beyond suspicion.

In the Hermitage at St. Petersburg is to be seen a scaraboid chalcedony found in a tomb at Kertch, carrying on it a flying stork, engraved in the shallowest Greek manner, and, at first sight, one would say almost entirely by the splinter. The pinions seem thus scraped out, and the cross lines indicating the feathers are apparently formed in the same way; yet a close inspection, with a moderate magnifying power, of the longer lines of the pinions, leaves it very difficult to believe that they were not worked by a wheel like the tool now in use. This gem is the more critical a test as it carries a signature—

ΔΕΞΑΜΕΝΟΣ

ΕΠΟΙΕΧΙΟΣ

—symmetrically written in two lines of large Greek letters, singularly recalling a similar inscription on a very large and famous amethyst, with a bust of Minerva, the original of which is among the Blenheim gems. It runs—

ΕΤΤΥΧΗC ΔΙΟСΚΟΥΡΙΔΟΥ

ΑΙΓΙΑΙΟC ΕΠ.

Both gems are indisputably antique—the former, Greek of the utmost purity; the latter, a Roman gem. Both alike set at flagrant defiance every one of the golden rules and criteria by which the German critics and Mr. King profess to determine the genuineness or otherwise of such an oft-forged enhancement of the interest and money value of a gem as the signature of the artist who engraved it. Even in this signature, however, it is impossible to believe that the lines of the Ε and Ξ, for instance, were not cut by a wheel, for they subside at their extremities in a concave curve. So, too, the O seems certainly the work of a tool in the form of a little pipe still used by the gem engraver for boring a hole or cutting in a circular line.

It is a hazardous thing to make these assertions in an absolute way, but, so far as comparison goes in observations of this kind, it seems to be as we have stated.

That Pliny does not mention the wheel—if, indeed, it as much as the drill be not implied in his language—would be little proof that it was not in use to anyone accustomed to the manner of the author of the ' Historia Naturalis.'

That Fronto, in his marculus or little mallet, may give us a fresh glimpse into the workshop of the gem-engraver, is not improbable. If so, his allusion is perhaps to some method of bruising the surface, where the design is to be sunk, by means of a blunt iron or copper tool, acting through the agency of emery dust, and tapped continually by a little mallet ; in short, abraiding the stone on a small scale, after the manner that designs are cut into granites and porphyries on a large scale— a manner certainly employed by the Egyptians in engraving on their monuments. The ' Meplat ' or flat shallow manner frequent with Greek artists may have been thus produced. It is often asserted that a modern gem may be discerned by a want of polish in its hollows. This may be true of gems cut within the last twenty-five years ; but, certainly, it is so far from being true generally, that the very perfection of the polish in the hollows of a gem by a Pichler or one of the great engravers of the cinque-cento period, is to the skilled eye condemnatory of the gem as an antique. The degree of polish in an ancient gem generally varies in different parts, and while penetrating every portion of the work, is never of the resplendent lustre of the modern sort.

Whether the ancient engraver availed himself of lenses has been often questioned; but this question can really have but one answer, and that answer is given by a lens now. Look into a gem with a moderate power, and you see detail in the work, and evidences of a mode of manipulation that could not have been there but for a power of vision in the artist that the unaided eye, except in the case of very short-sighted people, is not endowed with. Mr. King remarks truly that the actual incisions made with the instruments cannot be performed under the inspection of a lens, which is only of use in observing on a wax impression the progress that the tool has made. But the modern artists owe to the use of high magnifiers in this latter process the extreme minuteness in detail which they have been able to introduce into their works. The ancients had no such convenient means of using high powers; but it is quite impossible that an age which could cut crystal globes to cool the hands of luxurious ladies, and formed continually plano-convex gem stones of transparent materials, should have avoided making the simple observation that these lens-like objects magnified whatever was seen through them. Nay, Seneca even mentions the fact as regards globes of water. Here, as in the case of the wheel, Pliny's silence is interpreted as a negative argument of far more value than it is worth.

We are constrained, then, to conclude that, though the tools and appliances of the ancient engraver may not have been so convenient as those in modern use, they did not differ widely from these in their character ; only from some cause the Greek and the late or finer Etruscan artist depended little on the wheel, perhaps using it the less on account of some comparative inconvenience in his mode of mounting it. But also the cause of the wheel superseding other tools during the middle empire may have been due to diamond dust becoming an article of commerce only towards the decline of Greek art ; and though the wheel can be used with other dust, such as that of sapphire or garnet, it was the use with it of diamond dust that gave it such superiority as a tool. Sassanian and later Roman gems are almost entirely cut with it, aided occasionally by the drill.

Whatever at different times and among different nations may have been the forms into which the stones carrying intaglio may have been shaped, their purpose in all the earlier ages must have been the same. The gem was the 'signet.' It served the purposes at once of the seal and of the signature of the owner, from whose person it was inseparable, and with whose body it was often consumed or interred. Its impress was the ratification of his act and deed, as its impression was the guarantee and witness to his individuality. That a companion so important should soon become an ornament fashioned in 'costly sardonyx' or other stone precious and beautiful, and embody whatever art the particular age could impart to it, is the natural consequence of the functions the gem-signet had to perform.

Through long ages, with one branch of the human family, it was shaped as a cylinder or little roller, on which figures and legends were inscribed, and which served to impress those figures and legends on clay as the cylinder was rolled over the surface of the plastic substance. The axis was bored to receive the wire that fastened it to the arm or wrist of the wearer. With other nations, we find the form of the signet assuming such shapes as square or rectangular tablets, stones in the form of the beetle, conical stamps, spheroidal seals ; while among the Greeks, and those who borrowed their arts, the stone was usually cut with flat or plano-convex faces, and mounted so as to be worn in a ring on the finger.

In reviewing these various forms of signet in the order of the nationalities that made use of them, we shall be dealing with a subject that ranges over the whole period of authentic history. Indeed, in the gems that have been worn by any civilised people, we possess an epitome of that people's arts, their religion, and their civilisation, in a form at once the most portable, the most indestructible, and the most genuine.

We may begin with cylinders, the roller-like form which the inhabitants of Mesopotamia gave to their signets from before the days of Urukh (the supposed contemporary of the biblical Chedorlaomer, the Kudur-mapula of Sir Henry Rawlinson) to those of Xerxes—from at least 2000 or 2050 to 480 B.C.

This large portion of human history has been conveniently broken up into the following divisions :—

First Period, or earlier section of the Primitive Chaldæan Empire in Lower Mesopotamia. We may call this the Early Chaldæan Period—from about B.C. 2234 to about B.C. 1675.

Second Period, or later section of the Primitive Chaldæan Empire. The Archaic-Babylonian Period; the seat of government being fixed at Babylon—from about 1675 B.C. to about 1500 B.C.

Between the Second and Third Periods some 600 years elapse, during which we have as yet obtained but little knowledge regarding the arts of the nations in Mesopotamia. The evidences of them revive among the ruins of Nimrood, and we commence our next period in the mid-career of the great Assyrian empire, founded probably by Tiglath Pileser I., about 1110.

The Third Period, or Early Assyrian Period, will date from about 940 to 625 B.C. ; and

The Fourth Period, extending from the fall of Nineveh to the entry of the Persians into Babylon, will be the Assyro-Babylonian, or Later Babylonian Period—from 625 to 536.

The Fifth Period will be the Perso-Babylonian, or Persian Period, dating from B.C. 536, and extending to the time of Alexander.

The cylindrical signets which are so characteristic of all these periods are usually from one to four inches in length, with a diameter of about a third or fourth of their length. The collection of them which the British Museum owes to the zeal and energy of Mr. Layard is the most complete in existence. In what follows concerning these forms of signet, reference is made exclusively to this collection,* while nearly all that is known regarding the information conveyed by the cuneiform inscriptions on these cylinders is due to the patience and sagacity of Sir Henry Rawlinson. It may be well to go into some detail on the subject, as at present little has been written upon it, but in doing so it must be borne in mind that the precise dates assigned are subject to modification from the results of future research.

To the first period belong several cylinders, and among them one at least is said to bear a character still more archaic in form than that used in the days of Urukh. This is, therefore, far older than 2050 B.C. Like many others of the earlier dates, it seems to consist of a dark, compact, but not very hard serpentine. Others, again, of this first period, are formed of stones as hard, and indeed as beautiful, as those which the Greek and Roman sculptor delighted to engrave. Thus to the three centuries between 1700 and 2000 B.C. we may refer several beautiful dark-green jasper cylinders; a few also of a pea-green jasper, just like a variety greatly used in conjunction with lapis-lazuli in Egyptian ornamental work. One in the British Museum consists of a black jasper mottled with white; while another, apparently belonging to the earlier part of this period, is a ribboned jasper, so cut that the bands run as in a spiral of alternate stripes of a reddish-brown and white. Of these cylinders, many are composed of a stalactitic carbonate of lime, a few of quartz crystal, and about an equal number of lapis-lazuli. One of them consists of a fine translucent green chalcedony (a kind of plasma), containing a breccia of angular and rounded fragments of a similar green mineral, only just inferior in hardness to quartz crystal. The design engraved upon it represents, repeated twice, a bearded man in struggle with a wild bull, erect on his hind legs, and recognisable by his widely-spreading, knotted, curved and tapered horns, as the colossal wild buffalo, or arnee, of the Eastern world. In the field is a diminutive bull of apparently a different domestic species, that seems introduced to raise the other figures into heroic magnitude and dignity. An arrow-headed inscription completes the design, which is cut into this difficult stone by an art that had obviously triumphed over the hardness of the material. The moulding of the bull's carcass is strongly rendered, but its anatomy is

---

* We desire to express our obligations to Mr. Coxe, lately of the British Museum, now Professor of Sanskrit at Calcutta, for information regarding the inscriptions and dates on many of these cylinders.

admirable; even the legs are artistically finished in all their details of hoof and fetlock and muscle. One is tempted to contrast with this monument of archaic Chaldæan art, another, also with a bull for its subject, though at least six hundred years later in date, which is one of the oldest known gems of Egyptian workmanship on a stone of such hardness. It is a small rectangular slab of beautiful yellow jasper, carrying on one side a hollow-backed horse, fed by a Pharaoh, with the cartouche of Amenophis II.; on the obverse is a bull standing at rest. It is remarkable for being drawn in a delicate but still archaic manner and modelled in a flat shallow method, that contrasts strongly with the deep-cut workmanship and vigorous freedom of the archaic Chaldæan artisan. The drawing is not good enough for a fine period of art, the workmanship too careful for the gnostic age when this yellow jasper was much in vogue, and the cartouche presents an accuracy of type never met with in the later times. One can hardly, therefore, doubt the genuineness of this monument of Egyptian art.* In some of the most ancient cylinders, the deeper grooves seem to run in long sweeping lines, that look rather as if carved out by some sharp instrument than as if scraped out by a hard tool of steel or stone; and it is difficult to inspect some of these deep, long incisions, often narrowing as they shallow, without a belief that they were the work of a wheel-like tool—for it must be borne in mind that these jaspers and chalcedonies are far harder than any steel even of modern tempering.

When we come to the second archaic period—that, namely, when Babylon became the seat of the primitive Chaldæan or archaic Babylonian empire—the chief difference to be observed in the cylinders consists in the material being for the most part hæmatite : a pure oxide of iron, somewhat softer than the jaspers, and capable of taking a fine metallic polish. It is during the later part of these sixteenth and seventeenth centuries B.C., viz. in Khammu Rabi's reign (about 1517?) that these hæmatite cylinders seem most abundant. They are probably the seals of his chief officers. To this period, precise

---

* Objections may be raised to the genuineness of this stone on the ground that the Egyptians did not work on hard stones. The answer is that several other such signets are known—one notably in sard, also in the British Museum, of the reign of the same king, and carrying a horse exactly the counterpart of that on this jasper. Egyptian monuments everywhere refute the idea that this people was unable to cut such stones. The yellow jasper may have been chosen as nearest in colour to the usual material for such signets, gold.

dates in which are not as yet attainable, a beautiful little cylinder of smoky quartz, and another of amethystine quartz, would seem to belong; a pretty onyx, a cornelian, and a few jaspers may also be referred to it. The work on the hæmatites and later cylinders of the period often presents in the grooves a sharp angular section, such as might be cut by a tool (whether curved or straight) the edge of which must have been nearly square, and grooves worked by this tool may be seen running in successive ridges in ornamental parts of the design.

Leaving the history and the arts of Lower Mesopotamia, we leap the long gap in time that separates our second period from that of the great Assyrian empire. There exist, indeed, impressions on brick of a Shalmanassar and Tiglath Pileser I. (names that recur in later history); and they may serve to remind us that it is the monuments of art that are wanting, not that the art itself was in abeyance through these 600 years. We may hope that sites yet unexplored of ancient cities in Mesopotamia will one day yield up their records, and help to complete this great chapter in the history of Asia and of man.

Our third period, which succeeds to this historical gap, reaches from about 940, when Sardanapalus I. was king, and the capital was at Nimroud, down to the destruction of Nineveh, in 625. To this time belong a few pretty flesh-hued cornelians of a very wax-like texture, and in beautiful preservation; one of them is said to carry a date equivalent to 940 B.C. These are found mingled with a few of hæmatite, serpentine, jasper, and other stones; in all, some fifty or sixty cylinders that belong to this great period of the Assyrian empire. About one-half of them would seem to be confined in date to the years between 750 and 700, or rather later. Among these is one of amazon stone—a variety of felspar of a fine bluish-green colour, mottled with white, and described as the signet of Sennacherib, whose name it carries. It is remarkable that in later times the smaragdus, of which the amazon felspar may then have been considered a variety, was the material set apart for royal signets. The whole of these cylinders present purely Assyrian features, such as we see them in the larger monuments exhumed from their fossil state by Mr. Layard. The older ones are the more conventional; the later are the more free in their treatment, and are at once of a finer workmanship and generally on harder stones. The older cylinders of this group also often exhibit a style of ornamentation that recalls to our mind the different milled, guilloche, and other varieties of the so-called Etruscan borders on Phœnician, Etruscan, and Early Greek gems. On the other hand, the cylinders of a date subsequent to 700 begin to show the importation of Babylonian ideas.

The Medes and the Babylonians combined to destroy Nineveh in 625 B.C., and Babylon then emerged from her long historical eclipse, to shine as the resplendent capital of a new Assyrian empire. During this our fourth period, extending from the reign of Nebuchadnezzar to the entrance of the Persian in 536, Babylonian imagery is found blended with or superposed on the emblems and art of Assyria. The drapery becomes more elaborately finished; a feathery tiara-formed crown is frequent; while the lotus, the ibex, the sacred tree, the winged Presence—the 'Feroher,' something like that on Egyptian monuments—and a four-winged figure, are among the permanent but as yet uninterpreted or unsatisfactorily-interpreted emblems of Assyrian art that retain their places on the cylinders of this Assyro-Babylonian period. The stones of this time are always fine—generally chalcedonies—and often of that beautiful blue variety known by the epithet of sapphirine. Eyed agates and brecciated jaspers are also met with. It may be worth remarking, that the use of a shallow drill seems to have been not uncommon in the hands of the engravers of this Assyro-Babylonian period.

Before leaving the subject of cylinders, we must call attention to the last phase in which they presented themselves during the fifth, or Persian period. After the conquest of Babylon by Cyrus, this form of signet became less common; but if we may trust to the famous chalcedony with the portrait of Darius Hystaspis in his chariot, it must still have been the symbol and borne the warrants of sovereign authority. In point both of material and of workmanship, these Persian cylinders are the finest, as they are the latest, of this class of gems. Slightly barrelled in form — a peculiarity observable in one or two of the Assyrian period — they are made of beautiful stones, such as rich red sard, onyx, mocha-stone, agates, and jaspers, all selected for the beauty or contrast of their colours. The subjects on these Persian cylinders teem somewhat more with monsters than those of the Assyrian or Assyro-Babylonian periods; and one never-failing characteristic of their style consists in the dresses being looped up, whereas on the cylinders of the previous periods, extending over some 1,500 years, these long garments hang nearly to the feet. A few cylinders of somewhat enigmatical character—one or two probably Median, others of Parthian origin—and again a small number that seem to have been originally Assyro-Babylonian cylinders, on which Himyaritic inscriptions were afterwards engraved in South Arabia, cut on beautiful agates, nearly exhaust this important chapter in the history of gems, and of human art.

But there is still a class of gems that must be included in a survey of the Asiatic signets—that, namely, known by the name of stamps, or stamp seals. These, for the most part (so far as they are at present known), seem to belong to the Assyrian period subsequent to the middle of the eighth pre-Christian century, and previous to the destruction of Nineveh. They do not appear—so far, at least, as examples of them are known—to have been employed in Babylon previous to the Persian conquest; after which, however, in small numbers and in rather more diversified forms, they recur. The Assyrian stamps are usually in conical or conoid forms. The cone is truncated and generally facetted by planes tangent to its conical surface, so as to present a sort of octagonal slightly pyramidal handle for the seal, which was engraved upon its base. Sards, cornelians, agates, and quartz are materials of which these stamps are fashioned, but the favourite stone appears to have been the sapphirine chalcedony. Stamps of this material, of extraordinary beauty, may be seen in the Assyrian Gallery of the British Museum, one or two with a colour and lustre and a translucence that might well delude the eye into the belief that it was looking on a veritable sapphire. Among the more common subjects on these Assyrian stamps are to be seen priests making offerings before altars dedicated to different divinities, probably the ' patron saints ' or gods of the owner of the signet. An altar on one of them is surmounted by a dove—possibly an allusion to Semiramis ; while on others men wrestle with animals, or men and genii hold up the ' Feroher,' or winged Presence, over the sacred tree, the sun and moon often occurring in the field.

The few Persian stamps are cut on stones fantastic and pretty, of the onyx kind, and exhibit the same class of subjects as those seen on their cylinders, a lion and a man in combat being one of the most frequent on them.

We have dwelt at some length on this important though somewhat obscure period in the history of the engraver's art, partly because it is entirely new, and partly because Mr. King has unaccountably attributed the earliest engraving on hard stone cylinders, crystal, onyx, &c., to the ' engravers of Nineveh ' shortly before the time of Sargon,' who reigned in 720, just previous to the date of Sennacherib. He quotes the so-called Sennacherib's signet as an illustration of this early work, and he speaks of amazon-stone, of which it is composed, as one of the hardest substances known to the lapidary—unaware, it would seem, that a hard knife will scratch it. We have seen reason for declaring that human art had learnt the mastery over materials far more stubborn than this beautiful felspar at a period in Egypt probably 700 and in Chaldæa not less than 1,000 years earlier than the date of Sennacherib.

Of Asiatic gems during the Seleucid and the Arsacid periods, subsequent to the conquests of Alexander, we possess but little certain knowledge beyond a few portraits of the Syrian kings in a fine Greek manner ; but when, under the Sassanidæ, the exotic Greek art fostered by the previous dynasties gave way before the encouragement of native arts and the Parthian language, seals and stamps with oriental features again appear. The portraiture that had become a fashion soon after the days of Alexander, by the use of coins carrying a likeness of the head (but rarely, by the way, of the bust) of the sovereign, and repeated, of course, in the imitative art of the gem-engraver, continued in vogue ; but the treatment was Asiatic—not very refined in manipulation, though elaborate in details chiefly wrought by the wheel ; and the subject, especially where it is a royal head, often carries a circumscription in Pehlevi characters to which those of Greece had now yielded place.

The stamps of this Sassanian period—which, it is to be remembered, extended from A.D. 226 to A.D. 651—present singular rounded spheroidal forms, frequently pierced as a coarse but small ring. They differ much in shape and ornamentation ; are usually cut out of chalcedony, or carnelian, or jasper ; and in general the finer—or rather the less coarse— works would seem to belong to the earlier dates, down to about 300 A.D. But the finest relics of this latest phase of Persian art are the regular ring-stones, which, notwithstanding their Greek form and origin, the ' Parthian ' empire of the Shahpurs and the Chosroës must have consented to receive as an inheritance from the Greek taste of the days of the Arsacidæ. These ringstones are often beautiful specimens of almandine and other kinds of garnet—of amethyst, lapis-lazuli, nicolo, and all sorts of sard and chalcedony in large and rich variety ; and the seals vary in size from the minutest of carbuncles to the famous amethyst signet in the Devonshire Collection, of Bahrám Kermán Sháh, son of Shahpur (or Sapor the Great), which carries that prince's portrait, and a superscription recently read by Mr. E. Thomas.

We may now turn from the cylinders, stamps, and seals of the Asiatic world to the discussion of the beetle-stone, or scarabæus ; and to trace its history we must track back against the stream of time up to the early records of another people possessed of associations and arts not less venerable than those of the primitive Chaldæan empire; for the beetle form is met with among some of the oldest of the monuments of Egypt. It is usually carved out of a very soft steatitic or talcose stone, and glazed with a beautiful blue glaze (known to the Greeks as the ' artificial ' κύανος—a copper compound that formed an article of export to Greece, and of which, indeed, an exported cake was discovered at Camirus, and is now in the British Museum). As an ornament and as a symbol, the scarabæus existed as early and probably far earlier than the reign of Cheops, the founder of the Great Pyramid; for a steatitic beetle-stone of this kind in the British Museum has that sovereign's cartouche on its base, and another has that of a succeeding king. This would give the scarabæus a date of at least 2,300 years before our era—a date as early as that of Urukh in Chaldæa. But that this form of stone was in early times used by the Egyptians as a signet is doubtful, though long afterwards, in the age of the Ptolemies, certain seals still carry the marks of the beetle's feet round their edges, and were evidently impressed by beetle-stones.

The tablet of yellow jasper already alluded to, like a similar one of sard, belongs to the period of Amenophis II., about 1450 B.C.; and another in the British Museum, formed of a beautiful mottled maroon jasper, carries the cartouche of Rameses II., and would have an age, according to the chronology of the Egyptologers, of about 1320 B.C. These tablets would seem to have been true Egyptian signet-stones, for they are pierced by a hole to carry a fastening, in which a gold ring adapted to the size of the thumb was fitted. The Egyptian scarabæus was not, however, confined to small glazed steatitic ornaments; it was fashioned of many materials and of various sizes, from the colossal greenstone monster that now loads the floor of the British Museum, to the elegant green jasper, mounted in a plaque of gold, in the same collection; and numerous scarabæi occur in sard, in lapis-lazuli and amethyst, and, in short, in every material prized by Egyptian taste.

Nor was the scarab form confined to Egypt: it became, for some reason or other, the favourite shape of gem among races that were indebted to that nation for many, at least, of the details of their art. But with the Egyptian, the beetle or ' Kheper '—a word to which the German ' Käfer ' and our ' Chafer ' are probably allied—was the symbol of a worship; for this insect seems to have been looked on as a type of self-creative Power, and so of the Creator; inasmuch as to it was attributed (of course, erroneously) a faculty of self-reproduction—a sort of parthenogenesis, to use the language of modern physiology.

But for the Semitic races of Lower Egypt—branches of the same family as the Phœnician colonies of Palestine, and various islands and cities on the Mediterranean—the beetle had probably no superstitious significance, and yet both they and the perhaps kindred Etruscan race continually employed it; probably as a habit, acquired during the intercourse of the ingenious trafficking and industrious, but apparently not inventive Phœnician race with the civilisation of Egypt. The dark-green jasper scarabs found in the cemeteries at Tharros, in the island of Sardinia, are many of them undoubtedly Phœnician; and in workmanship, in material, and in subject, a little gem in the British Museum, found at Gaza, harmonises with these. This gem is mounted in a gold handle ornamented with the heads of gazelles, not unlike the mountings of some from Tharros, very Egyptian in their fashion. On the base of this jasper beetle is a figure of Baal (?) slaying an erect lion, like the subject so frequent on the monuments and on the cylinders and conical stamps of Assyria and of the Perso-Babylonian period. On these enigmatical scarabs, as on the other art-monuments of the world-wandering Phœnician race, we continually find Egyptian details mingled with art, mainly Assyrian or Babylonian, in its larger features. Artisans, but not in the highest sense, perhaps, artists, it is not improbable that their hands wrought the fictile vases and bronzes, if not the gems, in ancient use in Mesopotamia and in other parts of the world. Solomon employed a Tyrian, ' cunning to work in gold and silver, brass ' and iron, in purple, and in crimson, and in blue, and that ' could skill to engrave gravings with the cunning men that ' were with him in Judah and Jerusalem, whom David his ' father did provide.' May not many such Hurams have been known in the halls of Mesopotamian palaces, and were not the works in stone, in metal, in coloured fabrics, and in ivory, that adorned those palaces, made by Phœnician hands, and perhaps imported in Phœnician caravans? Their race had the command of the mines of Cyprus, that supplied the archaic world with copper, even as it would seem by a commerce that reached to India; and Phœnicians in that distant age reaped the golden wealth of the mines on the isle of Thasos and the adjacent Thracian coast.

Many of the copper vessels found in the North-West Palace at Nimroud present a close similarity, if not identity, in fabric and subject with those that have been found among undoubtedly Phœnician monuments in Cyprus and elsewhere, and are considered by Mr. Franks to be monuments of the handicraft and of the commerce of that people. They often, moreover, carry Egyptian symbols and hieroglyphics; but these, like the Cufic letters in some mediæval churches and monuments, are without other meaning than that of an exotic and ungenuine ornamentation. On the other hand, were the men that ' could skill to ' grave ' in hard stones, Phœnicians too ?

To this we must reply, that the cylinder form of signet is almost exclusively confined to Mesopotamia, and that the great antiquity of the art embodied in them, and the evident directness of descent of that art from the days of Urukh to those of Darius Hystaspis and Xerxes, alike preclude the idea of its being other than indigenous even on such stones as lapis-lazuli and amazon felspar, which were importations from beyond the confines of the Chaldæan, and probably also of the Assyrian empire.

Indeed, had these cylinders been wrought by Phœnicians, we should probably have found them among the tombs in Phœnician colonies. On the contrary, in the few cases where the gems belonging to this race have been met with, they are not cylindrical, but beetle-formed ; while a few cylinders inscribed with Phœnician characters seem to have had these characters cut on them in times long subsequent to the date at which the cylinders themselves were engraved.

How the scarab form came to be domiciled among the Etruscans is at present a mystery as dark as the origin of that people, their religion, and their arts. Like the Phœnician scarabæi, the Etruscan sort differed slightly in shape from the sacred beetle of Egyptian tradition : the favourite materials for the scarab also varied with the national tastes of the people who used them ; Phœnician gems being usually composed of a dark-green chlorite-jasper somewhat similar to the green base of the bloodstone, and (though rarely) also of a dark liver-brown jasper, while the Etruscan scarab was usually cut out of various kinds of carnelian and sard, and often also of veined and banded agates. Specimens also exist cut from amethyst, garnet, green chalcedony, and even emerald.

The ' Etruscan border,' to which allusion has just been made, was so called from the belief formerly held, that it was the characteristic mark of Etruscan work. It consists of an ornamental fringe or cordon engraved round the base of the beetle-stone, close to its edge, and forming a little frame within which the engraver usually confined his design. On one gem the border is ' granulated,' and looks like a string of beads ; on another— as the ' milled ' border—it consists of a sort of little ladderlike succession of cross-bars, uniting (generally at right angles; sometimes, however, obliquely) two parallel lines that girdle the face of the gem; while the 'guilloche,' again, is the most complex border of all, representing two wires loosely twisted. It is formed by a succession of *S*-shaped lines, in place of the straight cross-bars of the 'milled' border, and these are so neatly and regularly blent with the continuous lines that bound them, as to give to the whole the appearance of a delicate twist or plait. In all cases, save those of the poorest work, the finish of this little framework is most carefully elaborated, and the degree of elaboration is usually in some proportion to the beauty of the stone and finish, as well of the scarab as of the design it carries.

After examining these borders under the microscope, and especially the more careless ones, in which the artist was more liable to betray something of his method, one finds it difficult to believe that they were not the work of a revolving tool of the nature of, if not actually, a wheel.

That the scarab form ever became domiciled in Greece proper, or even in the more thoroughly Greek parts of Italy, is very questionable indeed, notwithstanding that a few such gems have been found in Ægina and in Greece. Gems certainly are not rare on stones of a scaraboid form; that is to say, on stones—usually chalcedony, lapis-lazuli, or amethyst—cut so as to have the general outline but none of the details of elytra, head, or feet of the beetle; and such stones, even of considerable size, are not unfrequently met with on sites as Greek as the work upon the gems themselves. But they are rarely, if ever, archaic; on the contrary, they often carry work of the best period of art. The chalcedony with a noble Victory arranging a Trophy, recently purchased by the British Museum from Signor Castellani, said to have been found in Sicily, and realising the description by Suetonius of the signet of Galba— 'Sculptura gemmæ Victoriam cum tropæo exprimens;' a fine lapis-lazuli Aphrodite 'anadyomene,' dug out at Athens, and belonging to Mr. Rhodes; the unique gem, a chalcedony with the signature of Dexamenos, found at Kertch, and now in the Hermitage, with other scaraboid gems exhumed at the same place, are among those that may be cited as grand examples of Greek engraving on stones cut into this form. Similarly formed stones are frequent with what appears to be Persian work on them; indeed, the form appears to be one fostered rather by Asiatic than by Greek tastes.

The presence of very fine Greek work within an 'Etruscan border,' upon ring-stones, finds its explanation in the probable supposition that the Greek, if he had ever borrowed the scarab form, soon discarded the beetle for the plain signet-stone calculated for mounting in that essentially Greek kind of signet, the finger-ring, whether the stone were sawn from a scarab or specially cut for the purpose. The scarab border, however, was for some time retained — more particularly in Italian-Greece — but that, too, was discarded when Greek art threw off all the other trammels of its archaic phase.

To distinguish Etruscan from other gems, though a task not exempt from the confusion introduced by forged imitations, is usually one of the least difficult presented by a collection. But to trace the connexion of Etruscan art with the early art of the Greek colonies of Italy; to seek an explanation of the use of the scarab-stone as a national custom; or to endeavour to unravel the threads, whether of ethnological relationship or of geographical accident, that had interwoven the myths and religion of Greeks with the worship of gods and an angelology possibly Semitic, but certainly of a type Greece did not know — these are tasks which the best archæologists have approached with modesty, and allowed to belong almost wholly to the regions of conjecture. That the Etruscan was personally indolent and voluptuous—' pinguis Tyrrhenus,' as we see him in his sepulchral effigies from Vulci and Tarquinii—is certain. That he gratified luxurious tastes, more particularly in the details of personal ornament, we find confirmed by the beautiful gold and gem-studded relics left in Etruscan tombs. That Etruria had arts of her own seems also evident, whether the artists and artisans who laboured on them were of native race, or Greeks working under Etruscan influences, or were both. That these arts extended beyond the confines of the Etrurian states also, there is some evidence to prove.

The so-called Etruscan fictile vases—the vases really of the whole Greek world—are indeed Greek, not Etruscan; the true fictile work of Etruria, so far as we at present know it, was to the last degree rude. And yet passages are not wanting in ancient writings to tempt us to give to this nation something of the place in the Greek and Roman worlds which we have just been assigning to the Phœnician in regard to the metallic utensils and smaller ornaments of Mesopotamia.

The ' Tyrrhena sigilla' of Horace would seem to allude to little statuettes after the Etruscan taste, and which, therefore, must have had artistic claims sufficient to fascinate and to satisfy the fastidious Roman. But Athenæus quotes Critias as averring that ' Etruria bore off the palm for gold-wrought ' bowls, and for all the bronze in use for economic purposes,' even in Athens herself, that 'nurse of arts and eye of Greece.' Indeed, the mines of Campania were celebrated for their copper produce from those days of old when, according to the tradition recounted by Pliny, the mythic Numa instituted a guild of brassfounders—the early days of an era during which a native Etruscan art had flourished that was well-nigh extinct in Rome when Pliny wrote.

It would probably be easy to exaggerate this Etruscan commerce. The Etruscans, however, were rich, and wealth indicates at least an industry and a commerce of some kind. It does not, however, follow that the artisans who developed that industry were Etruscan, though the maritime character of the people in early times is eminently in favour of their commerce having been so. The Greek lived near, and was of a versatile and enterprising nature; and it is not impossible that a class of artisan Greeks may have early settled in the land and become Etruscan in all but their religion, their mythology, and their arts, and these they may have engrafted on what they found in the Tuscan cities. Still, Etrurian art and religion never became wholly Greek. The one retained its style; the other, some at least of its characteristic forms and elaborate ceremonial, together with the names of certain of its divinities.

Thus the art of Etruria never quite loses a native quaintness; for we find stiff and serio-comic attitudes as well on the wall-paintings of late tombs as on the rudest types of early gems. The roughness of outline, the exaggeration in anatomy, the disproportion and incompleteness, or rather unrefined completion of delicate details, such as in the terminations of a figure, are other characters that it never quite shook off.

So, again, while the whole system of Greek mythology and tradition became naturalised in the Tuscan's household, it failed in entirely Hellenising his religion. The winged form of divinities—so rare in Greek art—was their habitual though not universal guise with the Etruscan; so that on two scarabs at Berlin and in the British Museum, Jove, with the thunder-bolt hurled from his hand, stands as a figure with vast wings over the object of his vengeance—a woman's form, called by the gem interpreters Semele. On other scarabs we see winged figures, silent monuments of a religion that is as lost to us as the language of the people who worshipped under it. And then, again, on how many gems as undoubtedly Etruscan, do we see the heroes of Hellenic myth represented on the little arena of the stone striving or acting there the oft-told deeds of Grecian story! An Italian cycle of myth collected, indeed, round

Hercules; but Theseus, Œdipus, Philoctetes, the thunder-blasted Capaneus, Othryades, Perseus, Ajax, Achilles—these are chiefly heroes of the Theban and Iliad cycles; Greek of the Greek, whence should they get any hereditary claim to an Etruscan domicile? Yet are they the subjects of the majority of Etruscan gems; and the gem-engraver, as if to tell the story of his work to a half-foreign people who might else mistake it, has on many of the finest of these gems inscribed the names of the heroes he represents on them—names that are nearly always corrupted forms of the Greek, except where, in the case of divinities, native titles have been applied to such Greek deities as the Etruscan had adopted as the representations or counter-parts of his own. In the famous gem at Berlin, found at Perugia, five of the seven heroes against Thebes are depicted in a carefully-finished but archaic guise, with the name of each inscribed by his side. That this feature is not confined to gems is shown by the beautiful mirrors from Etrurian tombs. In one of these, not the least valuable of the many splendid additions recently made to Mr. Newton's department at the British Museum, Menelaus and Helen are represented in an art exquisitely Greek in style but with names inscribed in Etruscan characters.

But whatever may be the true solution of the problems involved in the relations of Etruscan art and religion to the mythology and arts of Greece, and however profound the influence of Greek thought and technical method may have been on the artists who engraved the Tuscan gems and mirror-cases, it is certain that the engravers of Etruria worked in a style that retained its distinctive features, notwithstanding the near neighbourhood of the Greek artist of Southern Italy. At one time resembling the Greek art in its archaic phase, Etruscan gem-engraving seems to have retained its charac-teristics with but slight alteration, while the arts of Magna Græcia were being developed into noble beauty. It is as though the Etruscan had been cut off from the fountain-head of artistic nourishment, and retained in almost a stereotyped form the arts he had at some earlier time drawn from that living source.

Still it is probable that, if we could assign their dates to the Etruscan gems in our collections, we should be able to prove that the art embodied in them had not been entirely stationary. For we believe these gems may be classed into two or three broad divisions. First, there are figures, generally of ani-mals or armed men, unparalleled in rudeness by any known to Greek art. Formed of hollows sunk by an obtuse rotatory tool into the stone, they vary in crudeness of workmanship and rudeness of design from the coarsest attempts at an animal shape, to a class of work in which the engraving begins to take the form of art. This latter sort of gem is often carefully drawn, much as if it had been done by the hand of a vase-painter; and the interior is merely ground out by a drill, so as to represent the design somewhat with that kind of 'flat-tint' effect which characterises the vase-painter's art, and with very little attempt at rendering any of the inner markings of the anatomy. Besides animals and warriors, one sees satyrs and a few heroic and mythological subjects on such gems as these. The best of them may perhaps be compared to the rude attempts at animal representation on the most archaic bas-reliefs and fictile vases of Greece, the Archipelago, and Asia Minor. The next stage in excellence would be that wherein the inner anatomical markings are given with distinctness. This style represents the nearest approach that the Etruscan ever made to the Greek gem-engraving, as the works in it are often very similar to those archaic works which in Greece proper we should assign to an age of at least 500 B.C., while in Italian-Greece we might assume for them a somewhat later date. To this style of Etruscan gem, that probably retained its type for several generations, we should refer such scarabs as the 'Five against Thebes' at Berlin, the 'Ajax carrying 'Achilles' at St. Petersburg, and even the 'Perseus' at Berlin, and a similar gem in Mr. Bale's collection; indeed, a large proportion of the finest specimens of beetle-stones in the collections of Europe belong to this class. The sort of solemn grotesqueness so general in Etruscan art rises in these gems to its height. The area within the Etruscan border is usually overcrowded, by the figures labouring, as it were, to find room within it; but what distinguishes them particularly from the Greek works of the archaic style is the incompleteness of proportion and finish in the extremities, and an exaggeration in the delineament of the excellent but overwrought anatomy of the figures—a peculiarity which we have seen also to characterise the art of Mesopotamia.

But there is a class of Etruscan gems between which and the last no sharp line can indeed be drawn, though the more characteristic examples in either class are readily distinguished from those of the other. Here the area of the gem is no longer crowded; there is something like a margin between the figure—usually a single one—and the 'Etruscan border.' The grotesque element seems to be yielding place to solemnity of treatment; and if the drawing still wants the freedom and justness of proportion of the Greek, the technical process has been very carefully carried out, though with Etruscan incompleteness and the habitual rigidity of manner.

In entering on the somewhat bold endeavour of assigning some date to such gems as these, we may observe that their design is often eminently pictorial ; and in this respect they have much in common with some of the Roman consular coins of finer fabric. The Aurora leading out the Horses of the Sun, with the name of the moneyer Plautius Plancus, 47 B.C., is an instance in point. In subject, these gems now and then agree with such coins. An instance of this presents itself in a fine gem formerly in the possession of the Marquis de Dree, and lately in the collection of the Rev. G. Rhodes, but now one of that gentleman's liberal gifts from his collection to his friends. It is a rich banded sard agate, with a representation of Ulysses leaning on his staff, recognised and greeted by his faithful Argus. The subject might have been taken from a bas-relief, or a fresco ; hardly from a statue. But besides a smaller gem, with a similar treatment of the subject in the Etruscan manner, in the Hertz Collection, and besides a gem in the Berlin Museum, on a convex cornelian, in which the same subject occurs in an admirable Italo-Greek style, we have a consular coin of the date of 671 A.U.C., or 83 B.C., coined by the moneyer C. Manilius Limetanus, so like in its drawing, in its Etruscan style, and in the proportions of the figures, to Mr. Rhodes' Etruscan gem, that no one can doubt some well-known painting or bas-relief to have formed the original of them all. It is hard to believe that any very wide distance in time separated the period when this coin and that Etruscan gem were produced.

Among the finer examples of the highest Etruscan school must be placed the famous Theseus at St. Petersburg, once in the Orleans Collection, with the name inscribed on it in clear but rather Roman-shaped Etruscan characters: OESE(Whese). It is a sitting beardless figure, the head leaning on the hand, in such an attitude of solemn grief as might befit a mourner in Hades—

> ' Sedet æternumque sedebit
> Infelix Theseus.'

The figure spontaneously suggests the line ; nay, one can hardly forbear the thought that Virgil and the gem-engraver had looked upon and had drawn their pictures from one original.

A gem in the British Museum is singularly similar in treatment to this Theseus. It is a seated bearded figure in the act of adjusting an arm to a skeleton. Behind it in clear microscopic Etruscan characters, is a name that would read as *Pigitu*; possibly Pigmalion—or, it may be, Prometheus forming man. The work is even finer and more delicate than the Theseus; the dress, even the ornament on it, the chair, and the position of the feet, all are the same in both. Another noble gem of this class is the Tydeus, lettered *Tute* in the Berlin Collection—a lithe and sinewy form, using the strigil —and many others might be quoted from famous collections.

Is it rash to hazard a conjecture regarding the date of these finer Etruscan gems, and to assign them to a period that ranged from some 200 B.C. down to the influx into Rome of Greek artists at the beginning of the Empire? The speculative data on which this view is founded would give the Etruscan artist a home in Rome itself; even, perhaps, side by side with Italo-Greek artists during the later period. But why should not an art, in Rome half native because Etruscan, have lived on independently of the imported arts of Greece, even as we know the Etruscan language to have lived in the heart of the Eternal City down into her most splendid imperial age?

From the discussion of the scarab form of gem, we may pass on to consider the work embodied on stones habitually set in finger-rings—the form of gem habitually adopted by Greek and Roman civilisation. In archaic times these gems, often enclosed in the 'Etruscan border,' were carefully elaborated but stiffly drawn, and worked in the very shallow manner which characterised so much of the Greek gem-engraving of after-times, especially in Greece proper and the Levant. The Italo-Greek artists, on the other hand, gradually acquired great boldness in their execution, and in their finest and latest works plunged more deeply into the stone than was habitual with the engravers of Eastern Hellas. Still, gems of deep execution and of the finest workmanship have been found from Kertch to Athens, in Grecian cities that had little or no contact with the Italo-Greeks, and certainly did not learn their arts from them. The Etruscan gem, in its bold treatment of muscular prominences, exhibits incisions, never indeed very deep, but generally abrupt in their descent, and frequently steep, even close to the outline of the figure. In this they present a contrast with the more modulated surface of true Greek work, which, even in gems of the boldest relief, seems as carefully modelled close to the outline as on the middle of the design.

Of Greek work itself we may affirm that it was characterised by an artistic supremacy by which in its higher examples it may be everywhere recognised. A fine ease and dignity in the drawing, delicate and modulated treatment of surface, a crispness of touch in the lines of the diamond point that give lightness and elasticity to the hair, and a distribution of sentiment over the whole subject, are among these characteristics. Then, again, the sort of jealousy the antique artist felt lest his work should fail to fill the space allotted to it, and yet not to crowd that space to overflowing, but to occupy it completely, in a way which could not be defined by a rule, but was fulfilled by his taste, and entirely satisfies the eye,—this was characteristic of the whole art of antiquity, but rose into a noble harmony in Greek art. It is the charm of a Greek vase, a Greek gem, a bas-relief. The highest perfection in this just apportionment of space to design belonged to an age that had succeeded to one in which figures were closely, but still with a curious flexibility of art, compressed into a small gemstone, as if the artist wished no space to be left uncovered by his design ; and it preceded by long centuries that vanity of paper margins bordering closely-filled sheets of India-proof, the influence of which is felt in the finest works of the last three centuries : an age of art, that dealt in simple stately figures or groups, to which the artist sought to give all the dignity in his power, certainly not to take away such dignity as belongs to a figure filling, so to speak, its little world, and all the more of consequence when that little world is girdled by the tiny circle of a finger-ring.

Such are some of the chief characteristics of Greek work ; but would anyone see more nearly in what the Greek's supremacy consisted, let him hold to the light a ring set with one of those golden sards on which the Greek engraver loved to work —then let him with a lens look through the translucent stone, and trace the delicately-drawn outline of the design, just sunk as a depression, more or less shallow, below the level of the surface. That design at once starts into the proportions of life-sized bas-relief. Locks of hair fall elastically and freely ; there is a flesh-like texture and thoughtful modelling on the forehead and cheek ; while the mouth, that seat of passion and feeling, is —like the browless eye—somewhat overcharged with its burden of pride or passion, of joyousness or melancholy ; as though with the intent that the tiny actor on that little stage may speak the louder to the ear, and make his gesture the more visible to the eye of one gazing into his microcosm.

Anyone who will do this may learn how fraught with meaning is the phrase ' beautiful as a Greek gem ; ' for it is beautiful with such beauty as makes the fragments of the Parthenon transcend all sculpture—that gives to those little bronze heroic groups found in the bed of the Siris, a prerogative to challenge all works in bronze for all time : such beauty as only Greeks have imagined, and none but Greeks have in their works achieved.

In the Marlborough Collection is a fine pale sard, of great size for a Greek intaglio ; it has been repolished by some previous owner, who thought more of the lustre of its material than of the work it carried. Hermes is crossing the field of the gem, but, arrested by the power of music, he pauses in his advance. His cloak, the chlamys—for he is the type of the athletic youth of Athens—falls from his shoulders, and the wide picturesque hat of the Ephebi, the petasus, rests upon it. His ankles bear the talaria, and his left arm carries the lyre, from which the right hand is calling out the strains, to which he bends his ear in rapture. A graceful but manly figure, ' he ' walks a god,'—the god of rascals it may be, but a god of music too, and, as the Greeks always represented him, in air at least, every inch a gentleman. This is just one of those gems that does not give any very definite clue to its period by the particular action or attributes of the god represented on it. The skilled archæologist may often apply the touchstone of his experience in small details, and by a sort of mechanical method bring to light some anachronism in a garment, or in the form of an attribute, that shall betray the hand of a cinque-cento or even an eighteenth-century imitator, or may shift the date of a gem from Alexander to Hadrian.

But archæological criticism will here seek in vain to plume a shaft from the wing of its prey, for the mechanical treatment of the work, the style and exquisite drawing, may safely be our guides, and these in this Marlborough Hermes are far too simple even for an artist of Magna Græcia, much more for one of the Græco-Roman period. The features have the character of the Hermes heads on the exquisite Cyzicene electrum coins, and the whole figure, in its beautiful but living repose, breathes the free air of the early prime of Grecian art. Notwithstanding a certain depth in the technical treatment, its date can hardly be much later than the half century after Phidias. On the other hand, some one may ask why this Hermes should not with equal probability be assigned to the eighteenth century. Fortunately, an answer is at hand ; for this grand gem is one of those belonging to the Arundel division of the Blenheim Collection. But, as if to show the point of such a question, there exists also in the Blenheim Collection a copy on amethyst of this noble Hermes, made during the last century, most likely by the masterly hand of Natter—a copy so perfect that, but for the stone and a certain fresh look of polish, one might have hesitated as to its date. But between the first and the eighteenth centuries one might safely affirm neither the gem nor its modern counterpart to have been cut; even in the last century such a work could have been done only as a slavish copy from so transcendent an original.

A discussion on the various schools of Greek art would be out of place in an article on gems; on the other hand, it is essential that we should try to indicate the broader features which distinguish the gem-engraving of the Greek from that of the Græco-Roman and Roman artists. But in discussing this subject we have to bear in mind that this use of these very terms Greek and Græco-Roman implies a community in source, in feeling, and in process of execution for all these works; in other words, Græco-Roman art is Greek art modified by the requirements of Roman fashion and habits—and we must be prepared to find that the line of demarcation, especially in the early imperial time, cannot be abruptly drawn. Of the Greek gem enough has been said to describe its more important features, whether in the Greece of Italy or the Greece of the Levant. As regards the influences in Rome herself that guided fashion and impressed a peculiar character on Roman gems, we may suppose that Greek artists found themselves working in an atmosphere already charged with the traditionary sentiments of a quasi-native art—it may be Etruscan in source—but of which we now know almost nothing, though we may think we see the indications of its presence in the consular coins current in Rome in the century that preceded the Empire.

The characteristics of Greek and Græco-Roman gems may be divided into those of subjects, of manner, and of material.

With regard to the first—namely, the subjects depicted on these gems—we may quote from Mr. King some excellent observations bearing on the grand simplicity that characterised all Greek design:—

'All truly antique designs are marked by their extreme simplicity. Rarely does the composition include more than two figures; or, if others are introduced, they are treated as mere accessories, and only indicated by an outline. To this branch of art Horace's maxim can be strictly applied with but slight alteration—

"Nec quarta loqui persona laboret."

Except in the archaic work of the Greeks and the Græco-Italians, who preferred the representations of violent action of muscular exertions, repose is the characteristic of the productions of matured Hellenic and Italist taste.' (P. 173.)

'Gem-engraving, "Scalptura," being from the first ancillary to sculpture, and ever taking its larger productions for its models—the Etruscan his terra-cotta gods and masks, the Greek his bronze or marble statues—the gem-artist never attempted anything in miniature, the example of which had not previously been placed before his eyes on a larger scale. Another reason this for the simplicity of their compositions. Neither the one nor the other ever thought of representing events of contemporary or of actual history —an observation which applies invariably to Greek, and with the rarest exceptions to Roman works.' (P. 174.)

In fact, as Mr. King says a little further on, ' all truly ' antique themes are ideas hallowed by long use and reverence, ' or, so to speak, the " scriptural subjects of the age that embo- ' " died them as a gem." '

Hence the Greek and Italo-Greek—the former in a more severe, the latter in a more sensuous style—went for his subjects to the grand Homeric, post-Homeric, and tragic cycles of Hellenic myth. The Olympian gods are among the more ordinary subjects of the simple statuesque gems of Greece herself and the eastern Mediterranean; their retinues more often figure on the gems of Magna Græcia. The themes of love and wine—the Erotic and Dionysiac cycles, especially the latter, with its merry train of Satyrs, nymphs and Mænads, are favourite subjects on the Italo-Greek gems, as are masks, caprices, and some animals, in particular, perhaps as sacred to Proserpine, the swine. To both belong the head of Pallas, cold and severe in intellectual beauty; the Medusa head, in its earlier aspect of the horrid Gorgon, as well as in its later Lysippan phase of deathlike ' rapture of repose ; ' the veiled Persephone, type of maiden coyness and of Greek virginity ; and spirited representations of Victory or of Aurora urging on the divine coursers. Perhaps this distribution may have been rather one of time than place ; and we should attribute the more voluptuous designs to a later, the simpler ones to an earlier phase of Greek art as a whole. But having in view the coins of the whole Greek world, and the localities in which particular Greek gems have been found, and peculiarities in the stones that they consist of, we believe the former to be the more correct of two conclusions necessarily drawn from a somewhat incomplete induction.

The Romano-Greek and Roman gem, with so much in common with the Greek, especially in the earlier time of the Empire, yet shows a decided predominance of certain kinds of subject. The portraiture of imperial personages was not new to Greek art, for beautiful heads exist in fine Greek work representing Syrian and Ptolemaic sovereigns. But portraiture

took a new development under the 'Cæsars.' Innumerable
heads of the earlier, as well as heads with the busts of the
later emperors and imperial persons, were wrought during the
early and middle Empire.   In the first years of the Augustan
age, Brutus, Antony, and Cæsar are to be recognised on nobly-
cut gems ; the two former, for instance, as profiles in fine Greek
portraiture in the Marlborough Collection ; and Julius in that
deeply-cut gaunt head that frowns, from a sard, with the signature of Dioscourides, in the British Museum.   Other subjects were drawn from the hearth and altar of the domestic
Romans.   Sacrifices and forms of worship ; festivals ; animals,
chiefly as zodiacal or astrological symbols ; figures sometimes
of the greater gods, with their attributes carefully brought
in ; also of the minor and tutelary deities ; Roma, Victory,
Salus, Bonus Eventus, Æsculapius, &c. ; the head of Jupiter
Serapis, most frequently in front face, and cut in a noble manner ;
very rarely, too, a subject such as the Horatii, taken from
Roman history ;—these, with caprices of various kinds, form the
major part of the best contributions to our collections from the
hand of Græco-Roman and Roman gem-engravers.   And these
contributions to our knowledge help perhaps more to place
us ' at home' with the ancient Roman than any other material
things he has bequeathed to us.   It is from this point of view
also, as much as from that of art, that we have to enumerate
with actual gems the innumerable glass pastes—contemporary
copies in glass of ancient gems which subserved the purposes
of the gem to the citizen who was not rich enough to acquire
an original.
    Passing from subject to manner, it is to be observed that,
whereas the Greek technical treatment changed little from the
time of Alexander to that of Augustus, and presented features
of great similarity at the courts of the kings and princes
who divided the eastern world during those three centuries,
and drew to them great artists, no sooner had the Greek
engraving art become domiciled in Rome by the influx of
Greek artists in the early imperial or Augustan age, than it
began rapidly to undergo a change.   Deeper cutting—bold
rather than beautiful effect—a treatment of the hair as though
the locks were laid down in solid waves, no longer grooved out
and lined into crisp curls by the so-called diamond point—
drapery massed, but generally rather coarse in execution—the
features sharp and marked, but lacking the softer modulations
wrought by the fine hand of the purely Grecian workman ;
such were the peculiarities in style that overtook and transformed Græco-Roman art up to the time when it rapidly

degenerated into coarse drawing and almost barbarous execution towards the end of the middle Empire. The art underwent a temporary decline in the middle of the first century of our era, but rose again in the reign of Hadrian, and for a short time during the age of the Antonines retained that character for laboured but imperfect execution and florid character in design and in manner to which we have before alluded, and which seems to have been imitated by the cinque-cento artists.

As regards the gem-engraving of Egypt when under Roman sway, it is observable that Romano-Egyptian art generally retained for some time the manner that characterised that which prevailed under the Ptolemaic rule; while the incorporation in both of an Egyptian class of subjects with Greek art of a refined type produced splendid gems of which many a fine illustration might be quoted from among the royal portraits, the numerous representations of Sphinxes, of Serapis and Isis, Harpocrates, and other Græco-Egyptian subjects that are scattered through different collections.

We have sketched the salient features of Greek and Roman gem-engraving, as seen in the subjects chosen for designs, and in the technical treatment of them. The materials that were the fashion with different schools of gem-engravers remain to be considered. Nor is this part of the subject quite independent of those we have just discussed; for the translucency or hardness may have much influence in determining the degree of depth to which the engraver shall cut his design, or the manner in which he may treat it. Thus we can hardly look through one of those pale sards, with a fine and delicate Greek work upon it, without recognising the probability that the artist did not cut his intaglio merely to form an impression on clay or wax, but also with the intent of its conveying something of the effect of a transparency—in short, of a work of art that could be appreciated of itself without the necessity of its being reversed in a cast. The more opaque stones in vogue when jaspers began to be a fashion in Rome, or where the Italo-Greek artist had to work on deep rich sards (the morio of Pliny), or on 'tricoloured' or banded agates, would naturally make the engraver rather look to the impression yielded by a gem than to the effect of the intaglio as seen in the stone itself. Perhaps the deeper relief of the gems cut in Magna Græcia and Sicily and in Rome may be traced to this cause as much as to that more sensuous development of style which makes the great decadrachms of Syracuse a landmark in numismatic art.

We have said that the ruder Etruscan works are generally

to be found on cornelians and inferior sards, and on striped stones generally of the agate or jasper kind. In proportion as the work is finer, the material is generally more beautiful. The varieties of chalcedony that are met with as the materials of scarabæi would form a small mineralogical collection in themselves; indeed, almost every character this Protean mineral assumes may be illustrated in gems of this form. Garnets also, chiefly of the almandine kind, amethysts, even emerald and green turquoise, are among the rare and exotic materials that were employed occasionally by the artists who engraved them.

Those gems of the scarab class which we have assumed to be of the latest workmanship, and for which we have even suggested an Etrusco-Roman origin—rather stiff, though not archaic, in their style; carefully rather than correctly finished, and that with much use of the splinter; abruptly, though never at all deeply, incised; and for the most part representing deities or the heroes of Greek tragedy, in dramatic attitudes— are generally engraved on bright sards or on splendid banded stones, which are, in fact, the sardonyx cut athwart instead of parallel with its layers of white chalcedony and deep-hued sard. It is remarkable, as bearing on the question of their contemporary date, that on stones quite similar to these, and with subjects closely resembling them, we often find Italo-Greek work; and such rich sards and 'tricoloured agates' are then usually in the form of an elongated ellipse with a flat surface.

Besides the pale sard on which we have said that the finest Greek work was generally wrought, we meet with the blood-red sard and the brown sard occasionally so adorned. The beryl is rarer, and a pale prase (ὄμφαξ?) is among the rarest of the materials in use with the artist of Hellas proper. No gem, we believe, of Greek type is known on the green jasper, and indeed very few such occur on any of the three coloured varieties of that mineral. The elaborately helmeted but noble head of Minerva, at Vienna, signed ΑCΠΑCΙΟΤ, on a red jasper, can hardly belong to an earlier age than the close of the Augustan time. Greek work occasionally occurs on lapis-lazuli, and on amethyst and with Egyptian subjects also on emerald; while horny and sapphirine chalcedonies, especially of the scaraboid form, have already been cited as having been found in Kertch and in Sicily: the one with the purest Greek workmanship, the other with the rich and flowing and somewhat deeper work of the Sicilian Greek. There occur also what are usually called hyacinths, really hyacinthine garnets, and occasionally an almandine garnet may be seen charged with a message to our eyes from the veritable Greek engraver : but the work on it is seldom fine.

No doubt, most of these stones were only employed in the later years of true Greek art—at least the sard was the favourite in earlier times, and presented great recommendations, as well from its beautiful texture and softness under the engraving instruments, compared with most of the stones enumerated, as because wax does not adhere to it as it does to the garnets and several other stones. Furthermore, the sard was just sufficiently translucent to show the work on it in the greatest perfection when viewed as a transparency.

When we follow the course of the gem-engraver's art to the threshold of the Roman empire, we find the artists of the Græco-Roman school at first working on sards, amethysts, and occasionally on peridot—the topazius of Pliny—and a few other beautiful transparent stones: after a while, these begin to give place to red jaspers, and to plasmas, often of extraordinary richness and beauty. The nicolo (an onyx with a dark underlayer, and an upper bluish-white layer, ground to the thinnest film) also became fashionable early in this period, and maintained its ground by the side of the onyxes and sardonyxes that the growing taste for cameos brought more and more into fashion.

Garnets were now abundant, and the sapphire, even the ruby, were occasionally engraved down to at least the age of Caracalla, while the beryl was throughout the imperial time a favourite stone. The universal mediocrity of the workmanship where plasma and heliotrope and bloodstone are the materials of an ancient gem, may be traced to their coming about this time into vogue ; while the different jaspers of other striking but often beautiful colours will be found usually to carry only the most wretched products of the engraver's wheel. At times the designs on the finer plasmas and on some jaspers are admirable in drawing, but rough and poor in execution ; but more usually the design and workmanship on all these stones bespeak an art sinking fast into decrepitude.

ART. IX.—1. *Preussen als Militärstaat; eine historische Skizze.*   Vienna: 1866.

2. *Der einjährige Freiwillige im Preussischen Heere.*   Berlin: 1862.

3. *Allerhöchste Verordnungen über die grösseren Truppenübungen.*   Berlin: 1861.

4. *A Military Memorial*, translated from the German of Prince FREDERIC CHARLES.   London: 1866.

5. *Military Correspondence of the Times during the late Campaign.*   London: 1866.

'THE peace awakens universal joy.   For my own part, 'being but a poor old man, I return to a city where I 'now know nothing but the walls; where I cannot find again 'the friends I once had; where unmeasured toil awaits me; 'and where I must soon lay me down to rest in that place in 'which there is no more unquiet, nor war, nor misery, nor 'man's deceit.'   Thus wrote, more than a century since, a saddened philosopher-king, wearied, as he would have the world believe, of all earthly greatness and success; and if these reflections run too closely in the vein of the wise monarch of Israel, to give their author claim to originality, it must be admitted that Frederic the Great had as good reason as any one in Prussia for feeling worn out at the close of the Seven Years' War, having spared his own person as little as his suffering country.   The banded powers of half Europe had not indeed sufficed to tear from him any part of his dominions, or abated a jot of his pretensions, but the realm he ruled had paid dearly for his resolution.   'The nobility,' he tells us, 'is 'in the last stage of exhaustion; the poor man is ruined; 'countless villages are burnt; many towns destroyed . . . 'Prussia is like a man covered with wounds, who, weakened 'by severe loss of blood, is on the point of succumbing to 'the excess of his sufferings.'   Yet Prussia he had not allowed to rest until the objects of the war were fully attained. Wearied out by her lengthened and gallant resistance, the enemies who had leagued to reduce her limits to the original marquisate from which she sprang, had one by one withdrawn from the strife.   Last of all, even the bold Empress-Queen, who had entered on the contest determined not only to recover the province of Silesia, stolen by Frederic in the hour of Austria's weakness, but also to punish him for his personal share in opposing her imperial claims, had reluctantly resigned these objects to his fortitude, and left the real triumph of the war on the side of his exhausted but unyielding kingdom. Prussia was now the avowed rival and equal of Austria. Henceforth was established that extraordinary dualism in the government of Germany which has so powerfully influenced the politics of Europe for the past century, and ended only in thrusting out of the Empire the house which had presided over it for six hundred years, after a struggle of such dimensions as the world never witnessed save when all Europe armed to overthrow Napoleon.

The policy of aggrandisement by force or fraud which Frederic the Great had worked out in his seizure of Silesia was nothing new or original in the history of the state he ruled. The whole growth of Prussia from the rank of a petty border state of the Empire to the strong and independent kingdom which he handed his successor, is founded on the tradition of claim followed by conquest. It would seem as though from the time when the Elector of Brandenburg, at the beginning of the seventeenth century, found his hereditary dominions strengthened by the addition of the dukedom of Prussia—an unimportant territory then in European view—the process began to which the treaty of Nicolsburg, two hundred and fifty years later, gives the crowning triumph.

There is a theory favoured by many historians that the progress of empires and their decay can be little affected by the force of individual character. It may be true that revolutions are produced by an aggregate of circumstances independently of the men who take foremost place in them ; but it is surely more certain that a persistent family purpose handed down from father to son in a reigning house, through ages in which the sovereign has almost absolute sovereignty, may so tone the policy of a state as to influence its own fortunes and that of all its neighbours. Why did the people of Northern Germany long since fix on Prussia as the Power round which to hang for safety, when intrigues threatened from within or an invasion from without ? This land which, when first the Hohenzollern ruled it, was far more a Sclavish country occupied by a garrison of Teuton colonists than a truly German realm ; why did it gradually become the rallying point for those who believed in the coming unity of the Fatherland ? Why but that in the unchangeable purpose shown by the rulers of Prussia from the time of the Great Elector to advance the bounds of their dominion, and in their earnest attention to the material welfare of their subjects, there was foreshadowed the rise of a kingdom having within it the seeds of such growth and advancement as should place those it embraced in the security which the elements of the dissolving Reich had altogether lost. The Thirty Years' War and its attendant calamities had, indeed, at the cost of terrible sacrifice, given freedom to religious opinion; but the smaller states of the Empire had been so enfeebled by it that their lands were offered a helpless prey to foreign invasion, or to the newer civil dissensions which arose in the various Wars of Succession. French armies laid the Palatinate waste by royal decree; English generals fed their mixed levies from the fertile plains of Bavaria; Austria again and again made the western circles of the Empire the battle-ground of her pretensions; whilst the petty princes who had nominal sway within their borders could save their subjects neither by neutrality, nor by bringing their tiny contingents to join one of the contending forces. In the sufferings endured through these days, and in those which weighed more heavily still upon the minor principalities in the era of Napoleon, may be found the roots of that wish for a stronger nationality, and of the respect for Prussia as its only real representative, which have long been, in one shape or another, growing up in the German mind.

The Great Elector, Frederic William, is undoubtedly to be regarded as the real founder of the present grandeur of his successors. Under his able but despotic rule (1640 to 1688) the whole force of Brandenburg and Prussia, now welded into one power, and much enlarged by the treaty of Westphalia, was directed to the enforcing the acknowledgment of the independence of the latter dukedom, originally held separately as a fief from Poland. His success in this was soon followed by claims on Juliers, Cleves, and Berg, skilfully urged, and boldly supported by the sword; and the limits of the dominions handed his son were thus extended from the Oder to the Rhine. Lower Pomerania had been among the additions gained in the great European settlement above mentioned; and Frederic William used the opening thus obtained to the Baltic to lay the foundation of the navy which Prussia's statesmen even thus early regarded as a necessity to her claim of a distinguished place among the Great European Powers. The same policy, doubtless, rather than a love for Austria or hatred of the Turk, led to his sending a contingent to the relief of Vienna when threatened by the Sultan in 1683.

Under his successor, grandfather of the Great Frederic and first king, the land, although ruled on despotic principles where the monarch was personally concerned, enjoyed a degree of municipal freedom favourable to the growth of the sturdy German element which was already swallowing up the traces of Sclavonic rule. His troops were in constant service as allies of Austria in her Turkish and French wars; and various small principalities, obtained as reward or purchased, swelled his now extensive though scattered dominions. The resources he left to his son, in 1713, while receiving no further additions in land, were strengthened by the care with which the new king, more than any other of this military family, bestowed on the *personnel* of his regiments, and on accumulating treasure to support the war which for his day was deferred, though his chief business seemed the preparing for it. Indulging freely his singular passion for filling his regiments with the largest soldiers in the world, the administration of Frederic William I. was in all else economical to parsimony; and without straining the resources of his five millions of subjects, he left his son, the Great Frederic, the most efficient army of Europe, to be at once the temptation and the instrument for continuing the family policy. For exercising his tall battalions in petty conquests, he had not the opportunities of his father, the first Frederic; but such gain would have given the kingdom but little new importance as compared with a step which he took in her military organisation, in which we may clearly trace the origin of her present formidable system of recruiting. In 1733, seven years before his death, the whole of his territories were parcelled out by decree into cantons, to each of which was allotted a regiment whose effective strength was to be maintained from its limits; and all subjects, beneath the rank of noble, were held bound to serve if required. With this ready instrument for supplying the losses of a war, and with an army more splendidly equipped and trained than any other of the time, his son (known then as Frederic II.) stepped into the field of European politics.

Exceeding the two former kings as much in the extent of his desires as in the ability for accomplishing them, no petty lordship as that of Neufchatel or Tecklenburg lately added to the Crown would satisfy the new king, whose ambition was favoured by the stormy times in which he came to the throne. The very year in which he ascended it, saw all Germany distracted by the death of the last direct male descendant of the line of Hapsburg; and Austria herself, already weakened by long struggles against the encroachments of the Grand Monarque, and with the rights of her young queen challenged on all sides, seemed a victim ready to be spoiled. That

Frederic really believed in his own pretended claims on Silesia, it would be unjust to his clear sense to admit. It is better to say simply, with his latest and grossest panegyrist, that he knew what he wanted and was determined to have it. His first success only whetted the ambition of the young king-general; and Silesia once confirmed to him by treaty, he strove next to extend Prussian rule beyond the newly-gained mountain frontier into the northern district of Bohemia, where his successor's arms have lately won such signal success. Carlyle himself does not attempt to justify the greed which upon frivolous pretext brought him in arms into the coveted land when Austria seemed fully occupied with her Rhenish campaign against France in the year 1744. On this occasion, however, his strength proved unequal to the new task of spoliation. The king was fairly worsted and forced out of Bohemia by Daun and Prince Charles of Lorraine; and although the ready tactics of Hohenfriedberg and Sohr proved his increased dexterity in handling the machine-like army he had trained, he was glad to come soon to terms, and to resign the new attempt at aggrandising Prussia upon condition of her late acquisition being left her.

The ten succeeding years were busily spent in consolidating the scattered dominions he ruled, and in constant preparation for bringing their whole resources to bear on the further struggle which he long foresaw, with its issues all-important to his dynasty. Whatever were the ostensible causes of the Seven Years' War, the real one was, beyond doubt, the resolve of Austria to check at once by arms the formidable growth of this new rival for the dominion of Germany, whose power had already so thriven at her expense. The morality of his enemies was little better, it must be confessed, at this time, than Frederic's own; but in the gallantry of his defence against the coalition which strove to destroy his young kingdom, history is apt to forget or condone the doubtful means by which its power had been built up, and which gave occasion to the deadly hostility of the Empress-Queen. Various were the changes of fortune that befell. For the next six years, as he himself wrote in 1762, ' success alternated from one side ' to the other.' The glories of Rosbach, Prague, and Leuthen were overshadowed by the disasters of Kollin, Hochkirch, and Kunersdorf. Frederic himself at times seemed to despair of any issue but death for himself and dissolution for his realm. Yet his boldness as a general and readiness as a tactician remained undiminished by defeat, failure, or depression. These qualities, with the excellent training of his troops, his good fortune in possessing the two finest cavalry officers a single army has ever known, and, let us add in justice to our own country, the moral and material support consistently given by our own great war-minister, sufficed to save the struggling kingdom from the ruin that so often, during this tremendous struggle, seemed inevitable.   What Prussia suffered whilst it lasted, may be conjectured from the words which we have quoted in the first page of this article from the King's own correspondence.   On this subject he, above all men, would be little likely to exaggerate.   Yet her position was now assured; and the policy steadily pursued for three successive generations had attained its first end.   The principality, raised out of obscurity by the Great Elector, and made a kingdom by his son, was henceforth to hold a solid position as one of the first powers of Europe, and the admitted rival of Austria for the leadership of Germany.   Her land had indeed a long rest after the great strife for existence; but Frederic, whilst watching diligently over its internal improvement, took care to insure the independent position of his kingdom by refilling as soon as possible the gaps in his army.   The standing forces which he maintained and handed over to his successor were little less than those which Prussia, with more than three times the resources, kept in pay before the late war; and the greatness of the burden thus imposed is better understood when it is known that the 3 per cent. of the population which under Frederic were actively kept in arms, supply under the present system the whole peace army, its additions for the field, the Landwehr of the first call, and most of those of the second—a class but rarely embodied.

On Frederic's share in the first partition of Poland it is unnecessary here to enlarge.   The number and efficiency of his battalions, with his own well-won reputation as a general, made his co-operation necessary to the chief spoiler of the unhappy kingdom, and procured Prussia the addition of two considerable provinces; whilst their safe custody against Pole or Russian formed the best reason which could be assigned for the constant maintenance of the overgrown military establishment in which her king delighted.   Yet in the eastward extension of her limits Frederic never lost sight of his older objects, the advancement of her influence in Germany, and the humbling of her rival, Austria.   That neither the frontier limits of the latter, nor her authority, should be extended within the Empire, were cardinal points of his policy from the time that he had forced her before all the world to surrender Silesia to his claims; and when, in advanced years, he took arms for the fourth time against her, he found opportunity not only to assert these principles, but to appear as the champion of the rights of the lesser states, threatened by the son of Maria Theresa in the matter of the Bavarian succession.

The death of the Elector Charles Theodore in 1777, without direct heirs, produced a complication of claims upon various parts of his domains such as even the German Empire had rarely witnessed. The Elector Palatine was at first recognised as his successor; but his pretensions were disputed by Saxony, Mecklenburg, certain minor princes, and finally by Austria herself, whose Emperor, being collaterally connected with the deceased prince, prepared (at the instigation of his mother or his famous minister Kaunitz) to enforce by arms the rights he asserted. Frederic, either unwilling from growing infirmity to enter into a new war, or seeking to preserve to his side the appearance of moderation, engaged through the summer in negotiations; but not the less diligently did he prepare for the hostilities, which in July he suddenly commenced on its becoming apparent that Austria would yield to nothing else.

The campaign which ensued deserves notice on two grounds: its marked difference of character from the somewhat reckless strategy for which Frederic had been famed; and the striking parallel which its opening affords to that of the war of this year; for its scene lay on the very ground where Benedek was called to oppose the recent invasion of Bohemia. In 1778, Frederic entered that country suddenly by the same means as his descendants eighty-eight years later. Like them he had an army too large for a single movement over roads so difficult as those of the Giant Mountains. His commissariat was, for that age, a masterpiece of organisation; yet he could not safely entrust to it, even though starting from provinces blessed with fifteen years of peace and plenty, the supply of 200,000 men from a single base. For this reason, more than for the purpose of defence, he had distributed half his troops, previous to the rupture with Austria, on the Silesian side of Bohemia, and half in Saxony, whose Elector was now his natural ally. One army of 100,000 men, formidable for the vigour and size no less conspicuous then than now in the peasantry of Brandenburg and Pomerania; more formidable still in their perfect discipline and the reputation of their general; moved under the King from Glatz through Nachod and Skalitz. A second, of nearly the same strength, including a Saxon contingent, entered Bohemia by the line of the Elbe under Prince Henry, who had admirably seconded Frederic in the fiercest struggles of the Seven Years' War. The roads they followed were found open through the whole length of the passes, as open as when the Prussian armies trod them last June. Nachod and Skalitz were passed by the King without opposition, and the banks of the Elbe reached where the fortress of Josephstadt now commands the stream. In like manner Prince Henry moved on Münchengrätz and Turnau, his advance unchecked by a single Uhlan, and apparently unwatched. Another day of forward movement would have connected the two armies near Gitschin, important then as now for being the crossing-place of the roads converging from the passes, and 200,000 Prussians under the first general of the age would have been united for battle on the gently swelling hills which lie west of Horzitz and Sadowa. Such a movement, however, was not destined to be made; and the junction of the armies was to remain a problem even to Frederic insoluble. Rated (in Prussian history) as 250,000 strong, the Austrians, under Lacy and Laudon, were between them in a defensive position well chosen to prevent it. The design of the invaders had been sufficiently foreseen to prepare a vast line of rough entrenchments against which even Frederic's battalions might dash in vain. The Elbe, near Konig-gratz, covered the right or eastern flank; the central portion followed for five and twenty miles the higher part of the stream as it runs with eastward course after quitting the mountain chain at Hohenelbe; and from the latter place a line of hills was entrenched eastward until the Iser was reached above Turnau, whence that river made a chief part of the defence for the left or west flank, which stretched southward through München-grätz and the scenes of those affairs of the 27th and 28th of last June, which Mr. Hozier has so graphically described. The line thus held by the Kaiser's forces was nearly sixty miles long, covering a vast semicircle, each part being protected according to the formation of the ground with all that skill in the details of fieldworks which the ' Wars of Position ' of the seventeenth century had made familiar to Austrian commanders. Here was indeed the strong point of their school, and in this instance their training showed to special advantage. Palisades, escarpments, inundations, redoubts, covered doubly and trebly the weaker portions of the line, and everywhere bade defiance to the attack which Frederic, after long reconnaissances, found it inexpedient to attempt.

His conduct here was, in truth, very different from that of the Frederic of twenty years before. To account for it, we may adopt either the solution of certain plain-speakers of the time, and admit that his intellect and daring were dulled by coming infirmity, or we may follow that which his panegyrists

take from the personal memoirs with which he has striven
(whose pen was ever as active in his own cause as his sword)
to shape the opinion of posterity, and say that he believed the
objects of the campaign could be fully attained without the
risk and bloodshed of a great battle.   Certain it is that in this
the closing military adventure of his life, he appeared as though
utterly foiled by the adversaries he had so often in earlier
days worsted in fair field.   The next six weeks passed by,
spent chiefly in sweeping up supplies from the hilly district
which lay behind the Prussians between the works that stopped
them and the passes ; the only military operations being some
unsuccessful attempts of Prince Henry's light troops to break
the line of the Iser, and a movement of the King's army to its
right on Arnau, as though to make a flank march towards the
head of the Iser, and so unite his divided forces.   The difficulties of moving the trains over the bad cross-roads impeded this
latter design fatally ; and food and forage being soon exhausted
in the narrow slip of territory to which Lacy confined them,
the first week of September found the Prussians in retreat.
The King's army, having now got their backs on Trautenau,
retired by the pass through that place on Landshut, whilst
Prince Henry led his once more into Saxony by the line on
which he had advanced.

The Imperial generals made no attempt to follow up their
advantage by harassing the long trains which were with difficulty brought off over the steep roads that autumn rains had
already laid deep in mire.   In fact, though foiled for a time,
Frederic and his army were too formidable to be lightly treated,
whilst his position as defender of the rights of the minor states
promised, should they be compelled into an union against the
ambition of Austria, to give increased political weight to his
kingdom.   The Kaiser was loth, therefore, to push his late
success ; and his mother, seeing plainly the dangers which
lay before her son, urged him to come to terms whilst he could
do so with advantage.   The negotiations lately broken off were
renewed with the consent of all, and soon brought to a successful end.   Austria abandoned her general claims on Bavaria,
receiving in lieu of it a slice of the border territory on the
lower Inn between her hereditary states and the Electorate.
The latter remained under an independent line of princes ;
whilst Saxony and Mecklenburg were awarded compensation in
money.   The small though solid acquisition which the Emperor
thus gained corresponded ill with the previous largeness of his
claims and the success of his generals in the field ; and
Frederic, if losing some of his military prestige in the bloodless

campaign (known familiarly as the Potato-War) of his old age, found sufficient consolation in its political results, and the admission practically made by Austria, that her imperial power had sunk into the presidency of a confederation. Henceforth her differences with the lesser states were, like those with external monarchies, subjects for common diplomacy rather than for Reich-tribunals and high-handed assertion. Henceforth there was recognised in Prussia a Power whose consent was a first condition for any action of Austria within the Empire—a Power to whom every element hostile to the Kaiser would rally should the constant rivalry for the control of Germany break out into open hostility.

The military force so ably used by Frederic for enlarging his kingdom's influence at the expense of Austria, was for some time employed with scarcely less success in other quarters by his nephew and successor. Frederic William II. had not long ascended the throne when the civil war in Holland (1787) gave opportunity for the intervention of Prussia in the affairs of a neighbouring and hitherto independent state. Her well-drilled battalions without difficulty put down the popular party and restored his shaken seat to the Stadtholder; and the King had the double satisfaction of increasing the moral weight of his influence in Europe, and of asserting that principle of divine right, to him no less dear than to the first monarch of the line, or to their present successor. A more material gain was that achieved under the guidance of his unscrupulous minister, Herzberg, on the second partition of Poland. We have not space here to dwell on this, the darkest page in Prussia's history: her pretended alliance with Turkey and Poland against Russia and Austria; her use of the Swedes against the former, and of the Belgic insurrection against the latter; and the final sudden seizure, in concert with her late opponents, of the price of her double intrigues. Dantzic and Thorn, districts long coveted, as including the mouths of the Vistula, were the price of her complicity in this last spoliation, which was carried out with even more of diplomatic fraud than that in which Frederic had shared. Necessity, ' the tyrant's plea,' is the only justification which Prussian historians can offer for this stain on the annals of their country. To this day the wounds thus inflicted on their weaker neighbour remain unhealed, and influence for evil the foreign policy of their land.

Imitating his predecessors as well in the personal administration of domestic affairs as in their foreign policy, Frederic William was the unconscious instrument of restoring to his country's service one destined long after the King's decease to add new glories to her arms. Passing through Pomerania on one of his provincial tours, his attention was excited by the fine horsemanship of a country gentleman who rode a steed such as none of the royal suite could match, and evidently sought his notice. Blucher, for it was no other, had been dismissed by the Great Frederic from his troop of cavalry fifteen years before, for hot remonstrances at a promotion made over his head; but the dashing hussar had never fairly been reconciled to his civilian life, though seeming to follow its pursuits with energy. Inquiry on the King's part led to interest in the ex-officer, and, not long after, to his restoration to the service with the rank of major; and the service was thus provided with a leader for its squadrons fully able to maintain in the long wars to come the prestige established in Frederic's days by Ziethen and Seidlitz. No other army has been so fortunate as to produce within half a century three such matchless generals of cavalry as these.

The intervention of Prussia in the affairs of Holland had not long ceased to excite the observation of Europe, and the partition of Poland was still unaccomplished, when that mighty storm arose in the West which was destined for a time to extinguish the rivalries and animosities of German powers in their general humiliation, and to school them by common sufferings, by common hatred and fear of a foreign foe, into the Union which has just been dissolved after fifty years of life. The ancient empire of the Kaisers was to be laid prostrate by the blows of republican armies; the strong northern kingdom, got together with so much care and energy by the Hohenzollerns, to be brought lower still, and for years to bear the chain of the victor. A new general and a new system of warfare were to eclipse the achievements of Frederic, and to confound the armies he had trained. A bolder and more unscrupulous diplomacy than the Great Elector's was to change the whole map of Europe and to remove her most ancient landmarks. The Revolution came, and Napoleon; and the dial of Prussian progress was put backward until their final overthrow.

Herzberg, the able minister to whose care Frederic William left his foreign affairs, was for long unwilling to take any decided step against the new order of things in France. Prussia had as yet barely eight millions of population scattered over very divided territories. Her army, though inordinately large for defence, was yet insufficient to undertake single-handed that invasion of her dangerous neighbour in which

Marlborough, wielding far greater resources, had failed; and, moreover, it would soon be needed to secure further acquisitions on the Vistula. An alliance with Austria against the Revolution promised immediate advantage only to the new emperor, whose Belgic possessions had but recently been brought out of the rebellious condition in which Joseph had left them, and were laid open, in case of hostilities with France, by the dismantling of their fortresses. Not until the sacred rights of kings were attacked in the person of Louis XVI. after his flight to Varennes did Frederic William move to the rescue. Then, indeed, he roused himself from what for a Prussian monarch was almost an indolent life; mingled personally in the diplomacy of the time; brought on the famous meeting at Pillnitz (August 1791); and prepared to join Leopold in the armed intervention which the temporary release of the French King deferred until the following summer.

How great the influence of Frederic's name was on the armies of that age we have shown in a recent article in this Review.* His instructions were held to teach the perfection of tactics. His administration was copied servilely in its details, though its spirit had fled with the author. His generals, however old, were deemed of necessity masters of their art. It is not surprising that the Germans saw their emperor's troops moving for the first time under a Prussian commander; nor that the force which entered Champagne in 1792 was deemed by friends and foes irresistible because in the main composed of Prussian battalions. The new French levies had failed disgracefully in their first attempts against Belgium; and the emigrants who crowded into the allied head-quarters seemed not too sanguine when they promised their new allies an easy march into the rebellious capital which had driven them forth.

The arrival of Frederic William in Brunswick's camp was the signal for the advance, and for the issue of the boastful proclamation against the Revolution and its abettors, which, more than any other event of these strange times, threw absolute power into the hands of the reigning faction, that embodied at Paris the terror, wrath, and energy of the threatened nation. How completely the undertaking of the allies broke down in execution it is needless here to repeat at length.

The Prussian staff, relying too much on the promised support which they nowhere met, threw aside the prudent but

* Edin. Rev. Jan. 1866.

cumbrous arrangements of magazines by which Frederic had always prepared for his offensive movements; and their troops, plunged into an inhospitable district in unusually bad weather, perished by the thousand for lack of supplies. The sickness that ensued, and the unexplained vacillation of the King or of Brunswick at Valmy,* proved the ruin of the expedition, and the turning-point of the Revolutionary War. Thenceforth the Republican armies grew in morale as rapidly as in numbers, and a system of tactics was gradually formed by their generals, destined to replace that which Frederic had bequeathed to Europe, and to be brought to its perfection under Napoleon's master-hand in the grand camp of instruction at Boulogne. The failure of the Prussians in that campaign was as great a surprise to Europe in 1792, as the sudden collapse of the Austrian army in 1866. Goethe, who was in the camp on the morrow of the battle of Valmy at once discerned, with instinctive sagacity, the change which had occurred in the forces of the world.

Humbled bitterly by the disastrous result of Brunswick's expedition, the King of Prussia measured more truly than before the real strength of his kingdom, and repented of the temporary adhesion to Austria, in seeking which he had completely turned aside from the policy of his ancestors. Personal honour was, however, too deeply pledged to admit of his at once retreating from the alliance he had sought, and which appeared strengthened by the declaration of England and Holland against the Republic. Through the long bloodshed of the following years, Prussian armies were therefore engaged on the side of the Coalition; but the latter profited little by their aid. Europe watched with surprise a Power which had been deemed the most warlike of the century, conducting its share of great campaigns in a manner so feeble, as to make even the poor strategy of Coburg and York shine by comparison. To this day Austrian writers allege, and with good show of reason, that the defeat of the invasion of Northern France by those generals in 1794, and the subsequent loss of Belgium and Holland, were owing far more to the difficulties entailed by Prussian lukewarmness than to differences between themselves or the superiority of the enemy's manœuvres. These disasters were, however, a powerful motive for Frederic

---

* M. Mortimer Ternaux, although he has written a very interesting volume on this portion of the Revolution, and quoted many original authorities, has done little to explain why the action of Valmy was allowed to end in the cannonade with which it began.

William's withdrawal from a struggle in which there was now nothing for Prussia to gain, and which had brought a victorious enemy to the borders of her own western provinces. Ever since his first enthusiasm for the vindication of outraged majesty had passed away, the half-hearted nature of his alliance with Austria had produced increasing irritation in the correspondence of their diplomatists ; and he seized gladly the excuse offered by the insurrection of the Poles under Koschiusko in 1794 to withdraw his forces from the Coalition. The treaty of Basle soon followed, and Europe saw with dismay the great German Power whose arms forty years before had defied France leagued with half the Continent, now admit the claim of the aggressive Republic to advance her frontier to the Rhine.   Austria's cause was weakened further than by a single secession.   Bearing steadfastly in mind his family policy of rivalling the Kaiser in German allegiance, the King of Prussia offered a guarantee of neutrality to any States of the Empire which would join him in retiring from the contest ; and many of their petty princes were thus carried off to be followed later by others when Austrian arms met with further reverses.

The conduct of the war that Prussia thus relinquished had dimmed her former fame no less than the peace that closed it ; yet no administrator rose at this time competent to point out the causes of the ill success which had invariably attended her arms save where bold Colonel Blucher, with his cavalry (aided sometimes by a small force of infantry), harassed the enemy's outposts.   This officer from the beginning of the war showed such capability for detached service as marked him for future employ in higher grades, and made his name familiar to every man who served in the armies before which he held watch.   His activity was, however, exceptional; and the chief commanders illustrated every degree of military imbecility, whilst their troops retained only the form of the battalions of Frederic, the soldiery that formed them having fallen off from their model in every quality but stiffness.   In spite of the severe system of conscription by districts, enforced by every penalty which the law could employ, a trade in permits for absence had long been established as a perquisite of the captains.   Those who could pay well for the exemption were thus allowed to escape the allotted service ; the bribes received being used in part to attract an inferior class of recruit to fill the ranks of an army which an iron discipline maintained in every detail made thoroughly distasteful in time of peace.   Composed thus of indifferent material, brought together by a system of corruption, the companies were as ill commanded as formed. The captains and subalterns had served long with but little experience of war; and as a class had neither youth, hope, nor love of the profession which had become with them a mere trade. The higher posts of the staff were filled by veterans who were known merely as commonplace men who had served with Frederic, or by scions of certain princely houses among the minor States which Prussian policy strove to win. So trained, so enlisted, so officered, the army which had once been acknowledged the first in Europe was now behind others in fitness for the field. It was especially ill suited to meet the growing enthusiasm of the French soldiery, whose ardour, springing from political fanaticism, was sustained through the sternest want by the hope of professional advancement. The military prestige which had been handed down to Frederic William suffered therefore in this war against the Republic no less than the political influence of Prussia by his useless intervention and the inglorious peace which followed it.

His son, Frederic William III., succeeded in 1797 to the throne, which during his tenure was to know the greatest vicissitudes that modern history records. For nearly ten years he steadfastly maintained the policy bequeathed him; looking on with contentment at the repeated humiliations of Austria, and viewing in her losses the future gain of his kingdom. At length the time had come when this fatal neutrality could no longer serve the Court of Berlin. Russia had combined with Austria to check the growing power of Napoleon; and the rival emperors from East and West sought a passage for their legions through the straggling dominions of the Hohenzollern. What was refused to the Czar was forcibly taken by his opponent; and the march of Bernadotte through Anspach on his way to Ulm and Austerlitz produced such a fever of popular indignation through Prussia as shook the royal power, and showed alike the strength of the national feeling which had been roused in the whole German race by the progress of French influence within the Empire, and the necessity which henceforth lay upon the King to follow a policy not wholly disapproved by his subjects. The visit of Alexander to Berlin was naturally followed by the withdrawal of the French agent Duroc, and Napoleon was exposed to the prospect of finding the Prussians descending on his communications in conjunction with the allied corps which English means had brought together in Hanover. The sword of Brandenburg, in this hour of trial, proved rusty in the scabbard, and the maintenance of an overgrown standing army to have taxed the kingdom's strength without fitting it for ready defence. Before the needful preparations for taking the field were made—before the last vestige of the King's vacillation had been swept away by the entreaties of queen, ministers, and people—the great adventure of Austerlitz was made and lost by those who had grown tired of waiting for Prussian aid. ' Fortune has changed the address of your letter,' said Napoleon, when receiving the congratulations of the Berlin envoy Haugwitz ; but contented with sarcasm for the present, he deferred his revenge, and even feigned reconciliation and friendship. On the 15th December, the day that Frederic William had fixed for declaring against the French Emperor, his ambassador accepted at the latter's hands the gift of that coveted land of Hanover, which now, more honestly won, extends the limits of the once petty marquisate from Russia to the German Ocean. Haugwitz's master was scarcely ready to adopt the bold measure of annexing without provocation the territory of an old ally ; but Napoleon's instances soon compelled him to decide to retain the spoil thus offered, and openly declare to the world his acceptance of the Electorate as French spoil of war.

Not long was the degrading acquisition destined to reward this public avowal of treachery. Scarcely had the indignant fleet of Britain swept their new enemy's flag from the ocean, when Europe saw it raised by land in a brief struggle against the victorious legions which Frederic William had vainly sacrificed his honour to propitiate. The bribes of Napoleon Prussia found to be no free gifts. Bavaria was enlarged at her expense ; Cleves and Berg were surrendered to make the despot's brother-in-law a new duchy ; fresh humiliations were heaped on her by French administrators from day to day. From the rank of a Great Power she found herself suddenly fallen to the condition of an appanage, and her monarch treated as a vassal. Yet she had made no struggle and suffered no defeat ; had looked on unscathed whilst her neighbours bled ; and now, waiting for their loss to make her gain, found herself (is there no warning here for statesmen of other lands ?) isolated, exposed, humbled without pity. If the Court could endure this, the people would not. Alike the noble, the burgher, and the peasant felt the warlike thrill rush through them ; and that tempest of passion swept over the nation which is to individual fury as the trampling of a multitude to the footfall of a man. Without counting the cost or measuring the odds—without waiting for the aid of

Russia, still hostile to France—Frederic William was forced into the struggle he dreaded, and Prussia single-handed faced Napoleon and his vassals. Planted already by Bavarian permission within easy distance of the decisive points ; armed with the might of superior numbers,* long training, and accumulated victory ;. led by a chief whose bold strategy had not yet degenerated into limitless waste of men's lives, the French rushed on to the flank exposed by the rash ill-guided advance of their enemy.   Jena was fought and won almost within sight of the little hill of Rosbach which had given name to their defeat half a century before ; and Frederic's victory was avenged tenfold by the battle which laid Prussia prostrate at the conqueror's feet.

With a rapidity of which even Napoleon's troops were scarcely thought capable, the kingdom was overrun, the remains of its army annihilated, its cities occupied.   The hollowness of its military condition was manifested alike by the evil condition of the fortresses and the fate of the columns.   Blucher indeed fought fiercely to the last; but with this, and two other less noted exceptions to the shameful imbecility of the commanders, generals and governors seemed to vie with each other in surrendering their posts with the least effort at resistance.   The servile worship of Prussian models, which had prevailed through the armies of Europe, was changed into a contempt as ill founded as the opposite extreme ; and the officers whose system had so long been copied were now denied† even the common attribute of physical courage which soldiers are in general ready freely to accord even to the fallen.   Yet the last struggle of the King and the remnant of his forces by the side of the Russians in the spring campaign of 1807 showed gallantry of which their ancestors might have been proud.   Reduced as Frederic William was to a single city and a few square miles of his dominions, he refused to submit to `the harsh terms

---

* French historians (repeated too often by English writers who should have more care for truth) would make the Prussian forces that met Napoleon to number more than 150,000, against his admitted 190,000.   In fact Prussian authorities show that less than 120,000 men were on their side collected for the actual shock upon the Saal.

† Expressions of contempt for the personal conduct of Prussian officers abound in the works of the time.   It is sufficient here to point to those in the posthumous ' Memoirs ' (vol. ii.) of Sir R. Wilson, printed from his entries made in Poland in 1807.   Yet this same officer lived to witness. at Bautzen and Leipsic the magnificent valour and good generalship of these once despised allies.

required of him, whilst a gleam of hope was left. His troops gave valiant and timely support to their allies on the bloody field of Eylau. It needed, in fine, the fearful mistake of Benningsen at Friedland, and the disgust of Alexander at the disaster and subsequent retreat, to bring about the abandonment of the unhappy kingdom which followed on the celebrated armistice and interview of Tilsit.

Stripped of half her territory, the rest a mere field for French tax-gatherers, or exercise-ground for French troops, the policy of Prussia for the next six years to the outward world seemed to consist but in different degrees of servility to the master whose chains she had no power to shake off. Her revenues were swallowed up by foreign exactions; her army reduced to a mere corps by the decree of Napoleon; her means of rising against the oppressor seemed hopelessly gone. Yet there were those among her statesmen who never lost sight of her past greatness, and in these hours of darkness strove to fit her for a better destiny than that of a vassal province. Stein, her great minister, laboured indefatigably to prepare her recovery, by raising the legal condition of her peasantry, and to breathe in them the spirit of patriotism, by measures of domestic reform. Scharnhorst gave no less efficient aid by devising the system of short service in the regular army, with a constant supply and discharge of recruits, on which the existing organisation rests, and which gave, in 1813, to the allies four times the number of soldiers which Prussia had nominally counted. Patiently these great men bided their time, unmoved by the presence of calamity or by the dangerous ardour of such men as Blucher, fretting himself into illness in his inaction, and Schill, the gallant major, who rode forth with his squadrons to declare for freedom and meet death unflinchingly in the hope that all the chivalry of Germany would follow his devotion. They watched grimly the effect of the exactions of Daru, the brutal violence of Davoust. They saw the Tugendbund spreading its branches even through the very courts of princes who seemed true vassals of Napoleon. At last came the hour of his defeat, and Prussia's opportunity lay before her.

At first the King would fain have temporised. The conduct of York in abandoning the French side in Russia was disavowed; the general himself was spoken of as a traitor; a court-martial was promised as his reward. Then came, however, a torrent of popular feeling such as no nation in modern Europe, save the French in 1792, has ever known. By one far less the King had been urged on, in 1806, to his fatal war. By this he was fairly swept away; and, his choice once made, boldly and wisely he pressed on to head the new movement which no government could have stayed.   Blucher came forth from his retirement; and all eyes turned on him as the fit representative of the leading passion of the nation.   None of her soldiers had so openly cherished his hatred of the enemy, his hopes of revenge and triumph.   The command of the chief army fell naturally to his hands, and a staff was formed for him skilful to guide the sharp sword he drew, and to control the heat which might have exposed his force to danger.   Disaster and suffering had been no less useful in schooling Prussia's army than her people for greatness.   Her infantry had been trained to a light, mobile system of tactics, modelled on Napoleon's; their weapons modernised after the fashion of his army's.   The upper ranks of each department were now filled by men chosen solely for their efficiency.   England supplied the material wants of her soldiers. Russia placed corps of veterans beside the raw troops which swarmed voluntarily to the standards.   A long year of struggle and victory bore these once dishonoured ensigns into Paris. Another had scarcely passed away when Prussia was seen in the van of all Europe, striking a second time from his throne the general enemy.   Let those of our countrymen who think of 1806, recall with it the June afternoon of 1815, when our fainting line, weakened by the defection of half-hearted auxiliaries, looked and looked not in vain for the promised attack upon the flank of the foe, which was to give the Allies the completest victory that modern history records.

In proportion to the greatness of her sufferings and the magnitude of her efforts against the oppressor, was the reward that Prussia reaped on the new partition of Europe.   Recognised once more as one of the Great Powers, and the equal in all but nominal rank of Austria within Germany, she was no longer left with boundaries so ill-defined and broken as to call for constant preparation for war to maintain her security. Saxony paid dear for her firm adhesion to Napoleon; and the half of that kingdom, with considerable additions in Westphalia and the Rhine provinces at the expense of petty princes who lost their thrones, gave Prussia well-marked limits, extending (save where divided by Hanover and Hesse-Cassel) from the borders of Russia to those of France, with a population large enough to furnish without strain a standing army proportioned to her position.   Such a provision was not, however, sufficient for the designs of her rulers.   The presidency ceded to Austria in the new German Confederation, in virtue of her old imperial claims, was from the first distasteful to her former rival.   To restrain its authority within merely nominal limits being now, as under the Empire, a cardinal point of the Hohenzollern policy, a force was determined on as the future defence of Prussia, which, without crushing her resources, should, in case of need, give her military power beyond the natural importance of her territory. A foundation for this future system had been already laid by Scharnhorst during the years of her subjugation; and from 1806 to 1813, the actual service had been made but six months, with frequent calls of recruits succeeding each other in the ranks and thence returning to their homes to form part of the militia, so. as to spread through the suffering nation a general knowledge of arms against the day of need.

For the ease of conscription, Frederic William I., father of the Great Frederic, had (as before shown) divided the country into certain recruiting districts allotted to the regiments. To this arrangement, on which the landwehr system is still based, Frederic added certain further improvements; the chief being to distribute the various arms in due proportions over the respective districts, so as to make the force of each province independent in itself; and to abolish altogether the procuring of recruits from the neighbouring states, a practice much resorted to until the close of the Seven Years' War. The latter measure gave the Prussian army the strictly national character it has ever since maintained; the former prepared the way for the raising it by separate corps, each complete in itself, and capable of being put upon a war footing by the resources of the province. The materials of the patriotic army which Stein and Scharnhorst created were therefore ready in great part to their hands, and the feeling of the people did the rest. The bands of paternal government were, however, sensibly loosened by the presence of the foreigners who held all Prussia in their grasp; and her great minister took the occasion to encourage her sons in a spirit of national self-sacrifice by vast and far-reaching political reforms. The remains of feudal servitude were abolished. The peasant might in future hold and inherit land in his own right. The towns received increased political privileges. Taxation was made alike for all classes, and civil office thrown open to every native. The country during this period of apparently hopeless prostration made a vast political advance in its inner life; and though much of this liberal policy was reversed in the days of the Holy Alliance, enough remained to cause Prussian administration to be envied in the minor States, where the government, conducted by the caprice of the prince, made its despotism personally felt by changeful and petty interference with the subject. The immediate effect of Stein's reforms was a vast increase of national spirit and strength. The military service of the country was accepted by all without reluctance in tacit preparation for the day of reckoning with France; and the struggle of 1814 once over, the minister was encouraged by all classes to bring forth a complete project for the perpetuation of the system which had restored glory and freedom to his country. The foundation of the permanent constitution of the national force was laid by the remarkable law of the 3rd September 1814, which for more than forty years was the charter adhered to by the Government as binding on both sides, and which in its introduction is declared to be the product of the wishes of the whole people of the land.

'In a lawfully administered armament of the nation lies the ' best security of lasting peace,' is the principle proclaimed as the groundwork; together with the more immediate necessity of maintaining intact by the general exertions the freedom and honourable condition which Prussia had just won. All former exemptions from service in favour of the noblesse were from this time abrogated. Every native of the State, on completing his twentieth year, was to be held as bound to form part of her defensive power; and it was only with a view to the avoiding inconvenient pressure on the professional and industrial population that the armed force was to be composed of sections whose service should lessen in severity as their years advanced. The whole system comprised (1) a standing army; (2) a landwehr of the first call; (3) a landwehr of the second call; (4) and the landsturm. The constitution of these forces was laid down in detail as follows, and is still adhered to in principle, though altered in certain particulars to be hereafter noticed.

The standing army was to be composed of (1) volunteers desirous to undergo the necessary examinations for promotion with a view to adopting a regular military career; (2) of men voluntarily enlisting without being prepared for such examination; and (3) of a sufficient number of the youth of the nation called out from their twenty-first to their twenty-fifth year; the first three years to be spent by these latter actually with the colours, the other two as 'reserved' recruits, remaining at home but ready to join the ranks at the first sound of war. A further and most important provision allowed 'all ' young men of the educated classes, who could clothe and ' arm themselves, to take service in the rifle-corps and other ' light infantry; and after completing one year at their own ' expense to receive furlough to the end of their regular call, ' upon application.' This rule was no doubt introduced, to save the wealthy and wellborn the degradation which, in a country essentially aristocratic, the mixture in a barrack-room with recruits of the lowest classes would necessarily imply; and there has since been built upon it during the past half-century, the elaborate system of *Einjährige*, or one-year volunteers, which has solved at once two difficult problems. The universality of the conscription has been maintained without open opposition from that important middle order, the wealth and influence of which have grown in Prussia as much as in any part of Europe, and which, notwithstanding its claims, is excluded from the higher posts of the army; while a body of efficient officers, trained in all the duties of the line, has been provided for the staff of the landwehr without expense to the State. The process by which the latter object is accomplished will be traced hereafter. The regular organisation of the militia under the same fundamental law is thus described, together with its special duties.

The landwehr of the First Call is designed for the support of the standing army in case of war, and is liable to serve at home or abroad, though in peace only to be called out for such exercise as is necessary for training and practice. It is formed (1) of all the young men between the twentieth and twenty-sixth year who do not serve in the standing army; (2) of those volunteers who have been trained in the light battalions; (3) and of the rest of the male population up to the end of their thirty-second year, excepting only those who have sooner completed twelve years in this reserve and the army.

The landwehr of the Second Call is intended in case of war either to strengthen the garrisons and garrison battalions by detachments, or in special need to be used in its entirety either for corps of occupation or reinforcements to the army. It consists of all who have left the army and the First Call, and of any other able-bodied males who have not yet entered their fortieth year. Such cases include men who have begun the line service (as is permitted if the bodily strength be found sufficient) before the twentieth year, and thus been the earlier discharged their attendance on it, and their seven years in the First Call. The drill of the Second Call is in time of peace only for single days and in their own neighbourhood; and facilities are provided for their changing their residences and enrolling themselves in the nearest regiment to their new domicile.

The landsturm is only to be called out in provinces of the kingdom actually invaded, and then must be summoned by a special royal decree. It is, however, liable to be employed by the government for the support of public order in special cases. It includes (1) all the men up to the fiftieth year who are not regularly allotted to the army or landwehr; (2) of all who have completed their landwehr service; (3) of all the youth able to carry arms who have attained their seventeenth year. It consists of civic companies in the larger towns, and of local companies formed in the smaller towns, villages, and open country, according to the divisions of the districts for other governmental purposes. No provision, it should be remarked, is made for the exercise of these companies, which have in fact existed only on paper.

Further sections of the law direct the exemption (under careful restrictions) of candidates for the priesthood, and lay down certain additional principles. The most important of these is the declaration that the normal years for entering and leaving the standing army and reserves are valid only in time of peace, and in case of war may be altered so as the better to fill the gaps in such sections of the forces as are called under arms. All volunteers for the standing army have the option of choosing their own branch of the service. Soldiers who desire to re-enlist for a second term after the completion of their first three years, are to bear a distinguishing mark; and after a second re-enlistment are to receive a higher rate of pay, and the right to pension in case of being invalided. Similarly, those who desire to prolong their service in the First or Second Call, may do so, and are entitled to bear a distinguishing mark and to have a claim to higher rank in the regiment or company of the reserve thus selected, according to their qualifications. A special committee, composed of a military officer, a civil magistrate, and a local proprietor, is created in each district in the kingdom, to watch over the details of the administration of the recruiting within its limits, and to see that it is conducted with order and justice.

Such are the principal provisions of the law which the War of Independence bequeathed to Prussia. For more than forty years the compact was fairly maintained, although other legislation of the Stein Ministry suffered terribly at the hands of the reactionary party which rioted in all the Courts of Europe after the final fall of Napoleon. The people remained contented with the military administration, which was supported by a budget moderate for the resources of the country. 130 battalions of the line, 152 squadrons of cavalry, 112 companies of artillery, and a slender proportion of engineers formed the standing army. The exercise of the landwehr was of very moderate extent, and their only permanent staff consisted of a commanding officer and adjutant for each of the 116 battalions which were enrolled in the First Call. The *einjähriger* service of the line had been taught to supply the rest of the necessary officers; and although now recognised as a special personal tax on each male of the better class, the lightness of its practical working had (as before intimated) reconciled the majority to a system which would otherwise have been unendurable in time of long peace, contrasted as it was with the commutation of the conscript's service into a fine, practised in the neighbouring territory of France. The operation of the law and its results must now be more closely looked at.

It will be seen that no specific provision had been made for filling up the commissions in the standing army. The original exemption of the order of nobility from the conscription by Frederic William I. almost implied that many of this class would enter the service as officers. Practically no one of lower rank was considered eligible, until the War of Independence; and although the legal privileges of the nobles were then abolished, the system which was established has continued to the families which during the previous century had made arms their profession a monopoly of the upper ranks of the service. Any young man of means might indeed enter himself as a volunteer and pass the necessary examinations before his year was expired. This qualification and that of a university degree (a far more general possession in Prussia than in any other country) would give him the legal right to apply for an ensign's commission. Here, however, his prospects would end. The coveted appointment, which in England is the direct gift of the Crown, and in Austria of the honorary colonel of the regiment, is here subject, though nominally conferred by the Government, to the approval of a standing committee of the corps, whom the candidate must satisfy not only as to his professional qualifications, but as to his parentage and means. This committee has in fact just that power of rejection on personal grounds which custom has accorded the colonel in our own household regiments of cavalry; and the result has naturally been to make of the service the closest corporation which any profession in the world can show. Many of the noble families of Prussia are almost without means except as they may find them in the public service; and since the civil bureaux have been thrown open to other classes, the aristocracy are all the more tenacious of the supposed hereditary right of their order to the officering of the army. It should be added that a large part of the first commissions are given by the Crown, independently of these rules, to cadets who have completed their education at the royal military schools, and that the tendency of late years has been to increase this proportion, and thus make the upper ranks of the army more directly dependent on the king; but as the late monarch and the present have habitually leant for support on the nobles as against the trading classes, it is not surprising that the officers thus appointed from institutions entered solely by royal favour, are as separate from the bulk of the people as the rest of their cloth.

From the working of this system it has followed that not more than a twelfth part of the officers are of the middle orders. The Prussian military aristocracy have among them some men of local influence approaching that of the great families whose names from time immemorial are known in the service of Austria, men who, though loyal by descent, have other interests than those of the Crown. These, however, are the exceptions in a class composed too greatly of a needy noblesse, depending on the Crown for all hope of advancement, separate from the people by birth, habits, and profession, and apt in their self-assertion to increase, by offensive personal bearing, the distance which, in Prussia more than in any other country, divides the man of arms from the civilian. It needs no prophet to foretell the difficulties which this system will produce in revolutionary times. The endurance of such a military caste as has been described can only co-exist in modern society with the necessity of having constantly in view the use of the army against foreign enemies. Should Prussia's external horizon become clear, the first reform demanded in her domestic administration will be again, as it was not long since, the assimilation of the officering of the standing army to that of the landwehr; whilst the contempt with which the aristocratic soldiers of fortune regard all civil interference with their profession will tend greatly to precipitate a collision between crown and people.

From what has been said it will be seen that for all martial ardour in the middle classes of this great military people there has been no outlet for the last fifty years but the landwehr service. Promotion from the ranks of the line in Prussia, in the sense in which it is understood in our service and that of France, is a thing unknown. The actual performance of a private's duty by which a reformed scamp, often in the English army, an intelligent middle-class conscript much oftener in the French, wins his way to an officer's epaulettes, would never be the path selected there; nor would such temporary degradation (as Prussian opinion would regard it) be considered as a claim for advancement even in the landwehr. Here, indeed, the commissions are laid open without distinction of class, and the officers who hold them are a truly national body; but the preparation for them still requires considerable means and much pains, it being solely through the *einjährige* that its vacancies are filled up; while the system is worked so carefully that only those who have really a love for the details of the profession, and ability to master its theory, are finally selected out of the vast mass of unpaid volunteers who every year attend the colours. As a necessary consequence of the growing wealth of the trading order, the number of these has annually increased. The Government has done all in its power to encourage a feeling which has added constantly to the number of its intelligent defenders without swelling its military expenses; and it has long been a regular part of the education of the son of every manufacturer, proprietor, professional man, even of every well-to-do shopkeeper, to spend one of the three years between his seventeenth and twentieth birthdays in passing through his volunteer course. How greatly this differs from the idea of 'serving in the ranks,' as service is performed in other armies, will be best seen by following out in detail the life of the young *einjähriger* on entering his new condition.

Quitting his college, or counting-house, or home, he arrives at the head-quarters of the department to claim the right to take service as volunteer. A commission sits twice a year for a month each time to issue the necessary documents; and to this the candidate has already made his application in writing, supported by certificates of his birth, of the consent of his guardian to supply the necessary expenses, and of his conduct and attainments from his school or tutor—on which latter, be it noted, the insertion of any punishment for dishonourable conduct is fatal to the application. If these papers are all in due form, and properly attested, the certificate is granted at once, after a brief physical examination by a medical officer, to candidates from the universities, first-class royal schools (of which there are more than sixty in the kingdom), and certain second-class schools specially authorised; the commission seldom exercising the right which in theory at least it possesses of testing by written papers the candidate's knowledge. Indeed with this description of applicants a personal appearance may be dispensed with, at their own risk should the papers (including proof of physical fitness,) be found in any way incomplete. With the considerable class, however, who have not been educated at the prescribed institutions, an actual examination follows. The commission (consisting normally of a staff-officer, another military officer, and two civil officials of the department) calls in two or three extraordinary members from the heads of the nearest government college, and tests the candidates in their scholastic knowledge. German, Latin, French, mathematics, geography and history, and the elements of natural history and physics are the prescribed subjects; but the commission has very wide powers for varying them according to the future occupation of the candidate. Thus those who declare themselves designed ultimately for mercantile life escape the Latin; and the country squire's sporting son has his opening in a proviso which declares that ' youths who show ' special aptitude for riding and elect to serve their year with ' the cavalry, are to be very lightly pressed in the scientific ' examination.' On the whole, it may be assumed that the candidate, wherever trained, however taught, will in general find no practical difficulty in obtaining the desired permission to serve the State at his own cost for a year.

If not intended for the medical or veterinary professions, the candidate who has proceeded thus far is now considered as a combatant soldier yet untrained, and must apply for leave to defer his year of service, if not prepared to enter on it in the following autumn. In time of peace such leave is readily granted, and renewed until the twenty-third year is reached; but in most cases the service will naturally follow the procuring the necessary certificates. Quitting for a time his counting-house or other place of employment, the young volunteer prepares to join the regiment he has selected. If in the line, he may do this in the spring; but for the cavalry, artillery, and rifles, it is necessary to join on the 1st October, and on that day the vast majority of the new *einjährige* begin their twelve months of service, and report themselves to the commander of their battalion. If a citizen or university student of any garrison town, he need anticipate no rejection, provided the regimental surgeon be satisfied as to his bodily fitness for the arm he has selected, for colonels are authorised to receive any number of applicants who have this sort of local claim. Where none such exists the candidate has previously to ascertain that the battalion he would choose is not already provided with the full allowance of four volunteers per company which the regulations direct to be admitted by all commanders. This being seen to beforehand, and the candidate passed by the doctor, he becomes forthwith a member of the corps after the due verification of his papers. The fact of his enrolment as an *einjähriger* is reported to the local authorities of his district; the articles of war are read to him; and as soon as he can appear before his commanding officer in the proper uniform (prepared usually before the day of his admission to the service) he takes the oath of personal fidelity to the King, to which the reigning family of Prussia attach in these days a special importance.

Should the young cadet (for that is his real position) come from a rural district where the ways of the service are little known, and bring with him some lingering notion of hardships to be endured in his career, it will speedily disperse before the realities. From the time of his taking the oath and being posted to a company his attendance is strictly exacted at drills and parades ; but in all else his life is made pleasant enough. A neat but plain mark upon the shoulder distinguishes him from the genuine recruits, whose rough clothes the tailor, military or civil, may in his case replace by better material at the cost of his friends. If belonging to the mounted service, he may bring his own charger, or purchase one from the Government supplies at a nominal rate. Instead of sharing the coarse fare of the privates, he lives, according to his family circumstances, with his own friends, or in quiet lodgings, or perhaps in some grand hotel.* Although nominally subject to the garrison discipline as a soldier, (as in the matter of returning to his quarters at evening tattoo,) he may, with his commanding officer's sanction, replace his uniform by plain clothes when off duty, and for the hour lay the military life aside with its tokens. So far from being occupied for hours, like other recruits, with the care of his accoutrements, he is not merely allowed but recommended to employ a soldier servant to save him such menial labour, and leave his time to be turned to better uses. His parades are usually entirely in the first half of the day, so that he has the afternoon for his other employments. If studious, he continues his education. If still at the university, he attends such lectures as his attendance at drill allows, and counts the year as part of the triennial course which he must complete before taking his degree. If a young man of birth and fashion, he finds admission to all the gaieties of the place as readily as any officer or civilian of his own class. On the whole the twelve months will pass easily enough without other burden being felt than

---

* The delusion of English travellers as to the mixing of privates and officers in the Prussian service, arises commonly from ignorance of the real condition, civil and military, of the cadets whom they meet at their table d'hôte. Familiarity with the soldier is forbidden the officer alike by custom and military regulation, as well as by the difference of birth, which in no country draws a stricter line of demarcation than in Prussia.

the expense which his friends incur by this addition to his civil education; and many of those who begin with some passion for soldiering let it cool in the stress of other occupations or amusements, and allow the time to slip away without making an effort to raise their knowledge of the selected branch above the level expected in the average cadet. In such case they take their places in the ranks, when positively called out for training in future years; prepared, when the First Call service is performed, to lay aside the musket for ever.

Some there are every year, on the contrary, who desire to know more of the profession of arms; and to these every encouragement is given for forming themselves into the future officers of an efficient reserve. To do this is indeed, in Government phrase, the chief object of this volunteer service, grateful as its economy is no doubt to the ruler, and its ease to the well-born subject. For this end an officer is told off to every twenty cadets for the special purpose of superintending their military course, which for the first six months is confined chiefly to that prescribed for the recruit. At the end of this time the volunteer, if he is found perfect in the various drills, has performed the prescribed number of guards as sentry,* and passed a practical examination in swimming and gymnastics, will receive his grade of acting corporal, and thenceforward may direct his mind, if he so pleases, to the duties of an officer, and prepare for the required test. Three weeks before the end of the twelve months' service, a regimental Board of Examination sits, composed of a captain and two subalterns, who hold an examination of such cadets as, having already the rank of corporal, wish to proceed to proof of higher qualification. They are tested, first orally indoors; then upon the ground; and finally, by written papers, in all the ordinary duties of a subaltern in field and garrison: and the result, with the report of the board, is laid before the assembled officers of the corps, whose verdict on the examination, with their general opinion as to the personal qualifications of the cadet, determines the issue or withholding of the necessary certificate. This obtained, the applicant is entitled to the first vacancy as sergeant in the landwehr battalion of his own district, and in due course to a commission in that regiment; to which he continues attached until the period of his military service expires.

Many of the young nobility, who want either the interest or the inclination to devote their whole lives to the army, are

---

* In the Guards the cadet is allowed after his first three personal attendances, to pay a private for taking the sentry duties which fall to his turn.

among those who thus qualify as officers of a trained militia, superior in its composition to that of any other country. The majority of the landwehr commissions, however, fall to the sons of merchants, manufacturers, and proprietors; men of means and local influence, but outside the charmed pale of the 'Junker' class, which officers the standing army. It has followed as matter of course, that the growth of the mercantile order, and its increased influence in the state, have given a political character to the former force which very completely divides it in sympathy from the regular service, and is at times distasteful to the Crown. This militia, officered by men of more substance than the standing army, and with its ranks filled with old soldiers from the latter, became naturally the more popular of the two, and threatened at some future day to form a power within the state. A jealousy sprang up on either side, which mattered little whilst the landwehr assembled separately for their peace training, but seemed likely to paralyse the military machine devised in 1814, whenever called on for active service.

The tactical system bequeathed by that year was, in case of threatened war, to form the First Call of the landwehr (which numbered 116 battalions) into brigades; and to join to a brigade of the line a brigade of militia, to form each division of the army in the field. The reserve men of the standing army being at the same time summoned to fill up the numbers of the battalions and squadrons to which they belonged, the whole active force thus created would number 300,000 combatants. The ardent spirit of patriotism created by French occupation had, at the era of Leipsic, wiped away all class distinctions, and rendered this system fully practicable. Its retention long gave the landwehr regiments an importance justified by their gallantry in the War of Independence, and made their commissions worthy objects of ambition among the large class to which the *einjährige* belonged; but the growing political differences between this and the King caused a distrust of the force on the part of royalty which ended in its being thrust out of its former position, and made totally secondary to and separate from the standing army.

This great change, which, in place of a popular system of training based on the spirit of 1814, has given Prussia once more a vast military machine such as Frederic and Frederic's father loved to rear, was not brought about in a day. Three times the Government called out the field army before the decisive hour arrived. In 1850, when his dynastic traditions caused the late king to make the breach between the Elector of Hesse-Cassel and his subjects a means of extending the popularity of Prussia among the people of the Minor States, as Austria sought for the favour of the princes : in 1854, when pressed by the Western Powers to take part in the war against Russia, he armed to preserve his own neutrality : in 1859, when the indignation of all Middle Germany at the progress of French arms in Italy extended northward and moved William (then Regent) to place his contingent on the Rhine as a threat to Napoleon ; and though no hostilities followed to test the system by the stern proofs of war, the Government found it unready for action, and ill-suited to the needs of a bold policy. On each occasion it was observed that the tactical combination of elements so differently constituted worked badly in practice. The landwehr officers showed jealousy both of the assumed superiority of their comrades of the line and of the staff who controlled the whole.   Educated in a thorough military course; possessed generally of more means than the regulars ; and commanding soldiers as good at the least as the recruits under the latter ; endowed, moreover, constitutionally with a sort of military equality ; they gave plain signs of impatience under the actual demands of their call to the field, for the support of a policy which, in two of these instances, was not heartily favoured by the sympathies of the nation.

The royal government saw clearly enough that an army thus composed could not be relied on for accomplishing the scheme of German dominion bequeathed by the Great Elector and his successors as the hereditary legacy of the Hohenzollerns.   To advance beyond the dual system established by Frederic— to deprive Austria of the rights formally ceded to her on the erection of the Bund—to thrust out from the Confederation that ancient rival, and leave Prussia free to draw to herself its weaker elements by the gravitating force of nationality—these projects, long mooted in Berlin councils, required not merely bold statesmanship to devise but a strong and ready force to execute the plan.   The landwehr must be replaced in the field army, before the Cabinet could take the bold aggressive, for which the humbling of Austria in the campaign of Solferino paved the way ; and the alarming growth of French power, with the actual difficulties which arose from the old organisation when Prussia, in that anxious summer, mobilised her corps on the Rhenish frontier, formed opportune military reasons for the reform which had long been contemplated.   That this reform was distasteful to the representatives of the people was the natural consequence of its execution in open disregard of their right of granting supplies, and of their avowed leaning to the landwehr.   It is hardly less clear that it was thoroughly in unison with the wishes of the noblesse ; for their particular interests were involved in the coming enlargement of the regular army, whilst their natural sympathies were with the royalty that supported, rather than the middle class which threatened, the privileges of their order.   From the first, therefore, King William was sure of the support of his Upper House through the long parliamentary conflict which it needed victory in the field to close.

With this encouragement for reform, the impression produced by the palpable failure of the Prussian organisation in 1859, and its inferiority to that of France, was not suffered to grow cold. The following year saw the national force receive, by the mere will of the executive, a change as complete as any ever wrought by republican vote or imperial decree ; and notwithstanding six years of firm remonstrance on the part of the House of Deputies, the new system was maintained in every detail until the long-prepared-for war came to justify its authors in the eyes of the nation.   The yearly supply of recruits actually drafted into the line was raised from 40,000 to 63,000—a difference which the increase of population since 1814 prevented being specially burdensome.   The standing army was augmented by 117 infantry battalions, 72 squadrons of cavalry, 31 companies of artillery, 18 of engineers, and 9 battalions of train for the hitherto insufficient transport departments.   A far more serious innovation   was   the   prolonging   the   two   years   of ‘ reserved ’ service of the discharged recruits by two more. This class of men are so liable to sudden call, and so subject to government inspection, as to be(excepting such as have qualified as landwehr officers) but one degree more free than if still in the ranks. The unpopularity of the measure was complete when it appeared that the special use of this doubling of the line reserve was to exclude the landwehr from their former position as part of the field forces, and reduce their service to one of home garrison or similar duty.   In peace the standing army to be maintained was now as large as before it would have been with the addition of the whole First Call.   In war, when the reserved men are all called into the ranks, it numbered 300,000 ; or, including depôts and garrison artillery, 380,000 ; to which the First Call was to give* a second line of defence 100,000 strong.   The men of the Second Call were promised ex-

---

* This proved in the present year to be but a paper estimate : for on the mobilisation of the forces in the spring, the numbers were found incomplete in both army and First Call, and portions of the Second Call were very early drafted to take their places.

emption from duty except in the emergency of invasion, or of deficiencies in the other lists (a concession not ungrateful to citizens past their thirtieth year, and of whom five-sixths are computed to be married); and the service in it was shortened two years, in the First Call three, as some compensation for the additional time of attachment to the line reserves.

Into the history of the constitutional struggle which followed the promulgation of these ordinances it is not needful here to enter. The popular party failed to shake the position which had been taken up by the cabinet; and their efforts had little other effect than to hurry on the foreign policy of the government to that open rupture with Austria for which the change was expressly made. The Kaiser's vain attempt in 1863 to create a German parliament, prince-governed, and ready to prolong his presidency, furnished doubtless one strong motive to determine Bismarck (whose bold and successful conduct in the crisis made him thenceforward ruler in Prussian councils) to seize the first opportunity of testing the strength of the machine which existed only in open violation of the constitution. The Schleswig-Holstein question then arose; and Prussia was enabled, by the bold spring she took to the leadership in action against Denmark, to place Austria in the secondary position of a half-willing ally; and to show to the world the impotence of the Bund, apart from the Berlin cabinet, for action in Germany. Denmark once beaten into submission, it remained only to so carry on the system of joint occupation of the Duchies as to force Austria from one concession to another into hostility; and while degrading her first by policy, to feign just so much unwillingness to quarrel as might avoid giving pretext for foreign interference, or for the Kaiser to arm for war.

The present year found the military system of 1859 fairly complete in all its parts. The additions to the cavalry were not indeed wholly made; but in all other respects the active forces were complete in their cadres; the reserve lists full of trained men; and the whole could be made ready for the field at less than a month's notice. Provided thus with an army whose officers were utterly devoted to the Crown, the power of discipline was relied on for carrying its mass as boldly forward in the coming campaign as though the whole nation had urged the war. The landwehr in their second line could do but little by tacit disapproval; and in case of the field army's success, their military instincts would lead them to support their victorious brethren. The successful intrigue with Italy promised to reduce the Austrians to a numerical inferiority on the northern border. Their infantry, if better trained, was inferior in both composition and arms.   One single disadvantage remained in a military view in the supposed inferiority of the Prussian officers, those of higher rank especially.   Dependent as these are on a tedious and depressing system of seniority, the long peace had thrown commands into the hands of men respected for their connexion with the struggle against Napoleon, but past* the usual age at which a general leads his troops with vigour.   On the other hand, the recent wars of Austria in Italy and Hungary had given her staff experience, and raised up among them officers who had the promise of fame in the prime of life.   One of these especially had acquired a name beyond that of any other soldier in Europe, and with it the entire confidence of the military whom it would fall to his lot to command.

Here, however, came to the support of Prussia the instinct which had for generations led her princes to give to that profession of arms by which their house had risen, the chief place in their studies.   The King himself had served successfully as a commander in the short campaign of Baden.   His son and heir had been carefully educated in all the details of military knowledge.   His nephew, Prince Frederic Charles, had become known beyond the limits of Prussia as an earnest devotee of the science in which his ancestor had instructed all Europe. He had been ardent in the improvement of Prussian tactics ever since the year of Solferino brought their deficiencies to light; and in his celebrated pamphlet, the Military Memorial, published in 1860, had appealed to the martial spirit of the kingdom by showing how the ancient superiority of its army over that of France might be restored.   The events of the Schleswig campaign (in the latter part of which he commanded the Prussian contingent) made him known as a good practical officer, who had been hitherto regarded as a theorist, and gave him a foremost place in the military councils of Berlin.   To him the army naturally looked as their leader when the shock with Austria became inevitable; but the claims of the Crown Prince, no less than the vast extent of frontiers to be lined, caused the division of the forces directly opposed to the Austrians into the two great wings in which they afterwards acted; a third body being judged necessary for the seizure of Saxony from King John's contingent, so as to conduct this operation without uncovering the line of defence which guarded Berlin from the

---

* Of such are Herwarth, Steinmetz, and Vogel.   The former, with his younger brothers, left their school in 1813—the eldest being then but sixteen years old—to serve in the War of Independence.

Elbe to the Oder. This service was intrusted to General Herwarth, whose vigorous performance of it, coupled with the reputation already won by his passage of the Alsen Sound in 1864, fully justified his retention in a separate command to the end of the war.

This triple division of the force directed against Benedek would, according to former theory, have borne within it the elements of failure. The traditions of warfare are nowhere more modified, however, than in this matter. The Prussian staff had diligently studied the lessons given by the American War in combining field operations, however distant, by means of the electric telegraph. To this newly developed power, in the hands of a specially organised staff, the King trusted for the general direction of the whole scheme of the campaign, and secured the necessary singleness of will by intrusting the sole charge of its strategical execution to his valued adviser, Von Moltke. This general, son of a talented Danish officer, who enjoyed the peculiar confidence of the Berlin Court * forty years since, was little known before the war beyond the royal circle, and the office in which his whole life has been spent; and his success has singularly illustrated the truth that the larger operations of strategy may be—where sufficient talent and professional knowledge exist—in great part prepared in the closet, in these days of rapid communication. To the pen of Prince Frederic rather than to his, are generally understood to be due the ' Royal Ordinances for Exercises of Troops ' on a large Scale,' which were issued to the Prussian army shortly before the Danish War, and combine the results of close study of the theory of tactics with those derived from practical observation.

In this work, rather than in the private ' Instructions for ' Needle-musket Drill,' † we may expect to discern the value placed upon the new arm by the highest military minds in Prussia before the campaigns of 1864 and 1866 had tested it in practice. The first employment of the breech-loader against the Baden insurgents impressed unfavourably the officers of the troops engaged, and left a vague belief in the army (a

---

* Major Von Moltke was intrusted with the Prussian interests in Diebitsch's camp during the remarkable campaign of 1828–9, of which he has left a thoughtful and scientific history.

† The drill-book for the Prussian breech-loader, though nominally secret, has been read all over Germany for many years past. It is commonplace enough, and gives no clue to the field value of the weapon. The only real secresy observed has been as to the nature of the fulminating composition used in the cartridge.

belief which acted powerfully on those of other nations) that its wastefulness of ammunition would render it unfit for the uses of a hard-fought campaign.   There were men above these, however, more clear-sighted, as well as of more influence with the court.   They were able to distinguish between the misuse of the new ally by the raw half-trained recruits which followed the standards in the brief struggle of 1849, and its power when skilfully handled; and had discernment enough to lay, during the twelve years of peace that succeeded, the foundation of the successes of Nachod and Skalitz.   The Ordinances of 1861 may be held to sum up the results of their study; and as far as our present knowledge of the late war extends, there is no reason to believe that these results will be much improved on by the experience of the Bohemian War.

Taking for granted the probability of meeting an enemy armed solely with the minié in some of its varied forms, officers are reminded that the superiority of the fire of the breech-loader can only be shown on an exposed enemy, within moderate distance (shown by experiments to be not more than 500 paces), and by giving time for the rapidity of the fire to tell; and that under these conditions its effect will be threefold as severe as that of the muzzle-loader.   They are therefore taught that in all contests of infantry they must keep three objects in view; (1) to receive or approach the adversary on as open ground as may be; (2) to endeavour to keep him as long as possible engaged in a musketry contest; * and (3) *to handle their own troops in deep formation.*   The value of this last re-commendation is explained by the statement, that a line of 300 men firing in front will be equal at the least to 900 of the enemy; and that, when once he is disordered, the rear parts of the column, with their fresh men and full pouches, can be thrown out upon the flanks to drive in and turn those of the mass opposed to them.   This practice, no doubt, is the secret of those sudden flank attacks which surprised the Austrian officers, and caused them such severe losses in prisoners.

Had the Prussian staff, it will be asked, no reliance on the weapon for skirmishing, or driving the enemy from cover? Not

---

* It is here that the chief difference is to be found between these instructions and the principles laid down in the Military Memorial. The latter strongly insists on the necessity of constantly taking the offensive, in order to raise the moral power of the army.   It is evident that the royal writer, at that time at least, did not compre-hend the enormous advantage which the breech-loader gives for the defensive against the advance of an assaulting column attempting to close.

much, it would appear, from the theoretical views in this work : and the lesson which should have been taught the troops opposed is no less clear from this, than from the actual fact of the complete failure of Prince Frederic's attack at Sadowa on the very poorly intrenched position of the Austrians. For the defence of posts, on the contrary, it is specially noted in the ' Instructions' that the needle-gun will prove of much value— ' provided,' adds the unknown author, with a touch of hesitation, ' that there be cartridges enough.' In this part only is to be traced some lingering doubt as to the wisdom of putting in the hands of the soldier the means of so quickly getting rid of the contents of his pouch. This, doubtless, it was that prompted the Prussian staff to look, before war came, for the proper remedy to this one weak point of their system, by increasing and distributing the small-arm reserves of ammunition in the manner Mr. Hozier has described. The ascertained fact that a certain fraction of the privates engaged at Koniggratz actually got rid of ninety rounds, is proof sufficient that these precautions were not misplaced. It affords also some justification for the doubts which were everywhere expressed among military men, as to the difficulty of using so quick-shooting an arm with advantage, in the excitement of a prolonged action.

Much has been said of the superior intelligence of the Prussian soldiery, as bearing on the question of the new arm ; and it is quite true that, in the late campaign, the armies that invaded Bohemia brought with them a large leaven of the educated classes from their reserved lists—*einjährige* who had not passed as officers—equal in all social respects to those volunteers of whom our own nation is so justly proud. This peculiar condition once known, its advantages have been sung to the full by the mass of hasty writers who worship success in Bismarck's person, and gaze only on the bright side of the Prussian shield. History, however, should have clearer eyes in so grave a matter; and the truth, when fully apparent, if not quite new to certain of these ready penmen, will astonish those who have been guided by their teaching. It is natural, no doubt, that correspondents trusted, fêted, smiled on by the staff of an army, should adopt the views current at head-quarters, and give little heed to the gossip of the private's mess. Yet it is hardly credible that anyone of observation should have watched the armies prepared for the forward rush which was to end in so great a triumph, and have been ignorant of the deep-seated disaffection which, up to the hour of the first victory, threatened to baffle the strategy of Moltke and the policy of Bismarck. We speak not here on the

authority of single Prussians removed from the war, nor that
of the unanimous assertion of the liberals in the Minor States ;
but from the testimony of careful witnesses.   Murmurs and
threats against the then unpopular minister were no less plainly
heard in the camps around Glatz and Görlitz, than in the democratic circles of Frankfurt or the courts of Austria's allies.
Curses on the author of the ' One Man's War ' were as plentiful
in Herwarth's corps, even after the successful overrunning of
Saxony, as when the order came which dragged the *Reservisten*
unwillingly from their homes at the call of their ambitious
rulers.   Though ' thinking '—according to a remarkable expression in the preface of the original Frankfurt edition of the
Military Memorial—' is forbidden to the soldiers of Prussia ; '
though ' there be,'.according to the same authority, ' an im-
' passable gulf between the noble officer and the private ;' the
admixture of intelligence introduced by the volunteer element,
acting on the increased education of the mass of the soldiery,
gave promise of fearful danger to the government which had
provoked the war, had anything short of success, both speedy
and great, been its result.
   On such success Bismarck staked and threw.   Much of the
disaffection sure to be produced by the mobilising of the army
in its new form he was prepared for ; but with this danger the
measure brought in his eyes the remedy.   Austria, though
successful in deceiving her own wellwishers as to the extent of
her resources in Bohemia, had not blinded his keener observation.   Barely 200,000 men, and those with an incomplete commissariat, were all that her favoured general could command to
the north of Vienna ; so sorely were her resources taxed by
the attempt to maintain the hold on Italy which has cost the
Hapsburgs so dear.   It is true that from the lesser States a
diversion was hoped for against Prussia, which would give
time for the slower power to assemble reserves existing as yet
only on paper ; and enable her, as in 1813, to issue forth with
advantage from the great angle of Bohemia when preconcerted
delay had done its work.   Bismarck, however, was here more
wise than Napoleon.   Delay there was none on his side, save
just what was needed for bringing out the new Field Army in
its full strength ; and in view of the doubtful spirit existing
in its lower ranks, the magnitude of the stake which was to
be won by striking home against Benedek, and the danger of
relying for the main shock on any part of the landwehr, the
bold resolve was arrived at which gave Moltke the means of
success, by placing on a single frontier almost the whole of the
regular forces.   Almost the whole ; because thus only could

easy and complete success against Benedek be obtained: and yet not quite all; because the local circumstances of Western Prussia rendered it impossible to strip that district entirely of regular troops.

It must be remembered that the Westphalian and Rhenish provinces were divided from the rest of the kingdom by the interlying territories (now annexed) of Hanover, Hesse Cassel, and Nassau. Of these Powers, all favouring Austria, the first possessed an army of 20,000 men; formidable by its training, its traditions, and even its weapons, which were Prussian. If opposed by no troops but landwehr, it seemed probable that this force might maintain itself against their attacks; might even cut off all communication between the Lower Rhine and Berlin; and form a powerful advanced guard to the levies to be raised by Bavaria and her allies upon the Main; so that the latter might be enabled by a very slight advance to unite with the Hanoverians, and threaten that capital. To avoid this special danger, a full division, forming one-half of the 7th (Vogel's) corps, was collected under General Goeben at Minden. Vogel himself, a fierce old soldier of the Blucher school, was to command; and to aid him in the occupation of Hanover, the troops under Manteuffel (which had just driven the Austrians out of Holstein) were to move southward to his support; and the landwehr of the adjacent districts (most of them assembling at Wetzlar under General Beyer) were added to his command. Of the successes he obtained—extraordinary in their way, but derived chiefly from the divisions of his opponents and the moral support of the Bohemian victories—we have no space to speak. It is of more importance to observe that he was left to operate partly with the distrusted landwehr (whose recent mutiny at Frankfurt, in the hour of Prussia's rejoicing proves their sentiments far other than those of unreasoning loyalty); in order that the superiority of Moltke might be assured on the Bohemian frontier. Here the other half of Vogel's corps, added to Herwarth's, formed the third or Elbe army, which after occupying Saxony became part of the general force destined for the invasion. Deducting Goeben's division; and excluding also the garrison artillery, depôts, Holstein troops, and the necessary detachments, there were assembled, under the three commanders, eight and a half of the nine mobilised corps of the regular army, numbering, according to the lowest Prussian estimate, 260,000 fighting men.

To bring this great army over the mountains, and unite it before the enemy, was the problem to be solved. This once accomplished, the superiority of numbers, weapons, and physical condition would lie on the side of the Prussians; and the Austrian chief could hope only by some successful defensive scheme to prevent the threatened danger. It is easy to condemn defeat and criticise misfortune; and to speak briefly, Benedek's own generalship will not bear examination in detail. From the first, however, the rapid tactics with which the Austrians had of late years manœuvered their infantry, proved ineffectual (as the Prussians had plainly foreseen) in attacks made on open ground in face of the needle-gun. It would be interesting to know whether Gablenz used any better mode on the 27th, when he obtained his advantage over Bonin before Trautenau—the only success of his side during the campaign. Be this as it may, he was left unsupported; was turned next day by the advance of the guards through the unguarded pass of Eipel on his flank; and the progress continued, without further check, which united the Prussians around Horwitz. Benedek was less happy here than Lacy; although had he taught his troops to follow the lesson bequeathed by the latter, and to keep to the defensive, his success might have been the same as his predecessor's. A few days' arrest of the Prussian advance would have made a strange change in the tone of that triumphant army; as even the three hours of uncertainty at Sadowa showed by its serious effect upon their staff.

Even so late as that day of Austria's ruin, had Benedek guarded his right with the same care as his centre, who can say what would have been the result? It needed a gross tactical error, unequalled even at Austerlitz, to give the Prussians the victory, which their superior combinations as to numbers, and their moral advantage from the recent successes of the needle-gun, seemed to ensure beforehand. If here we condemn Benedek for his ill-fought battle, let us not forget that Napoleon fell before the same disproportion * of numbers at Leipsic; and that the Austrian general at least escapes the

---

* According to the fairest estimate (that of Cathcart), the numbers engaged on the great day of Leipsic were, on the side of the allies, 230,000, of the French, 160,000. At Koniggratz, the Prussians had 250,000, the Austrians, 185,000, by the most moderate accounts. It will be observed that this exceeds in dimensions the former—previously the greatest battle, as to mere numbers, recorded in any authentic history. There is a strange tactical similarity between these two gigantic conflicts; and in each the defeat, though not (as certain partisan writers allege) due to, was enhanced by, the defection of contingents fighting against their will.

censure which is fairly due to the French Emperor for an ill-secured retreat. That the army was brought across the Elbe the same evening, was due no less to his precautions as to bridges, than to the fine conduct of the Austrian cavalry. Had Blucher's spirit been with the pursuing horse, the war should have ended on the field without further effort. The prosperous staff of the victors, and the pens they have inspired, have done but scant justice to their opponents in this matter.

If it be asked what moral should our nation draw from the history of the recent war, the reply must needs be twofold. A military writer cannot but observe that the new Prussian system is not merely firmly established in North Germany by Bismarck's success, but that it is more than likely to become, with some modifications, that of the other chief Powers of the Continent. It behoves our statesmen to look closely to that of their country, and to see whether it may not, without increase of the paid staff, be made more elastic, in case of the sudden demands which war would inevitably bring. That our infantry must be not only armed with the breech-loader, but trained especially to its use ; that our light artillery must learn to put but little faith in the practical effect of fire at long ranges ; that cavalry are still essential to the service of an army in the field; are obvious lessons of detail. Not less so is it one, that whatever combatant force is maintained, the complete equipment and machinery for the service of a much larger one must be prepared and kept at all times ready for immediate use.

There are deeper and graver questions to be solved than these, since Prussia's success was won. It may be that those have truth on their side who say that Bismarck is but an instrument for working out the longed-for unity of the German race ; and that his task once done, the minister, with the monarch he guides, will sink into secondary positions before the progress of constitutional government. We confess that we are not so sanguine. It is too early by far to attempt to foretell the end of this mighty drama : but there are signs, in the threat lately hurled at peaceful Belgium ; in the dark allusions to the opening Eastern question ; in the demand for funds in hand against some new war foreseen yet not plainly spoken of, which may well make the greatest lover of the doctrine of nationalities doubt whether the new empire—founded as it was, and built up on Sclavonic spoils—will of necessity stay its bounds where the German tongue ceases to be spoken.

We have endeavoured in the preceding pages to trace the historical growth of the military power of Prussia, and to describe the present condition of the military institutions which have suddenly conferred upon her an indisputable supremacy in Germany, and one of the foremost political positions in Europe; and we have done no injustice to the patriotism of her princes, the dexterity of her statesmen, and the valour of her armies. But the triumphant success of a great military conspiracy against the existence of her own confederates and allies, who were ill-prepared for so fierce a contest, and the political results to Northern Germany, although in themselves advantageous, cannot efface the recollection of the scandalous duplicity and falsehood, on the part of the Prussian Court, which marked every stage of the late transactions, or of the mysterious and clandestine understanding which procured the neutrality of France. The unchecked success of Prussia in this enterprise has given an irreparable blow to political morality; it has shaken all trust in those public engagements on which the peace of the world depends; it has taught mankind once more the cruel lesson that strength alone, and not law, can give them security; it has placed all the smaller states of continental Europe at the mercy of three or four colossal empires; and it has compelled even these empires to augment their immense military establishments, and to press their whole adult male population into the ranks of their armies. Great indeed must be the advantages and political results of the new system to be established by the Prussian arms, which can compensate mankind for these positive evils. But what are these results? Let us try them by a single test.

Hostilities commenced in the Elbe Duchies because it was not to be endured by the German nation that two small provinces, in which the German race preponderated, should be cut off from the German Fatherland, and governed by a foreign sovereign. To win these Duchies back to Germany, the Danish Monarchy was dismembered, a solemn treaty was broken, and Prussia has now settled the question by annexing them to her own dominions. But the very same operations which accomplished this object, have produced contrary results at the opposite extremity of Germany. There, too, are German Duchies and German provinces, inhabited by eight millions of Germans, including the first of German capitals, and identified with the whole current of German history. Is it credible that the Duchies of Austria, Styria, Carinthia, the Tyrol, &c., have been ejected from the German State, by the very same policy used to bring the Duchies of Holstein and Schleswig into it? The Treaty of Nikolsburg has in fact dismembered Germany, and consigned these important German provinces to form part of a monarchy, now expressly excluded from Germany and linked to those non-German elements which numerically preponderate in the Austrian dominions. They are now, in fact, the German appendages of the kingdoms of Hungary and Bohemia. At the same time the independent States of South Germany, too large to be absorbed by Prussia, but too weak to stand alone, are left to form a pretended confederacy without the possibility of its duration. In other words, all that could add to the paramount force of Prussia has been seized and incorporated by her; but the remainder of Germany has been deprived of its former constitution, without even the liberty to form new combinations. These considerations suffice to demonstrate that the terms of the recent treaty of peace are insincere and incomplete. Germany cannot be really *one*, until North and South, Protestant and Catholic, Vienna, Munich, and Stutgard, as well as Berlin, Dresden, and Hanover, have a fair and equal share of national rights; and ere that end be accomplished the House of Hohenzollern may have to make the same sacrifices to the popular cause, which it has recently exacted from the allies it has betrayed and the adversaries it has conquered.

No. CCLV. will be published in January 1867.

INDEX.

———◆———

A

American Navy, in the late war, 185—in January 1861, 186—the 'Powhattan,' 190—Mr. Welles and Captain Fox, 192—the 'Iron-'sides' and 'Monitor,' 193—the navy in December, 1862, 196—operations against New Orleans, 198—bombardment of Vicksburg, 211—the battle of the 'Monitor' and 'Merrimack,' 213—the navy in 1863, 215—attack on Fort Sumter, 216—victory of the 'Weehawken,' 220—attack on Mobile, 222—Lieutenant Cushing, 223—capture of Wilmington, 224—the 'Miantonomah,' 226.

B

Baker, Samuel White, review of his 'Exploration of the Albert 'Nyanza,' 151—the natives of Central Africa, 152—the White Nile, 155—the Atbara and the Blue Nile, 156—Khartoum, 157—Captains Speke and Grant, 158—the Bari tribe, 160—Mr. Baker's difficulties, 160-1—the Latookas, 164—slavery and the slave-trade in Africa, 166—elephant-hunting, 167—the Obbo country, 168—the march to Albert Nyanza, 168—Mrs. Baker's illness, 174—the passage of the Cataracts, 180—results of Mr. Baker's expedition, 181-4.

C

Coinage, international, review of works relating to, 383—recent changes in the monetary system of Western Europe, 383—and in the United States, 386—Convention of December 1865, 388—suggestions for the English coinage, 393.
Cornwall, Barry, review of his 'Charles Lamb : a Memoir,' 261.

E

Ecce Homo, reviewed, 450, 467.
Eliot, George, review of her 'Felix Holt, the Radical,' 435.
Europe, state of, 275—war in Germany, 276—uncertainty of Continental affairs, 279—maxims of the Court of Berlin—280—projects of Count Bismarck, 282—his inconsistencies, 289-90—energy of Prussia, 291—battle of Sadowa, 293—foreign policy of England, 294.

F

Feuillet de Conches, M., review of his 'Variétés d'Histoire et d'Art,' 341—predatory habits of collectors, 344—early MSS. and autographs, 347—letter of our Saviour to Abgar, 347—letter of

Lentulus, 347—early portraits, 350—ancient autographs, 354—
ancient writing, 354—causes of the destruction of some of the
works of the ancients, 356—Chinese *causerie*, 358—use of collections, 360—collection of ropes, 361—walking-sticks, 364—garters,
365—wigs and hair-dressing, 366—buttons, 369—gloves, 370—
shoes, 371—flowers, 371—collections of autographs visited by the
Curieux, 372.

Froude, James Anthony, review of his 'History of England, from
'the Fall of Wolsey to the Reign of Elizabeth,' 476—peculiar
merit of the work, 476—the Simancas papers, 477—history of
Mary Queen of Scots, 479—and of Queen Elizabeth's treatment
of Mary, 487—conspiracies of Don Guerau, 492—and of the
Queen's own subjects, 494—influence of the Reformation upon the
character of the English and Scotch at this period, 495—the proposed marriage with Alençon, 503—Massacre of St. Bartholomew,
506—part played by Elizabeth in Scotch affairs, 509.

G

Gems, antique, review of works relating to, 511—cameos, 512—
intaglio engraving, 512—the dactylotheca, 513—rock crystal, 514
—counterfeit antiques, 516—collections of the last century, 517—
Pistrucci, 519—Lord Arundel's collection, 519—the public collections of Europe, 520—private gem cabinets, 521—tools used by
the modern engraver, 523—workshop of the ancient engraver,
524—Mesopotamian cylinders, 528—stamp seals, 533—the scarabæus, 534—the 'Etruscan border,' 537—Etrurian art, 539—
ancient finger-rings, 544—characteristics of Greek and Greco-
Roman gems, 547—Romano-Greek and Roman gems, 548—
ancient gem materials, 550.

H

Huguenots, annals of the, 86—commencement of the Protestant move-
ment in France, 88—Massacre of St. Bartholomew, 93—Henry
IV., 99—Edict of Nantes, 100—Daniel Chamier, 101—Louis
XIII., 102—siege of La Rochelle, 103—Louis XIV., 104—the
dragonnades, 107—the Huguenot exiles, 111—revocation of the
Edict of Nantes, 113—subsequent cruelties, 115—Louis XVI., 119.

K

Kaye, J. W., review of his 'History of the Sepoy War,' 299—causes
of the outbreak, 300—Mahomedan loyalty, 306—Nana Sahib, 311
—Behar, 313—case of Kooer Singh, 316—case of Gyah, 317—the
North-Western Provinces, 320—cases of the Southern Mahratta
country and of Oude, 324—question of mutiny or rebellion, 327
et seq.—our advantages in India, 337—lesson taught in 1857, 339
—opinions of Sir John Lawrence as to the cause of the mutiny,
340.

King, Rev. C. W., his works on Precious Stones reviewed, 228—
his work on Gems reviewed, 511.

L

Lamb, Charles, review of Barry Cornwall's Life of, 261—his early life and works, 263—the 'London Magazine,' 268—Lamb's cockneyism, 270—his jests, 271—his life at Enfield, 273—his residence in London, 273—his death, 274.

M

Mahomet, works relating to, 1—the Arabs of the time of Mahomet, 2—early Arabian commerce, 4—the Caaba, 8—Cossai, 8, 9—ancestors of Mahomet and their institutions, 9, 10—the Semitic mind previous to Mahomet's time, 11—Christianity and Judaism, 12–14—the Hanyfs, 14—Zeid ben Amr, 16—Mahomet's early life, 17—his physical and psychological nature, 19—his visions, 21—his converts, 24—persecution of him and his sect, 28—the city of Medina, 30—Mahomet's flight, 33—his new policy, 34—his destruction of the Jews in Arabia, 37–41—causes of the rapid spread of Islam, 42—the conquest of Mecca, 43—Mohammedanism as a religion, 47—character of Mahomet, 48.
Mill, John Stuart, review of his 'Examination of Sir W. Hamilton's 'Philosophy,'120—consciousness, 121—smell, 127—taste and hearing, 128—touch, 130—idea of time, 131—sight, 133—question of an outer world, 136—definition of mind, 140—memory, 141—the relativity of human knowledge, 145.

N

Napoleon III., review of his 'Histoire de Jules César,' 399—avowed object of the author, 401—the leading principle of Cæsarism or Napoleonism, 405—the Roman 'parliamentary faction,' 414—parts played by Cæsar and Cicero, 415 *et seq.*—the Gaulish wars, 420—estimate of the population of the Gauls, 422—account of Britain in the time of Cæsar, 425—Cæsar's invasions of Britain, and treatment of the conquered, 426–32—Cæsar's vicissitudes of poverty and wealth, 433.

P

Precious stones, 228—talismanic influences of gems, 230—Mr. King's treatise, 233—gems of the ancients, 234—the diamond, 241—corundum, 241—amethyst, 242—the spinels, 242—chrysolite, 243—beryl, 244—zircon and tourmaline, 245—topaz, 245—garnets, 246—opal, 250—chalcedony, 250—agates, 251—jaspers, 251—carbuncles, 254—lapis-lazuli and turquoise, 259.
Prussia, military growth of, 553—the Great Elector, 554—Frederic I., 555—Frederic II., 556—the first partition of Poland, 558—campaign of 1778, 559—Frederic William II., 562—war of 1792, 565—Blucher, 566—Frederic William III., 567—campaigns of 1806, 567–69—part of Prussia on the humiliation of Napoleon, 571—the Prussian methods of levying an army, 572—life of a young einjähriger, 578—Prussian military system, 582—the principal Prussian officers in the recent war, 586—Von

Moltke, 587—the needle-musket, 587—deep-seated disaffection of the Prussian soldiers, 589-90—problems to be solved, 590-91—effects of recent Prussian successes on public morality, 594.

R

Renan, 'Les Apôtres,' reviewed, 450.

S

Sprenger's 'Life of Mahomet,' reviewed, 1.

Strauss, Renan, and 'Ecce Homo,' review of, 450—attention paid to the life of Jesus at the present time, 450—examination of the views of MM. Renan and Strauss, 452—and of those of the author of 'Ecce Homo,' 467.

W

Weather forecasts and storm warnings, 51—signs of imminent changes and storms, 54-5—the winds, 57—the late Admiral Fitzroy's prognostications, 58—storm signals, 60—force and direction of winds, 67—practical utility of weather warnings, 69—recommendations of the Committee, 73—Russian observations, 74—those of M. Marie Davy, 76—cost and method of English observations, 79—text-book of Oceanic Meteorology needed, 84.

THE END OF VOL. CXXIV.

PRINTED BY SPOTTISWOODE AND CO., NEW-STREET SQUARE, LONDON.

THIS BOOK IS DUE ON THE LAST DATE
STAMPED BELOW

AN INITIAL FINE OF 25 CENTS
WILL BE ASSESSED FOR FAILURE TO RETURN
THIS BOOK ON THE DATE DUE. THE PENALTY
WILL INCREASE TO 50 CENTS ON THE FOURTH
DAY AND TO $1.00 ON THE SEVENTH DAY
OVERDUE.

LIBRARY, COLLEGE OF AGRICULTURE, DAVIS
UNIVERSITY OF CALIFORNIA
Book Slip—10m-8,'49(B5851s4)458

65845		AP4
Edinburgh review		E3
		v. 124

Edinburgh Review AP4
E3
v. 124

65845

Check Out More Titles From HardPress Classics Series In
this collection we are offering thousands of classic and hard
to find books. This series spans a vast array of subjects — so
you are bound to find something of interest to enjoy reading
and learning about.

Subjects:
Architecture
Art
Biography & Autobiography
Body, Mind &Spirit
Children & Young Adult
Dramas
Education
Fiction
History
Language Arts & Disciplines
Law
Literary Collections
Music
Poetry
Psychology
Science
…and many more.

Visit us at www.hardpress.net

Im The Story

personalised classic books

"Beautiful gift.. lovely finish.
My Niece loves it, so precious!"

Helen R Brumfieldon

⭐⭐⭐⭐⭐

UNIQUE
GIFT

FOR KIDS, PARTNERS
AND FRIENDS

Timeless books such as:

Kids

Alice in Wonderland · The Jungle Book · The Wonderful Wizard of Oz
Peter and Wendy · Robin Hood · The Prince and The Pauper
The Railway Children · Treasure Island · A Christmas Carol

Adults

Romeo and Juliet · Dracula

Highly
Customizable

Change
Books Title

Replace
Character's Names
with yours

Upload
Photos for
inside pages

Add
Inscriptions

Visit
Im The Story .com
and order yours today!